VIKING FUND PUBLICATIONS IN ANTHROPOLOGY
edited by SOL TAX

Number Forty-Two

THE PEYOTE RELIGION AMONG THE NAVAHO

The Peyote Religion Among the Navaho

By DAVID F. ABERLE

with field assistance by
HARVEY C. MOORE
and with an appendix on
Navaho Population and Education *by*
DENIS F. JOHNSTON

ALDINE PUBLISHING COMPANY / *Chicago*

This volume comprises one of a series of publications on research in general anthropology published by the Wenner-Gren Foundation for Anthropological Research, Incorporated, a foundation created and endowed at the instance of Axel L. Wenner-Gren for scientific, educational, and charitable purposes. The reports, numbered consecutively as independent contributions, appear at irregular intervals.

First published 1966 by
ALDINE PUBLISHING COMPANY

320 West Adams Street

Chicago, Illinois 60606

Second printing 1967

Printed in the United States of America

TO KATHLEEN

who listened

PREFACE

THIS BOOK deals with the history and nature of the peyote cult in the Navaho country, with the long-continued resistance to the cult of the majority of the tribe and the vast majority of the Tribal Council, and with the factors that promote individual acceptance of the cult and that account for variation in the level of acceptance of the cult in various communities. By and large, data were gathered from 1949 to 1953, and little attempt is made to discuss events since then. The book concludes by trying to put the peyote cult in general into the context of similar religious movements that have arisen among oppressed and deprived groups at many times and in many places.

It is addressed to several quite different audiences. Work started under the aegis of the Bureau of Indian Affairs, and so at various points policy issues are raised and discussed. The question of policy now lies largely in the hands of the Tribal Council and the Federal courts, however. It is hoped that this book may be of some assistance to officials of the Bureau of Indian Affairs at the national and local levels, and to Tribal officials and members of the Tribal Council. Since in fact I have not stated a policy position in the body of this work, let me say here that in my opinion the Native American Church of North America and its branches on the Navajo Reservation do not constitute a threat to the health, safety, welfare, or morality of the Navajo Tribe, and that, although the Tribe may have the right to legislate against the use of peyote—an issue still under legal dispute as I write— equity demands that the Native American Church be given that protection of freedom of worship normal in the larger society and written in the Bill of Rights.

Anti-peyotist Navahos have been eager to be heard and understood. Several of them asked me to make it clear that most Navahos are not peyotists. I have several times pointed out that when the peyotist population of the Navaho country was estimated in 1951, it is probable that well over 80 per cent of the Navahos were non-peyotists and strongly opposed to peyotism and the Native American Church of North America, the peyotist church. (In 1964, however, although a majority of Navahos remained non- and anti-peyotist, the peyotist percentage had grown considerably.) I have tried to describe the views of the anti-peyotists as clearly as possible. Whole sections of the book have been written with this group of Navahos in mind. Nevertheless, they will not be pleased at my assertions that many allegations against peyotism are unproved and that many more cannot be proved.

Navaho members of the Native American Church, and the few non-Navaho peyotists with whom I have talked, have been correspondingly eager to explain themselves and to present their views. I have tried to describe their beliefs, their ritual, their organization, and their strong commitment to the peyote way in painstaking detail. Many parts of this book have been written with this audience in mind. The members will not be pleased because I have not been willing to accept their testimony as regards the curative effects of peyote as evidence. Claims in this respect are unsubstantiated. The burden of their testimony in one respect, however, must be taken with the greatest seriousness: many Navahos who have felt unhappy and lost have gained a feeling of purpose in life and a remarkable serenity through their membership in the Native American Church, their participation in its meetings, and their use of peyote.

Peyote, its derivative mescaline, psilocybin, and lysergic acid diethylamide (LSD), all substances the ingestion of which causes changes in psychological reactions, have been of unusual interest to the public for some years. I have had this audience in mind in discussing the peyote reaction, and at various other points in this work. It will be evident that neither I nor my informants find the states induced by peyote as agreeable as they seem to be to some who have taken peyote, nor as sensational and startling, for the most part, as they seem to be to some others. In this public I include missionaries, physicians, and traders who deal with the Navaho, many of whom have expressed concern about peyotism in conversatons with me. I hope that this work will allay some of their fears.

Finally, however, my deepest commitment in writing this book is to other social scientists—to those interested in religion, in psychopharmacology, in the Navaho, in peyotism, and in religious movements among oppressed groups. The general form of this work has been determined by this commitment. But as I wrote it, I was keenly conscious that my effort to be meticulous in description, and particularly my effort to find the concomitants of membership in the peyote cult, necessarily made the book less useful and probably less clear to my other audiences. Even so, I am sure that there are many sections of the book oriented especially to other audiences which will seem extraneous to my readers in the social sciences.

To some readers my delineation of Navaho history from 1863 to the present and my history of Navaho livestock reduction will seem out of proportion. It is, however, my commitment to social science that is responsible for these sections. In my reading about other religious movements, I have discovered that the social background of these movements is rarely more than sketched in. It is, furthermore, often extraordinarily difficult—and sometimes impossible—for the reader to fill in this background without a major research undertaking. By the same token, I have found the materials on the social background of the Navaho peyote cult to be scattered, unorganized, and inaccessible—and it has been a major undertaking to assemble them. I have felt an obligation to do what I wish others had done for me, and to deal with this material in detail.

The last part of this book deals with relative deprivation and with the involvement or non-involvement of subordinate groups in the dominant society. I should not like the technical language of this section to obscure what is my major point. The peyote cult springs from human suffering, the suffering of Indians at the hands of American society. Some of this suffering has been occasioned by well-intentioned error, some by the obstacles and limitations placed by the larger society on those who work with Indians, some by neglect, and some by the intention of members of the larger society. I trust very much that this book leaves no doubt on this score.

Eugene, Oregon
December 1965

ACKNOWLEDGMENTS

SINCE FIELD WORK began in 1949 and analysis of data has been carried on intermittently ever since, my indebtedness is correspondingly extensive. I am deeply grateful to all of the people and organizations mentioned below.

FINANCIAL SUPPORT

My field work in the summers of 1949 and 1950 was supported by the Window Rock Area Office, Bureau of Indian Affairs, United States Department of Interior. In the summer of 1951, the Social Science Research Council and the National Institute of Mental Health, National Institutes of Health, Public Health Service (Grant M-463) supported my field work and Harvey C. Moore's. In the summers of 1952 and 1953 Moore's work and mine were supported by a grant from the National Institute of Mental Health, National Institutes of Health, Public Health Service (Grant M-513). This grant and a Ford Foundation Behavioral Studies grant supported Omer C. Stewart's work on the Utes in 1953, subsequently reported in Aberle and Stewart (1957). In the spring of 1954, my brief trip to a hearing of the Navajo Tribal Council on peyote, and a week's field work were supported by Grant M-513 and by a grant from the Wenner-Gren Foundation for Anthropological Research.

During the winters while field work went on, and for ten years thereafter, data collection from library sources, data analysis, mapping, and many other activities went forward. These activities usually required research assistants. Funds for this work came from all of the sources listed above except the Bureau of Indian Affairs and Grant M-463. In addition, there were funds from the Ford Foundation Behavioral Sciences Research Fund Program at the University of Michigan, and from Faculty Research Grants at the University of Oregon. The Center for Advanced Study in the Behavioral Sciences at Stanford supplied me with many hours of research assistance and statistical consultation, as well as providing a year of time freed from teaching during which part of the theoretical approach presented here, and part of the data analysis were completed. A small grant from the National Institute of Mental Health, National Institutes of Health, Department of Health, Education, and Welfare (M-2135) made possible the analysis of the Reports of the Commissioner of Indian Affairs respecting the Navaho, the Ute, and certain Apache groups, and of popular literature on the Navaho.

FACILITIES

A division between financial support and facilities is not always easy to make. For example, some of the help given at the Center for Advanced Study might well be listed in this section. The Window Rock Area Office provided an office for Moore and me, access to information, living quarters, telephone, some secretarial assistance, and in every way possible facilitated our research, both when I was an employee and subsequently. The Statistical Laboratory at the University of Michigan made machines available to me at various times from 1953 to 1960. The Statistical Laboratory and Computer Center of the University of Oregon provided computer facilities in 1964. In 1960–61, through the kindness of Professor Max Gluckman, I was Simon Visiting Professor for one term and Honorary Research Associate for two terms in the Department of Social Anthropology at Manchester University, Manchester, England. The leisure afforded by these appointments made it possible to complete a first draft of this book.

Many people have expressed a lively curiosity as to whether I expected to get a lot of money by writing a book about peyote. Perhaps this is the place to remark that I do not receive royalties on this book and that I consider myself fortunate that the Wenner-Gren Foundation for Anthropological Research has seen fit to publish it at no expense to me. In spite of the generous assistance I have received from so many sources, I have had to pay a portion of the research costs and typing costs myself.

RESEARCH ASSISTANCE

Harvey C. Moore worked with me for three summers in the Navaho country. His willingness to accept the framework of the project, fruitful suggestions, good humor, and painstaking field work made him an invaluable asset. He and his wife, Sarah Moore, dealt cheerfully with physically difficult and sometimes emotionally taxing field conditions, and I am deeply grateful to both of them. His specific contributions to the project are described in the body of this work. He is not accountable for the use I have made of his data, since he had no opportunity to participate in the analysis I have provided. He and Allen T. Dittmann did an analysis of Navaho dreams of which I have made use. The idea of collecting dream materials was Moore's, and he secured the information (see Dittmann and Moore, 1957).

Omer C. Stewart was uniquely qualified to study the inter-relationships of the Ute and Navaho cults. He has been a fine collaborator and a kindly and insightful critic. Our joint work appeared in Aberle and Stewart, 1957.

John Adair secured information for me from a retired Indian Service official in Albuquerque.

These were my field collaborators. The list of those who assisted in the collection of data from printed sources and in the analysis of data is more extensive.

The largest independent item of data analysis was Denis F. Johnston's work on Navaho population and education, presented in an appendix to this book. I stated the problem; the data collection and execution of the analysis was entirely Johnston's.

Pierre B. Gravel, Gerald Weiss, and Lewis Binford collected data from the Reports of the Commissioner of Indian Affairs. Gravel worked with popular literature on the Navaho as well. Gravel collected all the Navaho information and most of the Ute data. He subsequently supplied a painstaking analysis of the Ute data. Weiss collected and analyzed the Apache data. I am grateful to all these collaborators, and especially to Gravel, whose work was the most extensive and whose interpretative task was the most difficult.

Callista Farrell dug up most of the figures on Navaho livestock holdings from the beginning to the 1930's, prepared Tables 23 and 24, and located various Congressional hearings on the Navaho. If memory serves, this completes the list of people who gathered data for me, most of whom did data analysis as well. We turn now to technical and statistical consultation and assistance.

Consultation on a questionnaire on peyotism distributed to Navaho Agency personnel and on an interview with Agency personnel was supplied by John Clausen and Henry A. Riecken. The first map of the distribution of peyotism was constructed by my brother-in-law, George L. Levin. The final map was prepared by Arthur J. Jelinek. Maps showing communities mentioned in the text and showing the location of the Navaho Researvation in the context of other Southwestern reservations were prepared by William E. Taylor. Charles Miller drew the graphs. He also prepared the diagram of a peyote meeting.

William A. Scott initiated me in interview coding, was principally responsible for the development of codes for the 1952 and 1953 interviews, worked on the analysis of 1952 interviews, pressed me into random sampling in the summer of 1953, and developed the instructions for random sampling. He thus played a major role in the selection of research techniques. For this and for his gentle efforts to educate me I am grateful.

Coding of Moore's 1952 interviews was carried out by the coding division of the Survey Research Center of the University of Michigan. Leon G. Williams and John B. Cornell coded the 1953 interviews.

At various times I have profited from statistical consultation with John W. Atkinson, Charles W. Eriksen, Leon Festinger, Ray Hyman, Howard Raiffa, and John Johnston. I. Richard Savage developed the mode of analysis of data supplied in Chapter 17 and supervised the analysis. Judson Mills carried out virtually all of the statistical analysis in Chapter 17, although small portions were done by Manard Stewart and by the writer. The analysis of interview data in Chapter 16 (which consisted of the painstaking demonstration that there were no significant relationships between a large number of variables and peyotism) was done by Leon G. Williams. Subsequent efforts to improve on this analysis failed. John C. Scott did further analysis of the 1953 interviews, not presented here. I am grateful to all of these consultants and assistants, but I would be lacking in a sense of proportion if I did not express particular gratitude to Savage, Mills, and Williams.

Analysis of distributional data on peyotism and of data on Navaho communication patterns (presented in Aberle and Stewart, 1957) was carried out by Judson Mills, after consultation with Leon Festinger and Howard Raiffa.

The analysis of Navaho community differences and peyotism has followed a long and troubled course, and several analyses which seemed promising have been discarded for one or another reason, mainly technical. The first was carried out by Nicholas Longo after consultation with Charles Eriksen. The table in Chapter 18 which provides the community ratings was developed by John Caylor after consultation with Walter H. Crockett. Caylor, Mills, and the author made various attempts to analyze these data. My own work was aided by statistical assistance secured for me by John Johnston. The final analysis was done by Manard Stewart. Each of these assistants and consultants has shown great ingenuity and equally great persistence; I regret the fact that earlier analyses were superseded.

I am grateful to every technical and statistical consultant and data analyst not only for painstaking and ingenious work, but for partially successful efforts to educate me in the selection and use of the techniques involved. To this list should be added Hubert M. Blalock and Allan G. Feldt, whose impact on an earlier piece of research carried over into this one. As a result, a small portion of the statistical analysis is mine, largely in isolated tables here and there throughout the work.

To other assistants, whose names have disappeared from my mind into the mists of time, my gratitude is extended, with apologies for their inadvertent omission.

INTELLECTUAL STIMULATION

A fair account of my indebtedness in the approach I have taken in this work would require an intellectual autobiography, a course I must forego at the risk of failing to indicate some obvious intellectual debt. In Navaho studies, the late Clyde Kluckhohn first stimulated my interest and shaped my outlook. He retained a keen interest in my research on peyotism and supplied me with valuable data. Lee Wyman first introduced me to Navaho field work, in 1939. His work on Navaho religion has been a major help to me. The late Gladys Reichard and the late Father Berard Haile, O.F.M., have also affected my outlook on things Navaho. Walter O. Olson, formerly Associate Area Director of the Window Rock Area Office, and Robert W. Young of that Office, have been sources of constant stimulation. It is fair to say that my view of the contemporary Navaho situation was heavily influenced by many conversations with Walter Olson. Robert Young afforded many valuable insights and has been most patient in providing assistance in rectifying my tone-deaf transcriptions of Navaho terms and in translating terms for me. To return for a moment to anthropologists, Elizabeth Colson, W. W. Hill, Solon T. Kimball, Jerrold Levy, Elizabeth Clark Rosenthal, Katherine Spencer, and E. Z. Vogt are sources of valued discussions, communications and publications. Works by William Y. Adams (1963) and James F. Downs (1964) appeared too late to have their full impact on this work. Although my presentation would be improved in some respects by due use of their studies, I am happy to find that their data and interpretations support, rather than contradict, my interpretations of Navaho history and contemporary life.

I need hardly say that I have learned much from talking to Navahos. In the case of some Navaho friends, our discussions passed beyond the gathering of information into the realm of interpretation. My views have been permanently affected by the thinking of Sam Ahkeah, Thomas Billy, Anson Damon, Stewart Etsitty, Paul Jones, Carl Kinlicheenie, Mike Kiyaani, Howard Nalwood, Allan Neskahi, Albert G. (Chick) Sandoval, Sr., Dooley D. Shorty, and Hola Tso. Some of these men are peyotists; some are anti-peyotists. Some helped me primarily to understand the Navaho scene, and some primarily to understand peyotism. The atmosphere in the Navaho country when last I worked there makes it seem unsuitable to identify their affiliations. Each maintained a dialogue with me in which both of us reflected on the Navaho scene or on peyotism, and from each of them I have gained understanding.

In matters pertaining to peyotism in general, I have found the basic groundwork laid by Weston La Barre and the late J. S. Slotkin. Through his work and through our collaboration I have learned much from Omer C. Stewart. In Chapter

19 I have tried to indicate my indebtedness to various people, in discussion and through reading, for the theoretical approach adopted here. I will not repeat that list, but it requires some supplementation.

From my wife, Kathleen Gough Aberle, I have learned some things about social movements which have so affected my thinking that specific indications of influence are impossible. I have profited much from discussions with Bernard Barber, John Clausen, James Coleman, S. N. Eisenstadt, Leon Festinger, Max Gluckman, Louis Guttman, the late Alfred L. Kroeber, Philleo Nash, Thomas F. O'Dea, Robert N. Rapoport, David M. Schneider, Maurice H. Seevers, G. E. Swanson, Yonina Talmon, Victor W. Turner, and Abraham Wikler. In some cases these discussions preceded my interest in Navaho peyotism. Here too, Clyde Kluckhohn's influence, especially through *Navaho Witchcraft* (1944), is evident. I have also been helped by talks with Marshall D. Sahlins and Leslie A. White, although they may not recognize their influence.

HOSPITALITY AND ASSISTANCE

To acknowledge the aid of every employee of the Bureau of Indian Affairs and the Window Rock Area Office and of every interpreter and informant would require a small directory. Both Moore and I are permanently indebted to hundreds of people for information, help, hospitality, and friendship. Those whom we do not mention are not forgotten: our choice is between mentioning none and mentioning some, even at the risk of seeming to slight the help of others, in all cases essential.

In the early stages of this work, the late John H. Provinse, D'Arcy McNickle, and William C. Zimmerman, then Assistant Commissioners of Indian Affairs, were warmly supportive. Without their active interest this work would never have been initiated. Dillon Myer, the subsequent Commissioner, was also most helpful. I have had no contact with later Commissioners in connection with this work.

At Window Rock the late Allan G. Harper, Window Rock Area Director, facilitated my work and Moore's. Endless help and what must at times have seemed endless hospitality were provided by Betty and Walter Olson. Olga and Robert Young were fine hosts. The late Harry Spence and his wife, Gini, were my good friends, and Harry was one of several Agency physicians who provided emergency medical help. James F. Canan, Eloise Lovine Harper, and the late Richard Van Valkenburgh helped me in many ways.

The assistance of many elected and appointed officials of the Navajo Tribe eased Moore's task and mine. This assistance is the more appreciated because some of these officials were less than enthusiastic about a study of peyotism. Nevertheless, they helped us greatly, both in Window Rock and locally. The same is true of chapter officers.

Without the assistance and guidance of Hola Tso, Dooley D. Shorty, Anson Damon, and Stewart Etsitty, this study would have foundered. At Sawmill I often ate at the residence of Mr. and Mrs. Hola Tso. At Greasewood Springs below Ganado, I enjoyed the hospitality of the late Billy Pete and Mrs. Billy Pete, and of Mr. and Mrs. Carl Kinlicheenie. Otto Williams and Franklin Showa acted as interpreters, and Carl Kinlicheenie guided me about the community. At Piñon,

Howard Nalwood and Edgar Clark served as interpreters, and I repeatedly visited the residence cluster of the Silver family. At Sweetwater, I stayed in a household cluster headed by Old Lady John Yazzie and John Uncle (Hosteen Cedar). In that cluster I lived with Thomas Peters, who acted as interpreter and who also housed Maurice Benally, another interpreter, for me. Thomas Peters later traveled with me through District 8, as interpreter. At Shiprock I often enjoyed the hospitality of Mr. and Mrs. Allen Neskahi. Allen Neskahi and Richman Hobson interpreted for me. At Lukachukai I stayed with Mr. and Mrs. Allen Harvey. Allen Harvey served as guide, and the late Woody Harvey as interpreter. I enjoyed the hospitality of Mr. and Mrs. Albert G. Sandoval, Sr.; Albert G. Sandoval, Sr., and his son, Franklin, interpreted for me. At Red Rock I lived at the home of Mr. and Mrs. Morris Benally, and Morris Benally was my interpreter. At Crownpoint, John Perry interpreted for me. At Mexican Spings, I lived with Mr. and Mrs. Leroy Nez and also enjoyed the hospitality of his parents, Mr. and Mrs. Jim Etsitty. Leroy Nez served as interpreter. At Montezuma Creek I was welcomed by Thomas Billy and Cyrus Begay.

The simple question of a place to eat, to sleep, and to leave one's belongings can be a vexing one in the Navaho country—less so today than in 1949–1953, since several tourist facilities have been built in recent years. And so to each family with whom I stayed I owe a special debt. In every case friendship, and not merely convenience, was provided. Interpreters were not only conscientious translators, but guides, friends, and sure help in emergencies: when the car bogged down, broke up, or got hung up on a high center or a precipice. Virtually every day hospitality was provided by other Navahos too numerous to mention. Special thanks must go to those at whose homes I attended peyote meetings, those who conducted peyote meetings that I attended, and those who—often in spite of distrust of my intentions—provided information on the early history of the peyote cult. They cannot be named here.

In the field I am indebted for assistance, information, and guidance to a number of Agency employees: in District 17 to Mr. and Mrs. Ben Taylor, the District Supervisor and his wife, and Mr. and Mrs. Earl Jenkins, school teachers at Greasewood Springs; in District 12, to E. G. Jonas and Deb J. Victor; in District 4 to Paul Jones, District Supervisor, and Mr. and Mrs. Trellie James, school teachers; in District 14, to Mr. and Mrs. Marion South, the District Supervisor and his wife; in District 15, to Hugh D. Carroll, the School Principal.

Traders were, without exception, helpful and informative. Again a directory is out of the question. Only a few can be mentioned. Mr. and Mrs. Jack Hunt of Greasewood Springs were of great help to a neophyte. Mr. and Mrs. Edward Junker and Mr. and Mrs. George Junker of Mexican Springs were hospitable and helpful. Mr. and Mrs. Buddy Tanner of Aneth put me up for several days and provided particularly useful information. Mr. and Mrs. Ira Hatch and Mr. Sherman Hatch of Hatches Store pulled me out of a wash and supplied me with useful information. Mr. and Mrs. Burnham of Standing Rock, and Mr. Kenneth Washburn of Gallegos were also kind and helpful. Mr. and Mrs. Art Greene of Piñon boarded me and my interpreter at a time of particular inconvenience to them. Mr. Russell Foutz of Teec Nos Pas was helpful. And the list could be amplified greatly.

Several missionaries also aided this work. First among these is the late Fr. Berard Haile, already mentioned. Fr. Elmer of St. Michaels and Fr. Blase of Lukachukai supplied me with valuable information. All of these are members of the Order of Franciscan Monks. The Reverend and Mrs. David Clark, acquainted with peyotism among the Sioux and among the Navahos, of the Episcopalian Good Shepherd Mission, were hospitable and informative. So was Father James Liebler, of the Episcopal Mission at Bluff.

The Moores' acknowledgments include warm recollections of hospitality and help by Allan Harper, Betty and Walter Olson, Olga and Robert Young, and Brice and Judy Sewell at Window Rock. Advice, assistance, and often hospitality were also provided by the late John F. Carmody, Elvira Franchville, the Melvin Helanders, Eloise Lovine Harper, Rose James, William Morgan, and Hildegarde Thompson.

To signalize Moore's assistance in interviewing Agency personnel would require listing his thirty-three informants in various parts of the Reservation who subjected themselves to a strenuous interview in 1951.

In 1952, he was assisted at Tohatchi by Walter Steppe, Principal, McGee, trader, and Walter Francisco, interpreter. At Teec Nos Pas he received help from Bessie McEntire, Principal, the Lloyd Foutzes, traders, and James Clah and Howard Tsoh, interpreters. At Crownpoint he was assisted by Hugh D. Carroll, Area Principal, the Lloyd Washburns, traders, and Alfred Hogan Begay and John Perry, interpreters.

In 1953, he was assisted at Aneth by Stanley and Dorothy Rosenberg, Principal and teacher, Ralph Tanner and the Elijah Blairs, traders, and Sam Capitan, interpreter. Occasional interpreters at Aneth were Myron Poyer, Dan Weston, and Joe Merritt, the latter of whom was also a continuing source of good advice.

Moore's initial entry into the Tohatchi area was facilitated by Willis McNatt and into Crownpoint by Arthur Hubbard, District Supervisors of the respective areas. In both Teec Nos Pas and Aneth the good counsel and aid of Elvin G. Jonas, District Supervisor, and Deb J. Victor, Area Principal, were received many times.

And, especially, Moore is indebted to the assistance of his wife, Sarah.

Finally, Moore and I express our greatest appreciation to hundreds of Navahos, peyotist and anti-peyotist, and to scores of Agency personnel, who, almost without exception, answered questions which at times must have seemed peculiar and at other times naïve, and who struggled to convey to us their points of view in formal interviews, conversations, and group discussions, lasting from a quarter of an hour to a half a day. We have tried to be worthy of their trust by a faithful presentation of their views.

Dave Weber, the *Santa Fe New Mexican, Time* magazine, E. D. Newcomer, and the *Arizona Republic* (of Phoenix) have been exceedingly generous in making available to me their unique photographs of a peyote meeting. Some of these have appeared in the publications named. Specific attribution of photographs appears in the appropriate section of this work.

I am grateful to Elizabeth Slotkin for her generous permission to quote extensively from *The Peyote Religion,* by the late J. S. Slotkin. I thank Omer C.

Stewart and the University of Colorado Press for permission to reprint the three maps that first appeared in *Navaho and Ute Peyotism: A Chronological and Distributional Study* (Aberle and Stewart, 1957).

I am indebted to Alexander J. Morin, of the Aldine Publishing Company, for his sympathetic efforts to place the manuscript and to Sol Tax and the Wenner-Gren Foundation for its placement and for valuable assistance.

To all of those named here, and to those not mentioned specifically, my most profound gratitude.

It hardly needs to be said that ultimate responsibility for the presentation of interview materials, for the interpretation of statistical data, and for the theoretical approach adopted is mine. If I have unintentionally distorted the communications of informants, consultants, or assistants, or willfully refused to take their advice, mine is the error.

Mrs. Lloyd L. Armes typed the manuscript. Her good humor and painstaking care I value greatly. My mother, Lisette F. Aberle, provided sympathetic criticism of portions of this work, especially those dealing with beliefs and values. Garrick Bailey assisted in preparing the Index. Mary Knudson and Herbert Alexander assisted in the unhappy task of proofreading the tables.

The transcription system for Navaho words has been borrowed from Young and Morgan (n.d.).

A National Science Foundation grant to study Navaho family and kinship in the summer of 1965 provided incidental opportunities to gather certain additional information that appears at various points in this book.

TABLE OF CONTENTS

PART V. PEYOTISM AS A REDEMPTIVE MOVEMENT

APPENDIXES

BIBLIOGRAPHY

INDEXES

LIST OF FIGURES

(Facing page 134)

LIST OF MAPS, DIAGRAMS, AND GRAPHS

MAPS

DIAGRAMS

GRAPHS

LIST OF CHARTS

LIST OF TABLES

Part I

THE PEYOTE CULT

Chapter 1

INTRODUCTION

T HE PEYOTE CULT is the most popular, and one of the most durable of all the religious movements created by American Indian groups suffering from the effects of domination by American society. It combines beliefs tinged with Christianity and ritual distinctively Indian in character. Its members eat the peyote cactus, a substance with special psychological and physiological effects, sometimes including visions. For them, the cactus is the insigne of their religion, the basis for their communication with God, and their cure for all bodily and spiritual ills—a palladium, power, and panacea. Opponents of the cult fear and hate peyote. In spite of the opposition of the Indian Service, in times past, of both traditional and Christian Indians, of doctors, missionaries, and traders, the cult has spread from Oklahoma over the past seventy-odd years to embrace a territory reaching from Nevada in the west to Wisconsin in the east, and from New Mexico in the south to Saskatchewan in the north.

It reached the Navaho Indians, the largest tribe in the United States, in the 1930's, spreading in spite of the active hostility of the majority of the tribe, until in 1951 more than one out of seven Navaho families had joined the cult. In 1949, I was employed by the United States Bureau of Indian Affairs, Window Rock Area Office, to study the cult, at a time when the Navajo Tribal Council wanted the cult extirpated root and branch, whereas the Bureau held that this might constitute a violation of freedom of religion. Research continued into the summer of 1954— in 1950 under Bureau auspices, and thereafter with Bureau cooperation.

The results of the research are embodied in this book, which may be viewed as an effort to answer a number of questions about the peyote cult—factual, theoretical, and practical. To begin with, other post-conquest religions of American Indians do not use any pharmacologically active substance like peyote. What, then, is peyote, how does it act on the human system, and what is its role in the religion? What does the religion consist of: what is its ritual, its belief system, and its organization? Why has it been able to last so long and spread so far among Indians? The answers to these questions tell us what spread to the Navahos in the 1930's. They are found in Part I of this book.

But why did so many Navahos accept peyotism—particularly considering that the Navaho tribe is, or was in the 1930's, the least "acculturated" tribe in the United States, with a fully functioning native religion, and virtually uninfluenced by decades of Christian missionizing? And why did the Navahos accept peyotism when they did? Why did earlier nativistic movements like the Ghost Dance leave them virtually untouched, and why did not they develop their own nativistic movements in the past—as the Apaches did? Part II provides general background on the Navahos, from the time of their conquest by the United States in the 1860's to the present, so that the condition of the group receiving the cult can be clearly understood.

Part III describes the peyote cult as it is found among the Navaho. Since in each tribe there are minor differences in peyotist beliefs and rituals, the original description of the cult in Part I must be amplified with strictly Navaho information to understand exactly what the religion was that the Navahos received.

In Part IV, questions about the appeal of peyotism are raised and answered, in a discussion which lays heavy weight on the impact of livestock reduction on the Navahos.

Peyotism is called a nativistic movement, or a revitalistic movement. What does this mean? What is the place of the peyote cult in the family of nativistic or revitalistic movements? What are the conditions most likely to give rise to different kinds of nativistic movements? Part V discusses these problems.

Finally, peyotists believe that peyote is beneficial; anti-peyotists fear that it is dangerous. What evidence is there for either position? These and other practical issues receive attention in an appendix, but also at various points in the book.

We turn now to a brief discussion of peyote and the peyote cult.

Chapter 2

THE PEYOTE CULT

T HE PEYOTE CULT consists of rituals, beliefs, and organization.[1] But its rituals and beliefs center on the eating of the peyote cactus, and its organization first sprang into being to combat opposition to the eating of peyote. Believers and opponents regard peyote as central to the religion. So we will begin by discussing peyote itself.

Throughout the world, people use many pharmacological substances to create special psychological states. The opiates, marijuana, coca, fly agaric, psylocibine, alcohol, kava, caffeine, and tobacco come readily to mind. Many such substances are used in various magical contexts—as for divination—to create trance, stupor, visions, or dreams. But the peyote cult is the only religion known to me which uses a chemical substance to create special psychological states in the service of religious ends. Cult members face persecution and prison in order to use peyote for religious purposes. So it seems reasonable to assume that some characteristic of the peyote experience makes it particularly relevant for the religion of which it is a part.

PEYOTE

Peyote is a small, low-growing, hairy cactus, whose flesh and roots are eaten by members of the cult. The flesh looks like a small pincushion, and when dried rather like an overcoat button. It grows in Texas and Mexico, in an area approximately bounded by Corpus Christi, Texas, Deming, New Mexico, Durango, Mexico, and Puebla, Mexico (Rouhier, 1927, p. 12). It contains eight alkaloids, "the most important of which is mescaline. . . . Although this is the best known alkaloid, there is accumulating evidence that the other constituents contribute markedly to the effects of the total button" (Seevers, 1954, p. 14). There is a considerable literature on the chemistry of peyote and of mescaline and on their physiological and psychological effects on normals and on individuals with mental disease (cf. La Barre, 1960, for a review of some recent items). For present purposes, the chemistry and neurophysiology of peyote need not concern us. What is important is a phenomenological description of the core of the peyote experience.

The sequence of reactions which occurs in the course of using peyote has been described many times (e.g., La Barre, 1938, pp. 140–144). To begin with, there is wakefulness, mild analgesia, and a sensation of fullness in the stomach or loss of appetite. Some observers state that there is also a euphoric quality in the early phases of the peyote experience, but Navahos fail to mention this, and I have never

---

[1] The word "cult" is not used in a technical sense. Anthropological literature, however, has used the phrase "peyote cult" for so long that it does not seem worthwhile to drop it here for "peyote religion" or "peyote church."

felt it. If dosage continues, there may be active nausea, a feeling of tightness in the chest, some muscular tetany, often particularly evident in the jaw muscles, and heightened sensitivity to nuances of sound, color, form, and texture. These reactions are often reported. For some subjects, continued dosage or later phases may include "visions" with eyes closed, ranging from fairly elaborate scotomata to quite detailed pictures, and in even fewer cases there may be full-fledged visions with eyes open, including what are evidently major distortions of visual and auditory stimuli.

The emotional tone of the experiences is often one of mild to acute anxiety, sometimes of considerable duration, and often accompanied by depression. In a peyote meeting this normally passes off during the night, and in the early morning after a meeting, mild euphoria is common, although I cannot say whether this stems from peyote's processes or from the shared experience of having passed through a difficult and arduous ceremonial to its completion.

In all this, however, there is little to tell us why peyote should be so important for a religion—although I shall later indicate that I consider the anxiety and depression to be important. The visions are definitely *not* critical; they are rare or absent in a very large percentage of Navaho cases, and disvalued by many peyotists, although welcomed by many others.

After attending eleven peyote meetings at which I ate peyote, after discussing peyote experiences with a fair number of Navahos, after reading a good many clinical descriptions of the peyote experience, and after checking my own views against those of Dr. Abraham Wikler, who has administered mescaline to volunteers at the Federal Hospital at Lexington, I have formed a strong impression as to the core quality of the peyote experience.

In all but its mildest and most prodromal forms, the peyote experience is characterized by a feeling of the *personal significance* of external and internal stimuli. The user is prompted to ask of everything, "What does this mean *for me?*" We might use the clinical term "ideas of reference" to characterize this reaction, but it has too many pathological and paranoid overtones to suit the present context. Users may find personal significance in the events of the peyote meeting, the physical surroundings, their fellow participants and their behavior and expressions, scotomata, visions, nausea, indigestion, headache, backache, or simply in their own ruminations.

For example, an old Navaho ceremonial practitioner, much concerned because he was forgetting his chants, went to a peyote meeting to try to get them back. During the night, he said, he saw a yellow line. (This is quite a common visual effect of peyote.) As he watched it, it moved upward. Then he knew why he had forgotten his chants. He was an old man, and with the passage of the years, some of the people he had cured had died. They had "taken" parts of the chants with them. After he understood this, he began to remember his chants again. What he saw was commonplace enough, but he had endowed a rather neutral visual effect with personal significance: he had drawn from it an interpretation of the cause of his troubles.

Often in peyote meetings I told the members that I was obliged to be an impartial observer. One night I said that I walked a chalk line. In the morning the road chief (peyote priest) said, "I saw that line, a yellow chalk line, during the night." The visual stimulus must have been similar to that seen by the old singer. The road chief imposed meaning on it in the light of my words.

Peyote songs are in languages unfamiliar to the Navaho or contain only meaningless vocables. Peyotists say that if you listen to the songs while you are taking peyote, you will find out what they mean. They always say that peyote "teaches you," and that a person cannot discover the meaning of the cult from instruction, but only from experience.

They also say that when a man drums or sings with you, you can "read his mind," and that you can "read the minds" of other people in the meeting. If a drumstick breaks, it has a meaning. If many people become nauseated (or few), it has a meaning. And so on.

When we turn to the clinical administration of peyote, we find that it is very common for subjects to react to the "peculiar" experiences of taking peyote by asking the clinician, "What are you trying to do *to me?*" (Wikler, personal communication). The various temporal and sensory alterations, then, are not just experienced as peculiarities of the administration of a substance, but as having been supplied by the clinician with the intention of somehow affecting the subject. This happens as well with highly sophisticated psychiatric student volunteers, one of whom was convinced that the psychiatrist was attempting to make her psychotic (Beringer, 1927, p. 124). I think that this lies behind much of what excited Huxley when he wrote *The Doors of Perception.* "Draperies," he says, ". . . are much more than devices for the introduction of non-representational forms into naturalistic paintings and sculptures. What the rest of us see only under the influence of mescalin, the artist is congenitally equipped to see all the time. . . . It is a knowledge of the intrinsic significance of every existent" (1954, p. 33). Incidentally, I do not agree with Huxley that "the drug brings hell and purgatory only to those who have had a recent case of jaundice, or who suffer from periodical depressions or a chronic anxiety" (1954, p. 54), and I note that like many users before and since, he found himself "all at once on the brink of panic" (1954, p. 55).

With or without visions, with or without anxiety and depression, however, the peyote experience is one of an external and internal world of personal significance. And it is this which makes peyote religiously important.

Peyote is a religious adjunct—an aid to special experience. Other religions, for the same and other purposes, also have such adjuncts—although not all do, by any means. Fasting, repetitive prayer, trance, self-torture, techniques of withdrawal from external stimuli play their role in various religions. They share with peyote the provision of an other-than-usual experience which, in the context of religious ritual, is identified as having to do with the supernatural. Those religions which institutionalize such practices attempt to make religious virtuosi of the ordinary worshipper. But that is not to say that the experience sought is by any means identical with that of peyote.

The feeling of personal significance—in the context of peyote ritual—has broad application. If the worshipper is ill, he can ask his own bodily sensations and the events of the meeting for an understanding of why he is ill and whether he is likely to get better. If he is anxious, depressed, or guilt-ridden, he can ruminate over the reasons for these things and seek in his experience a clue as to whether he is forgiven, needs to worry, or can ever be happy. I do not claim that this experience is universal, but everything that I have heard leads me to believe that it is common, and that it is this quality which results in "revelations" of the utmost importance for the individual which yet have a banal quality when they are related. One of the commonest remarks made by peyotists is, "I used just to live from day to day, but now I *think*." When this comment can be elaborated—and often it cannot—it usually turns out to mean that one's self, one's aims, one's relationships, and one's ethics have become matters for reflection, and have somehow taken on a new dimension of meaning.

It has often been claimed that the primary appeal of peyote is its ability to provide people with visions (e.g., La Barre, 1939; 1960, p. 52). Yet many Navahos, and many other Indians for that matter, who are ardent peyotists have never seen a vision. For some peyotists, the vision is very important. But the vision is also an instance of the feeling of personal significance. Cult members do not take peyote to watch or listen to hallucinatory experiences for their own sake: they search for meanings in the visions, and it is the meanings that make them important.[2]

There are two other important elements in the peyote experience: the feeling of medical benefit, and the experiencing of the power of peyote. As to medical benefit, even relatively small doses of peyote have physiological effects which can be felt by the consumer. Since the user takes peyote in a therapeutic context, he seeks for evidence that peyote is curing him. It would seem—although the point is partly speculative—that there are two ways for the naïve observer to evaluate the supposed benefits of his medicine. One is to see whether it relieves symptoms. In short-run terms, peyote does have certain qualities likely to relieve suffering. It is mildly analgesic, and it promotes wakefulness, somewhat like benzedrine. Thus, as Dr. M. H. Seevers has suggested to me, small, frequent doses of peyote might well improve the physical comfort of an elderly, somewhat creaky individual, who would be relieved of pain and pepped up a bit. In addition, peyote has, at a minimum, *post hoc* benefits. As with other plants in the folk pharmacopeia, rituals, and modern therapies not yet subjected to precise, controlled studies, peyote benefits from the fact that virtually any therapeutic process which is not actually damaging is self-validating. No one has more than one fatal illness, whereas all human beings who live a few years have a good many transitory illnesses followed by full recovery—as in the case of many respiratory and gastrointestinal conditions and many muscular and nervous aches and pains. Thus either through its analgesic and stimulating effects or through ordinary recuperation, a peyote user is likely to learn to associate the physiological effects of peyote and his subsequent "cure."

A second way of judging the value of a medicine is to see how "strong" its

---

[2] I have heard reports, primarily from traders among the Navaho, of people who used peyote for the sake of the visions they would see—either beautiful pictures or erotically tinged ones. My own closest friends regarded erotic peyote visions as something utterly foreign to their own experience or that of others whom they knew, although they were by no means uninterested in sexual experience in ordinary life. As for aesthetic experience per se, one gifted silversmith told me that he got some ideas for designs by looking at the fire in peyote meetings. Otherwise I heard no comments of this sort.

effects are. Around the world, there seems to be a good deal of use of substances or procedures which have temporary effects on the system: purgatives, emetics, and irritants. The popularity of the more violent medications would seem to rest on the assumption that any change is for the better. And taking peyote does provide one with evidence that something *is* being done to one's system. For some people, the simple appeal of a "medical" experience may be sufficient, with no experience of personal significance whatsoever.

Peyote is also experienced as a "power." There are many reasons for this, but one phenomenological feature seems particularly relevant. When a person eats peyote, something external to him proves able to affect his thinking, his feelings, his perceptions, and his behavior, and to do so without his own volition. Not only that, but these effects are unpredictable: the individual does not know what will happen when next he eats peyote. One Navaho road chief asked me if I had taken peyote, and then asked how often I had eaten it. When I told him that I had done so several times, he asked me with great curiosity, "Does it affect you the same each time?" "No," I said. "Me either!" This external agent, whose effects on the individual cannot be predicted or fully controlled, is indeed a power.

In popular belief, the appeal of peyote is thought to be in the pleasurable experience it supplies, or in its addictive quality. Neither of these claims can be substantiated. Huxley's book at least suggests that the primary appeal of peyote is in the ineffable experiences it supplies. But the consensus among the peyotists with whom I have worked, as well as among those reported in some forty years of detailed anthropological field reports, is that taking peyote is hard: the taste is bitter, the nausea unpleasant, the anxiety and depression overwhelming, and the night's ritual performance taxing. My own experience is similar. The bliss reported by various western experimenters is incomprehensible both to me and to my Navaho friends. The feeling of personal significance, the successful grappling with unpleasant feelings, the group experience, the vision as a communication with deity—all these are positive experiences for the cult member, but they do not make peyote consumption a simple hedonic gratification. The relief from care provided by opiates and alcohol has no precise analogue in the peyote experience. As for the belief that peyote is "addicting," and that people take it because they "crave" it, evidence fails to support the claim. The term "addiction" itself has enough meanings so that it must be used with some care here.[3] It is fair to say that, at least for legal purposes, addiction is usually defined so as to permit the labelling of a number of substances considered noxious and "habit-forming" in the society in question as addictive, and to permit the exclusion from that category of various substances which are socially accepted. We will here use not legal definitions, but definitions primarily suggested by the work of Lindesmith (1947).

1. We may speak of *physical dependence* when the use of a substance over a period of time results in physiological changes such that *withdrawal symptoms* of a characteristic sort make their appearance if the substance is not available. These symptoms manifest themselves whether or not the individual is aware that they are expectable, and whether or not he is aware that the substance is no longer supplied

[3] Maurer and Vogel supply and evaluate three definitions in their work on narcotic addiction (1954).

(as when placebos are administered). The opiates give rise to physical dependence.

2. We may speak of *addiction* when a person knows that removal of the substance creates withdrawal symptoms and that these are alleviated by new doses of the same substance. A patient who has been given opiates to the point of physical dependence and who suffers withdrawal symptoms when the opiates are removed, but who does not know the cause of the symptoms, is *dependent physically* but not addicted. The person who knows that the removal of opiates is responsible is *addicted*.

3. *Tolerance* involves a diminished effect of the same size dose over time, or correspondingly, the maintenance of effect only through larger doses. It is found characteristically with the opiates and with various other substances.

4. *Craving* will be residually defined as a strong and compulsive desire for the substance in the absence of addiction.

There is no evidence for physiological dependence, and therefore there can be none for addiction, in the case of peyote. The ordinary animal experiments which are used to discover whether physiological dependence will occur with various substances (e.g., new analgesics) have been performed with peyote, with no positive results (Seevers, 1954, p. 14). No case of withdrawal symptoms has ever been observed in a human being, in spite of some seventy years of hostile, if unsystematic observation.

There is some very mild tolerance in the case of peyote. Repeated use over short periods of time seems to reduce nausea, for example. Peyotists themselves comment on this, although they believe that this is because they have been purged of their sins or of the causes of their disease in the first of a series of peyote meetings, and therefore do not suffer so much subsequently. This effect is transitory; abstinence removes it (Seevers, personal communication). The issue of addiction is discussed further in the appendix on health.

As for craving, subjective evidence is against it. As one long-time user of peyote said to me, "I understand a craving for cigarettes, a craving for coffee, but that is not what I feel toward peyote." All my efforts to elicit statements indicating craving failed, with this and with other informants.

Indeed, the pattern of use for peyote is not what would be expected with dependency, addiction, or craving. Use is typically highly irregular, and amounts consumed are highly variable. Men in their twenties, thirties, and forties seem sometimes to want to discover the power of peyote—or indeed as it were to duel with peyote to discover whether its power can overmaster them. Under these circumstances they may consume 40–60 buttons at a single meeting of 9–12 hours. In later years they content themselves with more modest doses. The figures commonly mentioned by informants range from 2 to 16 buttons at a meeting, and more buttons are considered a large dose. There are rare and questionable reports of consumption of 100 to 200 buttons at a time. There is no evidence in any case I have encountered of gradually increasing dosage, such as would indicate tolerance. In one Navaho community there is a group of peyotists who believe that one should eat peyote every day. But questioning revealed that few did so. When they were asked why, their casual reply was that it was not easily available in such quantities. There, too, there was no indication of craving; only of a firm belief that this procedure was desirable. Nor had any of these frequent users tended to increase their dosage over time.

On the basis of the experimental, observational, and field data now available, therefore, there is no basis for assuming that peyote creates physiological dependence, that it is addicting, or that it is the subject of compelling craving. There is some mild tolerance, a point which has pharmacological rather than policy implications. The peyote cult, it must be said, is not a religious mask for addictive behavior.[4]

In sum, peyote is not taken for simple, pleasurable kicks; it is not taken because the individual is unable to refrain from doing so, either from addiction or craving; it is taken because it supplies a feeling of personal significance which vastly heightens religious experience in the peyote meeting, because it supplies evident proof that something is being done to and for the human organism, and because it is felt to be a "power." We may now turn from peyote itself to the peyote ritual.

RITUAL

The ritual of the peyote cult lasts all night. For the believer, it involves communication with God and communion with his fellow worshippers. Prayer, song, drumming, and the eating of peyote are all regarded as forms of communication with God, and the peyote experience is thought to permit communication from Him—through reflection, illumination, or visual or auditory hallucination. But there is also communion with humans: in the joint eating of peyote at various points, in the drinking of water together at midnight and in the early morning, and in the ceremonial breakfast which closes the meeting. Furthermore, a peyote meeting must be held "for a purpose"—to cure, to avert evil, to promote future good, to thank God for past blessings. And it is the joint efforts of all those present through their prayers which may bring the meeting to accomplish this purpose. This, then, is the general atmosphere of a meeting. A full account of a Navaho peyote ritual will be presented in a later chapter. Here a short outline must suffice.

The participants assemble at about sundown to enter a round dwelling, in which the meeting is ordinarily held. Three or four major officiants are required: a road chief, who conducts the meeting, a drummer chief, who does much of the drumming, a fire chief, who tends the fire, and usually a cedar chief, who sprinkles dried cedar incense on the fire at some points.

Almost any one can learn the roles of drummer, fire, or cedar chief after a little observation. A road chief is trained more elaborately by another road chief.

The road chief, cedar chief, and drummer chief sit together opposite the door. In front of them is a raised crescent moon of earth, the altar, and on it is placed an especially fine peyote button, the chief peyote, which is not eaten, and which should be the focus of concentration in praying, singing, drumming, and smoking ritual cigarettes; it serves as a center for communication with God. The fire chief

[4] Peyote is sometimes called a "drug" or a "narcotic," and the anthropologist is asked why the Indian "takes drugs" or is permitted to take a "narcotic." These words vary enough in their legal, medical, and every day use so that endless confusion results from discussing peyote in those terms. C. Barber, however, takes a different position regarding the word "narcotic" (C. Barber, 1959). Questioners who speak of "drugs" and "narcotics" are usually asking whether peyote is a bad thing for the mind or body. This question is taken up elsewhere.

sits at the north side of the door. After a prayer which announces the purpose of the meeting, and private prayers by all, peyote is passed round and eaten. Singing and drumming begin, continuing until about midnight, when there is special ritual by the road chief and others, and a bucket of water is brought in and passed round, after prayers by various officiants. After midnight water, singing and drumming recommence, and specially prepared peyote is supplied to the person for whose benefit the meeting is being run. He and others offer lengthy prayers at this time. (Peyote is passed round at intervals through the night, and in some meetings road chiefs permit people to eat peyote they have brought, as well as to use the general supply.)

A morning water interval is like that at midnight and is followed by more singing and drumming, and often by prayers by various members of the group—for the patient or for themselves, or both. More singing and drumming is followed by a ceremonial breakfast of corn, meat, fruit, and water. The meeting closes a little after dawn. Sometime between about ten in the morning and one in the afternoon a large meal is served to all present.

During the night, there may be interpretation of the meaning of the cult or the ritual. In the morning, there may be discussion of the night's events and experiences, and often there is a good deal of joking. Some 9–12 hours, then, are spent in eating peyote, praying, singing, drumming, and acts of communion. Meetings have impressed all observers, from Mooney in the 1890's on, with the care and seriousness which characterize them.

A full treatment of symbolism must wait for a later chapter. Suffice it to say that the objects of peyote ritual are simple—a staff, rattles, fans, crescent moon altar, sage, cigarettes, and so on. They are endowed with multiple meanings, some widely shared, some private, but in general they seem to stand for the natural order, to express man's embeddedness in nature, and to stand for the moral order as well.

BELIEFS AND VALUES

For an account of the beliefs and values of peyotism, our best source is probably the writings of J. S. Slotkin, an anthropologist, whose book, *The Peyote Religion* (1956), was written when he was an official of the Native American Church of North America. He states that no "officially promulgated Peyotist doctrine can be presented, for the religion is relatively individualistic" (1956, p. 68), but points out that his account was "reviewed by all officers" of the church (*loc. cit*). I shall quote in part, since the statement is brief, but summarize in part, especially where Slotkin deals with variations in belief. I have corrected a few minor misprints without comment.

"Peyotist doctrine . . . consists [in] a belief in the existence of power, spirits, and incarnations of power. . . . [Power] is an immaterial and invisible supernatural force, which produces characteristic effects in things influenced by it, and can be transferred from one thing to another under the proper ritual conditions. Man needs power in order to be successful and healthy; without it he becomes unsuccessful and ill. . . .

"Spirits are immaterial personifications of power. The Peyotist pantheon consists of what may be called White and Indian spirits" (1956, pp. 68–69). White spirits include the Trinity, devils, who play a minor role, and angels. Indian spirits include

Waterbird, Peyote, and, in various tribes, various traditional spirits which are not in fact part of the central peyotist tradition. God, who is equated with the Great Spirit, is the "ultimate source of all power" (*loc. cit.*). Jesus' role is variable—sometimes equated with the traditional culture hero, sometimes an intercessor between God and man, and sometimes a symbol of a rejected man caring for the rejected Indian. Tribes vary in their beliefs on these points. The Holy Ghost is vaguely conceived.

Peyotists are more likely to think of devils as being evil spirits who harm people than of *the* devil as the source of evil and of temptation. The conception is not universal in any case. Angels, sometimes thought of as Indian and sometimes as whites in flowing robes, with wings, may be conceived of as "nature spirits, guardian spirits, intercessor spirits, or messenger spirits . . ." (1956, pp. 69–70).

The Waterbird is identified both with Thunderbird, the bringer of rain, and with the dove, as symbol of the Holy Ghost or of peace. It is also a messenger between man and God.

"In many tribes Peyote itself is personified as Peyote Spirit. Some tribes conceive of Peyote Spirit as generally similar to the guardian spirit aspect of Jesus in White Christianity; he is a compassionate being, always benevolent, sympathetic, and helpful. Other tribes conceive of Peyote Spirit as a messenger spirit between man and God" (1956, p. 70).

"Incarnations are material embodiments of power" (*loc. cit.*). Peyote, chief among these, "was given to the Indians by God because he took pity on them for being a subject people—poor, weak, helpless, and ignorant. . . . God made the Peyote cactus . . . , and put some of his power into it, in order to help the Indians. Therefore when one eats peyote he absorbs the power inherent in it, which he can then utilize. Thus it is a sacrament like . . . bread and wine . . . which are consumed in order to absorb the Holy Spirit inherent in them" (*loc. cit.*). In the perspective of the peyotist, the capacity of peyote to produce special psychological and physiological effects is based on (Slotkin says "consists of") the power within the peyote. Eating peyote results in the absorption of this power with corresponding effects on the user's spiritual and physical condition.

The midnight and morning water is the second most important incarnation of power. "Water is needed by all living things, and therefore all water is sacred. In addition, the water used in the rite is prayed over and 'blessed,' so that it acquires additional power. The morning water is particularly sacred because it is brought in, and prayed over, by the wife or other close female relative of the leader. She represents womanhood as the source of life (she symbolizes 'the mother of us all'), and in some tribes also Peyote Woman to whom the rite was revealed" (1956, pp. 70–71).

The foods served at the morning communion breakfast are also incarnations of power, representing the basic foods necessary for life.

"The Peyotist ethical code constitutes a way of life called the 'Peyote Road,' and conforming to the ethic is 'following the Peyote Road.' This ethic has four main parts. . . .

"(a) Brotherly love. Members should be honest, truthful, friendly, and helpful to one another. This is conceived as a spelling out of the Golden Rule.

"(b) Care of family. Married people should not engage in extra-marital affairs, and should cherish and care for one another, and their children. Money should be spent on the family as a whole, rather than selfishly.

"(c) Self-reliance. Members should work steadily and reliably at their jobs, and earn their own living.

"(d) Avoidance of alcohol. There is a maxim, 'Peyote and alcohol don't mix'" (1956, p. 71).

The Peyote Road is learned by informal indoctrination by older members, by formal preaching during rituals—in some tribes—and by revelation or reflection resulting from eating peyote, which is itself a teacher. Thus peyotists say, "Peyote enlights your heart and mind" (1956, p. 71).

The ethical code is supported by certain supernatural sanctions. "If a person follows the Peyote Road faithfully—with Peyote always ready to guide, help, and comfort him on the way—it will lead him to tranquillity in this life (and such material goods as health, long life, and the well being of children and grandchildren), and bliss in the next world (in association with his loved ones and God)" (1956, p. 71).

Although Slotkin does not mention them at this point, there are negative sanctions as well: a person who lapses morally will suffer in the peyote meeting, both spiritually and physically, nausea being a sign of punishment in the views of many believers. Hell plays little or no part in peyotist cosmology.

There are certain other points which Slotkin deals with in other connections which deserve treatment here. Slotkin emphasizes the belief that peyote is a power. In the view of the believer, it is a power which can produce a variety of tangible results: It can cure, bring good fortune, and ward off misfortune. I am reasonably certain that although believers do not think that it punishes by misfortune, at least it can withdraw protection from a person who does not behave properly, so that he is more vulnerable to illness and bad luck. It can also provide illuminations—through revelation or reflection—as to the causes of ill health or misfortune, and can induce a man to reflect on, and to alter an evil course of life. It can, as Slotkin points out, teach one—make one truly realize—the significance of one after another characteristic of the Peyote Road. "You can use Peyote all your life, but you'll never learn all there is to know about Peyote" (Slotkin, 1956, p. 76, quoting a stock phrase). Peyote permits communication with God. And it supplies information about the world, equal or superior to scientific truth. In sum, as one Indian woman said, peyote is "the comfort, healer, and guide of us poor Indians" (1956, p. 77).

Let us examine the appeal of this ideology. Perhaps the most striking thing about peyotism, in contrast with all but a few American Indian nativistic movements, is its durability. Of various Plains movements, it is the sole survivor, and only the Shaker Church and the Handsome Lake cult have a longer pedigree. Slotkin feels that its survival is to be attributed to the fact that it is a religion of accommodation—that it does not attempt to alter white-Indian relationships by force or supernatural power, whereas, for example, the Ghost Dance did seek for a supernatural change of the Indian's situation. This is true and important, in the sense that a militant religion could not have survived in the context of overwhelming white dominance. But Slotkin does not limit his view of the appeal of peyotism to this characteristic, and neither shall I, although my ideas on this subject were developed in

partial independence of his and will be set forth here without detailed comments
about correspondences and divergences.

There are certain chronic features of the contact situation faced by American
Indians from early reservation days to the present, which make peyotism an ideology of perennial appeal.

First, peyotism is a reasonable response to degraded status. Although American
Indians are by no means at the bottom of the American ethnic pyramid, they do
not occupy an enviable position in any perspective except that of those below them
in the pyramid. Individual Indians may become assimilated and receive recognition,
provided that they accept the values of the dominant majority, have educational
attainments, lack the cultural diacriticals which would identify them as Indian. In
this process of mobility, they are aided if their appearance, through genetic accident or admixture, resembles that of the white majority. Indian reservation populations, however, are subject to the full impact of invidious comparison, as are lower-
class enclaves in towns and cities. Peyotism supplies a goal of internal peace and
harmony, rather than competition or conflict, and provides a tight reference group
of other peyotists, within which approval and esteem can be sought. It also promises
ultimate heavenly rewards. Finally, it provides special gifts which compensate for
the Indian's lack of status and privilege. If the white man has the Bible and his
church, the Indian has direct access to God. If the white man has learning, the
Indian has revelation. Peyotism, then, provides mystical paths to knowledge equal
or superior to those enjoyed by the majority.

Second, peyotism supplies an ethical code peculiarly relevant to the Indian's
socio-economic situation. However much this situation has varied over time for the
same group, or varies for different tribes or sub-groups within tribes, it has had
certain constancies since the 1890's at least on the Plains and in other areas as well
today.

In brief, the Indian's economic situation is one in which both economically and
normatively he is torn between collectivism and a qualified individualism, while at
the same time he is threatened with anomie. Before conquest, the economy of
American Indian groups was based on some combination of communalism in the
family group and reciprocity and redistribution at the supra-familial level. Market
relationships were important external economic ties in many cases, but accumulation within the tribe was always ultimately in the service of status-maintaining acts
of generosity or conspicuous distribution—not in the service of still further profit, a
term meaningless in these tribal economies (see Polanyi et al., 1957, esp. pp. 243–
270 for definitions and discussion). Norms were supported in considerable part by
group approval and withdrawal of support, as well as by private justice.

After conquest and confinement to reservations, however, the Indian was under
some pressure to become individualistic. By providing jobs, artisan training, and
increasingly in the Plains, at least, individual farming allotments, the Indian Service
put pressure on the Indian to separate his economic fate from that of his fellow
tribesman and enter the market economy as farmer and as laborer. (This was not
true during the Collier administration and its immediate aftermath, 1933–1950.
Efforts to renew collective organization were a feature of Collier's policy.)

There were, however, certain major obstacles to individuation, variable in intensity from place to place. Sometimes—indeed, often—the farm land was marginal. The jobs offered minimal security, as is characteristic for ethnically marginal members of the American community, for reasons of education, and because of the prejudices of the dominant majority. These were external obstacles. There were internal ones as well. The impulse to cut one's self off from the Indian community was minimal so long as inalienable land was held by the tribe, and minimal for individuals who held such land in trust patent. It was also minimal so long as goods or services accrued or might accrue to those who maintained tribal membership: hospitalization, schools, issue, relief, per capita payments for resources or for successful suits, tribal loan funds, and so on.

Furthermore, insecure in relationship to the job or farm market, the Indian had to pay heed to the demands made on him for aid if he did accumulate. Now his accumulation could be invested, spent on such things as farm machinery, or used for the benefit of his children. But these possibilities competed only with difficulty with the needs for assistance of his less fortunate kinsmen and tribesmen. His own insecure position suggested that he might need assistance from the same sources in his turn. In spite of economic and political ties with the larger society, he lived in something very like a closed corporate community (Wolf, 1955).

Nevertheless, within this community, with the breakdown of most of the traditional structures which had regulated supra-familial life, there was a breakdown in morality which, in the past, had depended on group pressures mediated by these structures. There were tendencies, aggravated by multifarious frustrations and uncertainties, toward egocentric hedonism as respects work, sexual behavior, and indulgence in indiscriminate expenditure or excessive drinking. It could be argued that "laziness," extravagance, and excessive drinking were also products of a situation where what was accumulated could not, in any case, be enjoyed, but was dispersed to kin and friends. Be that as it may, it is quite clear that the breakdown in morality was not merely a threat from the point of view of white moralists, but a threat from the point of view of the Indians as well.

The peyote code, as Slotkin formulates it, seems to me to represent a delicate adjustment between individualism on behalf of one's family and collectivism. One should *care* for one's family and *help* fellow members (but not necessarily kinsmen). It is also responsive to a need for internalized sanctions, in its demands for honesty, truth, friendship, and temperance. Finally, it is attuned to the place of the small farmer and the laborer in a market economy in its demands for steady and reliable work and self-support. It seems to afford the possibility of a group within which families have different economic fates and yet retain an ethic of partial mutual support.

The third great appeal of peyotism is its polyvalent character. This, it seems to me, is another factor which accounts for its appeal to tribes over time, and to new tribes living under conditions rather unlike those of the tribes from which they adopted the cult. For some individuals, it can be primarily a religion of miraculous curing; for others, one of special and transcending knowledge; for still others, an incentive to work; and to yet others, a release from guilt. And this is merely a part of its multiple appeals. Indeed, two generations in the same family might attend meetings for somewhat different reasons, and both might be amply satisfied. The ritual itself, with its obviously Indian and its Christian features, is similarly multi-faceted. This polyvalent character is also found in Shakerism and the Handsome Lake cult, but not in some of the more transitory nativistic movements known in North America.

ORGANIZATION

Thus far we have dealt with what Slotkin calls "modern peyotism" as a fully developed religion. Before we can discuss its organization, some comments must be made as to its origin and spread. I will largely follow Slotkin in this matter, but with some use of La Barre (1938), especially for the early history of the use of peyote. In brief, peyote had been used by Mexican Indians for many centuries in the area where peyote grows, for divination, in pursuit of trance, for power, and probably for other supernatural aims, with some associations with the dance. Its use spread to certain Plains groups (Kiowa, Kiowa Apache, and Comanche), probably from certain Gulf tribes and from various Apacheans, some of whom may have been influenced by Gulf tribes.[5]

The origin of the ritual—as described quite consistently from Mooney's accounts in the 1890's (e.g., Mooney, 1897) to most recent descriptions—is unknown. Stewart (1948) suggests that it may have stabilized in Old Mexico, whereas Slotkin prefers a Plains origin. The ritual now crystallized with minor variations as *the* peyote ritual may have arisen before the modern cult; it certainly arose either before or with it, and not subsequently. The date of origin of the cult also remains unknown. Slotkin guesses that ritual and cult had taken on their essential characteristics by 1885, and were probably invented by Comanche or Kiowa Indians at the Kiowa, Comanche, and Wichita Agency. This guess seems perfectly sensible.

Wherever it originated, the peyote *cult* departed from earlier uses of peyote in its pan-Indian and nativistic character. There is some question whether it had Christian elements at this time. At least by 1892 Christian elements were present (Slotkin, 1956, p. 44).

Its spread in this new form was rapid. A minimum of 16 tribes are documented as having the cult by 1899, and an additional 61 had been added by 1955 (Slotkin, 1956, pp. 36–40). Peyotism reached from Alberta, Manitoba, and Saskatchewan to New Mexico, Arizona, and California, and from Wisconsin to Idaho and Nevada by 1955 (*loc. cit.*). The percentage of members varies greatly from tribe to tribe.

We will not here attempt to account for this variability, nor for the limits of spread at present. It is evident, however, that peyotism had enormous viability and appeal. It started on a small reservation in Oklahoma some 70-odd years ago and has touched at least 77 tribes—more than a tribe a year—in the United States and Canada in the interval. This appeal we have tried to locate in the peyote experience, in the polyvalent appeal of peyotism, and in its utility for Indians in a special socio-economic niche.

---

[5] Slotkin lists 29 theories or traditions of the origins of the modern cult—that is, the present ritual and ideology of peyotism—and concludes that these afford no reliable base for inferring its origin. This is true enough as regards the origin of the modern cult, but the convergence of many of these theories on Gulf and Apachean groups makes me think that the *use* of peyote spread to Oklahoma from these groups, even though the cult proper probably developed on the Kiowa, Comanche, and Wichita Agency. Cf. Slotkin, 1956, pp. 28–34.

It would, however, be a serious mistake to think of peyotism as merely "spreading," like a flow of oil. It met bitter opposition from the beginning, and opposition continues today. Peyotism has been and is opposed by traditionalist Indians, modernist Indians, and whites. The details of opposition will be reserved for a discussion of the Navaho case. Broadly speaking, traditionalists oppose it as a threat to traditional tribal culture, modernists oppose it as a combination of "heathenism" and misunderstood Christianity, and as backward, and so do whites. All three oppose it on the assumption that the consumption of peyote has evil effects, to wit: disease, death, sexual immorality, laziness, intoxication, mental disease, malformed or stillborn infants, and addiction. To date none of these claims has been substantiated by observations under properly controlled conditions.

Opposition has taken three primary forms: talk, unofficial harassment, and legal efforts. The first efforts at suppression date from 1888, in the form of arbitrary action by an agent; first organized efforts by the Indian Bureau in the absence of specific legislation began in 1908; and first efforts at federal laws against peyote commenced in 1907. No general law forbidding the use of peyote has ever been passed, but there are laws permitting the incarceration of peyote or mescaline addicts and making them eligible for treatment at United States Public Health Service Hospitals for narcotic addicts, although no one has ever entered a U.S.P.H.S. Hospital on this account (Maurer and Vogel, 1954, p. 114). From 1917 to 1940, there was a law forbidding the shipment of peyote through the mails (Slotkin, 1956, p. 56). The Bureau of Indian Affairs adopted a policy of non-interference with peyotism in 1934 under John Collier (Slotkin, 1956, p. 55). A good many state laws have been passed forbidding the sale, use, or possession of peyote, beginning in 1899 in Oklahoma. There was a rash of such laws in the period 1917–1923, when no less than 9 states enacted them. In recent years, however, the laws against peyote have been repealed in Oklahoma, Utah, Iowa, Texas, and New Mexico.

So far as I know, enforcement was no more than sporadic in any of the states which have, or have had, laws: Arizona, California, Idaho, Iowa, Kansas, Massachusetts, Montana, Nevada, New Mexico, North Dakota, Oklahoma, Texas, Utah, and Wyoming (Slotkin, 1956, p. 56, except for California and Massachusetts, which he fails to mention).

Only a few tribes, so far as I know, have enacted formal tribal legislation against peyotism. One is Taos Pueblo (Cohen, 1942, pp. 394–395). The White Mountain Apache Tribal Council passed an anti-peyote ordinance (No. 6, Law and Order Code, Ch. 5, Sec. 33), approved by the Secretary of the Interior on August 26, 1938 (Bureau of Indian Affairs files). The Tribal Council of the Colorado River Agency expressed itself as opposing the use of peyote on its Reservation on March 27, 1951, when an issue arose because some Navahos with farming allotments at Parker, Arizona, had peyote in their houses. Although a motion forbidding the use of peyote on that Reservation was suggested, no record of the motion can be found (Bureau of Indian Affairs files). And several Sioux reservations in the Dakotas have passed laws against peyote (Hurt, n.d.).

Slotkin considers that the first association of peyotist local groups began as part of the pan-Indian nature of peyotism and in connection with peyotist missionary activities. At any rate, a loose organization existed, covering several states, as early as 1906. Subsequently, however, defense against opposition became the primary interest. The Mescal Bean Eaters of 1906 changed its name in 1909 to the Union Church; from at least 1911 there was a Peyote Society, which may have been the Union Church renamed or a new organization. Local incorporation began in Oklahoma in 1914, with Koshiway's Firstborn Church of Christ. Directly connected with intensive Bureau efforts to pass a law against peyote was the formation of the Native American Church, partly stimulated by the advice of James Mooney, the anthropologist and first ethnographic recorder of the ritual. This was an Oklahoma organization, incorporated in that state. Incorporation, state-wide and local, followed in many other states, beginning in 1921 and continuing today. The pattern has spread to Canada, where a Saskatchewan church was incorporated in 1954. Oklahoma articles of incorporation were amended to permit the affiliation of out-of-state branches in 1934, so that a national organization achieved some formal status. Further changes in the Oklahoma articles of incorporation followed, with a change of name to The Native American Church of the United States in 1944. "At the end of 1946 a split arose in Oklahoma between the proponents of the national organization and those interested solely in state matters. The state group obtained the 1918 charter, which they amended in 1949 back to the original name of 'Native American Church.' The national group incorporated as 'The Native American Church of the United States' in Oklahoma in 1950, changed to 'The Native American Church of North America' in 1955" (Slotkin, 1956, p. 62; other data from *op. cit.* pp. 57–62). The most recent change of name is in response to the existence of Canadian peyotists.

"At present the international organization is a very loose federation. . . . Not all Peyotist groups are affiliated. Some affiliates are state organizations, others are denominational associations (i.e., based upon some Peyotist variant), and many are local groups.

"The current policy of the international officers . . . is to keep the organization a loose confederacy as is traditional to Indians. Its purpose is conceived to be the means of effective interaction between all Peyotist groups in North America, so that information can be transmitted, decisions reached, and collective action taken, in a coordinated manner. Only by such a combined and organized defense will Peyote be saved for the Indian" (Slotkin, 1956, p. 62).

The Native American Church of North America and its predecessors have, then, been quite loosely organized. At times there are dues drives; at times there are none. At times there are membership cards, and at others none are issued. The looseness and lack of definite structure is, however, no impediment to collective action in opposition to anti-peyotist activities. It serves under these conditions to channel information, collect funds, supply witnesses, provide petitions, and so on. Since there is no organized priesthood, since attendance at a particular meeting is a matter of local and kinship ties and of occasions, since there is no official creed, a more formal organization is unnecessary and redundant. The function of worship, reflection, revelation, and cure can all be handled by local road chiefs in local meetings. Peyotism has not been marked by numerous schisms; if "we all worship the same God and all eat peyote," this is sufficient.

On the other hand the formality of incorporation does provide the organization with a suitable dignity and legal status to act in opposition to legal machinery. If the ethic of peyotism is a response to the socio-economic condition of Indians, the organization of peyotism is a response to opposition between peyotists on the one hand and whites, modernist Indians, and traditionalists on the other. This, and not the regulation of belief or ritual (both subject to revelation, in any case), is its primary function.

This background regarding peyote, peyote ritual, peyote ideology, and peyote organization serves to show what kind of phenomenon was imported to the Navaho in the 1930's. We may now turn to the history and condition of the Navaho tribe.

Part II

THE NAVAHO

Chapter 3

THE NAVAHO: THE BEGINNING TO 1932

THIS BOOK will take the position—not entirely novel—that nativistic cults originate in experiences of relative deprivation engendered by the domination of one group by another which possesses an alien and more powerful culture. Similarly, when one group accepts a nativistic cult developed in another group, the same sorts of experience promote this acceptance. Finally, the type of movement which is engendered or accepted depends on the nature of the relationship of the subordinate group with the superordinate one, and particularly on the degree of involvement of the members of the subordinate group with the larger social system of which this group is a part. The details of this theoretical position are set forth elsewhere in this work. But within this theoretical context, it becomes important to inspect the conditions of life of the Navahos immediately before peyotism began to spread among the Navahos to see if significant deprivations occurred. This will be done in subsequent chapters. It is also important to examine the earlier history of the Navahos for signs of past deprivations or the absence of such deprivations, especially since the Navahos have been fairly free of nativistic movements in the past. It is necessary to examine the political and economic involvement of the Navaho social system with the larger society. Finally, it is necessary to understand the culture and social organization of the Navahos over time, to see what kind of cultural system it was that accepted peyotism.

These topics will be discussed in rather more detail than is sometimes done in presentations of materials on nativistic movements. The reasons for this are twofold: first, my conviction that whether or not the particular theory presented in this book is valid, these movements are almost unintelligible without historical and contemporary background information; and second, my recognition that it is extremely difficult to piece together this background where it is not supplied. If it has taken me months of work to assemble these data, it would presumably take others an equal amount of time. Hence a book on Navaho peyotism without this information, however intriguing, would be sadly deficient, except for people who already know this background: many Navahos, some officials and ex-officials of the Bureau of Indian Affairs, some traders and missionaries, and a few anthropologists.

This chapter begins with a short account of the early history and development of the Navahos, prior to their conquest in 1863. It then examines their post-conquest political organization, administration, economic life, kinship organization, and religion. The major source used for Navaho history from 1868 to the turn of the century is the Reports of the Commissioner of Indian Affairs. Biased and limited though the reports of agents to the Navaho may be, they afford an annual account of events and have value for tracing trends. Underhill's histories (n.d. and

1956) are valuable, and McNitt's book on traders in the Southwest (1962) contains materials elsewhere unreported on relations with agents and on violence.

EARLY NAVAHO HISTORY, TO 1868

The Navaho Indians are an Athabaskan-speaking group inhabiting a large tract of semi-arid country in Arizona, New Mexico, and Utah.[1] They numbered 70,000 or more during the period of this study and occupied a reservation of 23,500 square miles, and individual holdings of unknown size in northwestern New Mexico adjacent to the reservation.

The Apacheans arrived in the Southwest perhaps by A.D. 1000, entering the area as hunters and gatherers, organized in bands. To judge from the present slight dialect differentiation of the Apacheans, the Navahos did not then represent a discrete cultural unit. For at least 500 years, Navaho life has been characterized by rapidly changing conditions. The Navahos learned agriculture from the Pueblos, and religious practices as well. Borrowing was expedited by the Pueblo revolt of 1680, which led many Pueblo Indians to live with the Navahos. Probably the matrilineal clans of the Navaho developed in connection with agriculture, as a way of controlling small nucleated areas of land suitable for farming, and were localized and somewhat organized, like Western Apache clans. Since the Pueblos had occupied the bulk of the large nuclei of such suitable land, Navaho holdings could not, in most areas, develop into the large villages characteristic of the Pueblos. Conversion to agriculture must have occurred before 1541 ± 20, when definite, dated Navaho archeological sites are found.[2] Hunting and gathering co-existed with agriculture.

Livestock entered Navaho economic life as early as 1606, probably both directly from the Spanish in New Mexico, and indirectly from the Spanish of Old Mexico via other Indian groups. Both channels of diffusion provided Spanish patterns of riding, equipment, and animal husbandry. Horses were probably acquired first and used in raiding and war. Sheep came only a little later. By the first half of the eighteenth century, Navahos had modest herds of horses, sheep, goats, and cattle. By the second half of the eighteenth century herds must have been of fair size, since the Navaho were said to be extensive weavers. By 1795 their herds were described as "innumerable." So in two centuries the Navaho moved from agriculture, hunting, gathering, and raiding to herding, agriculture, hunting, gathering, and raiding. Presumably they became more mobile, seeking pasture for their animals and depending relatively less on farming; probably the dispersed clan arose at this time, as well as the diffuse but organized local clan element, the major unit of supra-familial kinship organization.

By the mid-nineteenth century, the Navahos were stratified by wealth. There

[1] Substantiation for much of the information in this chapter is given in Aberle, 1961. Documentation will not be repeated here.

[2] Hall reports a Navaho hogan, the wood specimens from which are dated by dendrochronology from 1491+ to 1541 ± 20 (Hall, 1944, p. 100). I associate the hogan, with its suggestion of partial sedentarization, with agriculture, a point of view supported by Forbes, who believes that the Querechos met by Espejo in 1582 four leagues from Laguna were Navahos. They brought tortillas to the Spanish (Forbes, 1960, p. 57). Nevertheless, Dolores Gunnerson holds that the Apacheans did not arrive in the Southwest until about 1525 (Gunnerson, 1956). I find the sequence, arrival about 1525, semi-sedentary 1541, maize agriculture 1582, a bit swift—although conceivably these Querechos were not Navahos or if they were, were cooking traded maize.

were the rich, the poor, and the "thieves." The thieves were those who raided or threatened wealthy Navahos and Mexican farmers and ranchers in the Southwest. The Navahos were raided by Utes, Comanches, and Mexicans. They raided Mexicans and Pueblos. They lost children and adults as slaves to the Mexicans and captured children and adults who became their slaves, but whose descendants seem to have been free, if of low social status.

Although the United States assumed nominal control of the area in 1846, after the Mexican War, agents of the government remained no more than a source of supplies in the form of Government issues, for nearly two decades. By this time there were more than 8,000 Navahos, with no organized over-all polity, grouped under local headmen, some of whom had influence over several groups because of their personal qualities. Typically, these headmen were not war leaders and could not control members of their own groups who wanted to raid—much less warlike members of other groups. Hence treaties signed with these leaders did not bind their followers. There was a tendency for the rich to want peace and for the more energetic poor to favor raiding.

American efforts to punish Navahos for raiding were ineffective. The Navahos retreated into the less accessible mountains and canyons, with little loss of life or property. In 1863, Kit Carson led a successful effort to subjugate the Navaho and end raiding—although he remarked that they were suffering more from Mexican slave raids than they were offending by raiding. Carson destroyed crops and drove off livestock. The Navahos were told that if they did not wish to starve, they should come to Fort Sumner, a considerable distance to the east of the Navaho country. By 1864, 8,000 had made the trek. A number hid out under severe conditions in the mountains and canyons, perhaps especially along the San Juan in Utah. These holdouts have been estimated at anything from a handful to 5,000.

Life at Fort Sumner was intolerable for the Navaho and enormously expensive for the Americans. A treaty was signed in 1868, assigning the Navahos a reservation, binding them to maintain the peace, and promising certain benefits as respects land, issues of goods, and education. The Navahos never broke the terms of this treaty, except that—so far as can be judged by the Reports of the Commissioner—some Navahos lived outside the bounds of the reservation from the beginning. They returned in 1868 to the reservation and its environs,[3] were issued livestock in small quantities, and began to build a new life, still based on herding and agriculture, with less hunting as the years passed, no raiding worth mentioning, and increasing sales of silver, weaving, meat, and hides, and increasing use of the job market. Between 1863 and 1868, they had passed from prosperity and independence to the cramped, hungry, and unhealthy conditions of Fort Sumner, and on to the poverty and freedom of the return to Navaho land. We now turn to Navaho life from 1868 to 1936 in somewhat greater detail.

LAND

The Navahos were returned to a limited portion of the country in which they had lived. According to Royce, in 1854 the Navaho occupied the territory from

[3] Although anthropologists customarily refer to the trek to Fort Sumner or the return as "the long walk," Robert W. Young informs me that he has never heard a Navaho use this term.

the Rio Grande to the Colorado, bounded on the south by the Zuni River and on the north by approximately the 37th parallel. An unratified treaty of 1855 provided for cessions on the east: the boundary was to run along the San Juan and Canyon Largo, and from the source of Canyon Largo to the Zuni River, straight in a southwesterly direction. The western boundary provided by this treaty nearly bisected the present Arizona portion of the Navajo Reservation with a line running north northeast from the Zuni River. An unratified treaty of 1858 supplied an eastern boundary only slightly east of the limits of the 1868 reservation. This reservation was a simple rectangle bounded on the north by the Arizona and New Mexico northern boundary, on the east by a line passing through Canyon Bonito, and

MAP 1

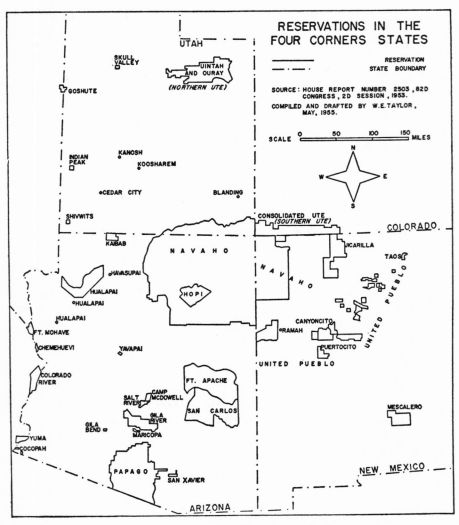

These maps reflect the situation as of 1951

MAP 2

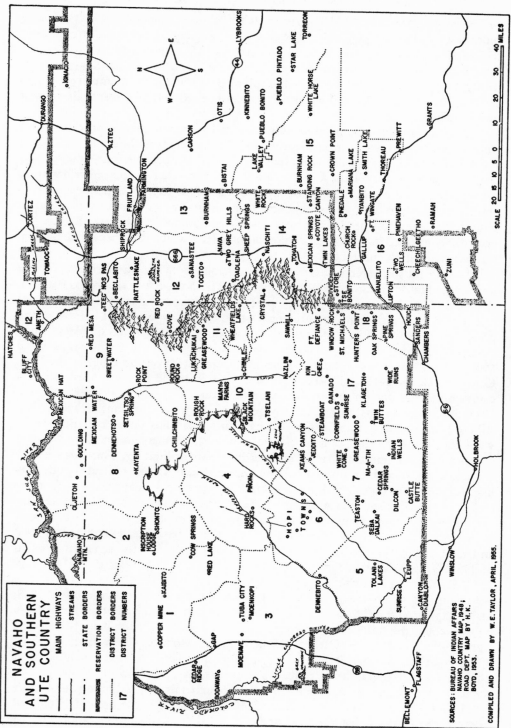

These maps reflect the situation as of 1951

on the west by the 109°30′ W. meridian. It was about 60 miles east to west and 85 miles north to south: about 5,100 square miles, by comparison with the present 23,500 square miles (Royce, 1899, pp. 848–851, Pls. CXI and CLI; the Navajo Land Claims case may be expected to shed further light on actual holdings prior to 1863). From the beginning the Navahos spilled over these borders into areas where settler pressure was low—and eventually began to meet settler pressure in the east and elsewhere.

If the Navahos had been effectively confined to the original reservation, this might have constituted a serious deprivation. As respects land, however, the Navaho situation differed radically from that of most other Southwestern tribes of any size. The holdings of all the Ute groups and all the other Apachean tribes were repeatedly reduced, and the entire group was often moved from one area to another (in law, if not always in fact). The Navahos, however, were assigned initially to a portion of their former territory—not to alien land—and were repeatedly confirmed in their control of additional land which they occupied. Seldom was the reservation contracted.

If we neglect some minor waverings and cessions from Navaho territory for the moment, additions took the following course. There were five accessions between 1878 and 1886. These supplied a large part of the territory between the boundaries of the 1868 reservation and the present western boundary and filled in most of the present northern boundary and virtually all of the present eastern boundary. They nearly quadrupled the initial holdings. Another group of four accessions between 1900 and 1907 mainly involved western extensions, with one addition in the Four Corners area. In 1913 and 1918, a small tract was added in New Mexico and a somewhat larger one on the extreme west, and three accessions between 1930 and 1934 filled out various corners and edges. This history of expansion can be attributed to several factors, in my opinion. First, Navahos occupied lands which were marginal from the point of view of American farmers and herders. Second, they utilized this land for farming and herding, not for hunting. Third, as we shall see, the Navaho country proved a disappointment in terms of mineral wealth—unlike, for example, the Black Hills. (Accessions based on Underhill, 1956, p. 149.)

The only major rollback suffered by the Navahos came after 1907. In that year the reservation was extended to the east to cover public lands in what is now "checkerboard" Navaho and white holdings. The extension was reduced in 1908 and cancelled in 1911. Efforts to restore some of this land to the reservation failed in 1936 (*Indian Affairs, Laws and Treaties*, pp. 669–670, 685; TNY 1961, pp. 258–262; *Survey of Conditions*, Part 34).

In sum, the greatest expansion occurred during the eighteen years after 1868; major expansion was blocked by 1911; but there were minor additions until 1934. Subsequently the tribe has purchased some land and Navahos have been given rights to cultivate land at Parker, Arizona, on the Mohave Reservation.

Nevertheless, the Navahos had reasons for apprehension about their lands at times and suffered transitory rollbacks at others. In 1874–1875 an agent tried to exchange a northern strip, supposedly rich in minerals, for extensions elsewhere (RCIA 1874, p. 307; McNitt, 1962, pp. 144–165). In 1882, the agent felt obliged to warn the Navaho that they might be expelled from their reservation (RCIA

1882, pp. 127–129). In 1884, a small strip of land east of Shiprock, importa[...] for irrigated agriculture, was removed from the reservation, but after some disturbance the area was restored in 1886 (RCIA 1886, p. L, for an accoun[...] disturbance). In 1896, a mineral lease was granted but was never worked [...] 1896, p. 39; 1897, p. 107). Lands added in northern Arizona and southern Utah in 1884 were partly withdrawn in 1892 and were not restored until 1933—although occupancy persisted. (All except the mineral lease are from Royce, 1899, pp. 916–917, 920–921, 944–945, and Pls. CX, CLII, and CLXVI; U.S. Laws, Statutes, etc. [1933].)

The area north of the San Juan in Utah has been subject to repeated negotiations and alterations. A cession in 1905 was cancelled the same year and other lands in the same general area were added; there was an addition in 1933 and exchanges of land in 1949. Undoubtedly there were many unrecorded efforts to achieve settlement for this area. (Exec. Order of March 10, 1905; Exec. Order of May 15, 1905; HR 11735, March 1, 1933; HR 53901, September 7, 1949.) There was a dispute between Navahos and whites over the use of public grazing lands in this area when this study was concluded in 1954. Navahos had suffered some violence.

There has been a long dispute with the Hopi over rights to the land around the Hopi towns. Whatever the pre-1868 occupancy, Navahos today live in large numbers on much of the Hopi Reservation established by Executive Order of December 16, 1882. (A 1962 decision has returned to the Hopi land now occupied by Navahos—Shepardson, 1963, p. 86; the Navahos are appealing the decision.)

There has been conflict with settlers over land: in 1882, when there was pressure from settlers and miners; in 1884, when two prospectors were killed; between 1884 and 1888, when the small corner of land south of the San Juan in New Mexico was under dispute; in 1889–1891, over mineral leases; in 1893, near Shiprock; in 1897, over lands in the Cohonino area in the west; in 1899, at Tuba City; in 1904, over grazing; and doubtless in many unrecorded instances. Conflict between Navahos and whites was probably endemic in the eastern off-reservation area as well (RCIA for relevant years).

The general trend of this history of expansion contrasts sharply with that for two groups of peoples with whom the Navahos retained contact: the Utes and Apaches. The various Apache tribes of New Mexico and Arizona experienced the beginning and end of seven reservations between 1860 and 1877, and the beginning and subsequent reduction of two others. Tribes were moved from one reservation to another, joined, separated, sent to Florida as prisoners of war, and so on. The Utes of Colorado and Utah suffered continuous reduction of territory and repeated relocation between 1856 and 1888, when they were more or less finally placed on two small reservations, one in northern Utah and one in southern Colorado. They had once ranged over most of Colorado west of the Rockies and a considerable part of eastern Utah (see Royce, 1899, and RCIA 1860–1893).

LIVELIHOOD

Navaho success with expanding tribal territory was paralleled by a reasonably good adjustment in the area of livelihood and an increasing population. Most of the trouble with livelihood for some decades was with agriculture. As for livestock, figures from 1868 to the mid-1930's are estimates and subject to rather wild fluctuations. Expansion of population must be discussed in connection with livestock holdings, since increased livestock does not always mean increased per capita holdings. The population was slightly under 10,000 in 1870, about 17,000 in 1890, over 25,000 in 1910, nearly 39,000 in 1930, nearly 68,000 in 1950, and over 90,000 in 1961 (based on research and estimates by Denis F. Johnston and TNY 1961, pp. 311–331).

In 1846, when the Americans first made contact with the Navahos, Calhoun estimated their stock at 500,000 sheep, 10,000 horses, burros, and mules, and 30,000 cattle. It took some years after the Fort Sumner captivity before the Navahos again reached this level.[4] After release from Fort Sumner, the Navahos spent some months at Fort Wingate en route to the reservation. They had only 1,965 small stock on hand (RCIA 1868, p. 165). Late in 1869, the Government distributed 15,000 small stock, or about two per capita (RCIA 1870, p. 145). In 1871, there were said to be 30,000 (RCIA 1871, p. 378). In 1872, the agent at Santa Fe reported that he had delivered 10,000 sheep to the Navaho in May, in lieu of a portion of their annuity—and that they now had 130,000 sheep (RCIA 1872, p. 296). The agent at Fort Defiance estimated 125,000 small stock at this time (RCIA 1872, p. 304), while a table in the Reports of the Commissioner lists 100,000 sheep (RCIA 1872, pp. 792–793). As in many subsequent years, one can speculate that perhaps goats were omitted from the table. A year later the agent at Santa Fe estimated small stock at 250,000; the agent at Fort Defiance, at 175,000; the RCIA table for that year also lists 175,000 (RCIA 1873, pp. 266, 272, table 80, insert between pp. 714 and 715). In 1874, the figure is 130,000 (RCIA 1874, p. 437). Quite apart from the discrepancies, this rate of increase is impossible. Either the estimates are in error or there were unrecorded issues of livestock. From 1869, when we know that the Navaho must have had between 15,000 and 20,000 stock, and the 1930's, when careful efforts at records began, it seems impossible to place reliance on published livestock figures.

There are no figures for 1875–1877; between 1878 and 1880 figures climb from 500,000 to 1,000,000 (RCIA 1878, pp. 802–803; 1879, pp. 115, 362–363; 1880, pp. 131, 390–391; in the *Navajo Agency Letter Book for 1880* the same agent, Bennett, estimates 1,500,000—TNY 1961, p. 146). This would supply between 66 and 100 sheep and goats for every man, woman, and child on the reservation, since the population was about 15,000 at this time, according to official figures.

Figures of about a million are entrenched from 1880 to 1884 (RCIA 1880, pp. 390–391; 1881, pp. 360–361; 1882, pp. 418–419; 1883, pp. 354–355; 1884, pp. 356–357; goats are apparently included in these figures).

In 1885, which was said to be a good year, the figure rises to 1,500,000 again (RCIA 1885, pp. 614–615). The years 1886–1888 demonstrate the problem of "where are the goats?" In his reports to the Commissioner, Agent Patterson supplies figures of 800,000 sheep and 300,000 goats; 750,000 sheep and 300,000 goats;

---

[4] Calhoun added that it was not rare for an individual to own 5,000–10,000 sheep and 400–500 head of large stock. But such holdings must have been rare unless Calhoun greatly underestimated the stock: it would have taken only 100 Navahos with holdings of 5,000 to make up the total estimated herd of 500,000. (Figures from TNY 1961, p. 145.)

800,000 sheep and 300,000 goats (RCIA 1886, p. 203; 1886, p. 171; 1888, p. 190). For two of these three years, 1886 and 1888, the goats are omitted in the tabular presentation of stock; in the middle year they are included (RCIA 1886, pp. 662–663; 1887, pp. 470–471; 1888, pp. 438–439). There is a slight drop in 1889 to 900,000 sheep and goats (RCIA 1889, pp. 522–523), carried forward in 1890 (RCIA 1890, pp. 472–473). But in 1891 and 1892, figures skyrocket—first to nearly 1,600,000 and then to more than 1,700,000—or in the neighborhood of 100 per capita (RCIA 1891, pp. 309, 776–777; RCIA 1892, pp. 802–803; p. 576 carries forward the 1891 figures). A year later the figures drop to 1,250,000 (RCIA 1893, 710–711), and are carried forward without change through 1899—from 1895 on, they are noted as taken from the previous year's report (RCIA 1894, pp. 586–587; 1895, pp. 582–583; 1896, pp. 538–539; 1897, pp. 498–499; 1898, pp. 616–617; 1899, pp. 582–583). In 1895, the agent notes that the figure is doubtless an over-estimate, since there was a great reduction in herds during the previous year (*loc. cit.*). In 1900, a new estimate appears—just over 400,000—after two bad years (RCIA 1900, pp. 658–659). The figures rise to 500,000 over the years 1901–1904 (RCIA 1901, pp. 708–709; 1902, 650–651; 1903, pp. 528–529; 1904, pp. 616–617). This would amount to about 18–23 per capita.

There are no tables from 1905 to 1911, and no complete tables until 1912. They then continue until 1920. These range from a high of over 1,800,000 (excluding Hopi) to a low of 1,100,000 (excluding Hopi). But the bulk of this change can be attributed to abrupt downward shifts of nearly 50 per cent for the Navajo (Southern Navajo) Agency, between 1915 and 1916, and the San Juan Agency, between 1915 and 1917. One might attribute these to war-time sales of meat, were it not that no such changes appear for the other reservations. (RCIA 1911, p. 223; 1912, pp. 252–253; 1913, pp. 223, 225; 1914, pp. 175, 177; 1915, pp. 189, 191; 1916, pp. 178, 181; 1917, pp. 184, 186; 1918, pp. 199, 201; 1919, pp. 189, 191, 192; 1920, pp. 180, 183.)

In connection with these dramatic shifts, it is worth commenting that in 1915, Peter Paquette, the agent for the Southern Navajo, carried out a livestock census, which showed just under 520,000 sheep and goats (TNY 1958, p. 375). His report to the Commissioner for that year showed 920,000, but in the following year he used the figure 520,000 (RCIA, *loc. cit.*). It seems safe to assume, therefore, that in 1915 he found a basis for changing his estimate.

Window Rock files supply a figure of 1,375,000 sheep and goats for 1927–28, but a note in the files states that these figures are dubious. For the period 1930–1932, just before reduction, figures of somewhere between 1,000,000 and 1,370,000 seem reasonable, the higher figures being based on dipping records (*Survey of Conditions*, Pt. 34, p. 17975; TNY 1961, p. 167). Presumably dipping records are likely to be underestimates, since some people avoid dipping—or did in the 1930's.

What is to be made of all this? It seems best to start with the most recent figures and work back. There must have been over a million small stock on the reservation in the early 1930's. At this time, when the reservation was badly overgrazed, there were about 29–33 small stock per capita (see below, Chapter 4). If Paquette's survey was indeed careful, and his family count of 2,400 equally so, then there were 38–43 small stock per capita in the Southern agency in 1915—allowing 5–5.5

members per family. The figures of 400,000–500,000 for the early 1900's, which allow for only 18–23 small stock per capita, seem far too low. Holdings of this order and smaller were realized during livestock reduction, but they caused anguish at the time, and it seems probable that the agent at the time was simply a low estimator.

On the other hand, the figures of 1,500,000 and upward for various years from 1880 on seem extraordinarily high, supplying, as they do, 75–100 per capita. And the rate of expansion from 1871 to 1873, and from 1874 to 1878, is simply impossible. It would seem to me probable that Navaho flocks reached and surpassed the optimum land-animal ratio by the 1880's, when comments on overgrazing first appear, but that the total herd kept growing rapidly through the 1880's as land was added. It seems possible that the herd reached a million or so by 1890, but it seems improbable that it ever exceeded a million and a half. This sort of growth pattern would allow for smaller herds than the published figures from the 1870's through the mid-1880's; it would disregard the peak estimates for 1885, 1892, and 1915; it would raise the figures for the early 1900's to something not too far below a million. From 1890 on, as population rose, per capita holdings probably levelled off and began to fall.

Any safer conclusions would have to be based on a study of the Navajo Agency Letter Books, which may contain information as to how estimates were made, and when—or whether—actual counts were carried out before Paquette's work in 1915.

It should be remembered that numbers of livestock are not a simple index of well-being. Once livestock sales began, increases might occur because of low prices, not merely because of good grazing conditions. Specifically, however, losses due to bad climatic conditions are recorded for 1874, 1882–83, 1888, 1893, 1895, 1899, and 1904. In 1881, stock failed to increase because of bad weather. There are many additional comments about dry weather which do not specifically mention stock. The first comment on overgrazing occurred in 1883; there were others in 1884 and 1892 (all from RCIA of the relevant years).

As in the days before Fort Sumner, livestock were distributed unevenly. On the Southern Navajo Reservation in 1915, for example, 24 per cent of families had no sheep; 42 per cent had less than 100, a meager holding today; 18 per cent had the modest holdings of 101–300; 14 per cent were well-to-do with 300–800; and 4 per cent could be called wealthy, with 800 or more (TNY 1958, p. 375; 2,400 families; percentages rounded).

Agriculture seems to have been a problem. In 1868, the Navahos could not plant because it was too late in the year when they arrived on the reservation. There was trouble with agriculture in fourteen years out of thirty-three between 1870 and 1902—drought, flash floods, frost, grasshoppers, and so on (Underhill, 1956, p. 167). RCIA reports of 1903–1906 have a similar story, and thereafter provide no information. Even in 1901 and 1902, livestock or no, rations were issued because of bad conditions (Underhill, loc. cit.). In 1883, the agent first mentions a need for irrigation. Efforts at water control by the Government apparently began in 1885. There was need also for stock water and hence for windmills (RCIA for relevant years).

Records on involvement in a cash economy are slim but show a clear trend. Sales of rugs are first mentioned, if ambiguously, in 1871. By 1873, they were definitely being sold. By 1880 there was a "considerable trade." In 1887, at least 1,800 blankets were sold, and in 1890, $24,000 worth (RCIA 1871, p. 367; 1873, p. 274; 1880, p. 131; 1887, p. 172; 1890, p. 162). Wool was being sold by 1876, and 800,000 pounds were marketed by 1880, although the railroad did not border the reservation for another year. Between 1886 and 1890, figures of three quarters of a million to a million pounds of wool are mentioned (RCIA 1876, p. 109; 1880, p. 131; 1886, p. 203; 1887, p. 172; 1888, p. 190; 1889, p. 256—no figure). In 1903–1906, sales of livestock, wool, and blankets rose from $500,000 to $1,000,000 (RCIA 1903, p. 126; 1904, p. 141; 1905, p. 167; 1906, p. 182). Amsden provides figures for blankets alone of $500,000 in 1913, $750,000 in 1923, and $1,000,000 in 1931 (Amsden, 1949, p. 182). There is little information on the value of silver or piñons sold.

Before 1898, the Reports of the Commissioner contain only casual comments on Navaho employment—work for the agency, work as teamsters, work with settlers. Between 1899 and 1903, there are reports of 300–400 men working on the railroad, but further systematic information is lacking. Apparently 1899 was the first year the railroads took on numbers of Navahos. Work in the beet fields is first mentioned in 1901. Undoubtedly employment rose steadily from 1899 on, with an acceleration during World War I (RCIA 1899, p. 157; 1900, p. 191; 1901, p. 180; 1902, p. 156; 1903, p. 125).

When we assay the livelihood situation of the Navaho for the years 1868–1932, several facts are prominent. First, unlike American Indian groups which depended mainly on hunting before conquest, the Navahos had a partly viable traditional technology to use on their return from captivity: farming, herding, and weaving. Raiding disappeared; hunting and gathering diminished; but sales of meat, wool, hides, blankets, silver, and piñons, and wages must have taken up a good deal of the slack as well as providing an opportunity to buy much-desired trade goods.

Livestock holdings must have shown some per capita decrease, on average, but the Navahos did not experience this loss as a result of American interference. There were wealthy and poor Navahos. Climatic fluctuations probably caused at least local hardship in some years. Involvement with the American economy steadily increased. No one source of livelihood was predictable from year to year. But all in all, no picture of severe deprivation emerges.[5]

POLITICAL ORGANIZATION, 1868–1907

The Reports of the Commissioner contain relatively little information on Navaho political organization, nor are other sources richer. Van Valkenburgh describes

[5] A better picture of Navaho livelihood will depend on future use of traders' records, diaries, and letters, and perhaps of the Navajo Agency Letter Books. Amsden provides no more, and McNitt little more information about the sheep, wool, blanket, and silver industries than is assembled here (Amsden, 1949; McNitt, 1962). McNitt and Underhill (1956) rightly insist on the importance of Navaho-trader relations. Traders were a major source for items of American culture, an enormous influence on the Navahos, often directed against the Government (and often rightly so), and through the system of pawn and credit a great incentive for production, and after the sheep were gone, for wage work.

a system far more structured than could be imagined from reading agents' reports —so much so that I am inclined to think that he has overformalized it. He reports that the head chief was selected by the agent and approved by the Secretary of Interior. Under him were regional leaders—*naat'áanii*, who received cards. In the event of some local fracas, the agent notified the head chief, who sent a notice to the local headman to come to the agency headquarters. There was a meeting of all local headmen and the head chief with the agent about once a year to discuss issues of tribal importance. This system was a residue of the administrative system at Fort Sumner. There were about thirty local leaders in 1900 (Van Valkenburgh as quoted in Shepardson, 1963, p. 78).

The picture which emerges from agents' reports is one of the gradual replacement of traditional leaders by police, courts, and the agent himself. At first there was an effort to formalize the organization, with twelve chiefs and ninety-four sub-captains, but no such clear-cut structure is mentioned after 1869. Government issue was of great importance in the early years. Apparently the agent wished to be the source of annuities and goods, whereas the chiefs' power flowed from their ability to control distribution of the goods to their followers. After 1877, there is no mention of the chiefs' role in distributing annuities. Although at first chiefs were coopted as policemen—quite early, in 1872—this system apparently collapsed in 1875 and new leadership came to the fore in the police force created about 1884. Comments about chiefs' lack of influence begin in 1870 and become more and more explicit. By 1889, the agent seems to have been an important force for the informal settlement of disputes. It may well be, however, that at the local level many disputes were adjudicated by headmen. The chiefs continued to play a representative role in external relations—negotiations about land—until 1888 or later, presumably because the American government had to deal with some individuals nominally capable of speaking for the tribe in such matters.

The police force seems to have been functioning adequately by 1885, and the court system was established in 1892. The chiefs were mentioned in RCIA for the last time in 1897. On the other hand, in 1892, Chee Dodge, an English-speaking Navaho, made his first appearance in official records—a new kind of leader, the person whose education makes it possible for him to mediate between his people and the outside world. By 1903, the agent reported that disputes were brought to him rather than settled among the Navahos themselves.

Thus, whereas it is highly probable that local leadership remained important, there was no development of a system of indirect rule. Far from it: the agent became the major superordinate political figure, and police and courts grew in importance (cf. Shepardson, 1963). The details of these changes are provided in Chart A, "Decline of Chiefs; Rise of Police and Courts."

This political change did not result in loss of well-defined native statuses for large numbers of people. Evidently certain major figures of influence, like Manuelito, suffered loss of status, but many informal leaders must have waxed and waned as in pre-conquest times. Nor does one get the impression, during these years, that the hand of the Government lay heavily on the Navahos in everyday affairs. But to round out the picture we must examine external relations and certain crises.

CHART A

Decline of Chiefs; Rise of Police and Courts

1868 Barboncito head chief, Ganado Mucho subchief for west, Manuelito for east (Underhill, n.d., p. 188).

1869 Chiefs intelligent, reliable (RCIA 1869, p. 531). Twelve "principal chiefs" and 94 "sub-captains" designated by chiefs (RCIA 1869, pp. 679–680), probably a paper organization (TNY 1961, p. 373), or one of very brief duration. Agent gives presents to sub-captains; says he will replace them if they do not support chiefs (RCIA 1869, p. 680).

First mention of need for police (RCIA 1869, p. 531).

1870 Barboncito d., Ganado Mucho head chief, Manuelito sub-chief (Underhill 1956, pp. 161–162). Chiefs have little influence (RCIA 1870, pp. 145, 150, 152). Goods issued pro rata, not through chiefs, who would fail to take care of half the people and make an unequal distribution for the rest (RCIA 1870, p. 148).

Further mention (RCIA 1870, p. 152).

1871 Chiefs advise agent (RCIA 1871, pp. 376, 378), decline to aid in rounding up stock thieves but accept agent's doing so with soldiers (RCIA 1871, p. 376).

Additional mention (RCIA 1871, p. 377).

1872 Chiefs and sub-chiefs meet Apache captains to make peace (RCIA 1872, p. 175).

Police force of 130 includes "all the principal chiefs of the tribe"; headed by Manuelito (RCIA 1872, p. 303).

1873

Force disbanded by Santa Fe superintendent over agent's protest; agent claims force success, controls stockraiding; chiefs cooperate when paid but unpaid would not (RCIA 1873, pp. 207, 273).

1874 Chiefs taken to Washington (Underhill 1956, pl. facing p. 81; see also discussion of Agent Arny below); discuss land questions

Force of 200 constituted, paid with annuity goods surplus (RCIA 1874, p. 306). Composition of this force not mentioned.

1876 Council of chiefs requests southern extension of reservation (RCIA 1876, p. 110).

1877 Twenty-six chiefs led by Manuelito are agent's main source of trouble. They attempt to control annuities and supplies and to prevent census which would allow issue to be regularized. Issue guarded, chiefs capitulate (RCIA 1877, p. 159).

1879 Council of 29 chiefs, sub-chiefs, and headmen request land on south and east (RCIA 1879, p. 116).

1880 Agent relies on chiefs, headmen, and peaceable Navahos to control restless young men (RCIA 1880, p. 133).

Agent authorized to create police force; pay too slim, none created (RCIA 1880, p. 133).

1881

Pay still too small (RCIA 1881, p. XX).

1882 Agent complains: no funds to entertain "my chiefs and their followings" when they stay overnight on monthly visits concerned with governing their "bands" (RCIA 1882, p. 128).

1883

Pay still too small (RCIA 1883, p. 121).

1884 Navahos lack "any political organization of their own. . . ." Their so-called chiefs amount to little; Ganado Mucho 75, feeble; Manuelito a drunkard and beggar without influence. Young, strong, progressive figures needed (RCIA 1884, p. 134).

Force of 15 police exists (RCIA 1884, p. 134).

1885
Force of 10, including "best and most influential young men of the tribe" who do their duty without "fear or favor" (RCIA 1885, p. 155).

1888 Agent calls council to meet special agent; a council requests land on south reaching to railroad (RCIA 1888, p. 191).
Police active (RCIA 1888, p. 192).

1889 Disputes referred to agent; advice of chiefs seldom sought and seldom accepted; influence of chiefs almost gone. Ganado Mucho 80, ill, but great influence for good (RCIA 1889, pp. 257–258). Agent speaks of 10 clans, each with a chief, further divided into bands (RCIA 1889, p. 256). This must be in error; no localized clans.
Force of 25 police headed by a Navaho adequate (RCIA 1889, p. 260).

1890 Dispute between Navahos and whites and subject of discussion at "all the councils of the older men, at their prescriptive gatherings" (RCIA 1890, p. 165). Three leading men to Albuquerque to see town and Indian Industrial school; returned "fully impressed with the greatness of the white man and fully believing in the importance of education" (RCIA 1890, p. 166).
Agent opposes Indian court—says it could not work because of clan partialities (RCIA 1890, p. 166).

1891
Force of 1 capt., 1 lieut., 14 pvts. too small (RCIA 1891, p. 310). Police successful in all later mentions (1892, p. 209; 1896, p. 113; 1897, p. 107; 1898, p. 123; 1903, p. 136—in the Navajo Extension).

1892 Agent attacked trying to send children to school; claims support by "best and leading Indians," including Chee Dodge (RCIA 1892, p. 156).
Court of Indian Offenses created (RCIA 1892, p. 200). Commended repeatedly thereafter (RCIA 1893, p. 111; 1894, p. 100; 1895, p. 118; 1896, p. 113; 1897, p. 107; 1898, p. 123; 1904, p. 145—in the Navajo Extension).

1893 Manuelito d. (Handbook of American Indians, Vol. 1, p. 803).

1894 Chiefs and leading men from all over sent to Chicago Columbian Exposition by private subscription; agent accompanies. They realize there are more whites than they believed and that war is impossible (RCIA 1894, p. 100).

1895 Twenty "most prominent chieftains of the tribe" oppose irrigation, fearing Ute raids or white expulsion if land improved (RCIA 1895, p. 26).

1897 Last mention of chiefs: chiefs and headmen exert good influence (RCIA 1897, p. 107).

1901 "Council" of 400 people (RCIA 1901, p. 180).

1903
Navahos unable to settle their problems as regards land, fields, water, stock, or marriage: prefer agent to settle (RCIA 1903, p. 125).

1907 Detailed reports by tribe discontinued.

EXTERNAL RELATIONS TO 1904

There was never a general Navaho uprising. There was never a serious effort to keep Navahos on the legally defined reservation. There was conflict with adjoining Indians, settlers, and miners. On the whole, however, the outcome of this conflict was fairly satisfactory for the Navahos.

In the early years the Utes and Apaches tried unsuccessfully to get the Navahos to join them in an uprising. Efforts apparently ended by 1885. Nevertheless, the Navaho leaders who traveled to the Chicago Columbian Exposition in 1894 were surprised to find how many whites there were; they had believed that the Americans could be expelled. The Navahos were raided for stock and for children for slavery by Utes and Spanish-Americans, and for stock by Anglos.

The Navahos spilled over the boundaries of their reservation throughout the entire period, sometimes to raid, sometimes for seasonal pasture, and sometimes to settle. Indeed, in 1875, three major leaders were living off-reservation and had never lived on it. In 1890, when the agent tried—not very hard—to get all non-homesteading Navahos back on the reservation, every Navaho brought in claimed between eleven and twenty-two years' residence off the reservation. Twenty-two years takes us back to the release from Fort Sumner.

The Navahos carried off stock from Utes, other Indians, Spanish-Americans, and Anglos, and children for slaves from Utes and Spanish-Americans. The agents did not call these raids, but referred to depredations, stealing, and thieving. By 1883, mention of disputes, as well as of thieving, suggests competition between rival Navaho and Anglo stockmen, rather than persistence of the old raiding pattern, and by 1886, these disputes and the mutual offenses of these competing stockmen dominated the scene. Navahos and whites were now trying to secure land by committing stock nuisances, rather than trying to build up their herds by theft.

The Navahos had some legal victories over settlers in conflicts over land. They lost a small valuable tract on the San Juan but regained it, and the settlers were expelled by the military (RCIA 1886, p. 204; 1887, p. 176; 1888, p. 193). They won out in a conflict in the Cohonino Forest area in the west after considerable livestock losses (RCIA 1897, p. 107; 1899, p. 157).

The Navahos profited by an apparent lack of valuable minerals. For it was supposed mineral wealth on the reservation that most often threatened the Navahos with loss of land. At various times, the agent and the commissioner suggested exchanges of northern territory for other, or cessions in the north, but once the agent was blocked (1874–1875—see below), and on other occasions, no minerals were found and these plans were dropped. The agent staved off invasions by would-be prospectors by threat and by force of arms in 1889 and 1890. In 1891, the agent forecast a fate for the Navahos like that of the Sioux after gold was discovered in the Black Hills. The northern cession of 1892 can be laid to plans for mineral exploitation. But no precious or industrial metals were discovered in workable quantities on the Navajo Reservation—a fact which partly accounts for the expansion of Navaho lands and the preservation of Navaho culture. In the end, of course, oil and gas strikes in the northern reservation brought wealth to the Tribal treasury—in the middle of this century. Detailed references substantiating all these trends appear in Chart B," Navaho External Relations, 1868–1900."

CHART B

NAVAHO EXTERNAL RELATIONS, 1868–1904

	Threaten to Raid	Depreda-tions	Raided	Urged to War	Outside Reserva-tion	Threat of Mining	Compe-tition with Settlers
1868	163	163, 169	....	....	678	....	....
1869	....	698	....	....	....	....	....
1870	145	144–45	151	....	....	....	....
1871	367	376	....	....	376	....	....
1872	296	175, 296 303	....	....	304	....	....
1873	267	....	....	....	....	....	....
1874	....	306	....	....	....	307	....
1875	....	....	....	....	834	....	....
1876	....	....	110	110	....	....	....
1877	....	....	....	....	....	....	....
1878	....	....	....	....	108	....	....
1879	116	....	....	....	....	....	....
1880	133	....	....	....	....	116	....
1881	....	....	....	....	....	....	....
1882	....	....	....	....	....	129	....
1883	....	121	121	....	121	....	121
1884	....	....	....	134–35	....	135	....
1885	....	....	....	153	155	....	....
1886	....	....	....	....	....	....	204
1887	....	174–77	174–77	....	174	....	175–76
1888	....	....	....	....	....	....	193
1889	....	....	....	....	256–57	260	....
1890	....	....	....	....	164–65	166	164–65
1891	....	....	....	....	309	45	310
1892	....	....	....	....	208, 579	75[a], 209	208, 579
1893	110–11	....	....	....	....	....	....
1894	....	....	....	....	....	....	....
1895	....	....	....	....	....	....	....
1896	....	....	....	....	....	113[b]	....
1897	....	....	....	....	....	107[b]	107[c]
1898	....	....	....	....	....	....	....
1899	....	....	....	....	157–58	....	....
1900	....	....	....	....	....	....	....
1901	....	....	....	....	....	77[b]	....
1902	....	....	....	....	....	....	....
1903	....	....	....	....	....	....	....
1904	....	....	....	....	....	....	146

[a] Not a threat: Commissioner reports no mineral wealth in Carrizos.

[b] Mining lease granted; never exploited or no report.

[c] See also 1899, p. 157.

Numbers in each column are page references for RCIA for that year. "Threaten to Raid" refers to any statement by agent or commissioner that the Navahos must be fed or they will raid or fight. "Depredations" refers to Navaho thefts of stock, in the main, but by 1886 at latest the reference is to disputes and stock nuisances against competing white stockmen. "Raided" refers to attacks on the Navahos for stock or slaves by Utes or Spanish-Americans, or for stock by Anglos. "Outside Reservation" refers to any comment that many Navahos are off the reservation, temporarily or permanently. "Threat of Mining" refers to any comment indicating possible or actual mineral leases, cessions of reservation for mineral exploitation, incursion of prospectors, etc. "Competition with Settlers" refers to comments about Navaho-Anglo conflict over land, water rights, etc.

CRISES

A series of crises sheds light on Navaho reactions to dominance. In 1872 a party of Utes killed Agent Miller. Navahos were not involved. The situation on the reservation was so pacific, only four years after Fort Sumner, that a traveler who was at the agency at the time did not hesitate to pass through the Navaho country to western Utah with only a Navaho guide for company. He had originally planned to go to the Ute country. He described the Navahos as grief-stricken (RCIA 1872, p. 303; TNY 1958, pp. 268–270, 274).

The Navahos drove Agent Arny from the reservation in 1875. Arny was trying to arrange to release a northern strip of the reservation, supposedly rich in minerals, in exchange for a southern or an eastern and western extension, much to the disadvantage of the Navahos. The Navahos had asked the Commissioner and President Grant to remove him, accusing him of coercing them to sign papers they did not understand, withholding annuity goods, enriching himself at their expense, and so on—accurate accusations. They came to believe he was trying to take away the reservation. When he returned from a trip to Washington, the Navahos threatened to kill him if he came on to the reservation. Traders seem to have assisted the Navahos, both in explaining Arny's devious plans and in drawing up petitions.[6]

In May of 1882, Ganado Mucho and other chiefs wanted to expel Agent Eastman from the reservation as utterly ineffectual, especially in securing sufficient appropriations (McNitt, 1962, pp. 174–176; this episode finds no place in RCIA).

In 1892 there was a fracas at Round Rock. A northern leader named "Black Horse" attempted to prevent Agent Shipley from collecting children for the Fort Defiance School. Shipley and his party were barricaded in Chee Dodge's trading post until a party of soldiers rescued them. Black Horse and his men were antagonistic to schooling, American culture, and the Government. "We ask nothing . . . but to be left alone . . ." (*Reports of the Board of Commissioners*, 1892, p. 134). There were also many pragmatic reasons for resistance. Conditions at the school were very bad and the School Superintendent was a brute. There was at least some sentiment favorable to education in the north, since a year later Agent Plummer said that the Navahos were eager to induce a woman missionary to open a school in the north (Young, 1952). Black Horse was one of a series of defiant leaders in the northern Navaho country. He hated white men. He made subsequent trouble for Shipley, Plummer, and Shelton (McNitt, 1962, p. 280; Young, 1952; Aberle, field notes).

There were two kidnappings whose causes seem somewhat obscure—one of a

[6] The Reports of the Commissioner are neither clear nor complete respecting these events, but McNitt's archival work is fully convincing (cf. RCIA 1875, p. 832; McNitt, 1962, pp. 144–165). Arny publicly laid his downfall to the conniving of "squaw men," by which he must have meant such major traders on the reservation as Thomas V. and William Keam, Anson C. Damon, and Daniel DuBois, who had helped the Navahos. The agent who followed Arny believed he had been expelled because he tried to take a census, rationalize the issue of food and goods, and undermine the chiefs (RCIA 1876, p. 109). Nearly fifty years later, Chee Dodge claimed that Arny was removed because he embarrassed the chiefs when they visited President Grant. He failed to tell them that Grant could not accept their gifts and removed a rug they had left for the President from his office and returned it to the Navahos (*Survey of Conditions*, Part 34, p. 17553).

.tendent of Schools on the Hopi Reservation and one of a Superintendent
_le, Arizona—the first time prior to 1905, the second in 1905 (RCIA 1905,
_5–117; McNitt, 1962, pp. 282–290).

_-a-lil-le, a major figure in the Aneth area, had a struggle with Agent Shelton
_he Northern Navajo Agency, culminating in violence in 1907. The episode
has some nativistic features. The name ba'álílii means "the one who has supernatural power," and he will be called Supernatural Power henceforth (Young,
1954, pp. 34, 108; cf. Haile, 1950b, pp. 9–10). Supernatural Power opposed Shelton
on a number of issues. He sold breeding stock and ewes when Shelton told people
to hold on to them; he refused to dip his sheep; he opposed sending his children
to school and seems to have persuaded others to keep their children at home. He
had the reputation of being a witch. He had a large following, reaching as far
as Black Mountain. Surprisingly enough, Black Horse was among the Navaho
leaders who tried to dissuade him from his opposition.

Supernatural Power did not feel that the agent had authority over him. He
rejected the common conception that because the whites had given the Navahos
livestock they controlled the Navahos' lives. Of stock and other goods he said,
"They were not given to us to become white men. You can tell for yourself that
our heads and our skins are different from the white people" (Dyk, 1947, p. 124).
He said that putting children into school was a way of killing them—and in the
past this had often been the case. According to official accounts, he threatened
with death Navahos who sent their children to school or took up white ways
and also threatened to strike with lightning any soldiers who might come after
him. Dyk, on the other hand, believes that the threat to kill by means of lightning
is not traditionally Navaho and is improbable. Be that as it may, Shelton, who was
an active and dominant man, seems to have decided to make an example of Supernatural Power. He called in the military and went to have him arrested. There was
a skirmish and some Navahos were killed. Supernatural Power and his followers
were jailed, and things quieted down. But the episode caused enough concern for
several congressional hearings (RCIA 1908, pp. 89–94; Young, 1954, pp. 34–38;
Dyk, 1947 pp. 111–113, 122–134, 201, 203–204; Kluckhohn and Spencer, 1940,
pp. 65–66).

Thus the beginnings of organized, active nativistic protest are evident among
the Navaho. Antagonism to education was to continue until after World War II
—for a variety of reasons. First, during the early decades schoolchildren suffered
from mistreatment, often became ill, and sometimes died. Second, their parents
lost their labor. Third, there was no obvious reason for the Navahos to believe
that education would have any benefits. Both Black Horse's and Supernatural
Power's campaigns against education undoubtedly were in reaction to increased
pressure from agents to put children in school. It is interesting that both men came
from the north—and thus from the area which, according to one agent, had benefited least from the work of the Indian Service (RCIA 1903, p. 127). Shelton had
begun a campaign for acculturation at least as early as 1905 (Dyk, 1947). He was
successful in the Shiprock area, but his opposition seems to have come from the
"back country" which was also under his jurisdiction.

In 1913, there was another blow-up in Shelton's jurisdiction, this one at Beautiful Mountain. Shelton brought in a polygynist's wives for questioning—he was actively opposed to polygyny—and the polygynist and his father brought a group of Navahos to free them from the agency. After the group returned to Lukachukai, a long wrangle followed, the Navahos refusing to surrender, Shelton sending for troops, and so on, until finally the resisters surrendered and were given nominal sentences (McNitt, 1962, pp. 347–358).

This is undoubtedly not a full account of all disturbances. For example, McNitt (1962) documents at least eleven cases of the burning of trading posts, assault on traders, or murder of traders. What is striking about all the cases I have discovered except for the expulsion of Arny and the plan to expel Eastman, is their local and transitory character.

This review of Navaho political organization and related issues makes it clear that Navaho history from 1868 to 1907, when the Reports of the Commissioner stop providing general coverage of events on the reservation, was by no means untroubled. But troubles between Navahos make up a strikingly small part of the record, and troubles with settlers were an accompaniment of an expanding, not a contracting Navaho population and territory. Considering the general record of other tribes, the backing of the agent for the Navahos in difficult situations is striking. An apparently successful system of internal control was established—though what sorts of problems were handled outside the courts we cannot know. Native political structure was shattered above the community level, but relatively few were adversely affected by the loss of status involved in the process. Signs of nativistic conservatism appear as early as 1892, with a definite suggestion of a relatively uncontrolled and antagonistic population in the more remote areas of the north. Suffering there was, but not in comparison to such groups as the Utes and the Apaches, near at hand, or the more remote Plains tribes.

POLITICAL ORGANIZATION, 1908–1932

As we have shown, by the early 1900's, the agent dealt directly with the Navaho, who used him to settle many disputes. RCIA reports by tribe are lacking after 1906, and I have not discovered other sources. There is a major lacuna for the years 1907 to 1923.

One major change, beginning a few years before 1908, was the development of what was eventually called the "six-agency system." Whereas the Navahos were originally administered from Fort Defiance, the growth of the reservation apparently led to its division. The final names for the six agencies were Northern, Eastern, Southern, and Western Navajo, Leupp, and Hopi. The Hopi reservation included many Navahos.[7] Each agency was directly responsible to Washington. There was no agent over all the Navahos.

This system supplied a responsible agent with considerable powers, close at hand

[7] The dates of establishing these reservations are as follows: Hopi, 1899, Western, 1901; Leupp, 1901; Northern, 1903; Eastern, 1907. These may be regarded as budding off the original agency area, much of which was contained in what came to be called the Southern agency. Since the alternate names for these agencies can be perplexing, they are supplied here: Northern—San Juan School and Agency; Eastern—Pueblo Bonito School and Agency; Southern—Navajo School, Navajo Agency; Western—Western Navajo School and Agency; Leupp—Navajo Extension, Leupp School and Agency; Hopi—Moqui School (all from TNY 1961, pp. 597–603).

and available to the Navahos. The administrative centers were at Shiprock (Northern), Crownpoint (Eastern), Fort Defiance (Southern), Keams Canyon (Hopi), Leupp (Leupp), and Tuba City (Western). Whatever the waste or lack of administrative coordination associated with the six-agency system, there is little doubt that by contrast with the consolidation of these agencies which followed July 1, 1935, the six-agency system was popular with the Navahos, and they felt distinctly disturbed by the later administration. The power of Navaho leaders must have been still further decreased by the division of the reservation and the proximity of the agent in each division. Nevertheless, Young says, "Before 1923, Navajo Superintendents periodically called Councils of Headmen to discuss matters of program and policy . . ." (TNY 1958, p. 192).

But from 1868 on there was no body with *de jure* authority to represent the tribe in external relations. ". . . From 1910 on there was a growing need for some type of Tribal organization to act for and on behalf of the Navajo Tribe, especially in connection with mineral and oil leases" (TNY 1958, p. 192). The discovery of oil in 1921 much increased the pressures for such a body. At first there were efforts to work with a "general council," an assembly of all the Navahos, in the Southern Navajo Agency. Then, in 1922, a small "Business Council" approved a mineral lease. In 1923, the Bureau authorized a Tribal Council. Its first act was to authorize oil and gas leases.

As finally approved in April of 1923, the Council included twelve delegates, twelve alternates, and a chairman. The delegates were elected from the six reservations, with rough proportionate representations. The delegates elected the chairman, who was not a delegate, and the vice-chairman, who was. The Council could not meet except in the presence of the Commissioner to the Navajo Tribe, a position created when the Council was established. He dealt largely with Council matters, although nominally maintaining general supervision over the six agencies. If the Navahos failed to elect delegates, the Secretary of the Interior could appoint them—so that the tribe could not withdraw from Council activities by passive failure to elect. Women were given the vote in 1928, when there were minor changes in term of office and the Commissioner of the Navajo Tribe disappeared from the organization, being replaced by an official designated by the Commissioner of Indian Affairs (all from TNY 1961, pp. 374–377, 393–400).

The Government's intention is clear: it was not to create a self-governing tribe, but to create an instrument which could be called at its behest to negotiate on behalf of the tribe in matters of property.

More important for Navaho local life was the chapter system, a bureaucratic substitute for the headman, developed by John Hunter, then Superintendent of the Leupp area, in 1927. A local community constituted a chapter. It elected a Chairman, Vice-Chairman, and Secretary. It met with the agent and dealt with a large number of local issues. Subsequently chapters were encouraged to send delegates to Council meetings, so that there could be discussions involving the entire local reservation (this was during the six-agency period). Hunter's system spread to the rest of the reservations, although it was not universally adopted. In the late 1930's, the chapters became foci of resistance to livestock reduction and lost agency support. Their great viability is attested by the fact that many survived without such support as late as 1949, when Kimball restudied them. The Council began to provide financial support in the 1950's, but there is no clear-cut structure articulating chapter and Council today (Young in TNY 1958, pp. 191–192; TNY 1961, pp. 335–339; Kimball, 1950; Aberle, field notes).[8]

The chapter provided a well-defined unit for the agent to deal with, while at the same time it did not depart from the Navaho pattern of prestige leadership. There are at least 96 chapters today (TNY 1961, pp. 335–339).

All in all, this was a period in which the agent's position was firmly consolidated and a relatively satisfactory organization was developed for the expression of community views and the organization of some community activities. A central organization for external relations was also developed.

KINSHIP

Anthropological study of Navaho kinship dates largely from the 1920's. Presumably kinship organization has changed over time and specifically during the period 1868–1932. Yet there are features of the Navaho setting which have been constant for a number of centuries. First, Navaho resources are fluctuating. From year to year the outcome of herding, farming, hunting, gathering, raiding, sales, or wage work remains uncertain. And the best locations for any of these activities shift from year to year. This fluctuation promotes flexibility in residence pattern and the composition of the local clan element. It also promotes a tendency to be unwilling to give up any single resource base, since it may be vital in a year when other bases are unproductive. Contributory to this flexibility were an expanding population and land base. Accompanying this fluctuating resource base was a pattern of inherited use ownership, rather than of fixed, hereditary estates in land.

Second, major differences in the accumulation of livestock, jewelry, and other valuables were possible and did occur. On the other hand, even though cash entered the economy early and wage work began in the 1880's or before, cash was rarely used for entrepreneurial activities. Navaho society remained organized largely in terms of kinship, and property was used for a comfortable style of life and for expenditure in status-maintaining activities. There was tension between the ethic of kinship and the possibilities for accumulation.

There was, however, one major change between 1868 and the 1930's: The penetration of the police and courts into native life much reduced the significance of the local clan element, as feud became insignificant. (On these points and subsequent ones see Aberle, 1961 and 1963.)

The skeleton of Navaho kinship organization may now be described. The largest unit was phratry, an un-named set of matrilineal clans viewed as connected rather than related, a unit of hospitality, exogamy, and aid when a man was far from home. Definition of phratries varied from locality to locality; some authorities

---

[8] Both Young (in TNY 1961, p. 327) and Shepardson (1963) attribute the beginnings of chapters to Agent John Hunter while he was at Leupp. Shepardson, however, dates this event at 1924 or 1925. If Hunter was at Leupp in those years, he was not agent. He was agent there in 1927–1928 and moved to Fort Defiance in 1928, where he remained until 1934 (TNY 1961, pp. 598, 601). A Navaho witness at Congressional hearings in 1931 speaks of the Leupp chapter system as originating "two or three years ago," which fits Young's date of 1927 better than Shepardson's earlier date (*Survey of Conditions*, Part 18, p. 8953).

prefer to consider that the Navahos have a linked clan system. Below this level came the clan, a dispersed, exogamic, unorganized, named matrilineal unit, again defining exogamy, hospitality, and aid.

The largest organized unit of Navaho kinship was the local clan element (LCE), a unit for which there is no distinctive word in Navaho: that group of local matrilineal clansmen who actually cooperated and assisted one another on a day to day and year to year basis.

The rules of exogamy forbade marriage into one's own clan and phratry and father's clan and phratry, although the last prohibition was probably least observed. In addition, two people whose fathers were of the same clan might not marry. Hence in the local community and its environs a network of cross-cutting ties developed among LCE's.

Both nuclear and lineal families were found. There was a matrilocal bias in residence.

Clans were not ranked in terms of possession of offices, powers, or prerogatives. The "original" Navaho clans were regarded as prestigious and clans of slave origin as of low status.

A man might lose his accumulated wealth through a bad winter or a dry summer. Hence an ethic of sharing was general, with primary dependency on matrilineal kin but secondary on many other kinsmen as well, including affines. The wealthy were supposed to be generous, the poor were unremitting in their pressures for generosity. Mutuality among kinsmen was reinforced by the tribal character of the process of regulating disputes: here self-help and compensation were the rule. A headman could only arbitrate, and kinsmen were needed for support in case of feud, pressure for compensation, or need to pay compensation. As has been said, this political aspect of kinship diminished in importance as the agent and police came to the fore.

Needless to say, the rich were not always eager to be generous, but there were levelling devices. Expensive ceremonies were likely to be prescribed for the rich when they fell ill. Old age, indeed, with its attendant ill health, might thus consume a wealthy man's entire livestock holdings. The aged poor were suspected of witchcraft, and hence their requests were heeded. The rich and stingy were likely to be accused of witchcraft, and hence were under pressure to be generous. The inheritance patterns provided for the dispersal of a man's estate among a large number of kin (matrilineal), rather than for its transmission, undisturbed, to a single heir.

Within the LCE and the family authoritative regulation was weak, and those in authority tended to manage their relations with their juniors with some delicacy. There were, however, marked tensions between father-in-law and son-in-law and between mother's brother and sister's son.

RELIGION

An outline of Navaho religion is provided here both to round out the description of Navaho culture and for subsequent comparison with peyotism. Little is known of changes in Navaho religion since 1868, and no effort at a diachronic treatment will be made.[9]

Navaho rituals are conducted by trained specialists, "singers," as they are usually called in the literature. A fully trained singer knows all the details of the ritual, including the many fixed chants and prayers, the rationale for these ritual practices, and the myth which justifies the ritual and explains its origin. Singers do not form an organized group. A new singer is created by a long apprenticeship to an established singer. He is likely to learn from a paternal kinsman, somewhat less likely to learn from a matrilineal kinsman or an affine, and still less likely to learn from a man with whom he has no tie of consanguinity of affinity. The learning process takes several years. His full validation as a singer requires that he perform the ceremony with his teacher as "patient" (see below for an explanation of the role of patient), and that he have the ceremony performed for himself, as "patient." Normally his teacher is the singer on this occasion.

Every performance of a ceremony requires a "fee," again a common term in the literature, and therefore in the process of becoming qualified to perform a ceremony, the learned must pay a "fee" to his teacher. If his teacher is not a kinsman, the apprentice must also pay at other times in the learning process. If he is a close kinsman, the "fee" for being sung over may be the only payment he makes. A more remote kinsman might demand more. Hence people tend to select kinsmen as teachers. A man may know one ceremony or several, learn them from one singer or several, and may learn only portions of some of the ceremonies—or indeed only portions of all. People who know only portions of ceremonies are sometimes called "curers" in the technical literature.

Virtually every ceremony requires a "patient." Much of the time, the "patient" is really ill, but after having one ceremony because of illness, a man should have three more performances of the same ceremony during his life. Hence the "patient" may be in flourishing health when the ceremony is held. It is also common to have several patients in a single ceremony. Some ceremonies are to bring good fortune or avert misfortune; here, too, the "patient" may be a well man. A ceremony is "put up" by the patient and his kinsmen. This involves procuring the singer, paying his "fee," feeding the singer, his assistants, and those who attend the ceremony. Most types of ceremonies are held at the home of the patient—in the case of a man, often at his mother's or sister's house. A square house will not do; only the traditional house (hogan) can be used.

Ceremonies last from two to nine nights and vary greatly in elaboration. Some of the "smaller" (and shorter) ceremonies are held with only a few kinsmen in attendance. Some of the larger ones, especially Enemy Way and the chants with masked god impersonators, assemble a thousand or more spectators for part or all of the time—and these spectators must be fed. Singers' "fees" range from nominal to quite high, but a "fee" there must be; otherwise the ceremony is not efficacious.

[9] This summary is based on a large number of monographs and papers, as well as on field experience. It would be nearly impossible to annotate every statement. References are supplied for only a few special points. The principal authorities whose works have been employed are Goddard, Haile, Kluckhohn, Matthews, Reichard, Spencer, Stevenson, and Wyman. References appear in the bibliography.

Depending on the type of ceremony, expenses may vary from $25 to several thousand dollars. (Foregoing paragraphs based largely on Kluckhohn, 1962, pp. 97–122.)

Although the word "fee" has been used for the compensation to the singer, following Kluckhohn and Wyman (1940), some other term should be found. The singer must be given *something*, or the ceremony will not be efficacious. Properly speaking, the chants belong to the holy people, and they would be displeased if nothing were given; the patient might come to harm as a result (Haile, 1943, p. 20). If a family is impoverished, a singer might ask for no more than an old arrowhead or a basket, but there must be some exchange of goods for his services if the ceremony is to be beneficial. I would suggest that the relationship between singer and patient is but another case of the general ethic of reciprocity discussed below.[10]

There are said to be twenty-six living Navaho ceremonies (Wyman, 1957, p. 13). A few are obsolescent or obsolete, and at least one is considered to be of recent origin, borrowed from Apaches at Fort Sumner. Since there is no priesthood, it can be assumed that variation develops among practitioners of the same ceremony. This variation is increased by the Navaho belief that it would be dangerous for a practitioner to teach everything he knew to his apprentice. Hence he holds back some elements until he is very old and often fails to pass them on at all. There are special features of many ceremonies which may or may not be performed. Since an apprentice, if he pays, must pay extra to learn these, he may not learn all of them.

Differences of opinion among specialists as to the classification of Navaho ceremonies is so great as to leave the reader with some skepticism about any of the proposed solutions. Wyman's (1957) will be used here.

A major dichotomy is that between Blessing Way ceremonies and all others.[10a] Blessing Way appears only in a two-night form. It is fundamentally a ritual for maintaining harmony and averting evil. Hence the traditional headmen were supposed to know Blessing Way, for the benefit of the community (Hill, 1940).

[10] Father Berard has translated the Navaho stem -*gheel* as "fee" in speaking of the ash-bread which is a ritually prescribed compensation for singers of Flint Way, as "offering" in speaking of the ash-bread and in speaking of various things given to the gods, in ceremonies and in myth, as "sacrifice" in this same context, and as "gifts" in referring to a -*gheel* given to Gila Monster which forced him to help the Twins (Haile, 1943, pp. 64, 93, 143, 272, 273, 281, 290). In all these connections the sense seems the same: a gift or offering which compels reciprocity from the other party, a required gift for required help. Father Berard also speaks of getting the help of Gila Monster as "hiring" Gila Monster (Haile, 1943, p. 61). The stem used here, -*kqqh*, he translates elsewhere as "to plead with, beg of one . . . he is usually begged to perform ceremonials. . . . I was begged, hired for a sing" (Haile, 1950b, p. 201). On the other hand "to beg for" and "beggar" employ other stems (Haile, 1951, p. 21, where -*kqqh* is translated "beg of, plead with . . ."). The stems for "hire" and "pay" involve *bik'éé* (Haile, 1951, pp. 153, 217). Young and Morgan supply *bik'é* as a post-position meaning "for it, in exchange for it" (Young and Morgan, n.d., p. 23). So Gila Monster and the singer are not hired, but besought to perform, in exchange for a gift, which is compelling. There may well be an additional element of pay involved in the cash that singers often receive in addition, but the ideology of reciprocity deserves stress.

[10a] Navaho specialists prefer "Blessingway" to "Blessing Way," etc., but this manuscript was completed before the author noticed this departure from standard form.

It is used to consecrate a hogan; portions are used in the girls' puberty rite; its songs and prayers appear in most other ceremonies, especially at the end, to avert the consequences of errors made in performing the other rituals.

Of the other ceremonies, the Holy Ways are the largest group. They correct the results of improper contact with supernatural forces, other than ghosts and witches. They treat the effects of lightning—not only of being struck by lightning but, say, cooking with wood struck by lightning, of improper contact with snakes, arrows, ants, horned toads, bears, porcupines, certain supernatural figures, and so on. They also correct the effects of excess—too much gambling, too much sex, or for that matter, too much weaving, and of incest.

The Ghost Way or Evil Way ceremonies fall into two sub-groups. One of these is represented by a single, popular ceremony, Enemy Way, which cures the effects of contact with the "Enemy" (gentile, non-Navaho) dead. This includes the effects of killing an enemy in war and such more remote effects as seeing a Pueblo mummy in a museum, washing clothes in an Anglo laundry, or having sexual relations with non-Navahos who may subsequently die, after which their ghosts may be troublesome.

The other sub-group takes care of the effects of Navaho ghosts: touching a corpse, seeing ghosts, washing sheets in a Navaho hospital, and so on. Some of these rituals are said to be effective for curing the effects of witchcraft, but Navahos are not too confident on this score.

Life Way ceremonies are performed after an accident—say, breaking a limb in a fall from a horse. Navahos clearly understand that direct physical treatment is required for the broken limb, but the chant is needed to correct the supernatural disharmony that caused the accident.

There once were rituals for hunting and warfare, and there is an obsolescent rain ceremony. These required no patient and are not grouped with the previous sets. Game Ways (for hunting) are also effective in gambling and in attracting women (Aberle, field notes).

If we omit Blessing Way, these major groups can be said to deal with gods and ghosts, fate and fortune.

Navaho religion is polytheistic with faint monotheistic overtones, immanent, and strongly magical. The universe is endowed with supernatural force, proceeding from many spiritual beings. It is not possible to draw a sharp distinction between Bear, the personification of all power inherent in bears, and a figure in the mythology, and bears as such, in whom such power equally resides. The same would be true of mountains, masks of gods, etc. In spite of the fact that these supernatural beings often work at cross purposes in the mythology, and hence have independent motivations and powers, there is a conception expressed in the views of some Navaho singers, that all these powers are manifestations of, or products of, a single power, whom Gladys Reichard has identified with Sun, perhaps himself identified with "universal harmony or destiny" (Reichard, 1950, pp. 75–76).

The single word that best characterizes man's relationships with the supernatural and man's relationships with his fellow-man is "reciprocity." If a favor is done, a favor can be expected in return; if an injury has been done, an injury can be expected in return, unless compensation is provided. In this context, gifts and offerings have compulsive force: they require a return. Even if the relationship is not one of equality as respects relative power and wealth, reciprocity is the rule, even if it is asymmetrical. A wealthy man who gives gifts expects returns in the form of labor. A man who gives a singer his "fee," however much it may be scaled down because of the man's poverty, has a right to expect the ceremony. The singer should never accept the fee if he cannot perform the ceremony. The gift, however, must be an appropriate one. The gods can be persuaded if one knows the appropriate offering—but they do not reveal it. A messenger, friendly to the protagonist, in many chant myths, tells him what the gods want; when it is brought, the gods are angry, because now they must act in accordance with the protagonist's own needs.

Man was given the land, the water, livestock, and farming by supernatural forces. His reciprocity for this is to care for what was given to him. Even obligation to obey the agent is sometimes phrased in terms of reciprocity: the white man protected the Navahos from the Utes, Apaches, and Mexicans; so he is entitled to expect us to do as he asks. Or, he gave us stock after Fort Sumner, and so he has a right to tell us what to do with them (cf. Dyk, 1947, p. 112). What Americans see as obedience to superior authority, Navahos see as reciprocity for prior favors. Reciprocity, however, is not nicely tailored and institutionalized as to time or amount, but meanness causes wounded feelings and sometimes disruption of relationships. Although asymmetrical terms like "offering" and "sacrifice" are used in the literature, "Offerings are exchanges, tokens to curry deific favor. In Navaho religion no service is gratuitous; it is interchanged, measured, traded, the benefits being reciprocal" (Reichard, 1950, p. 307).[11]

Misfortune, however, comes not merely from injuring supernatural forces, but through contagion, in all sorts of ways—as when one rests against a wall where, decades ago, a white man was killed, and hence becomes troubled by Enemy ghosts.

Recovery comes through sympathetic magic, contagion, and inducing the supernaturals to behave correctly. Thus "unravellers" are applied to painful joints, and as the specially wrapped cords are unwound, so the joints will be, as it were, untied. The patient is seated on a sand painting, and becomes himself a supernatural. The supernatural causing the illness is induced by proper offerings to restore health, or, in the case of enemy or native ghosts, more powerful supernatural forces are unleashed to combat and drive away the ghost.

Supernatural power pervades the world. It is not radically other than or alien to man. Men impersonate gods; men become as holy ones by sitting on sand paintings; plants, animals, mountains are endowed with supernatural power. In this sense Navaho religion is immanent.

---

[11] Evidently as a reply to Reichard, 1944, Haile translates certain prayers with the phrase, "I plead with you," noting that a petition is not compulsive. "The concept that a petition may not be refused in ordinary walks of life is present to a certain degree. . . . A stranger has no such prerogative and here, in prayer and song, strangers must be supposed to approach supernaturals by *pleading* with them. . . . The request is not compulsive" (Haile, 1950a, p. 262). I find Reichard's view, and a tremendous body of mythology, persuasive and not discordant with much of what Haile says. A stranger may indeed refuse a request, but if he accepts a favor or a gift, he lays himself open to a request for reciprocity.

Good fortune results from proper ritual behavior and correct performance of such ceremonies as Blessing Way. Bad fortune results from failure to know ritual ways of preventing it, from improper contact with objects endowed with power, from ghosts, and from witches. Even illness from ghosts comes largely from contagion. Occasionally it arises because burial ceremonies were improperly done —including failure to supply certain grave goods—but it does not seem to arise because of the bad relationships between the living. A man is not afraid that some one whom he mistreated in this life will injure him in the next; he is afraid of *all* ghosts.

Navaho ritual may be said to have strongly magical elements because all rites have fairly specific empirical ends in view. These are vaguest in Blessing Way, but an empirical state of good fortune is certainly the aim. The expression of Navaho values is present in all instances, but not in the forefront: proper harmony of the cosmos and of relations between men.

Punishment, suffering, or illness as a result of bad behavior toward one's fellow-man is not to be expected from the supernatural order. Murder, theft, adultery, cruelty, and meanness are not repaid by illness. Murder is, potentially, but only because one has had contact with the dead: the same results may accrue to a warrior or a laundress in a hospital. Although excessive gambling and sexual excess are subject to ritual curing, these activities are regarded as themselves a product of supernatural taboo violation or witchcraft; they are symptoms of disease, not sins. Incest does require a cure: it will otherwise cause illness and insanity.

The sanctions against transgressions of the moral code are shame and the loss of esteem of one's fellow-man (especially if one is caught), withdrawal of reciprocity, pressure from the community or from the kin-group of an injured man, and in some instances witchcraft (cf. Ladd, 1957, on Navaho morality).

The witch is hated and feared. He gains power through committing incest, through the use of such fearful substances as bits of the flesh of the dead, and through spells and the magical ability to project "darts" (e.g., beads, glass, wood, charcoal, etc.) into the body of an enemy. He is malevolent in general, but in particular the poor are thought to be witches—and hence there is an effort to help them to avert their malevolence, and the rich—and hence they try to avert the accusation through generosity. These attitudes become particularly comprehensible when we recall the generally egalitarian framework of relationships and ethics, and the context of marked inequalities of wealth in which it operates (witchcraft section based largely on Kluckhohn, 1944, and Aberle, field notes).

When a man falls ill, he selects his chant either because he "knows" what is making him ill (he recalls some specific taboo transgression), or he makes the selection after seeking the services of a diagnostician—a hand-trembler, stargazer, or listener—who determines the cause of the illness and hence the appropriate ceremony to be performed. More rarely, a singer will make a suggestion, but by and large he waits to be called by a man who says that he needs a particular ceremony. If the diagnostician suggests witchcraft, he ordinarily refuses to name the witch. Witchcraft is often regarded as difficult or impossible to cure. If an illness fails to yield to one after another ceremony, witchcraft is often suspected.

One of the devices for curing witchcraft is the "sucking cure." Fr. Berard Haile states that probably before Fort Sumner days, sucking was used to give relief to swellings and aches, with no theory of object-removal. He implies that both the witchcraft technique which claims the ability to throw "darts" and the sucking technique which claims to remove them were learned from Chiricahua Apaches at Fort Sumner (1950a, p. 297). I am unable to discover that Chiricahua Apaches were at Fort Sumner during this period. The Mescalero, however, were, and it is possible that the group included some Chiricahuas. The Navaho have terms which distinguish the two Apache tribes. According to Fr. Berard, the sucking cure is not a regular Navaho ceremonial, and such minor ceremonial activities as may be attached to it are neither essential nor firmly integrated with the practice of sucking to remove an object (1950a, pp. 294–297).

According to Young, accusations of witchcraft were used as a technique of political control in 1879:

> At this time the Navajos were increasing their raids on the Zunis and on the New Mexicans, stealing their livestock. Manuelito and Ganado Mucho, who were then Navajo leaders, became worried that these raids might get the people into serious trouble again. The police were unable to stop the forays, so these two leaders decided to take care of the matter themselves. They decided that witchcraft was to blame, so they made up a list of the men suspected of witchery. Then they told their men to find the men whose names were on the list and kill them. Over forty thieves and suspected witches were killed in cold blood. One of the men killed was Biwos, a leader over toward Chinle, and one of the Navajos who signed the treaty of 1868 as Muerto de Hambre [Young, 1952, pp. 7–8].[12]

To summarize the materials on religion: Religious practices are carried on by individual specialists for clients on occasions selected by the patients or their families. They center about the restoration of proper relations with the supernaturals, the exorcism of ghosts, and the cure of witchcraft. Relationships to the supernatural are those of reciprocity and depend on precise performance of ritual. Witchcraft is much feared and serves as a leveling device and source of social control. Public morality is enforced by public pressure and action by blocs of kinsmen. It is not supernaturally enforced.

ACCULTURATION

Changes in economic relationships and political organization from 1868 to the beginning of livestock reduction have now been dealt with. It is now time to take up individual acculturation: the assumption by individuals of culture traits of the dominant American culture.

Changes in material culture appear to have been extensive and, in most respects, eagerly sought after. Farm tools, wagons, foods, kitchen utensils, house-building equipment, nails, wire, etc., were taken on as they became available.

Missions proliferated, but securely converted Christians were few.

Certain cultural diacriticals, especially women's shawls and men's long hair, be-

---

12 The same episode is evidently referred to in Haile, 1950a, p. 297, with a later, and less definite date (scarcely twenty years after Fort Sumner); in Kluckhohn, 1944, p. 77 n., it is dated at 1884, on the basis of a communication from Haile. Other references to a rise in witchcraft after Fort Sumner and to this episode include Kluckhohn, 1944, pp. 77, 79, 93, 123, 124, 132. Kluckhohn believes that suspicion of witchcraft, witch-killings, and perhaps witchcraft reached a height between 1875 and 1890.

came centers for agency attention at various times and caused skirmishes. (Long hair is common in the Black Mountain [13] area today, regardless of early agency policy.) Use of hospitals increased gradually, but faith in native healers remained strong as well. New crops often passed away quietly as they proved unsuitable. Navahos believed their own sheep to be hardier than various improved breeds, but there is little doubt that new breeds were mixed in with the old.

In the area of education, the Navahos were most unresponsive, for many years, and Government development of schools was minimal. The data on this subject, and the statistical manipulation of these data, were assembled and computed by Denis F. Johnston, whose work is presented in an appendix. Between 1870 and 1900, no more than four per cent of the school-age population was ever enrolled in school in any one year. The percentage rises to nearly 6 in 1905, 12 in 1910, 18 in 1915, 25 in 1920, 37 in 1925, and 41 in 1930. The figures on numbers in school at any one time, however, are not too meaningful for an understanding of the level of education prevalent in the tribe. To calculate this, Johnston has made a cohort analysis, the assumptions of which are supplied in an appendix. Through 1910, the probable precentage of adults who had ever been to school ranges from none in 1870 to a gradual peak of a little less than 7 per cent. In 1915, nearly 10 per cent may have had some schooling, in 1920, nearly 17, in 1925, about 24, and in 1930, 32 per cent. Since some of these had had only one or two years, it seems reasonable to say that in 1932 a maximum of 25 per cent of the adult population had any usable English, much less ability to read, write, or calculate.

In important respects Navaho livelihood, kinship organization, and religion survived the post–Fort Sumner changes. This being the case, education appeared to the Navahos as an unnecessary frill, sought by a relatively small number of people. Many of those who got education later emerged in one guise or another as influential figures. Chee Dodge was the first, but, so far as I know, all chairmen of the Tribal Council have had some command of English—in some instances, an excellent command; major figures in the police force have been English-speaking for many decades; and the first appointments to significant posts in the local Indian Service were selected from this group as a matter of course. Barboncito, Manuelito, and Ganado Mucho were succeeded by a larger group of smaller leaders without education, but these were followed by such men as Chee Dodge, Frank Walker, Robert Martin, Henry Taliman, Jacob C. Morgan, Alfred Bowman, Albert G. Sandoval, Sr., Paul Jones—all except Chee schooled in the last decade of the nineteenth century or the first three of the twentieth.

[13] Except in Table 34, p. 288, "Black Mountain" is used to refer to the northern part of District 4, not to the community known as Black Mountain in District 10 (see Map 2, p. 27). In Table 34, a *portion* of the northern part of District 4 is shown under 4–8 as "Black Mountain"; the community in District 10 appears under 10–4.

Chapter 4

LIVESTOCK REDUCTION, THE FIRST
PHASE: 1933–1936

THE COUNTRY was in the grips of a depression in 1933. The Navahos depended primarily on subsistence farming and stock-raising, sale of animal products, and a little employment as unskilled laborers. There were about 40,000 Navahos, and they owned over a million sheep, goats, and lambs. Twenty years later, largely as a result of Government livestock reduction, livestock had been reduced by over 50 per cent. Meantime, population had nearly doubled. About 74,000 Navahos owned less than half a million small stock. And Navahos were primarily dependent on wage work. Later, I shall try to show that there was a connection between the deprivation which Navahos experienced as a result of livestock reduction and their acceptance of peyotism. First it is necessary to explain what happened: Why was it necessary to reduce the stock? How were the Navahos induced to do so? What means were used for reduction? How great was the reduction? How did the Navaho react?[1]

GENERAL SUMMARY

Although the range had been overgrazed for fifty years, the Navahos were psychologically little prepared for livestock reduction in the 1930's and had no realistic alternatives to a pastoral economy. The history of livestock reduction and regulation will be divided into five phases in the treatment which follows—some marked by changes in policy, others by changes in conditions for the Navaho.

The first phase, from 1933 to 1936, was the period of supposedly voluntary reduction. The second, from 1937 to 1941, was the period of setting up a systematic reduction and regulation program. The third, from 1942 to 1945, was the period of continued reduction in a war-time economy. The fourth, from 1946 to 1950, was the period of declining livestock numbers during a slump period. And the fifth, from 1951 to the present, was the period of rising impact of Federal funds and oil and gas revenues.

The general theme of the analysis which follows is best stated in the words of Sam Ahkeah, Chairman of the Navaho Tribal Council from 1946 to 1954, who

---

[1] There are three short histories of livestock reduction. One, primarily by Carl Beck, is in *Survey of Conditions,* Part 34, pp. 17985–17994, and covers the years through early 1936. A second, by Edward H. Spicer, with comments by John Collier, covers the years through 1950 (Spicer, 1952, pp. 185–207). A third, by Robert W. Young, goes through a part of 1960 (TNY 1961, pp. 143–176). Spicer's is the fullest as regards Navaho reactions and is inaccurate only in a few details; the other two are especially useful for sequences of administrative and tribal action. I have used all three, but in addition the wealth of materials in *Survey of Conditions,* Parts 18 and 34, and in various Minutes of the Navajo Tribal Council, data from Window Rock Area Office files and records, newspaper clippings, and my notes of discussions with members of the Indian Service and Navahos.

called the sudden reduction of Navaho livestock "the most devastating experience in [Navaho] history since the imprisonment at Fort Sumner from 1864 to 1868" (NTCR, pp. ii–iii).

CONTEXT

The Navaho range had been overgrazed since the 1880's. Nevertheless, for decades thereafter the primary emphasis in Navaho life was on self-sufficiency through raising livestock. Rapid growth of the reservation tended partially to compensate for increases in livestock, but major enlargements ceased after 1907. The fact that livestock reached a level in the 1880's which it seldom surpassed would suggest that during those years the optimum land-animal ratio was reached and passed. It is hard to determine when members of the Indian Service, members of Congress, friends of the Navaho, and the Navaho themselves first began to think of any remedy for the situation except more land.

In 1911 and 1914, for example, pleading for more land for Navahos in the eastern off-reservation area, Fr. Anselm Weber commented on the serious overgrazing of the range (*Survey of Conditions*, Part 34, pp. 17553–17575). But he sought more land, not grazing regulation. Apparently from 1923 on, the question of horse reduction was put to the Tribal Council, which was initially very resistant but less so later on (*Survey of Conditions*, Part 18, p. 9270). Some voluntary horse reduction had occurred (*Survey of Conditions*, Part 18, esp. p. 9277), and a number had been destroyed during a dourine epidemic in 1928 and perhaps a year or two earlier (*Survey of Conditions*, Part 34, p. 17986).[2]

In late 1928, the Tribal Council and the Bureau first formally discussed range conditions. The Council then agreed that the situation was critical. It resolved that any family with more than 1,000 head of sheep and goats must pay a grazing fee of 15¢ per head per annum or reduce. The aim was to induce large owners to cut down their flocks, but the resolution was never enforced. In 1930, in a hearing on the Paiute Strip, an official of the Southern agency said that livestock should be reduced (*Addition to the Western Navajo Indian Reservation*, pp. 19–20).

Many Indian Service employees believe that the turning point toward reduction came in 1930, when William Zeh, a forester, turned in a full report on Navaho range conditions. Yet this report has recommendations oddly at variance with its findings (*Survey of Conditions*, Part 18, pp. 9121–9132). Zeh estimated that the range was carrying a load of one animal per 9 acres when, under present conditions, it could only support one animal per 20–30 acres. He said that the range was being destroyed and that the future could bring only disaster to Navaho flocks as nature stepped into correct the balance. But his recommendations for livestock control were very mild: culling of flocks, reduction of surplus goats, and education of the young in range management and livestock control. The implications of "control" were not spelled out.

In February of 1931, there was a conference which Zeh attended, in which great urgency about livestock reduction and range control was expressed. The superintendents of the six agencies attended, but no Navahos seem to have been present.

[2] For details of chronology from 1928 on, see Chart C. Statements not annotated are substantiated in one of the three histories mentioned earlier.

The Director of Irrigation of the Indian Service wanted 900,000 sheep and goats out of an estimated total of 1,300,000 withdrawn from the reservation, relocation of numbers of Navahos to unused land on various Arizona Indian reservations, and great pressure on Indians to reduce stock. The agents believed reduction was possible and desirable; one favored speedy reduction. The Director of Irrigation asked the agents, "Is it true that there will be a reaction when they know they will have only half the number of animals as a matter of income?" And four of the six agents replied that the Navahos would cooperate. One other had been on the job only a few weeks, and still another said that his group was already fairly low in stock (*Survey of Conditions*, Part 18, pp. 9268–9293). So reduction was in the air; the agents had accepted it in principle, and the situation was seen as urgent.

Yet when the Senate held hearings on the condition of the Navaho in April and May of 1931, with Navahos present, there was little enough comment on livestock reduction. Every one agreed that the range was badly overgrazed, but the agents by and large did not discuss reduction, although they favored substitution of sheep for goats. Agents and Navahos alike pleaded for more land, more water for livestock, and more irrigated farm land. A few agents mentioned horse reduction. The Senators did not talk about general reduction, but of substitution of sheep for goats, and of horse reduction. Because of the depression and low livestock prices, the situation was rendered worse since Indians were holding stock instead of selling it. One would not judge from the Senate hearings *themselves* that either the Bureau or the Indians felt that reduction was urgent, although the *documents* inserted into the record—the Zeh report and the conference on overgrazing—make it clear that the Bureau, at least, saw the situation as an emergency.

After 1931 the situation became worse. Prices remained low. Stock was held. The range deteriorated. There were no concrete steps to improve the range or to regulate livestock. According to Beck, "When Mr. Collier became Commissioner in 1933, the Navajos and all of the men working with them were well aware of the fact that livestock reduction and range-management practices were more necessary than ever and that something would have to be done immediately to save the Navajo country from total destruction" (*Survey of Conditions*, Part 34, p. 17986). Somehow I doubt this. I think that most Navahos believed that nothing was wrong which would not be remedied by a few years of good rainfall.

Before we pass to the Collier administration, it is necessary to deal with the goat issue. Much of Collier's early efforts centered on reducing goats. Why were goats such a problem? From the point of view of a conservationist, goats on the Navaho reservation presented the following disadvantages. They crop closer than sheep and destroy the range that much more. They move faster over the ground than sheep do if sheep are left to their own devices. But if goats are herded with sheep, as the Navaho herded them, they lead the sheep at their pace, so that far more forage is trodden out than would otherwise be the case. They have little sale value, since the American public is prejudiced against goat meat, and their hair has little market value.

From the Navaho point of view the goat has a number of assets. It attains a larger portion of its full growth in its early months than does a lamb. Hence by keeping goats, a Navaho can kill and eat young kids, which are delicious, in the summer and fall, and still reserve his lamb crop for herd increase and for sales. Goat hair is valued for weaving, at least in some areas.

John Collier, Commissioner of Indian Affairs from 1933 to 1945, began his term of office in the first year of the experimentally-minded New Deal. He came prepared to implement the recommendations of the Meriam Report of 1928, and to go beyond it. He was distinctly "Indian-minded," favoring the strengthening of Indian community organization, respect for Indian tradition and religion, and the development of Tribal self-government and Tribally organized economic development. Conservation was in the air: Secretary of Interior Harold L. Ickes, Secretary of Agriculture Henry A. Wallace, and Collier himself were all conservation-minded.

At the time the reservation was divided into six agencies, and the Council, as has been said, was a unit primarily concerned with mineral leases. But these were the organizations available to Collier for work on stock reduction.

The Council was made up largely of relatively young men, most of whom spoke English, who were not very representative of the more traditional livestock-oriented, largely uneducated Navaho population. It included individuals of high ability—two future chairmen of the Tribal Council, several delegates to later Councils, and two men who had subsequent successful careers in the Indian Service. Later, one body of Navaho opinion was to regard the Council from 1933 until 1937, when the new and larger Tribal Council was created, as excessively compliant with Government wishes (names from Minutes of the Navajo Tribal Council, Oct. 30–31, Nov. 1, 1933; knowledge of English from *Survey of Conditions*, Part 18, since 10 members spoke at these hearings without interpreters—with no information on the other two; characteristics from my own field work).

GOVERNMENT AND COUNCIL ACTIONS, 1933–1936

The actions of the Council and the implementation of livestock reduction from 1933 to 1936 will be described; then the actual quantity of livestock reduction will be dealt with; lastly, reactions to livestock reduction will be discussed.

Collier was eager for livestock reduction, and eager to get Navaho assent to reduction. He first met with the Council in late October of 1933; within a year he had secured a reduction of nearly 300,000 sheep and goats. But he did so in an almost completely unplanned fashion, and one which deeply disturbed the Navaho. Apparently he moved hastily because funds were available to purchase the surplus stock of the Navaho. There was, after all, a serious problem as to how the Navahos could be compensated for the stock they were induced to surrender. In 1936, speaking of the first two reductions, he said, ". . . these opportunities to buy stock rose out of the availability of emergency funds in F.E.R.A. and A.A.A. funds—which had to be utilized then or not at all. We seized upon the funds" (*Survey of Conditions*, Part 34, p. 17801).

In late October of 1933, then, Collier first met the Council. He told the members that he had the legal authority to limit Navaho herds but that he did not want to use compulsion. He said that erosion in the Navaho country was damaging the Boulder Dam site. He said he could not undertake erosion control unless there were a reduction. And he proposed a reduction of 200,000 sheep and 200,000 goats, far less than the final scope of reduction established in 1937, and said that goats must be held at a level of 70,000–80,000 after reduction. Even though the Government was most concerned about the goats, he proposed that the Federal Emergency Relief Administration (F.E.R.A.) purchase 100,000 head of sheep at the present time, but no goats, since goat meat could not even be used for people on relief, who were ultimately the consumers of the purchase. The price was to be $1.00–$1.50 for ewes and $2.25–$3.00 for wethers. Chee Dodge prophesied correctly that at this price the Navahos would sell only culls, so that their herds would reach maximum productivity. This did not seem to concern Collier.

As compensation, Collier offered many things: more land, a large soil conservation program, many day schools, water development, and more irrigation. Navaho income per head of livestock would rise through stock improvement. Emergency Conservation Work (hereafter E.C.W.), which had already begun, would continue and would supply jobs to the Navahos. Wages would offset losses in livestock income, since the entire program involved work for Navahos. (Many Navahos believed that Collier promised indefinite employment if the livestock were reduced and thought that he broke this promise—one which he could not have made. The Navahos also complained—correctly—that those who got jobs were often *not* those who lost stock.)

Collier also asked for a resolution favoring a consolidated agency.

The Council was disturbed about the reduction proposals. At least one delegate had been asked to oppose reduction, so that there must have been some awareness on the part of the Navaho that reduction was in the air. There was a split on the issue of consolidation—of a kind which occurs on many Navaho questions: north against south. The northern delegates did not want consolidation. In the end, the Council voted 8–4 to endorse Collier's proposals. It promised to submit to the people "that part of the erosion-control program which has to do with overgrazing and stock reduction, urging our people to follow the counsel of the wise men who urge this step" (*Survey of Conditions*, Part 34, p. 17993). But the Council set up no mechanisms for reduction. It suggested, but did not resolve, that the reduction should be made up entirely of sheep from the herds of large owners. On the basis of this resolution expressing support for reduction, Collier took immediate action, following a quota plan which he had discussed: 20,000 sheep from the Northern agency; 32,000 from the Southern; 15,000 from the Eastern; 15,000 from the Western; 10,000 from Hopi (Navaho stock); and 8,000 from Leupp.

The question of reduction was taken to the people, first at a meeting in the west. Large owners were very resistive, and a formula was developed which was generally used for this reduction: a 10 per cent cut for every one, with 75 per cent of all sheep sold to be ewes. As a result, large owners culled effectively and achieved peak productivity, whereas small owners simply lost stock. During the discussion and reduction, some Navahos discovered the existence and power of the Council for the first time. Resistance was widespread, and women were especially resentful, complaining that they had not been consulted. A total of about 86,000 sheep were sold in the winter of 1933–1934, but because of culling and the new lamb crop, the total mature sheep a year later had dropped by only 8 per cent. Beck described the first sale as a total failure. Suspicion was rampant, and to the Navahos a future without adequate stock resources looked black.

In 1934, there were boundary bills before Congress, including the Eastern off-reservation area. In mid-March, Collier put new pressure on the Council. He said that unless reduction continued, Congress was not likely to give the Navahos more land. And without reduction, he was not willing to undertake land improvement, which would supply many jobs. Again he sought the voluntary assent of the Council. He was still talking of a total reduction of 400,000 sheep and goats. The Council was by now very sensitive about the views of the Navahos. The members were not willing to make a plan for the reduction without further discussion. They agreed to a goat reduction of 150,000, but did not mention it in their resolution. They passed a resolution favoring stock reduction which said that the planning of a reduction program must be discussed with their constituents. They added a "soak the rich" amendment to the resolution. Families with 100 sheep or less were not to be reduced. If such a family had a majority of goats in its flock, these were to be replaced by sheep taken from the flocks of the wealthy, who would receive and sell the goats as part of their reduction. This was never done.

In April, 1934, the goat question came to the Council again. If the Navahos were not confused, they should have been. On the one hand, they were assured that the 150,000 goats was the last reduction demanded, except for sale of 80 per cent of the lamb crop per annum thereafter. On the other, they were told that they must reduce by 386,000 sheep units, or nearly 50 per cent of their remaining stock, in the near future. Navahos kept insisting that their normal sales, consumption, and losses should be included as part of the numbers counted toward reduction. At this time the Council had a night session from which all whites except James Stewart of the Indian Service were excluded. In the end the members resolved to accept the sale of 150,000 goats, the details to be worked out in Washington and submitted to the Navahos. The source of payment for the goats was one topic of concern. The delegates were unhappy and upset about reduction.

On June 14, 1934, Congress voted certain additions to the reservation, not including the Eastern off-reservation area. On the same day, the Tribe voted not to organize under the provisions of the Wheeler-Howard Act, which would have given them a constitution and various other perquisites. The vote was lost by less than 400 ballots. Unquestionably, because of disturbance over reduction, it had come to seem to many Navahos that a vote for organization was a vote for Collier —and hence a vote for livestock reduction.

In July, the Council accepted the Government's mechanism for reduction: purchase of 150,000 goats with F.E.R.A. funds, and of up to 50,000 sheep, sales of sheep being optional. It also agreed to the castration of all goats during the period of the sale except those used to produce a milch goat strain. The castration was never carried out.

In Fall of 1934, about 148,000 goats and 50,000 sheep were sold. The sale was badly mismanaged. Agents in some areas put heavy pressure on owners, and often on small owners, to sell. It proved impossible to deliver all the goats to the railhead. So some were slaughtered and the meat dried and given back to the Navahos; others were shot and left to rot; still others were shot and partly cremated with gasoline. In one place, 3,500 goats were shot and left. To the Navahos this waste was appalling, and the attitude toward their valued resources was incomprehensible. Criticism and opposition, especially from women owners, was intense.

In April of 1935, the Council began its first discussion of grazing regulations, in

CHART C

Year	Event
1928	Dourine epidemic; many horses destroyed in Government antidourine campaign.
1928 November	First discussion of range conditions between Bureau and Tribal Council. Resolution: families with more than 1,000 small stock to reduce or pay 15¢ per head per year grazing fee. Never enforced.
1930 March 12	Senate hearing on addition to Western Navajo Reservation. U.S. Agriculturalist and Horticulturist at Southern Agency recommends stock limitation, culling, stock improvement.
1930 December 23	William H. Zeh, forester, submits General Report Covering the Grazing Situation on the Navajo Indian Reservation. Notes range disastrously overgrazed, recommends culling, goat elimination, education of young in range management and livestock control (*Survey of Conditions*, Part 18, pp. 9121–9132).
1931 February 19–20	Conference, directed by Special Commissioner H. J. Hagerman, attended by superintendents of the six agencies, Southern Pueblo Agency superintendent and extension agent, supervising engineer of the Navajo Reservation. William H. Zeh forester, 2 veterinaries from Bureau of Animal Industry, director of irrigation of the Indian Service, the superintendent of the six agencies, and others (*Survey of Conditions*, Part 18, 9268–9293). Very strong reduction measures recommended. No Indians present.
1931 April 27–30; May 16–20	Senate hearings on Navaho conditions. Little stress on reduction, much on land expansion. Indians present.
1933	John Collier becomes Commissioner of Indian Affairs.
1933 July 7	Tribal Council resolves to accept erosion-control station.
1933 October 30–31; November 1	First Council meeting with Collier. Council accepts reduction in principle, favors consolidation of six agencies.
1933–1934, early	86,000 sheep sold, purchased with F.E.R.A. funds.
1934 March 12–13	Council agrees to continue reduction. Accepts quota of 150,000 goats.
1934 April 9–11	Council again accepts goat reduction, 150,000 goats.
1934 June 14	Additions to reservation by Act of Congress—not including Eastern area.
1934 June 14	Tribe votes against organizing under Wheeler-Howard Act, 7992–7608 (TNY 1958, p. 193).
1934 July 10–12	Council accepts mechanism for reduction: F.E.R.A. purchase of 150,000 goats and up to 50,000 sheep (sheep sales voluntary).
1934 Fall	Sale of 148,000 goats and 50,000 sheep. Many goats destroyed by agency personnel after purchase.
1935 April 12	Council discusses plans for grazing regulations in Washington.
1935 May 28	Eastern boundary bill passes Senate; stalled thereafter.
1935 July 1	Consolidated Agency established.
1935 Fall	$250,000 in F.E.R.A. funds made available for purchase of sheep and goats. Council takes no action. About 16,000 sheep and 15,000 goats sold. Last step in voluntary reduction.
1935 November 6	Secretary of Interior approves regulations for Navaho range management: division into land management units, establishing of carrying capacity of units, working with Navaho organizations from the Tribal Council on down to secure satisfactory range management, and empowering the Commissioner to act without assent of the Navahos if they failed to cooperate (milder than general grazing regulations for all Indian lands, where no mention is made of working with Indian organizations) (*Survey of Conditions*, Part 34, pp. 17948–17950).
1936 January 25	Commissioner informs Council that Soil Conservation Service is not responsible for the initiation of livestock reduction, that it will remain, and that livestock control is essential (against widely prevalent Navaho view that expulsion of the S.C.S. would stop reduction).

CHART C—*Continued*

Year	Event
1936 March 16	E. Reeseman Fryer becomes General Superintendent, remaining until May 31, 1942.
1936 April 15	Shiprock chapter meeting over the question of acreage per family on the Fruitland Irrigation Project; Fryer present.
1936 March 18, 25; May 14, 25, 29; August 17–19, 21, 30	Senate hearings on Navajo boundary (Eastern extension) and New Mexico Pueblos.
1936 Spring	Based on grazing surveys, 1933–1935, land management units tentatively laid out.
1936 November 24	Council approves Committee on Special Grazing Regulations. Council requests its Executive Committee to call constitutional assembly for reorganizing Council; last meeting of 12-man council.

Washington. In May, the Eastern boundary bill passed the Senate but was never enacted into law—and in spite of full dress hearings in 1936, never again came close to enactment. In July, the Consolidated Agency was set up, later to become a focus of Navaho opposition. By Fall of 1935, livestock reduction had gone sour. The Government made available $250,000 in F.E.R.A. funds, but the Council did not pass any resolution favoring sale of livestock at this time, and only about 16,000 sheep and 15,000 goats were sold. This was the end of the voluntary reduction.

By now the Navahos were convinced that erosion control was somehow responsible for livestock reduction. Therefore, if the Soil Conservation Service could be removed from the reservation, livestock reduction would cease. The Commissioner informed the Council that he would not remove the Corps, and that reduction was essential, in January of 1936. In March, he appointed E. Reeseman Fryer as General Superintendent—the man who, with Collier, is most associated with reduction in the Navahos' minds.

Grazing surveys had gone on since 1933, preparatory to organized reduction, and in 1936, the 18 land management units connected with the future stock management program were tentatively laid out.

In November of 1936, the Tribal Council approved a Committee on Special Grazing Regulations and activated a constitutional assembly. The old Council was discredited, and plans for a new Council were under way.

LIVESTOCK NUMBERS

The question is: How many livestock were actually sold and with what effect on Navaho holdings? The fullest listing of stock sales to the Government supplies these figures in Table 1.

Over and above these sales, there was consumption of stock, sales to traders, sales to Indian Service schools for meals, etc. Yet the available figures indicate that mature sheep rose somewhat between 1933 and 1935; lambs dropped somewhat; and goats alone were markedly reduced. Table 2 supplies the data.

The accuracy of the dipping records may be questioned, but there are no better figures. The totals for 1933 precede the first sale, and I assume that those for 1935 follow the last sale, but it was small enough not to affect any conclusions. To the degree that goats were the primary target of reduction, the program was a modest success. The sale of 163,000 goats resulted in a total decrease of 184,000 goats, using 1933 as a base—or a drop of 56 per cent. One must assume that Navahos were eating their goats and selling them where they could, when the pressure to get rid of goats arose. But the sale of 153,000 sheep resulted in an increase of nearly 4,000, or a rise of over 7 per cent. There was a drop of 27,000 lambs, or 10 per cent, using 1933 as a base. All in all, the sale of 316,000 head of stock resulted in a decrease of only 180,000 mature stock and of a grand total of only 207,500 sheep, lambs, and goats. Considering that the Government started with the aim of reducing stock by

TABLE 1

EARLY REDUCTION FIGURES

Year	Sheep	Goats
1933............	86,517	....
1934............	50,000	148,334
1935............	16,225	14,760
Total........	152,742	163,060*

* Total stock units, 315,802.

Source: *Survey of Conditions*, Part 34, pp. 17806–7. Minor errors of mathematics are corrected. Elsewhere a figure of 90,000 sheep is supplied for 1933, and figures of 13,312 goats and 13,866 sheep for 1935 (*Survey of Conditions*, Part 34, p. 17988).

Different figures could be used: Collier claimed total purchases of 495,000 sheep units (*Survey of Conditions*, Part 34, pp. 17452–53), but also used the figure of 315,000 sheep and goats (*Survey of Conditions*, Part 34, p. 17537).

TABLE 2

LIVESTOCK HOLDINGS 1930–1935, SHOWING 1933–1935 REDUCTION

Year	Sheep	Lambs	Goats	Total
1930......	574,821	349,237	373,531	1,297,589
1931......	631,427	345,242	393,885	1,370,554
1932......	575,913	257,148	347,169	1,180,230
1933......	544,726	277,772	329,994	1,152,492
1934......	502,619	289,178	294,851	1,086,648
1935......	548,579	250,508	145,823	944,910

Compiled from dipping records (*Survey of Conditions*, Part 34, p. 17995. Other, slightly different figures can be secured elsewhere).

400,000 units, the program was a flat failure. And now the ultimate aim was to become that of a further reduction of 410,000 sheep, lambs, and goats—of 56 per cent of the remaining stock, with stabilization of livestock at that level, the supposed carrying capacity of the range. (Horses and cattle are disregarded for the present.)

The entire question of the impact of livestock reduction must be seen in a larger context—the over-all trajectory of Navaho livestock holdings over a number of years, along with the rise in population. Our aim is some sort of estimate of the per capita changes in holdings, in spite of having fairly bad figures to work with. However bad the figures may be, it is safe to assume that per capita holdings had been dropping for some time. In the Southern Navaho Agency in 1915, it is reasonable to assume that some 11,000 Navahos held 520,000 sheep and goats, or about 47 per capita.[3]

In 1930, there were 485,439 sheep and goats in the Southern agency, and the population was about 15,880.[4] Holdings had dropped to 31 per capita. Thus there was both an absolute drop in livestock holdings over 15 years and much larger drop in per capita holdings: 7 per cent over all, 37 per cent per capita. The absolute drop probably resulted from sales in boom years, losses in bad weather, and overgrazing. The per capita drop, of course, results from population increase and declining livestock.

In 1935, there were 341,753 sheep, goats, and lambs in the Southern jurisdiction, and the population was 16,611, or 21 sheep per capita, another considerable drop (*Survey of Conditions*, Part 34, p. 17978; RCIA 1935). Part of this must have resulted from a hard winter just before reduction, but part must be laid to reduction. We cannot be sure of the proportions, since I cannot find figures for Southern agency holdings for 1931-1934 inclusive. I have used the Southern agency up to this point because Paquette's survey provides an early base line.

Let us, then, turn to per capita figures for the total Navaho country, in 1930, 1933, and 1935. In 1930, there were 1,297,589 small stock and around 40,000 Navahos, or 32 sheep per capita; in 1933, small stock stood at 1,152,492, and population at something over 42,000, or 26-27 sheep per capita; and in 1935, there were 944,910 small stock and about 45,000 Navaho or 21 sheep per capita. (Livestock figures from *Survey of Conditions*, Part 34, p. 17995; census figures roughly based on RCIA 1930, 1933, and 1935; TNY 1958, p. 356; Denis F. Johnston extrapolations.)

Thus it is reasonable to infer that the long-term trajectory of per capita holdings was downward prior to reduction, that there had been a fairly marked drop in the period 1930-1933, primarily because of bad weather, and that reduction caused a further drop of about the same size.

In view of the Council's concern to reduce large rather than small holders and the claim that small holders were most severely affected by the reduction, it would be very worthwhile to know the change in distribution of holdings before and after reduction. Unfortunately, the only data I can find bearing on this point are for 45 owners in the Eastern off-reservation area, before and after the 1934 goat reduction. It shows that owners of less than 100 sheep lost 23 per cent of their

[3] Paquette, the agent, made a survey quoted in TNY 1957, p. 375, showing a total of 519,518 sheep and goats. The figures in RCIA for 1915 show 920,000 sheep and goats for this jurisdiction, however. Since Paquette's report shows a breakdown of livestock holdings by family, it seems probable that he made a fairly careful survey. RCIA figures for 1916-1919 use 520,000, which makes 920,000 look like a misprint. Paquette gives a total of 2,400 families, and RCIA for 1915 gives a figure of 10,000 population. But this figure had been in use since 1913 and was raised to 11,915 in 1916—an impossibly large rise. I therefore assume that, with 2,400 families and better than 5 per family, 11,000 population is reasonable.

[4] Figures from *Survey of Conditions*, Part 18, p. 9124. There is an error in addition in this source. Comparable figures are found in the same source on pp. 9112 and 9142. TNY 1958, p. 375, however, shows nearly 1,300,000 sheep and goats for the Southern agency, citing the same source I have used. No such figure can be found in *Survey of Conditions*, Part 18, but the precise totals which appear in TNY are given for the grand total of *all six* agencies (*Survey of Conditions*, Part 18, p. 9123).

herds; those owning between 100 and 250, 20 per cent; those owning between 250 and 500, 7 per cent; and those with more than 500, only 5 per cent (*Survey of Conditions*, Part 34, p. 17766). The trend is strong and clear, for this small sample from a special area. I am unable to put together any data showing the change in distribution of size of herds between the pre-reduction period and 1935. (Figures in TNY 1958, p. 375, in *Survey of Conditions*, Part 34, pp. 17994, 17995, 17772, 17754, 17766–67 are not genuinely comparable.)

To sum up, per capita holdings had been declining long prior to reduction. Reduction was sudden, cataclysmic, unrationalized, and unplanned. It caused a maximum disturbance and achieved a minimum reduction, but even this reduction, accompanied by steady population rise, caused a further decline in per capita holdings. And the small amount of data available suggests that during these years large owners were less affected by reduction than small owners.

NAVAHO REACTIONS

Perhaps the best way to assess Navaho reactions to the early reduction program from contemporary sources is to spend a few days reading the 900 pages of Part 34 of the *Survey of Conditions of the Indians in the United States* and comparing it with the 900 pages of Part 18 of the *Survey*. The Hearings in Part 18 took place in 1931; those in Part 34, in 1936. In 1931, there was a depression, the reservation was overgrazed, the Navahos wanted more land, they had no jobs, and livestock prices were very low. Yet in reading the hearings, which were held all over the reservation, one is impressed by a relatively high level of Navaho morale. Complaints were specific. Many were directed at traders. And there were insistent demands for more land.

In 1936, the Hearings were supposed to be concerned with the Eastern boundary bill, aimed at adding territory to the reservation. Collier was supporting the bill for all he was worth. All over the reservation schools were being built, erosion control was going on, jobs were being provided, and plans were being made for the Navahos' future. Yet in spite of repeated announcements by the Senators that this was not an investigation of general conditions, much of the hearings was devoted to an all-out attack on Collier and on Fryer. And virtually every feature of his program was attacked: livestock reduction, of course, but also day schools, soil conservation work, demonstration areas, the Wheeler-Howard Act, the Consolidated Agency, the eighteen land management units, and the plans to reorganize the Tribal Council. Often there were specific demands that Collier and Fryer be removed from office. (In 1931, there were a few requests that Governor Hagerman, Special Commissioner to the Navahos, be removed.) Every part of Collier's program had been contaminated by the livestock reduction.

Interpretation of this gross difference between the two hearings, however, is not quite so simple as it appears. In 1931, hearings were held all over the reservation, and correspondingly Navaho witnesses from all areas appeared. In 1936, virtually everyone who spoke or wrote to the Senate committee came from the eastern part of the reservation or from the eastern or southern off-reservation areas. Jacob C. Morgan of Farmington, a Navaho and a missionary, later to become a chairman of the Council, had become the manager of an active campaign against Collier and Fryer. Undoubtedly the campaign could not have gained support without the serious discontent which existed. But when one reads the barrage of letters from Navahos which he submitted to the committee and which arrived directly without his cover letter, the unanimity of opinion on some eight or ten points is so overwhelming as to indicate that Morgan focused the discontent on certain issues.

Indeed, of all the complainers against Collier, only one can be said to be independent of Morgan's influence: Scott Preston, of Tuba City, who lived far from Morgan's area and whose comments fail to show a nice parallelism with the others. And in his own words, he, too, rejected the Consolidated Agency, the land management units, and livestock reduction. Unlike others, he favored day schools, provided higher education was also supplied. In commenting on the destruction of goats by gasoline, he asked how the Senators would feel if he asked them for a five-dollar bill and then burned it up in front of them. That, he said, was what the Navahos felt when their valuable stock was destroyed (*Survey of Conditions*, Part 34, pp. 17912–16).

There was a small amount of comment favorable to Collier in the hearings. At Mexican Springs a demonstration area had been set up which many local residents felt was simply taking away their pasture. From the Mexican Springs Chapter came statements by its president and vice-president, favoring soil conservation, expressing guarded approval of stock control, and thanking Collier for his help to the Indians (*Survey of Conditions*, Part 34, pp. 17955–56, 18019–20).

A large group of Navahos from the southern reservation met at Ganado on August 8, 1936, while the hearings were going on, and expressed views set forth in a letter sent to the Committee. This group favored the Wheeler-Howard Act, asking for a fresh Navaho vote on the subject. This is a sort of support for Collier. Signers came from Cornfields, Greasewood, Ganado, Nazlini, Kinlichee, Keams Canyon, St. Michaels, Wheatfields, Jacob's Well, and Ple Yo Yo. They included Chee Dodge, former chairman of the Council, Frank Walker, a former police officer, Black Water, a respected large livestock owner from Greasewood, Jim Curley, an alternate on the Council, and Silver Smith, a member of the Council. In this, as in many other instances, the southern reservation adopted a moderately pro-Government position (*Survey of Condiitons*, Part 34, pp. 18035–36). But Chee expressed himself against livestock reduction at the hearings, and Shirley wrote a letter opposing many features of the Government's program (*Survey of Conditions*, Part 34, pp. 17905–06, 18017). One Navaho favored soil conservation and day schools; another spoke in favor of the Mexican Springs Demonstration Area (Paul Jones, later Chairman of the Navaho Tribal Council) (*Survey of Conditions*, Part 34, pp. 17956–60). And that was virtually every comment favorable to any feature of Collier's program which appeared in 900 pages of testimony and exhibits. Considering the caliber of the signers of the Ganado letter, however, it seems fair to infer that there was a little more quiet support than the record indicates.

The full flavor of these hearings cannot be judged from a summary. Two statements from letters illustrate the extreme tone sometimes reached.

One is a letter to Morgan from the Houck, Arizona, chapter organization on August 2, 1936. Speaking of Collier, the letter says:

He wanted to make us vote for the Wheeler-Howard bill and govern ourselves, and when we refused . . . he got very angry at us. He started a lot of new things; and now, when we want to do something like handling our own affairs and advising him what we want, he sayd, "No; but you got to take my advice." If he thinks we can be our own boss, why does he tell us what to do.

John Collier promised to help us more than any other white man, but before he made these promises he forced us to agree to some hard things that we didn't like. We tried it out, but Collier just fooled us. He only did some of the stock reduction. We know how many sheep we have now and how much our country will take care of, and we don't think we are overgrazed. We Indians don't think it is right for Collier to tell us we should govern ourselves, and then to tell us how to do it. Why does he want to fool us that way and make us believe we are running our country, when he makes us do what he wants.

The letter closes by saying that the Navahos have more worries than at any time since Fort Sumner (*Survey of Conditions*, Part 34, p. 18015).

Perhaps the most remarkable statement comes from Twin Lakes and surrounding areas (near the Mexican Springs Demonstration Area), undated, and addressed to Senator Chavez. Among other things, it says, "The sheep business . . . gives us the only decent living. When we have no more sheep then Mr. Collier will dance a jig and be happy" (*Survey of Conditions*, Part 34, p. 17972).

The Navahos were acutely disturbed, and reduction had just started.

Chapter 5

LIVESTOCK REDUCTION, THREE
PHASES: 1937–1951

CONTEXT, 1937–1941

THE GOVERNMENT attempted to compensate for losses in livestock by improving the quality of livestock and by employing Navahos in public works. The increased meat and wool yield per animal did partly offset the reduction in numbers—a point discussed in a subsequent chapter. But the Bureau's program of public spending declined, like that in the rest of the Government. Between 1936 and 1940, not only did Navaho income from livestock and agriculture decrease, but income from wages—mostly paid from Federal funds—also declined, so that total Navaho estimated income dropped from about five millions to little more than four (TNY 1958, p. 107). These were years of declining Navaho fortunes.

This was also the period of full development of the consolidated agency, which had been headed by E. Reeseman Fryer since March of 1936 (TNY 1961, p. 601). It was subdivided into eighteen Land Management Units. The Tribal Council underwent a complete and stormy reorganization during these years, finishing with 74 elected delegates, instead of 12. And there was a severe drought in 1939, forcing the sale of many sheep (Spicer, 1952, p. 198).

The Council reorganization must be treated in somewhat greater detail. The old Council was discredited because of its support for stock reduction—but the plans for a new Council which, Collier hoped, would be more broadly representative, were suspect because Collier wanted the new Council. The old Council appointed a committee to plan a larger and more representative Council in November of 1936. The committee developed a list of 250 or more likely candidates for the new Council. Seventy of these were selected as delegates to a Constitutional Assembly, to plan and adopt a constitution and by-laws. In the course of two chaotic days, in April of 1937, when the legality of the procedures was challenged by a faction headed by Jacob C. Morgan, the Constitutional Assembly reassembled as a Tribal Council and attempted to prepare a constitution and by-laws. In the end, it drafted only regulations for elections, which were held September 24, 1938. Jacob C. Morgan was elected Chairman. He was a northern Navaho, much opposed to Collier, Fryer, and livestock reduction. The new Council met November 8, 1938, for the first time. Efforts to create an Executive Committee at this time failed, as they were to fail for many years, until the Advisory Committee was created in 1947. As far as the Council was concerned, an Executive Committee was a group which could be expected to support the Commissioner on livestock reduction. (An Executive Committee had been created in November of 1936, to deal with the Commissioner regarding grazing regulations.) The stresses surrounding organization of the new Council, then, flowed directly from livestock reduction (Sources on Council: NTCR, Preface; TNY 1961, pp. 378–387, 400–411).

GOVERNMENT AND COUNCIL ACTIONS, 1937–1941

The Indian Service now began a program of systematic livestock reduction and regulation. The basic outlines of this program, developed between 1936 and 1941, remain as guides for livestock regulation on the Navaho reservation today. The basis for the new reduction program was threefold: to discover the carrying capacity of the Navaho range; to discover the amount of livestock on that range; and to arrive at a formula to bring the amount of livestock down to the carrying capacity and maintain it at that level.

There had been grazing surveys from 1933 to 1936. These served as the basis for dividing the reservation into 18 Land Management Units (Districts) and establishing the carrying capacity of each. Now, instead of dealing with all Navaho livestock as a unit, it became possible to work with smaller areas, some of which might be far more seriously overgrazed than others, and to try to adjust the herds to carrying capacity in each area.

There was a livestock census in 1937 and a second census of horses in 1939. These censuses served to establish how much the range was overburdened in each District. The census of sheep and goats was carried out by counting the sheep and goats as they were brought in for dipping (which rids them of external parasites). Horses and cattle were counted in 1937 by rounding them all up and holding them until the owners claimed them. In 1939, in the course of a horse reduction program, horses were again rounded up, and those in excess of a man's "permit"— see below—were disposed of, others being branded.

The 1937 and 1939 counts were supposed to establish not only how many stock were using the range in each District, but also who owned them. In fact, sheep at least were often tallied under the name of the person who brought them in for dipping, although they might be the property of several kinsmen and not of a single individual. Navahos were invited to correct the record, but they were already so concerned about livestock reduction that many would not do so. Hence the final records were often inaccurate as to ownership, and those which I have seen are particularly surprising in listing almost no women as owners, although it is well-known that Navaho women own livestock in their own right. The count itself may have erred on the low side, since some Navahos undoubtedly avoided dipping and counting.

Once the carrying capacity, livestock population, and livestock ownership of a District had been established, the reduction formula had to be chosen. The final choice was a levelling formula. It would have been possible to have cut all herds in a district on a flat percentage basis—as had been done in some of the earlier reductions. Or there might have been a graduated percentage cut, like the income tax formula. What was done instead was, at least in theory, to reduce the larger owners and to freeze the smaller ones at their current levels. The procedure was as follows.

Carrying capacity, actual livestock, and individual holdings were all expressed in "sheep units." A sheep unit is the equivalent of one sheep grazing yearlong. One sheep or goat equals one sheep unit; one head of cattle equals four sheep units; one horse equals five sheep units. These equivalents are based on the assumption that a horse eats five times as much forage as a sheep in one year. The "owners" were rank-ordered, on a roster which showed their total sheep units (S.U.), and the amount of units held in each kind of stock. On this basis a maximum permit was established for each District. The maximum permit was set at a level such that if every owner holding more than the maximum permit sold stock until he had only that amount, and if every owner holding only the maximum permit or less retained his stock at his current level, the District's livestock would be equal to its carrying capacity. As can be seen from Table 3, the maximum permit varied greatly from

TABLE 3

PERMIT SIZE BY DISTRICT

District	Maximum Permit	District	Maximum Permit
1	225	10	153
2	161	11	105
3	280	12*	104
4*	72	13	200
5	280	14*	61
6	(Hopi)	15*	88 (On-reservation portion)
			(Off-reservation)
7	237	16	275
8	154	17	238
9*	83	18	

* Special permits issued in these districts in 1941.
Source: TNY 1958, p. 380. Date of special permits, NTCR, p. 299.

District to District. In six districts, the theoretical maximum S.U. a man could hold was 105 or less. In three more, it was 161 or less. In seven, it ranged from 280 to 200. (Of the 18 Districts, one was off-reservation and not covered by these regulations, and one was Hopi, covered by other regulations.)

Then each "owner" was given a permit, which stated that he was entitled to, say, 96 S.U., of which not more than 10 could be in horses. This meant that he could have 86 sheep and 2 horses (10 S.U.), 91 sheep and 1 horse, or 96 sheep and no horses. Since any family would need at least two horses, he was likely to choose 86 sheep and two horses. These permits were issued in 1940, but some preliminary version must have been available in 1939 for the horse roundup and disposal of excess horses. The 1937 count served as the basis for the sheep permits. That is, if a man had held less than the maximum permitted number of sheep in 1937, he was confirmed in sheep up to the amount of his 1937 holdings. Thus the large owner was to sell off his stock; the small owner was to hold his stock constant and not increase it; and carrying capacity and actual livestock would be brought into line. The outcry in the Districts with small maximum permits was so great that in 1941 special permits of up to 350 sheep units were issued in 5 Districts, each of which had a regular maximum of 104 or less (see Table 3). A sixth District with a small permit, District 11, has always been a strong farming area and may not have protested quite so much. Since many Navahos had been selling off stock from 1936 on, because of Government pressure, the special permit was a legitimation of resistance to reduction: it was granted to individuals whose holdings had remained above their permits' maximum in every year since 1937.

The roster of permittees, then, was based on the 1937 livestock count, corrected in cases where individual Navahos took action. Any one omitted in error or through any other cause was excluded from the list of permittees, and minors not yet owning stock and children yet unborn were excluded from the permit list except as they might later inherit all or part of a permit from a parent.[1]

This, then, was the formula for reduction. What did the Government and the Council do? In July of 1937, the Executive Committee of the (old) Council approved of the reduction of surplus horses, which the Government was pushing, and again urged the Superintendent to expedite this reduction in January of 1938 (NTCR, pp. 247, 248). But the new Council too went after horses. In May of 1939, it endorsed the Government's livestock *improvement* program and pledged cooperation in the sale and removal of horses scheduled for summer of 1939. At the same time, it asked for extension of the date for compliance with grazing regulations until July 12, 1939. (I am unable to discover exactly what the form of the regulations was at this time.) And the Council agreed to assist in the distribution of permits, so that "every stock owner . . . will be assured of his rights and privileges" (NTRC, pp. 250–251). The Council renewed this pledge in June of 1940, but with the understanding that there would be no reduction until fall of 1941 in districts that proved cooperative. At the Council meeting, there was a good deal of discussion which bore on the aim of reducing large owners, perhaps turning over some of their stock to small owners who were below permit level. Large owners, the Council hoped, could be helped by leasing off-reservation land. Further reduction was opposed (*Proceedings of the Meeting of the Navajo Tribal Council, June 3–6, 1940*). In 1941, the Council pled for the special permits and pledged itself to support the grazing regulations and to work for removal of surplus horses. It withdrew its protection from violators of the regulations (NTCR, pp. 230–232).

The Council, then, unable to stop reduction, in effect swapped surplus horses for special permits, mercy to transgressors, and delayed deadlines in enforcement.

Exactly what the Government did during these years is by no means clear. The size of the permit to be issued in 1940 was known far earlier, and there were efforts to distribute them in 1939. But even before that, there were apparently efforts to prosecute stock regulation violators, although we do not know what the regulations were. Nor is the process of reduction at all clear. There are some indications that percentage cuts were still being applied as late as 1937 (Reichard, 1939, pp. 7–12).

[1] The foregoing is based primarily on TNY 1958, pp. 70–71; memorandum from Lyle L. Young, U.S. Dept. of Agriculture, Soil Conservation Service, Navajo Service, Window Rock, Arizona, June 15, 1940; Spicer, 1952; field notes; Aberle, interviews with Agency personnel. Spicer is in error in asserting that the maximum permit was equal to the carrying capacity divided by the number of owners in the District. This is impossible. The resulting figure would be the hypothetical mean holding for the District if all holdings equalled carrying capacity. Hence, if everyone were to hold stock at or below this hypothetical mean, the total livestock in the District would fall below carrying capacity.

LIVESTOCK NUMBERS, 1930–1959

It is now necessary to examine the changes in numbers of livestock over time in the Navaho country. I have brought together several sets of figures, if only to show that there are discrepancies of some magnitude in the official and unofficial records. On the other hand, even these discrepancies do not affect the general trends visible in each set of figures. No single set covers all years, and there are gaps in all tables for 1938 and 1939, and in most for 1942–1950. It is important to note that Tables 4 and 7 list all livestock, off and on reservation, whereas Tables 5 and 6 are limited to stock on reservation. (Off-reservation refers to the eastern and

TABLE 4

DIPPING RECORD CENSUS, 1930–1935

Year	Mature Sheep	Goats	Cattle	Horses	Lambs	Total (Sheep, Goats, Lambs)	Total S.U.[a]
1930...	574,821	373,531	26,075[b]	34,755[b]	349,237	1,297,589	1,575,644
1931...	631,427	393,885	....	....	345,242	1,370,554	....
1932...	575,913	347,169	....	....	257,148	1,180,230	....
1933...	544,726	329,994	77,500[c]		277,772	1,152,492	1,508,992
1934...	502,619	294,851	....	....	289,178	1,086,648	....
1935...	548,579	145,823[d]	19,020[e]	44,582[e]	250,508[f]	944,910	1,243,900[g]

Estimated carrying capacity, 1935: 560,000 S.U.[h]

Source: *Survey of Conditions*, Part 34, p. 17995.

[a] Includes lambs, includes horses @ 5 S.U., cattle @ 4 S.U., large stock @ 4.6 S.U. Totals supplied by DFA and not in sources.

[b] Estimates from *Survey of Conditions*, Part 18, p. 9123; the same source reports that the Bureau of Animal Husbandry estimate for 1930 for horses was 80,000, based on figures obtained in earlier years during dourine control work.

[c] Estimate supplied in *Survey of Conditions*, Part 34, p. 17995, for all large stock combined: "approximately 75,000 or 80,000 head."

[d] *Survey of Conditions*, Part 34, p. 17978, gives 92,222 goats. I assume that this is the count for mature goats and that the figure of 145,823 includes kids.

[e] From *Survey of Conditions*, Part 34, p. 17978. Sheep and lamb totals there correspond to those above. P. 17995, however, estimates 25,000 cattle and 45,000 horses, supposedly by count.

[f] TNY 1958, p. 383, supplies identical figures for mature sheep and for lambs for 1930–1935, except that lambs for 1935 are given as 252,554. Figures for horses and cattle vary widely from these.

[g] Using the estimate of 25,000 cattle and 45,000 horses. *Survey of Conditions*, Part 34, p. 17975, gives 1,269,910 S.U. It is evident that the S.U. count is markedly affected by the figures used to estimate large stock.

[h] *Survey of Conditions*, Part 34, p. 17975.

southern off-reservation area.) In spite of differences in figures, the tables within each set show a fair correspondence.

I have used Table 8 to bring together from several of the sources total mature sheep and goats, or total sheep, goats, and lambs, since these provide the best index for subsistence animals. In addition, cattle and horse figures are estimates, rather than counts, at least through 1934. Through the use of Denis F. Johnston's population extrapolations (see Appendix), it then becomes possible in this table to figure per capita small stock. If the total sheep, goats, and lambs are divided by the population, a per capita figure results which is at least 50 per cent larger than that from dividing mature sheep and goats by population. The figures for on-reservation small stock are not used for per capita estimates, since the proper divisor here would be on-reservation population only, and this is not available.

A final table shows percentage changes in total mature small stock or total sheep, goats, and lambs, using 1930 as a base and 1936, the first year after voluntary re-

TABLE 5

RESERVATION LIVESTOCK CENSUS, 1930–1959[a]

(Includes Navajo and Hopi Except as Indicated)

Year	Mature Sheep	Mature Goats	Mature Cattle	Mature Horses	Lambs	Total Mature Sheep, Goats[b]	Total Mature S.U.
1930.....	574,821	186,768	25,000	50,000	349,237	761,589	1,111,589
1931.....	631,427	196,945	25,000	50,000	345,242	827,373	1,178,372
1932.....	575,913	173,585	21,000	44,000	257,148	749,498	1,053,498
1933.....	544,726	164,999	20,000	42,000	277,772	709,725	999,725
1934.....	502,619	147,427	19,000	40,000	289,178	650,046	926,046
1935.....	548,579	92,222	19,020	40,270	252,554	640,801	918,231
1936.....	459,285	73,600	12,557	32,007	281,342	532,885	711,148
1937.....	391,103	57,819	18,053	39,835	295,802	448,922	720,309
1940[c]....	356,791	57,113	13,045	31,100	302,674	413,904	621,584
1941.....	433,733	72,018	....	....	....	505,751	....
1951[c]....	234,619	39,014	9,205	27,439	146,071	273,633	449,808
1952.....	220,476	41,997	8,847	27,802	162,739	262,473	433,983
1953.....	233,109	45,196	9,997	27,309	177,230	278,305	454,838
1954.....	252,261	52,678	11,149	26,972	173,393	304,939	484,395
1955.....	257,042	55,945	12,583	26,890[d]	172,408	312,987	497,769
1956[c]....	266,185	62,509	13,678	25,783[d]	180,268	328,694	515,965
1957[c]....	275,515	71,130	14,594	23,920	182,063	346,645	524,621
1958[c]....	287,785	77,000	14,590	23,051	212,623	364,785	538,400
1959[c]....	291,804	80,557	14,897	22,067	188,581	372,361	539,323

Source: TNY 1961, p. 167.

[a] According to TNY, early years are estimates. But sheep and lamb figures correspond with dipping records, *Survey of Conditions*, Part 34, p. 17995, with minor exceptions, 1930–1935. Goat figures 1930–1934 are apparently based on approximately half the figures for all goats in *Survey of Conditions*, Part 34, p. 17995. Goat figure for 1935 corresponds with *Survey of Conditions*, Part 34, p. 17978. Cattle and horse figures for 1930–1935 at least are estimates, differing from various other estimates in *Survey of Conditions*, Part 34, and *Survey of Conditions*, Part 18. Cattle figures for 1935 differ from count figures in *Survey of Conditions*, Part 34, p. 17978, as well as from estimates in *Survey of Conditions*, Part 34.

[b] Totals supplied by the author, not in original table.

[c] Figures for these years exclude Hopi stock and include only the reservation proper, according to source. Presumably, then, figures for other years include off-reservation stock.

[d] According to source, these figures include 768 yearling colts counted as mature horses.

TABLE 6

TOTAL LIVESTOCK NUMBERS, 1936–1947

(On Reservation Only, Hopi Excluded)

Year	Mature Sheep	Mature Goats	Mature Cattle	Mature Horses	Lambs	Total Mature Sheep, Goats[a]	Total Mature S.U.
1936........	408,500	66,000	12,000	23,500	....	474,500	639,000
1937........	380,000	55,000	17,000	41,000	....	435,000	708,000
1940........	357,000	57,000	13,000	31,000	....	414,000	621,500
1941........	357,000	52,000	9,000	27,500	275,000	409,000	585,000
1942........	362,000	52,000	8,000	27,000	290,000	414,000	583,500
1943........	338,000	47,000	8,000	27,000	253,000	385,000	552,000
1944........	344,000	42,000	8,000	26,000	236,000	386,000	548,000
1945........	284,000	32,500	7,000	26,000	212,000	316,000	477,000
1946........	257,000	29,000	7,500	26,500	189,000	286,000	449,000
1947........	245,000	29,000	8,000	27,000	183,000	274,000	440,000

Promulgated carrying capacity in S.U., 513,000 (on-reservation)

Source: Window Rock Area Office Files, transcribed by the author and rounded to the nearest 500.

[a] Not in source; supplied by author.

TABLE 7
TOTAL MATURE LIVESTOCK NUMBERS, 1930–1947
(Total Owned Off- and On-Reservation, Hopi Included)

Year	Mature Sheep	Mature Goats	Mature Cattle	Mature Horses	Total Mature Sheep, Goats[a]	Total Mature S.U.
1930.....	575,000	187,000	25,000	50,000	762,000	1,111,500
1931.....	631,000	197,000	25,000	50,000	828,000	1,178,000
1932.....	576,000	173,500	21,000	44,000	749,000	1,053,000
1933.....	545,000	165,000	20,000	42,000	710,000	1,000,000
1934.....	503,000	147,000	19,000	40,000	650,000	926,000
1935.....	548,500	92,000	19,000	40,000	640,500	918,000
1936.....	459,000	74,000	15,000	30,000	533,000	744,000
1937.....	476,000	64,000	20,000	45,000	540,000	846,000
1941.....	450,000	72,000	12,000	35,000	522,000	744,500
1942.....	449,000	74,000	10,000	36,000	523,000	743,000
1943.....	429,000	72,000	10,000	35,000	501,000	719,500
1944.....	350,000	69,000	10,000	35,000	519,000	736,000
1945.....	388,000	59,000	10,000	35,000	447,000	661,000
1946.....	355,000	55,000	10,000	35,000	410,000	628,000
1947.....	337,000	52,000	10,000	35,500	389,000	607,000

Source: Window Rock Area Office Files, transcribed by the author and rounded to the nearest 500.
[a] Not in source; supplied by author.

TABLE 8
COMPOSITE SMALL STOCK FIGURES; PER CAPITA FIGURES

Year	Total Sheep, Goats, Lambs[c] (1)	Total Mature Sheep, Goats[d] (2)	Total Mature Sheep, Goats[e] (3)	Total Mature Sheep, Goats[f] (4)	Population (5)[a]	Per Capita Small Stock Using Various Livestock Figures (1/5)[b]	(2/5)[b]	(4/5)k[b]
1930.....	1,297,589	761,589	....	762,000	38,787	33	20	20
1931.....	1,370,554	827,373	....	828,000	39,952	34	20	20
1932.....	1,180,230	749,498	....	749,000	41,117	29	21	21
1933.....	1,152,492	709,725	....	710,000	42,272	27	18	18
1934.....	1,086,648	650,046	....	650,000	43,437	25	17	17
1935.....	944,910	640,801	....	640,500	44,610	21	15	15
1936.....	....	532,885	474,500	533,000	45,949	......	14	14
1937.....	....	448,922	435,000	540,000	47,288	......	11	12
1940.....	....	413,904	414,000	....	51,306	......	10	14
1941.....	....	505,751	409,000	522,000	52,847	......	8	......
1942.....	....	....	414,000	523,000	54,388	......	10	10
1943.....	....	....	385,000	501,000	55,929	......	......	10
1944.....	....	....	386,000	519,000	57,470	......	......	9
1945.....	....	....	316,000	447,000	59,009	......	......	9
1946.....	....	....	286,000	410,000	60,781	......	......	8
1947.....	....	....	274,000	389,000	62,553	......	......	7
1950.....	....	....	....	....	64,553	......	......	6
1951.....	....	273,633	....	....	67,867	......	......	......
1952.....	....	262,473	....	....	69,973	......	4	......
1953.....	....	278,305	....	....	72,079	......	4	......
1954.....	....	304,939	....	....	74,185	......	4	......
1955.....	....	312,987	....	....	76,291	......	4	......
1956.....	....	328,694	....	....	78,395	......	4	......
1957.....	....	346,645	....	....	80,747	......	4	......
1958.....	....	364,785	....	....	83,099	......	4	......
1959.....	....	372,361	....	....	84,761	......	4	......
					87,302	......	4	......

[a] Population figures for 5-year intervals beginning in 1930 based on Johnson's extrapolations. Remaining years, extrapolated from these. 1956–1959 extrapolations at 3 per cent per annum.
[b] These three columns are per capita holdings in small stock, based on cols. 1, 2, and 4 divided by population.
[c] *Survey of Conditions*, Part 34, p. 17995.
[d] TNY 1961, p. 167. Includes Hopi stock and presumably off-reservation stock except for 1940, 1951, and 1956–1959.
[e] Window Rock Area Office Files. On-reservation only, Hopi excluded. Rounded.
[f] Window Rock Area Office Files. Includes Hopi stock and off-reservation stock. Rounded.

duction as a base. It also shows percentage declines in per capita holdings, using the same bases.

Whatever table is used, the general trend is unmistakable. There was a large decline between 1932, a peak year, and 1935, the end of voluntary reduction. Some of this decline occurred before reduction began. The Navahos lost somewhere between 16 and 27 per cent of their stock between 1930 and the end of voluntary reduction, half or more of it after reduction began. Between the close of voluntary reduction and 1940, when permits were issued, there was a considerable drop of 15 to 30 per cent. The decline continued throughout the war and thereafter until a low was reached in 1952. By then the Navahos had 36 per cent of their 1930 stock and 51 per cent of the stock which remained after the reduction of 1933–1935. Then a slow rise began, until in 1959 they held 49 per cent of their 1930 stock and 68 per cent of their 1936 stock.

This looks like a sizable rebound until it is examined in per capita terms. If we use the only table which runs from 1930 to 1959, it can be seen that per capita holdings in mature sheep and goats declined from 20 in 1930 to 14 in 1935, when voluntary reduction terminated, to 8 in 1940 when permits were issued, to 4 in 1951. The subsequent increase in stock was just sufficient to maintain the figure of 4 per capita, in the face of rising population. Clearly a family of 5 with 20 mature sheep and goats cannot make a living from livestock. Furthermore, in percentage terms,

TABLE 9*

PERCENTAGE DECLINES, TOTAL AND PER CAPITA

	1930 Base (1)	1930 Base (2)	1936 Base (2)	1936 Base (3)	1930 Base (4)	1936 Base (4)	1930 Base (1/5)	1930 Base (2/5)	1936 Base (2/5)	1930 Base (4/5)	1936 Base (4/5)
1930....	100	100	....	....	100	....	100	100	....	100	......
1931....	101	108	....	....	109	....	103	105	....	105	......
1932....	91	98	....	....	98	....	88	90	....	90	......
1933....	89	92	....	....	93	....	82	85	....	85	......
1934....	84	85	....	....	85	....	76	75	....	75	......
1935....	73	84	....	....	84	....	64	70	....	70	......
1936....	....	69	100	100	70	100	....	55	100	60	100
1937....	....	57	83	92	71	101	....	50	91	70	117
1940....	....	54	77	87	....	....	....	40	73	....	......
1941....	....	66	94	86	69	98	....	50	91	50	83
1942....	....	....	....	87	69	98	....	....	....	50	83
1943....	....	....	....	81	66	94	....	....	....	45	75
1944....	....	....	....	81	68	96	....	....	....	45	75
1945....	....	....	....	67	57	84	....	....	....	40	67
1946....	....	....	....	60	54	77	....	....	....	35	58
1947....	....	....	....	58	51	73	....	....	....	30	50
1951....	....	36	51	....	....	....	....	20	36	....	......
1952....	....	34	49	....	....	....	....	20	36	....	......
1953....	....	36	52	....	....	....	....	20	36	....	......
1954....	....	40	57	....	....	....	....	20	36	....	......
1955....	....	41	58	....	....	....	....	20	36	....	......
1956....	....	43	61	....	....	....	....	20	36	....	......
1957....	....	45	65	....	....	....	....	20	36	....	......
1958....	....	48	67	....	....	....	....	20	36	....	......
1959....	....	49	68	....	....	....	....	20	36	....	......

* This table is based on the previous table. Numbers at the heads of columns represent the numbers of columns for the previous table. Thus the first column shows percentage decline for the livestock totals in col. 1 of the previous table. 1930 and 1936 are used as bases for calculation of percentage decline of livestock totals and per capita figures, so as to make col. 3 of the previous table comparable with cols. 2 and 4.

Navahos had lost 80 per cent of their per capita holdings if 1930 is used as a base, and 64 per cent if 1936 is used. These figures, absolute, percentage, and per capita are essential for an understanding of the impact of livestock reduction on the Navaho.

REACTIONS TO REDUCTION, 1936–1941

Navaho hostility to reduction undoubtedly increased during these years. In 1937, the Bureau began the Human Dependency Surveys, a sociological and ecological survey of the reservation (Spicer, 1952, p. 190). In District 9, almost no one would cooperate with the field workers—because they associated the survey with livestock reduction (Aberle, field notes). In about 1936, a group of Navahos at Teec Nos Pas told Fryer, the Superintendent, that they would hang him if they found out he was lying to them about reduction (Kimball, Fryer, personal communications). It is possible that the Navahos were armed, and that Chee Dodge had sent his own private group of armed men to protect Fryer and Chee's son, Tom Dodge, who attended the meeting. In 1939, the Navahos of Districts 9 and 12 refused to round up their horses for the horse count, and Federal marshals were brought in. The Government began suits against some Navahos for non-compliance with horse reduction (Lyle Young, memorandum cited above; NTCR, pp. 251–252). After 1937, many Navahos refused to discuss the 1937 count with Government employees. Many refused to receive their permits in 1940, thinking thereby to avoid reduction. Many held their stock and forced the issue of supplementary permits.

On January 25, 1940, in Shiprock, four Navahos were on trial for refusing to cooperate in the 1939 roundup. Fifty Navahos assembled, it is said with the idea of tieing up the white officials there and preventing the trial. Some were armed. In the end there was only a fistfight, and by next day they were willing to let the trial continue. The same evening, a group of Navaho leaders meeting in Gallup wired the Commissioner to ask for an investigation of the reduction program (*Gallup Gazette*, Jan. 26, 1940). These episodes are undoubtedly only a scattering of the acts of resistance which Navahos carried out (see Young, 1954, for a number of poignant accounts of resistance to reduction and suffering through reduction).

Besides these acts of resistance and approaches to violence, there were visionary stirrings, some of which, at least, were clearly related to livestock reduction. In late 1936 or early 1937, a Navaho woman living near Farmington had a vision, followed by a dream, about "banded rock boy," a legendary Navaho figure. The "boy" told her, "Things are not good in the country. Times are bad; the people are bad. The rain does not come and the sheep do not increase. We do not live in the right way anymore. The whole world is the same. People have forgotten the right way to live and everyone thinks the wrong thoughts. It is not good. The people should hold ceremonies. They must pray for things to be good again." He described what seems to be a form of Blessing Way ceremony, including a prayer for rain, grass, and the well-being and increase of livestock, and said it should be held. This was the woman's vision. Thereafter ceremonies were held at Fruitland, Hogback, Redrock, and probably elsewhere. Then the "boy" came again in a dream. He praised the Navahos for performing the ceremony and said that things would improve. "He told the woman that all of the work being done on the reservation by the Government was for the best and that it would bring good sooner or later." He said he would give her special corn. Next morning she found a double handful of corn outside her door. She put it in a sack and later found the sack full. The corn had multiplied tenfold. She gave it to Navahos to plant for ceremonial purposes. But a singer at Two Gray Hills scoffed and said that the "boy" was an evil spirit. The singer died shortly afterward, which increased people's respect for the vision (Watson, 1937; he attests the ceremonies and the death of the singer).

It seems highly probable that this episode is connected with reduction, because of the references to the decline of the world and to future improvement through the Government's work. But the message is pacific. It seems to reflect the Navaho belief that there could be enough stock if there were more water and rain. It also stresses the value of agriculture.

In 1936, in the Huerfano district, not too far away, a young woman said she had been visited by White Shell Woman, one of the most important of Navaho supernaturals. She was given instructions for special Blessing Ways to be held (Kluckhohn, personal communication, based on *Farmington Times Hustler*, Feb. 21, 1937). There is no evidence here for connection with livestock reduction.

In the Shiprock area, probably between 1936 and 1941, a woman said that, even though the Navahos did not believe in Jesus Christ, she had seen him while she was herding (Kimball, personal communication). A Navaho, perhaps a woman, saw a Caucasian boy dressed in velvet, who was Jesus Christ and who said, "I will lead you out of these terrible troubles that the whites are making for you" (Kimball, personal communication; no date supplied, but during livestock reduction).

In 1941, in Largo or Blanco Canyon, a woman saw a vision of a field full of skulls of white men. The sons of Changing Woman, Born of Water and Monster Slayer, had come and killed them. These sons, she said, were the Japanese. The vision apparently occurred after Pearl Harbor (Kimball, personal communication).

Kimball gave his accounts to me in summer of 1949, from memory, so that it is possible that there is some overlap between the two visions of Jesus Christ. But the visions of Banded Rock Boy and White Shell Woman must be separate visions, but not necessarily separate visionaries, and both are clearly distinct in timing from the skull vision. The skull vision and one vision of Christ have clear anti-white elements. The Banded Rock Boy vision, the skull vision, and one vision of Christ carry a message of impending change through supernatural means, to help the Navahos. All the visions occurred in a limited area in the northern reservation, where hostility to livestock reduction and other features of the Government program were maximal.

Except for a flood prophecy some time in 1920 to 1922, discussed in a later chapter, this is the only occasion where I find any record of important Navaho visions or images of impending, supernaturally caused catastrophe.

In sum, as a result of the reductions of 1937–1941, there was conflict over the organization of the Council, distrust of the Council by others, distrust within the Council of a possible executive committee, open resistance, including minor violence, widespread feelings of helplessness and confusion, and a minor outbreak of visions and seeking after supernatural solutions. Violence and visions alike seem to have centered primarily in the north.

CONTEXT, 1942–1945

World War II had begun. The slump in Navaho income that had resulted from the tapering off of Government employment in the late 1930's was counterbalanced by the war situation. About 3,600 Navahos went into the armed services. The Army proved a significant source of cash for the Navahos, providing family allowances, and life insurance money. In the labor shortage of World War II, Navahos moved into the labor market on a considerable scale—into war industries, railroads, mining, and off-reservation agriculture. There is no information as to how many were employed during the war (TNY 1957, p. 281). Although some of the work was close at hand, in the bean, beet, and carrot fields of Arizona, New Mexico, Colorado, and Utah, and in the ordnance plants at Fort Wingate and Bellemont, many Navahos found jobs far removed from the reservation, especially on the West Coast. Hence, not only did more money come into Navaho economy, but less people had to be supported locally by livestock raising and farming.

GOVERNMENT AND COUNCIL ACTIONS, 1942–1945

Undoubtedly the Bureau suffered from a shortage of manpower, so that vigilant control of livestock may have become more difficult. But pressure continued. The Bureau threatened legal action against violators of regulations in March of 1943, and there were subsequent trials and jail sentences. Although there is no record available to me as to the precise nature of other Government action during these years, the actions of the Tribal Council clearly represent efforts to counter

CHART D
Certain Resolutions of the Navajo Tribal Council, 1942–1945

1942 Since small owners have always been dominated by large ones, since they cooperate with the grazing program, since they are poor and yet must furnish their children's clothing for day schools, resolved that within the carrying capacity of each District they be allowed to build up their herds, through special permits (NTCR, p. 234). Result unknown.

1943 Resolved to abolish all demonstration areas (NTCR, p. 172); rejected by Secretary of Interior. Equivalent resolution then passed (NTCR, p. 174). Result unknown.

So that Navahos might aid the war effort by eating home products, and so as to prepare for the post-war depression, resolved that special permits continue indefinitely and small owners keep sheep over permits, with continuous re-evaluation of carrying capacity. Rejected by the Commissioner (NTCR, p. 235). Second resolution to dispose of surplus horses by September 1, to retain all regular and special permits for 18 months; suggests that permittees keep food livestock over and above permit level (NTCR, p. 236).

Request community boarding schools, more medicine and irrigation, farming instruction, job training, and development of tribal enterprise—whatever happens to livestock (NTCR, p. 135). Result unknown.

1945 Since livestock numbers are now below the subsistence needs of most Navahos, and since the people cannot stand any more reduction, resolved to have a restudy of the range, a suspension of reduction, and continuation of existing permits (NTCR, p. 230).

1945 Resolved July 11 to abolish the consolidated agency, eliminate the Districts, and return to the six-agency system. Disapproved. Resolved again, December 20 (Minutes, Navajo Tribal Council, Window Rock, December 18–20, 1945). Result, nil.

Government pressures. And as time went on, the Council became more and more overtly opposed to the entire Government program. The resolutions were very much concerned with slowing or stopping reduction, with retaining the special permits, which had been granted originally for only a short time, with the development of alternatives to livestock raising for some Navahos, and with abolition of demonstration areas. The culmination came in 1945, when the Council twice asked for a return to the status quo ante Collier (Chart D).

LIVESTOCK NUMBERS, 1942-1945

Perhaps because of a shortage of personnel, there is little in the way of official records on livestock numbers between 1942 and 1951. No figures are published in TNY. Those I secured from files at Window Rock show a drop during these years, with minor waverings in 1942 and 1943, and an especially large decrease between 1944 and 1945. In 1945, for the first time, Navaho livestock holdings fell below the carrying capacity of the range established in the 1930's at 513,000 S.U. They stood at only 477,000 S.U. (Table 6).[2]

NAVAHO REACTIONS, 1942-1945

Navaho reactions during this period are scantily recorded. In March of 1943, there was a meeting on stock control at Shiprock, beginning at two in the afternoon and continuing until two in the morning. The Superintendent (J. M. Stewart) and the Council Chairman (probably J. C. Morgan) attended. The Government had announced the intention of bringing all holdings in line with existing permits. The prevailing tone of the meeting was a flat refusal to comply with regulations, although the Superintendent and the Chairman spoke in favor of reduction. The Navahos were told that refusal to comply would be met with action in the federal courts (*Gallup Gazette*, March 11, 1943).[3]

As has been pointed out, Navahos did violate the grazing regulations, and there were trials in March of 1944—and probably at other times for which I have no record. Defendants came from Twin Lakes, in the south, Fruitland, in the north, and other areas un-named. At this time, Chee Dodge spoke in favor of culling livestock, and the Government informed the Navahos that grazing regulations were definitely in effect—there was a rumor that they were not. Nevertheless, at about this time, Navahos at Aztec, New Mexico, said that they did not wish the Federal Government to remove its protection from them (*Gallup Gazette*, March 16, 1944).

[2] TNY does provide figures for total S.U. for each District and for the entire on-reservation area, for each year from 1936 on—excluding 1938 and 1939, and 1944-1949. These sometimes are identical with those which appear in previous tables, and sometimes vary. They do not add enough information to make it worthwhile to present them *in toto*. Figures for 1950, the only year supplied solely in these tables, are 460,526 S.U. (TNY 1957, p. 335, and comparable tables in other issues).

[3] Surprisingly enough, the newspaper article presenting this information states that in only four Districts was there any appreciable overstocking: Districts 2, 8, 9, and 10. Yet the official figures indicate that in 1942, when the count had last been made, Districts 2, 8, and 10 were little overstocked, whereas Districts 9, 4, 15, 14, and 12, in that order were overstocked 76 to 42 per cent (TNY, 1958, p. 335).

Perhaps the most serious episode of these years was the kidnapping of a Supervisor and a Navaho range rider at Teec Nos Pas in District 9. The Supervisor was knocked out and tied up, and when his wife refused to leave him, she was taken along. It seems probable that the Navahos wanted to kill the Supervisor. The Navajo Police retrieved the kidnapping victims with no trouble, taking some of the Navahos responsible into custody, but some of the Navahos fled. They shot at the Police when they were hunted down subsequently. All the Navaho participants were eventually tried, among them a Tribal Councilman.

Newspaper accounts at the time attributed the trouble to the fact that the Supervisor had ordered a Navaho to sell the stock he held over and above his permit. The Navaho claimed that the surplus belonged to his son and asked for a permit for him. The Supervisor refused—as indeed he had to, according to regulations (*New York Sunday News*, Jan. 28, 1945, and interviews).

Some years later, the Supervisor told me that the Government had been cutting down on special permit sizes in 1943–1944. In District 9, where the maximum regular permit was only 83 S.U., these special permits were of particular importance. He said that the Government had officially asked for the reduction but had unofficially asked Supervisors to take it easy. He had followed official orders and had found the contradictory demands confusing and disturbing. He felt that the kidnapping occurred because of the efforts to reduce special permits.[4]

Teec Nos Pas was a storm center throughout the period of stock reduction. Furthermore, it is said to be Black Horse's old stronghold, and a focus of opposition to the Bureau for decades. District 12 was another focus of resistance to reduction. It is therefore of interest to note that in 1943, both Districts shared the distinction of having *more* livestock than in 1936 after the voluntary reduction. This was true of no other Districts.

One final note on reactions to reduction will be made at this point, although I am not certain of its proper chronological placement. Sometime between the late 1930's and early 1940's, Jacob C. Morgan organized the Navajo Rights Association, which was active against the Collier administration on all issues: the consolidated agency, the day-school system, the livestock program, etc. Unfortunately, I have almost no information on this organization.[5]

CONTEXT, 1946–1950

These were years of increasing poverty and gloom in the Navaho country. With the end of the war, the soldiers returned and employment opportunities for the Navahos decreased (TNY 1957, p. 281). Population was rising not only through national increase but through the return of veterans and ex-war workers. Livestock continued to decline, and of course income dropped sharply. By 1947, the condition of the Navaho began to attract widespread public attention—in part be-

[4] The episode was dramatic—the aftermath was not. The Supervisor was transferred to another District and a more easy-going man brought in to District 9. In 1955, the kidnapped man became the head of one of the five new sub-agencies (see below).

[5] It was active in support of Raymond Nakai, who was elected Tribal Chairman in 1963, and remains active in 1965.

cause opponents of foreign aid found the plight of indigenous Americans a good platform from which to attack economic support for foreigners. In late 1947, Congress responded to the situation by providing $2,000,000 in direct relief to the Navahos and by asking for the development of a long-range plan for Navahos and Hopis. In 1948, the Department of Interior provided a plan, based on Agency and Bureau work going back as far as 1942. Congress passed an enabling bill for the $80,000,000 ten-year plan in 1950, and funds became available in fiscal year 1951 (see TNY, entire series, for the history of this plan).

In the winter of 1948–1949, there was a severe blizzard, which endangered Navaho livestock, which were starving for lack of fodder, but not the people themselves. But some whites on the reservation and the press took up the cry that the Navaho were starving. Operation Haylift was organized to drop needed fodder and unneeded food from planes. To some Navahos and whites, it was symbolic of American efforts to help the Navahos that a load of condensed milk dropped from a plane killed a Navaho woman (Young 1954, pp. 77–80). Drought began in 1950.

GOVERNMENT AND COUNCIL ACTION, 1946–1950

The Government tended to press for maintenance of livestock at permit level during these years. The Council continued to press for re-adjustment and re-evaluation. The general crisis was reflected in resolutions in 1947. In February a resolution remarked that "the patience and endurance of the Navajo Indians cannot be depended to remain calm in a time of adversity . . ." and asked for suspension of stock reduction for five years and a study of the range (NTCR, p. 263). In July, the Council stated that the Navahos could no longer sustain themselves by livestock because of reduction and range deterioration and asked for industrial development on the reservation (NTCR, pp. 143–144). In the same month, the Tribe hired a Tribal attorney, who was able to make the Secretary of the Interior agree that the livestock regulations were illegal. In October, ". . . enforcement was in practical effect suspended until the tribe and the Bureau could draft new regulations" (NTCR, Forward, p. ii; see also TNY 1957, pp. 242–243). So ten years of enforced livestock reduction and regulation were found to have no legal base. (The issue at stake was not the Secretary's right to control Indian grazing, but the mechanisms used in the Navaho case.)

Nevertheless, the Council agreed in March of 1948 that termination of permits would create chaos. Until new regulations could be developed, satisfactory to the Council and the Department of Interior, the Council suspended Law and Order provisions connected with reduction, thus removing legal penalties for transgression of the code. Some punitive provisions were re-established in 1949. At the end of 1950, the Commissioner and the Council were still negotiating to develop mutually acceptable regulations.

LIVESTOCK NUMBERS

Numbers continued to drop, until, in 1950, there were only about 40 per cent of the 1930 livestock count. Small stock per capita reached the low figure of 4 in 1947 and has never risen higher since then.

REACTIONS TO STOCK REDUCTION

No episodes of a dramatic character are known to me for these years; nor is there any published material other than the Council resolutions to give color to Navaho reactions. But in 1949, when I began my field work, the general mood was pessimistic and disgruntled. And again and again in my field work in this and subsequent years, Navahos told me that they must have more sheep to live. The promise of the ten-year plan was in the air in 1949, but there was considerable cynicism regarding its probable effect on local conditions—if it passed.

Chapter 6

STOCK REGULATION: 1951–1962

CONTEXT

ALTHOUGH I completed virtually all my field work in 1953, and this book is written primarily with reference to conditions up to that year, it is impossible to leave the Navaho story at that point. The Navaho scene changed completely. One factor in the transformation, and by no means the most important, was the expenditure under the ten-year plan of eighty-nine million dollars, of which twenty-five million went for school construction and thirty-eight million for roads (TNY 1961, p. 5). A second was the additional spurt of school development which took place between 1954 and 1958, using funds over and above the ten-year plan monies, which changed the percentage of Navaho children in school from 62 in 1954 to 93 in 1958 (TNY 1958, p. 356). A third was the development of mining and oil and natural gas, much of it on the reservation, with attendant jobs for Navahos and enormous increments to the Tribal treasury. A fourth, affected very much by the ten-year plan and the mineral and oil revenues, was the development of a far more bureaucratized Tribal Council with great financial responsibilities (cf. Shepardson, 1963). A fifth was the Glen Canyon Dam development in the west.

It must be emphasized that in 1953, when my field work stopped, only about $24,500,000 of the ten-year plan funds had been spent, and mineral resources had not yet begun to have their full impact. Thus uranium and vanadium revenues of the Tribe went from about $66,000 in 1950 to $470,000 in 1953, rising thereafter to between $550,000 and $755,000 per annum. Oil and gas income rose somewhat earlier—from $43,000 in 1946 to more than $1,000,000 in 1948—but after some fluctuations between $400,000 and $1,400,000, it rose to more than $5,000,000 in 1953 and 1954, dropped to $1,500,000 in 1956, but rose to nearly $35,000,000 in 1957, dropping gradually to nearly $12,000,000 in 1960 (TNY 1961, pp. 268–269).

The oil funds cannot be looked on primarily as income; much of them must be treated as capital. Furthermore, they are not used for per capita payments. And finally, if they were, it would not do very much good: the total revenues of nearly one hundred ten million, received since 1935, divided among ninety thousand Navahos, would give each a little more than twelve hundred dollars and would provide only temporary relief from their present problems.

The Tribe has used these funds in a variety of imaginative ways. The Council's budget, which ran between $500,000 and $6,000,000 in the years 1951–1957, has ranged between $15,000,000 and $35,000,000 in the years 1958–1962. The Tribe pays the costs of operating the Reservation court and police system. It purchases clothing for needy Navaho schoolchildren, whose parents formerly found the provision of clothing very burdensome, if not impossible. It set aside $10,000,000 of oil revenues, the income to be used for a scholarship program for Navaho college students. It supports the building of community centers associated with Chapter organizations. It provides eyeglasses, hearing aids, false teeth, wheelchairs, and layettes to the needy. It provides building materials for the needy to construct new houses, surplus commodities to Navahos on relief and other needy cases, and many other special welfare services.

In addition to these welfare provisions, it runs various agricultural, irrigation, and livestock improvement programs. It attempts to develop business and industrial units—thus far with little success. It pays for many other services. Between 1957 and 1962, it budgeted $12,000,000 for public works programs in economically depressed years (see TNY 1961 for a full account).

This is an opportune point to discuss the changes in the sources of Navaho income from 1936 to the recent period (Table 10). It must be remembered that in

TABLE 10

SOURCES OF NAVAHO INCOME IN PERCENTAGES

	1936	1940	1958 (est.)
Livestock and agriculture.........	54	58	10
Arts and crafts..................	6	9	1
Wages*........................	34	30	68
Miscellaneous...................	6	3	0
Mineral leases..................	....	....	5
Welfare, benefits, railroad ret.†	....	....	16
	100	100	100

* Most wages in 1936 and 1940 were from the Government.

† Split almost evenly between Social Security, other welfare and benefits, and railroad retirement act funds.

WAGE INCOME, FURTHER DIVIDED, IN PERCENTAGES

On-Reservation:		
Federal payroll......................	12	
Tribal............................	7	
Mining, uranium milling, natural gas (private) payroll........................	6	
Tribal public works payroll............	3	
Misc. (includes some small business income).............................	2	
Subtotal.......................	30	30
Off-Reservation:		
Railroad..........................	26	
Ordnance depots....................	3	
Agricultural wages..................	3	
Non-agricultural wages..............	3	
Miscellaneous......................	3	
Subtotal.......................	38	38
Total........................	....	68

Source: TNY 1958, pp. 100–109, esp. 107–108.

1936 there was a great deal of on-reservation employment supplied by the Government. Five years earlier, wages would have made up a very small percentage of the total. It can be seen that these very wages declined between 1936 and 1940, as public works spending dropped off. But in 1936 and 1940, most Navaho income came from livestock and agriculture, and only about a third from wages. In 1958, only a fraction of income came from these sources, and more than two-thirds was derived from wages, more of which were earned off-reservation than on. Indeed, welfare, railroad retirement act funds, and various relief and other benefits accounted for more income than did livestock. Total Navaho per capita income is only about one-third of that for New Mexico as a whole, and about 30 per cent of the American average (TNY 1958, pp. 100–109; 1961, pp. 228–229). Furthermore, however much Navaho income has been supplemented by funds supplied by the Tribe—as described above—it is increasing no more rapidly than the income of citizens of the surrounding states or of the United States. Since 1936, Navaho per capita income has stood at between one-third and one-quarter of New Mexico per capita income (loc. cit.).

Navaho sources of livelihood remain, as ever, extremely unstable. The Federal payroll was augmented from 1951 to 1960 with ten-year plan funds, which have now expired. The uranium finds are expected to deplete fairly rapidly. Railroads are reducing their needs for manpower by technological improvements—and in 1958, they were the major source of Navaho employment. Agricultural and non-agricultural wages from other sources are small in quantity and fluctuating in character. The income of the Tribe from oil and gas is primarily dependent on new finds, not on steady royalties. The Navahos themselves are probably aware of the relatively undependable nature of most sources of employment. For them, Federal, Tribal, and industrial jobs probably appear stable, but these are but a fraction of all jobs. Their unwillingness to abandon subsistence livestock activities seems eminently understandable under these circumstances.

The situation is not much ameliorated by the Government's relocation program, which settles Navahos in cities as far away as Chicago. By 1961, 3,273 people had been relocated, and about 2,000 remained relocated, the remainder returning to the Navaho country. This represents a little better than 2 per cent of the total population. On the whole, the numbers relocating have been increasing since the program started in 1952 (TNY 1961, pp. 235–236). There is no record of the number of Navahos who may have relocated without aid.

There was a major administrative change in July of 1955. The Land Management Units were grouped into five sub-agencies: Shiprock (Districts 9, 12, and 13); Fort Defiance (7, 14, 17, and 18); Crownpoint (15, 16, and 19—mainly off-reservation); Chinle (4, 10, and 11); and Tuba City (1, 2, 3, 5, and 8). This is a sort of return to the old "six-agency system" (TNY 1961, pp. x, 602). In the light of Navaho complaints of the 1930's, the present situation has its ironies. The major complaints which were made in Survey of Conditions, Part 34, were objections to livestock reduction, the consolidated agency, day schools instead of boarding schools, and soil conservation instead of water development. By the 1950's, the grazing regulations were found illegal, the five sub-agencies were created, stress on boarding schools increased, and the Tribe poured money into water development. Twenty years of Navaho tenacity in outlook finally found expression.

LIVESTOCK REGULATION, GOVERNMENT AND COUNCIL ACTION

There were two major struggles during this period: the first, to draft regulations acceptable both to the Council and to the Commissioner; the second, to bring the Tribe to enforce the regulations. It took from June of 1948 to April of 1956 to produce regulations mutually acceptable. During this time, the Commissioner tried several times to set a terminal date for revisions, but was not successful. Meantime, punitive provisions of the regulations were suspended in 1952, and permits were made negotiable (according to TNY, for the second time, but I cannot find when they first became negotiable). Local Grazing Committees were established in 1953 and met repeatedly with the Council to discuss the formulation of the new rules.

The new regulations were widely explained in the second half of 1956. Supposedly all stock above permit level were to be eliminated by April of 1957, but after much discussion there was an extension to April of 1958, and again to April of 1959. (The issue of compliance is still being discussed in 1965.)

Drought in the 1950's has further depleted the range, so that carrying capacity has declined from the 512,000 sheep units estimated in 1943 to a probable 387,000 in 1960. With at least 539,000 sheep units on the range (80,000 of them goats!), the range is badly overgrazed. The Department of Agriculture supplied emergency feed in the years 1957–1959 to attempt to save livestock perilously close to starvation. The Tribe dealt with the crisis in 1960 by appropriating purchase funds for livestock, to relieve the range, during a period when the market fell off. An extensive survey of the Navaho range is at present under way, and the Navaho head of the Tribal Division of Resources has begun to push for adequate livestock control (TNY 1961, pp. 157–172).

LIVESTOCK NUMBERS AND RELATED ISSUES

Livestock numbers continued to decline through 1952 but began to rise thereafter until, by 1959, they had nearly reached 1944 level. Per capita figures stayed stationary. The over-all decline in per capita livestock holdings is perhaps best seen in a comparison of 1915 holdings with those of 1940 and 1958 (Table 11). It must be kept in mind that Paquette's 1915 survey covered only sheep, that the figures cited by Kluckhohn are presumably sheep and goats, but that the 1958 figures are sheep *units*. Were the 1958 figures to exclude horses, burros, and cattle, the results would be even more striking—many a small permittee keeps only 2 horses, or 10 sheep units.

The median sheep holding in 1915 was less than 50 sheep; in 1940, the median remained somewhere in that range; in 1958, the median figure was *no* sheep units. One-third of the population had more than 100 sheep in 1915, more than 60 sheep in 1940, and more than 25 sheep units in 1958. The situation is even more striking in the west, where livestock is more important and farming less. There, in 1936, only 5 per cent of families lacked livestock: 24 per cent had 1–100 sheep units; 38

per cent held 101–300; and 33 per cent had more than 300 sheep units. In 1958, in the same western District, 70 per cent owned less than 100 sheep units, and less than one per cent held more than 300 (TNY 1961, p. 213). It is reasonable to estimate that a subsistence herd for a family of five should include a minimum of 250 sheep units—and the average Navaho family is at least five. Hence, even in Paquette's day, many Navahos must have had a thin time, supplementing livestock with farming, what little wage work there was, and labor for wealthy livestock owners. But by 1958, only ten per cent of all Navahos owned a herd sufficient for subsistence (TNY 1961, p. 214 for estimate of a subsistence herd).

TABLE 11

LIVESTOCK HOLDINGS, 1915, 1940, 1958

	1915	Cum.	1940	Cum.	1958	Cum.
None.........	24.2	24.2	26	26	53.9	53.9
1–25..........	16.0	40.2 ⎫	42*	68	⎰ 13.1	67.0
26–50.........	12.6	52.8 ⎭			⎱ 10.7	77.7
51–100........	13.5	66.3 ⎫	20†	88	⎰ 12.6	90.3
101–300........	18.4	84.7 ⎬			⎨ 9.0	99.3
301–500........	6.9	91.6 ⎭			⎩ 0.5	99.8
501–800........	4.4	96.0 ⎫	12	100	⎰ 0.1	99.9
801–1200.......	2.3	98.3 ⎬			⎨	....
1200——.......	1.5	99.8 ⎭			⎩	....

* Interval 1–60.
† Interval 61–500.
Sources: Paquette, survey of *sheep only*, Southern Navajo Agency, 1915 (TNY 1961, p. 212). Kluckhohn and Leighton, presumably using Government figures, all Navahos on and off reservation, probably including sheep and goats only, in 1940 (1946, p. 19). TNY 1961, total sheep units, all reservation in 1958 (TNY 1961, p. 212).
Only partially comparable, because of different intervals, are figures in *Survey of Conditions*, Part 34, p. 17840. These figures also omit non-owners. Among owners, 29 per cent held 1–59 units; 21 per cent held 60–99 units; 26 per cent held 100–199 units; 21 per cent held 200–499 units; and 3 per cent held 500 or more.

Still, these figures require some tempering. Although livestock were reduced, they were improved—as to weight, wool clip, and lambs produced per head of mature sheep. Indeed, the total wool clip for 1945–1947 was nearly as large as that for 1933–1935. The average wool clip per sheep increased 50 per cent (Spicer, 1952, p. 199). The average weight of lambs increased from 53 to 60 lbs. between 1930–1932 and 1942–1943 (Kluckhohn and Leighton, 1946, p. 35). Total income from livestock *increased* between 1933–1935 and 1945–1947, even if 1935 dollar values are used—increased by 60 per cent (Spicer, 1952, p. 199). So the total meat yield, important for diet and cash, and the total wool yield, especially important for cash, were affected far less than the numbers of livestock would suggest. But with a rise in population, even these gains were undoubtedly far more than offset.

The "numbers game" itself requires discussion as a social phenomenon. I have talked to many members of the Navajo Agency staff and to many Navahos about livestock reduction. In the years 1949–1953, the Agency staff members were typically concerned with the total number of sheep units on the reservation, or any section of it, and the total forage available. This lack of concern about per capita holdings seems to have been characteristic of Agency personnel from the very beginning of American domination. Indeed, except for Paquette's 1915 survey, there are no per capita or per family figures known to me until grazing surveys preliminary to livestock reduction began in the 1930's (cf. *Survey of Conditions*, Part 34, p. 17840). Data of this sort are available in the Human Dependency Survey made in the late 1930's, but thereafter published Government figures in TNY do not deal with per capita holdings until 1957. In a word, the primary focus of men concerned with stock regulation, erosion control, etc., is the land-animal balance, not the human-animal balance. If one argues that the per capita drop in Navaho livestock is alarming, they tend to respond that the yield of meat and wool per sheep unit has risen. It seems fair to say that their concern with conservation makes them obliterate from their minds any concern with per capita figures—since to do so would impale them on the horns of a dilemma which is actually obvious to them: if livestock are not reduced, the range will be ruined—and hence the Navaho; if livestock are reduced, the Navaho will be ruined.

Navahos may not talk in terms of numbers, but their discussion of livestock is largely with reference to per capita issues: how many sheep a family needs for a living; how should big and small owners share the range, and so on. They have a blind spot for increased yield in meat and wool. When they talk about carrying capacity, it is largely in terms of "hidden" carrying capacity—they claim that Navahos know and use places with good pasture which the range men overlook, and that the range is in any case not really eroded, just dry this year. These reactions were typical in the early 1950's. New developments, and local planning of grazing regulations, may have changed Navaho perspectives. And TNY from 1957 on has been much concerned with per capita holdings.

REACTIONS TO LIVESTOCK REDUCTION

During the summers of 1951 to 1953, I was on the reservation. The prevailing mood had shifted slightly from the profound discouragement just before the ten-year plan, but it was still fairly dark. This can be seen in Table 12, which shows Navaho reactions in two communities, one, Aneth, a long-term focus of anti-Government reactions; the other, Mexican Springs, within the southern, accommodative orbit, but the location of a demonstration area which has been a topic of conflict since the 1930's. Mexican Springs is clearly more cheerful than Aneth, but in both areas dissatisfaction with livestock holdings is the largest single source of discontent, and, where present, satisfaction with livestock or livestock and farm land is the single largest source of content. Both groups consider the period before livestock reduction satisfactory.

There were no particular crises over livestock between 1951 and 1953, and subsequent reactions are not relevant to the topic of this book.

Perhaps the final word on the subject should be spoken by a Navaho:

That is the way we were treated. A great number of the people's livestock was taken away. Although we were told that it was to restore the land, the fact remains that hunger and poverty stood with their mouths open to devour us. Before the stock that remained could reproduce, people slit the animals' throats to satisfy their starving children. Before the sheep could bear young the children's shoes would wear out. People would say, "Where can a sheep be sold?" When they heard of a place they would drive a couple of animals there. So instead of the stock increasing, it became less and less. And today one hears of many people who have come to possess stock permits for no reason at all (i.e., the permits are not filled or they have no more stock). There is no more stock with which to replace what is gone. It has come to the pass that there is not a place from which they can get a single sheep [Young, 1954, p. 71].

TABLE 12

REACTIONS TO LIVELIHOOD SITUATION

	Aneth (N 24) Per Cent	Mexican Springs (N 32) Per Cent
How are things going for you about making a living?:		
Badly, not very well............................	63	31
Fairly well, well...............................	37	69
What are the main bad things?:		
Not enough livestock, livestock and farm land, farm land alone (1 case)...............................	50	31
Other......................................	42	53
Nothing wrong...............................	8	16
What are the main good things?:		
Enough livestock or farm land or both.............	8	31
Other......................................	34	31
Nothing good................................	58	38
Was your livelihood satisfactory before stock reduction?:		
Yes..	75	91
So-so......................................	0	3
No...	12	6
Too young at the time, not ascertained.............	12	0

Random samples; standardized interviews, 1953, by Aberle and Moore.

COMPETING THEORIES OF NATURE AND ECONOMICS

Navaho attitudes toward stock reduction and grazing control have often been considered irrational, or governed by sentiments, values, or traditional beliefs. Some corrective to this view needs to be supplied. I shall attempt to contrast the Government and the Navaho points of view.

The Government attitude can be summed up more or less as follows:

1. There is an animal-plant cover ratio which cannot be transgressed. If there are too many animals, there will be erosion and down-grading of the quality of the range. Erosion in its milder forms involves loss of topsoil and range degradation; in its more severe forms it creates wastelands where once there were acres for forage and farming. Furthermore, by silting streams, it constitutes a hazard to major hydraulic projects outside the reservation. Downgrading the vegetation reduces carrying capacity. Thus it is not sufficient merely to freeze livestock at any given level: once the critical ratio is surpassed, stock must be reduced if the range is to recover. Unless the Navaho herd is kept in balance with the plant cover, there will be a natural catastrophe of incalculable harm to the Navahos.

2. The Navaho grazing territory has reached its maximum expansion, so that no reduction of animals per acre can be accomplished by increasing the number of acres.

3. Livestock raising is a commercial proposition. Horses are needed for riding, pulling wagons, farm work, and herding. Since they have little sale value, they should be kept at the minimum required for these purposes. Sheep are a source of meat and wool, some for consumption, and some for sale. It is far more efficient to feed large animals than to feed small ones, and far more profitable to raise animals with a good wool clip. It is also more efficient and profitable to keep herds at or below carrying capacity, since the lamb crop per head of sheep is thereby increased. It is profitable to eliminate culls and wethers, which have poor market value or are not reproductive stock, or both. It is vital to eliminate goats, which damage the range disproportionately and have poor market value.

The Navaho point of view differs from the Government one both in its beliefs about nature, which are partly erroneous, and in its understanding of the economy:

1. Overgrazing takes care of itself: if there are too many sheep, they will die. This is a risk that must be taken. The difference between what the Government considers dangerously overgrazed range and good range is merely a matter of rainfall: a year or two of good weather will restore bad range. (No account is taken of the cumulative effects of overgrazing.) Traditional Navahos believe, in addition, that the relationship between animals and the natural order is quite the reverse of that described by Government workers. Supernaturals gave sheep to the Navahos for livelihood. When the Navahos increase their flocks, the supernaturals see that the Navahos care for their gift and bring rain. When they use them improvidently or give them away, the supernaturals respond by failing to bring rain. Hence reduction brings drought, and drought damages the range. (Today, of course, there are a number of Navahos who do understand the relationship between overgrazing and range conditions in Western terms.)

2. There is no reason why the range could not be expanded, especially to the east, where the land traditionally belonged to the Navaho. This would reduce the pressure on forage.

3. Livestock raising is not a business matter. It provides subsistence, cash for consumer goods, and insurance. Sheep and goats provide food and bedding. The cash and credit gained by the sale of animals, hides, and wool, is used primarily to purchase needed goods—food, clothing, utensils, tools, wagons, trucks, etc. Cash and credit are intended for use, not for profit-taking and re-investment. Goats, wethers, and culls can be eaten, so as to save more valuable stock for sale—for more goods. Goats are especially useful in this respect. Kids, which have a low market value, come to full use for meat when lambs are still reaching market weight.

Every available basis of livelihood is uncertain. A farm, dry or irrigated, may fail completely. Then more stock are needed for consumption. Jobs are unpredictable. So was the pinon crop, when Navaho pinon gathering was a significant source of cash. The only basis that permits accumulation is livestock raising. Herds, however, can be catastrophically affected by drought or a heavy winter, or utterly consumed if some one falls ill and expensive ceremonies must be given. Hence it is best to increase the number—in case.

Furthermore, surplus livestock can be converted into storable wealth—jewelry in the main, which can be pawned with the trader, but buckskins and baskets as well, which can be used to pay a ceremonial practitioner. As a form of accumulation, jewelry has advantages over money. It is easily identified, virtually indestructible, and, used for pawn, serves to enforce savings. If a man pawns his jewelry, he will try to get the cash to pay off the pawn. If he does, he gets the jewelry back, although the cash is gone. But if he pays his debt in cash in the first instance, he has no cash and no jewelry and no special incentive to save. Surplus stock can also be turned into credit, for the long winter months.

In addition, livestock can be used to pay off reciprocities and to validate status. It can be used to maintain a following, since poor people can be induced to be loyal supporters of the wealthy in return for mutton and the chance to herd a portion of a wealthy man's flock. Whereas cash can be used to a minor degree for reciprocity, it is rarely so used even in societies where money is in extensive use. In Western culture, we do not give cash presents to equals in years or status, nor are we as likely to ask a friend for money as for time. The same is true for the Navaho.

Horses are a means of transportation. They are the traditional gifts of bridewealth. In some areas, they have an insurance function. Old horses can be eaten in case of a hard winter. They are also status symbols.

Navaho sheep must be able to withstand bad climate and forage and long treks to water. Past experience with quality breeds has been discouraging. Many die under even moderately adverse circumstances.

New resources are also unstable. Experience shows that mass employment by the Government, as in the case of Emergency Conservation Work and Soil Conservation Service jobs, waxes and wanes. Mines open and close. Railroads and off-reservation farmers need many laborers at one time and few at another. Education and job-training are seldom adequate for a stable job in a city. Stable jobs on-reservation are few in number, whether Government-paid, paid by the Tribe, or paid by private corporations. Though herd size can be radically affected by climatic conditions, these other resources fluctuate more. When a job is gone, it is gone; when a herd is decimated, it can still be built up again.

This, it seems to me, is the Navaho position. It is least rational at certain points: its theory of nature, its attitude toward surplus horses, its attitude toward improved breeds, and its attitude toward culls. These are precisely the points where the greatest change has occurred over the past twenty-five or more years. There are an increasing number of Navahos who understand the relationship between grazing and range conditions, though they maintain that the Government underestimates the range. From the beginning, surplus horses have been the focus of least resistance on the part of the Tribal Council, and they remain so today. Culling has been carried out. As breeds have been created which can withstand Navaho conditions—and produce a wool that can be woven—they have been adopted, if slowly. But these breeds did not exist early in the reduction program.

Which is the rational view? Neither, or both. The context of livestock reduction was that of an uneducated population with no alternative means of livelihood, and of Navahos and Government workers forced to work within the limits set by the American economy and polity. It seems perfectly rational to ask the Navahos to give up some of their sheep lest they lose them all, but in 1933 this was a little like telling a man who is hanging by his fingertips on the edge of a steep cliff to release his grip—or he will make the edge crumble, fall, and be killed. Today the image is a little different. But with multiple, unstable sources of livelihood, the Navahos are not likely to accept with equanimity the loss of *any* source. This, not sentiment or tradition, seems to me to be the source of the realistic Navaho unwillingness to give up his sheep.

SUMMARY: LIVESTOCK REDUCTION AND LIVESTOCK CONTROL[1]

The first period of so-called voluntary reductions (1933–1935) affected especially small owners and subsistence stock: goats and culls. Its effects were partly cushioned by employment on the reservation, but often those who benefited by employment were not those most hurt by reduction.

The second period of enforced reduction backed by legal action (1937–1947) affected larger owners especially but froze smaller owners at levels which were partly a product of the earlier reduction. Since in some districts the ceilings were low, many of the relatively larger owners had quite small permits. Culls and horses were particular targets, but needs for cash accelerated sales of other stock, including breeding stock. This period was somewhat cushioned by on-reservation employment until 1941, although Government appropriations dropped as the defense effort began. The Navahos were aided from 1942 to 1945 by high levels of employment.

The third period was one of control by suasion and by need for cash. A crisis created by lack of employment came to a head in 1947, with minimal relief until after 1950. Large and small owners remained more or less frozen, larger ones in some districts anxious over special permits subject to revocation. Non-permittees could not get a legal start in the livestock business.

A new era begins with Navaho Tribal administration of stock regulation—but this regulation still occurs within a context of low carrying capacity and rising population.

The cost to the Navahos was untold anguish and material hardship. They reacted to the Agency and the Bureau with hostility, non-compliance, physical resistance, and legal action. There are signs that acceptance of regulation may be beginning, but I hesitate to add my voice to the chorus of Bureau and Agency personnel which has asserted at intervals since the 1930's that the Navahos have started to agree to reduction and regulation.

The reduction program has been used by Collier's opponents as one more basis for attacking him. I also do not wish to join *that* chorus. He has summarized his own views of what happened in the Navaho country. Livestock reduction, he said, was vital. He could have used direct compulsion to reduce—the old Indian Service method; he could have thrown "the whole staggering responsibility onto the

---

[1] The periods used here do not correspond with the phases used in Chapters 4 and 5. Here the focus is on mechanisms of control—"voluntary," enforced, through suasion, and tribal. In Chapters 4 and 5 the focus is on mechanisms of control, but also on economic conditions. Each set of divisions is for convenience only. Thus reactions in 1936 to the voluntary reductions of 1933–1935 are considered in Chapter 5, rather than Chapter 4, because of their special importance in establishing an atmosphere of hostility preceding the systematic reduction program of 1937 and subsequent years.

Navajo Tribal Council . . ."; or he could have gone to the local community and undertaken a long program of education. He rejected the first choice on moral grounds and the third because it seemed impracticable. "In this rejection we may have erred profoundly. . . ." He chose the second. (In fairness to Collier, where I have written "he," he has written, "we": the Bureau and the Agency.)

"The Council accepted and affirmed the conservation program . . . because its intellect and conscience required it to. The Council's constituency . . . resisted [the program] with a bitterness sometimes sad, sometimes angry and wild." When Councils supported reduction, they were voted out of office, but new Councils re-affirmed reduction. "They did it out of a political virtue of a high order, and under no compulsion except that of an overwhelming reality which they acknowledged after they entered on responsibility. They were helpless to communicate their understanding to the mass of the Navajos . . ." (Collier, 1962, pp. 65–66; compare also Spicer, 1952, where Collier's comments appear).

In my opinion, Collier over-rates the voluntary assent of the Council and under-rates the suasion he applied. The Bureau had been, as Collier points out, an authoritarian agency since its beginnings. In the first half-year of his incumbency, whatever his desires to be democratic, he presented the livestock issue to the Navajo Tribal Council. After eighty-odd years of compulsion, the Navahos were not likely to hear his voice as that of *primus inter pares*. It was the voice of the Government. Furthermore, Collier used pressure: cooperation was required if the boundary bill was to pass; if reduction was not undertaken now, there might be no funds for purchasing livestock, and so on. Furthermore, how was the Council to interpret Collier's remark that he had the authority to reduce them without their assent, but that he wanted their assent? Finally, when arrests were made, Navahos were tried in Federal, not Tribal, court. Unquestionably the Tribal Council did, as Collier says, recognize that reduction was necessary for the sake of the range. But it must have acted as well with a perception of another iron necessity besides the law of nature: the power of the state to compel. Perhaps this is one reason why, in 1948, the Council expressed its hostility to E. R. Fryer, a man of conscience and high ability, but the man who administered the Agency during the height of livestock reduction (NTCR, pp. 60–62).

Chapter 7

THE NAVAHOS IN THE 1950'S

IT IS TIME NOW to look at the Navaho people as they were in the 1950's, some twenty years after livestock reduction began and more than eighty years after they were first placed on a reservation. The primary data for this examination are interviews with small samples of Navahos from only two communities, Aneth and Mexican Springs. But since systematic information on many salient characteristics of the contemporary Navaho population is impossible to come by, these data have their value.

The communities themselves differed in important respects (all statements refer to 1953). Aneth was the more remote of the two communities. The major road to Aneth passed through the Ute Mountain Ute reservation from the highway between Cortez and Shiprock. It was a killer. Aneth could also be reached from Red Mesa, in District 9, by crossing the San Juan on horseback. There were other ways of getting there by horseback and other, far more roundabout and difficult, automobile roads that touched various parts of the community. Access to the job market was correspondingly difficult. Transportation within the community was also difficult, so that the day school was virtually useless until the American Friends' Service Committee built a dormitory there in the late 1940's and improved the accommodations for the teacher.

Disputes over the land on which Aneth is located, and over the adjoining land, go back at least to the early 1900's. The border of the reservation in this area was settled in 1933, without consultation with the people of Aneth. They, and the people of Bluff, maintained that they had use rights to pasture and homes beyond these borders. The fight was still in the courts. The people were always more than a little antagonistic to surrounding whites and to the Indian Service. Aneth is the site of the Ba-i-lil-ley uprising, and hostility to livestock reduction was very strong in the 1930's.

Medical facilities were remote. The nearest ones were the nurse at the Episcopal Mission at Bluff and the hospital at Shiprock. It was fifty-five miles to Shiprock, half of it on unpaved bad road. Neither facility was easily available for quick treatment.

All in all, Aneth was one of the more isolated communities in the Navaho country. There were others more cut off from contact with the outside, but it was certainly below the average.

Mexican Springs, on the other hand, was only three miles from the highway. Its day school could be used as such, in spite of poor roads. From the highway, it was nineteen miles to Gallup, thirty-two to Window Rock, and thirty-eight to Fort Defiance—all by paved road. People living in the more remote mountain pastures, and many living in the flats were, of course, further from these centers. But it was possible for a man to take a job in Gallup and return every evening to his home in Mexican Springs.

There was a fenced Demonstration Area in the community which pastured the cattle of the local Cattle Cooperative. There was intense opposition to the fencing and to the Cooperative, but there was also strong support for both: the community was virtually deadlocked on this issue. There were a number of resident Agency personnel, and (a rarity) a privately run, Navaho-owned and staffed garage which could manage major repairs.

Mexican Springs was well above average in terms of amount of outside contact. There were more acculturated areas—Shiprock for example, just as there were more isolated and less acculturated communities than Aneth. But the two communities covered the range of most Navaho communities to be found in 1953.

Navahos were told that the interview concerned how they were getting along and what they thought about their present situation. In spite of our efforts to find neutral words to describe the purpose of the interview, it probably tended to evoke complaints, since people were well aware that their condition was not good and that publicity to this effect might be helpful. Harvey C. Moore interviewed at Aneth, and the writer interviewed at Mexican Springs.

A random sample was drawn in each community. We began with the school census and went over this list with several local informants, white and Navaho, to eliminate duplications and to add any names that might have been omitted. We also eliminated all respondents living away from the community for the summer or for a longer period, whether they were on reservation or off: it would have been impossible to track them down. We also eliminated all respondents under twenty-five, because experience indicated that it was difficult to get younger people to express opinions.

The result was undoubtedly a sample lower in education, higher in age, and with more women than a random sample of all individuals who had their base in the community.

Every *k'th* individual on the final list was drawn for the random sample. (Names were rostered by family, which reduced the likelihood of having two interviews in a single family. Experience had taught us that such interviews created difficulties.) When people on the final list proved to be away from the community or under twenty-five, they were eliminated from the sample. If they were in the community but could not be found, would not be interviewed, or could not be interviewed (one was nearly stone deaf), they were still considered part of the sample. Additional samples were drawn randomly as the summer wore on to make the sample as large as possible within the available time.

A number of cases on the original sample lists were later eliminated, because they were too young, or because they proved to live in adjoining communities, or because they were gone from the community during the summer. These cases should not have been included in the original roster, but our information about them was incomplete. From the final list at Aneth, only two were not interviewed. One refused; the other could never be reached. From the final list at Mexican Springs, ten were not interviewed. Three were too deaf for communication; three refused to be interviewed; four could never be reached. Thus the rate of failure at Aneth was two out of twenty-six, or eight per cent, but the refusal rate was only four per cent. The rate of failure at Mexican Springs was ten out of forty-two, or twenty-four per cent. The refusal rate was seven per cent. Contrary to our expectations, the primary difficulty with the use of a random sample was not failure to cooperate, but our inability to locate these mobile respondents in a limited time.

We used interpreters for most interviews. Although the English form of the interview was standardized, the Navaho version was not. Although there is a simple system for writing Navaho, few Navahos can read it. Since we could not prepare a text which our interpreters could read, we could not make our interpreters stick to an absolutely fixed wording in Navaho.

The statistical results of this work appear in Table 13. In the text I shall discuss the general picture that emerges. For the reasons mentioned above, it is not a picture of the entire Navaho population, but it is a good representation of the "core" reservation community. And it is a sad picture, in many ways.

This core population consisted primarily of women. Over half the people were aged 51 years or more. The majority were married and living in nuclear families.[1] And only a few had any education whatever. (The total reservation population, of course, was much younger, with an approximately equal sex ratio, and with rather more education.)

Although certainly not trained for jobs, only a minority of the people claimed that their primary dependency for livelihood was traditional—herding, farming, or weaving. (None claimed to earn most of their living from silversmithing.) The majority depended on cash, derived from jobs, various forms of welfare payments, and children's employment. Yet their livestock holdings in 1953, though small, were well above the reservation average for 1958. The median holding was 26–50 sheep units, whereas the reservation-wide median for 1958 was no stock at all— and this despite the fact that the maximum regular permit in both areas was small. These small, but above average livestock holdings undoubtedly reflect the high mean age of the sample.

Educated or not, most of the men had been employed at least some of the time during the years 1938–1953. The greater availability of employment for the Mexican Springs group is apparent. By and large, the men were employed seasonally, with more steady employment at Mexican Springs. And of course jobs were overwhelmingly common labor and semi-skilled.

Nearer to the job market, the men of Mexican Springs worked near home, whereas those at Aneth worked far away. Both communities depended heavily on railroad gang labor over a period of fifteen years, but in Mexican Springs there

[1] The statistics indicating that a majority of respondents in each community live in nuclear families are likely to be misleading. The sampling was so carried out as to minimize the possibility that two respondents would come from the same family unit, because after one respondent in a family has expressed himself, it is hard to induce a second one to do so. Hence the sample does not accurately reflect the percentage of persons living in nuclear or extended families, but is perhaps an approximation, instead, of the percentage of nuclear versus extended families. It is probably legitimate to conclude from the figures that there are more nuclear than extended families in each of these communities. Since there are more individuals in extended families, on average, than in nuclear families, however, no inferences should be drawn as to the percentage of Navaho individuals to be found in each family type.

TABLE 13

CHARACTERISTICS OF TWO GROUPS OF NAVAHOS IN 1953

	Aneth	Mexican Springs
Sex:		
Male..	33	41
Female..	67	59
Age:		
25–50...	46	46
51 plus...	54	55
Marital status:		
Married...	75	84
Other...	25	15
Family type:		
Nuclear or living alone...	62	53
Extended..	38	41
Not ascertained..	0	6
Education:		
None..	75	66
Through 4th grade..	8	19
Through 8th grade..	17	6
At least some high school......................................	0	9
Livestock:		
None..	14*	9 (9)†
1–25..	18	19 (16)
26–50...	27	28 (22)
51–75...	9	16 (19)
76–100..	9	13(19)
101–150...	18	9 (9)
151–200...	0	6 (6)
201–250...	0	0 (0)
251–300...	5	0 (0)
Farming:		
Farm some land..	16	84
Do not farm..	84	16
Primary source of income claimed:		
Herding...	38	28
Farming...	4	9
Weaving...	0	3
Job (own or spouse)..	25	34
Old age pension, relief, aid to dependent children..............	25	12
Children's jobs...	8	12
Secondary source claimed:		
Herding...	21	9
Farming...	4	50
Job...	25	9
Old age pension, relief, aid to dependent children..............	8	9
Children's jobs...	0	3
None or none mentioned..	42	19
Number of respondents mentioning any *support from each of these sources (does not total 100%):*		
Herding...	58	38
Farming...	8	59
Weaving...	0	3
Job...	50	44
Old age pension, relief, aid to dependent children..............	33	22
Children's jobs...	8	16
Primary source of income, classified:		
Traditional...	42	41
Job...	25	34
Dependent..	33	25
Secondary source of income, classified:		
Traditional...	25	59
Job...	25	9
Dependent..	8	12
None mentioned..	42	19

* Aneth, N is 22; 2 other cases, not ascertained.

† Mexican Springs, numbers in parentheses include Cattle Association livestock; numbers without parentheses exclude this stock.

TABLE 13—*Continued*

	Aneth	Mexican Springs
Employment of men respondents, of husbands of women respondents, 1938–1953:		
Employed at some time	79	91
Never employed	17	6
Inapplicable: unmarried or long divorced or widowed woman	4	3
Amount of employment:		
None	17	6
Little	21	16
Moderate	38	25
Much	8	41
Employment, no other data	8	6
Inapplicable	4	3
Not ascertained	4	3
Duration of employment, longest single job:		
None	17	6
Less than nine months	71	50
Nine months or more	8	34
Inapplicable	4	3
Not ascertained	0	6
Number of years 1938–1952 during which men respondents were employed part of the year (8 men, Aneth; 13, Mex. Spgs.):		
3 years or less	25	15
4–6 years	12	23
7–10 years	25	8
11 years or more	25	54
Not ascertained	12	0
Duration of employment in years when employed, men resps.:		
Three months or less per annum, average	88	46
Up to six months	12	15
Over nine months	0	38
Duration of husband's employment as reported by wife (16 women, Aneth; 19 women, Mex. Spgs.):		
Rare, short jobs or widely spaced jobs	19	16
Moderate steady employment or considerable intermittent employment	38	21
Considerable steady employment	0	32
Employment, no other data	12	11
Never employed	25	11
Inapplicable	6	5
Not ascertained	0	5
Duration of husband's employment as reported by wife:		
At least one job lasting longer than one year	12	32
No job lasting that long	56	42
Never employed	25	11
Inapplicable	6	5
Not ascertained	0	11
Type of job as reported by men:		
Labor, service, or semi-skilled	100	85
Skilled or civil service	0	15
Predominant location of jobs over last 15 years, men respondents (defined in terms of number of years employed in various locations):		
Mostly on-reservation, or mixed on-reservation and in adjoining communities, or mix on-reservation, adjoining communities, and more distant communities	12	69
Mostly more distant communities, mostly adjoining communities, or mixed adjoining and distant communities	88	31
Main source of employment, men respondents (defined as the source providing most years of a man's employment history):		
Railroad	50	38
Seasonal agricultural gang labor	38	8
Indian Service	0	38
Other	12	15
(Second most important source provides little additional information.)		
Predominant family situation for men with jobs (defined by number of years in each situation):		
Mostly away from family	62	38
Family came along	38	0
Lived at home and worked outside community or worked outside community and visited home frequently	0	62

TABLE 13—*Continued*

	Aneth	Mexican Springs
Reactions, all respondents, about husbands' going away to work:		
Pretty good	33	31
Mixed	8	6
Not so good	21	25
No job, no job away	38	38
Reactions, all respondents, to family accompanying husband when he works away from home:		
Pretty good	38	12
Mixed	0	3
Not so good	8	3
Inapplicable	54	81
Speaks English:		
No	67	62
A little	8	16
Yes	25	22
Uses English to talk to other Navahos outside home:		
Speaks no English	67	62
Uses it seldom or never	17	19
Sometimes	12	9
Usually	4	9
Speaks English in the home:		
Speaks no English	67	62
Uses it seldom or never	21	12
Sometimes	8	19
Usually	4	6
Did education help you?:		
No education	67	66
No	0	9
Yes	33	22
Don't know	0	3
Ways in which education helped:		
To get, hold, or improve a job	13	13
Other or unspecified	13	9
No education or education is no help	75	78
Do you feel satisfied with your level of education (or undisturbed by your lack of education)?:		
Satisfied, or mixed feelings	12	12
Dissatisfied	79	88
Don't know and not ascertained	8	0
Reasons for not attending school (uneducated only), Aneth N 18; Mex. Spgs. N 21:		
Wanted for work at home	39	57
Other parental opposition	33	19
Parents did not mention or did not urge school	11	10
Did not want to go	6	0
No schools then, or none where I was	11	5
Other	0	10
How did parents (or surrogates) feel about school?:		
In favor	12	22
Indifferent or did not mention it	12	19
Opposed	58	50
One favored; the other did not	12	6
Not ascertained	4	3
Do you mainly follow the Navaho or the white way?:		
Mostly Navaho	71	50
Mixed	25	16
Mostly white	4	31
Not ascertained	0	3
Is the Navaho way of life changing?:		
Dying out, changing fast, changing in most ways	42	69
Changing (no further amplification)	29	25
Changing in some ways but not in others	4	6
Not changing	0	0
Don't know and not ascertained	24	0

TABLE 13—Continued

	Aneth	Mexican Springs
If people no longer followed the Navaho way of life, would that be good or not?:		
Good, or good with minor qualifications	33	28
Mixed or acceptable	8	9
Bad, or bad with minor qualifications	17	34
Bad if they gave up their religion	4	12
Don't know or not ascertained	37	16
Claims knowledge of private Navaho ritual (songs or prayers):		
Yes	42	16
Learned but forgot	4	3
No	50	81
Refused to answer	4	0
Transmits this knowledge to children:		
Yes	21	6
No	75	91
No children or none old enough	4	3
Avoids mother-in-law or son-in-law (excluding unmarried or those with no mother-in-law or son-in-law) Aneth N 19; Mex. Spgs. N 21:		
Yes, yes when she was alive, or yes to some degree (1 case)	11	11
No, but I used to	16	0
No	73	89
Believes a person should move out of a hogan (house) after a death there:		
Yes	33	56
No	33	38
Don't know	21	6
Not ascertained	12	0
In religion, respondent follows:		
Only or mostly Navaho way	46‡	28
Both	50	53§
Only or mostly the white way	4	19‖
Membership:		
Catholic	4	47
Protestant	12	41
Mormon	4	6
Christian (unspecified)	4	0
Navaho religion or no church	46	0
Peyote religion	17	0
Some combination, or not ascertained	12	6
Attends church:		
Frequently or regularly	12	12
Occasionally, rarely, when I am where there is one	34	88
Not a member	46	0
Not ascertained	8	0
Health:		
Good, good qualified	38	59
So-so	0	3
Poor, poor qualified	62	37
Health history:		
Good	71	88
Bad	12	12
Not ascertained	17	0
Special health problems (e.g., bad eyes, deafness, lameness, etc.):		
None	33	56
Some	67	44
Family's health:		
Good, mostly good	58	62
Mostly good, but some ill or dead	29	34
Bad, mostly bad	12	3
What do you do when some one in the family gets sick? (Spontaneous mentions only):		
Mentions only Navaho medicine	17	3
Mentions only white medicine	38	47
Mentions both	33	50
Mehtions both and Ute or other sucking cure	4	0
Mentions Navaho medicine and peyote	4	0
Not ascertained	4	0

‡ 1 case mentions Navaho religion and peyote religion.

§ 2 cases mention the hospital in connection with white way.

‖ 2 cases mention the hospital in connection with white way.

TABLE 13—*Continued*

	Aneth	Mexican Springs
Which curing technique do you prefer? (Some respondents refused to choose only one):		
Navaho medicine	12	9
White medicine	4	47
Both	12	31
Peyote	8	6
Peyote and Navaho medicine	12	3
Peyote and white medicine	4	3
Peyote and both	25	0
Peyote and both and Ute and/or other sucking cure	21	0
How many of your children were born in hospitals?:		
All	4	19
Some	21	47
None	75	34
Do you own a radio?:		
Yes	12	66
No	88	31
Not ascertained	0	3
Do you listen to radio programs in Navaho?:		
Yes, has listened	54	88
No, has not listened	46	6
Not ascertained	0	6
Do you own a car, pickup, or truck?:		
No vehicle	75	66
One vehicle	25	25
Two or more vehicles	0	9
Number of living children:		
1–2	17	9
3–4	17	25
5–6	38	47
7–8	17	6
9 or more	12	12
Maximum level of education achieved by children (omitting families with no children eligible for school), Aneth N 22; Mex. Spgs. N 31:		
Some children have gone beyond high school	0	6
None have gone beyond high school but some have completed high school	0	6
None have completed high school but some have completed eighth grade	0	42
None have completed eighth grade but some have completed fourth grade	41	35
None have completed fourth grade but some are in grades one through four	18	0
None have completed fourth grade or are attending school	41	10
Number of children 8 or older who have completed 4 grades or are now in school:		
All	4	44
Half or more	21	28
Less than half	29	16
None	38	9
No children over 7	8	3
Number of children 8 or over who have completed 4 grades and who are also attending grades 5–8 or have completed them:		
All	4	44
Half or more	8	19
Less than half	4	3
None	21	16
No children who have completed 4 grades	62	19
Number of children who have completed 8 grades, who have also completed grades 9–12 or are now attending school:		
All	0	22
Of these 7 families (22%), 1 has all children who have completed high school in some post-high-school educational program; 1 has less than half the eligible children in such a program; 2 have none of their eligible children in such a program; and 3 have no children eligible—they are still in high school.		
Half or more	0	0
Less than half	0	0
None	0	31
No children who have completed 8 grades	100	47

TABLE 13—*Continued*

	Aneth	Mexican Springs
Respondent's attitude toward children's schooling: how far should they go in school? (Parents with some children of school age—Aneth N 17; Mex. Spgs. N 25.):		
It's up to them, with generally positive attitude but no plans............	31	8
As far as they want to, or as far as they can.........................	44	4
Finish grade school.....................................	0	4
Finish high school, or finish school.........................	6	64
Go beyond high school.........................	6	16
Not ascertained.........................	13	4
Which way should your children follow? (Parents with children under 18—Aneth N 16; Mex. Spgs. N 25.):		
The Navaho way, or mostly the Navaho way...............	6	7
Both the Navaho and the white way.........................	19	4
The white way, or mostly the white way......................	62	76
It's up to them.........................	12	8
Don't know#.........................	0	4
What do you want your children to do when they grow up? (Parents with children under 18—Aneth N 16; Mex. Spgs. N 25.):		
Mentions traditional occupations only.........................	6	0
Mentions these and jobs.........................	31	16
Mentions jobs exclusively.........................	6	16
Mentions jobs, not ascertained whether intention is exclusive............	37	68
It's up to them.........................	6	0
Don't know.........................	13	0
In 6 cases expectations about children, but no preferences were expressed..		
How do you feel about your children's holding full or part-time jobs? (Parents with children under 18—Aneth N 16; Mex. Spgs. N 25.):		
Positive.........................	69	88
Neutral.........................	25	8
Not ascertained.........................	6	4
Which way did your children follow (for respondents all of whose children are over 18)? (Aneth N 8; Mex. Spgs. N 7.):		
Mostly Navaho.........................	38	14
Mostly white.........................	62	86
Did they go as you wanted them to (for respondents all of whose children are over 18)? (Aneth N 8; Mex. Spgs. N 7.):		
Too much in the Navaho way.........................	0	14
Acceptable, or as I wanted them to, or up to them...................	75	86
Too much in the white way.........................	25	0
Attendance at chapter meetings:		
Frequently or most of the time.........................	17	47
Sometimes.........................	25	16
Rarely or never.........................	54	37
Not ascertained.........................	4	0
Voting in the previous tribal election:		
Yes.........................	67	66
No.........................	33	34
Voting in the previous Presidential election (U.S.):		
Democratic.........................	0	22
Republican.........................	0	44
Non-voter.........................	100	34
Membership in Navajo Rights Association in the past:		
Yes**.........................	62	25
No.........................	38	75
On the whole, is the Tribal Council doing a good job?:		
Yes, yes qualified.........................	8	47
Mixed.........................	0	6
No, not qualified.........................	58	44
Don't know.........................	33	3

2 respondents at Aneth and 7 at Mexican Springs began by saying, "It's up to the children." But 5 of the Mexican Springs respondents were then willing to state their own preferences.

** 1 case of "No, but I contributed."

TABLE 13—*Continued*

	Aneth	Mexican Springs
What do you think of the Tribal Council (first thing mentioned)?:		
Helps us or tries to help us	8	13
Miscellaneous positive things	4	13
Does not help us, or does not help me	21	31
It is responsible for stock reduction or for grazing regulations (negative implications in all cases)	21	3
The members don't work together; they are divided	4	13
Other	8	9
Don't know, no comment, not ascertained	34	19
(Two-thirds or more of the respondents in each community mentioned only one thing. The second thing mentioned was negative in the majority of cases where there was additional comment.)		
Is the Indian Service helping the Navaho, or not?:		
Yes, it is; yes, qualified	21	62
No, it is not; no, qualified	46	38
Don't know	29	0
Not ascertained	4	0
What do you think of the Indian Service (first thing mentioned)?:		
It helps us	4	28
It provides medical facilities	0	9
It provides education	13	3
Other positive things	0	6
It doesn't help us	25	12
Livestock reduction hurts us	8	3
It does not keep its promises	0	12
Other	13	19
Don't know, no comment, not ascertained	37	6
In response to question, expresses need for help with current problems:		
Yes	88	84
No	12	12
Not ascertained	0	3
Respondent thinks that help should come from:		
Federal or state sources only	33	28
These sources and Navaho sources (Tribal Council and Chapters)	21	6
Navaho sources only	4	34
No need for help expressed	12	16
Source not ascertained	29	16
Where did you grow up?:		
Same or adjoining community (an adjoining community is one bordering on Aneth or on Mexican Springs)	92	91
Other communities	8	9
Do you have many relatives here?:		
Many	83	62
Some or few	4	25
Relatives, no further specification	0	9
None	12	3
Do you get all the help you want from your relatives?:		
They help when I ask, or "Yes."	50	41
They would help if I asked	8	12
Neutral, or some do, some don't	8	9
They help less than I want, or very little, or they ask for pay	29	38
No relatives claimed	4	0
Do you get help from your friends instead? (Asked only if dissatisfied with help from relatives—Aneth N 12; Mexican Springs N 19). Is that help adequate?:		
Satisfied	8	5
Neutral	8	5
Dissatisfied	42	58
Don't want help; don't need it; don't ask for it	8	5
Not ascertained	33	26
Do relatives help each other as much now as they used to?:		
Situation static or improving and adequate (they helped each other in the past and still do; they help more nowadays; don't know the past but help nowadays)	21	9
Past and present bad	0	3
People help less (or not at all) nowadays	67	88
Don't know	12	0

TABLE 13—*Continued*

	Aneth	Mexican Springs
Reasons why they don't help (asked of respondents who say they do not):		
They do not have the means to help.................................	50	28
They expect pay, like white men.....................................	4	9
Both..	4	3
Other...	0	16
Inapplicable and don't know...	42	44
Is this a community where people work together and get along together pretty well?:		
Yes, yes qualified..	54	19
Yes and no, fairly well..	4	3
No, no qualified...	33	75
Don't know...	8	3
What seem to be the sources of troubles in the community?:		
The Cattle Association and Demonstration Area........................	0	47
Nothing can be decided, or the people are too confused..............	8	6
No Chapter meetings..	4	0
Other...	8	0
Don't know...	21	25
Nothing..	58	16
Not ascertained..	0	6
Involved in Aneth land suit:		
Yes...	12	....
No..	75	....
Not ascertained..	12	....
Member of Mexican Springs Cattle Association:		
Yes...	....	41
No..	....	59
Why are you better or worse off now than before stock reduction?:		
More livestock or more livestock and more farmland before	42	75
More rain or better natural conditions of any sort..................	8	0
Other things (higher income, no need to take a job), better before..	12	0
Although I lost livestock, it was compensated by a job or my children's help; about the same now as then	0	6
Stock loss was more than compensated for by job, relief, or other income; other things better now...................................	8	15
Not ascertained and don't know......................................	29	3
What worries you most nowadays?:		
Not enough livestock...	50	56
Not enough farmland; deteriorated farmland; not enough irrigated land...	12	3
Other (natural conditions, physical disability, old age, job troubles, children's lack of education, not enough relief, etc.)................	33	31
No worries...	4	9
How much livestock did you have before reduction? (Aneth N 23; 1 not ascertained. Total S.U.):		
0...	0	0
1–25..	4	0
26–50...	4	6
51–100††..	0	16
101–300...	39	41
301–500...	13	16
501–800...	9	3
801–1,200...	17	16
1,201 plus..	13	3
(Intervals comparable with figures for 1915 and 1958 cited in Chapter 6.)		
How much livestock did you have before reduction? (Aneth N 23; 1 not ascertained. Sheep and goats only):		
0...	0	0
1–25..	4	0
26–50...	4	13
51–100††..	22	13
101–300...	22	44
301–500...	17	13
501–800...	9	6
801–1,200...	9	9
1,201 plus..	13	3

†† Between 51 and 60, Aneth none; Mexican Springs 3 per cent. (Intervals comparable with figures for 1915 and 1958 cited in Chapter 6; also, using information on interval 51–60, figures for 1940 cited in Chapter 6.)

TABLE 13—*Continued*

	Aneth	Mexican Springs
How does the future look to you, for yourself?:		
Good, pretty good...	50	59
Mixed..	8	6
Bad, pretty bad..	12	22
Don't know..	29	9
Not ascertained..	0	3
How are things now for the Navaho people as a whole?:		
Good, mostly good..	21	28
Medium, mixed...	12	34
Bad, mostly bad..	17	34
Don't know..	42	3
Not ascertained..	8	0
Some respondents felt that things were good (or bad) for some people but not others; others felt that things were good, or good qualified, or bad or bad qualified for the people as a whole.		
What should be done to improve things for the Navahos? (First mention):		
More irrigation, water, or farmland................................	17	44
More stock, eliminate reduction, improve stock......................	21	19
Better housing...	0	9
Other..	25	22
Don't know, not ascertained......................................	37	6
Who should do these things?:		
Mentions Federal or State sources only.............................	29	19
Mentions Federal or State sources and Navahos (Council, Delegates, Chapters, and/or the people themselves)................................	17	25
Mentions only Navaho sources (Council, Delegates, Chapters, and/or the people themselves)..	21	50
"Somebody"..	4	0
Nothing mentioned, or not ascertained..............................	29	6

were Indian Service jobs available as well. In a majority of cases, Mexican Springs men could live at home when they took jobs, whereas Aneth men had to leave their families—or, in the case of agricultural gang labor, sometimes took them along. By and large attitudes toward the husband's going away to work were not too negative, and the few families that went to work as a unit seemed to like it.

In spite of this rather high frequency of employment, much of it off the reservation, only about a third of the group spoke any English at all—and some who never attended school claimed to speak some English. English was a language to use with Anglos, not with fellow-Navahos or in the home. Those who were educated felt that schooling helped them, often in connection with employment, and most, educated or uneducated, regretted their relative or absolute lack of schooling. Those who never went to school were most often held back by their parents, who were indifferent to school or opposed it.

Nearly three-quarters of the Aneth Navahos and half of those at Mexican Springs claimed that "they mostly follow the Navaho way of life." Nevertheless, they tended to feel that the Navaho way of life was changing, or even dying out. (The tendency at Aneth to avoid questions with "I don't know" is visible here and at other points in the interview.) The idea of giving up the Navaho way, however, met with a mixed reception and was unimaginable to some people.

There was evidence of loss of certain elements of traditional culture. Relatively few people still knew private ritual—or would admit to it, but the more culturally conservative character of Aneth is visible here: more than 40 per cent of the sample claimed to know some such ritual.[2] Even those who had the knowledge, however, were not passing it on to their children.

Two tabu which have been ridiculed or criticized for decades by whites are the mother-in-law tabu and the tabu on living in a hogan where some one has died. These two items were therefore employed as markers of individual acculturation. It is apparent that the mother-in-law tabu had virtually disappeared, whereas breaking the death tabu was acceptable to only about a third of the people in each community—nor did respondents like to be asked the question.

But movement toward Western religions was not vigorous. Most respondents felt that they followed both Navaho and Anglo religious practice, but only in Mexican Springs were there many who considered themselves largely or wholly followers of Western religions. Missionized for many years, Mexican Springs had far more nominal church members, but in neither community was church attendance characteristic.

Relevant to individual acculturation are health practices, since Navaho religion centers on curing, and for many years rejection of American medicine was characteristic. These Navahos tended to feel that their past health record was not bad. The people of Aneth, far from clinics, felt that their present health was poor, whereas those in Mexican Springs felt that it was fair. Many claimed special health problems, such as poor eyesight, lameness, deafness, and so on—especially at Aneth. Yet they thought their family members had reasonably good health.

In pursuit of health they tended to use—or say they used—Western medicine or a combination of that and Navaho curing. Only a minority failed to mention Western medicine. If this was a bow to the interviewers, it was not evident in other parts of the interview. Eclecticism continued to feature their comments when they were asked to express a preference, as between Navaho curing, the doctor, peyote, and sucking cures. Mexican Springs showed a general prefrence for Western techniques. And, as might be expected, the women of Mexican Springs were far more likely to have their babies in the hospital.

From all this emerges a general impression of the loss of portions of Navaho culture with only incomplete and imperfect replacement with corresponding features of Anglo culture.

In consumer goods, Mexican Springs led the way. Far more people owned radios there. (Aneth was out of reach of good radio reception, and specifically out of reach of Navaho programs.) Many people without radios listened to Navaho programs on other people's radios, and even at Aneth more than half had heard these programs at one time or another. Whether because of better roads or higher income, Mexican Springs had more cars and trucks per capita, but few enough Navahos had either. (Again, those not in the community probably had more vehicles per capita.)

[2] Fr. Berard Haile later told me that a man who has such knowledge will deny it until he has been asked four times—something which I failed to do. I suspect that this taboo on admitting sacred knowledge must be breaking down, since so many people made the admission after only one inquiry.

The situation as respects education of the younger generation gives promise of troubles for the future. We asked for a complete list of all living children, of whatever ages. The median number of children for this sample is 5–6, and the families in many cases are not yet complete.

At Aneth, the school was open only some years after it was built in the 1930's, whereas at Mexican Springs it was open continuously—and schools at Tohatchi were not too far away and much older than at Mexican Springs proper. The effects are evident. At Aneth, no child had completed eighth grade. At Mexican Springs, more than half the families had at least one child who had completed eighth grade. Families were not necessarily consistent in the education of their children. Even in Mexican Springs, where there was some consistency, many families put only some of their children in school. Forty-four per cent of Mexican Springs families put all their children in school, and were keeping them there in 1953, whereas this was true for only four per cent of Aneth families.

Educational objectives were clearer at Mexican Springs. Parents wanted their children to finish high school or go beyond it. Aneth parents were likely to say that the child should decide, or simply that the child should go as far as he wanted to or could. Partly, this may be due to less understanding of the school system. In part, however, it reflects a traditional Navaho attitude: that the child is an autonomous person for whose decisions no one else, not even a parent, can be fully responsible.

However much or little education their children were receiving, the parents' attitude toward education was wholly positive. Similarly, parents said that their children should follow the white way, or mostly the white way, when they grew up. They expected them, by and large, to hold jobs, as their sole source of support, or combined with farming and herding. Furthermore, they favored jobs for their children. Those who had grown children thought that the children had followed mostly the white way—although an observer would probably not agree. And the parents approved of this.

So the respondents expected further change, along the lines of present change. They saw education as important in this new world, in which jobs were necessary, but their performance in sending their children to school was not fully congruent with their expressed attitudes. (It should be remembered that in 1953 the crash program for Navaho schools had not begun, and that at no time since 1868 had there ever been enough schools to absorb the Navaho school-age population.)

Navahos are willy-nilly involved in national politics, state politics, Agency administration, Tribal administration, and Chapter organizations. The people of Aneth showed a lower level of national and tribal participation than those of Mexican Springs (indeed no one in Aneth voted in the presidential election of 1952). It seems probable, however, that they were alienated rather than apathetic. They did vote in the tribal elections, at least as frequently as the people of Mexican Springs, and in the past they were active in the Navajo Rights Association. They did not think that the Tribal Council was doing a good job, whereas in Mexican Springs opinion was divided. The commonest specific complaint against the Council was that it was responsible for livestock reduction or grazing regulations.

Similarly, Aneth people were far less positive in their attitudes toward the

Indian Service than those in Mexican Springs. Oddly enough, however, in neither community did complaints about livestock reduction have any saliency.

It is not surprising that almost every Navaho in the sample felt that he had problems requiring help. But most Navahos favored assistance from the Tribe only, or from a mixture of Federal, State, and Tribal sources. Only a minority favored help solely from the Federal or State governments. This suggests a desire for active participation in the solution of these problems. The people of Mexican Springs were most likely to want Tribal assistance only.

Navahos live in a network of kinship—which I assume to be declining in importance—and of organized, quasi-organized, or unorganized community relationships. Navahos have the reputation of being great wanderers. It is interesting, therefore, to note that virtually every Navaho was born in the community where he was interviewed or in one adjoining it, and most had many relatives nearby. There was some dissatisfaction with the amount of help supplied by relatives. Those who were most dissatisfied did not feel that their friends were any special help. By and large, they believed that help from relatives had declined over the years, and the commonest explanation for this was that people no longer have the means to help. Alienated though they were from the Council and the nation, Aneth people considered that their community was reasonably harmonious—perhaps because they stood in opposition to the Tribe and to surrounding whites on so many issues. At Mexican Springs, where there was a sharp division over the Cattle Association and Demonstration Area, most people thought the community was riven.

Since this book deals so much with relative deprivation, the Navahos' general attitudes toward past, present, and future were of special interest. Some of these were discussed in the concluding chapter on livestock reduction. Most people felt that they were worse off than before livestock reduction, and worse off because of livestock reduction—not, say, just the passage of time. Their present worries were largely about livestock. The pre-reduction holdings that they reported were well above the figures for sheep in Paquette's 1915 survey, and for livestock figures in any subsequent survey. Furthermore, not a single individual admitted to having held no stock prior to reduction, although we know that there were a considerable number of non-owners in those years. Perhaps this is retrospective falsification, but perhaps it reflects the character of the sample, which omits some of the younger people and perhaps omits some of the non-owners of the past, still non-owners and hence assiduous in wage work.

In spite of their grave worries about livelihood and expressed needs for help, the Navahos were fairly optimistic about their personal futures. They varied considerably in their views about the general condition of the Navahos. When they were asked what should be done for the Navahos, they mentioned giving them more livestock only in one-fifth of cases, although if the Aneth "Don't know" cases could have been induced to talk more freely, this percentage might have been higher. And, as in the question about help for their own problems, they believe that Navaho organizations or the Navaho people should be active in bringing about improvement, with or without the aid of Federal or State agencies. Mexican Springs people stand more for Navaho activities than do the people of Aneth.

This is a sad picture not so much in terms of Navaho reactions as in terms of this country's dealings with them. For decades they were encouraged to increase their herds. For decades they had insufficient and inadequate schools. And because the livestock industry appeared to be viable, they had little incentive to go to school. When the livestock were reduced, an undereducated population was forced into marginal participation in the job market. Considering the handicaps, this participation was surprisingly high. And twenty years after livestock reduction began, the education of the younger generation lagged, even though further involvement in the larger economy was certain.

Navaho preoccupation with stock reduction, anxiety, and such hostility as emerges in these interviews, seem quite realistic.

Part III

THE PEYOTE CULT AMONG THE NAVAHO

Chapter 8

THE STRUGGLE OVER PEYOTISM

UNTIL THE ORDINANCE OF 1940

THE PEYOTE CULT has been described, and relevant features of Navaho history, culture, and present conditions have been discussed. With this chapter, we begin to deal with the peyote cult among the Navaho. Specifically, we now describe the history of the spread of the Navaho peyote cult and the struggle over peyotism between cult members and other Navahos. Much of this struggle centers on Tribal Council legislation against the sale, use, or possession of peyote in the Navaho country.

Navaho peyotism took its origin from the Ute peyote cult at Towaoc. Through contacts with the Utes and with Oklahoma Indians who visited the Utes, a small number of Navahos came to take up peyotism, and some of these became priests. The transmission of the cult from Utes to Navahos was facilitated by close relationships between Navahos and Utes in this area since as early as 1910—especially for Navahos from Aneth, Teec Nos Pas, Beclabito, Shiprock, and Mancos Creek. At Mancos Creek, Navahos live on the Ute reservation and in particularly close relationship with Utes. From Mancos Creek came a number of the earliest Navaho users of peyote, including at least five men who were the first Navaho peyote priests. By 1935 at the latest, several of these men could run a peyote meeting. By the early 1930's, there were sporadic meetings here and there over a wide strip running west of the Shiprock-Gallup highway. Sometime shortly after May of 1936, a Navaho from Shiprock, converted to peyotism, began to use his automobile to take various of these early priests south of Shiprock, and meetings seem to have become more frequent.

Thereafter the cult continued to spread from the north, and a secondary center of diffusion arose in the south, where new priests were created. This center probably existed by 1938, and certainly by 1940, and included Tohatchi, Crystal, Sawmill, Fort Defiance, and Window Rock. By 1940, the cult had reached at least the following communities, moving more or less from north to south and then west: Aneth, Teec Nos Pas, Shiprock, Red Rock, Lukachukai, Crystal, Naschitti, Red Lake, Sawmill, Tohatchi, Fort Defiance, Twin Lakes, Divide Store, Canyon Bonito (not Pueblo Bonito), Lake Valley, St. Michaels, Greasewood below Ganado, Steamboat Canyon, and the northern part of District 4.

By 1951, it had touched many communities in the eastern half of the reservation. Districts 9, 10, 11, 12, 13, 14, 15, 16, 17, and 18 were affected. In the west, there was a sprinkling of members at Grey Mountain in District 3, at Dinnehotso in District 8, throughout the northern part of District 4, and scattered about District 7. The relative frequency of cult members was higher in the north. A majority of the people at Aneth and in District 9, about half the people in the northern part of District 12, about half the people of Lukachukai and Many Farms, and about a third of those at Greasewood below Ganado were members. Elsewhere, participation was lower. In all, in 1951, I estimate that 12–14 per cent of the Navahos, or 8,400–9,800 out of 70,000, were cult members. By 1954 the cult had grown greatly in District 4, but I have no further detailed information on growth or decline elsewhere (all based on Aberle and Stewart, 1957, which supplies sub-stantiating data).[1] Frank Takes Gun, President of the Native American Church of North America, estimated that there were 22,000 Navaho members in 1956; Dustin that there were 30,000 in 1960 (Dustin, 1960). I doubt that membership is this high, but I have no detailed information later than 1951.

This chapter will take up the public, and especially the legal struggle over peyotism. But this struggle had its counterpart at the local level in factionalism and bitterness, gossip, and occasional physical encounters. The public record opens on January 25, 1938, when two of the early peyote priests were arrested and "charged with the offense of possessing dope (peyote) on the Navajo Reservation" and sentenced to 60 days in jail (Law and Order files; first date of record for Navaho peyotism). Since there was no law against the use of peyote on the Navajo Reservation at the time, it seems reasonable to assume that the activities of these pioneers had aroused a good deal of hostility.

I have no record of other arrests, nor of other special crises until June 3, 1940, when the Tribal Council took up the question of the peyote cult. According to E. Reeseman Fryer, who was Superintendent in 1940, the campaign against peyotism was sparked by Jacob C. Morgan, the Chairman. Morgan was a Navaho, a Christian missionary educated at Hampton Institute, and a bitter opponent of

[1] Various items pertaining to Navaho peyote history that were not dealt with in Aberle and Stewart, 1957, should be mentioned:

a) In a letter of March 16, 1956, Clyde Kluckhohn provided additional chronological informa-tion. His field notes for 1936 have no references to peyote. In 1937, Ramah Navahos had heard of it, but no more; in Chaco Canyon, the Navahos knew a little more about it but there was no indication of actual participation. In 1942, neither Dorothea Leighton nor Kluckhohn heard anything about peyote at Navajo Mountain, in spite of specific inquiries.

b) In 1942, a man in Kayenta was arrested for the use of peyote.

c) In order to clear up a possible future source of confusion, De Huff's and Grunn's publica-tion of a "Peyote Drinking Song (Navajo Indians)" in their 1924 publication (pp. 7–9) should be briefly noted. If this song indeed authenticated Navaho use of peyote at this early date, it would change the history of Navaho peyotism remarkably. The fact is that the song was recorded by De Huff "as sung by two Lujan girls of Taos pueblo" (Rhodes, 1958, p. 45). De Huff continues, "According to their statement (the two Lujan girls), which was corroborated by several other Taos and Navaho pupils at the Santa Fe Indian School, where I collected it, the song originated among the Navajo and was adopted by the Taos Indians to use in their peyote ceremony. At that time, the Government was opposing the use of peyote and I could not find out whether or not the Navajos used the song in a peyote ceremony. That is still a moot ques-tion" (Rhodes, 1958, pp. 45–46). It should be added that the song as transcribed by De Huff and Grunn became popular among schoolchildren and seems to have become a secular song as a result (Rhodes, 1958). Furthermore, whether Grunn or the Lujan girls changed the tune, and in spite of De Huff's claim that it was transcribed "as it was" (Rhodes, 1958, p. 46), it is recog-nizably different in the published version from the several varieties of the peyote opening song (which it copies) that I have heard or seen transcribed by musicologists. Peyotism existed among the Taos by 1919; learning of the peyote opening song by schoolchildren of various tribes, not themselves peyotists, is a definite possibility. It is highly improbable that the peyote cult flourished among the Navaho prior to 1919 and that the Navaho transmitted the cult or the song to the Taos (Aberle and Stewart, 1957).

Collier's, as has been brought out in the history of livestock reduction in Chapters 4 and 5. Indeed, the principal leaders of opposition to peyotism at this time were all Christian: Morgan, Howard Gorman, Vice-Chairman of the Council and a Presbyterian, and Roger Davis, a delegate to the Council and a Christian missionary.

It is not clear to me exactly why the issue came up at this point. One distinct possibility is that Morgan raised it because *Indians at Work*, a Bureau publication edited by Collier, had published an article by Petrullo strongly favorable to peyote in April of 1940 (Petrullo, 1940). Morgan must have known that Collier himself was favorable to peyote, since there is a great deal of evidence to this effect in *Survey of Conditions*, Part 34. This Morgan must have seen, since his own testimony and submissions make up so much of these hearings. A section of Part 34 deals with the fight over peyote at Taos and includes large quantities of anti-peyote propaganda, as well as a good deal of neutral and positive material, and a solid anthropological summary by Donald Collier, John Collier's son. Furthermore, in April, 1940, *The Christian Indian*, a Christian Reform missionary magazine dealing with the Navaho missionary field, published an article attacking Collier for circulating Petrullo's material. Morgan, although an independent missionary, had a Christian Reform background and must have seen this article. It seems probable that the combination of Morgan's Christian position, his hostility to Collier, the Petrullo article, and the counterattack in *The Christian Indian* may have precipitated his action in June of 1940.[2]

A reading of the minutes of this meeting (hereafter TC 1940) makes it clear that some members of the Council were familiar with a pamphlet published by the Indian Bureau several years before, which was an anti-peyote tract—*Peyote: An Abridged Compilation*, prepared by Newberne and Burke (1925). Burke was a Commissioner of Indian Affairs. Morgan and another Council member showed a knowledge of this work, and Davis mentioned the anti-peyote literature he had read.

Morgan laid out the agenda for the meeting and put the peyote issue first. Nearly half the time was used by Howard Gorman, who had carried out a field investigation of the cult on the Navajo Reservation. The Council members who spoke most were all English-speaking: Gorman, Davis, Frank Bradley (who had discussed peyotism with Morgan), Morgan himself, John Curley, and Sam Gorman.

The Superintendent did not take an active role in the discussion, but he told me that at the time he was, in fact, opposed to peyotism on the basis of what he had heard. The presentation by Gorman and the comments by other Navahos were unequivocally opposed to peyotism, on every ground. The following beliefs and values were invoked. Peyotism was regarded as foreign, as leading to extravagant expenditures for peyote, as accompanied by gross sexual misbehavior (especially since peyote was said to enlarge the prostate gland), as a cause of insanity

[2] Curiously enough, in the *Proceedings of the Meeting of the Navajo Tribal Council . . . June 3–6, 1940*, Gorman commented that the Indian Bureau in Washington had requested a report on peyote in the Navaho country—but this seems odd, in view of Collier's tolerance for the peyote cult.

and death, as similar to the dangerous mind medicines, and as a danger to traditional Navaho religion. For some Christian Navahos, it was a threat to Christianity.
The character of some peyote priests was castigated. Claims of the curative value
of peyote were ridiculed, as were claims that it stopped people from drinking.
There was also concern over rumors that schoolchildren were being given peyote
and that Navaho employees of the schools were cult members. And there was
anxiety that peyote would cause the birth of crippled, deformed, or otherwise
unhealthy infants.

The discussion of peyote threatened at one point to become very much en-
tangled with the general issue of religious novelties on the reservation. Some delegates expressed a strong desire to see the "new" way of doing the "squaw dance"
eliminated—by law, and to see other ceremonial innovations, probably Chiricahua
Wind Way, eliminated as well.[3]

Several members of the Council said that the peyotists claimed that the plant
was curative, whereas the speakers claimed that it was dangerous. In the face of
this contradiction, they asked for medical testimony—and these were not pro-
peyotists. In answer, Morgan quoted Newberne and Burke.

There was then only one man on the Council who was a peyotist, Hola Tso
(Tsoi, Tsoh), of Sawmill. He defended the cult. He asked for more evidence, for
an analysis of the plant, and for medical testimony. He informed people that he
had gone to a peyote meeting run by Alfred Wilson (the respected Cheyenne
peyotist) and implied that he spoke with more authority than others present. He
commented with irony, "Since Howard [Gorman] has gone into it so thoroughly
I suppose he is the main priest in it. I am . . . telling . . . about what I have seen
myself, not simply going around and questioning about it. . . . Therefore, I think
I know what I am talking about." He said that he had quit drinking, and indeed
had been forced to do so before the peyotists would admit him to a meeting, and
listed other former drinkers who were now teetotalers. He said that the harm
done by alcohol was obvious to all, and for this reason it was forbidden to Indians.
He implied that outlawing peyote could occur only if it were equally harmful,
but acknowledged the Council's power to act. He implied that fear that peyote
would damage Navaho ceremonies was exaggerated, particularly since the Navaho
singers themselves exposed their ceremonies to the public and failed to keep them
sacred. Hence he could not expect respectful treatment of peyotism in this meeting. His was the sole speech in favor of the cult. Its brevity probably resulted
from his perception that there was massive opposition from many Council members and ignorance and dawning disapproval in the minds of others.

[3] The "squaw dance" is a part of the Enemy Way ceremony, a popular Navaho ritual for
exorcising the ghosts of aliens—non-Navahos. Girls pick their partners and drag them into the
dance; subsequently the partner is expected to pay the girl. About 1910, the girl stood behind
her partner, grasped his side and completed a circle or two with him, reversing occasionally to
keep from becoming dizzy (*Franciscan Fathers, 1910*, p. 370). By 1923–1925, some couples
danced pivoting in a circle and facing one another, with the man's hand on the girl's shoulder
—a style brought back by schoolchildren and disfavored by the older people (Reichard, 1928,
p. 121 and Plate Ia). By 1940, and probably well before, the couples formed a large, circular
double file, all facing the same way, and shuffled forward. Often a young man wraps his partner
about with his blanket and whispers to her. Some of my informants believe this dance comes
from the Chiricahua Apaches and consider it a serious corruption of ceremonial life. In 1949,
one old man told me that its importation was the cause of the deterioration of Navaho life.

There were also a few statements supporting the cult in the testimony that Gorman had amassed.

During the meeting, Morgan drafted a resolution for the delegates to consider. After debating whether there was any way to make penalties more severe and arguing about including a ban on other foreign ceremonies, the delegates passed it with only one dissenting vote—Hola Tso's. Since this resolution has been the center of a legal battle for more than twenty years, it is worth quoting in full.

RESOLUTION No. CJ-1-40

To prevent the introduction in or the use of peyote on the Navajo Reservation.

WHEREAS, during the last few months great quantities of peyote have been brought into the Navajo Reservation, and

WHEREAS, its use is not connected with any Navajo religious practice and is in contradiction to the traditional ceremonies of the Navajo people;

THEREFORE, BE IT RESOLVED that as far as the Navajo people are concerned peyote is harmful and foreign to our traditional way of life;

BE IT FURTHER RESOLVED that the introduction into the Navajo country or to the use of peyote by the Navajo people be stamped out and appropriate action be taken by the Tribal Courts to enforce this resolution;

BE IT FURTHER RESOLVED that there be added to the Code of Tribal Offenses, approved by the Secretary of the Interior on June 2, 1937, the following section: "Any person who shall introduce into the Navajo country, sell, use, or have in possession within said Navajo country, the bean known as peyote shall be deemed guilty of an offense against the Navajo Tribe, and upon conviction thereof shall be sentenced to labor for a period not to exceed nine months, or a fine of $100.00, or both";

BE IT FURTHER RESOLVED that any person having a peddlers license who is found trafficking in peyote shall, in addition to the above sentence, have his peddlers license forever cancelled;

BE IT FURTHER RESOLVED that the Tribal Council hereby petitions Congress to enact a law to supplement the above addition to the Code of Tribal Offenses to the end that peyote shall never be permitted in the Navajo country.

CERTIFICATION

I hereby certify that the foregoing resolution was passed this 3rd day of June, 1940, by a 52 to 1 vote of the Navajo Tribal Council in assembly at Window Rock, Arizona, at which a quorum was present.

WITNESSED:

HOWARD GORMAN (Sgd.)
Vice-Chairman, Navajo Tribal Council

J. C. MORGAN (Sgd.)
Chairman, Navajo Tribal Council

(From NTCR: 107-108)

The form of the resolution is not without its ironies, when one considers that it was drafted by a Christian missionary—although only peyotists seem to notice this. Peyote is condemned on two grounds—that it is harmful, and that it is foreign to the traditional Navaho way of life. The resolution had teeth—a fine of $100.00 was not a small matter.

UNTIL THE HEARINGS OF 1954

It seems to me quite possible that if the Council had not been headed by a man who was both a missionary and a bitter enemy to Collier, there might have been no Council ruling against peyote. Peyote has been opposed in many tribes, but legislated against in relatively few. It is also true that the resolution was passed in one day, with no medical or other scientific testimony, before a Council many of whose members had probably never seen a peyotist. But, as we shall see, with whatever additional experience or testimony, successive Councils have invariably backed up the 1940 resolution.

This resolution left Collier, as Commissioner, in a curious position. He believed that Indians should be given maximum opportunities for self-government. He also believed that Indians should have freedom to worship according to native rituals, specifically including the peyote cult. At this point, the principles of self-government and religious freedom came into conflict. In December of 1940, Collier recommended that the Tribal ordinance be approved. He seems to have done so because he thought the principle of self-government was overriding. He certainly did not act out of opposition to peyotism, since both before and after 1940 he repeatedly put himself on record as favoring freedom for members of the cult to follow their rituals and practices (Collier, 1952, summarizes his actions and his attitude).

Having upheld self-government and accepted the anti-peyote law, Collier tried to soften the blow. In mid-1941, the Superintendent wanted to enforce the law, but Collier was becoming uneasy at the idea of Federal intervention in a religious issue—and since the Navaho police were paid with Federal funds, this was Federal intervention. But at first he asked only that the police take a minimum of initiative in enforcing the ordinance. By April of 1944, however, he had come to take the position that no Federal employee (which meant no Navaho policeman) could enforce the ordinance. In his view, tribal employees paid by tribal funds could act, but in 1944 there were no such police.

In effect, Collier was telling the Tribal Council that they had every right to the law but no way to enforce it. The result of this was a situation unsatisfactory to most people. The Superintendent and other members of the Agency staff had to tell the Navahos that the Agency could not help them to enforce what was now Tribal law. When members of the Council pressed for enforcement, the Superintendent tended to sympathize with them. The result was a sort of intermittent and haphazard enforcement unsatisfactory to the Council. Needless to say, any enforcement was unsatisfactory to the peyotists.

The actions taken at various times included: (1) arrests, trials, fines, and jail sentences; (2) arrests, trials, and probation; (3) arrests, followed by release without trial; (4) arrests, including illegal confiscation of peyote equipment—followed, whatever else, by an urgent and usually effective appeal by the peyotist for the return of ritual equipment.

I have only incidental and unsystematic information about arrests. I have used Agency files, newspaper articles, and my own correspondence with Navahos as sources.

In early 1944, there were three arrests, convictions, and sentences. The Superintendent, who had been in office since June 1, 1942, said that these were the first peyote cases resulting in court action since he took office—but there might have been other arrests without trials. It was these cases that prompted Collier to take his anti-enforcement stand. In addition, a Navaho woman was arrested in Colorado for shipping peyote through the mails—something that has been illegal in various states at various times. These arrests seem to have followed a period of some tension. The three arrested were all from District 9, and the Supervisor there sent to the Superintendent a list of 45 Navahos who had protested against non-enforcement.

In 1946, pressure apparently built up again. A prominent citizen of Gallup wrote to a mission organization complaining of non-enforcement. There were a series of complaints and arrests in January, 1946. There was one complaint and arrest, and there were five complaints. All but one seem to have been in Districts 9 and 12; the remaining one was in Lukachukai. In March, a peyote priest was arrested in District 17 when a patient died a few days after a meeting. In June, there were at least three peyotists in jail, and an officer of the Native American Church, from the Plains, was threatening legal action on behalf of Navaho peyotists and complaining to the Secretary of Interior.

In 1947, night raids by private individuals began in District 9 and at Cove in District 12. In these raids, a gang of anti-peyotists would descend on a peyote meeting and attempt to break it up, often trying to destroy the altar, seize ritual paraphernalia, and, it is said, to grab jewelry from peyotists. There were two complaints of raids in District 9 in February, 1947, and one in Cove, not too far away. There was some overlap in the lists of raiders supplied by the complainants in District 9. And among the raiders were four of the people who had complained about non-enforcement in 1944. Probably more of the raiders than that had been involved in drafting the complaint, since some of the raiders were apparently husbands of women who complained about non-enforcement in 1944. (At least two of the 1944 complainers about non-enforcement were among those who kidnapped the Supervisor in District 9 in 1945, and at least two of the 1947 raiders were involved in the kidnapping.) In one case the peyotists were ready, tied up the raiders for the night, and continued the meeting. The Agency took steps to try to end such private action. Morgan, however, defended the raiders in the *Farmington Times-Hustler*.

In November of 1948, a report by three physicians evaluating medical care of the Indians in the upper middle west was circulated by the Bureau. It later appeared in the *Journal of the American Medical Association* (Braasch *et al.*, 1949, p. 225). Although it contained no evidence, it condemned peyote roundly. As a result, many Navahos believe that the American Medical Association has officially condemned peyote. The rumors of the report gave ammunition to anti-peyotists and worried peyotists.

In 1949, I believe because of tension over the peyote issue, I was hired by the Bureau to do a study of Navaho peyotism. To be precise, I heard that the Bureau wanted an anthropologist to do such a study and solicited the job. The policy of minimal enforcement continued. Also in 1949, Dr. Clarence Salsbury, medical missionary and then head of Ganado Presbyterian Mission, provided anti-peyotist statements to the press.

In May of 1950, the Advisory Committee of the Tribal Council took a look at the enforcement issue. There had been an arrest in District 17. The Chief of Law and Order on the reservation, himself a Navaho, wanted to be told whether to enforce or not. He said that in this case he had acted on a complaint, using three policemen paid out of Tribal, not Federal, funds.[4] The Advisory Committee did not lay down a policy line. It clearly favored enforcement but was concerned about factionalism on the reservation.

In 1951, Dr. Salsbury became Commissioner of Public Health in the State of Arizona. In this capacity, he made a series of statements opposing Navaho use of peyote—newspaper articles in Arizona in April, May, and June. An article in *Time* based on his views appeared in the issue of June 18. The Indian Office put out opposing news releases. Five anthropologists published a statement in support of peyotism in *Science* in November, and Collier made a similar statement in *Science* the following year (La Barre *et al.*, 1951; Collier, 1952). In October of 1951, five people were arrested and put on 9 months' probation.

In early January of 1952, a respected trader among the Navaho addressed the Advisory Committee and made a short statement opposing peyote. In August, an article depicting peyote as a dangerous and highly gratifying drug appeared in *Sir!*, a popular magazine whose general tone can be grasped from a list of the contents of other articles in the same issue—the sexual habits of the brother of Louis XIV; prostate trouble; and the fighting stallions of the Philippines (Francisco, 1952). There was another article in another, similar publication about the same time. Both articles circulated widely in the Navaho country and upset peyotists considerably (both were hideously inaccurate).

In early 1954, there was a sudden rash of arrests, thirteen in all. All of those arrested were jailed. By now the Tribe was paying a good deal of the Police salaries. Hence Collier's objection was met. The Navaho head of Law and Order, who had learned to be cautious about peyote arrests through many disappointments, was no longer in office. The Police asked the temporary head whether the peyote law was to be enforced—and he said it was. There had been some precipitating incident leading to complaints about peyote rituals, but I have not been able to find out exactly what happened. At any rate, the thirteen arrests jarred the peyotists.

They asked for a hearing on the law at a Tribal Council meeting. This was the first full dress discussion since 1940. The Government requested that Dr. Maurice H. Seevers, of the Department of Pharmacology at the University of Michigan, as a pharmacological expert on peyote, and I as an anthropological expert, attend the hearings. We both accepted.[5]

The hearings occurred et the Navajo Tribal Council meeting of June 1–10, 1954.

---

[4] TNY 1958, p. 140, states that the police were not paid out of Tribal funds until 1953. This would seem to be an error.

[5] Since the Advisory Committee meeting of 1950, some members of the Council had known that the Bureau set some store by the outcome of reports expected from Dr. Seevers and myself. When both of us appeared at the hearings (wearing, as it happened, tropical worsted suits of identical color and pattern), both from Michigan, there was some feeling that we were conspiratorial, in some sense or other. In fact, when I began my work in 1949 I was at Harvard, and Dr. Seevers' research was already under way. Later, it chanced that I went to Michigan—in 1952. Thus the Bureau developed its connections with Dr. Seevers and with me quite independently. Because of mutual interests, we exchanged ideas several times, but we have never done joint research.

It lasted two and a half days, from Tuesday morning, June 1, to Thursday noon, June 3. It frayed a good many tempers and resulted in no action. There were many spectators, most of them cult members. Additional cult members waited outside the Council chambers. The then President of the Native American Church of North America, Allen P. Dale, came to Window Rock for the hearings, but in the end the Council would not allow him to speak.

There were three technical presentations—Seevers', my own, and that of Norman Littell, the General Counsel of the Navaho Tribe. Littell pointed out that a tribe has special rights to limit freedom of religion which the Federal Government does not possess. If a tribe were to adopt a constitution (and the Navajo Tribe did not yet have one), it might well include a replica of the Constitutional guarantee of freedom of religion. Even so, such freedom is absolute as respects belief but not as respects practice. Freedom of practice has always been constrained by considerations of the moral code, public order, public interest, and health. The Council could not, under a guarantee like that in the Bill of Rights, forbid a religion because it was foreign or for any other reason of prejudice, but could forbid it on these other grounds. Thus far, Littell.

Seevers stated that peyote was non-addictive and that experiments showed no evidence of damage to the nervous system. He said that the best opinion as to mental effects was that peyote did not cause insanity, although it might make insanity visible. He said that in small doses peyote acted as a stimulant and in large ones as a depressant. He said that in massive doses it could kill experimental animals but that this was true of such innocuous substances as baking soda, salt, and water. He considered peyote to have less risks for health than either barbiturates or alcohol, neither of which were illegal according to Federal code. He believed that individuals might, in a few instances, behave badly under the influence of peyote, but he thought the risk small by comparison with alcohol. As a medical man he considered it bad if a man used peyote when he should be using Western medicine.

In his initial presentation, the anthropologist stressed the religious character of peyote, described the ceremony, told the origin myth of the cult, gave a history of the cult in the United States, and supplied estimates of the percentages of cult members in each District and for the Navahos as a whole.

There were few other witnesses: a peyote priest of some years' standing, a Navaho who complained that his wife went to peyote ceremonies and took his daughter with her, and Hola Tso of Sawmill, head of the Native American Church in Arizona. Like the anti-peyote witness who preceded him, Hola Tso was told that he had five minutes to speak. He argued that he should have more time and, when it was not granted, he said that he would not talk, "and we will go on home and let it stand as it is." He walked off the witness stand before the interpreter could finish translating his statement, and a large number of the audience left with him. No member of the Council made any comment when this occurred.

At the Council meeting were three Councilmen publicly identified as peyotists and a fourth who was said not to be a member but to favor toleration of peyotism. There may have been another pro-peyote delegate. Only one of these spoke during the hearing. The rest of the Council was completely antagonistic to peyotism.

The same issues arose as in 1940, and a few new ones. Peyote was foreign and non-traditional, dangerous to mind and body, allied to the mind medicines, etc. It was given, they believed, to schoolchildren and made them sluggish and unable to perform properly in school. Employers at the Bellemont Ordnance plant did not want peyotist employees. What the Navahos needed was something to advance them. There was no evidence that peyote did so. There was criticism of the selection of witnesses: why had Dr. Salsbury not been called; why had not a teacher who had comments on the effects of peyote on schoolchildren not been called? Was the hearing rigged in advance? There was comment on the fact that the peyote priest claimed that peyote was not given to children, whereas the anthropologist said it was. If peyote was so good, why *not* give it to children? One peyotist delegate spoke to this point: peyote *was* given to children occasionally, but in any case, not everything good for adults is also good for children, he said.

There was a rather complicated discussion of peyote as religion and as cure. It was said that peyotists talked of curing to Navahos and of religion to whites. If peyote was a cure, evidence of its curative properties was needed. If it was a religion, then it should petition for mission sites, operate like any other church, and hold open, not secret meetings.

The anthropologist was criticized sharply. Perhaps, it was said, he was a member of the cult. His information on ritual and cult history was familiar enough—what about information on the social and health effects of peyote?

He replied that there was no evidence to show that peyotists differed significantly from non-peyotists in livestock holdings, educational level, education of their children, quality or duration of employment, or comments of employers about their abilities as workmen. The Council clearly regarded these findings as no conclusion at all. When he said that he had thus far found no evidence that peyote caused insanity, disease, or death, he was asked if he had examined records at the Ganado mission hospital (not available to him). Since this was Dr. Salsbury's former location, it was evident that Council members thoughts that it was not sufficient to check records in Government medical facilities.

Seevers was castigated because, it was said, he might understand a lot about drugs but he knew nothing about Navahos.

As the hearing drew to a close, there were voices favoring further investigation —a hearing at which Salsbury and others would appear. Other voices favored confirmation of the 1940 vote. The Chairman favored further investigation and said that it had been claimed that the 1940 law had been railroaded through. He did not want a similar charge to be made against him. No motion was made, the meeting was adjourned for lunch, and, after two days and a half, no action was taken save for a subsequent vote to release the proceedings to the press.

Thus the 1954 Council, few of whose members had been present in 1940, refused to act or to overrule the 1940 Council. It would seem that the Council wanted more evidence of damage from peyote before it would vote to reaffirm, and more assurances than could be supplied that peyote had positive effects religiously and medically before it would reconsider. Perhaps stimulated by the Council hearings and the expert testimony which did not take a stand against peyote, the *Santa Fe*

New Mexican (July 14, 1954), the *Arizona Republic* (July 11, 1954), and *Time* (August 9, 1954) presented articles favorable to peyotism, with pictures of a peyote ceremony. The peyotists were not discouraged by the outcome of the hearing, interpreting the Council's failure to reaffirm the 1940 law (an affirmation which was unnecessary) as a fairly favorable sign.

FURTHER COUNCIL HEARINGS

But in 1955, arrests continued. In late 1955, the peyotists were said to be preparing a petition for a hearing at the Council. There was a small rash of arrests in late December of 1955, with probationary sentences in at least a few cases.

In 1956, as a result of pressure from the peyotists, a new Council hearing took place. It must be recalled that both in 1940 and in 1954 the Council had asked for more data on the effects of peyote. In May of 1956, the discussion centered about a proposed resolution to instruct the Health Committee of the Navajo Tribal Council to investigate the peyote problem and secure adequate medical evidence from "independent experts" and to hear witnesses, pro and con, thereafter to report to the Council with a recommendation as to whether the peyote ordinance should be kept or repealed. The Chairman indicated that there had been difficulties in getting an investigation by the Council under way. He was opposed to changing the law, since there were laws against peyote in Arizona, New Mexico, and Texas. Furthermore, he was informed by the Area Solicitor that Federal funds *could* be used to enforce the regulation. Whereas he regarded it as conceivable that the Council might vote to change the law, he saw no basis for such action without further evidence.

In the course of the discussion which followed, the resolution was read, but was neither moved nor seconded. There were signs of a very small shift of attitude favorable to the peyotists. Three principal issues were discussed: whether there should be an investigation, whether there should be a popular referendum on peyote, and whether law should be made stiffer. Six people spoke in favor of an investigation, only two of them peyotists. Three spoke in favor of a referendum, only two of them peyotists (the others came from communities with a number of peyotist constituents). Two non-peyotists spoke in favor of a laissez-faire policy for peyote. One of these had been in the 1940 and 1954 Council meetings, where he had opposed peyotism. Now he said that there was no evidence that peyote caused death or moral deterioration, or even that peyotists ran about in the nude, as some alleged. There was, however, evidence that alcohol was deleterious, for anyone to see. Furthermore, the issue of the foreign-ness of peyote was scarcely germane: many Navaho ceremonies were of Pueblo origin but were accepted. There were, in any case, too many peyotists to think of cutting the cult back now. This was the most striking shift of position that could be seen.

All other speakers opposed an investigation—either because there were enough facts known or because an investigation would be too costly or too difficult. Some wanted peyote ritual equipment confiscated. Opposition to the cult remained strong, on the usual grounds: the danger of peyote to health and morality and its foreign origins. On May 25, 1956, the Council voted to amend the 1940 regulations so that peyote confiscated by Law and Order officers must be destroyed—a point not covered by the law. There was no motion on ritual equipment and no vote on the proposed health investigation. I am informed that ten or twelve Council members abstained from voting on the new clause. The final vote on confiscation was 54 to 5. Thus the outcome of the 1956 hearing was quite similar to that in 1940 and 1954.

I know of no subsequent Council hearings on peyote. From this point on, the issue came to the attention of State and Federal courts and State legislatures.

As might be expected, peyotism was an issue in the Tribal Council elections of 1959 and 1963. In 1959, the peyotists strongly opposed the incumbent chairman, Paul Jones, but he was nominated without opposition and elected. The peyotists, however, are said to have placed a dozen cult members on the Council, and to have influenced the election of other delegates, not members, but sympathetic to the peyotists' wish for religious freedom.[6]

In 1963, Raymond Nakai was elected chairman. He had stated during the campaign that he was in favor of religious freedom and that he did not know anything about peyotism. This was undoubtedly widely interpreted by peyotists as support for a less stringent policy on peyote, and it can be assumed that Nakai got some peyotist votes on this account. This was but one of many issues in the election, and it is impossible to decide what the significance of the peyote issue may have been. There were additional peyotists elected to the Tribal Council, although as always they constituted a small minority of the delegates. (I am indebted to Mary Shepardson for information on this subject.)

STATE ACTION; LEGAL CASES

Immediately after the 1956 hearing, the Native American Church of North America began a legal campaign on behalf of Navaho peyotists. Frank Takes Gun, a Crow Indian, active in the Native American Church, who had attended the 1956 hearings, began legal action two days after the Council vote. He filed a restraining order against the enforcement of the law against peyote.[7]

Suit was filed by August 5, 1956 (*Arizona Daily Sun* of that date), in the United States District Court, by the Native American Church, contesting the right of the Tribe to prohibit peyotism. In February of 1957, the United States District Court of Appeals refused a writ of *habeas corpus* sought on behalf of a Navaho peyote priest arrested under the Tribal ordinance. The Court asserted that the peyote ordinance was reasonable and that the limitations found in the first and fifth amend-

---

[6] Of course peyotism was an issue in prior elections as well. Peyotists normally tried to discover the views of candidates for the chairmanship, and there was some voting on the basis of a candidate's possible leniency toward the cult.

[7] By his own account, he had complained to Secretary Ickes immediately after the 1940 ordinance was passed, and had subsequently complained to Secretary Krug. He was Vice-President of the Native American Church 1944–1952 and was elected President on July 1, 1956. At the same election, Hola Tso of Sawmill was elected Vice-President, the second non-Plains member to hold so high an office in the Church. (Teles Romero of Taos was Vice-President in 1954–1956.) The election of Hola Tso was undoubtedly a recognition of the importance of the Navaho membership in the Church, and probably a reaction to the difficulties faced by Navaho peyotists. (Data on officers to 1954, Slotkin, 1956, pp. 63–64; on Takes Gun's campaign from the *Quarterly Bulletins of the Native American Church of North America* and from mimeographed letters circulated by Takes Gun. Other sources indicated in text.)

ments held here. This was apparently in response to Takes Gun's suit of 1956. The Church appealed to the 10th Circuit Court of Appeals. (Cf. Stewart, 1961, p. 15. There was also a suit in Arizona, dismissed because the State judge said he had no jurisdiction over the Council.)

In 1957, the New Mexico Legislature passed a bill legalizing the use of peyote for religious purposes. Takes Gun led the peyotists in support of the bill; the Tribal Council opposed it. Governor Mechem vetoed the bill. In 1959, the Legislature passed the bill again, and the new Governor, John Burroughs, allowed it to become law without his signature—over the vigorous objections of the Tribal Council.

In 1959, the United States Court of Appeals upheld the Tribe's right to its anti-peyote ordinance (U.S. Court of Appeals, Tenth Circuit, 1959, Native American Church of North America vs. The Navajo Tribal Council. No. 6146). In brief, the Court held that the Tribe had the right to have, and to enforce such an ordinance, because of the special status of Indian tribes. Other grounds were also mentioned (Stewart, 1961).

In 1960 the American Civil Liberties Union (A.C.L.U.) assisted the Native American Church in a case involving the arrest of Mary Attakai, a Navaho peyotist, off the reservation. She was arrested by Arizona law officers. The A.C.L.U. retained an attorney; Omer C. Stewart appeared at Takes Gun's request as an anthropological expert; and a psychiatrist from Phoenix also appeared on behalf of the peyotists. On July 26, 1960, Judge Yale McFate declared the Arizona law against the use of peyote unconstitutional. He stated that the issue was whether a prohibition on the use of peyote was "reasonably necessary to protect the public health" (Stewart, 1961, p. 13). He stated that peyote was not a narcotic, was not habit-forming, and had no harmful after-effects. He argued that the use of peyote was essential to the religion and that use of peyote by non-cult members was insignificant. He argued that the Arizona law prevented worship by members of the Native American Church. "The manner in which peyote is used by the Indian worshiper is not inconsistent with the public health, morals, or welfare" (Stewart, 1961, p. 14). And so, he concluded, the Arizona law was unconstitutional. This, however, affected only the situation of Arizona Indians using peyote off the reservation.

Faced with the Court of Appeals decision, Takes Gun had to decide whether to appeal from this court to the Supreme Court. In consultation with the A.C.L.U., he decided instead to start a new suit in the United States Court of Appeals, District of Columbia Circuit. As I understand it, the suit was directed at the Secretary of Interior, on account of the Secretary's approval of the Navaho ordinance. The A.C.L.U. supplied an attorney. This suit was lost July 26, 1962, when the court ruled that the Secretary had merely approved action which the Tribal Council was entitled to take (*New York Times*, July 28, 1962). I assume that the Native American Church will attempt further appeals.

In April of 1962, three Navahos were arrested near Needles, California, and charged with violation of the California Narcotics Law. On November 29, the Superior Court ruled against their plea of religious freedom, upheld the California law, and gave the defendants suspended prison sentences. The American Civil

Liberties Union had entered the case and planned to appeal, first to the State Court of Appeal, and beyond, if necessary. Omer C. Stewart appeared as an expert witness in this case. Thus diametrically opposed conclusions were reached in Arizona and California (based on *Arizona Daily Star*, Tucson, November 15, 1962; *New York Times*, November 30, 1962; Stewart, personal communication).

SUMMARY OF STRUGGLES

To sum up, the struggle against peyotism, which must have begun in the form of local and spontaneous actions of individual Navahos and groups of Navahos, directed against peyotists and peyote priests, moved to police action as early as 1938 —two years before there was a law to serve as the basis of arrests—and to legislative methods in 1940. Efforts to enforce the law have varied in intensity over time, and there have been occasional outbreaks of illegal, organized, local action against the peyotists.

The peyotists themselves have similarly moved from spontaneous efforts at self-defense to increasingly organized efforts, pressing for hearings, attempting to achieve greater representation on the Council, and ultimately involving the national organization of the Native American Church and the American Civil Liberties Union. They have tried to influence State legislation and have tried for redress through the courts. The New Mexico law against peyote has been repealed; the Arizona law has been declared unconstitutional; but the Tribal ordinance has been repeatedly upheld by the courts.

The central legal issue at stake is that a tribe has certain sovereign powers that have never been removed. As Cohen puts it,

Indian self-government . . . includes the power of an Indian tribe to adopt and operate under a form of government of the Indians' choosing, to define conditions of tribal membership, to regulate domestic relations of members, to prescribe rules of inheritance, to levy taxes, to regulate property within the jurisdiction of the tribe, to control the conduct of members by municipal legislation, and to administer justice.

Perhaps the most basic principle . . . is the principle that *those powers which are lawfully vested in an Indian tribe are not, in general, delegated powers granted by express acts of Congress, but rather inherent powers of a limited sovereignty which has never been extinguished.*

. . . .

The powers of sovereignty have been limited from time to time by special treaties and laws. . . .

. . . .

What is not expressly limited remains within the domain of tribal sovereignty [Cohen, 1942, p. 122; italics in source].[8]

And thus it has been held that the Navajo Tribe has the power to enact a resolution against the sale, possession, or use of peyote, without respect to the Bill of Rights. Needless to say, however, the peyotists have always found it bewildering, that, as they see it, the Constitution does not protect them. They are not prepared

8 Among the relevant cases are Worcester v. Georgia, 31 U.S. 350; United States v. Kagama, 118 U.S. 375; Williams v. Lee, 358 U.S. 217; Talton v. Mayes, 163 U.S. 376; Barta v. Oglala Sioux Tribe of Pine Ridge Reservation, 259 F.2d 553; and Toledo v. Pueblo de Jemez, 119 F.Supp. 429 (cited from the 10th Circuit Court of Appeals decision against the peyotists, from Stewart, 1961, pp. 15–17).

to believe that use of peyote is contrary to public morality, health, or welfare, and they do not understand the legal peculiarities of tribal status.

ARRESTS

We have seen that arrests have occurred ever since 1938. Only for the years 1952–1959 is there any systematic information about them. Through all the legal struggles, convictions for violation of the law against peyote have run close to 100 per annum throughout these years. Yet during the same years, virtually all other categories of offenses tried in Tribal courts have shown a considerable increase. Thus illicit cohabitation has doubled, assault has more than doubled, etc. Whereas the increase in other categories may well reflect only an increase both in population and in the police force and its efficiency, the static character of peyote arrests is curious.

CHURCH ORGANIZATION

Before we close the account of the struggle over peyotism, it is necessary to discuss the organization of the Native American Church among the Navaho and its connection with the national Church. The Navaho system follows the general lines of the Church elsewhere. There is a state organization in Arizona, New Mexico, and Utah. (So far as I know, the Colorado state organization is primarily for Utes. Cf. Stewart, 1961.) There are local organizations as well, but I do not know how many exist. Each state organization has filed papers of incorporation at the State Capital. Such papers always include a statement which speaks of the right to use peyote as a sacrament—even in states where the possession, sale, or use of peyote is an offense under state law. After incorporation is completed, it is possible for individuals to get certified copies of these papers, which they call a "charter." Peyotists show these papers to their antagonists, in good faith, to show that they have the legal right to use peyote. This sometimes confuses, sometimes intimidates, and sometimes merely irritates the opposition. The Native American Church was incorporated in New Mexico on June 15, 1945, the Native American Church of the State of Utah on June 23, 1945, and the Native American Church of the State of Arizona on February 28, 1946. The New Mexico group includes Taos members. I do not know whether its incorporation was inspired by Taos peyotists, Navaho peyotists, or both. The Arizona and Utah group are entirely Navaho (dates from Slotkin, 1956, pp. 60–61).[9]

In 1955, there were said to be ten local groups of Navahos using peyote (*Quarterly Bulletin of the Native American Church*, Vol. 1, No. 1, Jan.–March 1955). Those listed were: Fort Defiance, Indian Wells, Kayenta, Tuba City, Winslow, Aneth, Shiprock, Thoreau, Crown Point, and Gallup. The Indian Wells group is undoubtedly located at Greasewood below Ganado, where there are many peyotists. There are few at Indian Wells. It is probable that some of these "groups" are simply individual peyotists. And, on the other hand, organized groups known to me at Sweetwater and Black Mountain are omitted from the list.

[9] The Ute group in Colorado, first incorporated in 1926 as the Native American Lodge, changed its name to the Native American Church and filed new papers in 1946. According to Stewart (1961), the incorporations in all the Four Corners states were stimulated by Frank Takes Gun, preparatory to efforts to change state laws, and as part of a general drive.

Both state and local organizations always include at least one literate member. Officials need not be road men but often are. Efforts are made to send men from the state organizations to the national convention of the Church, sometimes by taking up a collection to pay his way.

The national Church has been interested in the Navaho situation from an early date. Alfred Wilson, the distinguished Cheyenne peyotists, visited the reservation a number of times, beginning in 1937 or 1938, often advising Navahos about their legal and public problems. Allen P. Dale, President of the Church in 1954, visited the Council hearing in that year. Frank Takes Gun was active on behalf of the Navaho from 1940 on and has been especially active since 1956, when he became President. As member of the Board of the Church and editor of its quarterly bulletin, J. S. Slotkin, anthropologist, and as he called himself, quasi-Menomini, visited Sawmill and Shiprock in 1955 (*Quarterly Bulletin*, Vol. 1, No. 3, July–Sept., 1955). Navahos have contributed to the national organization, and members of other tribes have contributed funds for the Navaho legal struggle. The Navaho situation has been reported in the Bulletin, by Navahos, and Takes Gun has circulated letters describing it (*Quarterly Bulletin*, 1955–1958—when it was discontinued, and associated letters).

Undoubtedly the struggle over peyotism still continues on the Navajo Reservation.[10]

[10] *Postscript, September, 1964.*—Utah, New Mexico, and Arizona organizations of the Native American Church are now centralized to some degree under a coordinator who works fairly closely with the President of the Native American Church, Frank Takes Gun. There are continuous efforts to develop effective local ("chapter") organizations, and to collect dues. Dues are needed to pay the travel expenses of local officials for meetings of the Navajo Native American Church. The coordinator estimates membership at 25,000 to 40,000 Navahos, and several people believe that the Church has close to a majority of the Navaho population. Under the new Chairman of the Navajo Tribal Council, Raymond Nakai, arrests for peyote offenses have stopped. He is not a member of the Church, although some anti-peyotists believe he is. Peyotists believe that there are members all over the Reservation. A missionary in Monument Valley, where there were almost no members in 1952 (DFA, field notes), reports that about half the Navahos are members (*New York Times*, Sept. 12, 1964). According to the missionary, there were almost no members in 1959.

On August 24, the Supreme Court of California ruled favorably on the Navaho case. It decided that the use of peyote in religious ceremonies does not violate a California law forbidding the use of peyote (*New York Times*, Aug. 25, 1964). This ruling is consistent with the Arizona ruling. A case before the Supreme Court of the United States, challenging the right of the Navajo Tribal Council to legislate against the use of peyote, on grounds of religious freedom, is still pending.

Further postscript, September, 1965.—The coordinator of the Native American Church in the Navaho country says that there are 35,000 Navaho men, women, and children now members of the Native American Church. He states that membership cards substantiate this figure. Since the total Navaho population is 90,000–100,000, this estimate would mean that 35–39 per cent of Navahos are now peyotists, as compared with Aberle's estimate of 12,000–14,000 peyotists in 1951, in a total population of 70,000, or 17–20 per cent. Thus, if both estimates are accepted, there has been a marked absolute and relative rise in membership.

Two Navahos have been appointed to the Executive Board of the international Native American Church, and Hola Tso continues as Vice-President of the international organization. Frank Takes Gun has been active in Washington in hearings on federal drug legislation. Further efforts to remove legal obstacles to members' use of peyote in the Navaho country are contemplated.

Chapter 9

THE RITUAL OF NAVAHO PEYOTISM

EYOTISM among the Navaho is like peyotism elsewhere. Every American Indian group probably has some minor variations in ritual and ideology, depending on the culture of the group receiving peyotism, the specific peyotist tradition or traditions introduced, and local innovations. But these variations are small enough so that if James Mooney were alive today and attended a peyote meeting anywhere in North America, or discussed peyotism with leaders and followers, he would not find things too different from his descriptions of matters in the 1390's on the Plains. But in a book on *Navaho* peyotism, it is necessary to deal with Navaho ritual and ideology in detail.

We will begin by discussing the purposes for which peyote meetings are held, proceeding thence to a detailed description of the ritual of a peyote meeting supplied by one Navaho road man. Then variants of ritual, major and minor, and the question of syncretism with Navaho practice will be dealt with.

PURPOSES OF MEETINGS

Peyote meetings are held most often for the sake of curing. Most such meetings are for every conceivable variety of physical complaint, but meetings are also held for people suffering from mental illness. I know of at least three instances in which psychotic individuals were treated in peyote meetings. Some Navahos believe that there should be four curing meetings for complete recovery—a belief which has its parallel in Navaho ideology.[1] It also has Plains analogues (La Barre, 1938, pp. 86–87). And a meeting may be held to give thanks for being cured.

People sometimes hold ceremonies in hopes of deciding whether a person should be treated with a Navaho ceremony or sent to the hospital. They hope that someone in the meeting will have an insight as to what should be done. Or, if a peyotist is planning a Navaho ceremony, he may have a peyote meeting to pray for its successful outcome.

Late in the summer, there are many ceremonies to insure that children going to school will have good health, learn a lot, and return safely in the spring. There are also meetings of thanks in the spring when the children return.[2]

There are birthday meetings, usually for young children, which presumably aim at securing good fortune for the child.

[1] Navaho non-peyotists claim to be baffled by the claims of peyotists that their meetings are to cure patients, since they know that sometimes the "patient" is not ill. They do not seem to recognize the parallelism with Navaho belief.

[2] Curing meetings are serious matters, and there was not too much enthusiasm about my attending them. Meetings for schoolchildren are less serious, and so I have attended far more of these, particularly since there were so many during the summer, when I was there.

There were meetings during World War II and the Korean War to pray for departing soldiers and soldiers away from home, and to give thanks for returning soldiers. Meetings were also held for victory.

There are holiday meetings. Christmas, New Year's, Easter, Fourth of July, and Thanksgiving are the days most commonly mentioned. These meetings begin the evening before the holiday. Thanks to God and prayers for guidance in the future, not jollification, are the keynotes of these occasions.

Peyote weddings occur. A peyote button is divided and the bride and groom each eat half—a practice reminiscent of the traditional Navaho wedding, where a basket of mush is shared. Whether there are also peyote funerals, baptisms, or naming ceremonies I do not know.

Meetings may also be held to bless a new hogan, to keep things running right, or to bring health, good luck, and good fortune to a family.

Some peyotists claim that in order to join the Native American Church formally, one should put up a peyote meeting. Others say that this is unnecessary.

In one area, it is said, an effort is made to hold a meeting regularly once a week, usually on Saturday night, without any special aim for any particular meeting. As in other areas, the meetings are in various hogans, not in a fixed place, and special good accrues to the family that puts up the meeting.

Most commonly, then, the meeting has at least one fairly specific aim. A particular family is responsible for "putting up" the meeting, and there is at least one "patient." The patient is often a member of the family putting up the meeting. Double-barreled meetings are common. In one meeting the prayers of which are presented elsewhere, the aims included blessing some children before their return to school and curing the wife of the road chief. In another, there were four patients. And, in the course of the meeting, some of those present may seek God's help and the help of participants' prayers for still other problems.

There are parallels to Navaho chant practice in these matters. Most Navaho chants are held to cure specific patients of specific ills (or to round out the cycle of four chants toward this end), but the commonest Navaho chant, Blessing Way, may be held to bless a new hogan, to seek good fortune, to maintain harmony, and so on. But before attributing Navaho peyotist practice to syncretism, we should note La Barre's comments on the purposes of Plains peyotist meetings. They include curing, rain-making, divination, baptism, marriage, funerals, birthdays, celebrating desired events, seeking of good fortune, and holiday meetings for Easter, New Year's, Thanksgiving, and Christmas. Death anniversary meetings are also mentioned; I do not know whether they occur among the Navaho (La Barre, 1938, pp. 58–60). Hence, although there are parallels with Navaho chant practice, there are even more precise parallels with Plains peyotism as well.[2a]

2a Postscript, 1965.—In conversations with me, some English-speaking Navahos have described meetings held to seek God's blessing, to gain or maintain good fortune, or to give thanks for good fortune, as "hózhǫ́ǫ́jí way," and those held to cure, to deal with catastrophe, and so on, as "hóchǫ́ǫ́jí way." These mixed Navaho-English phrases are apparently redundant, since "hózhǫ́ǫ́jí" means "Blessing Way," and "hóchǫ́ǫ́jí" means "Evil Way," but they are best understood as signifying "in the manner of Blessing Way" or "Evil Way." The same individual might have a peyote meeting first in the manner of Evil Way, to overcome bad fortune, and then in the manner of Blessing Way, to give thanks for the successful outcome of the first meeting. There is, then, some mild syncretism with traditional Navaho orientations here.

This list of the purposes of meetings leads to several conclusions: (1) Peyotists, like other Navahos and like all traditional North American Indians, see illness as a product of spiritual forces, and the cure of illness as a part of man's dealings with the supernatural. (2) Like other Navahos and traditional North American Indians, they believe that a good life depends on proper relations with supernatural forces. (3) They refuse—as a group, though not as individuals—to cut themselves off from recourse to Navaho ceremonies or western medicine. (4) They show an explicit awareness of their involvement with an extra-tribal world, in their celebration of national holidays and in their stress on education. (5) They wish to be on a par with traditional Navaho religion and with western churches in carrying out such life-crisis acts as weddings.

With this background, we present the account of a ceremony provided by Mike Kiyaani, a road man from Piñon, Arizona. He supplied this account to me verbally in May of 1954. In 1957, I provided him with a transcription of our discussion from my notes, and he returned this with emendations which have been incorporated without notation. At some points, I have shown that questions were asked, to indicate that the flow of the materials was guided, rather than spontaneous, with respect to some topics. Mike Kiyaani began running peyote meetings in 1947 and was taught by Truman W. Dailey, an Oto Indian (cf. Slotkin, 1956, p. 63). Kiyaani says that the ritual is that of Quanah Parker (d. 1911), a Comanche on his father's side, a white on his mother's (Slotkin, 1956, p. 79). Accounts supplied by other road men would differ in details from this one, because of different apprenticeships and individually introduced variations. We proceed with the transcription of the interview with Kiyaani and will indicate the end of these materials, but without using quotation marks. Parentheses are his; square brackets are questions directed at Mike Kiyaani or comments by the anthropologist to elucidate the text.

MIKE KIYAANI'S DESCRIPTION OF RITUAL

Before the meeting, the family or the person who wants a meeting asks the road chief to perform it. Either the road chief or the family can set the date. [At this point a question was asked about paying for a meeting.] We road men do not usually take an offering of money to run a meeting. We do not really "perform" a meeting—peyote performs, and we serve. So we should not take money or things as payment from the person who puts up the meeting. It is a sacred thing and not to be paid for. We human beings can help one another; we road chiefs should help others. If a road chief cannot run a meeting at the time [requested by the patient or his family], he should postpone it until later, when he can, or refer the person who wants the meeting to some one else [some other road man]. When the meeting is over, we can take an offering, but that is not a payment. If there is no offering, that is all right, too. The most I ever got was $20.00. Five dollars of that came from the family that was putting up the meeting, and the rest came in small amounts from the other people there. [A question was asked about rumors of very large payments, including gifts of jewelry and sheep.] At first there were some gifts like that [among the Navaho], but it is not true any more. [Should a man pay for special prayers he requests from the road man?] No, there is no special money for a prayer. Someone at the meeting besides the patient might ask me to do a special prayer for him, and I would have to do that. There would be no payment. Once in a great while someone like that might give the road man a dollar as an offering on account of that prayer. [Does the road chief keep the various offerings, or what happens?] About $2.00 each would go to the fire chief, the drummer chief, the cedar chief, and the woman who brought in the morning water, from the road chief. I have seen offerings running from about $10.00 to about $30.00, and $20.00 is about the average.

[Who furnishes the peyote?] The road chief might, or the patient, or his family. Or everyone coming to the meeting might contribute for a poor person. [If the road chief provides the peyote, does he get paid for it?] No. [Where do you get peyote?] Either by having it shipped to me from Texas or by going to get it in Texas. I have done both. I got 60,000 buttons once in Texas. I offered a prayer when I cut it. You can do that either with a cedar incense offering or by smoking a cigarette. [It will be seen below that smoking a cigarette handrolled in cornhusk or paper is a way of making an offering to God.] [What does it cost in Texas?] I sold it and I gave it to people who needed it. It used to cost 10¢ a button out here, but now I sell it for 5¢. [How much peyote is needed for one meeting?] Between 200 and 400 buttons, depending on the size of the meeting. [What else does a family need to put up a meeting, and what does it cost?] It would take a sheep, worth about $15.00, about 24 pounds of flour, a pound of coffee, five pounds of sugar, about a dollar and a half of canned fruit, some bread—it depends on how many people are coming. It would probably cost about $50.00 or $75.00, but other people help out with the food; so the entire amount does not come just from the family putting up a meeting. [How many meetings would a family have in a year?] Two or three.

[What should the road chief do to get ready for the meeting?] He should bathe and put on clean clothes. The people coming to the meeting should put on good clean clothes, too—no special type of clothes, just clean and good. [Should they bathe, too?] That is not necessary.

[The remainder of the discussion concerns the meeting itself. The account was supplied with few interruptions for questions.]

The meeting starts about 8:00 P.M., regardless of whether that is before or after sundown. I do not make a prayer just before I go into the meeting, although some road chiefs do. The people go into the meeting in the following order: the road chief enters first, with his kit; then the drummer chief; then the cedar chief; then the patient; the rest come in any old way, but the fire chief comes at the end of the line. They enter clockwise.

[What has been done before that, and who brings the equipment?]

The road chief provides: the drum, the eagle feather for the fire chief; the fan of two eagle feathers that goes around the meeting, with the cane; an eagle tail fan that I keep with me all the time; the bunch of sage that goes around with the cane; another bunch of sage from which people take pieces early in the ceremony; the cane itself; a gourd rattle; the parts of the drum [an iron or brass pot, a buckskin drumhead, a rope for tying the drum, pebbles to press into the buckskin and tie the rope around, and a drumstick]; a whistle of eagle bone; the chief peyote [a fine specimen put on the altar and not eaten, used by the road man as an altar piece in all his ceremonies; some are decorated with white paint, but Mike's is plain]; corn husks; cigarette papers; tobacco. [What about a piece of deer horn to tighten the drum rope?] The drum can be tightened with any stick, or with a piece of horn, which some people have.

Before the meeting the road chief supervises the fixing of the earth or sand crescent moon altar. He is also there when the drum is bound. He does not supply the firewood, the fire stick or poker used to light the ceremonial cigarettes, the pieces of charcoal for inside the drum, or the water for inside the drum.

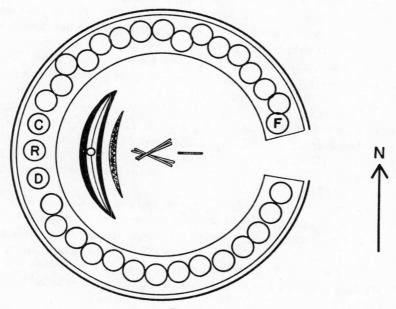

DIAGRAM 1

Arrangement of a Navaho Peyote Meeting. Outer circle represents hogan or teepee. Small circles represent participants (not segregated by sex). Lines inside outer circle represent area spread with blankets on which participants sit. R is road man, D is drummer man, C is cedar man, F is fire man. West to east in center appear: crescent moon earth "altar" with "peyote road" line down center and "chief peyote" on top; ash crescent; fire; "poker"; entrance. Not shown: road man's kit, drum, water bucket, dishes for peyote breakfast, woodpile.

[Since I had heard some argument as to whether it was proper to supplement the light of the fire with kerosene lamps, I asked a question on this point.] There is no need for lamps. If it is a sick person, you should use only the fire for light; if it is a less serious meeting, like for schoolchildren, lamps might be all right.

Four sticks of wood are used to make the fire. They are laid in a crib construction in the form of an X with the arms of the X nearest the altar very short, and those away from the altar very long. Any stick could be used for a smoke stick [fire stick, so-called poker], but for a special meeting you might have a specially decorated stick.

The hogan should be cleaned out and places to sit should be prepared—places big enough to sit, but not big enough to lie down. [Could you stretch your legs out in front of you?] Yes, but not for long. And for prayers you should sit right [that is, kneel]. You should keep yourself off the ground, by sitting on a mattress, a blanket, or a pad. You should keep yourself reverent and think of good spirit. Spirits will be coming round as the meeting goes on, and you should sit up and not be sprawled out, so that the spirits can go round the center track of the meeting, on the ground, as the cane, the drum, and the water do.

Every one is now in the meeting and they should sit down. The men are paired off so that a man has someone next to him who can sing while he drums and drum while he sings. [Where should the women sit?] It doesn't matter. [What about a mother-in-law and a son-in-law—could they sit next to each other?] They could if neither one minded. [Can a woman ever take the staff and fan and sing?] I don't want them to, but I couldn't stop them.

Now the road chief takes out the chief peyote. He puts cedar incense [dried and crumbled cedar leaves] on the fire and smokes the chief peyote four times in the cedar smoke: he puts the chief peyote in the smoke and then moves it toward its place on the altar. He repeats this four times and then puts the chief peyote on the moon [altar], on a bed of sage that he has prepared. The sage bed is in the form of a circle. [Do they ever make a bed shaped like a cross?] Yes, I have seen that, but I make a round one. [Does one part of the chief peyote have to go in a particular direction, like East or West—that is, is the chief peyote considered to have cardinal orientation points?] No.

Then I smoke the whistle in the fire four times and put it at the foot of the moon. [All references to "smoking" that do not involve cigarettes refer to the putting of an object in cedar incense smoke, fanning the smoke toward a person, etc.] The whistle can be lying down with the mouthpiece south, or standing, leaning against the moon. [If it stands, is the mouthpiece up or down?] Up. [When would you choose to lay it down and when would you stand it up?] Just whichever way you would like it to be.

The fire chief's eagle feather is now smoked once and is passed to the fire chief, clockwise. He keeps it all through the meeting. He can fan the fire with it, or smoke himself off, fanning the smoke of cedar incense on to himself with it.

[Why are these things smoked in cedar smoke?] The cedar smoke is an offering to God and a blessing. It purifies the instruments. [Why is the peyote chief put on a bed of sage?] That is the custom. [Why is the altar shaped like a moon?] There are different stories. You may say that it's the universe. [And the road on the moon?] That's *the* road, the peyote road, our path.

[Later, written addendum by Mike Kiyaani:] Any living creatures depends on certain things in order to be on this earth. We use fire, water, etc., earth shaped like a moon. The moon represents the universe.

[Do you use a big moon altar or a small moon altar?] It depends on the size of the hogan. [Is that the only reason to pick one or the other?] Yes.[3] [I have seen a

3 Petrullo (1934) and La Barre (1938) follow their informants in distinguishing between Big Moon and Small Moon. Big Moon has an elaborate altar with many markings on the ground to the east of the altar; Small Moon is a simple crescent of earth with a line running from point to point, dividing the crescent. The Small Moon is classical for Plains peyotism and is found

ditch dug on the east side of the moon for the ashes. Do you do that?] No, I don't use that. [I have also heard about a way with no moon, just a "V" of ash.] I don't use it. [Where did you get your way of running a meeting?] From Truman Dailey. He got it from a Kiowa who died last year [1953] at the age of 100.

Now Bull Durham tobacco is circulated to the participants. No Indian tobacco is used, only Bull Durham. Cigarette papers are sent around too—but not corn-husks. The road chief starts with the tobacco and papers and then gives them to the drummer chief, and then it goes around clockwise. Or they might use two sacks and two sets of papers. Then one would start with the road chief and the other would start south of the door entrance and go clockwise. [How would it get to the person south of the door to start with?] Any items being passed around should go clockwise. [That is, since the road chief supplies these items, the second sack would be passed without being used from the road chief, clockwise to the person on the south side of the door, where it would begin to be used for cigarettes, returning to the road chief. The use of two sacks reduces the time required for everyone to procure tobacco and roll a cigarette.]

Before they went into the meeting, the fire had been started. If there are small children, they do not smoke. When everyone has rolled his cigarette, they are all lit. The fire chief puts the fire stick in the fire to get a glowing end on it and brings the fire stick around, clockwise and gives it to the road chief. Then it goes to the drummer chief, and then it goes around clockwise, hand to hand. [See below for completion of this routine.]

Then the person who is putting up the meeting tells the purpose of the meeting. He tells what the meeting is for, and after that, people must think and talk that way—think and talk so that the purpose of the meeting will come about. And the medicine [peyote] must be used that way—for a purpose. [Who decides who should come to the meeting?] People can come of their own accord, but the man who is putting up the meeting would tell his relatives about it and he would get the road chief and tell the other officials.

Now the road chief talks and says, "I am glad for this meeting. Think of me. I will help the best that I can; I don't know how, but I can help you." This talk by the person putting up the meeting and the road chief can go on until about halfway through the cigarettes. As soon as they are lit, a person should puff four puffs toward the chief peyote, and then one puff toward mother earth, and then blow two or three puffs on his own body.

[What happens to the fire stick?] The fire chief goes clockwise from his place and hands it to the road chief. He returns counterclockwise to his seat. The fire stick itself goes from the road chief to the drummer chief, and then clockwise to the end [which will be the person on the drummer chief's right hand]. Then it

among the Menomini, Washo-Paiute, Ute, and many, many other tribes (cf. Slotkin, 1952; Stewart, 1944, 1948). Petrullo's and La Barre's "Small Moon" is the only moon found among the Navahos, but Navaho peyotists distinguish between "big moon" and "small moon" on the basis of the size of the crescent. In addition, the points of the crescent are more likely to be sharply pointed for "big moon" and blunted for "small moon." There should be no confusion between Navaho simple crescent "big moon" and variants on Moonhead Wilson's elaborated "Big Moon" altar.

goes back hand to hand counterclockwise to the fire chief. The packages of tobacco and papers are returned to the road chief, clockwise, before the lighting of the cigarettes begins, but the lighting and the talking can go on together. When everyone has his cigarette lit, it is time to pray. The road chief prays and the others can pray according to what the man who is putting up the meeting or the patient has told them about the purpose of the meeting. If the cigarette goes out while you are praying, that is OK. This smoke and prayer is the beginning of the ceremony: a short, general prayer for the purpose of the meeting. The prayers people make are related to the purpose of the meeting. All in all there are four special smokes and prayers during the night for the purpose of the meeting.

[I asked Mike for a later written comment as to the important divisions of the ceremony. He replied:] 1. The Starting Ceremony. 2. The Midnight Water Time. 3. The Morning Water Time. 4. The Closing Ceremony.

When they are through praying, the fire chief gives his smoke to the man on his right and starts taking up the cigarette butts beginning at the south side of the door, moving clockwise, laying them on the palm on his hand, all the same way, with the mouthpieces all in the same direction. [In response to questions, he said that it did not matter which way the butts were laid, just so they were all laid in the same direction. They did not have to be kept in order, first worshipper's first, etc. Indeed, it did not matter which hand was used.]

He collects the butts as far as the drummer chief and puts them at the south end of the moon. He then goes counterclockwise to the road chief and goes clockwise from there to the end, picking up his own cigarette butt last. These butts are placed at the north end of the moon. Then the fire chief goes back to his place and sits down. [I neglected to ask, but assume that he proceeds counterclockwise from picking up the last cigarette butt, his own, held by the man on his right, to the north end of the moon and clockwise to his place.] The fire chief keeps tending the fire and the charcoal. He keeps things in a straight line: from the door to the poker to the fire, to the moon and to the chief peyote on the moon.

Now sage is passed. The road chief takes the sage and the medicine [peyote] and puts cedar in the fire and puts the medicine and the sage in the smoke of the cedar four times. He sits down and passes the sage. It goes to the drummer first and then clockwise. When the sage passes the road chief it is medicine: something for the Indians to use in a ceremony. [Presumably it is medicine when it leaves his hands, rather than after the drummer uses it, when it "passes" the road chief.] Each person takes a little sage off the bunch. After the sage has gone around it is put away. Each person rubs the sage in his hands and then rubs it over his head and body. Then the road chief starts the peyote around. Each person takes what he wants. In my way of doing things the road chief does not tell people how much to take [as some road chiefs do]. It would usually be one or two to start with. The medicine passes around clockwise and returns to the road chief. [Individuals now scrape the cotton fuzz from the peyote button and eat the button, usually offering it toward the chief peyote first, then eating it, then spitting in the hands and rubbing them over the head and body to get the virtue of the medicine over the body.]

Then the road chief sets out the instruments: the cane, the sage (a different bunch from the one that was passed around before—four nice pieces), the two-feather fan, and the gourd [rattle]. The drummer brings out the drum. Cedar is put in the fire, and all these instruments are smoked four times and put down, and then the drum, which was not smoked before, is smoked four times.

The road chief now starts singing a special song, the opening song, and the drummer drums for him. The road chief sings four songs. One is the opening song, but the others can be any songs. When the road chief is done singing, the cane is passed to the drummer. It is passed around the drum—between the drum and the altar. He takes the drum from the drummer and now drums while the drummer sings four songs. Now the cane goes to the cedar chief and the road chief drums for him and four songs are sung. Then the drum and cane pass on to others. The drum can go back—counterclockwise, but the cane never goes back [except for the occasion just mentioned when the cane goes from the road chief to the drummer chief]. And the drum always goes behind the cane—that is, the cane always passes between the drum and the altar if the drum is going back, and it passes ahead of the drum if they are both going forward.

At this time, when the singing has started, people may still be eating peyote, but the sack has been returned. People should remove the fuzz from the peyote, but some don't. [Does it matter?] No, it is OK either way. The fuzz should go under the seat, the place where you are sitting, and not lie around. [Why?] Because it would not look good. [Can you use a knife to scrape the button?] Yes. You should eat the peyote you take [that is, you should not take peyote from the store for the meeting and carry it away]. [Why do people spit on their hands and rub them over themselves?] To get the good of the peyote into the person. [What about the various ways that peyote is prepared?] Whether it's whole, green, dried, or soaked, or ground, or boiled, it's OK. [Why is the drum used?] To get a good effect from peyote. [Why do you use an eagle feather fan?] Because this particular fire place is originated from an eagle clan [not among the Navaho, of course].

There are two prayers before midnight. In the first, the road chief rolls a smoke and lights it: the fire chief brings the fire stick to light it. [Going which way?] It depends on which side of the path is clear. [That is, if there is drumming and singing on the north side, the fire chief goes and returns on the south side, and vice versa, so as to avoid passing between the drummer and singer and the altar.] The road chief, the drummer, and the cedar chief smoke this cigarette. It is a corn-husk cigarette. [Does it have Indian tobacco?] If there is some available. This is a prayer for the four officials. I mention the bad dreams I have had and talk about the shortcomings of the people as a whole, so as to make the meeting run well.

About a half hour before midnight, I make a second prayer, just before the cane gets back to the road chief. That prayer is for the feathers to be used in the cere-mony—all the fans that people use, and for all the instruments being used. I ask God to carry this midnight prayer, for it to go right. These special prayers are with cornhusk and Indian tobacco. After this prayer the drum stops and stays where it is; the drumming and singing stop briefly.

I put cedar in the fire and put the feathers—the eagle fan I will use now—in the smoke. The patient is smoked off with the fan. [That is, cedar incense is put in the fire, the fan is put in the smoke, and then the patient is fanned with it.] I smoke myself off with the fan. There is no singing. Then a little more cedar is put in, and other people smoke the fans they have brought. The fire chief can smoke himself [in the same way as above], but he should not do it close to the fire. Now that people have smoked their own feathers they can use them.

Now the singing can start again. And while the singing goes on, the fire chief fixes things for the midnight ceremony. He fixes the charcoal first. He changes it sometimes from a heart-shaped pile to a crescent, or a circle [moon], or even a bird—an eagle—by adding a bird-tail of ash below the crescent. Or he may leave it in a heart shape. Then he fixes the fire. Then he sweeps the floor. When he gets to the cigarette butts, he puts them into the fire, first on the north; then he goes back to the door and sweeps the south and burns the butts on the south. A person's sickness and shortcomings and prayers went into the cigarettes. They are all in the cigarettes, and they are burnt. [Would it be correct to say that the burning gets rid of the sins and shortcomings and makes the prayers reach God?] Yes.

Now there is no singing. The drum has come back to the drummer chief. Now the road chief sings again, the midnight water song. First the road chief puts cedar all over the charcoal, takes his fan, smokes all along the ashbird and up to the chief peyote, and on to himself. The others smoke themselves. Every one should sit up and be reverent. Now comes the midnight water song and two other songs. Then the road chief picks up the whistle, sits down, kneels, and blows four times. He puts the whistle down again. The water is brought in by the fire chief as the road chief finishes whistling. It is carried round the room clockwise and is then put in line with the poker, the fire, and the chief peyote. The fire chief kneels behind it [to the east]. The road chief sings one more song. He holds the cane. The fire chief takes the water pail and cup and puts it in front of the road chief, facing "the same way" [that is, the side of the pail that used to face east toward the fire chief now faces west toward the road chief]. The handle of the pail is on the east side of the bucket. The fire chief takes Bull Durham, Indian tobacco, and cornshucks from the road chief, passes between the water and the altar, and goes back to his place. He gets back and fixes a cigarette. This is the second time that he has gone around the fire. [The first time was when he brought the water in.]

When the bucket is brought to the road chief, the cane, sage, feathers [those travelling with the cane and those kept by the road chief], and rattle are brought around the bucket from the south, between the bucket and the altar, with this equipment lying diagonally, the head ends facing the north end of the moon. The drummer puts his drum and stick between himself and the altar.

The cedar chief now prays. He says a few words first, and then he prays. He encourages the patient. The patient might now thank the people. The cedar chief prays for the cedar and the water. The water is used for thirst and for curing. Cedar is put in the fire to smoke the water. Fans can be used. Then cedar is put into the fire, and the fire chief brings the smoke to himself, and then everyone brings smoke to himself. Then the fire chief lights his cigarette and prays. First he speaks and encourages the patient and thanks all the people there and starts pray-

PHOTOGRAPHS OF PEYOTE MEETING

INTRODUCTORY COMMENT

The photographs of a peyote meeting that follow were taken by Dave Weber, of the *Santa Fe New Mexican*, and E. D. Newcomer, of the *Arizona Republic*. Mr. Weber's work was also made available to *Time* magazine. The pictures are identified in each case by the name of the photographer. It should be understood that those by Mr. Weber are published by the kind permission of Mr. Weber, the *Santa Fe New Mexican*, and *Time* magazine. Those by Mr. Newcomer are published by the kind permission of Mr. Newcomer and the *Arizona Republic*.

These photographs were taken at a single peyote meeting near Sawmill in late June or early July (cf. *Arizona Republic*, July 11, 1954, for approximate date). Although I did not attend the meeting, the major participants are all known to me, and this makes it possible to say where the meeting was held. The feature stories that followed, in the *Santa Fe New Mexican*, the *Arizona Republic*, and *Time* (see Bibliography), were favorable to the Native American Church. They were probably stimulated by the publicity given to Tribal Council hearings on peyote, at which Maurice Seevers and I testified, and by the Church members' desire for a favorable press.

Whereas it is not possible to put the photographs into perfect sequence, the smaller sequences presented are largely accurate. Thus Figures 5–10 form a singing-drumming sequence in which the staff approaches and reaches the road man. No cigarette butts are visible leaning against the altar in Figure 6, and the ends of the altar are not visible, so that it cannot be seen whether there are piles of cigarettes there. This sequence, therefore, might be before the midnight water, or just after the fire man swept before the midnight or the morning water ceremony. The fire-tending sequence, however, in Figures 11–16, shows the piles of cigarette butts at the ends of the altar and should therefore represent the preparations for midnight water. It is evident that Figures 17 and 18 belong to the morning water sequence.

Fig. 1.—Hogan in which meeting will be held. It is quite new, with composition roof. (Weber.)

Fig. 2.—Entrance to hogan, which faces toward the rising sun when the hogan is built, according to Navaho custom. Neat stack of firewood for peyote meeting, slightly to the north of the entrance, behind table. (Weber.)

FIG. 3.—Last participants enter the hogan after sundown. (Weber.)

FIG. 4.—Fireplace. Note sticks in a V, with smaller sticks to serve to start the fire in the cleft of the V. Behind is the small moon altar, with a cross of sage in the middle, on which the chief peyote will later be placed. On the floor are quilts on which the participants will sit. The walls are entirely covered with hangings: Navaho blankets, Pendleton blankets, bedspreads, etc. On the double-weave Navaho blanket directly behind the position of the road chief is hung a picture of a biblical scene. Covering all the walls with hangings is an embellishment not found in most meetings, but very much in the spirit of the Native American Church, which would seek to have all meetings neat and proper. This photograph was taken before the participants entered. (Weber.)

FIG. 5.—Singing and drumming. Singer holds staff and fan. Drum is approaching drummer man (*right*). Can (*left*) is used to spit in, for the sake of neatness and sanitation. (Weber.)

FIG. 6.—Singing and drumming. Drummer man holds staff and fan. Bird-bone whistle leans against altar (moon). Road man at right wears special peyote necktie. (Weber.)

FIG. 7.—Singing and drumming. Drummer man holds staff and several fans in right hand, rattle in left. Road man is reflecting or praying. Prayer with hands in this position is not characteristic, but road man is a Catholic. At road man's right knee can be seen cedar box, in which equipment is kept. Detail of drum clearly visible: iron kettle with buckskin head, rocks used for purchase in tying drum bulge out between loops of rope used to tie. (Newcomer.)

FIG. 8.—Singing and drumming. Drummer man drums, road man sings. Road man's tie depicts peyote fireplace. Biblical scene visible above. Cedar man on right closes eyes, sings along, shaking his left hand as if he held a rattle. Chief peyote visible on altar (*moon*). (Newcomer.)

FIG. 9.—Road man receives ceremonial cigarette (probably cornhusk) from some participant who has just finished a prayer. He will smoke it and "second" the prayer. This is not one of the fixed prayers (beginning, midnight or morning water, closing), because he still holds staff and fan. (Weber.)

Fig. 10.–Cedar man listens while smoking and prayer (*above*) go on. No drumming is going on at this point. (Weber.)

Fig. 11.–Participants at south side of entrance. Water bird painted on door. (Weber.)

Fig. 12.—Fire man approaches fire to tend it. Eagle feather in left hand, poker at knee, crooked stick for arranging coals in right hand. (Weber.)

Fig. 13.—Fire man shapes coals, beginning ash bird. Long box contains camera man's light. Participants' cigarette butts (from opening prayer) at ends of altar. Cigarette butts from other prayers lean against center of altar, near bird-bone whistle. (Weber.)

FIG. 14.—Fire man uses whisk broom to tidy up ash bird. (Weber.)

FIG. 15.—Fire man uses crooked stick to smooth bed of coals. (Weber.)

Fig. 16.—Fire man uses large broom to sweep altar area. Cigarette butts have been put into fire. (Weber.)

Fig. 17.—Dawn lady has brought in morning water. She kneels before water bucket, on blanket, directly in front of the door. (Weber.)

Fig. 18.—Fire man sits with eagle feather and fan while dawn woman kneels before water. He wears a special peyote necktie. (Weber.)

Fig. 19.—Morning water songs have been sung. Road man deposits equipment near altar, preparatory to dawn lady's prayer. (Weber.)

FIG. 20.—Cedar man sprinkles cedar incense on fire (sequence of scene not certain). (Newcomer.)

FIG. 21.—Road man sprinkles cedar in fire while dawn lady stands next to him (placement of scene not certain). (Newcomer.)

FIG. 22.—Dawn lady drinks water. Bucket has been turned. Water bird painted on bucket. She is using paper cup, not dipper cup (reason unknown). She wears much jewelry and a fine blouse decorated with coin buttons. (Newcomer.)

Fig. 23.—Participants emerge from meeting shortly after sunrise. Smiles and cheerfulness are typical. (Weber.)

Fig. 24.—Ash bird in the morning. Drum water has been poured along altar, on outside. Chief peyote and sage have been removed. (Newcomer.)

Fig. 25.—Peyote dinner, held sometime between 9:00 A.M. and noon after the meeting. In this case it was provided at about 9:00 A.M. Tablecloths have been spread and quilts and canvases laid out for people to sit on. This is not the ceremonial peyote breakfast held inside the meeting. (Newcomer.)

Fɪɢ. 26.—Two fine feather fans. (Newcomer.)

ing: "I brought water from the dark. Let it be medicine to cure the patient." He blesses all the officials to help the patient, and blesses the patient and his house and his surroundings, his stock, his farm, his relatives, and he works from there out in his prayer—to the Navaho tribe, mother earth, and some of those that help out. And when he is done, he relights his smoke and passes down the south side to the road chief and returns on the south side [bringing the cigarette to the road chief and returning].

The road chief smokes [the cigarette], toward the peyote chief, the earth, and himself. The drummer chief and cedar chief do the same, in that order, and then the cigarette goes back to the road chief. The road chief may speak and thank people, and then comes his prayer. He prays as road chief, asking a blessing on the water, the patient, his relatives, his hogan, his livestock, his land. The other prayers should be shorter than his—15 to 30 minutes. Short prayers are best. Long ones tire people. Then he takes his smoke [the cigarette butt] and puts it straight over the peyote chief into the charcoal and puts cedar on top. He picks up his whistle and goes north both times [twice?] around the instruments and the water [this would be clockwise]. He kneels and makes the sign of the cross with the whistle in the water, blowing at the same time. First he moves the whistle from east to west, then from south to north, then from west to east, and then from north to south, while blowing the whistle in the water. [Thus the starting point moves clockwise.] He puts the whistle back. Then he takes the fan and makes the same motions with it. Each stroke of the fan in the water goes from the outside to the center, thus making the four arms of the cross. He takes the fan out and sprinkles the water that is on it in the four directions, east, south, west, and north. After that he sprinkles himself without dipping the fan again. The fan is now dipped into the water and handed to the drummer chief, who sprinkles himself, and the same is done for the cedar chief. He dips the fan again to sprinkle the patient. He takes the fan, goes north past the patient, turns clockwise, and sprinkles the patient: forehead, right side, forehead, left side. Then he returns to his place.

It is time to water the drum. A half-cup of water is poured over the drum [and soaks through the buckskin drum head], and the drum stick. Then the drum and stick go back to their place.

At this time I try to teach the people and talk about what is being done—tell them to be reverent, and so on. I tell them that this ceremony is for our own good and explain what is happening—especially for the new members.

I drink water and set it down, and put water on myself (that is, I pour the last few drops out of the cup on my hands and then put my hands on my forehead, top of my head, trunk, and legs). Then the water goes to the drummer, then to the cedar chief, and around. If the patient is very sick there is no talking while the water is being drunk. If it is a birthday meeting, a meeting for schoolchildren, or something of that sort, there is talking. It should be good talk only. By the time the water has gone round, it is about one o'clock. The water returns to the road chief. The road chief and the drummer pick up their instruments. The fire chief goes clockwise and picks up the water and goes the rest of the way clockwise and goes out. This is his third trip. Now he comes back in without the water, goes round the altar again, clockwise, and sits down. This is the fourth time. [There was some confusion in the discussion and correspondence over the four complete clockwise circles of the fire chief, which has been "smoothed" in the above account. When asked to outline the four clockwise trips in our correspondence, Mike mentioned: (1) when he first comes in—entering last but proceeding to the north side of the door; (2) when he brings in the water; (3) when he comes back in after midnight water; (4) in the morning after taking out the instruments before breakfast. Probably both sets of four are viewed as cycles of four, and are contrasted with the many occasions on which the fire chief works first at the north side and then at the south, or vice versa, without making a complete clockwise cycle—as in sweeping the room before the midnight water.]

It is now time for the road chief to go out. He picks up the cedar, the feathers, and the eagle tail fan. He puts cedar on the fire. He smokes the equipment. He goes outside, just past the woodpile, and blows the whistle four times, facing east, and prays a little. Then, still facing east, he prays for the south, the west, and the north. Then he walks south to the south side of the hogan and blows the whistle four times facing south. Then he goes to the west and blows the whistle four times facing west. Then he goes to the north and blows the whistle facing north four times. He prays only at the first position. Then he goes around the woodpile and back in. The whistle is a blessing and calls the spirits down—four kinds. While the road chief is out they fix the charcoal inside. The drummer now puts cedar in the fire, and the road chief smokes the feathers, and the whistle and smokes the patient with the feathers and the whistle and smokes himself off, and puts the whistle down and takes his place.

Just before midnight people can take a stretch—a few at a time and not for long; any person who wishes to step out may do so when the road chief is not busy.

While the road chief is outside with the whistle, a singer may sing. When the cane and drum pass the patient, it is time for the patient to smoke—time for the real purpose of the meeting. He rolls his own smoke, using cornhusk and Indian tobacco and Bull Durham. Some one might be singing at the time [but not during the prayer]. The fire chief lights the cigarette. The patient smokes to the chief peyote, then to mother earth, then to himself. He can speak before he prays—give thanks to the road chief, cedar chief, fire chief, and then he prays. That prayer must be said for the purpose of the meeting. It must be short. He can go further in his prayer: he may pray for the hogan, the fire in the hogan, for the poker, food, water, bedding, valuables—whatever he has—for pollen and other Navaho instruments used for ceremonies, for other hogans around him, land, livestock, goats, cattle, sheep, the mountains and springs, the roads, and his relatives. Some go further and pray for the road chief, the fire chief, and people far away, but that is not necessary. [Does a man confess his sins during his prayer?] If he feels like it. Others can hear what he has to say, but they should not resent it [if he confesses something he did that was hurtful to another person there]. The confession wipes out the sin, and there is no more to be done [that is, he is not to commit that sin again]. His cigarette is relighted if it is necessary during the prayer. He then goes up to the chief peyote and holds the smoke [cigarette] out to it, and then to the road chief, who takes it. The patient's wife could take the cigarette before it went to the road chief, or a woman patient's husband. The road chief now smokes to peyote, the earth, and himself. The cigarette goes to the drummer and cedar chief and back to the road chief, and the singing may start. During the patient's prayer the drum and singing stop—all the people there sanction his prayer, which they hear.

The road chief now prays. He prays to support the patient's prayer, like an interpreter speaking to God for the patient. When he is through, he puts the cigarette in the fire, puts cedar on the fire, and puts the patient next to the moon, facing the chief peyote, and the road chief fans the patient. The patient turns clockwise at the altar and then sits down. His sins are now all gone, and he uses medicine [eats peyote—see below]. Sins cause illnesses and accidents, and so do bad thoughts. The thoughts of adults affect children, too. Bad dreams result from bad thoughts. [Is this just the peyote idea, or is it the Navaho idea?] It is the peyote idea, and the Navaho idea, and the white man's idea and [later addendum] the Indian idea. The road chief takes the disease of the patient on himself. [What if the patient's trouble came from someone's witching him?] He should not think about that. He should think about the medicine and not worry about it. He should pray to the Supreme Being—He doesn't consider witchcraft.

The road chief chews some peyote to fix it for the patient. We are not afraid of germs. At such a time, the road chief, his whole self, is medicine. There are no germs involved. While he is chewing the medicine, he should think of the purpose of the meeting, and the moon, and the universe. He should think of God.

Then the road chief puts cedar in the fire, walks past the patient, turns clockwise, and gives the peyote to the patient, placing it on the patient's right hand. He gives him one medicine [one bolus of chewed peyote]. The patient should swallow it without chewing. The road chief fans the patient on his chest, head, arms, and limbs, to get the medicine all the way through. The road chief goes back to his place. More cedar is put on, and the patient draws the smoke to himself.

Now people can go out. Before that they should be thinking and helping and being reverent. The road chief can call for attention and assistance [not further elucidated]. In smoking cigarettes and praying for the patient, the patient's relatives come first [that is, other worshippers may now pray for the patient with cornhusk cigarettes]. When the road chief sings, no one should smoke. A man can ask the road chief to smoke after him [that is, to second his prayer].

The peyote goes round at the start of the meeting, and about two peyotes are taken. When the cane gets to the leader again, the peyote goes round again. Every time the cane comes round, the peyote can go round again—so it depends on how often the cane goes round [that is, how many rounds of singing are done—a function of the number of men present]. It would probably go round about three or four times.

[Can a man bring his own medicine to the meeting and use it?] No—this medicine is a special medicine that has been purified [smoked at the beginning]. There may be peyote tea, and the road chief can use it. The road chief himself eats peyote before every smoke and prayer and for the midnight and morning water ceremonies. The road chief, drummer chief, cedar chief, and fire chief can take peyote as they wish from the road chief's supply, but others can ask for more.

After three or four people have prayed for the patient, it is morning. Each of these prayers has to do with the patient. By now it is about 4 A.M.

The fire chief gets ready. He fixes the charcoal. The drum and cane might have come back to the drummer's place, or they might still be singing. He spreads live coals all over, adds more wood to the fire, and sweeps. He fixes the charcoal on the south side first and sweeps there, and then on the north side. At midnight he did it in the reverse order. He finds the dawn lady [the woman who brings in the water in the morning]. If I am running a meeting, the dawn lady would be my wife, according to my teaching. Other women might make a mistake.

The whistle is blown by the road chief as a signal, and then the morning water song is sung. It is time for the water. This is a new ceremony [begins a new section of the ritual]. The road chief puts cedar in the fire and smokes himself. Then the rest smoke themselves. He takes the instruments in his hands. The drum is put down. He takes the whistle, kneels, blows four times, and sings the water song —just that one song—and the water comes in. [There is drumming at that time.] Then there is no singing. The water is lined up as before, at midnight. This time the dawn lady brings it in and sits behind it. Now the road chief sings three more songs, and then puts the cane, sage, feathers, gourd, and fan down. The whistle is next to the altar, straight north and south, with the mouthpiece toward the north. Then there is a little space, and the other objects are placed at a slant, butts south and tips north, but slanting north northeast. Next to the road chief is the cane. Then comes the sage, then the feathers, lying on top of the sage and across it, then the rattle, the same way, and then the eagle tail fan separated. [I am unable entirely to follow this.] The road chief gives the dawn lady a parrot feather. The cedar man now prays. The water is in the middle of the room, in front of the dawn lady, not in front of the road chief. The cedar man might ask someone else to say this prayer. If so, that person would pray from where he ordinarily sits. Short prayers should be used. The bad things are past now. He should talk about good things, and about the future, and how to live, and so on. Either the cedar man or someone prays that way.

Cedar is put in the fire. The water woman takes the feather and moves it toward the chief peyote and the smoke, and then over the water, but not in it, four times. Other people smoke themselves with their hands or with their fans. The materials for a smoke are passed to her. She rolls a cornshuck cigarette, using Indian tobacco and Bull Durham. She passes the tobacco back clockwise, gets a light from the fire chief, puffs twice toward the chief peyote, and down the line to the water. She can speak if she wishes and express her appreciation. The fire is fixed before she prays. There is no fire tending during the prayer. She prays for the water, and the morning water, and she says the patient is to take it for his future and for a long life. She prays for the road chief, the drummer, the cedar man, the fire man, and the others there, and when she is through her smoke may be out. It is relit, and the drummer comes on the south side and she gives the cigarette to him, and he takes it to the road chief after a gesture to the chief peyote. The road chief smokes, and then the drummer and cedar man smoke, and the road chief prays again—the last prayer. He prays according to the whole night's events. He sanctions all the prayers of everyone there, and the water, and prays for the future and quits. The smoke [cigarette] is put over the chief peyote into the fire.

He takes the fan, the gourd, the feathers, the sage, and the cane, in that order. The drummer takes the drum. The lady fixes her blanket, the cup, the handle, and the pail, and without turning the bucket around, sets it before the road chief, returning on the south side. First, however, she pours water on the ground for mother earth. The road chief takes the instruments around the south side of the pail, between the moon and the pail—the cane, sage, feathers, gourd, fan in that order—it is always that way. He puts cedar on the north side into the fire, takes up the whistle, goes back to his place, makes the sign of the cross four times, as before, blowing into the water, and then the whistle is put back in place to the north. Then the same with the feather [fan] as before [in making the sign of the cross at midnight], and he sprinkles east, south, west, north, and then himself. The feather is then used to sprinkle the drummer chief and cedar man, and is redipped into the water and the patient sprinkled with it as before. He puts the feather down the way he did at midnight. The water goes to the drummer for the drum and drumstick, and then the road man drinks first. Then the drummer, cedar man, and then everyone straightens up and kneels, and the water goes round, and as before people drink and put some on their bodies. Then when the water reaches the drummer again, the water passes in front of the instruments, and the dawn lady goes south, picks up the water, and goes out clockwise. If she has been in the meeting all night, she must come back in after she takes the water out.

Now they are singing and getting ready for the breakfast. The charcoal is fixed again and people sing. The water, corn, fruit, and meat are all set, outside, and when the song is over the dishes are brought in. The drummer rolls a cornhusk cigarette. The fire chief brings in the breakfast: water, corn, fruit, and meat, in that order. He takes a light, goes between the bucket of water and the fire, and around the south end of the altar, and goes to the drummer, lights his cigarette, and returns the same way—round the south end of the altar, back between the fire and the water, and back to his place. Everyone may sing. The drummer smokes, and then the road man and the cedar man. The drummer prays as long as he wants for the food. He puts in the purpose of the meeting and gives thanks for it. When he is done, he puts the cigarette in the fire. Then cedar is put in the fire, and then the road man has to decide to let more singing continue, or not. He can let it go on, or he can call the drum and staff back to him and start the closing song. He sings three songs of his own choosing, and then he sings the closing song last of all. This is at 6 or 7 A.M.

Now the drum is untied. The rope is taken off, and the skin, and the pebbles are removed from the buckskin, and then the drumstick is put in the kettle. The road chief has the canes and feathers. He picks up the whistle, takes the peyote chief from the altar, sits back and puts the peyote chief to his body. Then he hands it to the drummer, who hands it back to the road chief. From him it goes around the instruments [between the instruments and the altar] to the cedar man. Each presses it to his body. The peyote chief may or may not be passed around any further. The whistle is passed around next. The fans are separated and put in the instrument box. The cane is put away, the two feathers, and the gourd. Only the drum kettle, with water and ash in it, and the drumstick in it, and perhaps the chief peyote, are passed around. Everyone can drink a little of the drum water; everyone can touch it. After they have gone around, they are all put away. First the chief peyote, then the whistle, cane, gourd, feathers, and sage, in that order. Then the drum, hide, rope, and pebbles. The drum water is put along the moon on the outside. The ashes that were in the drum are put back in the fire. Leftover peyote is put in the drum. The road man asks the fire chief for the poker. The fire chief comes on the north side, the road chief gives him cedar, he puts cedar on the fire, and smokes the instrument box, the kettle [drum], and the poker, and goes out on the north side again. The drummer takes the sage cushion that was under the chief peyote and gives it to the patient for himself. The fire chief comes in, between the fire and the water, and goes back to his place. Then he goes on the south side of the breakfast to the water and the corn, and takes these two dishes to the road chief and returns counterclockwise to pick up the next two dishes [fruit and meat] and take those to the road chief, and returns counterclockwise to his place. The order remains: water, corn, fruit, and meat. The road man drinks and eats first; then the drummer, then the cedar man, and around clockwise. At that time the patient or a relative might say something. People can talk. Everything must be eaten. The talk may go on. The dishes sit by the road man, having gone round. Everything is done; it is time to go out. The fire chief comes in on the north. The road man gives him cedar. He smokes the dishes once. He goes out with the dishes, and the people go out in order. It is now 7 or 7:30 A.M. There is no need to wait for sunrise. Some people might get cedar smoke from the fireplace at this time. Then the ashes are taken out. The poker is saved after each meeting until it is too short and then it is burned. The room is swept. The moon is taken out and the earth put by the hogan or disposed of as one wishes. The offering to the road chief, if there is one, is made after the dinner, which comes about noon. There is a prayer before the dinner. The one to pray is chosen by the people who put up the meeting.

[What is the significance of the fire?] Fire is a person who doctors. There is a fire in every home, and fire is like a person. We cannot live without it. And the poker, too, is like a person. Peyote is a woman; mother earth is a woman; and water is a woman. I have had no visions during peyote meetings, but some people do. They are disturbing.

[Mike Kiyaani began running meetings in 1947. He went to Oklahoma to visit Truman Dailey, his teacher, and learn how. Truman came to Piñon for a visit, and then Mike went back to Oklahoma again to learn. He learned how to run a meeting during meetings that he attended, and then Truman watched him run a meeting and told him that he knew how. Truman ran a meeting for his benefit. He plans to go back to Oklahoma to learn more: instruction is given to people bit by bit. Truman has told Mike the main part of the ceremony. You have to rise toward it. If you are inspired to do so, you can make changes in the ceremony. You need not follow exactly what your teacher did: respect and reverence are the main things, not the details of the ritual.]

[To all of this, after a careful reading of my preliminary record and the questions I asked of Mike, he appended the following typed note:] Brother Dave, what I told you the last time we met on how a meeting should be run isn't the only exact way that I run my meeting. There are in places that I do things different now. But I wouldn't advise you to change the whole story, Dave. What you got down on papers now is good enough.

[This concludes Mike Kiyaani's text.]

RITUAL IDIOM

There are a few points of ritual idiom which should be mentioned. One is that a series of virtually identical ritual acts are varied in such a way as to indicate progress from beginning to end of the ritual. Thus the first song of the ceremony is the opening song, followed immediately by three more, freely chosen by the road chief. The second fixed song is the midnight water song, followed by two more, freely chosen; then the water is brought in and the final free song of this set of four is sung. The third fixed song is the morning water song, the water is brought in and thereafter three more free songs are sung, in contrast to the midnight water pattern of three before the water and one after. Finally, the last fixed song is the closing song, which appears at the end of a set of four, the others freely chosen, in contrast to the opening song, which initiates a set of four.

Similarly, the whistle mouthpiece is pointed south at the beginning of the meeting and north at the midnight water ceremony. (Further changes are not indicated in my text.) Finally, the midnight water bucket is turned so that what was the side facing the door now faces the road chief, whereas the morning water bucket is not turned. The fire chief cleanses the north side first before the midnight water, and the south side first before the morning water. These "mirror" variations on a common pattern suggest movement from beginning to end of the ceremony.

A second "topic" of ritual idiom has to do with completed clockwise movements versus ritually incomplete movements which do not close a complete clockwise circle.

Roughly speaking, full clockwise movement of persons (not objects) begin and end the ceremony and parts of the ceremony. Thus we find the fire chief's entry at the end of the group and his progression to his seat at the north side of the hogan begins the ceremony; there are clockwise circuits (four in all) by the fire chief in the course of the midnight water ceremony; there is at least one such circuit by the dawn lady during the morning water ceremony; and, according to Kiyaani's comment, but not his text, there is a final complete clockwise circuit when the fire chief removes the instruments at the close of the ceremony.

There is a generally held belief that worshippers should focus on the chief peyote during the meeting and send their prayers through it, and that this contact should not be interrupted. In addition, Mike Kiyaani holds that there must be a "track" open for spirits to move about, between the altar, fire, etc., and the worshippers.

It seems to be in accordance with this that the fire chief, with the exceptions noted, always maneuvers so as to perform less than a complete clockwise circuit. When he provides the fire stick for an official to light a cigarette for a prayer, or for the patient or some one else to do so, he advances clockwise but returns counterclockwise, never, as it were, cutting off the participant from the altar by a complete circle. By the same token, he collects cigarette butts, beginning with the person on the south side of the door, advancing to the drummer chief, and putting the collected butts at the south end of the altar. He then proceeds to the road chief (counterclockwise), passing clockwise to the man sitting next to the fire chief's own position, who is holding the fire chief's own cigarette butt, counterclockwise to the south end of the altar, and clockwise to his own seat. He never passes behind the altar between the drummer chief and the road chief, so that the circle is never made complete. And there are many other instances of this.

Worshippers desiring to go out do so at some peril. First, they must find a time when a path is clear, one way or another: when they will not step between a singer, a drummer, a smoker, or one chewing peyote, and the altar. Second, they must return under the same conditions. It is preferable that both moves be clockwise, but frequent difficulties are encountered. Thus their exit and entry do normally complete a circle.

Something should be said of the meticulousness of the fire chief: of his constant effort to keep fire sticks, poker, and chief peyote in a straight line, his neatness in shaping the coals, etc. The work of the fire chief demands constant and careful attention.

Finally, it should be noted that there are two types of ritual situations: four group occasions when there is no group singing and drumming, and when either the equipment has not started to circulate or it has returned to the road chief, and all other occasions, when the drum and cane are circulating. The patient's prayer is intermediate, since singing and drumming stop, yet the instruments are not returned to the road chief. Each of these four group situations is concerned with the central purpose of the meeting, and each involves an act of communion: the group smoking of cigarettes at the beginning, the water drinking at midnight and in the morning, and the peyote breakfast. The other activities, although deeply concerned with the major focus of the meeting, are also acts of communication with God by individuals or pairs. To eat peyote, which is done at other points besides the beginning, to drum, to sing, or to pray, are all "prayers"— communications with God, and in addition, of course, much of the night when one is not singing, praying, drumming, or eating peyote, is given over to reverie and rumination. There is a certain individualistic quality involved in these activities, during which a person may seek illumination, guidance, health, and good fortune privately, even though in a group. It would be unwise to overstress this, since the purpose of the meeting should be at the heart of a person's concern, and since the act of singing and drumming together is itself a sort of sharing. Indeed, it is believed that singer and drummer can read one another's minds, and that if they are unfriendly they should not attempt to pair off. Nevertheless, there may be some opposition between the sharing of group purposes in the periods of what I have called communion[4] and the individual differentiation of

___

[4] The language used here is not that of the peyotists, who customarily compare the eating of peyote with the taking of communion.

the remainder of the service. (I am indebted to Louis Guttman for discussions which developed this point.)

This opposition, in turn, may be a reflection of a feature of the lives of many American Indians since peyotism first began as an organized cult: the sharing, egalitarianism, and mutual help required by reservation life, and the individualism created by involvement with the wider economy.

As to the avoidance of closing the circle and the meticulousness of the fire chief, certain other comments seem appropriate. Peyotists again and again emphasize that "mistakes" in ritual do not matter, and that prayers are spontaneous and not fixed. Freedom for innovation by individual road chiefs is also recognized—even though there is often criticism of such innovations. Navaho peyotists compare Navaho religion and its preoccupation with ritual errors unfavorably with peyotism in these matters. Yet we have the clockwise and counterclockwise concerns of the ritual, and the care of the fire chief to keep things lined up. It seems as if the concern were not so much with the automatic effects of ritual accuracy—as is the case with traditional Navaho ceremony—as it is with keeping the "mind" straight. La Barre has noted many comments that peyote is tricky (La Barre, 1938, pp. 93–104). Many of my Navaho friends have said that they cannot tell how peyote will affect them, and I have heard many comments about keeping one's thoughts in the right direction. The emphasis on not breaking the circuit which permits communication through peyote with God, and on keeping things in line seems to be an effort to control thought processes which, under the impact of peyote, may not go as they should, with resulting misery for the worshipper.

PRAYERS

From Kiyaani's account it is evident that there are a number of lengthy prayers in the course of a ceremony. He has briefly sketched their content. In the ceremonies I have attended, almost all these prayers have been in Navaho, and the conditions of the meeting made it impossible to ask for translations at the time. Ordinarily it was also awkward or impossible to ask afterward. On two occasions, however, I was able to secure accounts of these prayers subsequently from my interpreter, and it seems worthwhile to present these, since, with the notable exception of Slotkin (1952), there are relatively few in print. It will be recalled from Kiyaani's description that the prayers are as follows. There is a group of four prayers for fixed points: an opening prayer by the road chief, a midnight water prayer by the fire chief, a morning water prayer, ordinarily by the dawn lady, and a closing prayer by the drummer chief. The omission of the cedar chief from this set is probably one reason that his services can sometimes be dispensed with. In addition, before the midnight water there is the road chief's prayer for the general purpose of the meeting, the road chief's prayer for his equipment, and the cedar chief's prayer just before the midnight water, and just before the morning water. There is the patient's prayer, sometime after midnight. The road chief "seconds" the fire chief's midnight water prayer, the patient's prayer, and the dawn lady's prayer.

The first meeting the prayers of which were translated for me was held on August 24–25, 1950, near Walker Creek in District 9, at the hogan of *Nat Kearney, whose wife was sister to my interpreter's wife.[5] My interpreter, *Fred Goodman, was also resident in the same cluster of hogans. There were 26 people present, not all of them known to the interpreter. The meeting was conducted by *Nat Kearney, and one of the patients was his wife—a practice unthinkable in Navaho chant practice unless he were prepared to treat her henceforth as a sister, which was not *Nat's intention. His wife sat next to him, in what should have been the cedar chief's position, with her young son next to her. Next to them was the wife's father's paternal half-sister, who had brought a young baby. Next came another such half-sister, who was later to bring in the morning water. Next to this woman was her own daughter, a young girl. Other close kinsmen of the patient's family included two brothers of the sick woman, one quite young, her mother, her father, and her sister's husband (my interpreter). The connections of other members of the group are unknown to me. Excluding the baby, there were 18 men and boys and 7 women and girls. At my request *Fred Goodman recalled the content of the prayers beginning in the late afternoon of the 25th, some 10 hours after the meeting finished. Where the interpreter paraphrases briefly, parentheses are used. Brackets are used for comments.

[The road chief explained the purpose of the meeting.] He thanked the people gathered there, all coming from far off for the meeting, and said that people were there to help each other out by prayer, singing, and doctoring, if they knew how, or by thinking toward good judgment sense. Four days ago he went to *Alfred Sarton's place, and they had a meeting there. *Sarton called his name and said it was a good idea to have a meeting for school children going off the reservation, to protect them from sickness. And so he is having a meeting for them. Also, his own wife has been sick since last Spring. He asked that they mention her in their prayers. He would be thankful for that. He mentioned DFA, our white brother, who has permission from Washington and Window Rock to come out all the way to investigate peyote and the welfare of the tribe on both sides [peyotist and anti-peyotist]. He was thankful that DFA was there at the meeting, and he mentioned that the others at the meeing were glad too, and that's about all.

[Now the sick girl's mother, mother-in-law of the road chief, and member of the family sponsoring the meeting, spoke.] "I would like to say a few words. I thank each and every one in this house for coming, for their long journey even

---

[5] As in Aberle and Stewart, 1957, I have used pseudonyms for most Navaho peyotists. Undoubtedly, many of these men would be quite willing for their names to be used, but since I am not certain about this in many instances, since anonymity was promised to many, and since peyotism is, as I write this, still illegal on the Navajo Reservation, I have preferred to err on the side of caution. In dealing with summaries of minutes of the Tribal Council, I have used actual names, since these are a matter of record. In quoting Mike Kiyaani's account of a peyote meeting, and elsewhere in quoting Mike Kiyaani, I have used his name, since I am certain that he is willing for me to do so. In acknowledging assistance I have used real names, but I have not indicated the peyotist or non-peyotist position of the people involved. All pseudonyms are marked with an asterisk, thus: *Orrin Musgrave. Names are consistent with Aberle and Stewart, 1957, but new names have been added. Individuals with the same family names are consanguine kin if men or unmarried women. Husbands and wives are given the same family name.

if they had something else to do, other work to do, and because they gave their time I really appreciate it." She mentioned the road chief and *Fred Goodman [another of her sons-in-law, my interpreter] for suggesting the meeting, and thanked them for that, and thanked the visitors there, and is thankful to have DFA in the meeting. And she hoped that someone might suggest this meeting for our schoolchildren and their benefit, for good health in school.

[The entire group rolled and lit their cigarettes, and the road chief delivered the opening prayer.] "Thank God Almighty and thank the atmosphere we breathe (*nitch'i*) and our spirits [?] and the earth." And he started his prayer from the beginning, thus: "Almighty made the heavens, the earth, moon, sun, stars, and the purposes of the moon and sun, and He made the waters—the bodies of water on the earth and around the earth, and the springs, and all the plants. They all live from water and are made by God in that way, and He made men with five fingers, of different breeds, colors, and tongues. And we are wet with water [made partly of water], and in that time the Lord was with us, and only yesterday with us, and tonight we gather in the house, a house of earth and wood." And he prayed for the whole house and the chief peyote button and for the ground and the feathers, the drumstick and the drum, the stones binding the drum, and the water—the holy water. And he explained it all. "The drum is to hear our voices and have them received in heaven. The rope is a holy road, a path, a true way of life to the Almighty. And the rock [stones used to bind the drum] is for protection, to be unharmed. The drumstick is for lightning. And the staff is for old age: in this worship we come in young and leave old." And he prayed for the holy fire. "The Almighty cares for us every day. It cooks our meals and keeps us warm—Mother Fire. And the poker [fire stick], it is placed straight, and while it is straight our minds are straight, our thoughts are straight, and our whole body is straight. And that [stick] represents it." And he prayed for the chief altar [moon and peyote button on top of it]. "And through this we pray to the Lord Almighty. And peyote is the Lord's medicine, He put it in the ground for poor and rich alike. God put it in the earth and predicted that My children will pray to Me by it, to be used as a prayer to remember Me by, to Me in heaven."

And he prayed for the drummer, to keep him in good health and strong, make his work lighter and easier, protect him from evil, and get his mind straight, and make his religion strong, his songs and prayers, and keep them and his mind straight, and for the drummer's father and mother, and he prayed for the drummer's wife and children, and for them to have enough to eat and to care for them, food, water, livestock, and the farm and its surroundings, and livestock and friends and relatives of his. And the fire chief, he prayed for him the same way—himself, his wife, neighbors, in-laws, those living with him, his stock, horses, and his possessions.

Then he prayed for himself: a clear mind, strength, his conscience, and he prayed for his wife, explaining that his wife got sick last spring and is still sick, and with God's help to cure her, and prayed for her mother, father, sisters, and the people living here [at his wife's sister's hogan], the farm, the springs where he gets water, his stock, and the car which helps in making a living, and his son to grow strong and a healthy body.

And then he prayed for peyote buttons. "Bless them, put all good thoughts in peyote, and eat it with good thoughts, that we [participants] may have strong body and veins, able to think straight, to help one another." And he prayed for peyote, and for those who don't know how [to use it], and that they may learn how through eating peyote. And so he prayed for the cedar and for the sage, and for all the individuals gathered there, and their fathers, mothers, and children at home or away at work. And he told peyote that the Lord knows each and every one inside and out, and helps those who need help through the Lord's power, and so on.

Then he prayed for all the members of the [Native American] Church, and for men running meetings, and for the fire chief, the woman who would carry the water [during the morning water ceremony], and for those who eat peyote and for the non-members, though they argue against you, and bless and care for them and what they want to say. And for all the people in the world, for the U.S. soldiers in Korea, it's best for them under the U.S. flag, and he prayed to stop all wars and to live in peace. And for those in Washington—the President, Congress, and those who plan for the good of the people—to keep them in good health, and those who plan for the people of the U.S. to be in prosperity. And for DFA, coming for a long ways, for his father, mother, family, and friends, the loved ones close to him, and for the Almighty to be with him in his work and guide him home safe and sound.

And he thanked the sun, earth, and atmosphere we breathe, and God Almighty that all prayers are through the altar of this peyote, and all good will be toward man from the East, South, West, North, and from the heart of mother earth and from above [the sun], and he asked all of these things in the name of Jesus Christ our Lord, Amen.

[The fire chief prayed after bringing in the water at midnight. There was no cedar chief. The fire chief had lost a half-brother in an automobile accident less than a month before. He was so choked with emotion throughout his prayer that he could only jerk out half-sentences. Then his voice would catch, and he would continue.] He prayed to the Lord, thanked the Lord and peyote and the peyote chief, and thanked his Lord and Savior (*nihítaa' diyin yisdá'iiníłii*), and he prayed [back to] the beginning, ever since peyote meetings started and gave the law that people are to drink blessed water. He prayed that at the beginning God put water around the earth and inside the earth, holy water, medicine water, which washes any ailment, and he blessed the water, and he brought in water for the instruments they use: for the drum and the gourd, and for the poker, and for the chief altar, and for the earth. He brought in water to bless and keep all these wet, and all the earth wet, that we may have rain and when we have it we have wool and are happy for our livestock, our farms, and we raise vegetables with it [water], and eat the vegetables, and that keeps us healthy, and so we are happy to live by it, and stronger in body, and to carry out our work whatever it may be, and prosperity, nourishment, and clear conscience are in this water. He prayed for those gathered here and the house, and let them drink, and those gathered here, and their fathers and mothers and wives and children, as they may have them, and for those away at work, and our white brothers all over the earth, and for the Marines [in Korea], and for all different ways of worship. "You made it that way to worship You in their own tongues." And he thanked God. And he said, "A dear friend with whom I worked closely for several years at the Wyoming Ice Plant, my brother [name], came to visit here, and on the way [back] he drove off [the road], and his spirit is with You, and his body is made into earth such as I sit on, and his body is turned into flowers and vegetables and something beautiful. And I am just a humble person, my heart is weak and my body is weak and my mind is weak and I am just humble. I need God's strength. Give me strength. My beloved brother is gone to Your place for everlasting life. I ask that my brother's spirit with the Almighty's permission might be with me and that I might have strength in body and mind, to help me to think straight and help me to plan to make a living, and that is to be always that way [that is, his brother's spirit is always to accompany him], and that my brother will always be remembered in prayers, and I will always mention him as long as I can live." And [he prayed for] DFA, his mother, his sister, his father, and that the holy water may keep him strong and keep him in good health.

[The road chief now prayed in response to the fire chief's prayer.] He went over the same thing. He told the Lord that Your baby asked You for this and that, like an echo. [That is, the road chief repeats the fire chief's prayer in detail and affirms its contents.]

[In this meeting there was quiet talk during the circulation of the water bucket. This is common in many meetings, but there are some road chiefs who do not want conversation at this time: they consider concentration on drinking the holy water more important.] There were various thanks. People said that water would be in our blood and veins. "We pray for our children to learn, and all that. And some day they will be in the way to learn and to earn a living and understand their white brothers (nihik'is bitsį' daalgaii)." They thanked the road chief, the fire chief, and everybody in there, and they told them all, "Yá'át'ééh, good." [Also a standard Navaho greeting.]

Then the road chief said, "After the fire chief carries out the water, I will go out and blow the whistle in all four directions, and when I return I will roll peyote for the schoolchildren and for my wife. I want you to remain sitting and don't go out until I am through doctoring, and then if you want more peyote it will be available, and if you wish to smoke [offer a prayer cigarette], there is lots of tobacco, open to everyone."

[Before he administered rolled peyote to the schoolchildren, the road chief prayed for them.] "Our Father Who art in heaven (nihitaa' diyin yá'ąąshdi honílóonii)," and he went on to speak of God (są'ą naagháí and bik'eh hózhóón), referring to His immortality and saying that He made things beautiful, blessed, and good [these phrases are the traditional conclusion of many songs in Navaho chants]. "The holy house [this house is holy]. Thank God for the privilege of running the meeting, through this peyote. And you will receive what I have to say through the altar, and I pray for the rolled peyotes, [that they may put the children] into the ability of learning, for learning in school, and also [that they may have] a shield, the Lord's hand, which will protect them from any sickness, and from all the evils, and I also pray for the peyotes [that I am giving them] to give them nourishment, food, and water in school, to keep, protect, and guide them, so that they will learn and that they will remember their instructions that the [Native American] Church taught them and follow those rules, and when peyote enters their bodies, these things will build up their veins, minds, body, and entire strength, and they will love one another and cooperate with their teachers, and pray for their white brother teachers, and that they will take care of the children, and in the spring they will return home safe and sound."

This was a short prayer. Then he put down his cigarette, called the children one by one, and sat them in front of the altar with water to sip. He breathed on the rolled peyote with a holy breath, and they swallowed it, and he lined them up and smoked them [with cedar incense]. During the night four other people prayed. They all prayed for the meeting, for the schoolchildren, and for the Navaho people, members and non-members, for our white brothers, for different tribes, for our parents and loved ones, and they all prayed for DFA, and they always prayed for the schoolchildren. They prayed after that for themselves, their families and their parents, and all the people here—it gets wider and wider, out to Washington and the entire world. It is like whirling something, and it is called a prayer circle (*sodizin náházbąs*). You must never forget yourself, your wife, and your children in your prayer. Some people confessed, but if they did, they did so in a low voice. If you confess, you should vomit afterward or you are not forgiven.

[The road chief prayed before incensing the morning water.] "I thank the Lord Almighty for being with us and caring for us throughout the night, and the Holy People have been with us [*diyin dine'é*, the Holy People of Navaho religion, is the term used, but some reference to saints and angels is intended] with their strength, building up our prayers and songs, and I give them thanks for carrying out the meeting, and for the night and for the early dawn, and for these schoolchildren, and for my wife, and (mentioning them) for all the people here praying for help, perhaps their prayers are answered. And Your baby [the woman who brought in the morning water] brought in the water into this meeting and I pray for her, to be strong, have a healthy mind, and for her children, and for those she lives with, and for all that she has to make a living with, and grant her the power to have a clear mind and pray for us [to deliver the next prayer, that is]. I pray for the cedar to purify the water, and I give it to the holy fire, and the smoke arising will purify the water and the woman, and all her prayers will be like crystal, like inside, and her thoughts like crystal, and I thank the peyote chief [on the altar] and the Almighty."

[The woman who had brought in the morning water now ritually purified it and herself in the smoke of the cedar incense, rolled a cigarette, and prayed.] "Our Heavenly Father, thank You for the privilege of bringing in the water, thank mother earth and mother peyote that all the prayers went through her all night to the Lord Almighty. Thank Him for His blessing, for strength, prayers, our songs, and that we fill up our bodies in good condition, that we are well. I pray for the water, blessed water, and all the instruments in the meeting, and I thank the Almighty for this meeting through the night for the schoolchildren and for [the road chief's] wife, and for the men and women here, for their children, their wives and husbands, parents, relatives, livestock, houses, farms, and surroundings, and for those who are leaders [of peyote meetings], the drummer chief, his wife and children, father, mother, brothers, and sisters, relatives, for the road chief, his wife and children, father, mother, brothers, sisters, relatives, the fire chief, his wife, children, loved ones, father-in-law, mother-in-law, the children of his in-laws." And she prayed then for each person in the meeting, his brothers, sisters, father, mother, prayed for each of them one at a time." And I pray for the water, too, for all blessings, for the nourishment to get well, and for the water [to help us to] carry on our work, and for our bodies and systems, that it [water] should make us strong, healthy, with clear conscience, and [help us with our] way of making a living. I pray for all non-members, and for the people of the U.S., and for those in Washington, and for the U.S. soldiers in Korea, and for all the people of the world, and for myself and my children—and some of my schoolchildren and some are working far off—that they may be taken care of, and pray for the details of what we do daily, and for DFA and the purpose of his being among the Navaho, from his shoes to his head, and for his parents, and for his family, and for his car, to make the car run in good order, and for all those interviews, that people may tell their stories, and that it may be easy for people to explain the main points. And for the summer, and for the crops ready to harvest, and thank God Almighty for that, and for each and every home to have food and water, to be cared for and guarded by God Almighty."

[As at the midnight water ceremony, there was quiet discussion, initiated by the road chief.] "It is morning already," he said. Then he thanked the lady who had brought in the water. He just talked; he didn't pray. He spoke of the homes and the children and thanked her for praying for all these things. "We will try to live up to your prayers," he said. And then he thanked every one for their cooperation and their prayer, songs, and thoughts. He said to give them thought. He put down his cigarette and then they all drank. [I failed to inquire why he did not pray.] Then there were thanks. They thanked the woman with the water for her blessings, and said that the water would be their veins and their body. They thanked the road chief for the meeting and were thankful for his peyote. And everybody said, "Yá'át'ééh, good," and they thanked DFA. Then a man and two women thanked everybody. They were thankful for the meeting. The mother of some of the children said that she, too, was thankful for the meeting, and that it helped a lot to pray for her children. And the old lady [grandmother of the sick woman] said "Thank you," and "Thank you," to the woman who brought in the water, to the road chief, to each one of those present. She was thankful that the meeting was held in her hogan. And *Vic Ames [the local Tribal Delegate] said thanks to everyone, and he said we should not forget that that old lady was the mother of all these hogans [her children and grandchildren occupied this hogan cluster]. He suggested that people should realize that an older woman should be mentioned in a prayer, as well as your wife and children and so on, and in that way, he said, "You will learn how to pray and think about these things. You forgot," he said, "to pray for the dishes and bedding and wealth. Pray and little by little you will add to them."

Then DFA spoke. Then the ceremonial meal was brought in, and the closing song was sung.

[After the ceremonial breakfast was brought in] the road chief prayed for the food, the schoolchildren, and mentioned everybody, each and every one, and their surroundings, and their food, water, and their wives. He prayed for people all over. And he said, "That's the close of the meeting. That's all I know."

Thus far *Fred Goodman. Although there was a blessing over the food at a later morning meal and discussion of events of the night at the meal, I did not ask *Fred to go over these with me. Ordinarily any further treatment to be sought for the patient (the road chief's wife) would be discussed during the morning. In this case the road chief's wife was suffering, as I have said, from St. Vitus' Dance, a sequel to rheumatic fever. Since I decided to observe and question her the morning after the meeting, in an attempt to discover what was wrong (I had seen her during the night only in the relative darkness of the hogan), I unwittingly fell into the pattern of the meeting. I suggested sending the patient to Fort Defiance, to an Agency hospital, and her parents decided to do so and had her sent a few days later. My initial impression as to her illness was confirmed there. A year later I discovered that the girl's father had prayed all night that I would find out what was wrong with her. By the time of my second visit she had recovered from her condition and had been safely delivered. The father, although most grateful to me, regarded my clinical impression and her cure as proof of the wonders of peyote.

A second meeting for which there is a record of the content of prayers was held July 26–27, 1952, in the Red Rock–Cove area, and was a curing meeting. Again the interpreter's recollections of the prayers were taken down a few hours after the conclusion of the meeting, beginning at 2 P.M. *Joe Sherwood was the interpreter. The meeting was run by *Ben Eastman, also a Navaho singer, and a long-time peyotist. He was assisted by *Henry Hague, as drummer chief, also a Navaho singer. *Ben's wife sat in the position usually accorded the cedar chief, but did not act as cedar chief. She brought in the morning water. Next to her was a man related to the drummer chief, who was described as "acting cedar chief." Next to him was the patient and the patient's wife. The fire chief was *Tom Sumner, one of the first Navahos to use peyote—as a sheepherder among the Utes. Probably because of *Ben Eastman's close connections with people in District 9, there was a man there from Sweetwater and another from near Emmanuel Mission. The rest of the participants were from the Red Rock–Cove area. A special round summer shade had been constructed for the meeting, but it grew so crowded that some eight people were sent out of the meeting before it got under way, at the road chief's request. These were young men.

Disregarding these, there were 35 people present, 6 of them women. The meeting was put up by *Steve Brooks, and although the meeting, was in the main to cure *Al Conrad, *Steve's daughter was a supplementary patient, as was still another man. *Al's wife and *Steve's wife are clan sisters and close, and *Steve calls *Al sik'is (brother, friend).

The interpreter, *Joe Sherwood, asserted that the meeting was a "big moon" meeting, and probably run according to the practice of Alfred Wilson (the famous Cheyenne peyotist). He stated that a big moon and an ashpit were used if the person had been sick for a long time, and big moon for the more acute illnesses. This may be compared with Mike Kiyaani's remark that the size of the hogan is most important in deciding between big and small moon. In response to other questions about specifics of the ritual, *Joe made the following comments. The peyote was supplied by *Steve, who had arranged the meeting. No cornhusks were used for smoking ceremonial cigarettes simply because none were available. As to the order of the peyote breakfast, water is always first and corn second, but either fruit or meat may be the third dish, the order of prayer for the items being altered to fit. He also asserted that there was no prayer before people entered the meeting. It should be said that the road chief had had a difficult time getting to the meeting because of muddy roads. *Joe Sherwood's account follows.

First the road chief spoke. He spoke about the hard trip and the rain and said that even if it was raining we would still pray for rain. He spoke of taking care of the Church. "All you members in the Church, go carefully, watch whatever you say, and think it over, and then you will have no trouble." And he spoke of the purpose of the meeting—of all four of the people involved. He explained *Al's trouble [the principal patient], of his long illness and his pain, and of his wife's illness too, and he turned it to all the members to help him out with prayers, songs, and thoughts. "And the prayers are before the chief medicine [chief peyote on the altar]. A man is to remember his prayer and what he said, and when he rolls his cigarette, lights it, and speaks to the Lord, the Lord knows every word and what kind of person he is, and each person's mind and thought and feeling. So you are 'branded' by your smoke. If you really tell the truth in your prayer, remember the prayer. A true believer should remember his prayer. But it is hard for a person who understands little. If it's a hard case, then with the drum and the songs strong, if you have faith in the Lord, the Lord will help you out. So try your best to be a good believer." He wished the patients the best luck and appreciated the members' coming in spite of the steep hill and the mud. Even if he had to send some people out and bring others in, it should be peaceful; we should help each other and get along fine.

Then *Steve Brooks [who had put up the meeting] spoke of putting up the meeting and the shade house, of getting the things together; he wanted to help *Al and his wife out in a peaceful and friendly way, and his own daughter too. He was glad the road chief and his wife had come in spite of the road and was glad many people came to the meeting. He also spoke to the same point about prayers as the road chief did. And he wished that some day they [Navahos? peyotists? both?] could live good and overcome their troubles and enjoy their families and children and their country and honor the flag of the United States, the President, the Congress, and the leaders. And those who are in the [Korean] war: think of that in your prayers. And pray for DFA, trying to help him out with prayers, to do his work right, to enjoy his work, for him to make friends among the Navahos and for them to learn how to get along with him in the Church [Native American Church] or wherever he goes; to treat him right and help him wherever he goes. And everyone needs help. Help and love each other as brothers. And DFA's ear trouble, pray for him to get well. And pray for his car, for his tires, air, electricity, gas, water, and oil, so that it goes safely. And for his father, mother, brothers, sisters, and all his family, for his home and his belongings.

Then *Dave Runyon, one of the patients [not the main one] spoke briefly about his illness and asked for help with prayers.

Now *Ben Eastman prayed [the prayer with the first cigarette]. He prayed for every single person in the meeting and on the reservation and on earth. [In answer to a question:] At this time only *Ben prayed, as leader. He began, My Father in heaven, and so on. *Steve said a prayer, about like the speech. [This must have been at another point in the night, after the patient was doctored.]

*Tom Sumner, the fire chief, supplied the midnight water prayer. It was a long prayer, too, for everybody, and how they are going to live in the future, as long as they are living on this earth. He spoke of *Al's troubles, and of *Dave's and *Steve's daughter's troubles. [Instead of seconding these prayers at length] *Ben said, "The words have been heard, there is no reason to repeat them. The Lord understands."

Asked to describe the talk during the midnight water, *Joe said that there were expressions of thanks by various people, and people said they were glad to have an "American" [DFA] there, although they do not think of DFA as an "American" because he is too dark.

During the night there were prayers by *Tim Redding, *Dave Runyon, *Ed Regent, *Steve Brooks' daughter, and *Al Conrad, but not by his wife—her mouth tightened up. *Al's confession was brief. He said he had done wrong, but you *should* say what it was. *Fred Minor prayed, and so did *Brad Councilor. [This is a large number of "supporting" prayers and reflects a "serious" curing meeting. Since *Joe Sherwood's own special brand of peyotism stresses confession, I asked about whether all of these confessed.] Confession need not be every time. [I asked whether I had been prayed for again.] Every one prayed for you. [I said I had heard nothing in *Ben's prayer about me.] *Ben put you in a general category—everybody having trouble.[6]

*Bertha Eastman [*Ben's wife] prayed over the morning water. She prayed for Alfred Wilson's family and his memory. This meeting was learned from him. His prayers, drum, and instruments are still going on.

During the morning water, nothing special was said, just thanks.

Nothing was said during the night about the causes of *Al's illness. Maybe he was told privately. They said he would be OK.

At the breakfast, the prayer for food was by *Steve Brooks. He was to appoint a man, and asked for the drummer chief, but he was untying the drum; so it came back to *Steve. The same things were said, and there were thanks to God for everything coming out all right.

[Since *Ben has repeatedly shown his antagonism to whites, and since peyote meetings with me present rarely pass entirely without anti-white comments, I was intrigued to know whether *Ben or others had made any such remarks; none was made in English, from beginning to end. *Joe, who seems reliable and was certainly not perturbed by the question, said that there had been no such remarks nor speeches on the virtues of the Indian and vices of the white man—another common theme.] This concludes *Joe Sherwood's comments.

[6] What seems to be my preoccupation with the attention paid to me in peyote meetings derives from the fact that comments about me and prayers about me often illuminated attitudes toward peyotism and toward whites.

It will easily be seen that *Joe's account is far more abbreviated than the one supplied by *Fred Goodman. It is, however, evident that the pattern of the prayers is similar. More extensive collection of prayers would seem worthwhile.

ANALYSIS OF PRAYERS

These two accounts of the prayers in peyote meetings, one lengthy and one brief, suffice to show a common pattern of the content of prayer. I should now like to comment on the style and significance of peyote prayers and other behavior during the meetings. For these purposes, a contrast with Navaho ceremonial behavior is particularly illuminating.

The peyotist's prayers combine a stress on spontaneity with a relatively stable pattern within which this spontaneity is sought. There is no fixed order in the sequence of blessings requested, and of course what is sought varies from meeting to meeting and from speaker to speaker. There are, however, many routine phrases: Our Heavenly Father, Our Lord and Savior, etc. The gradual spread of the blessings from the immediate group of those present to the whole world is fairly typical; some informants call it a "prayer circle." There are frequent references to God as "Our Father," or even as "Our Father and Our Mother," and to the participants as "Your children," and "Your babies." Tears are usual in the course of the prayers. The person praying usually cries, and often so do listeners. The fire chief's prayer for his dead friend was an occasion for much weeping. In this connection one leader (*Bill Conroy) said, "We are like children, asking our father for candy, and so we cry as we ask Him." Since peyote produces depressive reactions in many people, it would be easy to assume that this crying is a product of the ingestion of peyote. Peyote may well facilitate weeping, but it should be observed that the initial prayer, which occurs before the first peyotes are passed around, is often accompanied by tears. The name of Jesus may or may not be used. Mary and the Heavenly Angels are sometimes mentioned. The use of the words God, Jesus, Mary, and the Heavenly Angels in a prayer otherwise wholly in Navaho is not uncommon. On the other hand, Mary may be referred to in Navaho by the term for Changing Woman, so prominent in Navaho mythology, who miraculously gave birth to Monster Slayer, a culture hero (or twin heroes—versions vary, and the second culture hero, Born of Water, is sometimes endowed with a different mother). To anticipate the discussion of belief somewhat, it is difficult to discover from textual analysis or by any means the degree to which a single spiritual force is intended. Thus, God is sometimes called *nítch'i diyiní*, which is simply holy spirit, with no indication as to whether the spirit is sole or one among many. He is called *diyin 'aláájí'*, or first holy one, the qualifier here being the one which is ordinarily used to refer to the first among many, as a firstborn child. He is called *diyin binant'a'í*, or "boss holy one," where the possibility of a world of spirits He commands cannot be eliminated because of the ambiguity of the term.

Traditional Navaho prayers, on the other hand, have a rigidly fixed formula. Errors and departures from that formula may result not only in the failure of the prayer to achieve its ends, but in damage to the patient or to the singer. They are compulsive formulae, the correct use of which compels the favorable action of spiritual powers. They are not accompanied by tears. Although spiritual beings may be addressed as "Our Father," the singer does not refer to himself as "Your baby." Navaho ceremonies, like peyote ceremonies, have such specific aims in mind as the cure of a patient. They are certainly considered to have wider functions of maintaining harmony in the human and cosmic spheres. But there are no prayers for the Navaho tribe, for other tribes, the Government, American soldiers, or the people of the world. Navaho religion is tribal.

The prayers of the peyotist, then, express a feeling of helplessness. The language and the tears clearly indicate this. But the prayers are intended to alleviate the anxiety of helplessness through the aid of an all-powerful God. The ritual incantations of traditional Navaho ceremonialism, however, compel, rather than appeal to the spirit world. We will later return to discuss the radically different states of mind thus reflected.

For some Navahos, one explicit appeal of the peyote prayer is the impossibility of making a mistake. Navaho prayers, they think, can have evil consequences through error; fundamentally there is no fatal error in peyote prayers.

The prayers clearly reflect an increased orientation to the extra-tribal world, a feeling of kinship with other Indians, and have as one of their themes the common humanity of man.

Predominant anxieties are evident throughout the prayers. They are concerned with stock, farming, water, health, far away friends and kinsmen at work off the reservation, schoolchildren away from home, the need for education in the contemporary world, and the problem of understanding "our white brothers." The locus of power is quite clearly Washington.

The prayer of the fire chief for his dead half-brother in the first group of prayers is most astonishing for a Navaho. Navaho fear of the body and ghost of the dead, of a house where some one has died, of the belongings of the dead, of graves has often been observed. Yet here we have a man praying for the support of his dead brother's spirit. An old woman at that meeting spoke to me on another occasion of the fact that she would not know what to do or where to turn were it not for the support of church members and the guidance of her dead husband's spirit. This is a startling transmutation of Navaho attitudes.

Along these same lines, one road chief (*Ben Eastman) has, as I have seen and as he proudly informed me, a small cemetery, well-tended, near his hogan, where some of his kin are buried. Nevertheless, he still sings Evil Way, or Ghost Way, as it is sometimes called, *hóchǫ́ǫ́ji*, which is commonly used to cure diseases resulting from contact with the dead or the spirits of the dead. When I asked him about this, he said that the members of the Native American Church had immortal souls (*niłch'i*, breath or spirit) which returned to God, but that non-members had ghosts, and people still had to be cured of sicknesses resulting from contact with them. Needless to say, traditional Navaho aware of the practice of burial in state near the hogan are horrified.

A reverence for nature and proliferation of symbols of nature and of man embedded in nature is evident in the prayers: the virtues of water, the repeated concept of man as the child of earth, and of peyote as a product of the earth used by man to reach God, run through the prayers. One peyotist, *Dan Pritchard, states that one can pray from the earth to the heavens, since we are creatures of earth, or from the heavens to the earth. Since he himself knows the Ten Commandments, he prays from the heavens to the earth: it is said, Thou shalt have none other Gods before Me.

In the prayers to sun, moon, earth, the atmosphere (or winds), in the reference to the four cardinal directions, the zenith and the nadir, are to be found elements which make it possible for traditional Navaho to find anchoring points in the new prayers. Peyotist singers sometimes comment that the Native American Church prayers are "no different from the Navaho prayers" for this reason—though in other contexts they would recognize definite differences. Thus the God prayed to may to some people represent the missionaries' God, the God of the Bible, the sole and only One, and the Savior, while to others he is but the chief among many figures, including the Navaho Holy People and various aspects of nature. In such ways may peyotism serve its diverse audience.

The references to a clear mind, to the straight thoughts achieved through keeping the poker straight, to a "clear conscience," all deal in part with matters related to the peyote reaction itself. (By a clear conscience the interpreter means both a clear mind and freedom from guilt.) These remarks seem to me to refer to the serious problem of thinking one's way through to an understanding of life, both from a practical and from a meaningful point of view, under the conditions of contemporary Navaho existence. References to shields, protection, and the like bear witness again to feelings of helplessness. In the reference to a road of life, and to old age we find echoes of that preoccupation with setting the ends of existence and achieving a new perspective on the future, rather than "living from day to day" which so many peyotists mention.

Rolled peyote is peyote which has been chewed by the road chief and rolled into a pellet, and breathed on, prior to being given to the patient. It has special virtue, it is believed. The use of cedar smoke purifies and makes the mind clear. It relieves the participants when peyote works on them too hard (its effects are uncomfortable or painful).

The number of relatives mentioned in prayers shows the strength of Navaho family solidarity, while at the same time the frequent references to the help given by those present reflects the strength of the solidarity between members of the church, as opposed to the weaker solidarity between members and non-members.

In connection with kinship, the data raise some interesting points about mother-in-law avoidance. In traditional Navaho culture the preferred pattern is for mother-in-law and son-in-law to avoid one another: never to be in the same room, never to look at one another, never to address one another directly. This pattern has never been observed by all Navaho and is today rejected by an increasing number, including both peyotists and non-peyotists. In the first meeting described one of the women who put up the ceremony and who was present throughout is mother-in-law to the road chief, who conducted the meeting, and to my interpreter, both of whom she addressed directly. My interpreter considered this behavior part of the "modern" code of the peyotists, in spite of the fact that similar behavior can be observed among non-members. At Piñon, a more conservative community, the avoidance pattern is still quite strong, but it is considered proper for a mother-in-law and a son-in-law who avoid each other at other times to attend the same peyote meeting.

The crying during the prayers and the crying of women, and sometimes men, in the morning after the meeting (which can be called "a good cry," one that makes you feel good) is absolutely atypical for traditional Navaho. It astonishes non-members, and often surprises novices, who consider it unmanly. Similarly the myriad "thank you's" are atypical. I have known a roomful of peyotists each to thank me separately for the cigarettes I gave them, whereas traditional Navahos thank each other, or whites, only for major favors.

It should be noted in passing that similar prayers for the anthropologist are recorded by Stewart (1948, p. 18).

The evidence of the prayers, here exemplified by two complete sequences, enables us to say, then, that peyotism appeals to feelings of need for support, that it encourages the expression of such feelings and affords an opportunity to overcome them through prayer. Furthermore, it encourages an emotionality not typical for the Navaho, and creates a radical, but not complete, alteration in attitudes toward the dead. It lays heavy stress on reciprocity, cooperation, and solidarity among members. It also stresses family solidarity. It encourages identification of Navahos with other American Indians, with their country, and with humanity. And through the insights afforded by peyote experiences it affords an opportunity to see one's path in a world of baffling perplexities.

Chapter 10

VARIATIONS IN RITUAL: V-WAY AND OTHERS

THE RITUAL DESCRIBED by Mike Kiyaani, as I have pointed out, varies slightly from each of the many versions of the peyote ritual already published—and as Mike indicates in a letter, varies slightly from his current practices. Before taking up these minor variations, we will consider a major variation on peyote ritual current at least as late as 1952, and a series of minor variants current at the same time. The first of these, called "V-way" by its innovators, involves both ritual and ideological changes. For three other innovations, water way, star way, and eagle way, information is scanty. A fifth innovation, which I have called "sanitary way," involves only certain additions to the usual ritual.

V-WAY

V-way departs in three ways from normal peyote ritual as described in all sources familiar to me: it dispenses with the moon altar and uses only the coals of the fire shaped in a "V"; it lays special stress on confession; and its participants believe that one should eat some peyote every day, as a prayer. I now supply the account of one of the innovators of this way.

*Joe Sherwood,[1] the innovator, was aged about 40 in 1952, a quiet, unobtrusive, amiable man, born, reared, and living at Red Rock. He had ten years of schooling at Shiprock and Ft. Wingate, quitting at a time when he was ill and the superintendent said he could discontinue. His father did not teach him much of Navaho religious ways until he returned from school. His father was strict and was a president of the local chapter (Navaho community organization). His father was not a singer. *Joe regards himself as affiliated with the Mormon Church, which he attends, and which has recently started proselytizing in his area, although he attended Presbyterian services in school and formerly attended the Catholic Church (long represented at Red Rock). Of his Presbyterian exposure he says that it didn't mean much to him except for, "And God so loved the world. . . ." Inasmuch as peyote, Navaho ceremonies, and Western medicine are all regarded as curing agents by Navahos, he was asked about his attitudes toward other cures. He replied that he has had only one Navaho ceremony since he began using peyote, in 1946. He has quit attending Navaho ceremonies. He also is willing to use the Government medical facilities, but has not done so. He uses aspirin and Akla-Seltzer, and his wife has been to the hospital since she began her use of peyote.

Incredible though it seems to me now, I did not pursue *Joe's life history more intensively. His livestock permit indicates only modest holdings: the top regular permit in the area is for 104 sheep units, and he has a permit for only 67. In the

[1] See footnote 5, Chapter 9, for explanation of asterisk here.

light of his stress on confession, I asked him, in effect, whether he had been a great sinner. He says that he did not drink, gamble, or play around with women much in his pre-conversion days, but that he did race horses—a point which does not seem to weigh on his mind.

I have chosen to reproduce my interview with *Joe in full for several reasons. It exemplifies an extreme of the visionary development in peyotism; it retails the common pattern of seeking one cure after another; it shows something of the legal difficulties of the peyotist; it tells a little about peyotist factionalism; and finally, it includes an account of *Joe's own ritual innovation and allusions to several more, all from the same general region.

The interview began with a request that *Joe tell me how it came about that he began to use peyote, and proceeded toward the discussion of V-way, since I knew before I visited him that he was its inventor. In view of the preoccupation with visions and inner life which is manifest in this interview, it is well to remember that the interview was supplied quietly and consecutively, and that *Joe acted as my interpreter for five days after this interview, a shy but fully adequate interpreter and guide.

Until further indication, *Joe speaks, without benefit of quotation marks. Parentheses are his; square brackets are questions directed at *Joe or comments by the anthropologist to elucidate the text. The interview was mainly carried out on July 20, 1952, in English.

My wife was sick. She had eye trouble—she was blind. She tried the medicine man [singer], and all kinds of remedies, and the hospital, but it was no help. She could see nothing. There were a few [peyote cult] members here. Her uncle said this medicine [peyote] was all right, and so we went to Towaoc, Colorado. Ute Indians run meetings over there, and one told us how to run a meeting [see below]. She took the medicine, and then one Ute Indian, an old man, Herbert Stacher's father, he uses the sucking cure, and he worked on the back of her head and above her eyes and removed white stuff, like paper, a big wad of it, and from above her eyes, something red and black, two finger-joints long [cf. Aberle and Stewart, 1957, pp. 34–40, for uses of the Utes for sucking cures].

She took the medicine, but she didn't see anything, she just cried, and I don't know why she was crying. And we bought some medicine, and Herbert Stacher and his wife told us how to use it and how much to take, and to pray to God. "You will find out and know for yourself, depending on how much you take," he said, and we did what he said, and then she began to get better in a month, and she wanted to go back and put up a meeting—the other time was not a meeting, just medicine and doctoring—and so we went again, and then Herbert Stacher ran the meeting for us, and then he gave me rolled medicine [chewed peyote bolus], and that's the first time I went to a meeting.

And so we went into a hogan and three of them were running the meeting: the chief, drummer, and fire chief, and that night we took medicine, and there were Utes there, but only four Navahos. I knew only one, from Shiprock. I ate rolled medicine that Herbert Stacher fixed. All the Utes were singing, but I didn't know what they sang, and they prayed in Ute, but Herbert Stacher prayed in English. He said, "Pray to God to find out where you're at," but I didn't know how to pray or sing, and I sat until midnight examining it. And an hour before morning,

Herbert Stacher prayed thirty minutes or more and passed the instruments to me. The medicine had been working on me. I just sat there. There were the moon and fire, and I was looking at them, and it was different.

I saw the ashes as if there were machine guns, tanks, and planes—that's what the ash turned into [World War II was still going on]. And the ground I looked at— I saw horse heads, cattle heads, sheep heads, and on top of the moon were soldiers lined up, coming back from the war, I figured out. And Herbert handed me a feather [fan] and it was as if it were alive, with blood in it, and as if there were a whistling in the wind, and he handed me the cane, the rattle, and the feather, and I tried to pass it [on], and I couldn't, and started to rattle, and was asked if I were going to sing, and didn't answer. The drummer came to me, and my ears shut off and everything turned red, and I sang four songs, and passed it on, and a Ute said, "Four is all, pass it on," and he gave me more rolled peyote, and told me, "When the drum passes the door, you go out." Yet I felt as if I were up in the air, having trouble walking, and I got out, and I could not see to walk outside, but the ground seemed covered with the medicine, and I came back in. And it was morning.

They called for breakfast and brought the water in. I drank water and ate the breakfast, and the meeting closed. And we went outside and everyone looked different from what they had during the night, and I was scared of that. I thought the medicine must be pretty strong, but "Whatever I see is alive and true," that's what my mind said. When I held that cane and shook that rattle, it was just going by itself. I didn't even know the words of the song I sang. And it [the cane] was like a post, in front of the fire—the fire purple, and a black and white post like a high-way post in front of the fire—and my mind said, "You've got to think straight and smooth if you really want to believe the medicine and God; you've got to be clean." And the chief peyote started to talk to me: "Put away the bad things." It told me what I did. I didn't know what to say. I thought, "That medicine must be strong and must be good. As long as I live I will believe it is God's medicine."

And I made up my mind to come to the church and to the meeting to find out what this medicine is. "I don't want all kinds of sickness any more. I want to live good, and desire to learn more about this medicine." And then Herbert told me, "This medicine is good medicine, and strong. Believe it, use it in a clean way." He told me that. If I was to be a member, I should have a membership card. He showed me the charter, but it was too strong for me to read it. And then we said, "We're ready to go home. We'll try our best." [Although peyotists regard the charter as a legal shield, and with some reverence, I have not elsewhere found it regarded with real awe.]

But I was afraid, because they didn't want it on the reservation—they were strict at that time—and then we came home, and I went to another meeting alone, run by *Ben Eastman. There were just older people there, with five younger ones. He told us to stay out during the night, and I said, "I came to this meeting for a pur-pose; so I don't want to go out. I want to stay in and watch to see how the Navahos are running the Native American Church." And by that time Roosevelt had died. [Since World War II was not yet over, this second meeting must have been in spring or summer of 1945.] And I learned more that night, what the Navahos were praying for and what they were saying, and how it was going.

I came home, and right after that I went to Towaoc to Herbert Stacher. I got some medicine from him. I brought it home and learned a little, how to use it and how to pray, and whenever I pray it gives me a good feeling and new thoughts. And then in that way I keep going and keep learning, and buy medicine, and I went to several meetings and studied this church, and it was like starting a new way, learning new words, learning new things, and I was not good at talking English and I learned lots of new words. From there, they caught me using it.

The police came to my home and searched my home and suitcases [a stack of these serves as a storage place in many Navaho hogans], and there were 2, 3, 5 medicines [pieces of peyote] in my suitcase, which they didn't find. I showed my feathers and rattle, but they said they were just looking for medicine. I was taken to jail for two days, and came home after signing a bond, and stayed seven days. I think someone was against me and signed a complaint, and the police came again at night and took me to jail and showed me seven medicines and said it was mine, that a man had gotten it from me. Yet I had none, and he probably bought it from X and accused me, and I said it was not mine, but they didn't believe me, and so I was put in jail and stayed there. [According to court records, this was 1946.]

[The legal story is summarized more briefly. Two members, both V-way adherents when I knew them, and probably at the time of the arrest, signed a bond and got *Joe out again. It was four months before he got a hearing. He was sworn, felt the court to be very hostile, says that two witnesses were prevented from speaking, and was given a 10-month sentence, 5 on each of two complaints— possession and sale?—and a $200.00 fine. He was sent to Ft. Defiance and put on a gravedigging detail, and then made a trusty. After further complications tending, he believes, to show a judge's animus against him, he secured leave for 15 days to attempt to get his fine. His friends said they would recommend an appeal for a second hearing, but he would have none of it. He assembled $180.00 from his nephew, his mother, and his own cash, and returned to Window Rock. Since he had worked 20 days, he was then released and went to work in the bean fields and then to Colorado to herd sheep for 6 months to collect the repayment, which he made with interest.]

And from there I started off differently and did not go to meetings for a long time; in fact I didn't go among the people here at Red Rock. But anyhow I used the medicine and prayed. [He then began to go to meetings again, trying to learn, and was often asked to speak. He became well-acquainted with a New Mexico official of the Church, and with Taos boys. He and some of his friends asked the official for a charter and got one, and later, after learning more about peyote, he requested one for himself—one which was secured from Phoenix, Arizona, in 1950.]

From there I go by the charter and its articles. And I was elected Secretary of the Red Rock Chapter Organization [not the peyote church, the community organization]. Yet they did not want me because I was a member of the Native American Church, and yet I just try to help, and I was re-elected last spring and they said nothing about peyote, and they elected three peyote members as President, Vice-President, and me as Secretary. [An anomaly, since the majority of the community does not belong to the peyote church, and there are other English-speakers who could fill the secretarial position. The President does not speak English, but the Vice-President is fluent.] And we work together and straighten things out. According to that church I am not to be disrespectful to any one; I am to treat every one equally. And so I pray for all nationalities, for [tribal] councilmen, senators, soldiers, armies. I pray to God for them to win victory [Korean War], and I feel that this medicine is all right, and if you really believe the medicine and serve God and use peyote as a sacrament, you will help one another and love one another.

[We turned now to his wife's health. She recovered sufficiently from her blindness after two weeks so that she now weaves. Although she is said to have a medical record at the Shiprock Hospital, I could not locate one—either because there is none or because old records there are hard to locate. Also, she was at Ft. Defiance Hospital, but there again I find no record. Since, in fact, peyote was known in the Red Rock area and widely available at Shiprock and Teec Nos Pas by 1945, I asked how he had happened to go first to Towaoc for his peyote. This was strikingly frequent at Red Rock (see Aberle and Stewart, 1957, pp. 34–40). He said both that he had not heard that there were peyotists nearby at the time, and that in fact he went for the sucking cure. Since use of the sucking cure normally indicates a belief that one has been magically "shot" by witchcraft, I asked about the cause of his wife's illness.]

The tears she shed on her dead infants were what caused her eye trouble. And behind her head, that was caused by lightning. Sucking cures are not used just for witchcraft. The object removed from her had a head and limbs, a ch'įindii [spirit of the dead] perhaps. The Ute pulled it right out, and so she believed it. She had had a sucking cure at Dulce, among the Jicarilla. The Jicarilla said she would go blind after two years. [Any Navaho ceremonies?] Evil Way, Male and Female Shooting Way, Blessing Way, Blackening—Evil Way we tried three times and Shooting Way twice, one male and one female, mountain tobacco, and a hand-trembler. But that was no good. The hand-trembler recommended Night Way. She tried drug-store medicine, eye drops. While taking the peyote she found out the sings were against her—they were turned around to kill her, due to the intention of the singers. Three of them died; they were the ones working against her. She was a widow then, during part of this. We married in 1940. She had trouble before and got blind after three children by her previous husband died. She had trouble for a year, but was not blind, but had been blind a week when we went to Towaoc. We feared the medicine. I wanted to find out. [Note that although the cause of her illness is said not to be witchcraft, the witchcraft theme emerges thereafter in the reference to singers who worked against her and are now dead—inferentially because their power turned back against them when she recovered.]

[We now turned to the theme of visions—did he have them? Many Navahos flatly deny ever having visions during peyote meetings and of these, many seem utterly sincere.] I see visions in every meeting, for example money and paper. Or I hear voices singing. I see things if I take peyote and pray at home. If I take only two peyotes I see nothing; I just have good feelings. I take twenty or forty to see and hear. If I am interrupted, I know where I am and can talk, and then can turn back, but I may have to take more medicine. [Does it ever make you sick?] I have vomited only once. I vomited four or five colors. It was a tough one, at home. And that was after the meeting was over. And then I threw up black blood and my heart closed up, but I was not afraid of dying—it was only a cure. The vomit became clear, and empty, and then I was OK. I was as good as a little kid. It made no trouble.

[Only now did I turn to ask him about V-way, since I knew there had been some trouble about it.] It is still in use, but the two sides got together and there is no trouble. The President and the Vice-President of the Native American Church of the United States were brought in, and they say, "It's all the same— the same fire, medicine, prayer, food, and earth, all the same. So the V-way is the short way. The Cheyenne and Taos had a diagram of what they see. [Apparently the Cheyenne and Taos draw diagrams of what they see insofar as it dictates ritual innovations, but this passage is obscure.] Act according to the medicine, that's what to do. I run a V-way ceremony myself. I just learned from the medicine.

At that time there was a war, and the medicine showed me how to set the fire [arrange the coals from the fire], with "V" for victory. And we found out that a victory was to come, and a month later there was victory, over Germany and Japan. [If this is correct, V-way followed hard on his second peyote meeting, which occurred after Roosevelt's death.] The fire is like the regular fire, but there is a V of ash where the moon would ordinarily be, with the chief peyote behind the V. The fire can be lighted with a match. It takes four officials as in other meetings. If there is an acute illness, you could use V-way. [Less preparations are required than for a typical meeting.] Or you could just have the fire, in which case it would just be for a prayer.

The reason for the V is to confess all one's sins. In moon way one can confess some sins. In V-way, one or two in a meeting confess, everything, back to twelve years of age. They do so before all the members. You cannot hide things before the V. V-way is pretty strong. We don't talk bad stories, or talk about people, or about what we don't know. [This may be a hint that they do not talk about witchcraft.] We want to be clean and straight. Some people go to moon way and drink afterward, and they give trouble if they go back into the meeting; so some quit and some come back, and that's a lesson for them. But in V-way you can't. If you go back [backslide], you can't stand it, you can't sit in the meeting.

[He does not run a moon way meeting, and knows only one man who may possibly run meetings both ways. V-way members are found mainly at Shiprock, Red Rock, and Cove. He lists two men who also run V-way.] Then *Randall Bruce runs star way. And there is a man with water and no fire at all, up in the mountain, *Irwin Michaels.

Some of the songs are Navaho—new words and old tunes. I was the one to start V-way. The V stands for wings, and for victory over temptation. I started in 1945, before the war was over. I saw how to run it in the meeting, by taking medicine. [From what follows, he must mean that he learned how to run it as a meeting while taking peyote.] Before sunup, sitting there, I rose, got outside, brought in eight sticks and an ash shovel, and put ash in the middle, walked around, took a cigarette and prayed, and repeated this. I took the fire stick and set a V, and brought in water, rolled a smoke, prayed for the water—just the two of us, me and my wife, and took the stick and pointed toward the V, and went round again and just sat there. I had no chief medicine or drum or feathers, just medicine, and I prayed, and that was the beginning. And then a few days later I took more medicine and prayed, and everything looked different—the world, and my flesh, and the food tasted different, and the water.

And I took more medicine and kept on until I found out everything. Sometimes everything looked dirty and sometimes it all looked clean. Sometimes I couldn't even eat, everything tasted bad. And I found out everything that was wrong, the bad words and so on that make things not right. And I decided to be good and clean all the time, and straight, and everything was OK. I found out that way. All this was in family meetings here. My wife was not yet much improved; after that she got well and can see clear, and we cleaned it all up. And our neighbors—my cousin was having trouble with her hurt, and she wanted to get well, and they asked "How did you get well?" At first I did not tell. We spent money and did work and travel and had hard luck and faced temptation and learned. But they kept asking me. *Hugh Scammon came to me and spoke about his heart trouble, and he took medicine, not going to a meeting, and they asked me, and I told them. I was afraid to run a meeting for them, but relatives asked, and they found it out—and that's how I got jailed. [Presumably publicity came from this.] *Larry Hawkins helped me.

And more and more came in and asked me for help, and V-way grew and got going, and we had no drum, just prayer, and then we got feathers. Stacher gave me a gourd and his brother gave me a cane. And we organized it and started praying together, and I took more medicine. And another man, *Orrin Musgrave, had the same thing—just the fire—and *Orrin said to come here and have a prayer meeting, and he had full equipment, and the question arose as to who is to run the meeting. And he said, "You must, the medicine showed you how." And so I did, ran a V fire all night long.

And I saw another way. Lots of feathers, cane, drum, rattle, and whistle, were about 5 feet high in the hogan, above my reach, and therefore I was not to run the meeting, but it came down gradually and came between *Orrin and me. "You should run the meeting," I said to *Orrin. "And don't worry," he said, "and we will pray and it will straighten out." And two weeks later I had a pain in my heart, and I made tea [peyote tea] and took two full dippers, and the medicine worked on me, and right there I learned a song, water song, quitting song, and starting song, and we started from there. [In other words, when he started, he had neither paraphernalia nor knowledge of certain standard items, such as the fixed songs. He felt that this way was inspired, but was apparently unable to keep from feeling that it was incomplete and did not constitute a meeting properly speaking. Further revelations are filling out the ritual repertoire.]

Even the ones who run moon way come to V-way. They say, "I can learn nothing more from moon way; I must come to V." And so they got together, and they all quit talking about it. There is no use to talk against it they said. And so when there is a meeting [moon way], I go, and follow that way and say nothing, and they come to me. There are no more politics. [He then lists prominent leaders who have, and have not attended his meetings.]

[In response to questions:] V-way is an all night meeting. Yes, there is a short way, with fire and ash, and cedar, and you pray and give medicine, plain or rolled, to the sick person, and leave the fire there. There is no singing, no drum, and no cane. And if the patient wants to pray, OK, and if he wants to sleep, OK. Just put the ash in the fire. It is just with a singer and a patient or other members of his family, lasting one or two hours. They do the same in moon way. [In fact, peyote can be taken and a prayer said at any time.]

[Why are the non-peyotists hostile to the peyotists?] Because they want to hold on to their sin. [Any recent trouble?] No trouble this past year; they help each other out.

I keep learning all the time and got it all straight. And people talked about it and said it was not right, and one member was an officer of the Church in Arizona, and I told him what was being said, and there was another man running V-way at Naschitti, *Randall Bruce, and *Sam Thatcher saw *Bruce's meeting, and a crazy woman was treated; the moon didn't help her, but V-way did. Now she is OK. I heard at Naschitti that *Randall Bruce is running star way [this is not entirely clear], and *Thatcher saw it. An old woman got about half-way toward recovering and started confessing, but she couldn't. *Sam Thatcher said, "OK, I can say nothing against it, because I don't know." Then I was called to Rattlesnake for a V-way meeting, for a woman with stomach trouble, ready to die, and *Sam followed this meeting. I told him all about it. And he said that some Oklahoma Indians run it that way.

And talk started. People wanted to cut it out. There was a gathering at Rattlesnake at *Louis Dayton's, and *Thatcher was there and said "I have seen it, and the meeting is OK, the prayer is the same, we who use peyote must not fight. Meetings must run as the medicine tells people. There will be many ways." And the meeting was cut off. And Sam Standing Water of Hammond, Oklahoma, saw it, and he said it was OK, and he said that some run a meeting one way and some another—there are always differences. He could say nothing against it, he said. This concludes *Joe Sherwood's account.

People who participate in V-way ceremonies seem to have special attitudes and values as compared with other peyotists, attitudes readily apparent in the interview with *Joe Sherwood. There is more stress on confession, and on confession of all sins from childhood on. There is more emphasis on ecstatic and elaborated visions. And there is more stress on a total transformation of personality, on total purity of thought and deed. These generalizations are based on a comparison of interviews with V-way participants and others.

I interviewed fourteen people who had had some contact with V-way, but with four of these the discussion centered on other topics. Of the remaining ten, six could be regarded as strongly committed to V-way. They either use nothing else or express a strong preference for this ritual. Four of the six run V-way meetings: *Joe Sherwood, the innovator, *Larry Hawkins and *Hugh Scammon of Red Rock, and *William Budd of Shiprock, *Stephen Cooper of Shiprock and *Larry Hawkins' wife make up the remaining two. The remaining four include *Sherwood's half-sister, her husband, her daughter, all of Red Rock, and *Cooper's half-sister's daughter, also of Red Rock. Five of the ten stress the importance of confession, three of confession from childhood (or from twelve years of age). All have seen visions or had auditory hallucinations, save *Cooper, where a full and elaborate dream seems to have served the same purpose. In three cases the visions were among the most elaborate and ecstatic I transcribed in five summers of field work; *Cooper's dream falls into the same category. In the remaining six cases the visions are briefer and more mundane.

For comparison, I have taken a sample of interviews from nearby areas. I made a list of all interviews with peyotists in District 9 that were sufficiently full for analysis, selecting every other one beginning with the first, a total of seven. I also listed all interviews secured in the Lukachukai area (which included one case from Cove, near Red Rock and one from Red Rock itself), choosing every other one beginning with the first, for a total of six. Of these thirteen interviews, none mentions confession; none mentions confession from the beginning of one's sinful life; only two claim major vision experience; four others mention single unelaborated visions;

TABLE 14

VISIONS AND V-WAY

	Major Visions* or Dream†	Minor Visions*	No Visions	None Mentioned
V-way only or preferred..................	4	2	0	0
V-way and moon way equally valued.......	0	4	0	0
No V-way..............................	2	4	5‡	2

* Visions or auditory experiences.
† One elaborate dream included.
‡ Includes 1 case from Red Rock and 1 from Cove, where V-way is found.
A test of the extremes: V-way only, or preferred versus no V-way, major visions versus none, is significant at better than the .05 level, Fisher's exact test, one-tailed.

five explicitly deny visions; two fail to mention them, but there seems to have been no explicit question on the point in the interview (see Table 14).

The failure of so many peyotists to mention confession does not, of course, mean that it is unimportant in usual peyotism; confession is at least supposed to feature the patient's prayer in an ordinary meeting. It does mean, however, that confession has a degree of saliency among V-way members that is lacking elsewhere. By the same token, the vision, unimportant to many peyotists and important to others, is of great importance to V-way members.

There is one other point worth stressing: the notion of a total transformation of personality found among five V-way members, four of them V-way priests. They believe in total purity, and in the banishing of all sin and hate from their hearts. They aim at an almost ecstatic state of happiness. Since many peyotists are likely to say that they have given up sin and make comments on their changed state, the emphasis here is difficult to bring out by any mechanical coding such as I have attempted above. The tone, however, does differ in the V-way interviews from most others that I have recorded. The emotional intensity of these interviews, least marked in the case of *Joe Sherwood's, is also striking.

As illustration of these points, *Cooper's account of his transformation, and

*Scammon's of his vision are supplied. *Scammon's comes first. Both were recorded in 1949.

I kept on using peyote, and as time goes by I wonder if this God I am praying to is the God the missionaries preach of. Could I use the word God? And the word came to me, "Yes, you are under one heaven and on one earth. It is your home. You are *all* My children. God is your Father, Jesus your Brother, Mary your Mother. It makes no difference about denominations. You are all My children. At that time I saw myself in the Church of God, the Heavenly Church, and though I was strong, I was not then strong in the sight of God. When I entered this church, there were two white doors, high-class doors, with gold plates, and the gold was so shiny that I couldn't stand it, it was so shiny. But I went in. And there were two angels on each side of the door, and as I went in, a table. And God Himself was behind the table, and Jesus Christ, and Mary, and I was weeping. And I was told to sit down. And I was told, "If you really want to know the truth about the Church, here it is, so you know it for your people, your property, and future generations. And the teaching is endless and you cannot learn it all in your life."

I was thinking: I am an earthly man. I ought to learn how to live on the earth and set an example. And They knew before I said it. And then I said to myself, my father is gone, and is dead, and my mother, brothers, sisters, and relatives. I want to know if there is a second life. And I *saw* them. They were living. And then They said there is a second life. "I am the light. My heart gives light to man. You are going to know about this later on," He told me. And then Jesus spoke to me. I asked Him, "What is this peyote?" And Jesus Christ said to me, "Today when many are against this, and many are for it, Me, too, those who hated Me crucified Me on the cross. And then after My blood dropped to the earth from My heart, and there grew up from the earth vegetation, and that was peyote, and peyote is My blood," He said.

He said, "You cannot see all these things unless you are purified and give up all your sins. You can't see anything but dark if you don't give up your sins. This peyote, as I describe it, is the everlasting life and will lead you toward everlasting life and lead you in the right way of living. It's hard to be a true Christian. You have to teach others the true way and it is a hard job to do so. But you must remember Christians must live, so long till God Almighty calls them from earth to heaven, and there everlasting life will be given to you."

When I went to school I was small and didn't learn the word of God, but I *did* learn it through peyote. I learned His words, and what He is and what it's for, and what it means to be a Christian, and *how* to be. I learned *that* through peyote. The white missionaries teach from the Bible, but I am not that way. The peyote showed me how, and that's how I make my testimony. In the next peyote meeting from today we will find out what your [DFA's] real purpose is and whether this report will be OK. Thus far *Scammon.

*Scammon was forty-five in 1949. He had three years of school, one of them off-reservation. He was never formally allied with any church and maintains that his early Christian training made little impression on him. The interpreter, *Dan Pritchard, acted as interpreter for a missionary for seven years. This accounts for some of the Biblical turns of phrase. But *Cooper spoke in English. His account follows.

I started five years ago. I used to be against Christ and anyone who preached Christianity. I worked for a missionary. I would pretend I believe the Bible, but now I can pray any time. That [the ability to pray from the heart] made me believe in a God and a beloved Savior Jesus Christ that made this wonderful and powerful medicine. The Protestants don't believe in Mary, but she's in heaven, and we each have a Guardian Angel—there are millions of them. It [peyote] teaches you, and you know what you are doing. God sent it to us poor Indians. We have missionaries, but they don't believe what they are preaching. *They* get mad, and God and Jesus never got mad. Moses said, "Forgive your brother seven times," but Jesus said, "Forgive him seventy times seventy times." My heart is OK and you can't make me mad. And *God* answers my prayer. After I start praying to God I gave up my sins, and He agreed. "From now on, never sin again." Peyote bothered me before [when he began using it] but now it does not.

The Protestants, Catholics, and Mormons hate each other, and they are not to do that. The Catholics respect Mary and the Angels, and we do. [His earlier affiliation had been Protestant.] We uneducated Navahos can pray to God better than the missionaries. The missionaries don't get the Navahos to believe, but they take peyote and believe and see. They give up drinking, swearing, and bad things, and know they were sinning. If you are an unbeliever [and take peyote], it will turn you upside down and tie and bind you. If you are sinless, you will get *happy* [that is, beatific]. That woman you told me about [who became frightened at the sound of the drum at a peyote meeting and wanted to leave], she was wicked. If she took more peyote, she would be OK. She's afraid of her sins. If we misbehave, lie, or steal, we have no fear to pray or talk to God. We love the wicked, like God. God shines on all. When I first heard the drums, I could not stand it because I had sinned. I confessed *all* my sins from my childhood on and was forgiven. They can read your mind in the meeting [that is, they can tell whether you are really confessing your sins]. We are not doing this for fun. We believe in God. The medicine is powerful and wonderful, given to our uneducated people to know God for themselves and to see Him. But the missionary can't make the Navaho believe.

[Nowadays] I sing in the field. I don't feel tired, even if I go to meeting at night, though at first I was afraid. . . . I pray in English, I am just catching on how to pray. At first you are like a child and you recall all your sins and vomit them all up. Now I could eat as many peyote buttons as I want and they don't bother me. In the morning we are all quiet and kind to one another. That's how we are. . . .

The Old Testament says the world is 6000 years old. The Jews were 2000 years [in duration before the coming of Jesus]. And from then on there were no prophets but the Mormons. Peyote is the New Generation, one hundred per cent believers. They can tell you just what the Lord is saying, and He is talking to us all the time. . . . As Jesus said, He cured them and said, "Sin no more." If you pretend to believe and break the commandments, the whole thing goes back on you and you feel bad. You must pray and pray, the honest way.

This concludes *Cooper's statement. I am at a loss to know why in these, and other interviews, there is some tendency for Catholic elements, notably the concern with Mary and with angels, to appear, even when the individuals have Protestant backgrounds.

OTHER SPECIAL DEVELOPMENTS

With these fervent statements we leave V-way for another variant, water way, used by *Irwin Michaels of Sanastee. Only a few details are available. According to a woman informant from Red Rock, *Irwin sits on a chair on the south side of the doorway of the hogan, with the patient at the west side of the hogan (opposite the door). The patient unbuttons his (her) shirt, and *Irwin stands at the door and examines him, and can see what is wrong. There is no moon, but he uses corn pollen and has two bowls of water. He uses no drum, but a fan, a rattle, and singing in the language of the Oklahoma Indians. The informant's son, who went to *Irwin separately, also mentions pollen, which *Irwin uses because it is an ancient Navaho custom; *Irwin claims that the Navahos once used peyote (in the mythical past) but somehow lost it. *Irwin, he says, looks at the sky and tells you your sins, and then asks Christ for forgiveness and looks again, and the sin is gone. Peyote is used in this ceremony. *Irwin will not use the moon because it doesn't work. This fragmentary account is supplied to stimulate further research on this and other variants.

*Orrin Musgrave and *Randall Bruce are said to use star way. Both men live somewhere in the Sanastee–Red Rock–Shiprock area. I have also heard mention in this same area of eagle way, but I do not know who practices it. *Orrin Musgrave claims joint credit for inventing V-way, as discussed in *Joe Sherwood's interview. I assume that both star and eagle way involve special manipulation of the ashes and coals during a peyote ritual.

Thus, between Shiprock and Sanastee, and between 1945 and 1952, at least the following variants on traditional peyote ritual have arisen: V-way, water way, star way, and eagle way. I have no clue as to why so many innovations should have occurred in so small an area, but these new ways have certain features in common which should be mentioned.

1. All of them dispense with the moon and thus require less elaborate preparations.

2. It is highly probable that all of them can be run with only a practitioner and a patient or with only a practitioner and a small family group.

3. The first practitioners claim peyote experience as the total validation of the ritual; they have not undergone the apprenticeship typical of "moon way" practitioners.

In all these respects they seem to be a reaction against the fully developed cult, its large meetings, and its routinization of charisma, its transmission of the grace of leadership both through learning and through inspiration.

It should be noted that Oklahoma was for some time the site of various elaborations of ritual equipment, but that by the time La Barre did his field work in the 1930's, the general mood was one of return to simplicity—to the basic ritual which was eventually transmitted to the Navahos (La Barre, 1938, p. 76). Hence this tendency toward variation has certain parallels in the history of peyotism.

It is probable that these innovations among the Navahos are in some ways syncretic with Navaho practice, as well as divergent from standard peyotism. The proliferation of "ways" suggests this, and *Irwin Michael's practice seems to overlap with Navaho divinatory practices.

Finally, it is notable that, as so often in the past, the ritual divergences of V-way were not permitted to develop into full-fledged schism: that Oklahoma peyotists accepted the V-way ritual as a permissible variant, since the fundamentals of the use of peyote and belief in and prayer to God were not violated.

A minor innovation of some interest is that of *Edgar Meridith, a former Marine, from District 9. *Edgar introduced the following innovations: (1) He did not "roll peyote" in the usual fashion, which is to chew it into a pulp, spit the pulp into the hands, and roll it into a bolus. Instead, after washing his hands, using ground peyote, clean water, a clean cup, and a clean spoon, he made ground peyote into a paste with the water and rolled this. (2) Although he used the customary common cup for drinking the midnight water, at the peyote breakfast each person was served with individual paper cups and plastic spoons. Each dipped his own fresh cup into the common bucket and drank from it, using a serving spoon thereafter to dish out a helping of the peyote breakfast dishes into the paper cup, and eating the helping with his own plastic spoon. (3) At the feast which follows a peyote ceremony about noon, huge white cloths were laid down to keep off the dust, and each place was provided with a plate, two bowls, a cup, a spoon, a fork, and so on, so that eating utensils need not be shared. The food was dished out in these containers before people started to eat, and there was no eating from common containers. These variations were *Edgar's own idea, derived from military experiences, and were explicitly aimed at sanitation. He feared spreading tuberculosis to children and explicitly rejected the chewing of peyote to be given to patients. He enforced these practices on those to whom he taught the ritual. His own teacher was John P. Hart, the Cheyenne. These features were *Edgar's own addition. It might be said that *Edgar's respect for Western sanitation was greater than his respect for Western medicine. He claimed to be a diabetic, but said that peyote kept him well. He did not use insulin. *Edgar was interviewed in 1950. He died sometime between 1954 and 1963, I believe in the 1960's, but I do not know the cause of death. I do not know whether his way is still observed.

COMPARISON OF NAVAHO AND OTHER RITUALS

We come now to minute variations of ritual among Navaho practitioners, and resemblances of Navaho rituals to those of other tribes. Omer Stewart's check list of 265 traits relating to peyote equipment, ritual, and belief, is useful for inter-tribal and inter-individual comparisons (Stewart, 1948, pp. 19–30). Chart E presents the results of comparison of Navaho rituals with Stewart's check list. I used the list in only four instances: a meeting held by *Bill Conroy, Oto-trained, in 1949; another by *Conroy in 1952; one by Mike Kiyaani, a pupil of Truman Dailey's (Oto) in 1950; and one by *Edgar Meridith, a pupil of John P. Hart's (Cheyenne), in 1950. I also compared the list with Kiyanni's oral account of how to run a peyote meeting, presented above.

I was not able in all instances to observe, nor in all to remember all of these details. Items thus fall into four possible categories: (1) no information; (2) fits the item as listed by Stewart; (3) differs for all cases from the item as listed by Stewart; (4) differs among Navahos. Wherever there is at least one observation or a comment by Kiyaani, this is considered an item for which there is information.

Items relating to knowledge and belief are omitted. All items where there is complete agreement with Stewart's list are passed over without comment. (Stewart's items are in simple declarative form, e.g., "After midnight individual fans, rattles, etc., used." He then indicates whether this trait is present, absent, or no information for various tribes.) Essentially, then, Chart E provides details on some variations of Navaho practice not dealt with explicitly elsewhere, as an aid to comparative work.

CHART E

NAVAHO RITUAL IN THE LIGHT OF STEWART'S TRAIT LIST

Item No. (from Stewart, 1948, pp. 19–30)	Comments
15. Individual rattles used in addition to leader's.	Sometimes; probably depends on acquisition of rattles.
19. Each feather of leader's fan tied separately.	Not *Edgar Meridith's.[1]
24. Individual fans used only after midnight.	Kiyaani says after a special prayer by road chief, before midnight water.
26. Eagle-bone whistle.	Kiyaani used bamboo but mentions eagle bone.
32. Cloth on which to place paraphernalia.	Lacking in all meetings observed; seen at preliminaries to meeting conducted by *Mal Hancock.
35. Iron kettle drum.	Iron, brass, aluminum.
36. Pottery jar drum.	Never observed or mentioned.
47. Individual drumsticks in addition to leader's.	In some meetings; probably depends on acquisition of drumsticks.
48. Used only after midnight.	At any time according to Kiyaani.
51. Drummer usually at right of singer.	Men tend to pair and exchange, each drumming for the other, without shifting places.
55. Cedar sprinkled on fire usually by cedar chief.	Much done by road man.
56. Only one bag of cedar used.	I have seen two.
58. Tobacco rolled in maize.	Ordinarily only for prayers of officials, patient, and those who deliver special prayers. *Meridith uses none.
59. Tobacco rolled in oak leaves.	Not found.
60. Tobacco lacking.	Never.
63. Peyote furnished by leader.	Passed by leader, but not necessarily furnished by him.
65. Chief peyote decorated with white lines.	Undecorated in one of *Conroy's meetings; Kiyaani says his undecorated.
69. Artemisia leaves under chief peyote form cross.	Circular bed; cross.
71. Only leader's peyote used until after midnight.	According to Kiyaani, no one should eat any peyote except that passed by the leader, through the night.
73. Leader named "chief" or "peyote chief."	Never called "peyote chief." Road man, road chief.
76. Assistants; 77 2 Ass'ts; 78 3 Ass'ts; 79 4 Ass'ts or more.	Minimum 2 (drummer, fire); cedar chief usual, not required; dawn lady may be used or morning water brought by fire chief. Range, 2–4.
83. Drummer chief drums for each singer in turn.	Variable; pattern differed in 2 of *Conroy's meetings.
94. Bathing before meeting.	No observations; Kiyaani once said that leader should, others need not; once said that those who could, should.
103. Sticks making fire form right angle.	More nearly acute.
104. Old methods used to start fire.	No special requirements mentioned.
105. Four sticks.	Eight observed in 1 meeting. In some meetings on hot nights fire kept outside and coals brought in on shovel. Then lamps sometimes used for additional light.

[1] Asterisk preceding a proper name indicates a pseudonym.

CHART E—*Continued*

108. Preference for Indian dress.	Not observed. Stress on neat, good clothing.
110. Leader prays before entering.	Kiyaani denies this; no observations.
114. Men precede women and children entering meeting.	No.
115. Women prohibited.	No.
118–119. Men either side near leader; women either side near entrance.	Observed only once.
120. Separation of men and women.	No.
122. Women sit back of men.	No.
125. People sit on artemisia.	Not observed; it may have been under blankets and mats; Kiyaani says yes.
130–131. After initial cigarette rolling, leader prays aloud, others silently.	Others likely to pray aloud.
135–136. Artemisia leaves passed clockwise, rubbed on hands, clothes.	In all but one meeting; preparations there perhaps incomplete.
137. Artemisia chewed.	Not observed; Kiyaani says it should be.
141. All take 4 buttons at start.	Variable.
142. Each button chewed, spit into hands, rolled, offered to altar, swallowed.	Offered first, chewed, swallowed; then worshipper spits in hands and pats head, chest, body.
161. Rule against women singing.	Denied; many sing softly when men lead; a few women take the staff and sing.
174. Midnight water brought by woman.	Never observed.
194. All urged to eat as much peyote as possible.	Denied by Kiyaani; no other data.
195. People urged not to eat too much.	No information.
201–205. Outlines disposition of cigarette butt after individual prayers.	Not followed in *Edgar Meridith's meeting.
206. No one to leave meeting while others sing, pray, or eat peyote.	Not followed by *Meridith. Kiyaani permits exits during singing.
217. Parched maize at peyote breakfast.	Only canned or fresh corn observed.
220. Candy included in breakfast.	Lacking.
222. Ablutions precede breakfast.	Lacking.
229. After drum disassembled, objects used to tie drumhead passed and touched to body.	Not always.
230. All parts of drum passed, handled.	Not always.
233. Food dishes for peyote breakfast placed in reverse order before door for removal.	Sometimes stacked; stacking order not observed.
235. All go outside about 9 A.M.	About 7 A.M. in summer.
239–250. As I understand these items, they describe the position of paraphernalia during the meal which follows a meeting (not the ceremonial peyote breakfast).	No ceremonial layout for this occasion. There is for the ceremonial breakfast (peyote breakfast) described elsewhere in the check list.

Navaho departures from Stewart's basic pattern seem to be of three varieties. First, they circumscribe the position of women less carefully than do many other tribes. This undoubtedly results from the past and present position of Navaho women. Thus women may become traditional ceremonial practitioners among the Navaho, although few do, and the right of such a woman to take the leader's staff and sing in a peyote meeting is not challenged. Second, certain items have special nativistic significance for the Plains but not among the Navaho: native techniques of making fire, traditional costume, parched corn, and avoidance of cigarette papers are among these. Third, certain refinements have not yet developed. Some people do not have rattles or drumsticks, although they would like to; a cloth for the leader's paraphernalia is not used, etc.

Navaho features sharply diagnostic of affinities for particular Plains groups do not emerge from the use of this check list. On the contrary, the Navaho ritual shares certain features with the Washo-Paiute. Some of these center on the position of women; others, rather than pointing to a common origin, seem to result from the fact that, like the Navaho, the Washo-Paiute started peyotism in the mid-1930's and hence had not yet acquired certain refinements of ritual.

There are some items not in Stewart's check list which discriminate among the rituals of various Navaho road chiefs, and even among rituals of the same road chief on different occasions, which are regarded as important by Navahos. Some road chiefs require that the water bucket be passed first to the road chief; others start it on the south side of the door. The first group considers its procedure dignified; the second considers its procedure democratic. Talking at midnight water may or may not be permitted. Lounging may be permitted (by *Edgar Meridith) or avoided (by Mike Kiyaani). Late comers may be welcomed (most road chiefs) or excluded (*Edgar Meridith once refused entry to men coming all the way from Taos). Some road chiefs have the fire chief lean each cigarette butt against the moon in the order in which the smokers sat; others have them all placed against the ends of the moon. For some people, the "big moon" (large altar) is a more important or serious meeting than the "small moon." For others, it is a matter of the size of the room. For still others, it is a choice for the road chief. All these details greatly interest Navaho peyotists.

La Barre provided a fine 35-page variorum of Plains peyote ritual (1938, pp. 47–92). Chart F presents comments on some of La Barre's headings, dealing with topics not treated elsewhere in this work, again for comparative purposes. Inspection of La Barre's variorum does not indicate Navaho affinities with any particular Plains group. Furthermore, it yields very few special Navaho developments.

Although trait analysis does not highlight Navaho ritual affinities, we know, of course, what the sources of Navaho peyotism are. This topic has been dealt with in Aberle and Stewart (1957). We will summarize here. Initial Navaho use of peyote stems from the Southern Ute, and in particular the Towaoc Ute. The Ute were stimulated initially by the Oglala Sioux, and subsequently by a variety of Plains Indians, principally Cheyenne, but including Kiowa. Navaho contacts with the Southern Ute were followed at once by contacts with Oklahoma Indians. The pattern of influence in 1952 was as follows. In the northern part of the reservation, in Aneth, District 9, Shiprock, Red Rock, Cove, Lukachukai, and Mexican Springs, the dominant external influences are Ute and Cheyenne (and priests trained by Ute and Cheyenne practitioners or by other Navaho priests so trained). In Lukachukai and Mexican Springs, relations with neighboring communities are important and outside priests of little importance. In Tohatchi, Divide Store, and Sawmill, Oto contacts become more prominent, and one Yuchi was active. Greasewood similarly shows an Oto impact, and in Black Mountain, although initial influences were Cheyenne and Ute, Oto contacts were at least as important in the 1950's.

Ultimately, then, Navaho peyotism has been most strongly influenced by the Cheyenne and the Oto, Cheyenne influence being prominent in the north and Oto in the south.

CHART F

COMPARISON OF NAVAHO PEYOTISM WITH LA BARRE'S PLAINS VARIORUM
(1938, pp. 57–92)

Item (La Barre Paragraph Heading)	Comments
Vowing of meetings.	Unknown.
Time of meetings.	Commonly Saturday night.
Purpose of meetings.	Discussed elsewhere. No objection to white participants on ideological grounds. Whites should be well disposed. Attendance at curing meetings sometimes discouraged.
Visiting.	Navaho peyotists enjoy visiting other tribes and being visited.
Place of meeting.	Hogans principally, canvas tipis rare but prestigious, meeting in summer shade (ramada) observed. Special buildings, meeting in unroofed canvas circle, or circle of sticks or windbreak not observed.
Painting.	No face- or body-painting observed.
Clothing and headdress.	Treated previously. Peyote jewelry and beadwork often worn, Plains or Navaho manufacture.
Economics.	For 1930's La Barre cites $2.50–$5.00 per 1,000 from Laredo dealers. 1950's prices $10.00–$12.00 per 1,000. For 1930's La Barre cites $6.00–$10.00 for groceries for meeting, $15.00 for meeting. Navaho estimates for 1950's are $50.00–$75.00. Rises undoubtedly affected by increase in cost of living.
Feathers.	Peyotists are eager to own their own fans and rattles.
Ashes.	Elaborate ashbirds built by the fire chief are much admired.
Smoking.	Among the Oto peyotists there was an early anti-smoking movement, but Jonathan Koshiway later returned to the use of tobacco. The Oto influence on the Navaho is not anti-tobacco.
Prophecy.	Peyote used for divination: to discover whether someone will recover from illness, to find a lost horse, and, during livestock reduction, to discover what the Bureau's plans were.

Much of this chapter has dealt with special variants of peyote ritual in a restricted area—Shiprock, Red Rock, Cove, and Sanastee. In that area there seem to be certain minor syncretistic trends, movement of peyote ritual in the direction of Navaho ritual. The emphasis of the chapter should not obscure the fact that the ritual of Navaho peyotism resembles very closely that of various Oklahoma peyotist groups. It is the identity of Navaho ritual with what might be called standard peyote ritual which should be stressed.

Chapter 11

SYMBOLISM; BELIEFS AND VALUES (I)

W**E TURN NOW TO THE SYMBOLISM** of various objects used in the peyote ritual, a topic to be dealt with cautiously. Sometimes a road man—the principal source of information—claims not to know the meaning of a ritual object because he regards himself as genuinely ignorant on this point. Sometimes he feels that the anthropologist is not ready for knowledge. Sometimes he would prefer that the anthropologist, like cult members, should discover meanings through eating peyote and reflecting on the ritual or having a vision. Road men may have more information on one occasion than on another, as a result of visits to Oklahoma and instruction there, or as a result of their own illuminations. Meanings are not regarded as standardized and official: the private illumination of road man or lay member has validity. Finally, as in other religions, the simple objects of the peyote ritual can be invested with a complex of multiple meanings. In this inheres part of their appeal. (I am indebted to Victor Turner for discussions on this point.) Water, fire, earth, herbs, and food are materials which can be invested with many symbolic meanings. The more numerous the meanings, the richer the ritual for the participants. So a point-for-point exegesis of the meaning of ritual objects or rituals is not to be expected, and further information would have emerged from further field work.

The discussion that follows is based on the comments of road men. It is not legitimate to infer that the meanings discussed are all known to the average member of the cult.

One complex of ideas associates the ritual with nature, and, as it were, embeds the worshipper in the world of nature. Mike Kiyaani says in his account that there are various stories as to why the altar is shaped like a moon: "You may say that it's the universe." Ambrose Lee speaks of man as having come from the moon ("Proceedings of the Meeting of the Advisory Committee, Navajo Tribal Council" [that part of the minutes of the meeting dealing with the Native American Church], Window Rock, Arizona, May 16–18, 1950, mimeo., p. 36), but this interpretation is challenged by Hola Tso (*loc. cit.*). As has been said, Howard Gorman, non-peyoist, prepared a report for the Tribal Council in 1940 which appears to contain an account of a peyote meeting dictated by a road chief (TC, June 3–6, 1940, pp. 13–17). The account seems to be of a Cheyenne meeting in the style of John P. Hart, since cigarette butts are placed against the moon by each worshipper, rather than collected by the fire chief. The account says, "The symbol of the quarter moon typifies the female from which all things come; the mother earth; Navajo mothers; female rain" (p. 13). These statements alone suffice to show that *the* meaning of the moon cannot be pinned down; it is far too variable. Inspection of peyotist sources for other tribes would increase the variability.

There would, however, be general agreement on the line which is drawn from tip to tip of the top surface of the crescent moon: it is the peyote way, the proper path of life and conduct which a man should traverse. It is also identified with human life, from birth to old age.

According to Mike Kiyaani, we depend on fire and water; so they appear in the ritual. According to *David Morton,[1] sage appears because it is an old American Indian remedy; Indians once doctored just with sage. According to *Edgar Meridith, peyote, sage, and cedar are all green; they don't die; they keep you going, keep your flesh from withering. The prayers in Chapter 9 stress man's dependency on water, water as the source of all life, and the identification of water with purity. As for the feathers, *Charlie Rodman says, "We use fans and blow the whistle and think that there are four great birds at the four directions which bring power into the meeting. The ashbird is tied up with the four birds of the directions. The chief peyote is his eye, the sticks of the fire his tail, and the poker his legs."

*David Morton says that the gourd, staff, and sage (which pass together around the meeting) are like a person who talks to you. Mike Kiyaani also says that the fire is a person who doctors, and that fire is something on which we depend. Peyote, mother earth, and water he identifies with woman.

*Fred Goodman says that the drum helps to have our prayers received in heaven, that the rope signifies a holy road and true way of life, the rocks used to bind the drum are for protection, the drumstick for lightning, and the staff for old age. In the meeting he describes, water is also identified with blood and by clear implication with the life principle.

It is worth mentioning that virtually every comment about the meaning of the ritual and of the equipment in my notes stems from my records of the eleven peyote meetings I attended. Each such meeting was regarded by the road chief as an occasion to instruct me; other occasions were not.

It would undoubtedly be possible to discover a great many more standardized, private, or even disputed meanings of the items of peyote equipment. The examples supplied are illustrative, not definitive. What seems to be important is that by its symbolism peyote religion is made a part of nature, that the Indian participant is seen as a "natural" man of this earth, not an artificial product—like a white man, and that the peyote way is associated with this natural order. A peyotist may not take a clear philosophical position that the peyote way of life is part of a harmonious moral and natural order, but there is certainly a strong and indissoluble association between nature, the Indian, and the ritual and morality of peyotism. In this connection, *Leonard McKenzie's remark is appropriate. He said that non-peyotist people said that the religion was all right, but the peyote was not. But he said that the peyote is the very center, the way we reach God. It sits on the altar, and without it we would become confused. We are humble and sit upon the ground, whereas the white man has fine churches, and gold and silver.

Within this framework of the Indian as a part of nature, and peyote ritual as associated with the natural order, the individual is clearly free to seek his own interpretations regarding the ritual and its objects. On several occasions I have

[1] Asterisk preceding a proper name indicates a pseudonym.

been asked to deliver one or another prayer at or after a meeting; on such occasions I have used the symbols that came to my mind to join the occasion and the ritual, and in each case my interpretations have been accepted.

A few other comments on ritual meanings may be added. The burning of cigarette butts seems to convey both the meaning of the destruction of past sin and the "delivering" of a prayer. Brushing with a fan, smoking with cedar smoke, and drinking water are all associated with purification and cleansing—although for some people it may be purification from sin, and for others from ritual pollution or witchcraft. Singing and drumming are considered equivalent to prayers. One man states that the hogan may be divided into quadrants, but the seating arrangement suggested thereby is not followed. In the southeast quadrant are probationers, those still "being examined" by peyote. In the northeast are "students." On the northwest are "patients," the "death chamber" from which people hope to emerge. And on the southwest are cured patients. This is probably a private interpretation.

Whatever the past symbolism of peyotism, Navaho peyotism is explicitly Christian. The sign of the cross is used in the road chief's gestures with the midnight and the morning water. Although Navahos have not mentioned it, the passing of a cigarette butt from fire chief to road chief to drummer chief, back to road chief and cedar chief, makes a cross (cf. La Barre, 1938, p. 51). Prayers mention God, Jesus, Mary, and the Heavenly Angels. For individual Navahos this may be unimportant; for some, these beings may be syncretized with Navaho sacred figures; but for road chiefs, in the main at least, peyotism is Christian.

We come now to the difficult question of the chief peyote itself. Its meaning in the ritual is highly variable. It is, without doubt, the center of the meeting. *Dan Pritchard, a road chief who had worked many years for missionaries, says that *Edgar Meridith, another road man, prays to peyote as a divinity. But *Edgar told me that he prayed to God, but not to Jesus—he went direct to the source of power. I did not ask him point blank if peyote were a divinity. For some Navahos peyote is an intermediary; for some it is an independent power. For at least one, peyote is "nothing," just a sign, and God is everything. I have been told on two separate occasions that the chief peyote (on the altar) is like a telephone switchboard, or a telephone operator, through which a connection with God may be achieved.

I think that it would be inaccurate to attempt to set forth *the* meaning of the chief peyote for Navahos. It can be *the* power, with God a dim and shadowy figure, *a* power, a means to power, a means of communicating with God, or a sacrament and symbol only. Answers would vary both among road chiefs and among the laity. For some peyotists, peyote is the blood of Christ: they believe that the plant first grew where His blood fell from the cross.

By the same token, the power of the peyote consumed during the meeting would be subject to divergent interpretations: a medicine, a power, a crucial accompaniment to prayer and reflection, a path to communication with God, an aid to prayer answered by an all-powerful God. *Dan Pritchard, who believes in the value of peyote for curing illness, has been pestered by people who wish to be forced to give up drinking by using peyote. He answers, "I cannot stop you from drinking, peyote cannot stop you from drinking; only *you* can stop yourself from drinking."

It is certain that had I questioned more, I could have accumulated more elaborate interpretations of ritual and ritual equipment. The key point, however, is the open, flexible, and multiple nature of the interpretation of these matters. Peyotism has among its members people who have spent seven years interpreting for missionaries and those who have never been inside a church, Navaho singers who know several chantways and people who say they know nothing about any Navaho ceremonial, young college students and men in their seventies who speak not a word of English, people who wish only to continue Navaho farming and herding and people whose income is based only on employment. Its flexible and multivalent symbolic system permits the cult to satisfy all of them without too much conflict.

We have examined the peyote experience, the occasions for peyote meetings, and peyote prayer and ritual for the light they cast on the beliefs and values of peyotists. When we turn to direct verbal expressions of these beliefs and values, the data become more difficult to deal with. For one thing, beliefs vary among members. For another, most peyotists—at least when they talk to an anthropologist through an interpreter—are not too concerned with detailed philosophical discussions of beliefs. Often I asked Navahos, "What are the main teachings of this Church?" or "What are the main things you have learned from this Church?" or, in desperation, "What are the main things you like about this Church?" The answers were brief and simple, although much can be learned from them. English-speaking peyotists, on the contrary, would discuss beliefs and values at length. Not only was there no severe language barrier between us, but in addition many of these informants had close contact with Oklahoma road men and had heard a lot from them.

So, at the simplest level, there seem to be some Navaho peyotists for whom it is sufficient that they "got well on peyote." It is a cure and a protector, and that suffices for them. At the most complex level are peyotists who are concerned to decide whether the peyote chief on the altar is a symbol, a power, or a spiritual being, and who know that prominent peyotists differ on this question. Hence I cannot state *the* beliefs of *the* peyotists. I shall begin by presenting a general description of beliefs and values synthesized from discussions with my most articulate informants and from comments made at peyote meetings I attended. This general description, then, is more a summary of the view of leaders in the Navaho cult than of the view of followers.

1. *The nature of the supernatural.*[2]—The cosmos is ruled by God, a Supreme Being above all other spiritual beings such as Mary, the Heavenly Angels, the Navaho Holy People, and so on. The peyotist believes in an omnipotent spiritual force and, following Swanson, I shall refer to this as monotheism (Swanson, 1960, pp. 55–56).[3]

[2] I am indebted to Thomas F. O'Dea for discussions which brought out the immanent character of Navaho supernaturals by contrast with the transcendent nature of the peyotists' God. The treatment which follows has also been influenced by Florence Kluckhohn's approach to value orientations, although I have not used her categories systematically (F. Kluckhohn, 1961).

[3] "Judaism, Christianity, and Mohammedanism are monotheistic beliefs, not in the sense that God is the only supernatural being, nor in the sense that God forces all supernatural beings into a monolithic uniformity of desire and function. Instead, they are monotheistic religions in specifying God as the first cause of all effects and the necessary and sufficient condition for

The terms used for God in prayers reflect this monotheistic trend (see Appendix, Vocabulary). He is called by the term used by the Franciscans for God, the Supreme Being or the Supernatural Who is the Great One; the Leader of Supernatural Beings; the First (Foremost) Supernatural Being. He is also called the Holy Spirit, and Our Holy Father Who Saves People (but in the sense of saving them from danger, not from sin). And He may be called, "My Mother and My Father," by a worshipper who will speak of himself or of the group as "Your infant(s)" or "Your child(ren)." Several of these terms approach as closely as the Navaho language now permits to the conception of a Supreme Being. And He is also called "God," even by Navahos who speak no English.

There are other spiritual beings: Jesus Christ, the Virgin Mary, and the Heavenly Angels. I have not heard the Holy Ghost discussed, but He may appear in prayers. Navaho and English terms are used for these beings, but Navahos who do not speak English sometimes use English terms. And the Navaho Holy People are undoubtedly still a part of the world of spirit for many Navaho peyotists. When they are asked about the relationships of these beings to God and the Christian spiritual beings, they reply that they are all the same thing, or all part of the same thing. No further elucidation is forthcoming.

Peyote is a spiritual entity. Sometimes it is called Holy Spirit, the same phrase used for God but presumably distinguished by context. It is also called Holy Medicine, or just medicine. It must be remembered that in Navaho the word for medicine refers primarily to any herbal medicine, but also to any ceremony and to any material used ceremonially: charcoal for blackening the patient, the singer's paraphernalia, and so on (Haile, 1950b, pp. 22–23). Traditional Navahos and peyotists alike view "medicine" as something that sets right a disturbed state of functioning for the individual by means of both spiritual and organic processes—difficult to separate in any case. In a peyote ceremony various descriptive terms for peyote are used, some of which carry the sense that peyote is all-seeing.

God is over all. He is transcendent, not immanent. He is above nature and controls it. He created the world and man. The God worshipped by the peyotists is the same one worshipped by Catholics, Protestants, Mormons, and Jews—and, for Navahos who know of non-Western creeds, the same God as is worshipped by people all over the world. For most Navaho peyotists, peyote is a substance, a power, and a being given by God to the Indian. There is some difference of opinion on this point, however. A very few peyotists seem to regard peyote as the Supreme Being; a few see it as a symbol. Some road men are concerned to deny that peyote itself is worshipped.

In addition to the supernatural, personal powers of God, other spiritual beings, and peyote, there is the supernatural power of witchcraft. Although no Navaho

---

reality's continued existence" (Swanson, 1960, p. 55). It should be noted that Judaism has angels and devils as additional supernatural beings, and Catholicism angels, devils, and saints. Whereas I have not interrogated peyotists as to whether God is "necessary and sufficient condition for reality's continued existence," they certainly conceive of him as creator and as omnipotent in man's affairs. I regard this as implicitly fitting Swanson's criteria, and so regard peyotism as monotheistic, even though (as in other Judaeo-Christian religions) there are other spiritual beings. Christian missionaries would not accept this definition.

has thus described it to me, this must be conceived of as impersonal power manipulated by malevolent human beings (rather than, for example, power derived from a satanic, personal figure and used by human beings). Many Navahos believe that peyote can overcome illness caused by witchcraft, and they are encouraged in this belief by at least some peyote priests, who will diagnose witchcraft and sometimes name the witch for a patient. Some peyotists hold that a person who takes peyote cannot remain a witch. And some peyotists claim that through peyote they have learned that there is no such thing as witchcraft. At any rate, in one way or another, peyote controls the effects of this power or eliminates the fear of it.

There is one more significant type of supernatural power: the ghost. According to traditional Navaho belief, all, or most, people give rise to a ghost when they die. Since both experts and Navahos disagree about the characteristics of ghosts, the topic cannot be handled definitively. Apparently ghostliness inheres both in a spirit entity which remains on earth after a person dies and in the corpse and its clothing. At any rate, persons and things may become contaminated by contact with a corpse, a grave, etc., or may be undesirably affected by wandering ghosts. These may be the ghosts of anyone, although sometimes ghosts trouble those close to them if they are not buried properly or with sufficient grave offerings. But a ghost's capacity to do harm is not a function of his mortal personality nor of his kinship connections with the living nor of his friendly or unfriendly relationships when he was alive. Ghosts of Navahos can cause illness and death, as can ghosts of aliens ("enemies"—non-Navahos), and different chants are used for the two types of ghosts. In one way or another, peyotism removes the potency of these ghosts—whether by assuring the peyotist that there are no ghosts, but only souls, or by giving assurance that the power of God and peyote can remove ghost sickness, like all other sickness.

2. *The nature of man.*—Man is neither good nor evil. He is all too human—he is weak. Perfect behavior is not to be expected of him, since he is human. (There is variation in belief here. The V-way practitioners seem to believe in the possibility of absolute purity. Some road men, however, have no concern about sexual misdemeanors—it is normal for weak humanity to err.) Some peyotists seem to believe that Indians are particularly weak. Rom. 14:2–3 is often cited to justify the use of peyote. "For one believeth that he may eat all things: another, who is weak, eateth herbs. Let not him that eateth despise him that eateth not; and let not him which eateth not judge him that eateth: for God hath received him." Peyote, they say, is a herb.

Man has an immortal soul, which returns after his death to God and a heavenly dwelling place, or perhaps to a new life on earth. But some peyotists believe that peyotists have good souls that go to heaven, whereas non-peyotists have ghosts that go around making people ill. I have heard no discussion of hell, damnation, or eternal punishment.

Indians are a part of nature, close to it, embedded in it. Whites have separated themselves from nature.

3. *The relations between the supernatural and man.*—God, who created the world and man, is God for all men, loves all men, and cares for all men. As there is but one Supreme Being whom all humans worship, so all men form a unity:

men of all colors are all human and all equal—"God created man with five fingers." Man exists because of God's will, not through some casual act of a demi-urge. God put man on this earth for a purpose. Man fulfills this purpose by good and careful behavior; specifically, men fulfill it by taking care of their bodies, their material possessions, and their families. Aimless or careless behavior, which shows a lack of care for one's own future or the well-being of one's family, is purposeless and bad.

There is a special relationship between God and the Indian, and specifically between God, peyote, and the peyotist. Peyote and the peyote way were given to the Indians as their path to God, as other ways were given to other people. Through peyote man communicates with God. God and peyote are to be approached humbly and besought for help. The peyotist recognizes that he is helpless and that God is all-powerful. The peyotist is like a child crying to its parents for something it wants. But, given God's purpose for man, the peyotist is not to wait passively for God's help, but instead to recognize that he is on this earth for a purpose and strive to fulfill that purpose.

Unless the peyotist is good, peyote will "work hard against him" during the peyote meeting—the effects of peyote will be unpleasant. Some peyotists would say that vomiting in the meeting is a sign of sin. Others would say that it was rather a purge of "bad stuff," such as sickness, effects of witchcraft, etc. Still others would say, more prosaically, that vomiting is a result of eating too heavily just before a meeting. Although, as I have said, I have heard no mention of hell or damnation or of punishment more severe than discomfort in a peyote meeting, it is clear that God will not favor the sinner, but instead the peyotist who tries to be good and who seeks His help.

Peyote is sacred and not to be used for curiosity or amusement, nor casually by people who are not members of the church. It is to be taken ritually, in the right place, at the right time, in the right manner, and for a purpose. It is a sacrament. A member may take peyote outside of meetings for curative purposes.

Through eating peyote, participating in the ritual, praying, and concentrating, the peyotist gets access to supernatural power. This power will cure the sick, ward off misfortune, give insight into the future, and supply knowledge about the world and the cosmos such as a white man gets through education and reading. Through this power he may be cured of ills caused by witchcraft—or may learn that witchcraft has no power or that there are no real witches. Through the teachings of the Church he also learns not to fear ghosts.

4. *The relations between man and man.*—A peyotist should take care of himself and of his family. (This follows from the fact that he was put on this earth for a purpose.) Therefore he should not drink, since he may injure himself or neglect his family. He should work hard and plan for the future. He is responsible for his family. Most members would say that he should not commit adultery. He should train his children in the peyote way, since it is not just a teaching for today but for coming generations.

He should help his fellow church members of whatever tribe, when they are in need of assistance. Differences of ritual should not become a serious issue, since all cult members eat peyote and worship the same God, and these are the essentials.

He should be a man of peace. One of the good results of a peyote meeting is the feeling of fellowship which prevails the morning after a meeting. A member should not quarrel, fight, or backbite. He should turn the other cheek when he is criticized by non-believers. Since all men worship the same God, it is acceptable for a peyotist to join with any congregation in their worship of God. Exclusive membership in the Native American Church is not demanded. When he prays, a church member should not seek good only for himself, his family, or even his church or his tribe. His prayers must widen out, beginning with himself, to include his family, his church, his tribe, all Indians, all Americans, and all mankind—even his enemies (the so-called "prayer circle").

5. *Some supplementary comments.—*

a) *Sin and moral responsibility.—*In discussing bad behavior, many peyotists speak of sin. In the peyote meeting, one confesses sins. The very notion of sin is non-traditional. In 1949, *Dan Pritchard, a road man who had had the experiences of starting an apprenticeship as a singer and of working many years as an interpreter for a missionary, said to me, "It's a wonderful thing to see old Navahos on their knees, praying—praying for salvation and forgiveness of sin." Navaho religion, he said, lacked the conception of sin, and traditional Protestantism, in his experience, led Navahos neither to the conviction of sin nor to the search for salvation. (Later, however, in 1953, he said that he had become disturbed because he worked all night as a road man for the salvation of young Navahos, who went out and got drunk the following Saturday. Subsequently he left peyotism for the Baptist Church.) Most Navahos, whether or not they speak of sin, would agree that through peyotism they should come to moral reflection and moral action. Yet there is another, more magical and compulsive view of peyote: some Navahos believe that taking peyote will remove the desire to drink, or perhaps the possibility of drinking—since "peyote and alcohol don't mix."

b) *Universalism and Indianism.—*In theory, peyotism preaches the equality and humanity of all mankind under God, and seems to teach that all religions worship the same God and are therefore equal—although peyotism is peculiarly appropriate for the Indian. In practice and for entirely understandable reasons, peyotists tend to have very strong anti-white feelings. The white man's materialism, greed, and domination of the Indian, the Indian's poverty, misery, and oppression, are frequently described—especially to the anthropologist. The white man is also seen as daring to penetrate too far into nature's secrets, and as war-like—because of his greed. This theme was especially prominent during the Korean War. Some peyotists believe the whites will eventually destroy themselves, but the Indians will survive.

One Navaho from Montezuma Creek, in close contact with Mormons but hostile to them, seems to combine Mormon and peyote themes. In 1952, he wrote me to ask whether it were not true that the Navahos were the lost ten tribes. He wanted to know whether the domination of the "gentiles," the whites, would not eventually terminate, and whether the Korean War was not caused by the gentiles.

c) *Peyote as cure.—*It would be a mistake to think of peyote curing as operating only through the spiritual power of peyote, only through communication with God through peyote, or only through peyote as a substance. Peyote is a power;

God is a power. In a curing ceremony the prayers of the officiants (road chief and others), of participants, and of the patient; the singing and drumming; and the ingestion of peyote by the patient and the others are all contributory to a cure. The special rolled peyote prepared by the road man is particularly efficacious because it has been sanctified. After eating peyote, participants are likely to spit into their hands and then rub and pat the head, chest, and limbs to absorb the virtues of the medicine. Peyote was used by one woman as a poultice for her son's open sore, the result of osteomyelitis. Thus its effects are achieved by ritual, by ingestion, and by absorption.

Because peyote's powers are thus broadly conceived, it is thought of as a catholicon. Among the conditions for which cures have been claimed by my informants are insanity, tuberculosis, diabetes, high blood pressure, appendicitis, blindness, rheumatism, general malaise, colds, localized aches and pains, and ill-defined nervousness, anxiety, and depression. Yet in most cases peyotists do not refrain from the use of Western or Navaho curative practices.

d) *Activism and dependency.*—The peyotist acknowledges that he is as helpless as a baby, crying to its mother or father for candy. When he prays, he cries in recognition of his dependency. It is therefore worth stressing that no peyotist has ever said anything to indicate that he expects to sit back and let God take care of him. On the contrary, the necessity to strive is emphasized repeatedly, and the capacity to gain a sense of purpose in life from peyotism is often stressed. There are certainly lazy peyotists, as well as energetic ones, but retreat into reflection and passivity is not found in my experience; nor is God's help ever used as a rationalization for inactivity.

Chapter 12

BELIEFS AND VALUES (II)

THE PREVIOUS CHAPTER dealt largely with the views of sophisticated peyotists. The sophisticated peyotists are, however, a relatively small proportion of the cult's Navaho membership. There are a very large number of peyotists who are less sophisticated and who have incorporated only a part of this system of beliefs. It proved difficult to elicit their views by direct questioning. I shall attempt to state something of the range of views here and will then pass on to other sorts of evidence for beliefs.

These peyotists would agree that peyote is a great power, not only for curing, but also for understanding the world and one's place in it. Peyote is thought to be superior to Navaho ceremonies, since, by their own claim, so many peyotists have entered the cult to be cured after every effort to cure them by Navaho ceremonies had failed. The same attitude is found in most instances toward American medicine. There would be belief in a Supreme Being, but Navaho spiritual beings might well be considered to be much the same as this Being, and issues of a hierarchy of beings would be of little concern. The view that helpless man implores peyote and God for help and receives it would be widespread, and acceptance of some conception of sin, confession, and purification would be common, since these are expressed in ritual. Belief in peyote as protection against witchcraft would be widespread. Pan-Indianism would be weakly developed, but visiting peyotists from other Indian groups would be much respected.

REASONS FOR FIRST USING PEYOTE

We may approach the issue of the ideology of the ordinary peyotist in more detail, and with more supporting data, first by a consideration of the reasons for recourse to peyotism, and then by considering the reasons given for its sustaining appeal.

In the vast majority of cases, initial recourse to peyotism is for the purpose of being cured, or occurs when a member of one's family of orientation or of procreation is ill and is taken to a peyote ceremony. This is true of both members, former members, and people who tried peyote only once or twice. Curing one's self or a family member accounts for about three-quarters of all instances. Since cases where it is not clear from the interview whether curing was involved are tabulated as other than curing, the percentage may in fact be higher—perhaps 80 per cent or so. There is some variation among communities, but the only striking deviation is found in Black Mountain, where an unusually large number of individuals joined for other than curing reasons—a point discussed in somewhat more detail below. The figures do not vary greatly between the non-random samples from more than 7 areas and the random samples from two communities.

In cases involving curing, a fairly common narrative is of this sort: "I (or a relative of mine) was very sick. I (he) was getting down; I (he) had tried all sorts of sings and they did no good. I had spent (we had spent) everything on these ceremonies, and our livestock was getting down to nothing." Sometimes a Pueblo sucking doctor had also been used. At this point, the subject decided to use peyote. Perhaps he knew of it, perhaps someone now suggested it to him. He might attend a ceremony in his home community or a neighboring one, might arrange for one at his own home, or might go to the Utes, since their use of peyote is known. In some cases, however, he might go to the Utes for a sucking cure and be induced

TABLE 15

REASON FOR FIRST USE OF PEYOTE*

COMMUNITY	CULT MEMBERS		FORMER MEMBERS OR CASUAL USERS	
	Curing Self or Family Member	Other or NA	Curing Self or Family Member	Other or NA
Greasewood.............	18	3	5	3
Black Mountain..........	19	9	1	1
Teec Nos Pas............	13	3	0	1
Lukachukai..............	8	0	3	0
Red Rock–Cove..........	19	5	5	1
Dinnehotso.............	5	2	0	0
General Northern........	7	4	0	0
Aneth†..................	13	5	0	2
Mexican Springs†.......	5	1	4	1
Miscellaneous...........	3	0	1	0
Totals................	110	32	19	9
Per cent..............	77	23	68	32

* Key: Tally of virtually all interviews among peyotists, non-peyotists who tried peyote, and casual users of peyote. Communities listed in order in which field work was done, except for General Northern (which includes Shiprock and environs and non-random interviewing in Aneth). Greasewood is Greasewood Springs, below Ganado. Percentages shown in tables are for Member and Former Member, etc., categories, separately. For all cases, 76 per cent entered the cult to cure themselves or a family member.

† Random samples.

by the Utes or by Navahos visiting them to try peyote. Members usually report that recovery followed.

In some instances, further interrogation reveals that the respondent now believes that witchcraft was responsible for the illness. Sometimes, indeed, one or more of the people who performed Navaho ceremonies is accused of witchcraft.

My informants mentioned witchcraft as the cause of the condition that led them to try a peyote cure in 13 per cent of all cases tabulated. I omit from the tabulation cases of former members and people who tried peyote briefly; witchcraft is mentioned in none of these instances. I also omit some interviews so brief that the issue could not have been raised. The range among communities is from none to as high as 50 per cent, in Lukachukai, where we are dealing with only 8 interviews. A larger sample might have lowered the percentage for Lukachukai. In three communities, there were interviews with several members of some families. Recomputation of percentages to show the number of families where witch-craft was involved supplies a somewhat higher percentage in each instance.

These figures, however, must be interpreted cautiously. Questions on this subject are delicate and could not be asked in all cases. Furthermore, my interest in this topic differed from summer to summer. Thus I was interested but cautious in 1949, when 9 per cent of all interviews involved mention of witchcraft; was not following up on this problem in 1950, when 10 per cent show such concerns; and was following the issue with some care in 1951 and 1952, when percentages rose

TABLE 16

CULT MEMBERS MENTIONING WITCHCRAFT,
NON-RANDOM SAMPLE*

	Witchcraft not Mentioned	Witchcraft Mentioned	Total	Per Cent Witchcraft Mentioned
Greasewood.............	18	3	21	14
Black Mountain..........	28	0	28	0
Teec Nos Pas............	15	1	16	6
Lukachukai.............	4	4	8	8
Red Rock–Cove..........	20	4†	24	17
Dinnehotso..............	5	2	7	29
General Northern........	11	0	11	0
Miscellaneous...........	2	1	3	33
Total................	103	15	118	13
1949 interviews.........	29	3	32	9
1950 interviews..........	47	5	52	10
1951 interviews..........	12	3	15	20
1952 interviews..........	15	4†	19	21
Total................	103	15	118	13
Lukachukai families.......	4	3	7	43
Red Rock–Cove families..	14	4†	18	22
Dinnehotso families.......	3	2	5	40
Totals................	21	9	30	30

* Key: Includes cult members only.
† One case of illness of livestock caused by witchcraft. Question not pursued in random samples, which are not tallied here.

to 20 and 21. These figures, then, must be taken as representing a minimum number of instances where the peyotist considers that witchcraft was at the root of the troubles that led him to peyotism. During the summer of 1952, some informants told me that in the course of their first peyote treatment, the road chief—or sometimes a Ute shaman who had induced them to try peyote—had informed them that witchcraft was at the root of their troubles. Hence we cannot now say with security that all of these individuals thought that their illness was caused by witchcraft *before* they attended their first peyote meeting.

It can be said, however, that Navahos tend to begin to make a diagnosis of witchcraft when a succession of cures has been attempted without success; so it is likely that in a good many of the cases where witchcraft was mentioned, and in a good many others, this suspicion was present.

Another attack on the question of the connection between suspicion of witch-craft and resort to peyotism is examination of the use of sucking cures by peyotists and non-peyotists. When a Navaho resorts to a sucking cure, he seems often to suspect that "dart-throwing" witchcraft has been practiced against him (Kluck-hohn, 1944). Not all cases of witchcraft require sucking cures, and not all use of sucking cures reflect a fear of witchcraft. Nevertheless, in many cases where I questioned further about the use of sucking cure, the informant indicated that it was used for relief from illness caused by witchcraft. It therefore seems probable that many of the Navahos who claim to have used a sucking cure before they turned to peyote—or in the process of first use of peyote among the Utes—con-sidered themselves at the time to be victims of witchcraft.

I have elsewhere presented evidence for a statistically significant association of resort to the sucking cure and use of peyote (Aberle and Stewart, 1957, pp. 37–40). This test, however, demanded that both peyotist and non-peyotist subjects be asked whether they had ever used a sucking cure, and that this question be asked of every subject. Correspondingly, it was impossible to raise the question of witchcraft with every subject, regardless of rapport, without running the risk of trouble in the community or in the remainder of the interview. Hence in the cases where a significant association was shown between resort to sucking cures and use of peyote, we cannot be certain that witchcraft was suspected, but we can be reasonably sure of this through Kluckhohn's work and through the considerable number of other cases where this connection was found.

On a number of occasions, non-peyotist Navahos informed me that the reason Navaho singers so disliked peyotism was that peyote "priests" were all too prone to accuse singers of witchcraft. One particularly reliable Navaho informant told me with bitterness and passion that when his daughter was dying of tuberculosis, the peyote "priests," summoned against his wishes, had informed him that such and such a man was bewitching his daughter. After she died, he asked them to leave. He thanked them for their efforts but asked them to go quickly, saying that an accusation of witchcraft such as they had made could have resulted in murder—and would have, if it had been believed. Hence in some cases the Navaho may learn as a result of peyotism that witchcraft was the cause of his ills. There are some peyote leaders who believe that this sort of talk about witchcraft should not occur, but it is by no means clear that in all instances this results from a rejection of witchcraft beliefs. In some cases, it certainly indicates only that the man be-lieves that such accusations make trouble and should not be uttered, even where witchcraft is suspected by the priest.

Thus far, then, it becomes evident that the initial appeal of peyotism is as a cure, that this cure is sometimes sought in desperation after all else has failed, and that suspicions of witchcraft are sometimes involved before the cure is tried, and are sometimes produced in the course of the cure. Other appeals become important as the individual gets indoctrinated in the beliefs and values of the cult, but it is safe to say that every peyotist whom I have ever encountered believes in the curative importance of peyote.

A statistical breakdown of the remaining reasons for entering the cult would not be particularly convincing, few as they are. One of the two commonest reasons other than curing is the desire for relief from some pressing personal misery. Especially at Black Mountain, but elsewhere as well, the individual may say that he "felt just lost," "didn't know what he was living for," "had no purpose," and so on. Some hoped to be stopped from drinking. One man entered in a mood of black despair after his son died. Some became disturbed as one after another member of their family died. The second common reason is simply a matter of family influence. It is not that the individual is urged by his family to enter and be cured or enter and be saved; rather, other family members indicate that they use peyote and it is good, and the respondent should do likewise. One man married into a peyotist family, and his father-in-law told him at the time that some day he would ask him to attend a peyote meeting. Subsequently he did so, and the young man began his participation. Other reasons are many but infrequently represented; perhaps curiosity is the commonest of these. "I went to see what it was like." Many of the "curious" satisfy their curiosity and attend no longer, but some remain to pray.

Since peyotism has now been present in the Navaho country for long enough so that some young people are raised as peyotists from childhood, we can expect more and more often that the reason for entry into the cult will be a matter of parental choice for children. At the time of the study, however, most entries were for crisis reasons—health or personal. The existence of even a small percentage of cases where a personal crisis provoked first attendance indicates, however, that dominant though curing may be, some non-peyotists were aware of other aspects of peyotism before they attended their first meeting.

SUSTAINING APPEALS OF PEYOTISM

Apparently, once people have entered the cult—in most instances for curing purposes—its meaning becomes much more differentiated for them, and its appeals more diverse. In my interviews, I asked most peyotist Navahos what were the principal good things about the Native American Church. The results do not lend themselves to any such straightforward tabulation as that previously presented. If one asks how it came about that a person entered the Native American Church, the result is a reasonably consecutive narrative, in the course of which the ostensible reason for the choice of peyote therapy emerges clearly. Seldom are compound reasons presented. If one asks about the principal good things connected with the Native American Church, the answer can be a sentence or a paragraph, can include one reason or a dozen, depending on the expansiveness of the informant, the quality of communication—a good or a mediocre interpreter, an informant with good or poor command of English, the time available, etc. Furthermore, the most pressing concerns of the informant may be expressed elsewhere in the interview. Coding presents parallel difficulties. Hence I shall not attempt a full and detailed analysis, but only a brief one which gives at least some picture of saliency.

To this end I have examined 104 interviews from 7 areas. (This disregards interviews with peyotists where no information on this score was secured.) I have eliminated Moore's interviews in Tohatchi and Teec Nos Pas, since the question used in his interviews does not distinguish between initial and sustaining appeals of peyotism. I have presented separately a random sample from two communities, where the coding differs slightly from that used in non-random interviews, but the results nevertheless are similar in general to the 104 non-random interviews.

A set of relatively limited categories useful for most interviews was developed empirically. In Table 17 I have included every case where any given reason was mentioned. Since some informants mention more than one, percentages are not cumulative: a man might praise the curative properties of peyote and say that it prevented people from drinking. His answers would appear in both categories.

Curing one's self or one's family, maintaining good health or a good mind are mentioned by a great many people, as are the anti-alcohol views of the cult and various other moral teachings. (Some of those who are most concerned with drinking are former heavy drinkers by their own account; some are light drinkers; one

TABLE 17

PERCENTAGE OF INFORMANTS IN 104 NON-RANDOM INTERVIEWS
MENTIONING VARIOUS "GOOD THINGS" ABOUT THE
NATIVE AMERICAN CHURCH

Item No.	Item	Percentage*
1........	Curing self	39
2........	Maintaining good health	7
3........	Keeping a good mind	7
4........	Curing family members	27
5........	Prevents drinking, teaches not to drink	45
6........	Various moral teachings	36
7........	Purpose in life	11
8........	Improving livelihood, including getting more stock or other direct aid from the Almighty	24
9........	Other	34

* Since informants might mention one or several of these, percentages are not cumulative.

young man had never tasted liquor.) The other moral teachings include sexual restraint, control of temper, and many other issues. A smaller number mention gaining a sense of purpose in life. Somewhat more mention improving their livelihood—a near-allied concern, since for most it involved a realization of the need to work harder, plan ahead, and take care. A few believed that God would send more stock or otherwise aid them. There were a very large number of other appeals, too diverse to categorize, such as the road chiefs' pleasure in curing other people, gaining knowledge, thinking, thinking about the future or about one's children's future, etc.

These responses may be grouped into exclusive categories, first by using a broader classification: any mention of curing (items 1-4 in Table 17); any mention of morality, including abstinence from alcohol (items 5, 6); any improvement of aim, including gaining a sense of purpose, focusing on improved livelihood, and some of the miscellaneous items (items 7, 8, some of 9). Informants can then be classified as to whether they mention one, or more than one of these major classes (Table 18). And non-cumulative totals of *any* mention of the broader categories are supplied (Table 19).

It then becomes apparent that whereas a majority of all informants are concerned with curing as a benefit of peyotism, only a minority are exclusively concerned with curing. On the other hand, relief from anomic feelings of aimlessness and of economic helplessness, is less frequently mentioned but is found in more than a third of all cases.

The two random samples contain somewhat different categories (Table 20), since the questions and the coding differed slightly. Curing bulks larger, if anything, and morality smaller. The random samples contain more new members than the non-random.

These tables justify the inference that most peyotists enter their first meeting to be cured, and nothing more. Thereafter, as they become involved in peyotist activities, they come to see the Native American Church as a combination of cure, ethical code, and inspiration for life.

TABLE 18

PERCENTAGE OF INFORMANTS IN 104 NON-RAN-
DOM INTERVIEWS MENTIONING VARIOUS
COMBINATIONS OF "GOOD THINGS" ABOUT
THE NATIVE AMERICAN CHURCH

Curing (1, 2, 3, 4)*..................	21
Morality (5, 6)*....................	22
Improved aims (7, 8)*...............	8
Curing and morality................	15
Curing and aims....................	8
Morality and aims..................	10
Curing, morality and aims..........	10
None of these.....................	7
Total...........................	101

* Numbers refer to items in Table 17.

TABLE 19

PERCENTAGE OF INFORMANTS IN 104 NON-
RANDOM INTERVIEWS MENTIONING VAR-
IOUS CLUSTERS OF "GOOD THINGS" ABOUT
THE NATIVE AMERICAN CHURCH*

All curing.........................	54
All morality.......................	55
All improvement of aims............	35

* Non-cumulative.

TABLE 20

PERCENTAGE OF INFORMANTS IN TWO RANDOM SAMPLES MENTIONING
VARIOUS "GOOD THINGS" ABOUT THE NATIVE AMERICAN CHURCH*

Item	Aneth (N = 20)	Mexican Springs (N = 9)
Curing (self or family, or curative value)...........	75	33
Appeal of ritual, belief, mystical experience, etc......	40	44
Magical powers of peyote other than curing.........	20	0
Morality..	10	11
All other..	5	6

* Non-cumulative.

AREAL DIFFERENCES IN IDEOLOGY

A further point in discussing the ideology of peyotism has to do with differences of accent in this ideology in different areas. I have not found a satisfactory way of coding interviews to bring out the differences. Where interviews are free, a topic may not be touched on by the interviewer in several interviews, may come up spontaneously in some of them, and thereafter may be elicited in still others if it becomes a focus of the anthropologist's attention. A quantitative analysis of this state of affairs is conceivable, but too laborious to be attempted for present purposes. The regional differences that I observed were primarily between northern and southern peyotists. These differences were called to my attention in the summer of 1950, when I worked first in the northern part of District 4 and then in Sweetwater and Teec Nos Pas in District 9. I have some faith in their validity for two reasons. The first is that one of my key informants subsequently volunteered the information that there was a major difference in outlook between the two areas and the second is the observation that non-Navaho peyotists of different tribal background are popular in the two areas.

In brief, northern Navaho peyotism stresses particularly the mystical and the magical aspects of peyotism. It is interested in revelations and mystical insights into the nature of the world, and there is more belief in the power of peyote to bring good fortune unaided by human endeavor. (I do not wish to imply that there is any tendency to wait apathetically on this account.) There is a much stronger anti-white sentiment—although it is hard to live for any length of time with peyotists without encountering some anti-white sentiment. There is less discussion of morality and more of the power of peyote.

Southern peyotism stresses contemplation and introspection, rather than revelation. It would not deny that God and peyote can bring good fortune, but its tenets favor learning that one must work hard to achieve success. There is less anti-white sentiment, and much more focus on the "teachings" of peyote, rather than just on its power.

I had formed this impression at the end of the summer of 1950. In July of 1951, I had an opportunity for a long talk with *Job Linnfield,[1] a key informant—the first peyotist I had ever talked to in the Navaho country, in 1949, and a man who had subsequently become a close friend of mine.

A sensitive, highly intelligent man and a gifted silversmith, he has a very good command of English. He was born in about 1913 and grew up in Cornfields, near Ganado, attending St. Michaels (Catholic) school and Government school. He completed the eighth grade at Santa Fe Indian School. He spent one year in the army during World War II. He regards himself as a Catholic and tries to send his children to St. Michaels for at least part of their schooling. He therefore resents the comments of some nuns there who criticize peyote. Since 1940, or perhaps earlier, he has held Government jobs, mainly in the schools, and most often as teacher-interpreter. Since around 1950 he has been employed in this capacity in an off-reservation school remote from the Navaho country. But he returns frequently to the reservation, where he travels widely during his vacations, and

[1] Asterisk preceding a proper name indicates a pseudonym.

he travels to Oklahoma as well. Although he had been instructed as a road chief, he had not begun to run meetings in 1954, saying that he was not yet ready. Thus he is an informant of broad background and experience. He speaks as a southern peyotist, and not as a detached observer, but his remarks are most illuminating.

According to *Linnfield, the northern peyotists follow Ute and Cheyenne ways. He thinks that these ways stem ultimately from Alfred Wilson. (From what I have seen elsewhere of Wilson's views, I would think it incorrect to attribute some of the northern attitudes to Wilson.) The northern group emphasizes the value of visions. They are much interested in seeing what bad things their fellow-members in a meeting may be doing to them, or thinking against them. (This is a not very veiled allusion to witchcraft.) There is a good deal of stress on arbitrary rules. These rules are not essential to a peyote meeting; it seems as if they just make them up. Thus *Edgar Meridith of Teec Nos Pas once refused admission to a man who had travelled all the way from Taos to attend a meeting in District 9 or District 12, because the man arrived late. *Edgar maintains that he is the only person who knows how to run a meeting properly, but when he is challenged to demonstrate, he fails to appear. There is relatively little emphasis on teaching and instruction in ethical standards in northern meetings.

The southern group is principally influenced by Oto road men (Jonathan (Jack) Koshiway and Truman W. Dailey in particular). It stresses good teachings and does not regard visions with enthusiasm. Indeed, *Job himself disapproves of visions. It accepts brief illuminations as of possible value, but believes that they must be carefully considered and thought about. Thus, *Job once got an idea during a meeting that he should not use much peyote that night because he was tired. He "was told" that he was just punishing himself, and that he should not do that. So he quit taking peyote for the rest of the night. This was not a voice or a vision, but an idea or illumination. "Something seemed to tell me." The southern group disapproves of thinking about what other people may be doing to you, and the associated suspiciousness that this implies. There is far less concern with "rule." According to *Job, the only important rule is not to step between the altar and a man who is singing, praying, or eating medicine. (Since this rule is designed to promote concentration and communication with God for the worshipper, it is highly relevant to the meeting, and not merely an arbitrary rule or item of etiquette.) The thing that keeps the meeting going is the drum; hence the drummer must not hit on the edge of the drum, he believes. It is important to keep one's mind on the right track. Talking, and walking between a worshipper and the altar confuse people.

The northern influence runs from Aneth and Shiprock, into District 9, and finally into District 4, through *Mal Hancock, taught originally by Navahos and subsequently by a Cheyenne. Tohatchi is also influenced by this style. The southern influence includes Gallup, Divide (near Window Rock, not Divide east of Gallup), Greasewood, and District 4 as well.

When the two groups get together, the meeting is likely to go badly. The northern group accuses the southern of being "half-white" in their ways. This concludes *Linnfield's remarks.

The division is not clean-cut, either as regards tradition or general attitude. Thus *Job mentions among the "northern" group *Ben Eastman, *Edgar Meridith, and *Charlie Rodman. *Charlie, one of the original Mancos Creek peyote priests, lives today at Crystal and thus provides a "northern" focus in the south. *Bill Rodman, *Charlie's older brother, another of the pioneers, lives at Divide. *Dan Pritchard of Shiprock conforms in general to what has been described as a "southern" attitude—indeed he has these attitudes more strongly entrenched than some of the southerners. He is particularly concerned with morality and teaching and has a minimum of interest in visions. (He left the cult in 1961 or before.) But the trend is there. Oto influence is on the increase in District 4, which could be described today as largely "southern" in attitude. The cleft does not merely appear when the two groups join for meetings. In a letter to me, a major organizing figure in the Native American Church of Arizona remarked at a time when peyotism was under serious pressure from the Tribal Council, that at last the northern and the southern groups had managed to "get together" to decide on action.

I would now be inclined to divide peyotist orientations into three approximately regional groups. The northern group would include Aneth, most of Shiprock, Beclabito, and much of Red Rock and Cove, all of District 9, and a small part of District 4. Probably part of District 10, where *Mal Hancock is influential, should be included. The southern group would include Divide Store, Window Rock, and most of Districts 18, 17, 7, and 5 (moving from east to west). Tohatchi, Naschitti, and Crystal would be mixed.

A third group, however, would be the V-way group, which combines a strong mysticism and concern with visions, a special ritual, and an intense preoccupation with moral purity. This includes a part of Shiprock, "Little Shiprock," portions of Red Rock and Cove, and Sanastee. It has no region which it dominates exclusively, but it is nevertheless fairly narrowly localized.

The place of District 11, much of District 10, and those portions of District 8 affected by peyotism is not clear to me. On areas further west and north I have no information.

The choice of Cheyenne and Ute, versus Oto guides appears to me to be selective and not to be determined by factors of geography. Early influences on Navaho peyotism were largely Ute and Cheyenne visitors to the Ute. Alfred Wilson (d. 1945) was active in this area and as far west as Lukachukai and as far south as Districts 14 and 18. When, how, and by whom Oto contacts were made, I do not know. But the Cheyenne influences are largely or wholly Southern Cheyenne, stemming from Oklahoma, as do the Oto contacts. The Oto group lives slightly further east in Oklahoma (around Red Rock), but access to the two Oklahoma groups is equally convenient from north or south in the Navaho country. Hence this pattern of selection, in which early Cheyenne and Ute influence in the south was replaced by Oto, must be a matter of local preference and mutual compatibility.

The Oto group has a long history of influence from fundamentalist Protestantism (Russellite and Mormon—cf. La Barre, 1938, 167–172). The Cheyenne group shows less of this impact.

Northern Navahos have a history of more marked direct opposition to whites and to the Indian Service, and southern Navahos of more acceptance of the situation in which they find themselves, with efforts to work within the framework that is given. It seems symbolically appropriate that the area which produced Black Horse's unprising, Ba-i-lil-ley's uprising, and a large number of arrests in the period of stock reduction should also be particularly interested in mysticism, magic, and especially strong nativism, whereas the area which produced Chee Dodge and which has experienced most benefits from its relations with the Agency and with the job market should produce a more moralistic, and more reflective peyotism.

Even departures from the general norm vary between the two areas. *Mal Hancock stems originally from District 9, but now lives at Rough Rock. He learned peyotism first in District 9 and then from a Cheyenne. I once saw him quite drunk at a squaw dance and was malicious enough to comment on his behavior to a peyotist friend who was with me. My friend was embarrassed, since he believed that peyotists should not drink, but he remarked that *Hancock's teacher did not preach abstention from alcohol. My friend implied that *Hancock's behavior was excusable, although my companion also insisted that abstention is a cardinal principle of peyotism.

In the south, however, sexual peccadilloes are more likely to be excused by the road chief than drinking. People whose record for wenching is considerable are very proud of their record of non-drinking.

By way of illustration of the differences between sophisticated and unsophisticated members, and between north and south, I have supplied four interviews—in an appendix—with a northern and a southern road chief, and with a northern and a southern layman (see Appendix, "Four Interviews").

SUMMARY: THE OSTENSIBLE APPEALS OF PEYOTISM

In concluding the treatment of beliefs and values, I shall summarize the ostensible appeals of peyotism to the Navahos, organizing in skeleton form the product of interviews, conversations, public records, and observations of peyote meetings, and including only conscious appeals mentioned by at least a few informants. Not all Navahos would find all these appeals important, but it is the multifarious nature of the appeals of peyote which has helped to maintain the religion as a viable and growing one over a period of more than seventy years.

First and foremost, peyotism supplies access to supernatural power. This power can be used to combat misfortunes, including illness, mental distress, poverty, and so on. It can be used to maintain good health and good fortune, and to seek good fortune in the future (for example, one may pray that one's children learn a lot in school). It can be used for access to knowledge: to diagnose the causes of illness and misfortunes, find lost objects, foretell the future, and guide man's actions toward the future. Furthermore, it can be used to understand the universe and the world. It can provide security against two of the most anxiety-provoking features of traditional Navaho belief—witches and ghosts.

Second, as an ideology, it assures some Navahos that Indians are at least equal to, and in some ways superior to whites—in knowledge, in wisdom, in spirituality, and in possession of a good religion—and superior to traditional Navahos. It supplies an ideological basis for antagonism to whites. It defines a purpose in life and meaningful relationships to fellow-men and the supernatural. It supplies a morality, including abstinence from alcohol. It insures a happy afterlife; but few Navahos stress this.

Third, the peyote experience serves to validate this conception of access to power and, through the feelings of personal significance, to underscore the ideology.

And so peyotism appeals to the person who seeks only cure after a crisis, to the disorganized and unhappy, to the alienated and marginal, to the philosopher, to the mystic, and to the person who seeks guidance and a sense of purpose and sustaining motive in the difficult situation that faces Navahos today.

Chapter 13

NAVAHO AND PEYOTE RELIGION CONTRASTED

IN SECTION II of this work, Navaho religion was briefly described; subsequently, the Native American Church has been discussed in detail. It is now necessary to compare the two religions at certain points to see the major differences in orientation between traditional belief and peyotism.

1. *The supernatural and man's relationship to it.*—Supernatural power is imma-nent in Navaho religion and largely transcendent in peyotism. The animals, plants, minerals, and mountains of the Navaho country are endowed with power: the world is endowed with spirit at every point. Man, nature, and supernatural are in-extricably interwoven. Spirit suffuses nature, and when a man undergoes a cere-mony he becomes, temporarily, a Holy Being. The powers of the Navaho super-natural system do not form a well-ordered hierarchy, even though Reichard could suggest that a sun-cult might underlie everything.

But for the peyotist, God is above all and controls all. *He* is not *in* nature, but man is embedded in nature. God rules both man and nature.

In Navaho religion, man's relationship to supernaturals is fundamentally one of reciprocity. By and large, if one can discover what gift will establish reciprocity with a spiritual being, and supply the gift, the being must respond. Hence super-naturals are angry in Navaho myths when a messenger spirit tells a man seeking help exactly what gift is wanted. Religious belief parallels traditional social life. One's existing relationships involve continuous reciprocity. To fail in reciprocity may be to terminate a relationship. But if no prior relationship exists, to accept a favor is to engender an obligation and start a new set of reciprocities. Therefore one should carefully consider such favors to others. A request from a stranger is not a demand and can be refused (save where a claim of kinship or clan kinship can be made). Since relationships involve continuous reciprocity, thanks are un-necessary: there will later be a return for any favor, voluntary or sought. Only un-usual favors merit a "thank you."

The peyotist deals with his all-powerful God by beseeching Him in humility: he can give Him no better gift than a contrite heart and the act of worship.[1] God re-plies to man's prayers because He is good and merciful and man is helpless and

[1] By implication I have defined reciprocity as an egalitarian relationship and thereby excluded hierarchical relationships from the sphere of reciprocity. This, however, is a matter of labels. In the transactions between superordinate and subordinate, the element of mutual constraint by prestation is weaker; rather, the superordinate can often constrain the subordinate by doing something for him or giving something to him, whereas the subordinate can merely hope to influence the superordinate.

Specifically, in the peyote ritual, every ritual cigarette is an offering to God. At certain points in the ceremony mother earth is given water. To me there is more of a flavor of reciprocity in the offering to mother earth; the cigarettes seem to be offerings, not gifts requiring reciprocity nor returns for favors.

God's child. No compulsions can be laid on God. Parallel to this is the peyotist conception that one cares for one's family and aids one's fellow-man. Although undoubtedly there is a great deal of reciprocity involved in this aid, the peyotist would like to think that his help is given voluntarily and received with gratitude (and peyotists thank profusely), rather than constrained by previous reciprocities or by kinship.

The traditional Navaho fears error in his rituals, and particularly error in the fixed prayers which the chanter and patient must repeat in the course of a ceremony. Error may not only render the ceremony ineffectual but may cause illness to the patient years later. The peyotist values spontaneity in his prayers. Although the observer can see patterns in them, the peyotist insists that they have no fixed formula—and certainly they are never rote prayers. Thus the traditional Navaho tries to bind power by formulae, while the peyotist tries to sway God by his fervor.

Navaho supernatural power is likely to harm man when man breaches various tabus, but these tabus have almost nothing to do with the moral order. If a man were to commit murder, he might have ghost trouble—but so might he if he worked in a hospital or happened to burn wood from a hogan where some one had died. His ghost trouble stems from ritual contamination, not from God's curse or the ghost's vengeance. Theft, adultery, deceit, assault, and rape have no supernatural sanctions. Sexual excess is a symptom of supernaturally caused illness, not the result of sexual misbehavior. Only incest is supernaturally punished. True, ceremonies are impaired if the singer becomes angry or there is quarreling at the ceremony. In this sense, there are supernatural sanctions against misbehavior—but only while the ceremony continues. On the other hand, the Navaho must fear the consequences of many accidental breaches of tabus—contact with lightning-struck wood, with anything somehow contaminated by the dead, with snakes, bears, etc.

The peyotists' God is interested in morality. Confession of sin is necessary to gain God's blessing and aid. If He does not punish, peyote at least "works hard" on the sinner during the peyote meeting. And God does not favor the stubborn sinner.

The traditional Navaho fears the body and spirit of the dead and fears witches. He is uncertain how he may cure witcraft-caused disease. The peyotist in theory believes in a heavenly spirit, does not fear ghosts (at least of peyotist dead), and, though he often fears witches, is sure of curing any witchcraft-caused disease.

2. *Purposes of ceremonies.*—The parallels regarding the aims of ceremonies are more striking than the differences. Both attempt to overcome misfortune, avert misfortune, and secure good fortune. Both use divination, but this is a part of peyote ritual, whereas it is separate from Navaho curing ceremonies. Both traditional and peyotist ceremonies ritualize marriage; both care for schoolchildren going away and returning, and for soldiers. I have never heard of a peyotist girl's puberty ceremony, whereas Navaho religion supplies one, and I do not know what is done by peyotists in connection with burial.

But peyotism has birthday and holiday meetings, which have no Navaho parallel, and ceremonies to thank God for past favors, a practice which again has no traditional analogue.

3. *Practitioners.*—There are similarities and differences in the nature of practi-

tioners—the Navaho singer, the peyote road man. The singer's power derives from learning, and from making an obligatory prestation to the man who teaches him the ceremony. (See Aberle, 1965, for a discussion of this point.) If, as is sometimes the case, a man has "picked up," or as some would say, "bootlegged" the ceremony by learning through observation and without prestations, his ability to produce results is in doubt. The critical prestation is made when the candidate has the ceremony performed with himself as patient and his teacher as practitioner. His subsequent effectiveness depends upon his replication of the sing without changes and upon his receiving a prestation whenever he performs.[2]

The peyote road man may just "pick up" the ceremony, but he certainly is held in higher regard if he has learned it with care from an experienced road man. He may return repeatedly to this road man to learn more. He does not "pay" for this, but he gives gifts out of gratitude, paralleling exactly the attitude of the patient and participants in the peyote ceremony. He also should have a ceremony performed for his benefit by his teacher to solemnize his full qualification as a road man. His teacher also "holds back," because it is not fitting that a man should learn all at once. But fundamentally, it is thought that peyote, not man, is the real teacher. By the same token, a man is free to vary the ceremony according to his own inspiration. Nevertheless, Navahos are concerned, at least initially, to get the ceremony "right" by repeated training with a particular road man, and some Navahos seem to collect "moons"—different rituals according to different traditions—just as a singer may collect chants. I do not know if this attitude is found among other peyotists. Certainly learning a peyote ceremony is far less demanding in time and sheer memory work than learning a Navaho ceremony.[3]

4. *Membership.*—Traditionally, to be a Navaho was to follow Navaho religion. Undoubtedly many non-Navahos who married into the tribe came to follow it as well. But Navahos have sung over Caucasians as patients—Reichard, Wyman, Matthews, and Roman Hubbell, at a minimum. And the Navahos seem to have thought of Washington Matthews as a man who learned the Night Chant as a singer would learn it, and who became paralyzed because he pronounced the prayers incorrectly, as a Navaho learner might have. Navaho Christians sometimes reject Navaho religion partly or *in toto*. In sum, normally Navahos follow Navaho religious practices and non-Navahos do not, but there are exceptions. There is no "membership." One uses, or does not use the ceremonies.

[2] He may delete portions, but he should not change portions. By the same token, he may, by persistence and payment, break down his teacher's tendency to "hold back" portions of the myth, ritual, song, and prayer. The teacher holds back partly to get such payments, partly to test his pupil's acuteness in seeking more information, and partly out of fear that when all his knowledge is transmitted, he will die.

[3] There is a source of anxiety for the potential road man that is lacking for the traditional singer. There is a quality of personal charisma in the role that is less developed in the case of the singer: the road man must be capable of taking the patient's pains into himself and must have confidence in his capacity to cure. Although he would claim that peyote brings about the cure, curing occurs also through the efforts of participants in the meeting, not least among these the road man. He must feel confidence in order to assume the role. Hence, I believe, *Job Linnfield's unwillingness to perform, several years after he had learned the ceremony. The salient contrast referred to above, however, is the difference in the amount of time it takes to learn to perform a Navaho ceremony correctly, as opposed to a peyote ceremony.

There is no organization of Navaho singers or diviners. Some singers know certain chants, others know others. The formalized role relationships in Navaho religion are the stable relationship between a singer and his apprentice (past or present), and the transitory relationships between a singer, his helpers, the patients, and the participants that arise for each ceremony and terminate at its conclusion.

There is an idea of membership in the peyote cult. Among other things, members of the Native American Church refer to themselves as "medicine eaters" ('azee' deiyání), and non-members are "non-medicine eaters" (doo'azee' deiyání). Consequently, when the anthropologist says, "I have eaten peyote but I am not a member of the peyote cult," his words are translated more or less as "I have eaten peyote but I do not eat peyote," or even, "I eat peyote but I do not eat peyote," statements which confuse his audience. The peyote church is called 'azee' bee hoogáałii, or "the peyote (lit. medicine) movement" (see Appendix, Vocabulary).

But membership and non-membership are not clear-cut categories. Some members believe that there should be a formal ceremony of joining the cult: a special peyote ceremony to signalize this act. Others say that this is unnecessary. Some have membership cards, depending considerably on whether the national organization has recently held a membership drive. Some Navaho users of peyote have no clear conception of membership in the Native American Church. They use peyote when the occasion arises. Some members divide the local group of peyote users into "real" members and others. "Real" members seem to combine advocacy, understanding of peyotism, and some conviction about following the moral teachings of the cult.

The Native American Church poses a problem for the Tribal Council, which does understand the idea of organization. It deals with mission organizations, granting or refusing mission sites, and thereby in theory controlling mission activities. It is very much put out by peyotism, an outside organization operating on the reservation, seeking no mission sites, and under no Tribal control save through raids and arrests. Similarly, in 1952 at least, the Council was disturbed by a few Mormon missionaries who traveled in trailers and sought no mission sites.

Finally, peyotism, with a transcendent God approached by his dependent worshippers and taking an active interest in their moral behavior, stands point for point contrasted with Navaho religion, with immanent spirit approached in reciprocity and punishing only for the transgression of tabus. Peyote prayers are spontaneous, Navaho prayers are compulsive spells. Peyotist dead have spirits which go to heaven; Navaho spirits stay around and make trouble or go to a drab and little-described afterlife. Both peyotists and Navahos fear witchcraft, but peyotists have a sure remedy. Peyotists are organized, Navaho religion is not. Both peyotists and traditionalists maintain for the most part that the two spheres of religious activity are distinct. Is there any evidence of syncretism?

SYNCRETISM

There is a little. Navaho singers in small numbers have taken up peyotism and in a few cases have become road men. They hold that there are many evidences of similarity between Navaho and peyotist ritual—a syncretism of a purely ideological character. They point to singing, drumming, use of feathers, plants, the all-night ritual, and so on, as similarities. They hold that the God of the peyotists and the holy beings of Navaho religion are "all part of the same thing" and for the most part are uninterested in further theological elaboration. They are undisturbed by the fact that peyote is not Navaho. I was eating lunch with one old singer, a peyotist, when I asked him how he felt about the importation of peyotism, since it was not "the old ways." He snorted. "I suppose you think these canned tomatoes are part of the old ways," he replied. Needless to say, non-peyotist singers challenge this view at every point. Peyotist singers have been known to mix peyotism in their own chants in the following ways: (1) in one case, providing peyote during a Navaho ceremony to a patient at the patient's request—which would normally occur only with a peyotist patient; (2) in at least one case, having the singer's pouch blessed at a peyote ceremony. Peyotist opinion on the whole favors keeping the two spheres absolutely distinct.

Road men, whether they are singers or not, claim that they do not import Navaho ceremonial devices into peyote ceremonies—songs, prayers, or ritual patterns. I have seen two road men who were also singers perform, and they did not deviate in any respect from normal peyotist practice. One of these was the man who gave peyote to patients at sings if requested to do so.

The learning of many "moons" may be a syncretic feature, borrowed from the Navaho practice of learning many chants.

"Pollen way," "star way," and "eagle way" are probably syncretic, but I have not observed them.

I am in no way inclined to believe that the focus on curing found among the Navaho is syncretic. It parallels the emphasis of Navaho religion, but curing is a very strong element in peyotism in every tribe and has been important from the 1880's on (cf. Schultes, 1938). The relative lack of stress on visions among southern peyotists also has many parallels elsewhere.

PEYOTISM AS A MEANINGFUL IDEOLOGY FOR SOME NAVAHOS

The contrast between peyotism and Navaho religion in many respects is marked. There are, however, a variety of reasons why this new religion is meaningful to some Navahos under present-day conditions, attracting them even though their traditional religion, quite different from peyotism, is still very much alive.

At the end of Chapter 12, the ostensible appeals of peyotism were described, in a summary based on direct statements by Navahos. The discussion of the meaningful appeal of peyotism which follows here is not a simple effort to summarize the conscious views of peyotists, but is far more interpretative, and correspondingly, more speculative.

Peyotism came on the scene when the natural and the social order among the Navahos was gravely disrupted. The natural order was disrupted as respects the balance of population, herds, and forage. The Navahos increased in numbers, herd-size, and area until little further expansion could occur without displacing Anglo and Spanish-American populations that had been filling in the same general semi-arid, pastoral niche. Population and herd-size continued to grow. The administrator's answer was to reduce herds and supply alternative modes of subsistence. The Indian Service was successful in reducing herds, in spite of Navaho opposition, but minimally succesful in finding other satisfactory modes of livelihood for Navahos. It was successful to the degree that Navahos were not starved to death.

From the Navaho point of view, the balance of nature was seen in different terms. Stock was given to them by the supernaturals. If they cared for their stock, the supernaturals would provide rain and thereby, pasture. Most of them argued until fairly recently that they were not over-grazed, but that when the livestock were taken away, the supernaturals also withheld the rain. Hence pasture also declined. From any point of view, something had gone dreadfully wrong. From the Navaho point of view, man, nature, and supernatural power were no longer in a relationship of mutually satisfying reciprocity.

Disruption of the social order followed both from livestock reduction and from decline in the external job and wool market. A man could not by effort, foresight, and ritual knowledge, support his family on the reservation. Of course, in the past by no means all Navahos could in fact support themselves, but failures were not attributed either to something generally out of kilter or to the Government. Improvidence, ignorance, laziness sometimes impoverished a man. So did the caprices of nature. So did such hazards as illness or a childless old age. But now through Government intervention the people were prevented from maintaining themselves.

The loose web of reciprocities had supplied economic aid in crises, had held together some of the larger aggregates within the community, and had supported ethical standards. Stock reduction damaged the network of reciprocity and thereby all these other features of social life.

In theory, and to a considerable degree in practice, kinship at its most extended range provided a cushion against all misfortune. If a man needed food, help, a horse, assistance in giving a ceremony, or anything else, he turned to his kin— immediate kin, members of his own clan, his father's clan, or his clan group, or even to his affines, close or remote. During periods of acute crisis, Indian agents sometimes commented that the needy would arrive at the home of someone with food, continuing there until there was no more. The major sources of supply for this reciprocity were farming and, much more important, herding. Now the herds were reduced, and the very materials for this reciprocity and mutual aid were done away with.

A man with many sheep gathered around him as informal dependents other families, who took a portion of his herd to manage, and in return were given part of the yield of the herd. They could be called on for cooperative ventures. The basis for these large units no longer existed. And at the same time, very large differences in status—between the man with a thousand head of sheep or more, and the man with no sheep, became very small differences—between the man with at most three hundred fifty stock units and the man with none. In most cases, the biggest difference was between those with just enough to live on by sheepherding and those with not enough to live on in this manner.

Navaho ethical standards were formerly supported to an amazing degree not by internalized sanctions, but by fear of reprisal, fear of withdrawal of support, and fear of shame. This state of affairs is found in its purest expression in Ladd's Structure of a Moral Code. Ladd's principal informant was the former leader of the Ramah community, a man who enjoyed the respect of Navahos and whites alike, a man honorable and upright in his dealings, and one who has given us a moving account of the standards his father held up for him to follow, and his acceptance of his father's values (Ladd, 1957; Kluckhohn, 1945). Yet whenever he was asked to justify his ethical standards, or given an opportunity to assert an absolute moral imperative, he replied only in terms of the immediate effects of misbehavior: it would make trouble, it would cause a man to lose support, it would cause a man to lose face, or it would affect his economic well-being (as in the case of laziness or gambling).

One basis of community moral control was already impaired: local clan elements could no longer operate in the more extreme situations—such as murder—as agents of justice. (For the sake of brevity, I shall use the term "clan" to refer to local clan elements in the discussion that follows.) American law and order was a partial substitute for this. But clans continued some of these functions for lesser offenses, and were themselves held together by the reciprocities of economic aid. Clan cohesion was impaired as the possibility of mutual aid was reduced. Fear of loss of support in the community also became a lesser threat. And fear of loss of face or shame depended on the degree of involvement in the face-to-face community.

Not only was intra-community interdependence lessened, and enforcement of morality thereby impaired, but extra-community dependence—on wage work, and familial economic autonomy, was increased, still further lessening the interdependencies. The decrease in reciprocities and increase in familial autonomy, then, very much affected the eminently practical re-enforcement of Navaho norms.

An additional feature of the scene was a probable reduction in the number of singers being trained. There are suggestions that this had been going on for some time. As early as 1910, the Franciscans asserted that many chants were becoming extinct, and spoke of "inferior and ignorant apprentices," stating that the conservative singers regarded the extinction of the existing chants as inevitable (Franciscan Fathers, 1910, pp. 361–362). On the other hand, the Wyman-Kluckhohn list of chants published in 1938 includes virtually every chant mentioned by the Franciscans and adds few to the list of obsolescent or obsolete chants (Wyman and Kluckhohn, 1938). Reichard's list (1950) does not differ too much from either of these, but she does not discuss obsolescence or extinction. It seems probable that there has been a reduction in the quality of singers since the early twentieth century, less of them learning the legend associated with the chant, but certainly in the 1930's there was little or no decrease in the chants actually sung. In the 1950's, I continued to encounter approximately the same chants as those listed by earlier workers, but my identifications are not always complete, sometimes failing to distinguish male and female branches of a type of chant, or other types of subdivisions, so that a lapse of some sorts of ceremonies would not be distinguishable in my notes.

There was, however, general agreement among most singers to whom I talked that they lacked apprentices. The reasons for this are straightforward. To learn a chant requires that a man be on the reservation, especially during the winter, for long periods of time. It also requires leisure, and the ability to pay the teacher. With more and more employment and less and less herds, these conditions were not fulfilled—though summer remains the peak employment season. Furthermore, the attitudes that might lead to becoming a singer were not being established: school-children were not at home in many cases during the critical winter months, when myths can be told. I found few young men learning to be chanters, but this is not absolutely conclusive, since Reichard asserts that people who start to be singers usually do not begin until middle age (1950, p. xxxiii). In sum, there is probably some decrease in the number of singers per capita, the number of trainees, and the amount of knowledge of the traditional religion among younger Navahos.

The ideology of peyotism helps to cope with some of these disruptions. For a system of balanced relationships among men, and between man, nature, and the supernatural order, it substitutes a transcendent God not a part of nature, whose power is not impaired even if the natural order is upset. For a system of reciproci-ties which compel the deities, it substitutes prayers to an all-powerful deity. And in Navaho life, we find that traditional, reciprocal, non-hierarchical relationships were supplemented by Governmental hierarchy in 1864, after conquest, with pervasive penetration into daily life beginning with livestock reduction in 1933, and further hierarchical development in 1938 and following, with the reorganized Tribal Council. One beseeches superiors and puts pressure on equals. Although Navaho gods were not equals, they were treated like other Navahos in the stress on reci-procity in religious practice. The God of peyotists is not.[4]

Peyotism supplied internalized sanctions which replaced pervasive social pres-sures. It taught people to "realize who they were," to think about the "purpose for which they were put on earth," to feel responsible for their families, to be con-cerned about sin whether it came to public attention or not. In a world in which traditional norms were still important but traditional sanctions had lost their force, this regulation by internalized sanctions had important functions.

Peyotism also permitted men to feel a little less bound by kinship and a little more responsible for their own immediate affairs. This situation must be stated with care. Contemporary Navahos do not, for the most part, live in a world where they can stand alone. As has been said before, no resource on which they depend is stable. Anyone, through no fault of his own, can be thrown back on family, kin, or neighborhood for help. When men leave the reservation to work, those who re-main at home need help from outside the family—even in such matters as hauling wood and water. The man who is financially ahead can seldom afford to cut his ties with others who need his help—he could need theirs in the near future. Indeed, the only family where a Navaho (in this case a woman) told me that she didn't want help from her relatives, was one in which the wife had a steady Government job as a matron in a school, while her husband ran a garage in a community where there were many cars and trucks and his services were in constant demand. Yet there is more individuation of the economic fate of family units than there used to be—through wages and through social security funds. Navahos want to be able to use cash for consumer goods and to save some of it, and kinship reciprocities are a

---

4 This approach to hierarchy rests on Swanson's treatment of monotheism in Birth of the Gods (1960, pp. 54–81), and specifically on his theory that three levels of authoritative organi-zation—three "types of groups arranged in a hierarchy"—are critical for the genesis of mono-theistic belief.

drain on this. Hence a religion which preaches primary responsibility for one's family and secondary responsibility to help other peyotists supports a more familial economy and loosens kin ties. It does not totally extricate the individual from kinship and community; this would be impossible at present.

The anti-alcohol position of the cult is also significant for Navahos in the modern world. There can be little doubt that Navahos have not been socialized in middle-class American patterns of drinking. There is a decided tendency among many Navahos to start drinking and continue until they are unable to drink any more. Federal laws prohibiting the sale of liquor to Indions are partly responsible for this state of affairs; isolation from other patterns of drinking, an accompaniment of prohibition, is partly responsible; and the difficulties of policing the reservation are also responsible. In the event, drinking among the Navaho is often accompanied by pugnacious behavior, by unconsciousness, which sometimes leads to death if the individual passes out out of doors on a cold winter's night, by traffic accidents and fatalities, by arrests, and so on. True alcoholism, in the sense of a compelling need to drink, is rare, nevertheless. Drinking is one major factor which leads to failures to report on time for work and to inadequate work performance, so that its consequences have become increasingly serious as the importance of wage work has risen. It also leads unquestionably to expenditure of funds which are needed for other purposes, destruction of valuable property, such as cars, and losses, as when drinking in town leads to a person's being "rolled" by a thief.[5]

Peyotism, with its message that alcohol is evil, and its insistence on the importance of hard work and care for one's family, is hence meaningful in the present context.

Witchcraft accusations, in my view, have come to play a special role in the contemporary situation. Swanson has shown that the prevalence of witchcraft is associated with what he calls important "unlegitimated" ties—ties between parties where no sovereign authority can adjust differences between them. Such is the case, for example, in the marital exchanges between Dobuan settlements, where there is no authority above the community level to adjudicate conflicts if one or the other party fails in its obligations (Swanson, 1960, pp. 137–152). With a decrease in the power of the clan, an incomplete penetration of American law and order to establish rules for many situations or to enforce the rules in others, and with a disturbance in reciprocities and in consensus as to when reciprocity is enjoined, it is expectable that witchcraft anxieties and accusations should increase. Witchcraft, as Kluckhohn has pointed out, was a significant levelling device in traditional Navaho life (Kluckhohn, 1944). The poor were treated with generosity lest they bewitch, and the rich acted with generosity lest they be accused of witchcraft. The contemporary situation provides new pressures for reciprocity, but new needs that oppose these pressures, as family economies become to some degree individuated. There is correspondingly a need to be "shut" of witchcraft, and peyote meets this

---

[5] Prohibition for Indians was repealed in Arizona and New Mexico after all field work had been completed except for two weeks in summer of 1954. The Navajo Reservation remains nominally dry today. There is no reason to believe that drinking is less of a problem now than it was during the period of field work.

need. Only peyote supplies, in one form or another, a guarantee that one need not fear witchcraft—paradoxically by promising to some that it can cure witchcraft disease and by telling others that witchcraft does not exist.

This brings us to another major difference between peyotism and traditional Navaho religion: the attitude toward ghosts. I do not find that I can bring this difference under the general rubric of social disruption. Navahos do not fear those ghosts whom they injured or failed in life. They fear ghosts to whom they did not give enough grave goods, or ghosts who are injuring them, whose identities they may not even seek to know. Thus fear of ghosts is not a factor which exerts pressures for socially approved behavior, as does fear of witches. There is one connection between witches and ghosts: witches use corpse poison as one device for lethal witchcraft. But this does not seem to me to provide a reason why Navahos would like to be "shut" of the fear of ghosts. Yet they find profound relief in the beliefs of peyotism, which tells them to have no fear of ghosts but to believe in an immortal soul. I can think of a variety of possible explanations why this belief is acceptable in modern Navaho life, but I have no special conviction about any of them; so I leave the topic as a loose end.

Finally, peyotism, with its simpler ritual, appeal to inspiration and feeling, lack of dependence on elaborate learning, and lack of dependence on elaborate training in Navaho mythology to engage the worshipper, seems to have an appeal for untrained worshippers and for those who wish to become ceremonial practitioners in a world in which Navaho mythology is less often taught and the training of singers is increasingly difficult.

Many of the features of peyotism which make it meaningful to Navahos in the contemporary situation are shared with orthodox forms of Christianity, but on the whole the traditional Christian religions have not spread with the speed of peyotism, nor been accepted with such fervor. For this at least two factors are responsible. First, peyotism is an Indian, not a white religion—a point to which we will later return. Second, it permits greater leeway. It does not absolutely insist that belief in ghosts and witches is nonsense; its Puritanism is more limited and far less consistent than that of Christianity.

Chapter 14

BASES OF NAVAHO OPPOSITION TO PEYOTISM

IN 1951, peyotism had no appeal whatsoever to more than 80 per cent of the Navaho tribe. Furthermore, those who were not cult members were bitterly opposed to it. Neutrals were rare; people opposed to peyotism but feeling no real intensity about the issue were as rare; there was only a handful of people who felt that regardless of their own opinions of peyotism, those who wished to use peyote should be allowed to do so.

Leaders, such as chapter officers and tribal delegates, were sometimes more lenient in private discussion than in public meetings. In talks with me they sometimes said that it was impossible to uproot peyotism, and that since there were so many members, it would be better to let the practice continue than to create endless conflict by attempting to enforce the law. This more moderate opinion seldom found public expression. And the leniency never went to the point of expressing any positive attitudes toward peyotism. I was often asked to make it clear, in any publication that I might produce, that most Navahos were not peyotists: non-peyotists felt that the tribe was disgraced by the existence of peyotism on the reservation.

By and large, neutrals were to be found among highly educated Navahos. Thus one Navaho with an MA degree and two with partial college education regarded peyotism as an interesting curosity and took an almost academic interest in the reasons for its appeal. By no means all highly educated Navahos were neutral, however. There were also a few people who had entered the cult for a cure and had been cured, as they saw it, but had then stopped participating in cult activities because of public pressure. They were likely to refute the more astonishing rumors about peyote's bad effects, but sometimes displayed mildly negative attitudes.

The anti-peyote resolution of 1940 stated two grounds for hostility to peyotism: that peyote was foreign and non-Navaho, and that it was harmful. These continue to be among the four major bases for the rejection of peyotism.

GENERAL BASES FOR REJECTION OF PEYOTISM

To provide some picture of bases for rejection of peyotism, I have coded 66 interviews with non-peyotists (including a few former peyotists), from eight areas, collected between 1949 and 1952. These do not constitute a random sample. The results appear in Table 21. Since individuals might name more than one reason for rejection, the percentages are non-cumulative.

Two-thirds of the respondents show some concern for the effects of peyote on physical or mental health. They think that peyote causes illness, death, or insanity, or they stigmatize it as habit-forming, or they refer to specific individuals who, they believe, fell ill, became insane, or died from using peyote.

Other major bases of opposition to peyotism were each mentioned by more than a third of the respondents, but are about equal in frequency. One major basis is the fact that peyotism is regarded as "not the Navaho religion," or not native, or unknown to the Navahos.

Another major basis is the belief that the entry of peyotism has caused disruption of community or kinship relationships. It is asserted that religious factionalism prevents the community from working together, or that peyotists fail to assist their non-peyotist kinsmen.

A final major basis is the belief that peyotism is associated with behavior which the respondents evaluated negatively. Some of these items of behavior were believed to result from peyotism, but others were regarded by anti-peyotists as illustrations of the fact that cult membership is connected with moral offenses. The most frequent reference was to the supposed capacity of peyote to induce sexual misbehavior (a topic further discussed below). Another type of comment dealt

TABLE 21

BASES FOR HOSTILITY TO PEYOTISM: NON-RANDOM INTERVIEWS

Reasons	Number	Per Cent*
Health	44	66
Foreign religion	27	41
Bad relations in community or among kin	26	39
Bad behavior	24	36
Total interviews	66	

* Percentages non-cumulative.

with the supposed tendency of peyote priests to profiteer through the gifts they received from their followers. Still another comment was that peyotists failed to care for their stock or gave it to peyote priests, and that as a result these peyotists were going downhill economically.

In sum, these data indicate concerns with the supposed physical and behavioral effects of peyote, the non-traditional character of the peyote religion, and the disruption of kinship and community solidarities attendant on cult formation.

I shall now try to sketch in more detailed fashion the beliefs of non-peyotist Navahos about peyotism. To do this, it is necessary to deal with certain Navaho beliefs as a background for attitudes about peyote and peyotism.

First, Navaho ideology and religion are thoroughly ethnocentric. Navahos are "the people," and other peoples are "enemies" or gentiles. The only word for "Indian" is simply a corruption of that word: 'íílzhin or 'íínlzhin people (Haile, 1950b, p. 166). The Navaho country was given to the Navahos by the supernaturals and is bounded by four sacred peaks. Navaho ceremonies were given by supernaturals and work only within the confines of the area bounded by the sacred peaks. The origin story of each ceremony prescribes the details of the ceremony and provides it with validity. Other tribes are different from Navahos, or inferior, or both (cf. Haile, 1938). There are, however, hints in a myth of the material superiority of the Mexicans (Matthews, 1889). Many Navahos believe that the identity and continuity of the Navahos is mystically bound up with the continuity of Navaho ceremonials, although in one case at least, the whites were viewed by one major singer as the heirs to Navaho knowledge (Reichard, 1950, p. 25). Navahos do use ritual or curing practices from other tribes; they go to Pueblo diviners and Pueblo and Ute specialists in the sucking cure. This seems to be a matter of last resort, to some degree associated with the cure of witchcraft-caused disease. Some Navahos, as has been said, view Chiricahua Apache Wind Way ceremony and a new feature of Enemy Way as foreign and injurious to Navaho ceremonies, Navaho tribal life, and so on.

Exactly how Navahos view Christianity is not so clear. Reichard believed that the Navahos viewed Christianity, essentially, as the tribal religion of whites—proper for them, as the Navaho religion was for Navahos—but that they were unable to understand the very notion of proselytizing (Reichard, 1949). Rapoport's work also includes a number of Navaho comments indicating a rejection of Christianity as foreign (Rapoport, 1954). There is no doubt that in the past some Navahos looked on Christianity (and on American medicine) as forces inimical to the continuity of Navaho culture, and some still do. It is my impression, however, that after many years of missionary endeavor, Christianity is put in a different category from the "foreign" religions of other Indians. It is seen, rather, as one element in that larger society to which Navahos must somehow develop an accommodation.

Second, there is a body of Navaho lore which has to do with magical ways of affecting people's mind, will, and conduct. Much of this is connected with a group of plants thought to have effects on the mind. These techniques are used by the person who knows them to secure luck in gambling, trading, and hunting, and irresistibly to attract someone of the opposite sex. The core concept is that of making someone else's will powerless. The desired sexual partner cannot control himself and is drawn to the magician. The gambling partner becomes reckless and loses caution. The animals are magically attracted to the hunter and are oblivious to danger.

In its sexual aspect this type of magic is called 'ajiłee, as is the chant used to counteract its effects. Kluckhohn has called the magic "Frenzy Witchcraft" and the chant "Prostitution Way" (Kluckhohn, 1944). In this he follows Fr. Berard (cf. Haile, 1950b, pp. 29–30). Reichard objects to this, both because the chant is used for overcoming all kinds of "rashness" and for ensuring a variety of kinds of luck, and also because the sexual activities involved are not properly defined as prostitution. I shall follow her in speaking of "excess magic" and "Excess Chant" (Reichard, 1950, pp. 139–140).

A number of plants are supposed to be effective in thus bending the mind. Perhaps the one most often mentioned is ch'óxojilghéí, "madness producing," one or another species of datura (cf. Wyman and Harris, 1941, plant no. 128, pp. 25, 29; Kluckhohn, 1944; Hill, 1938). Datura is a plant empirically known to create hallucinations, and capable of producing convulsions and death. It is used for divination, poulticing for wounds and broken limbs, and perhaps for pleasure by some Navahos. In theory, it can be used for excess magic. But it should be made clear that the empirical and magical uses of this and other plants are not sharply distinguished. Small amounts of the pollen of such plants, blown on a person, are thought to be effective in excess magic. Or a portion of the plant might be rubbed on gambling equipment and take effect. Thus some Navaho women were afraid to handle an old set of three-stick dice colored with ochre which I had in my possession, lest they become the victims of excess magic.

A variety of other plants, some unidentified, some identified with several different species, have similar effects. Among them are *'azee' dlo'í*, laughing medicine, *shílátsoh*, my thumb, *toohjí' hwiidzo*, a narrow line extends as far as the water, *k'ishishjíízh*, smashed down sumac, *'azee' nchíí'ii*, irritating medicine, and others. (For further discussion and identificatons see Kluckhohn, 1944; Wyman and Harris, 1941 and 1951. I have followed communications from Young for some transcriptions.) All these are regarded as dangerous, capable of creating mental disturbance for the victim and quite possibly for the magician. Thus the person magicked may first obey the will of the magician but may subsequently simply behave in an uncontrolled fashion—victim of uncontrollable lust, or simply insane. The magician may have the power turned back on him.

On the other hand, like most things in Navaho life, these plants are susceptible of producing good for the person who has been taught their proper use—as when datura is used for divination or for a poultice.

These various substances and other ways of affecting the mind appear in a variety of Navaho chantway myths and in the legend of the Great Gambler of Chaco Canyon (cf. Spencer, 1957; Wetherill and Cummings, 1922).

With this background, we can approach Navaho beliefs about peyote and peyotism. In connection with each allegation against peyotism, the facts will be discussed, insofar as they are available. This manner of presentation is adopted because of the importance of the facts for an interpretation of opposition to peyotism. Thus, for example, if individuals oppose fluoridation of water in American communities and allege that the practice is dangerous, we would evaluate the sources of their hostility to fluoridation quite differently if there were ample evidence that it did cause death and disease than if there were no evidence that it did.

With some exceptions, I have not attempted a similar evaluation of the evidence for and against the claims of peyotists. In some instances I have not done so because the claims cannot be evaluated, in some instances because evaluation would be extraordinarily difficult, and in some instances because I do not have the information, although it could be gathered. Thus, if peyotists claim that through peyote they communicate with God, there is no empirical technique to evaluate the claim. If they claim that peyote cures, validation is extremely difficult without a mass of medical data and the application of careful controls. If they claim that peyotists on the whole are less likely to use alcohol than non-peyotists, this claim can be evaluated, but with some difficulty. Such data as I have are presented.

On the other hand, if non-peyotists claim that peyote is lethal or causes insanity, the general claim cannot be assessed. But if they claim that peyote drove X insane or killed Y, then in those instances where there is medical information, it is sometimes possible to decide whether or not peyote did play a role in the event.

After the allegations against peyote have been assessed, it will then be possible to venture an interpretation of the opposition to peyotism.

PEYOTISM VIEWED AS FOREIGN

Peyotism is not acceptable because it is foreign and non-traditional. Supernatural power, whether embodied in ritual, in plant or animal substances, or in a combination of these, depends on knowledge. This knowledge involves the mythical pedigree of the ritual or substance. Ultimately this pedigree is based on the contact of a mythological protagonist with Navaho supernatural beings (cf. Spencer, 1957). The validity of all practice, then, depends on its derivation from Navaho supernaturals within the area of the sacred peaks. Hence the extreme irritation of Navahos when a history or myth of peyote's origin is given. They already know that it is foreign; the details of its derivation make it no more acceptable. (I was not fully aware of this during the Council hearings of 1954.) Navaho singers comment that "there is no name" for peyote, or that they "know no name" for it. In fact, of course, there is a phrase which designates peyote, 'azee' yit'aałii, "chewing medicine." There are also a variety of derogatory terms for it. But the names of Navaho medicinal plants are conceived of as given by the supernaturals and as having mystical significance. This name is as modern as chidí bitoo', car its water, for gasoline, and as little sanctified. (Peyotists never use the term "chewing medicine" to refer to peyote. For them it is simply "medicine.")

Peyote and its ritual are regarded, then, as foreign, dangerous, and uncontrolled.

At this point, however, it might be as well to discuss the mythological and historical traditions now current among both peyotist and non-peyotist Navahos regarding peyote. First, everyone recognizes a factual story, according to which peyote came to the Navahos from the Utes, and many people know as well that it came to the Utes from Oklahoma or from the naa'łání, often translated "Comanche" but literally, "many enemies" and sometimes applied to Oklahoma or Plains Indians in general. Those who know of its use in Oklahoma also know that it comes ultimately from Old Mexico.

Second, some peyotists know one or another of the origin stories of peyote and its ritual current in Oklahoma, most of which are connected with a woman, or a woman and her child, wandering alone and starving on the Plains—who finds and eats peyote and through supernatural means discovers the appropriate ritual for its use.

Third, some Navaho peyotists whose background in Navaho ritual and myth is extensive, provide peyote with a Navaho pedigree: some claim that the old singers spoke of a plant more powerful than all other medicinal plants which the Navahos would know some day.

Fourth, some antagonists of the peyote cult provide peyote with a special Navaho mythological pedigree. The myth of the Great Gambler of Pueblo Bonito is much concerned with a powerful plant which the Gamble used to achieve his ends: he gained virtually all the women and all the property of the denizens of the Pueblo. The people who lived in Pueblo Bonito were the Snake People. According to some anti-peyotists, peyote was the plant that the Great Gambler used. It was known to the Snake People. Their use of it resulted in the death or expulsion of the people from Pueblo Bonito, and it is hence forbidden to all Navahos. Thus if peyote is given a mythological status by anti-peyotists, it is one which derogates the plant.

PEYOTISM VIEWED AS INJURIOUS

Navaho religion is concerned with curing. So is American medicine. These are regarded by an increasing number of Navahos as alternatives or as complementary. The skill of doctors in operations is known and accepted; the skill of singers in dealing with ghosts is also accepted. One disease requires one cure; another, another. Or a stay in the hospital may be preceded by an effort at cure by Navaho techniques, or followed by a chant to remove the supernatural causes of the illness or misfortune and make the person wholly well. The claims of peyotism to cure are regarded with suspicion. This follows from the fact that peyote is foreign, has no pedigree, and cannot be controlled. Hence there is a strong, deep fear that peyote will affect its users adversely.

I will later take up the question of the medical effects of peyote. Suffice it for the time being to say that *post hoc* reasoning supplies Navahos with sufficient support for their belief in the negative qualities of peyote. For one thing, among the early users of peyote were many people who thought that they were *in extremis*—and some of them probably were. Some of them died, and the deaths were laid to peyote. People in their early and mid-seventies were among those who died some time after taking up peyote, early in the history of the cult in several communities, but since they were alive before they used it, and dead some time afterward, the deaths were unhesitatingly ascribed to peyote. By the same token, if an individual who had used peyote had a malformed or mentally defective child, or one who died—and Navaho infant mortality rates remain high—peyote was, and is, blamed.

One of the special beliefs about the damage caused by peyote is that it "grows in the stomach" and packs the system. Navahos have told me firmly that doctors in the hospital have told them of performing operations or autopsies in the course of which large amounts of peyote were found in the intestines. Peyote is eliminated like any other vegetable substance. It is possible that if someone died after eating peyote, some might be found in his stomach or intestines.

In sum, peyote is rejected as a cure because it is foreign, and suspected as a cause of disease, death, still-births, abnormal infants, and the death of infants.

SUPPOSED BEHAVIORAL EFFECTS

Peyote is also associated with a variety of mental and behavioral effects. It is associated with the mind medicines previously discussed, those used in excess witchcraft. It is a substance that "affects the mind," and so are these. The Navaho mind medicines can, in theory, be used to induce sexual excess, and, it is believed, peyote can be used in this way. This belief has several strands.

First, it is believed that a peyote meeting is a gigantic sexual orgy. In this orgy, people are said to "act just like dogs," which turns out to mean that promiscuous sexual relations occur which disregard incest prohibitions. If the anthropologist states that he has seen no such thing, the anti-peyotist has one of two responses. One is to say, "Well, you don't suppose they would do that with *you* around, do you?" The other is a veiled or open assertion that since the anthropologist indulged in such behavior himself, he will not admit to the truth. Fundamentally, there is no way for the observer to extricate himself from the dilemma posed by either assertion. He can never observe a meeting without being present, and he cannot *prove* that he did not indulge in promiscuous sexuality without the evidence of peyotists, who are also suspect. For what it is worth, I should like to point out that peyote meetings were not specially arranged for my benefit, and that at least on one occasion, at Montezuma Creek, I arrived at a meeting on the most pressing invitation of my host, who had known nothing of my plans to visit him. I will also assert that I have never observed any sexual misbehavior at a peyote meeting.

Second, it is asserted that through peyote the road man—or others at a peyote meeting—work something very like excess magic on girls or women present, and subsequently work their will with the girls. There are known and verified cases where road men have in fact committed adultery or seduced and taken away girls. In such cases, the non-peyotist often claims that the sexual misbehavior occurred through the influence that peyote had on the girl. In spite of Navaho reports to the contrary, there is no verified instance where such a thing occurred at a peyote meeting.

This belief, however, has material on which to feed. At Lukachukai, quite early in the history of the cult, one man's wife left him for a peyote priest, a second man's wife made a trip without him to the Ute country and was suspected of adultery—denied by all parties concerned, and a third man's daughter was abducted by a road man, who later abandoned her. There are other peyote priests who have similar episodes on their record.

In this connection, it should be observed that there is no medical evidence to support the view that peyote is an aphrodisiac. There is evidence that a small number of road men have exploited their position as interesting strangers with powerful cures in order to have sexual adventures.

The question might be raised whether any peyotist has ever *tried* to use peyote for excess magic or its equivalent. On this point there is, and can be no conclusive evidence. I once asked an experienced peyotist to give me his word that no such thing had ever occurred. He replied, quite properly, that peyote had no such effects and was not intended for such use. But, he said, there is no predicting what young men will do. He could not give me a blanket guarantee that no one had ever *tried* this, because of his inability to know the intentions of all peyotists at all times in all places. He could only assure me that it was both an ineffective and an improper use of peyote.

Some peyotists assert that the patient should observe four days of sexual continence after a meeting, a practice comparable with the restrictions imposed by Navaho ceremonial rules.

Peyote is also held by some anti-peyotists to be a sexual rejuvenator, a stimulus to perverse heterosexual activities, and to inflame the prostate and thus lead to sexual excitement. There is no supporting evidence, medical or other, for these assertions.

Thus, for many Navahos, peyotism arouses concerns about unbridled sexuality and loss of control, both of which are traditionally associated with the "mind medicines."

Another set of beliefs regarding supposed mental effects of peyote includes the belief that it makes one "drunk" just as alcohol does, that it induces "crazy" behavior during meetings, and that it causes insanity.

The charge regarding the supposed intoxicating effects of peyote has a special significance in the light of peyotist ideology and Navaho attitudes. The peyotists hold that it is bad to drink, and in some instances that peyote's power will stop a man from drinking. Not every peyotist has permanently stopped drinking, but there are a considerable number of total abstainers among church members. Peyotists hold that Navaho ritual is vitiated when participants, and even in some instances the ceremonialist himself, drink at Navaho ceremonies. They hold that this impairs the value of the ritual and shows a lack of seriousness about a sacred occasion. They claim for themselves the virtue of sobriety. There is no doubt whatsoever that at large, public Navaho ceremonies there is drinking, and that the police attend in an effort to control bootlegging and lock up the staggering drunks and aggressive drunks. This is a matter of record in the Law and Order office. In my experience, there is some drinking at some smaller ceremonies, and doubtless there are occasions when the singer drinks as well. Many traditionalists disapprove of all of this, and at the large ceremonies, public speeches urging people to behave are a normal part of the occasion.

The anti-peyotist reply to this charge is that peyote is a "worse" intoxicant than liquor. Charge and countercharge go on indefinitely, each group maintaining that the other gets "drunk" and both attacking drunkenness as such. The use of alcohol has become so much a symbol that the anti-peyotists are sometimes called the "bootleggers" or the "drinkers," and a man who refuses to take a drink may be thought to be a peyotist. By the same token, in a few instances, individuals who have left the peyote cult have signalized this by taking a drink in public.

Navahos are in general most reliable and truthful informants, but they are often not reliable as respects their own drinking habits. Hence testimony regarding sobriety might be suspect. I have made fairly careful observations at rodeos and "squaw dances" in communities where I was reasonably well acquainted. I am prepared to say that on these occasions, when there is a great deal of public drinking and drunkenness, very few peyotists show any signs of drinking. There are exceptions, but the peyotists' claim not to use alcohol seems fairly well supported.

We now come to the supposed intoxicating effects of peyote. Many peyotists would agree that peyote does affect mood and mental state, although some would claim that no matter how much they ate they felt "normal." Some acknowledge effects on motor coordination. Indeed one road man informed me that he ate very little peyote because he was afraid of stepping on the altar through these effects. In some instances, the consumption of peyote results in a lethargic and apparently comatose state. The individual can apparently be aroused, but lies down, curls up, and closes his eyes as soon as he is permitted to. I have seen two such cases in attending eleven peyote meetings, at each of which twenty to forty people were present. Thus they do not appear to be too common. Experienced peyotists claim that this condition is likely to be found in young people (in their late teens or early twenties) who have taken peyote very seldom. The comatose effect is regarded as a result of the young person's sins, and it is said that more experienced—and more purified—peyotists do not suffer in this way. Both cases I saw were young people of the age-range mentioned.

Some non-peyotists claim that a group of peyotists who have been eating peyote resemble people who have been drinking. My own observations do not support this. Occasionally I have found that conversation outside, during a break in a peyote meeting, involves a slight repetitiousness, but I can find no other features that resemble alcoholic intoxication—except for motor incoordination, which is rarely evident and slight in degree.

In sum, the charge is made that peyotism is just another type of intoxication. Reported and observed behavior suggest that the effects are, for the most part, very different from those of drinking.

Although claims have been made of extravagant behavior during peyote meetings, no reliable, attested reports of this sort are available. It has been said that peyotists tear off their clothes and run about naked, or that they rush to a hill to dig up objects in a grave, shouting, "Someone has been working witchcraft against me," etc. It is asserted that a young woman rode wildly by Drolet's Trading Post (Nava) under the influence of peyote. My efforts to recheck the story were ineffectual: the supposed witness became exceedingly vague. At any rate, such stories have wide currency.

Many circumstantial accounts are given of how a person went insane after using peyote. Almost all such cases reduce to a limited number of types. In some cases, it develops that the person never took peyote but did go insane. In others, the person showed obvious signs of insanity either shortly before, or shortly after, taking peyote. The insanity ordinarily resembles schizophrenia. The best psychiatric opinions that I can secure are that peyote is not capable of causing a full-blown long-continued psychosis but is capable of precipitating symptoms in a person already headed for a psychotic breakdown. In a handful of cases, a transient psychotic episode has occurred, but there is no information for deciding whether a toxic psychosis occurred or whether the cause lay in other conditions. In a limited number of cases, peyotists themselves have described for me transitory disturbances of a few hours' duration during a peyote meeting which were, in all probability, effects of peyote on a particular personality type.

Be that as it may, since peyote is regarded as a mind medicine, any user who goes insane—and many people who go insane are not users—is thought to have become insane through the use of peyote. (See Appendix, "Peyote and Health.")

Two other classes of effects attributed to peyote itself deserve mention. A small number of Navahos hold that it is a "habit-forming" drug and therefore fear it. We have already pointed out that there is no evidence to support this view. Some Navahos hold that peyotists can be recognized by physical stigmata. These include "peculiar-looking" eyes, grey skin, and other things. The first may arise from the fact that peyote does cause some temporary dilation of the pupils. The other "stigmata" do not seem perceptible to the non-Navaho observer, or very clearly connected with peyote. Thus one singer in the Shiprock area informed me that he knew from the way I smoked that I was a peyotist. I have, in fact, been a heavy smoker since 1946 or 1947. I had taken peyote one time (in the summer of 1949) a few weeks before I was observed by the singer.

It is clear that fear of the effects of peyote is very deep in the Navaho population—as reflected in these comments, in the original resolution, and in the two-thirds of non-peyotists who commented about the theoretically damaging effects of the cactus.

We come next to a set of behaviors and attitudes attributed to peyotists but not necessarily thought to be connected with the use of peyote itself. The first of these has to do with the costs of using peyote, the supposed greed of the road man, and supposed extravagance of peyote users. It meets peyotist attitudes about the costs of Navaho ceremonies and the supposed greed of Navaho ceremonialists.

PEYOTE VIEWED AS COSTLY

In Navaho ceremonies, the singer must be paid. The fee must be agreed on in advance.[1] If there is no pay, the ceremony is regarded as having no efficacy. The payment is graded according to the scope of the ceremony and the wealth of the patient and his family. In 1946, fees for a ceremony were said to range from five to five hundred dollars. Special rituals which may be added or omitted from a ceremony require additional fees for their inclusion. Certain assistants receive fees, ritual equipment must be purchased, and those who attend must be fed. In the Ramah area in the 1940's, about 20 per cent of total family income went for ceremonies (Kluckhohn and Leighton, 1946, pp. 160–161). It would probably be safe to say that the total expenses of ceremonies in the 1950's ranged from about twenty-five dollars for a two-night ceremony involving only the family to perhaps a thousand for an enemy way and more for a nine-night winter chant.

A common peyotist story is that of being beggared by having to give ceremony after ceremony because of illness unrelieved by rituals. The costs of ceremonies are seen by peyotists as prohibitive. Some peyotists murmur that the singers probably know witchcraft, or deliberately do things "wrong" in the ceremonies in order to be able to give more ceremonies and earn more fees. Non-peyotists make the same allegation in some instances.

They contrast the peyote ceremony. The road chief asks for no fee, they say. One does not have to give him anything. Peyote ceremonies do not ruin or beggar a family.

Traditionalists, and especially chanters, have a different point of view. They claim that the chanter's fee is graded to family fortune: one singer said to me that just an arrowhead would suffice if a man had nothing. They claim in addition that any given family has more peyote ceremonies in a year than he would have Navaho ceremonies. Finally, they claim that the road man seeks out the rich and encourages large offerings, and that the users of peyote, in their intoxication, shower the road chief with valuables.

Essentially, anti-peyotists claim that it costs more to be a peyotist and that a road man makes more profit than a singer. Peyotists make the reverse claim. Both sides were understandably eager to convince me, and both Navahos and interested whites felt that I should ble able to evaluate these claims. Unfortunately, although the critical data could be gathered, they have not been. Nor would it be easy to carry out the task. Here are the questions at issue. (1) Does the average traditional Navaho pay more for ceremonies over, say, a year, than the average peyotist? If this question is to be answered, the problem of controlling for general health arises. If, for example, people tend to enter the peyote cult because of health problems, it might be that a sample of peyotists would have worse health than a sample of

---

[1] Although I consider the "fee" an obligatory prestation rather than a payment, I have used the terms ordinarily employed in Navaho ethnography.

non-peyotists. If use of ceremonies is a function of health, then our figures on costs would be deceptive. (2) Does the average Navaho singer receive more, or less per annum from those whom he serves than the average road man? (3) Do local singers and road men tend to receive less per annum than far-travelling singers and road men? None of these questions can now be answered. All that can be said is that, since most types of sings are two nights or more, it is likely that most types of sings cost more than does the average peyote ceremony, and that most types of sings produce a larger fee for the singer than does the average peyote ceremony. This tells us nothing, however, about the usual costs per annum or gains per annum for peyotists, non-peyotists, road men, or singers. And the question of costs is still further complicated by the fact that Navahos help their kin with the costs of sings, and peyotists help their friends with the costs of ceremonies. What information I have on contributions at peyote meetings is supplied below.

After a peyote ceremony is over, a blanket is spread in front of the road man, in the hogan. He may comment on the amount of peyote used or on his expenses in getting to the meeting, or both. After this has gone on for a while, the participants get up, one by one, and go round the circle of those sitting in the hogan. They shake hands with each person and, as they pass by the blanket, some of them lay money on the blanket, but others do not. I have seen only small change and bills contributed, and I have seen many non-contributors. Those responsible for putting up the ceremony may also make private gifts to the road man. I have attended eleven peyote meetings. I have figures on total visible contributions in five cases and partial figures for one more.[1a]

These figures suggest that the average member is likely to contribute less than a dollar per meeting. How much the sponsoring family may give is quite uncertain. The road man's gross does not seem very large.

The price of peyote on the reservation was 10¢ a button, according to all peyotists with whom I discussed the matter (1949–1953). The price in bulk from Texas was $10.00 to $11.00 a thousand, or 1¢ or so a button. This does represent a markup of considerable size. On the other hand, by no means all peyote circulated on the reservation is bought and sold, and it is not just road men who supply peyote. There are other Navahos who send direct to Texas for peyote. Some is supplied from Oklahoma. I do not know what the costs are from Oklahoma, but I assume there is some markup. Some Navahos travel to the "peyote gardens" in Texas and gather or purchase peyote there.

Road men give some peyote away, and sometimes the family giving the meeting secures its own supply. Thus at a meeting on July 26–27, 1952, which I attended, *Steve Brooks[2] put up a meeting for a sick man and supplied the peyote for it himself. Hence the cost of peyote for a member may vary from nothing at all to

---

[1a] *Postscript, 1965.*—It is common for the patient or his family to provide an offering to the road man, privately or publicly, whether or not a collection is taken up at the meeting from the participants. Figures mentioned in 1965 ranged from $5.00, which was considered small, to $20.00, for such offerings. At least one road man refuses offerings from close relatives. Sometimes there is no collection from the participants. Sometimes the collection is intended for the Native American Church, to sustain its activities.

[2] Asterisk preceding a proper name indicates a pseudonym.

10¢ a button, and it would be unwarranted to conceive of road men as enjoying a straight markup of 9¢ or so a button.[3]

Non-peyotists often say that the price of peyote is 25¢ a button, but this is certainly not true today. When peyote first came on the reservation, when a very small number of people controlled the supply, and when they themselves did not

[3] In the Quarterly Bulletin of the Native American Church of North America, Vol. 1, No. 4, for October–December, 1955, dealers' prices were listed. At that time, prices for dried peyote, varying in size, ranged from $9.50 per thousand to $15.00 per thousand. Dried, cup-shaped peyote was $20.00 per thousand. Ground peyote varied greatly, from $25.00 per thousand to $50.00 per thousand. Green peyote was $25.00 per thousand and was listed by only one dealer. The Native American Church did not act as an intermediary in the purchase of peyote; it only supplied names, addresses, and price lists of five dealers.

CHART G
CONTRIBUTIONS AT SIX PEYOTE MEETINGS

Date[1]	Place	Gross	No. Adults	Per Capita	Comments
8/8/49	Greasewood	$16	12	$1.25	Conducted by *Bill Conroy.[2] He claimed 150 buttons had been eaten. Cost at local prices, $15. Cost to *Conroy, unknown. Buttons consumed by 12 Navaho adults, 6 children, 1 anthropologist; per capita, 7.
7/28/50	Black Mountain	$12	16	75¢	Conducted by *Barney Strong. $4 split evenly between drummer and fire chief. 5 children, 1 anthropologist, besides 16 adult Navahos.
8/19/50	Rattlesnake	None	(?)	None	Conducted by *Edgar Meridith. No public collection. *Edgar and anthropologist left immediately after end of meeting.
7/29/51	Sawmill	$22	15+	See comments, note 1.	Conducted by John James, Yuchi, from Oklahoma. Total announced. Included two $5 bills, presumably contributed by sponsors. Omitting this, the per capita is about 75¢; with it, it is about $1.50 or less. Mention made of a subsequent gift to be sent to Oklahoma.
7/7/52	Sawmill	$10	25	40¢	Conducted by *Charlie Rodman. Entire collection to a member, to repay him for contributing to costs of sending a delegate to Native American Church annual convention.
7/12/52	Sawmill	See comments, note 1.	....	....	Conducted by *Bill Conroy. A donation of $10 or more was given privately; I did not find out the size of the collection.

[1] Key: Date shown is date of evening when meeting began. It was incumbent on the anthropologist to contribute at these meetings; his contributions are omitted from the calculations. Private donations may well have been made in all cases; I observed this only on 7/12/52.

[2] Asterisk preceding a proper name indicates a pseudonym.

know how to get it in quantity from Texas, it is possible that a few road men did receive this price. Indeed, the report to the Tribal Council of 1940 quotes a price of 50¢ a button (TC, 1940, p. 20). Whether in fact such prices were paid as late as 1940 I do not know. By 1949, when I started field work, the price for peyote *sold* on the reservation was, as I have said, about 10¢ a button. The Greasewood meeting, with its collection of $16.00 and its consumption of about 150 peyote buttons realized slightly more than that amount.

In addition, it is charged by anti-peyotists that extravagant donations, of jewelry, blankets, sheep, horses, and cash are made to peyote priests. The implication, or direct accusation, is that these contributions are made "under the influence" of peyote, and in response to the greed of the road man.

It is evident from my accounts of eleven meetings that no such lavish contributions occurred at these meetings. I do not have a record in dollars and cents of the contributions at five of these meetings, but certainly no pile of valuables or unusually large stack of cash or bills was to be seen. Peyotist informants state that such lavish gifts did occur in the past but claim that they no longer occur. Some peyotists admit that greed for goods and money was characteristic of some of the first road men, but they do not approve in principle of such behavior. My own view of the matter is that there are a limited number of road men, especially those who travel widely and minister outside their home communities, who are very decidedly interested in the financial gains which can be realized through the gratitude of those who consider that peyote has cured them. There is another, and more sizable group of road men whose ministry is local and who have no special interest in gain. There is no question that the ideology of peyotism is opposed to large profits from ceremonies, and that both Navahos and old Oklahoma peyotists with whom I have talked disapprove of profiteering. Nevertheless, the reputation of the road man among non-peyotists is that of greed and operation for gain.

VARIOUS CHARGES REGARDING BEHAVIOR

There are a series of other allegations made against peyotists respecting their behavior. It is asserted that some peyotists, who boast of not drinking, do drink. I have already stated that in a limited number of cases this is true. It is further alleged that some peyotists, who preach against drinking and do not drink themselves, nevertheless engage in bootlegging. (Some road men travel widely and own trucks; they are thus in a position to bootleg.) Some peyotists have admitted to me that this is true. Some do not seem to consider this undesirable behavior—they say, simply, that a man has to make a living somehow. Others are concerned and would like to see this sort of behavior eliminated, but are unable to police these activities. There is no question that the existence of bootlegging by people who inveigh against the evils of alcohol is disturbing to non-peyotists, who see it as the height of hypocrisy.

Some traditional Navahos are disturbed by the peyotist attitude toward burial and the corpse: the fact that peyotists claim not to fear the ghost or the corpse, sometimes burying the body close to the house and in a well-marked spot. To traditionalists, who fear both body and spirit, such a change from custom is a matter for concern. To peyotists it is a matter of pride.

Quite apart from the belief of non-peyotists in the analogy of peyote and excess magic to secure sexual favors, some anti-peyotists charge peyotists, and particularly leading peyotists, with adultery on a large scale, and home-wrecking. It should be said that changes of marriage partners with little formality, small numbers of plural marriages (forbidden by the Tribal code of law and order, though not regarded with great seriousness by the Navahos), and casual adultery on a fair scale are features of Navaho life today and probably have been for some time, if we are to take the evidence from life-histories seriously (cf. Dyk, 1938, 1947). Thus, using figures for the Ramah area, Leighton and Kluckhohn assert that "only about one woman out of three and one man out of four reaches old age with the same spouse . . ." (Leighton and Kluckhohn, 1947, p. 83). Most of these changes result from divorce, not from the death of one partner. More than four-fifths of these broken marriages occur within the first three years of a marriage.

It has already been pointed out that in the early history of peyote, a small number of men were involved in quite a few escapades of this sort. At present, there are peyotists—and non-peyotists—involved in one or another scandal. The difference is that the religion, or the plant, is blamed when the peyotist misbehaves, and the man himself when the non-peyotist steps out of line.

We come next to a set of complaints that center around peyotist reactions to witchcraft. It is alleged that peyotists are unduly concerned with who may be a witch, or who may be witching them. The allegations include several kinds of behavior. It is sometimes claimed that peyotists dig into graves to find materials buried there, with the aim of terminating witchcraft directed at them. Navahos believe that one way of witching a person is to insert something of his in a grave—clothing, hair, nail clippings, etc. Naturally enough, if one does dig up a grave, clothing will be found in it, since the dead are buried fully clothed. It is asserted that peyotists use peyote meetings to discover that someone has done this to them, and the location of the grave, and then go there and dig to get at the objects. In spite of the fact that most Navahos believe in this technique of witchcraft, the peyotist is somehow thought to be credulous in doing this digging.

It is also said that peyotists use their visions to see who is witching them. According to one Navaho, there was a peyotist who spoke so much about seeing witches that the non-peyotists finally asked him if he had seen his own grandfather yet—since the old man was widely thought to be a witch. Probably this use of visions would create less concern were it not that the witch is sometimes named. This creates considerable disturbance in the local community. It is further said that peyote priests tell the patient that he is bewitched and name the witch. As to the digging in graves, I have no information. As to charges of witchcraft that name the witches, by laity and road men, these have undoubtedly occurred, and have occasioned trouble. The most sophisticated peyotists disapprove of such behavior, but it goes on. There is also little doubt that for some road men, witchcraft accusations and profiteering are linked: they tell the patient that he is bewitched and assert that they can cure the effects of witchcraft by a peyote meeting. One peyotist of my acquaintance with an exceptionally broad understanding of the issues and individuals involved, asserts flatly that this was done in some instances for the sake of money.

It should be made clear, however, that both peyotist and non-peyotist Navahos believe in witchcraft and fear it greatly, and that peyotism as a cure for witchcraft is believed in by laity and many road men.

In this connection, road men have sometimes named singers as witches or made sweeping charges that singers in general practice witchcraft so as to make money —by making more sick people, who need traditional cures. These accusations have been particularly disturbing to Navaho singers and account for a part of their marked antipathy for peyotism.

The subject of witch-finding[4] leads to a brief consideration of traditional attitudes toward peyote visions. Fr. Berard has pointed out the general distrust of visions in Navaho culture (Haile, 1940). Nevertheless, divination by jimson weed vision does occur (Hill, 1938).

In fact, I have rarely heard Navahos deprecate peyotism because people *have* visions. Rather, they are likely to complain that they tried peyote and had *no* visions, a not uncommon complaint among people who have used it once or twice and then quit, or that they had *evil* visions. A man who sees skeletons, owls, or snakes is not likely to consider the vision a very gratifying experience, unless he came to the meeting to discover the cause of an illness, or unless the vision is interpreted to him in such a way as to supply it with positive meanings. Otherwise, he has simply seen evil things, and finds this objectionable. So the visionary experience is not rejected in and of itself.

Another set of objections to the behavior of peyotists centers on effortful adjustment to current conditions. It is asserted that peyotists do not work as hard, do not care for their livestock adequately (or dissipate it in ceremonies, as discussed above), do not send their children to school, and—in the view of a few anti-peyotists—are not "progressive" or "don't give us anything [beliefs, practices] to help us with our livelihood." It is of interest to note that the charge of inadequate economic adjustment is also made by Rimrock Navahos against members of the "Galilean" church, a fundamentalist Protestant sect (Rapoport, 1954).

The fact is that few statistically significant differences in economic adjustment or pattern of education can be observed as between peyotists and non-peyotists. In Mexican Springs and Aneth, in two random samples, peyotists had on average more sheep, goats, and cattle, and more total stock (including horses) than did non-peyotists. Thus, if anything, peyotists have slightly more stock today than do non-peyotists. These findings are discussed subsequently in considerably greater detail.

No significant differences can be demonstrated as between peyotists and non-peyotists in these samples, with respect to: own education, ability to speak English, children's education, job history, or acres farmed. Unless we assume that the

---

[4] It would be worthwhile to compare peyotism and the various African witch-finding movements and new religions which include witch-finding elements, but this would be a major essay in itself. There are parallels between the general explanation of the prevalence of witchcraft provided by Swanson (1960) and the approaches of Africanists to this subject (cf., for example, Marwick, 1952 and 1958; Middleton and Winter, eds., 1963). For a skeptical attitude toward the linking of increases of witchcraft fears with modern changes, see Goody, 1957. In this study I have not made a distinction between what British anthropologists call witchcraft and what they call sorcery.

peyotists were once superior to non-peyotists on all of these indices but are grad-ually declining, so that they are now equal to non-peyotists, it seems fair to say that peyotism is not marked by poorer than average economic adjustment, effort (measured by acres farmed and employment history), or planfulness for children.

PROBLEMS OF KINSHIP AND COMMUNITY SPLITS

There is also a set of negative reactions directed at peyotists because of troubles among kin and within the community over the peyote issue. Two issues are raised as regards kinship. The first is that families are divided on the issue and that hus-band and wife sometimes break up over the question of participation in the Native American Church. The second is that more extended kin stop helping each other once the peyote issue divides them. A common phrasing of this complaint is, "I once had relatives, but it seems as if now they are not my relatives at all."

Such divisions and ruptures occur. It is impossible to segment a Navaho com-munity without cutting across either ties of consanguinity or ties of affinity, or both—and indeed, impossible to divide adjoining communities without cutting across both sets of bonds. When one considers the relative fragility of the marital bond, it is surprising that so few cases of division between husband and wife are found.

At Greasewood below Ganado, the chapter chairman supplied a complete list of families in the chapter, a total of 133 families. Of these, 99 did not belong to the cult, 31 did, and 3 were divided. In each case, the wife was a member and the husband was not. Thus less than 3 per cent of families were divided. One family had been divided previously: the husband was a member and the wife was not. They were divorced at the time of my visit to Greasewood, but many dis-satisfactions were responsible for the breakup.

I do not have a similarly complete census of peyotist and non-peyotist families for other communities, but in every area I inqured particularly about split families and was never able to get the names of more than two or three; so the percentage is probably comparable elsewhere. In most such cases, it is the wife who is a mem-ber and the husband who is not. There are reported cases in which the husband issued an ultimatum: either the wife must leave the cult or he will divorce her. In all such cases, the wife left the cult. I do not have records of similar demands made by wives. Thus, in fact, the divided family is a rarity. Each such case, however, does create considerable disturbance. The husband in a divided family reported his views in the Tribal Council hearings on peyote in 1954 (TC 1954, pp. 81–86).

Splits between the members of an extended family are also relatively rare, but not always attended by discord. My interpreter at Lukachukai, his wife, and all his children were members of the cult. In an adjoining hogan lived his parents-in-law, non-members, who were having a sing when I was living there. The singer whom they had chosen was a well-known member of the peyote cult and a road man as well. The interpreter reported that no trouble had occurred on account of peyote.

Far more common, of course, are divisions between consanguine kin residing in different families: between siblings, between parents and children, and between clan relatives. The peyote member finds new solidarities and sources of aid as a result of his membership. The non-peyotist suffers a loss. How serious this loss would be if joining the cult did not cause bitter feelings between the new member and his kinsmen, it is hard to say. It is typically the non-peyotist who complains of loss, not the peyotist. It is my impression that after membership becomes an accepted fact, some of these wounds between member and non-member begin to heal. The period of greatest tension occurs during a period of rapid cult growth in a community, and in the first few years after any given individual has joined the cult.

Within the community, peyotism becomes a center for factionalism. There are sometimes disputes over election of tribal delegates—as happened at Greasewood —or over election of chapter officers—as happened at Sweetwater. It is often charged that one or the other side has acted illegally in calling the election or in presenting a particular candidate. Sometimes there is failure of cooperation over joint enterprises. Sometimes there is merely division of opinion on issues at stake. Non-peyotists universally deplore this situation. Some express genuine concern over the probable divisive result of any effort to uproot peyotism. They seem, however, to think that the only possible resolution of the conflict is for the peyotist to abandon his religion.

This brings us to the last in a long list of complaints against peyote, peyotism, and peyotists. The non-peyotists complain that the cult members take a lofty attitude, seem to think that they "know it all," and show disdain for other members of the community. Since peyotists do believe that they have access to superior knowledge, and since some pride themselves on a somewhat barbed style of speech, this accusation is undoubtedly true.

SUMMARY AND INTERPRETATION

In sum, the anti-peyotist's hostility to peyotism is expressed in the following allegations: (1) it is not traditional; (2) it is dangerous in its effects on mind and body; (3) its use is associated with uncontrolled behavior and specifically with uncontrolled sexual behavior; (4) it is a sort of intoxication; (5) it causes declining economic adjustment in one way or another; (6) it makes people lazy and careless about their children's educaton; (7) at least some of its members behave in ways not consonant with their ideals, committing adultery, bootlegging, and drinking; (8) peyotists create disturbance by making accusations of witchcraft; (9) peyotism causes divisions among family members, among kinsmen, and within the community; (10) peyotists are arrogant and sarcastic in manner.

The charge that peyotism is not traditional is correct. The medical evidence has not yet been discussed, but suffice it for the moment to say that there is little support for the theory that the effects of peyote include serious hazards to health or sanity. Allegations regarding health, orgiastic behavior, declining economic adjustment, or declining attention to well-being or children's education, can be seen to be founded on no evidence, or inadequate evidence. Allegations regarding the behavior of some members, the disturbance caused by allegations of witchcraft, divisions among kinsmen and within the community, and the "know-it-all" attitudes of peyotists are founded on fact. In the case of kinship and community divisions, however, it must be pointed out again that it takes two to make a quarrel.

It is easy to see why Navahos believe that peyote causes death and insanity. After all, some users of peyote have died or gone insane. They have not done so, in my judgment, *because* they used peyote, even though they did so *after* using peyote. But non-peyotist Navahos are not the first to make the error of confusing *post hoc* and *propter hoc*. It is not so easy to see why Navahos believe so firmly that sexual orgies occur in peyote meetings. There is no supporting evidence, and there are many reputable Navahos ready to deny that such events occur. Denial, at least in the years 1949–54, however, was countered by disbelief.

It is my general interpretation that peyotism is resisted by most Navahos because it represents both a significant threat to Navaho ways today and a significant deviation from many Navahos' expectations about the future of the tribe. It is further resisted because of an experientally based, but false, deep anxiety about its effects on health and sanity. I do not think that the anxiety about the effects of peyote itself is a purely secondary rationalization based on hostility to a non-traditional religion. My principal reason for this is the fact that debate on peyotism so often returns to the question, Does medical opinion show that peyote is injurious, or doesn't it? (It is true that authorities who say that it is are heard more willingly than authorities who say that it is not.)

Let us now return to peyotism as a perceived threat to Navaho ways.[5] It would be a mistake to think of Navahos as attempting to cling desperately to every traditional feature of life and to avoid every novelty. Theirs has been a record of borrowing since first they arrived in the Southwest, and eager borrowing continues today. But by and large, their borrowing has undoubtedly appeared to them to be something that would enhance, not destroy their current way of life: more elaborate ceremonials, probably borrowed at a time when the Pueblos were more numerous than the Navahos and had a higher standard of living than the Navahos; new crops, new animals, new tools, new machines—everything but new words. The record is almost endless. The record of resistance is far more limited. The Navahos resisted new crops, such as wheat, when the outcome of planting them was uncertain or the techniques of use were still unfamiliar. They resisted schooling when it seemed to have no obvious benefits—and thronged to the schools when the benefits became evident. They resisted new breeds of sheep when the evidence seemed to indicate that they could not survive local conditions—and adopted the improved breeds even during stock reduction when they proved viable. They resisted, if quite passively, conversion to Christianity, which seems, on the whole, to have had little message for them until recently. They were disturbed by recent ceremonial innovations, and they resisted stock reduction as long as they could and by every means save widespread organized violence. They seem today to vary in their outlook for the future: some seem to think that traditional ways—which means both traditional livelihood and traditional religion—can continue indefinitely, if incomes are augmented by wage labor. Others seem to think that some sort of gradual conversion to the "white way" in livelihood, medicine, and religion will occur. What they do not envisage is becoming just "Indians." What this word can

[5] I am indebted to Mr. R. Abrams for a helpful discussion of this subject.

mean to many, it is hard to say. The tribe is enormous; most Navahos know it is the most numerous "Indian" group in the United States. They have direct contact only with Pueblos, Apaches, and Utes. The Pueblos, like themselves, each think of themselves as a people with a way of life, not as a mere segment of a heterogeneous minority. Navaho views on the Apache I do not know. The Utes they regard as a deplorable example of what can happen. They see them as impoverished, reduced in number, and in no sense an example to follow. (Furthermore, many of them think that peyote caused the decline of the Ute.) The limited contacts of a few Navahos and some Tribal Council members with people at Parker, Arizona, is also with groups which seem to regard themselves not as generic Indians, but specifically as Mohave, etc. (The Mohave have also passed a Tribal regulation against the use of peyote.)

To many, what contributes to their economic welfare but allows them to continue as Navahos is acceptable; hence, on many issues, such as water development, irrigation, etc., they are "progressive." To a smaller number, what contributes to taking them into the larger community and polity is acceptable. Hence in education, religion, employment plans, etc., they are "progressive." Even the traditionalists accept education, since they know that it is necessary to cope with life since livestock reduction. To both types of "progressives," traditionalists and modernists, peyotism represents something utterly alien—something that neither perpetuates the old nor aligns them usefully with the new. It is a threat to Navaho religion as Christianity is not, because it is a curing religion. It is a threat as well because it introduces something Indian but not Navaho.

It thus appears as a foreign body, and efforts to extrude it occur. These efforts occur through beliefs that it is antagonistic to either Navaho or "modern" life on every front: it is thought to lead to breaches of the incest tabu, to loss of stock, to improvidence, to failure to educate, etc. Since it is foreign, as seen by the Navahos, it is transformed by anti-peyotists into an inversion of every Navaho value. I assume that Christianity is not seen as "foreign" in the same sense, but as part of the larger community with which the Navaho must somehow articulate.

To this is added a real anxiety about the health effects of peyote, and some fuel for the more extreme beliefs of anti-peyotists in the form of actual misbehavior of some road men, especially during the period of peyote's introduction. Given these negative attitudes, divisions of opinion regarding religious participation become bases for splits among kin and community factions—for which peyote gets the blame.

It must not be forgotten that antagonism toward peyotism is continually reinforced by Christian Navahos, missionaries, medical missionaries, traders with strong Christian commitments, and some doctors. These people oppose it both because it threatens the spread of orthodox Christianity and modern medicine and because it appears to them a step backward—or sideways—since they regard themselves as apostles of modernism. Thus peyotism is caught in a pincer movement in which extreme traditionalists and extreme modernists with Christian orientations form the two arms.

Part IV

THE DIFFERENTIAL APPEAL OF PEYOTISM
IN THE NAVAHO COUNTRY

Chapter 15

THE COURSE OF RESEARCH

ALTHOUGH I HAVE DISCUSSED the meaning of the cult to its Navaho members, and the major reasons for opposition to the cult given by non-members, I have not thus far attempted to account for the differential appeal of the cult, either in terms of individuals or of communities. Yet from the beginning of my research, the question of differential appeal was a primary preoccupation. Ultimately this led to the formation of a theory of relative deprivation, to be discussed subsequently. But an honest account of how this theory came to be formulated requires a description of the course of my research, including the blind alleys into which I travelled and the errors that I made. My role in the field should be made clear, and this will be my starting point.

ROLE OF THE ANTHROPOLOGIST

In spring of 1949, I was informed by another anthropologist that the Bureau of Indian Affairs was interested in hiring an anthropologist to do research on the peyote cult among the Navahos. He had been approached to take the job, but was unable to do so. Since I had done field work among the Navahos in the summers of 1939 and 1940, the idea was attractive, and I began negotiations with the Bureau which resulted in my employment in the summer of 1949. At that time I understood my role to be that of independent researcher, obligated to report my findings to the Bureau and to the Navajo Agency. I requested assurances that I need not supply information about specific individuals. These assurances of anonymity were granted and never violated. I realized, however, that I would have to try to track down the truth about the more spectacular rumors about peyote and peyotism, in the event that I had to give testimony at some future date. I did not interpret my role as that of supplying policy recommendations.

Nevertheless, in autumn of 1949 an Assistant Commissioner of Indian Affairs requested me to incorporate policy recommendations in my first report for the Bureau and the Agency, and I acceded to this change of role then and on many subsequent occasions. The definition of my position as research worker and casual source of policy suggestions was generally accepted in the Window Rock Area Office. But the Area Director (also General Superintendent of the Navajo Agency) took a somewhat different view, one which was to create difficulties from time to time. He held that I must turn in a final and decisive report, which could be released to the Tribal Council, at the earliest opportunity, since he believed that without such a mandate I was likely to spend an indefinite amount of time in research and writing—an assumption which proved correct. Furthermore, he held that a religion could be judged by its fruits—by the behavior of its adherents, and that it should be possible therefore to decide whether peyotism was worthy of protection. He believed that either the Tribal law should be upheld in its full rigor by the Agency, or peyotism should be fully allowed. My report, he held, should supply evidence for the decision. He did not press for a final report the first summer, but at the end of a second summer the pressure began, partly in the form of refusal to supply further research funds—although I was subsequently afforded every assistance short of funds that could be supplied: room, office space, access to files, etc. The third summer (1951) he requested an official report as soon as possible, for public release. Since, however, the Commissioner of Indian Affairs did not consider that such a report would be advantageous, the issue was dropped. And so I maintained a position as researcher and advisor throughout the years 1949–1953.

During these years, I had no official relationship with the Tribal Council as such. Many members knew of my research among the Navahos and of the research on the chemistry and physiology of peyote, under Dr. M. H. Seevers at Michigan. Some knew me. My work had been discussed with the Advisory Committee of the Council.

Furthermore, in every community where I stayed for any length of time, I discussed my work with either the local Tribal Council member or with the chapter officer, or both. It was these people who were most likely to want to know whether the Government knew about my work. Other members of the local community sometimes asked whether the chapter officer or councilman knew about my work and seemed satisfied if they knew that I had spoken with, or was going to speak with, one or the other. In only one community did either Navaho official express any concern over my doing research, whatever his views on peyote. In Greasewood, my first location, the chapter officer (with whom I lived) said that my interviewing was stirring up the controversy between peyotists and non-peyotists. And later he came to feel that I was encouraging the peyotists, or siding with them. Nevertheless, we remained on fairly good terms.

Among the Navahos, my role as an earnest seeker after truth was never accepted. Or, perhaps better, the kind of truth they thought I should pursue was different from my own interpretation—and far closer to the Area Director's. Without doubt, no matter what I said, I was seen by both sides as a judge—one come to find out the truth as to whether peyote was a good thing or a bad thing, and to report my findings to the Government, which would then make a reasonable solution. Needless to say, both sides knew the truth on this score, in advance. Both sides were disappointed in me, in the long run. The peyotists expected me to become a member of the Native American Church, and indeed I was given a membership pin on one occasion—which I said I could accept as a gift but could not wear, since I was not, and would not become, a member. They also expected me to find that their religion was revealed truth, and they supplied testimonials as to the curative effects of peyote in part to attempt to bring about a favorable verdict for peyote. The non-peyotists expected me to discover the awful truths about peyote and to take the position that it must be stamped out. Their disappointment was greater than that of cult members, since my eventual stand in favor of religious liberty seemed—and seems—to them to be a stand in favor of peyotism.

In the beginning, then, the peyotists were apprehensive about me, uncertain about talking to me, and unsure about permitting me to attend meetings. They were also unable to understand why I felt I could find out anything about peyote through discussion, since only peyote itself could teach about peyote—through eating it and attending meetings. In one of my first meetings with a Navaho peyotist, I told a man, "I want to talk to you about this peyote business." Although he talked to me, and eventually became a friend, the word "business" disturbed him very much indeed. It was four years before he found that he had no basis for suspicion and before he told me how the word "business" had upset him. (Peyote, after all, is not a "business" in standard English.) As time passed, all but a few came to trust me. I was admitted to peyote meetings on arrival in strange communities and found access easy almost everyhere. A handful of peyotists, however, made no secret of their continued distrust of me—and of all white men. One peyotist believed that I was secretly doing a medical study.

In the beginning non-peyotists were very willing to talk. As time passed, they continued to be willing, but those who knew most about my activities began to assume that I must be either a knave or a fool. If I had attended peyote meetings and had no horrors to report, I was either concealing my complicity in these horrors or I had been completely hoodwinked. If I recommended tolerance, I was promoting evil for the tribe. Nevertheless, only two people refused to talk to me. (From time to time the rumor spread that I was selling peyote, and some people believed that I was a bootlegger.)

During the last full summer of research (1953) I had to define a different role. I felt that I had gone as far as I could with direct investigation of peyotism, and that I must talk to both peyotists and non-peyotists about a variety of subjects without biasing responses by announcing my interest in peyotism. I had extensive interviews in Mexican Springs on the question of the present condition of the Navaho, presenting myself (truthfully) as an anthropologist interested in this subject. Toward the end of the summer, my interpreter, not a cult member, discovered my unusual interest in peyotism and found out that I had attended peyote meetings—in the course of an interview with an old friend of his who was a peyotist I had known previously—the only man in the community with whom I had had prior contact. This discovery did not impair our relationship or his acceptance of my mission for that summer. Harvey C. Moore, who was associated with the project in the summers of 1951–1953, always worked on general Navaho conditions, and was accepted in this role. Indeed, any interview with Navahos which dwelt on livelihood proved reasonably acceptable to the Navaho, since the subject was for them a very serious one and they easily understood a serious interest in it on our part.

In the early summer of 1954, my role was re-defined for me. I was asked by the Navajo Agency to appear at a Tribal Council hearing as an expert witness. The hearing was called to determine whether the law against peyote should be maintained or done away with. There is no doubt that both peyotists and anti-peyotists perceived me as a witness for peyotism on this occasion.

From the beginning of my work, most peyotists seemed to feel a genuine responsibility for facilitating my research. Indeed they would sometimes speak of "sending" me to a particular location. Since I did not like to make my appearance in a community without the name of some initial contact, the word is perhaps not misapplied. Thus, I besought *Leonard McKenzie[1] of Sawmill for suggestions as to where I might find a community in which I could find housing and work easily. He gave me a number of names, but did not seem too enthusiastic about any of them. When I mentioned the list to another peyotist—my first contact among the Navahos—he became quite excited at one of these names. "That's my uncle," he exclaimed. "We could find him at a squaw dance at Greasewood Springs, tonight." And so at 8:30 in the evening we started on a 120-mile round trip to find his uncle, returning at 3:00 AM with all arrangements made for my housing and for an interpreter at Greasewood Springs. And when, after two years, I visited Lukachukai and discovered a series of minor scandals of the 1930's concerning early peyote priests, my earliest informants were ready to admit that they had concealed this information earlier because they thought I would be disturbed, but had "sent" me to Lukachukai—recommended a visit there—"because you had to find out *some* time." I was readily admitted to peyote meetings—indeed pressed to enter them—attending eleven over five summers. In some instances I arrived in a community to find that one was to occur that night, so that I can fairly claim that I attended meetings arranged with no thought or knowledge of my presence. There was reluctance to have me attend curing meetings, since these were thought to be serious and tasking for those in attendance. But I attended one meeting whose primary purpose was curative and others where curing rituals were performed.

Twice I lived in the house of a peyotist while interviewing non-peyotists, and on one of these occasions my non-peyotist interpreter joined me in the household.

Non-peyotists were also very hospitable. At Greasewood Springs, the chapter officer found room for me and for a non-peyotist interpreter who came from another community. He even tolerated my going to a peyote meeting while I lived in his house, although this event did disturb him.

Interpreters were difficult to find, because English-speaking Navahos tended to be working off-reservation during the summer. Whenever possible, peyotist interpreters were used with peyotist informants, and non-peyotist with non-peyotist informants. It was almost impossible to discuss peyotism otherwise. Peyotist or non-peyotist, they worked hard and faithfully, as interpreters and guides, securing lodging and food for both of us when we worked out of home territory—in spite of shyness and lack of contacts in some instances. In five summers, only one failed to appear for work on an agreed-on day. Most were not trained as interpreters. My limited knowledge of Navaho served to check on marked simplification or omission, but in my judgment seriousness and care to repeat as much of what was said as possible was characteristic. Men in their forties, or older, some of limited education, proved more satisfactory than young men. Indeed, in one case the chapter officer accompanied my youthful interpreter, who did not know the community, guiding us to houses and then breaking down the streams of Navaho of voluble informants into bite-sized chunks, since the young man simply could not retain extended discourse.

Had I spoken fluent Navaho, the work would have gone better. As it is, my most intimate friendships and most detailed information comes from English-speaking Navahos. But I think I was served well by every interpreter I worked with.

[1] Asterisk preceding a proper name indicates a pseudonym.

Interpreters were paid by the day, and, after one painful experience, they were paid approximately the wage they could have received by working off-reservation. Informants were not paid. Gifts of cigarettes or food were made at the end of a discussion; meals received were recompensed by cans of food. A relationship with an interpreter, and sometimes with an informant, often passed beyond the point of pay for services or gifts for talking: the Navaho would come to feel that I owed him a favor beyond this, and would then make his claim. Once I was asked to take my host's insane brother-in-law to the hospital; once to take my interpreter's parents-in-law more than a hundred miles to visit their son, who was living alone on an Anglo ranch at the bottom of a canyon off the reservation. In both cases the feeling of claim was amply justified, and I fulfilled the requests. By contrast, a stranger asked me for a ride when I was working at a squaw dance. "What shall I do?" I asked my interpreter. "Tell him you're busy; there are lots of other people here with cars; he doesn't know you." Thus, by and large, individual relationships seem to have been interpreted in terms of a sensible reciprocity.

WORK, 1949–1950

Let us turn now to the formulation and reformulation of research problems, beginning with prospectuses written prior to field work in 1949 and concluding with the results of preliminary data analysis after the termination of field work in 1954. Before I started field work, I prepared two prospectuses for the Bureau of Indian Affairs, and an additional document for my own use. All three selected as two major problems the explanation of the differential appeal of peyotism to Navaho communities and individuals. The one prepared for my own use had hints of a conception of relative deprivation, but no more. Thus four types of strains were considered to be likely factors in promoting a high level of peyotism in some communities (but the term "strains" was undefined). (1) Economic strains: disruption in economic life through greater than average competition with whites, greater impact of livestock reduction, more erosion, etc. (2) Political strains: prior existence of marked factionalism. (3) Solidarity strains: breakdown of extended families, which would create emotional strains and deprivations (and this term, too, was undefined). (4) Strains of acculturation: education, training in guilt, training in Christianity, and exposure to religious enthusiasm would create emotional needs unsatisfied in traditional Navaho life. Communities with more of these strains should be more likely to accept peyotism, assuming equal availability of the cult to communities with more and with less strains. (The problem of availability was to plague me ever after. Cf. Aberle and Stewart, 1957.) In addition, the status of those who brought peyote to the community, and the apparent success or failure of early curing effects, might add complications.

In terms of individual differences, "strains" and "tensions" (undefined) were made the basis for two predictions. (1) In part because tensions were greater for men than for women (and in part because men were more acculturated), men should be more receptive to peyotism than should women. (2) The poor, who suffered more strains, should be more receptive than the rich. Other predictions were that the acculturated (except for the almost completely Americanized), the old (because they were less acculturated), the status-deprived and marginal men, and young men unable to achieve status in the traditional system should be more receptive to peyotism. Among ceremonialists, full-fledged singers should be less receptive than curers and diviners, and singers who did become peyotists should be those previously suspected of witchcraft. For Christians, the attitude of the local missionary toward the cult would be a determining factor.

The Bureau stated that it was particularly interested in factors leading to continued or increasing use of peyote and in the effects of peyote (and peyotism) on individuals or groups, and especially on family organization and wider social organization. I myself was convinced that I would have to investigate some of the more spectacular rumors about peyotism to prepare for questioning on this score. I had also, of course, set myself the task of finding out the sources of the Navaho peyote cult, the means of transmission, and the distribution, as well as of examining the Navaho cult for changes in ritual or ideology by comparison with the cult as received by them. In addition, these early prospectuses correctly anticipated that peyotism would not appeal to the majority of Navahos and would be resisted by political leaders and by ceremonial practitioners. I was not aware at this time of the importance of the Tribal Council in the peyote issue nor of the significance of Christian leaders in that Council for the law against peyotism.

So I went to the Reservation in 1949 and, after making my initial contacts, spent about four weeks at Greasewood Springs, talking first to peyotists and then to non-peyotists. I attended two peyote meetings. During this time the main outlines of the materials previously presented regarding the attitudes and beliefs of peyotists and opponents of peyotism were laid down. Subsequent work did little but confirm and refine them. My search for individual differences, however, did not seem to make headway. Using very rough procedures, I could not find differences in level of acculturation or between veterans and non-veterans as respects cult membership. Ceremonialists did seem less likely to participate in the cult than laity.

My anti-peyotist host at Greasewood maintained stoutly that important men (which for him meant relatively well-to-do Navahos with relatively large herds) did not join the cult. Furthermore, like most non-peyotists, he was convinced that cult members were destroying their herds by giving ceremonies and making extravagant gifts to peyote priests. Peyotists, on the other hand, maintained stoutly that traditional Navaho ceremonies had nearly reduced some of them to beggary and that peyote ceremonies were far cheaper. In an effort to check on this, I went over livestock records for some members of the community over a five-year period. The results were inconclusive at the time, but the effort was the beginning of my collection of data on livestock and livestock reduction.

By this time I had come to view peyotism as one of several individual and collective responses to current Navaho frustrations. Other responses included drinking, increased use of traditional ceremonies, and direct efforts to deal with economic problems. I also came to feel—on no very rational basis—that I needed to see peyotism in other communities, and in particular in communities where it had been established longer than at Greasewood, where it had entered about 1940.

A trip to the northern reservation gave me new information on peyote history, my first exposure to V-way, and experience of a level of antagonism to peyotism more extreme than I had hitherto recorded (this was at Shiprock). Various discus-

sions led me to believe that peyote, far from being strongest in the most acculturated communities, was strongest in communities of little acculturation. In the
end the information on which this belief was based turned out to be incorrect, but
before I discovered this, I had formulated new theories about the spread of the cult.

At the end of the summer a report was submitted to the Bureau and to the Window Rock Area Office. It described peyotism as a response to a situation of "cultural deprivation." It asserted the importance of discovering whether the Navahos
had accepted peyotism as soon as it became available, or whether there had been a
"lag," a period when it was known at Towaoc, among the Utes, and to adjoining
Navahos, but did not spread. If this were the case, a stronger argument could be
made for associating the spread with "deprivation" (undefined). The report found
no evidence that peyotists were declining economically, that they were more
acculturated, or that peyotists and non-peyotists differed in the education of their
children. I suggested that perhaps the very poor tended to accept peyotism and the
very rich to reject it—an idea which subsequent research has failed to support.
Peyotism and anti-peyotism were described as alternative responses to a single set
of pressures and dilemmas, such as traditionalism versus assimilation, anomie associated with acculturation, difficulties in understanding white ways, economic
problems, including fixed livestock holdings, health problems, and witchcraft fears.
The guilt implied by the peyote confession and the dependency on the peyotist's
relationship to God had been topics of interest throughout the summer, especially
by contrast with traditional Navaho belief. I suggested that guilt reactions and dependency both stemmed from the Navaho's relations with the dominant culture.
The report concluded with a plea for more research, and it was agreed that field
work would continue with Indian Service support in the summer of 1950.

WORK, 1950–1951

In May of 1950, a new prospectus was presented to the Bureau, outlining several
problem areas, most of which had been mentioned in the concluding section of the
1949 report. I planned to work on the development of relations between peyotist
and anti-peyotist factions in different communities over time (an eminently practical topic for the Bureau, in view of the conflict between the two groups), the history of the cult, more data on ritual, prayers, songs, and V-way, more information
on peyote leaders and on the organization of the Navaho peyotists and the distribution of the cult. I also planned specifically to work on the apparent paradox that
the cult was strongest in unacculturated areas, and so wanted to work in such areas.

Things were a little tense when I arrived in the field in 1950. One peyote leader
told me that there were "rumors" against me from Greasewood—but my supposed
antagonists proved friendly when I saw them and have remained so ever since. The
Council wanted to discuss peyote at a meeting and bring pressure to bear on the
Government to enforce the law. At this particular time, however, the General
Superintendent and the Commissioner opposed the discussion—the Superintendent
because he rightly assumed he would get no other business discussed if this issue
arose.

I wanted to go to Black Mountain, where, I was told, the community was little
acculturated ("they wear their hair long and eat mutton three times a day," said

my Navaho friends), and where 75–90 per cent of the group was said to have joined the cult. Six days after I arrived at Window Rock, a peyote priest from Window Rock (who was supposedly "mad" at me) came to tell me to come straight to Piñon. He could recommend two interpreters, one of whom was with him at the time, and could even suggest people who would lend me a truck if my car wouldn't work. So I went. (Thus my location at Greasewood and in the Black Mountain area was arranged for me by peyotists.)

The Black Mountain area (the northern portion of District 4) proved indeed to be the least acculturated area I was to visit in all my field work—although communities further north and west would undoubtedly have been even less acculturated. There were more "long hairs" among the men, more silver hat bands, more big hats, more mother-in-law avoidance, less education, and there was more mutton to eat than I was ever to see again. I attended two peyote meetings there.

But I soon found that the peyotists in District 4 were in a minority. Estimates must be rough, but somewhere between 10 and 25 per cent of the population were cult members. Almost all of these were north of Piñon, in the mountains, not south, on the flats. They included a group of fairly closely connected, well-to-do families (by Navaho standards).

Indeed, the District Supervisor, himself a Navaho but not a cult member, spoke of the Black Mountain peyotists as a "rich man's club," and one of these rich men told me that he had joined the cult because of his disturbance over livestock reduction. Unfortunately I did not pay enough heed to these bits of information. The "rich," it should be said, were people who held at most a little more than 300 head of sheep. They all held special permits, since the regular permit was for only 72 sheep units. They lived north of Piñon in the mountains, where the pasture was best but where farming was not easy because of frosts. My journal at this time suggested, without further elaboration, that the predominance of the rich might result from the fact that road men visiting the community might well proselytize among the rich because of desires for gifts and comfortable hospitality, or from the fact that whereas the Navahos south of Piñon were poorer, the rich above Piñon might be more "deprived."

The Black Mountain experience also led me to have a general impression about the typical sequence of events in communities where peyote entered, which was reasonably well-corroborated by subsequent information from elsewhere. But I was uncertain then, and I still am, as to why the entry of the cult was accompanied by so much more trouble, over so much longer a period of time, in some communities than in others. I was at a total loss to account for community differences in the acceptance of peyotism. I had abandoned the idea that less acculturated communities were more peyote-prone. And I had become interested in the history of livestock reduction. I had the impression that areas with special permits tended somewhat more toward peyotism than other areas.

At this point I moved to Teec Nos Pas. Although I failed to note why I did so, it must have been so that I could see an area where peyotists were very numerous. In the event, I settled west of Teec Nos Pas at Sweetwater, where I remained for ten days. There I attended two peyote meetings. I discovered a history of physical fracases over the peyote issue and found a bitterness between the two factions of a most extreme nature, but was unable to find any way of explaining this. I also began to encounter differences in attitudes toward peyotism among cult members from Sweetwater on the one hand and Black Mountain on the other—differences which eventually led to the formulation of the views about northern and southern peyotism presented earlier. I revisited Greasewood briefly, did some work on peyote history, and spent a good deal of time chasing down medical cases. On almost the last day of my 1950 field work I wrote, "Is there a fit between stock reduction tensions and peyote?"

In September of 1950, I submitted a second report to the Bureau and to the Window Rock Area Office. In this report there was an attempt to account for the level of disturbance which arose in communities after peyotism entered, and to account for the acceptance or rejection of peyotism. Six factors promoting or inhibiting troubles over peyotism were mentioned. Early efforts to enforce the regulation in the community, missionary antagonism, and the antagonism of medical authorities were three "exogenous" factors considered to promote strife (although legal action in fact ordinarily results from local efforts). A strong chapter organization and a high general level of "tension" prior to peyotism were two internal factors promoting factionalism and trouble. (A "tense" community was one which had been a trouble spot in the past—as was the case for Teec Nos Pas, for example.) On the other hand, a "strong" kinship system was thought to be an internal factor tending to heal factionalism. Impressionistic ratings of three communities on these six variables gave them scores which corresponded with their rank order when they were rated on the amount of disturbance over peyote described by informants.

Three factors were suggested to account for the level of peyotism found in communities. The first was "tension"—again, tendencies toward disturbance and hostility toward whites evident before peyotism entered. The second was acculturation, which was assumed to have a curvilinear relationship to peyotism: the most traditional and the most acculturated communities might be resistive to peyotism, whereas intermediate levels of acculturation might promote it. The third factor was availability: geographical proximity to a center of distribution, position in the communication system, time of exposure. The report discussed various findings of the summer's work, including a rather lengthy treatment of Navaho reactions to livestock reduction, a subject which had become obtrusive when I worked in District 4. But finally I was unable to decide why peyotism, rather than various alternative responses to current problems, was elected by some communities or individuals.

By this time I was somewhat overwhelmed by the variety presented by the Navajo reservation and by the job that confronted a lone investigator. So I proposed, among other enterprises, questionnaires about various Navaho communities, to be distributed to Agency personnel, which would deal with factors promoting or inhibiting the spread of peyotism and those promoting or inhibiting trouble in the community.

There was an emerging division of opinion at the Agency regarding the utility of further research. The General Superintendent felt that I would continue work well past the point of practical return. He wanted a definitive, public, final report, to serve as a basis for settling the issue. Others wanted more research and also considered that a public report would be disadvantageous. Sometime during the academic year 1950–1951, it was decided that I would be given full Agency cooperation, but no funds, if I wanted to continue. Support for the research was provided by the National Institute of Mental Health and the Social Science Research Council. Dr. Harvey C. Moore joined me to assist in the research in the summer of 1951.

WORK, 1951–1952

Meantime, after consultation with Dr. John Clausen and Dr. Henry A. Riecken, plans for questionnaires and structured interviews were completed. In May of 1951, the General Superintendent circulated questionnaires to a large number of Agency employees, dealing with the level of peyotism to be found in various Districts and communities and the date of introduction of peyotism (results in Aberle and Stewart, 1957). During the summer, Moore interviewed more than thirty Agency employees, asking them to describe certain characteristics of communities with which they were particularly familiar, and to rate these and other communities on a series of variables. The interview attempted a general survey of conditions in the area, and was not presented as primarily concerned with peyotism—both because the section on peyotism formed only a relatively small part of the total and because it was thought that a discussion of general conditions oriented specifically to the question of why peyotism spreads might bias the replies. The interview dealt broadly with political organization, troubles in the community (termed "tension"), reactions to livestock reduction, level of acculturation, and trouble over peyotism. These topics represented a reworking of the list of variables which had appeared in my 1950 report as possible facilitators and inhibitors of the spread of peyote and of trouble over peyote. It was hypothesized that peyotism would be associated positively with troubles in the community and with antagonism to livestock reduction. Trouble over peyotism, it was hypothesized, would be associated positively with trouble and with evidence of early enforcement efforts. Acculturation was introduced because of the long history of considering it to be an important variable in the genesis of nativistic movements, but no definite hypothesis was made about acculturation in the prospectuses for that summer.

Agency personnel proved highly cooperative both in turning in questionnaires and in completing what turned out to be a very lengthy interview. This interviewing occupied Moore full time during the summer.

My own work was considerably less satisfactory. A good deal of time was spent in two communities trying to find an interpreter and failing in both. Eight days were spent at Lukachukai. There I first was able to get detailed information on certain disturbances which occurred quite early in the history of Navaho peyotism and which undoubtedly accounted in part for its bad reputation among some Navahos. Lukachukai also provided an anomaly: a community where the membership reached the high level of 40 per cent, but where there were no peyote priests in residence and most meetings attended by local members were held outside the community. The remainder of the summer was spent on the distribution and history of the cult and involved extensive travelling on the Reservation.

Between my return from the field in early September and the end of October, it became necessary for me to submit research plans to the National Institute of Mental Health, to secure continued support. This resulted from the fact that I was planning to move from Johns Hopkins to Michigan in September of 1952. The questionnaires and ratings Moore had secured could not be analyzed fully in the time available, and the new prospectus was largely a re-working of the 1951 plans in terms of my own experiences during the summer. A general hypothesis about factors inhibiting and promoting the spread of peyotism was advanced: that acceptance of peyotism varied directly with tension, inversely with secularization, and directly with availability.

Tension was defined as "a function of the discrepancy between legitimate expectation and actuality"; discussion of the concept indicated that what was meant was a situation where legitimate expectations were not fulfilled. "Secularization" was defined as a tendency to strive to relieve tension by empirical, rather than non-empirical means. And "availability" referred to access to agents of the cult. I attempted to operationalize the three variables and to apply the hypothesis to eleven communities, nine of them places where I had worked and two of them communities on which I had a reasonable amount of information.

Although my definition of tension was clearly virtually identical with my later definition of relative deprivation, the indices of tension I used were based on the items selected for discusison in Moore's interview: various sorts of trouble, such as drunkenness, fear of witches, threats against witches, efforts to kill witches, above-average divorce rates, wife-beating, numerous separations, high frequency of use of Navaho ceremonies, acts of violence, etc. Livestock reduction was considered as a cause of tensions. But the causes of tension were not important, only the manifest level to be found. Tension—as defined—was thought to promote peyotism because (1) peyotism supplied mystical knowledge when practical knowledge failed; (2) it promised God's help when the individual felt helpless; (3) it was a source of self-respect when the outside world generated feelings of inferiority; and (4) it provided moral guidance in an anomic world—although I was not certain that this point belonged in the "tension" group.

As for secularization, I proposed, in the absence of direct evidence, to use level of acculturation as equivalent to a measure of secularization. (The relationship between a direct measure of secularization and peyotism need not have been tautologous, since the measures subsequently proposed involved an evaluation of the individual's approach to solving a variety of problems in his life.)

For availability, the number of years that had elapsed since the introduction of peyote into the community was taken as a rough index. Certain difficulties with the hypothesis could be seen, especially since one might expect that relatively acculturated areas (hence secularized, so that peyotism should be low) were likely to be relatively tension-laden, simply because they were acculturated. It seems clear at this point that my discussion was wavering between tension as defined, and tension as operationalized. The communities I called "tense" were, in each instance, trouble-spots. My own ratings of the eleven communities on all three variables and on level of peyotism, done fairly subjectively, tended to support this three-factor theory, although no statistical test was attempted. With these results from an admittedly rough and ready test of the hypothesis, I now proposed to have Moore work in at least two communities on the general question of secularization, selecting two with high tension and different levels of acculturation, and perhaps a third. My own work would have to continue along previous lines, because, I thought, I was too much identified with the peyote issue to begin studies of problem solution. The proposal had to be tentative, however, because Moore's ratings and the questionnaires had not yet been analyzed.

Statistical work during the winter of 1951–1952 supported this set of predictions for one area of the reservation, but not for others, for three separate time periods. In spite of the lack of confirmation for other areas, I tended to place great weight in these findings. (Ultimately, for technical, statistical reasons, this entire analysis was set aside.) The analysis was completed only in June of 1952. For this one area, Districts 9, 11, 12, 14, and 18, where peyote had first appeared, there were positive correlations between Moore's "tension" ratings and peyote level and between trouble over livestock reduction and peyote level. There were negative correlations between acculturation and peyote level. These correlations held for each of three time periods. They heavily influenced plans for research for 1952. I had already planned to study "tension" and to study "secularization" directly, instead of using acculturation as a measure of this variable. Now reactions to livestock reduction also became a topic for separate consideration.

WORK, 1952–1953

It was planned to go to two or three communities, communities which differed from each other on the ratings Moore had secured, and to interview a supposedly representative sample of Navahos in two or three communities: to wit, a sample which would include a fair range of age, wealth, and education, some peyotists and some non-peyotists, some heavy drinkers and some light drinkers or abstainers, and a few ceremonial practitioners. (This is not, of course, a representative sample in the technical sense.) Moore was to do the interviewing, using an outline of topics to be covered, rather than a scheduled interview book. The communities would be selected because they fell at certain extremes on the variables rated by Bureau personnel. I was initially tempted to select communities where the variables "worked against" each other: where, for example, tension was high but acculturation was also high, or where tension was low and acculturation was also low. But for reasons to be discussed shortly, instead we selected two communities where the ratings fitted my hypothesis and one where they did not. Tohatchi showed relatively high acculturation, relatively low tension, relatively little hostility to livestock reduction, and, as expected, was low on peyotism. Teec Nos Pas showed relatively high tension, relatively great hostility to peyotism, relatively little acculturation, and was high on peyotism, thus fitting the hypothesis. Crownpoint was relatively high in acculturation but moderately high in tension and hostility to stock reduction. It should have had a moderate level of peyotism but at that time it had almost none.

The selection of the first two communities was based on a fundamental misconception on my part. Much though I later regretted the error, not only did I overlook it, but so did a number of anthropologists and other social scientists with whom I discussed my plans. In my view, the community, not the individual, was to be the unit of analysis. The people selected for interviewing were to stand as representative of the population of a given community. If the interviews showed that Tohatchi was in fact highly secularized and suffering from little tension, then—since Tohatchi was known to have few cult members—this would support the theory. If Teec Nos Pas proved similarly to be little secularized and suffering from much tension, then—since it had many cult members, this would support the hypothesis. And, since I fully expected the relationships to work out this way, we could go further in the case of Crownpoint by exploring some possible reasons why the theory did not predict peyote level correctly there. Only after the conclusion of field work in 1953—a year later—did I come to realize that, if the community were indeed the unit of analysis, my approach was far more a check on the validity of Indian Service ratings than on the verification of my hypothesis. In the case of Tohatchi and Teec Nos Pas I had selected communities where the Indian Service ratings provided results which *did* fit the hypothesis. If interviewing were to provide comparable ratings on secularization and tension, this would merely prove that interviews provided an assessment of the community which paralleled that of the raters. Indeed, only if interviews failed to corroborate the ratings, and if levels of peyote differed from those we assumed to be correct, and if the variables *still* predicted the level of peyotism, would we have had any additional corroboration of the theory, and then, of course, only for three communities (including Crownpoint).

This study went forward in the summer of 1952. Moore described it, correctly, to Navahos, as a study of how things were going with them and what they thought of various matters. In addition to touching on many "trouble" areas, peyote cult membership, and reactions to livestock reduction, it dealt with reactions to a variety of problems and the solutions adopted by the Navahos for each. It also dealt with general mood, and with orientations to past, present, and future situation.

Yet in spite of my intention to use the entire body of interviews from a given community to represent that community as a single instance, I also had plans to use individual interviews to compare peyotists and non-peyotists. We hoped to explore a variety of factors which would lead to an individual's choosing or rejecting peyotism. By now the variables had proliferated a good deal. In addition to pragmatism ("secularization"), I was considering confusion or clarity about the future, feelings of inferiority, anomic reactions, etc. I was by no means ready to stake everything on tension, reactions to livestock reduction, and acculturation or secularization.

My own work continued with discussions of peyote with peyotists and non-peyotists. A part of the summer was spent at Red Rock and Cove, where there were a good many peyotists, and much time was devoted to getting new information on V-way. I revisited Lukachukai briefly and spent the remainder of the summer travelling widely in an effort to learn more about the history of the Navaho cult. During the summer I spoke with Solon T. Kimball, who talked about acceptance of peyote in District 4 in terms of relative deprivation: the "rich" there were also those most hurt by livestock reduction—a point which I had noted in the course of work there in 1950.

In September of 1952, I moved from the Johns Hopkins University to the University of Michigan. Confronted by a large stack of Moore's interviews, I turned to the Survey Research Center of the University of Michigan for help in the analysis of these data. With the assistance of William Scott, a code-book was developed, and the interviews were dealt with by the coding staff at the Center. This operation was subsidized by a Behavioral Studies Grant from the Ford Foundation. The analysis of the data, once the interviews were transferred to IBM cards, gave rise to a variety of problems and questions. First, the question of whether the community or the individual was the unit of study—or both—became pressing. Second, Moore had been unable to secure any peyotist interviews at Crownpoint because of problems in locating interpreters. Third, there were very few peyotists in the Tohatchi sample. Initial runs, using all Tohatchi and Teec Nos Pas interviews as a single sample, showed relatively few sharp differences between peyotists and non-peyotists, and when there were differences we were not at all sure when we were measuring associations between peyotism and the variable in question and when we were measuring associations between the variable and the community. Thus, since few people in Teec Nos Pas had automobiles and many people in Tohatchi did, and since many people in Teec Nos Pas and few in Tohatchi were peyotists, a table which combined data from the two communities would tend to show a negative association between automobile ownership and peyotism— an association which might not hold within each community. Fourth, because we had used an interview outline rather than an interview book, we found many items which had to be coded "not ascertained." And fifth, affected by my contacts with sociologists and social psychologists, I had begun to become uneasy about the failure to use random sampling.

WORK, 1953–1954

The fatal difficulty of using the community as the unit of analysis had not yet become clear. Some of the tables looked interesting, and it was decided to try to get random samples, using a standardized interview dealing with materials like those in the 1952 work, and working in two new communities in the summer of 1953. William Scott developed a plan for random sampling. We intended once again to select one community with high acculturation, low tension, low antagonism to livestock reduction, and low cult membership, and one community with low acculturation, high tension and antagonism to livestock reduction, and high cult membership. Eventually Mexican Springs and Aneth, which adjoined Tohatchi and Teec Nos Pas, respectively, were selected.

A revision of the 1952 interview schedule was undertaken. The interview was to deal with Navaho adjustment. Plans for data analysis still involved "validating" the tension-secularization hypothesis. But in addition, there were plans to compare the peyotists of the two communities, and the non-peyotists of the two communities. Peyotists and non-peyotists were to be compared by lumping interviews for 1952 and 1953.

In the summer of 1953, we decided that samples of any reasonable size could be gathered only if both of us worked, rather than leaving standardized interviewing to Moore. So Moore went to Aneth and I to Mexican Springs, where, as I have said, I was able to dissociate myself almost completely from the study of peyotism as such. Random sample lists were developed from the school census. It should be emphasized that both of us found that our interpreters and respondents accepted the idea of random sampling as a suitable way of ensuring a cross-section of community views. Indeed, at Aneth, where Moore was unable to reach some of the more isolated households, some of his designated respondents came to visit him at his living quarters toward the end of his stay, saying that they had heard he wanted to talk to them and were afraid he might leave before they could be interviewed.

The interview was long, the roads were formidable, cars broke down, and interpreters were not always available. As a result, only 24 interviews based on random sampling were secured at Aneth, and only 35 at Mexican Springs (where the roads were better). Some substitute interviews were gathered where individuals on the sample list could not be reached, but they were not used for data analysis. The Aneth sample had an alarmingly small number of non-peyotists—6. The Mexican Springs sample had only 6 peyotists initially; so a special random sample of 3 peyotists was added, from a list of people regarded as peyotists.

The small number of peyotists in one community and of non-peyotists in the other led to a vacillating attitude toward the use of individuals versus communities as units of analysis when work began in the fall of 1953. The small samples and skewed distributions in each sample made it difficult to find significant results within each community, but treating the two communities as a single sample proved impossible for reasons already discussed: it tended to produce artifactual results. And finally, the conception of treating the community as a case to prove my hypothesis was abandoned when I came to realize through discussions with Clyde Coombs that my design was suitable as a test of the validity of Moore's ratings, not as a test of my theory.

Hence I finally came to the realization that my two random samples could be used only to explore the bases for individual adherence to peyotism and that the two samples had to be treated independently. At this point, I decided that my hypotheses had proliferated so greatly that it was necessary to do a full job of analysis of these data, rather than to return to the field for more, even if the samples were small. I was by now interested in "secularization," acculturation, anxiety, resentment, participation in community, tribal, and national affairs, attitudes toward whites, toward culture change, general livelihood conditions, past livelihood conditions, and so on. A return to the field would undoubtedly have multiplied, not reduced, these possibly significant variables, unless a careful analysis of existing data were completed.

WORK, 1954–1956

In the summer of 1954, I made an appearance at the Tribal Council hearing on peyote and did a short piece of field work dealing with the growth of the cult in District 4 and Greasewood, and with peyote history. No further field work was done. Statistical analysis continued throughout the academic years of 1953–1954, 1954–1955, and 1955–1956. Some of the results are to be found in Aberle and Stewart, 1957. The rest appear in this work. Gradually a rule of thumb emerged:

CHART H

Field Work Schedule

Summer of:	Field Worker	Locations	Activities and Aims
1949	Aberle	Window Rock area	Initial contacts.
		Greasewood near Ganado	Initial understanding of cult.
		Shiprock and Aneth	Early cult history; information on V-way.
1950	Aberle	Piñon	Attitudes and experiences of cult members and non-members; comparison with Greasewood; exploration of relatively unacculturated community.
		Teec Nos Pas	Examination of a community where peyotists were in the majority. Exploration of different attitudes toward peyotism among cult members in different areas.
		Greasewood	Maintaining relationships; checking on cult stability, growth or decline.
1951 (May)	Aberle	Reservation-wide	Questionnaires prepared by DFA circulated to field personnel by Area General Superintendent.
1951 (Summer)		Crownpoint	Trying to find an interpreter.
		Tohatchi	Trying to find an interpreter.
		Lukachukai	Attitudes and experiences of cult members and non-members.
		Montezuma Creek, Bluff, Mexican Hat, Kayenta, Dinnehotso	History of the cult; current distribution.
1951	Moore	Reservation-wide	Interviews with Agency field employees regarding general conditions in various Navaho communities.
1952	Aberle	Red Rock–Cove	Attitudes and experiences of cult members and non-members; V-way.
		Shiprock, Fruitland, Farmington, Cortez, Montezuma Creek, etc.	History of the cult.
	Moore	Tohatchi, Teec Nos Pas, Crownpoint	Systematic interviews on general adjustment of peyotists and non-peyotists.
1953	Aberle	Mexican Springs	Systematic interviews on general adjustment of a random sample of 35 Navahos.
	Moore	Aneth	Systematic interviews on general adjustment of a random sample of 24 Navahos.
	Stewart	Consolidated Ute Reservation	History of the Ute and Navaho cults.
1954	Aberle	Window Rock	Expert witness on the peyote cult at Tribal Council hearing. Discussion with key informants regarding growth of cult at Piñon.
		Shiprock	History of the cult.

findings would be used only if (*a*) the trends were the same in the two communities, and (*b*) the combined significance for the two communities was .05 or better. In the end, the only clearly significant variables associated with peyotism had to do with livestock.

Acculturation, secularization, future-orientation, helplessness, dependency, adequacy, mysticism, attitude toward culture change, and many other intriguing variables had gone by the board. The findings that were significant led, gradually, to the formulation of a relative deprivation theory, centering on livestock reduction. This theory was firmed up more than six years after I began field work, although it was one of many possible approaches I had flirted with from at least as early as 1950.

In addition, in 1955–1956, Omer Stewart and I completed our collaboration on Navaho and Ute peyote history. Prompted by Stewart, I came to see that the communications factor did account for some of the variance among communities as respects the level of peyotism found.

This painful excursion into the course of research is necessary to show what was done, why it was done at particular points, and why apparently obvious things were overlooked. If I had not been so attached to the problem of differences between communities—which I cannot fully explain even now—I would have settled down to work in one or two communities intensively. If I had done this, my knowledge of the history of the cult would have suffered, but my understanding of the network of social influence and its impact on acceptance of peyotism would have been much enlarged. Whether I would have arrived at my present formulation, I do not know. It is possible that the rickety scaffolding provided by the "tension" theory was a necessary step to later theory-building. I turn now to the results of the 1953 field work.

Chapter 16

SOME NEGATIVE RESULTS

IN MY INITIAL APPROACH TO PEYOTISM, I was governed by the widely held anthropological view that peyotism is a religion of transition, something that eases the adjustment of Indians who are uprooted from tradition but incompletely acculturated in American ways and unassimilated into the larger society. Thus La Barre remarks that "the cult is a compromise solution between Christianity and older native religions . . ." (1938, p. 93). In 1937, a series of anthropologists supplied statements on peyote in connection with a Senate Bill (1399) to outlaw its use. I quote from a mimeographed copy of these statements ("Documents on Peyote," 1937). Boas said, "peyote has been one of the means which has facilitated the transition from primitive beliefs to an amalgamation with Christianity." Kroeber said that peyote "represents a way out of a difficult problem to certain elements of our Indian population: their particular adaptation to an inevitable adjustment. . . ." M. R. Harrington, after saying that the physiological effects of peyote required medical study, went on, "In other respects I think the use of peyote and the rites and teachings accompanying such use have been of great benefit to the Indians with whom I came in contact during my Oklahoma work. This is especially true of tribes whose organization and native life were breaking down with the consequent loss of morale and pride in their racial heritage." Petrullo said, "The religious cult built around the Peyote represents, on analysis, an attempt on the part of our Indians to adjust themselves to modern conditions and to bridge the gap that exists between their ancient cultures and the modern American." These statements are, I think, a reasonable sample of the general view of peyotism in anthropology when I began my work, and indeed subsequently. In 1952, Spindler and Goldschmidt proposed to use cult membership to define a stage of acculturation among the Menomini (Spindler and Goldschmidt, 1952).[1]

For this reason, I continued throughout my work to be interested in age, education, livelihood base, knowledge of traditional ways, attitude toward culture change, attitude toward whites, and many similar features as they pertained to the "transition" theory. I also became interested in a large number of other considerations, such as relations with the Indian Service and attitude toward it, activism-passivism, orientation toward the future, resentment, and so on. It would be only a slight exaggeration to say that, beginning with any dysphorias I could think of

[1] Later, Spindler discovered that Menomini members of the peyote cult did indeed occupy an intermediate position on the acculturation continuum, using his indices of acculturation. More precisely, they were closest to Spindler's least acculturated and intermediate group and shared fewer traits successively with his lower-status acculturated and elite acculturated groups (Spindler, 1955). In terms of Rorschach characteristics, however, they differed in a number of respects from the other groups, which formed more or less of a continuum as respects Rorschach results (Spindler, 1952 and 1955).

in connection with acculturation, I went on to any dysphorias I could think of in any connection, provided that these were not wholly idiosyncratic. And the progression from the first, already very broad frame of reference to the second occurred because I was having serious difficulty with the acculturation approach, beginning with my first summer, when my rough figures failed to indicate a clear connection between education and peyotism. Indeed, for several years I thought of inverting the normal theory and using "secularization," a product of acculturation, as a process inhibiting peyotism.

It is in the light of this general approach, evident in the previous chapter, that my negative findings should be understood. I regard the variables I selected as plausible in most instances, and I think that most anthropologists would so regard them. In the event, these variables did not show a significant relationship with peyotism. I reiterate that a significant finding has the following criteria: the association of the variable with peyotism is in the same direction in both communities (i.e., it is not a positive association in one community and a negative one in the other), and the combined significance for the two communities is at the .05 level or better. In some instances the results may be significant at the .05 level in only one community, or in neither, provided that the combined significance for the two communities is .05 or better.

I might add that the initial exploration for relationships that obtained in both communities was done with less rigorous criteria: we used the .20 level of significance—and even then we were unable to get parallel findings for the two communities. It is possible that where my data show parallel trends but no significant findings, a larger sample would show significance. That, however, remains a subject for later investigation. I present some of the tables, but not all, since the examination of a series of non-significant results in tabular form is wearisome and their presentation expensive (Table 22).

Nevertheless, some of these findings are important precisely because they are not significant. Both administrators and Navahos, peyotist and non-peyotist, often ask whether peyotism leads to improvement or ruination, or indeed to any sort of differential behavior, important from the point of view of welfare and progress as seen by the questioners.

It must be recalled that we excluded from the sample all Navahos under 25, since in the past it had proved very difficult to elicit opinions from this group. We also excluded all people working off-reservation for the entire summer of 1953, but included those who lived at home but worked in town or who returned to the community regularly for weekends. For this reason, the sample is skewed in the direction of a relatively older population, with less education, and with proportionately fewer males than the total Navaho population, including off-reservation workers. On the other hand, the bias is the same for the two communities. There are, however, more "commuters" and weekly returnees at Mexican Springs. We have no reason to believe that those off-reservation are proportionately more inclined or less inclined to peyotism.

In discussing findings, I shall use the expressions "no significant difference," "no difference," "similar," "the same," or "negative findings" to mean "no significant

TABLE 22

SOME NEGATIVE RESULTS

	ANETH		MEXICAN SPRINGS	
	Peyotists	Non-peyotists	Peyotists	Non-peyotists
DEMOGRAPHY:				
Age:				
50 or less..........................	8	3	4	13
51 or more..........................	10	3	5	13
Sex:				
Male...............................	8	0	2	11
Female.............................	10	6	7	15
Marital status:				
Married............................	14	4	6	22
Other..............................	4	2	3	4
Family type:				
Nuclear or living alone.............	11	4	6	12*
Extended (some kin other than spouse and children living in household)........................	7	2	3	12
Education:				
Any................................	6	0	2	10
None...............................	12	6	7	16
LIVELIHOOD:				
Occupation after livestock reduction:				
Traditional........................	3	1	0	3
Mixed and non-traditional (1 case)	14	3	6	21
Women without husbands.............	1	2	3	2
Predominant source of livelihood:				
Traditional........................	8	2	5	10
Dependent.........................	6	2	2	7
Job................................	4	2	2	9
Job history:				
Good...............................	8	2	3	15
Bad................................	8	2	3	8
Inappropriate question..............	2	2	3	3
Occupation before livestock reduction:				
Traditional only....................	12	3	5	10
Traditional and non-traditional......	3	1	4	13
Too young, unmarried women, etc.....	3	2	0	3
Change in occupation after livestock reduction:				
Traditional before and after.........	3	1	0	2
Mixed (traditional and job) before and after.............	3	0	2	11
Transitional (from traditional to mixed, traditional to job, mixed to job)........................	8	1	4	7
Inappropriate (women without husbands; 1 case of movement from mixed to traditional)....................	4	4	3	6
Farming:				
Below median acreage (Aneth, no acres; Mexican Springs, 2 acres or less)...................................	14	6	5	13
Above median acreage (Aneth, any farming; Mexican Springs, 3 acres or more)...........................	4	0	4	13
How are things going for you as regards making a living?:				
Predominantly good.................	6	0	3	20
Medium, or some good and some bad things.............	2	1	2	0
Predominantly bad..................	10	5	4	6
ACCULTURATION:				
Do you follow the Navaho or the white way?:				
Mostly Navaho.....................	12	5	6	13
Right between the two...............	5	1	2	3
Mostly white.......................	1	0	1	9
Not ascertained....................	0	0	0	1
Which way do you follow as respects religion?:				
Navaho way, only or mostly.........	9†	2	2	7
Both Navaho and white way.........	8	4	5	14
White way, only or mostly...........	1	0	2	5

* Two cases not ascertained.

† One case of "Navaho way and peyote way."

TABLE 22—*Continued*

	ANETH		MEXICAN SPRINGS	
	Peyotists	Non-peyotists	Peyotists	Non-peyotists
Mother-in-law or son-in-law avoidance:				
Yes; yes, when she (he) was alive; yes, qualified..........	2	0	1	3
No, no but formerly did........................	14	3	6	14
Inappropriate: unmarried, or never had son-in-law or mother-in-law..........................	2	3	2	9
Should people move out of a hogan when someone dies in it?:				
Yes..	4	4	5	15
No...	8	0	4	9
Don't know and not ascertained....................	6	2	0	2
Do you own a car, truck, or pickup?:				
One or more................................	5	1	4	9
None.......................................	13	5	5	17
Do you own a radio?:				
Yes..	2	1	3	20
No...	16	5	6	5
Not ascertained.............................	0	0	0	1
How many of your children were born in the hospital?:				
Some.......................................	4	2	5	18
None.......................................	14	4	4	8
HEALTH:				
How is your health?:				
Pretty good, pretty good qualified, so-so (1 case).........	6	3	4	17
Not so good, qualified........................	2	0	0	1
Poor.......................................	10	3	5	8
How is your family's health?:				
Pretty good.................................	11	3	3	18
So-so......................................	5	2	6	7
Not very good...............................	2	1	0	1
CHURCH:				
Are you a member of any church, Catholic or Protestant?:				
Protestant..................................	3	0	1	13
Catholic....................................	1	0	7	10
Christian, Mormon............................	1	1	1	2
None of these...............................	12	3	0	0
Not ascertained.............................	1	2	0	1
How often do you attend church?:				
Regularly, frequently, occasionally..................	4	0	4	7
Rarely, or when I am near a church..................	4	3	5	19
Non-member (some non-members attend church rarely)...	8	3	0	0
Not ascertained.............................	2	0	0	0
CHILDREN'S EDUCATION AND FUTURE:				
Number of living children:				
1–5..	10	4	5	15
6–9 or more................................	8	2	4	11
Education of children:				
All children over 7 have completed 4 grades or are in school	1	0	3	11
Half or more children over 7 have completed 4 grades or are in school.........................	4	1	6	6
Less than half of children over 7 have completed 4 grades or are in school.........................	5	2	0	5
None of children over 7 have completed 4 grades or are in school.......................................	7	2	0	3
No children over 7............................	1	1	0	1
How far do you want your children to go in school?:				
Go beyond high school or to college..................	1	0	0	4
Finish high school or "finish school"..................	1	0	5	12
As far as they want to or as far as they can, or finish grade school (1 case)................................	4	3	1	1
Generally positive attitude, no specific plans, or "it's up to them," unqualified..............................	5	0	0	2
No children, or all children have finished school..........	5	3	2	6
Not ascertained.............................	2	0	1	1

TABLE 22—*Continued*

	ANETH		MEXICAN SPRINGS	
	Peyotists	Non-peyotists	Peyotists	Non-peyotists
Attitude toward children's taking jobs:				
Positive	9	2	5	18
Neutral, mixed	3	1	0	2
No children under 18	5	3	2	6
Not ascertained	1	0	2	0
PARTICIPATION:				
Do you attend Chapter meetings?:				
Most of the time or frequently	3	1	4	13
Sometimes, not very often	5	1	2	4
Rarely or never	9	4	3	9
Not ascertained	1	0	0	0
Did you vote in the last Tribal Council election (1952)?:				
Yes	13	3	6	17
No	5	3	3	9
Did you vote in the last Presidential election (1952)?:				
Yes, Democratic	0	0	2	5
Yes, Republican	0	0	4	11
No	18	6	3	10
Are you a member of the Mexican Springs Cattle Association?:				
Yes	....	....	5	11
No	....	....	4	15
Did you ever belong to the Navajo Rights Association?:				
Yes, or no but contributed (1 case)	10	5	3	6
No	8	1	6	20
COOPERATION:				
Do you get as much help from your relatives as you want?:				
Get the help I want; would get it if I asked	10	4	4	15
Neutral or mixed reactions	2	0	1	2
Dissatisfied with help; they ask for pay, etc.	6	1	4	9
No relatives	0	1	0	0
Is this a community where people work together and get along with each other?:				
Yes, yes qualified	10	3	0	6
Mixed	1	0	0	1
No, no qualified	6	2	9	18
Don't know	1	1	0	1
COUNCIL AND AGENCY:				
Is the Tribal Council doing a good job?:				
Yes, yes qualified	2	0	4	12
Neutral, mixed	0	0	1	1
No, no qualified	11	3	3	13
Don't know	5	3	1	0
Does the Indian Service help the Navaho people?:				
Yes, yes qualified	5	0	5	16
No, no qualified	8	3	4	10
Don't know, and not ascertained (1 case)	5	3	0	0

difference" as defined above. I shall speak of no significant difference "between peyotists and non-peyotists" to mean "between peyotists and non-peyotists within each community," whether we used intra-community medians or the median for the entire sample. For simplicity's sake it should be said now that the remainder of this chapter is devoted entirely to non-significant results.

Whereas in the earlier chapter on the contemporary Navaho, figures were based on a random sample of 24 for Aneth and 32 for Mexican Springs, the Mexican

Springs sample here is expanded to include a special over-sample of 3 peyotists (selected randomly from a list of peyotists). In the original samples, 75 per cent of the Aneth sample and 19 per cent of the Mexican Springs sample were peyotists, figures which fit very well with earlier estimates for the two areas.

Age distribution is similar in the two communities. Women predominate among non-peyotists at Aneth and among peyotists at Mexican Springs. This and some other findings of opposite trends in the two communities led us to explore the possibility that peyotists, as a majority at Aneth, might resemble non-peyotists, as a majority at Mexican Springs. Some ingenuity and time was spent with this approach in mind, but to no good end.

There are no differences between peyotists and non-peyotists in marital status, most people in the samples being married, and no differences as to whether they live in nuclear or extended family units.

There is a slight but not significant tendency for peyotists to have more education at Aneth and non-peyotists at Mexican Springs. Probably this reflects the sex distribution of peyotists and non-peyotists in the two communities. Here and at many other points the analysis is handicapped by the lack of male non-peyotists at Aneth and the virtual lack of male peyotists at Mexican Springs: it is impossible to control for sex and examine the impact of other variables on peyotism.

In the area of livelihood, we find no significant differences. For further details regarding the questions, the reader is referred to Chapter 7 on the contemporary Navaho. Peyotists do not differ from non-peyotists as to their dependency on traditional or non-traditional ways of making a living, or as to their predominant livelihood base. It is worth while expanding somewhat on the table regarding job history, since peyotists claim that they perform better than non-peyotists as regards employment, and non-peyotists claim the reverse.

Men were asked about the frequency and length of their employment. Women were asked roughly comparable questions about their husbands' employment, but in far less detail. It was necessary to combine the answers for statistical analysis. Job histories were then categorized as "good" and "bad." Women long widowed were classified as "other," as were a few instances where the data were inadequate.

If a man reported at least part-time employment for 7 or more years between 1938 and 1953, or a woman reported that her husband had a considerable or a moderate amount of steady employment, or considerable or moderate amounts of intermittent employment, the job history was classified "good."

If a man reported part-time employment for 6 years or less between 1938 and 1953, or if a woman reported that her husband had had sporadic employment or none, the job history was classified "bad." Peyotists and non-peyotists do not differ in job history.

It seemed possible that a person's occupation before livestock reduction, or changes in livelihood base after reduction might be predictors of peyotism. They did not prove to be.

We asked a number of questions about reactions to a man's going away to work, and about reactions to an entire family's going away to work, but statistical analysis of these items proved unprofitable. No tables are presented.

Peyotists do not differ from non-peyotists in number of acres farmed. Differences in livestock holdings are discussed in another chapter. The two groups do not differ in general attitude toward their present livelihood, although peyotists at Mexican Springs and non-peyotists at Aneth tend slightly toward the gloomier answers. In sum, none of these items respecting livelihood discriminates between peyotists and non-peyotists.

The same is true of items relating to acculturation. No differences emerge as respects global attitudes as to whether respondents follow mostly the Navaho or mostly the white way, nor as respects church membership or church attendance. No significant differences appear with regard to knowledge of Navaho religion, transmission of Navaho religion, or being a singer or diviner or having one in the family. Tables are not supplied. The groups do not differ respecting two major tabus, mother-in-law avoidance and moving out of a hogan when someone dies. The results for the death tabu are particularly surprising, consider the difference between Navaho and peyotist ideology as respects ghosts and the dead.

Attitudes toward whites, attitudes toward culture change, etc., did not discriminate, either because there was no variation in the answers in one or both communities or because there were no differences between peyotists and non-peyotists. Tables are not supplied. There were no significant differences in use of English in general, use of English with traders, with other Navahos, or in the home. Tables are not supplied. Such material items as car ownership and radio ownership did not discriminate.

Various health items also failed to show significant differences: number of children born in the hospital, the individual's own health, or his family's health. There is a slight but not signficant tendency for peyotists to claim poorer health. Use of peyote, of course, does distinguish the groups, as does use of sucking cures, discussed earlier (no tables).

Actual educational practices and attitudes toward children's education did not distinguish the peyotists from the non-peyotists—again a matter of interest, since each side accuses the other of negligence in matters educational. Tables are supplied for number of living children, education through fourth grade, and attitude toward children's education. Tables for further education are omitted. Nor do the groups differ in their reactions to their immature children's taking jobs when they grow up.

In sum, as respects acculturation, peyotists and non-peyotists do not differ significantly from each other in self-image, church membership, adherence to traditional tabus, education, material possessions, children's education, plans for children's education, or attitudes toward children's subsequent occupation. We made a variety of complicated analyses combining various acculturation factors, with no results. An acculturation index, which summed some of these traits, was also unproductive.

It seemed conceivable that peyotists might be people seeking individual solutions to contemporary problems, whereas non-peyotists might be people seeking organized solutions. Or that peyotists might be alienated non-participators and non-peyotists, participators. Or even that peyotists might seek to change things, because they were organized, whereas non-peyotists might be passive non-participators. At any rate, a whole series of types of participation were explored: attendance at chapter meetings, voting in tribal and national elections, membership in the cattle association (at Mexican Springs), and membership in the Navajo Rights Association. No significant associations emerged.

Attitudes toward various sources of help—kin, community, Tribal Council, and Indian Service—do not discriminate between peyotists and non-peyotists.

Various questions about the individual's own future, about the future of the tribe, about needs for help failed to discriminate. Fairly elaborate efforts to pick out activists and passivists, the most discontented, optimists and pessimists, etc., by combining various items produced no results (no tables supplied).

All in all, many plausible topics were explored, some stimulated by the "transition" or "acculturation" theory of peyotism, but others stimulated by events in the field. None did any good. It would be helpful if I could guarantee that none of them would discriminate with a larger sample, but of this one cannot be sure. I can only say that working with small samples on other problems in the past, I have had rather more positive findings than were located in this study: the number stands at zero so far as the discussion has gone.

Chapter 17

PEYOTISM AND LIVESTOCK

THE POSSIBLE CONNECTION BETWEEN PEYOTISM AND LIVESTOCK REDUCTION had occurred to me many times in the course of my field work, but only as one among many issues to be explored. In the end, it was the only factor that was significantly associated with cult membership. In broad terms, membership in the cult was associated with the amount of livestock lost in the process of reduction, and with pre-reduction holdings. Furthermore, there was an association between the time of joining the cult and the amount of livestock loss (with certain qualifications supplied below). This finding is interpreted in terms of relative deprivation: of a negative discrepancy between legitimate expectation and actuality. As between any two individuals suffering the same type of deprivation, the individual who experiences the larger discrepancy is the more deprived. This approach will be more fully discussed subsequently.

The association between loss of livestock and peyotism was first observed in the course of analyzing the Mexican Springs and Aneth data. But the finding emerged out of such a large number of non-significant tables that it could well be regarded as accidental. Hence it became vital to replicate these findings in other populations. Let us now turn to the data, beginning with the random samples from Aneth and Mexican Springs.

BASIC DATA

All the basic data for these communities are supplied in Tables 23 and 24. These tables show, in columns 5, 6, 7, and 8, the Navahos' own reports of the numbers of livestock they held before livestock reduction. Column 5 shows the number of sheep and goats, column 6 of cattle, and column 7 of horses. Column 8 supplies total sheep units. (It will be recalled that the official Government system considers one cow to be equivalent to four sheep units, and one horse, mule, or burro to five sheep units.) In one case in Aneth there is no information on pre-reduction holdings. In another, the respondent reported "a little bunch of sheep and goats." In this case the arbitrary figure of 75 sheep and goats has been supplied as a quantity which would have been regarded as "a little bunch," in those days. The respondent was quite specific about cattle and horse holdings.

We cannot, of course, be sure that every individual used the same year in reporting on his pre-reduction holdings: he may have referred to the year before the "voluntary" reductions, the year before systematic reduction, or some good year before reduction. Some individuals explicitly noted that they were talking about the holdings of an extended family, but such cases are not numerous enough for separate analysis.

TABLE 23

Basic Data: Aneth

Interview No.	Peyote Status	First Use	CA	Before Stock Reduction				Reported Total Permit	Reported Horse Permit	Official Total Permit	Official Horse Permit	After Stock Reduction				Better Off Before Stock Reduction
				Sheep and Goats	Cattle	Horses	Total Sheep Units					Sheep and Goats	Cattle	Horses	Total Sheep Units	
501	P	1936	PP	3,000	65	60	3,560	73	4	(73)	(4)	0	0	2	10	B
502	P	1939	CA	860	0	47	1,095	128	5	120	5	248	0	4	268	B
503	NP(T)	1942		75*	0	8	115	45	9	45	9	0	0	0	0	B
504	P	1939	CA	100	0	10	150	83	3	83	3	105	0	4	125	B
505	NP			180	0	16	260	(27)	(5)	27	5	22	0	4	22	B
508	P	1942	PP	1,000	0	50	1,250	0	0	0	0	19	0	2	29	B
509	P	1946	PP	133	2	10	191	30	5	30	5	15	0	2	25	B
510	P	1939	CA	207	0	12	267	0	0	44	4	5	0	1	10	B
511	P	1941	PP	500	0	7	535	(79)	(6)	79	6	50	0	5	75	B
512	NP(Pr)	1941		30	0	4	50	77	9	77	9	22	0	5	47	DK
513	P	1942	PP	590	1	13	659	75	5	75	5	65	0	5	90	B
514	NP(Pr)	1951		265	0	20	365	65	5	94	5	42	0	5	67	B
515	P	1941	PP	20	0	1	25	7	3	32	3	15	0	4	35	A
516	NP			98	0	20	198	33	6	34	6	0	0	0	0	DK
517	P	1935	CA	770	70	12	1,110	40	1	56	3	0	0	0	0	B
518	P	1946	CA	NA	0	NA	NA	NA	NA	NA	NA	NA	NA	NA	NA	DK
519	P	1934	CA	69	25	10	119	109	8	109	8	68	0	4	88	NA
520	P	1948	CA	1,610	0	30	1,860	100	(5)	75	5	3	0	8	48	B
521	P	1937	CA	105	40	7	140	20	3	20	3	23	0	3	38	B
523	NP(T)	NA		500	40	40	860	25	3	33	4	DK	0	1	DK	B
524	P	1938	PP	1,500	0	40	1,700	106	5	213	5	83	0	5	108	B
525	P	1943	PP	400	0	20	500	104	8	104	8	100	0	5	125	B
526	P	1937	CA	75	15	8	175	140	4	135	4	108	0	1	149	B
527	P	1938	CA	340	0	10	390	0	0	0	0	26	0	0	26	DK

Notes:
* "A little bunch."
CA = Contact affected peyotist
PP = Pure peyotist
P = Peyotist
NP(T) = Has tried peyote but non-member
NP(Pr) = Private use, non-member
NP = Non-member, unqualified, or non-member no other data

NA = Not ascertained
DK = Respondent does not know
B = Better off before reduction
A = Better off after reduction (in 1953)
S = Same before and after

Where data are lacking for cols. 9 and 10, they have been supplied from cols. 11 and 12. Where data are lacking for cols. 11 and 12, they have been supplied from cols. 9 and 10; such cases are indicated by parentheses around the figures thus supplied.

TABLE 24

BASIC DATA: MEXICAN SPRINGS

			Before Stock Reduction								After Stock Reduction				
1	2	3	5	6	7	8	9	10	11	12	13	14	15	16	17
Interview No.	Peyote Status	First Use	Sheep and Goats	Cattle	Horses	Total Sheep Units	Reported Total Permit	Reported Horse Permit	Official Total Permit	Official Horse Permit	Sheep and Goats	Cattle	Horses	Total Sheep Units	Better Off Before Stock Reduction
402	NP(T)	1941	120	15	15	255	61	4	61	4	18	(3)	3	33+(12)	B
404	P	1942	575	54	11	846	90	6	95	6	74	8	6	136	B
405	P	1941	900	48	32	1,252	104	5	74	5	44	42(2)	5	85+(8)	B
406	NP	.....	130	20	12	270	0	0	(0)	(0)	0	0	0	0	A
407	NP	.....	1,000	40	5	1,185	0	0	(0)	(0)	30	0	1	35	B
408	NP	.....	400	5	50	670	61	7	100	7	61	0	7	96	B
409	P	1938	575	0	5	600	268	5	161	5	238	(3)	5	263+(12)	B
410	P	1944	400	0	12	460	61	5	97	9	28	(1)	5	53+(4)	B
411	NP	.....	55	2	4	83	50	4	50	4	0	2	4	28	B
412	P	1940	1,009	0	16	1,089	25	4	76	4	84	0	1	39	B
414	NP	.....	37	0	3	52	17	2	17	2	0	0	0	0	B
415	NP	.....	210	0	6	240	54	3	54	3	40	2	3	63	B
416	NP	.....	800	16	8	904	73	3	73	3	20	0	3	35	B
417	NP	.....	147	0	5	172	15	3	15	3	8	0	3	23	B
418	NP(T)	NA	2,070	42	23	2,353	45	3	45	3	18	2	3	41	A
419	NP	.....	130	19	4	226	52	4	52	4	41	16	4	84	A
420	NP	.....	185	0	9	230	54	3	54	3	0	2	3	64	B
421	NP(T)	1950	30	0	0	30	0	0	0	0	0	0	0	0	B
422	NP	.....	100	0	3	115	10	2	10	0	5	(1)	3	5+(4)	B
423	NP	.....	30	0	0	30	25	3	35	2	0	0	3	15	B
425	NP	.....	110	0	5	135	90	3	90	4	74	0	3	89	B
427	NP	.....	170	0	6	200	58	4	58	0	67	1	4	91	B
428	NP	.....	120	2	19	223	0	0	61	4	5	(2)	2	15+(8)	A
429	NP(T)	NA	120	15	15	255	61	5	72	5	148	0	5	173	B
431	NP(T)	1943	200	8	30	382	61	5	61	4	15	0	3	15	B
432	P	1953	130	0	3	145	50	3	(61)	(3)	70	14	3	141	S
433	NP	.....	400	7	4	448	61	5	61	5	80	0	5	105	B
434	NP	.....	35	0	6	65	18	0	18	0	18	(1)	0	18+(4)	B
435	P	1951	350	0	12	410	15	3	15	3	30	(1)	3	45+(4)	B
436	P	1946	300	0	2	310	53	3	40	2	25	2	5	50+(8)	A
437	NP	.....	72	0	5	97	107	5	107	5	128	4	7	179	B
438	P	1937	975	11	3	1,034	35	4	(35)	(4)	8	5	2	38	A
439	NP(T)	1939	61	0	0	61	192	4	89	8	55	0	4	75	B
440	NP	.....	325	0	11	380	192	4	89	8	55	0	4	75	B
441	NP(T)	1952	150	0	17	235	130	2	63	2	40	1	2	54	B

NOTES: Key to abbreviations: See Table 23. Col. 14, figures in parentheses are cattle held in Cattle Association; col. 16, figures in parentheses are cattle held in Cattle Association converted to sheep units. These are not counted against permits.

Precisely comparable data for 1953 are reported in columns 13–16: sheep and goats, cattle, horses, and total sheep units. In Mexican Springs, some cattle were held in the Cattle Association. These are shown in parentheses, in column 14. They do not count against a person's permit, but they do contribute to his livelihood. They are converted into sheep units and shown, again in parentheses, in column 16. In one case at Aneth we have no data on 1953 holdings: the same one who gave no information on pre-reduction holdings.

NAVAHOS' REPORTED LIVESTOCK VS. OFFICIAL RECORDS

It is clear that one can arrive at various measures of deprivation by subtracting current from past livestock holdings. But reports both of present and of past holdings are subject to conscious or unconscious distortion. As respects past holdings, for example, there may be a tendency to exaggerate, to recall a golden age. The obvious way to check this is to compare the individual's own report of his past holdings with the Government reports. But it would be a great mistake, in doing so, to assume that the individual's report is subjective and open to distortion, and that the Government report, based on a physical count, is objective and valid. First, the earliest Government figures available are for 1936, before systematic reduction, but after "voluntary" reduction, whereas the respondent may have had in mind an earlier date. Second, it is plain that the Government tallies did not necessarily assign sheep to their real owners. They tend to assign herds to "heads of households," ordinarily the senior male appearing with the livestock at dipping time. This eliminates some actual owners from the record and attributes more livestock to some owners than they actually held. (In spite of the fact that many women were owners in 1936, few appear on Government rosters.) Third, by 1936 the Navahos were suspicious of livestock counts. Some failed to bring part of their herds for dipping, when the records were made, and some failed to appear. Government reports at Window Rock made it clear that officials were aware that the 1936 count, and many later ones, were incomplete. Hence, both memory and record are subject to error.

On the whole, however, it seems reasonable to assume that people who told us of very large holdings in the past probably had more sheep than those who reported smaller holdings in the past. And by the same token, probably people who were listed with much stock in the 1936 rosters had more livestock than those who were listed with few. A well-known wealthy owner could not easily claim to be radically impoverished, since agents knew something of his standing in the community. Either such people had to bring a fair number of sheep to be tallied, or they had to choose open defiance. These assumptions would lead to the expectation that if a group of people were to be rank-ordered according to their reported holdings, and again rank-ordered according to the holdings shown in official records, the two rank-orders would tend to coincide. Furthermore, it is to be expected that the holdings reported to us would be larger than those appearing in the official records.

Working with our samples and with Government rosters of 1936, we discovered 16 cases in our samples where the 1936 figures were available. This is a small proportion of the total sample, but there is no reason to believe that it is biased in such a way as to affect the comparison. The small number results from such things as the death of a 1936 owner and the dispersion of his flocks among his kin, changes of names, and failure to appear at the 1936 count. Three additional cases were located at Tohatchi, using 1952 interviews and Government rosters. Holdings in sheep, goats, and cattle are available for all 19 cases; total holdings are available for only 16 of them.

The rank-order correlations between reported and official holdings are fairly high (Table 25). They are also significant. (See Chart I for a list of statistical techniques utilized in this and other chapters, and for a comment on significance levels. The .05 level or beyond was selected as the criterion for significance.) But whereas the rank-order correlations are fairly high, there is a considerable difference between the absolute figures reported by Navahos and those recorded by the

TABLE 25

NAVAHOS' REPORTS AND OFFICIAL RECORDS OF
EARLIER LIVESTOCK HOLDINGS

1. Spearman rank-order correlation of official permit and official holdings before reduction.

	Greasewood	Aneth, Mex. Spgs., and Tohatchi
Sheep, goats, and cattle........	.66** (N 18)	.57* (N 16)
Total holdings.................	.66** (N 18)	.61** (N 16)

2. Spearman rank-order correlation of official holdings before reduction and reported holdings before reduction.

	Aneth, Mex. Spgs., and Tohatchi
Sheep, goats, and cattle........	.68** (N 16)
Total........................	.72** (N 16)

3. Spearman rank-order correlation of reported loss (reported holdings minus reported permit) and official loss (official holdings minus official permit).

	Aneth, Mex. Spgs., and Tohatchi
Sheep, goats, and cattle........	.67** (N 16)
Total........................	.73** (N 16)

4. Size of discrepancy between official and reported holdings in absolute numbers, Aneth, Mex. Spgs., and Tohatchi, measured by reported holdings minus official holdings.

	Median of Difference	N
Sheep, goats, and cattle........	339	19
Total........................	452	16

* Significant at the .05 level.
** Significant at the .01 level.

Government. Individuals recall far larger holdings than are shown in 1936 Government records (Table 25).

Thus the comparison fits our expectation. Relative rankings are reasonably similar. Those who report that they were once large owners tend to rank high on official rosters; those who report that they were small owners are similarly ranked on the official roster. Individuals' reports are large by comparison with official reports. Neither is a necessarily valid report of actual holdings prior to reduction, but they are rough measures of the same thing: of the individual's actual holdings. So it seems fair to assume that when we use the individuals' own reports of past holdings, we are not measuring merely subjective deprivation and that when we use official records we are not measuring merely ingenuity in dodging the count.

CHART I

STATISTICAL TECHNIQUES

1. Summed Ranks Test (Siegel, 1956, p. 123, formula 6.8).
2. Spearman Rank-Order Correlation (Siegel, 1956, p. 204, formula 9.7 and, where necessary to correct for ties, p. 203, formula 9.4).
3. Significance levels for Spearman Rank-Order Correlation up to N 30 (Siegel, 1956, p. 284; Dixon and Massey, 1957, p. 469). Beyond N 30, computed (Blalock, 1960, p. 319).
4. Test for the Significance of the Difference of Two Means (Dixon and Massey, 1957, p. 123).
5. Fisher Exact Probability Test (Siegel, 1956, p. 97, formula 6.1).
6. Chi-square Test (Siegel, 1956, p. 107, formula 6.4).
7. "Stouffer" Method for the Combination of Probabilities (Mosteller and Bush, 1954, p. 329). This method was considered appropriate (a) because of the large samples, from the point of view of the technique employed and (b) because the hypotheses were one-sided. In Table 28, Wallis' method was also used (Wallis, 1942).
8. In Chapter 18, a linear multiple regression model was used (Blalock, 1960, pp. 326–346).
9. The .05 level and beyond was selected as significant throughout this work. Findings between .11 and .05 are regarded as of borderline significance, and sometimes receive comment when they are in accord with a number of significant findings.

It may also be asked whether individuals' reports of their 1953 holdings have any validity. For some years after livestock reduction began, Navahos were extremely touchy about responding to any questions on this score. They did not object to these questions in 1953, and it is notable that in a number of cases they admitted to having more sheep units than were allowed by their permits. (They were first asked about holdings and then about permits.) This also occasioned no special disturbance. Their apparent frankness leads us to some confidence in the figures they supplied.

MEASURES OF DEPRIVATION

The measures of deprivation used here are far short of the ideal. One useful measure would be the difference between holdings prior to livestock reduction and holdings immediately afterward, but we did not ask for a report on holdings immediately after the reduction. If we had, it is probable that individuals would have selected different years as appropriate for "after" reduction or would have had trouble remembering the holdings for a fixed year supplied by the interviewer as a measuring point.

Another reasonable measure is the difference between pre-reduction holdings and a man's livestock permit. These permits were issued in 1940 and were intended to set a ceiling on holdings. Hence the difference between pre-reduction holdings and permits reflects the discrepancy between what a man once held through his own efforts and what he was allowed to hold by official edict. The use of the permit as part of a measure of deprivation would not be acceptable if Navahos had taken a casual attitude toward the permit—an attitude suggested by the fact that today some people hold stock without a permit and some hold more than the permit allows. But at the beginning of livestock reduction the permit was viewed almost magically: many people felt that by refusing the permit they might be able to keep their sheep. Subsequently some were prosecuted for failure to obey the regulations, and it became clear that permits were a serious matter. Navahos pressed continually to have special permits issued, and to retain them—behavior which does not suggest a casual attitude. In 1957, only 6 per cent of all livestock operators lacked permits (TNY 1958: 390), so that there was a surprisingly small number of "illegal" operators.

Permits take the following form. They allow an individual a given number of livestock units, not more than a given amount of which may be in horses. Thus a permit may be for 75 stock units, of which 10 may be in horses. This allows a man 65 units in sheep, goats, and cattle, and 2 horses (10 units), or 70 units in sheep, goats, and cattle, and 1 horse, or 75 units in sheep, goats, and cattle, if he elects not to keep a horse.

In columns 9–12 of Tables 23 and 24, the data on permits are supplied. Column 9 shows the total number of sheep units allowed the individual by his own account, and column 10 shows the number of horses (not horses converted to sheep units) allowed him. Column 11 shows the number of sheep units allowed the individual according to Government records, and column 12 the number of horses allowed him according to Government records. In some cases, the individual could not recall his permit; in others, we could not locate the record. Since it was desirable to fill both columns as completely as possible, a comparison was made between rank-orders of permit size according to the individual and the Government record, where both figures were available. The correlation for total permit was very high (Table 26). There was also a correlation for "residual" permit (total permit minus horse permit), which was nearly as high (Table 26). Inspection alone indicates that discrepancies between reported and official permit are small. Hence, where official permit data were lacking, the reported permit was entered in the official permit column (in parentheses), and where reported permit data were lacking, the official permit was entered in the reported permit column (in parentheses).

One last step may be taken to check on the value of the permit as a ceiling: a check on the relationship between a man's permit and his holdings in 1953. The rank-order correlation between the two figures is fairly high, ranging from .55 to .80, for various measures, using total permit or residual permit, total holdings or sheep, goat, and cattle holdings, in Aneth and Mexican Springs (Table 26). Hence the permit, which established a theoretical ceiling, seems to be a good figure to use in estimating the difference between past holdings and Government-established post-reduction levels. And for these purposes, either official or reported permit can be used.

Under some circumstances, a man's past holdings alone are a reasonable measure of deprivation. In the past, there were very large differences between the stock holdings of big and small owners. According to the respondents at Aneth, for example, there was a range from 3,560 sheep units to 25. Twenty-six per cent held more than 1,000 sheep units, 34 per cent held between 250 and 499, and 39 per cent

TABLE 26

SPEARMAN RANK-ORDER CORRELATIONS OF STOCK MEASURES

	COMMUNITY	3 Reported Permit (SG&C)	5 Official Permit (SG&C)	7 Reported Loss (SG&C)	9 Official Loss (SG&C)	11 Present (1953) (SG&C)
1. SG&C before reduction	A	.33	.23	.98**	.98**	−.01a
	MS	.34*	.51**	.91**	.98**	.46**
3. Reported permit, SG&C	A		.91b**	.20	.22	.62a**
	MS		.73c**	.17	.22	.71**
5. Official permit, SG&C	A			.11	.13	.55a**
	MS			.42*	.40*	.67**
7. Reported loss, SG&C	A				.999**	−.14a
	MS				.92**	.31*
9. Official loss, SG&C	A					−.12a
	MS					.38*

	COMMUNITY	4 Reported Permit Total	6 Official Permit Total	8 Reported Loss Total	10 Official Loss Total	12 Present (1953) Total
2. Total before reduction	A	.11	.10	.98**	.99**	.04a
	MS	.38*	.51**	.98**	.99**	.44**
4. Reported permit, total	A		.92b**	.02	.04	.74a**
	MS		.83c**	.28	.31*	.80**
6. Official permit, total	A			.02	.02	.74a**
	MS			.40*	.44**	.74**
8. Reported loss, total	A				.999**	−.05a
	MS				.99**	.35*
10. Official loss, total	A					−.04a
	MS					.39*

NOTES: Except as noted, Aneth N is 23; Mexican Springs N is 35. aN is 22; bN is 19; cN is 31.
Numbering of rows and columns corresponds with items in Table 27.
* Significant at the .05 level.
** Significant at the .01 level.

held less than 250. After reduction, this pyramid was very much flattened. The range was from 268 to 0, and 70 per cent of the people held less than 84 units allowed by the maximum regular permit (Table 23). Permits themselves range from 213 to 0. Hence the difference between present holdings and past holdings correlates almost perfectly with past holdings alone, and the same is true for the difference between present permit and past holdings. This situation is likely to prevail where the maximum regular permit is small—as is the case at Aneth and Mexican Springs—but not so likely to prevail where the maximum permit is large, say 225–275 sheep units.

It would be desirable to assess separately the effects of losses of sheep, goats, cattle, and horses, because of the different parts they played in traditional economic life and in the reduction program. Sheep were a "cash crop," since the sheep themselves, wool, hides, and Navaho rugs were all sold. They were also a "subsistence crop," since mutton was eaten and wool and hides were used. The reduction program aimed to cull flocks, reduce herds to carrying capacity, and improve the meat and wool yields. Goats were primarily a "subsistence crop," with little market value, enjoyed as food and eaten while the lambs were still maturing. Government programs aimed at reducing goats drastically because of their bad effect on forage and minimal commercial value. Cattle were uncommon and could not be killed for day-to-day use. They were never a special target for reduction. Horses were clearly vital for transportation, hauling, and farm work. They were also used for bride-wealth and kept for prestige: a man with many horses was highly regarded. They were a special target of the reduction program because they were kept in excess of needs. They had no commercial value. Many whites say that the Navahos were more disturbed by horse reduction than by sheep reduction.

Nevertheless, in the analysis of the data, no separation of sheep and goats is possible. Navahos rarely gave separate figures for sheep and goats in recalling pre-reduction holdings, and the permit shows no division into "sheep units" and "goat units." Furthermore, there is no separate permit for cattle. There are figures for horses prior to reduction and for the horse permit; hence losses could be estimated for horses alone. So, in estimating deprivation by subtracting permit from pre-reduction holdings, three figures can be computed: total loss, horse loss, and residual loss. "Residual loss" is estimated by subtracting "residual permit" from past "residual holdings." The residual permit is the total permit minus the horse permit. This is a construct, since the Navaho is not required to use his horse permit: he may elect to keep sheep instead. Nevertheless, it can be seen in Tables 23 and 24 that Navahos tended in 1953 to take advantage of the full horse permit— a tendency less marked at Aneth than at Mexican Springs. The "residual holdings" are total holdings minus horses: holdings in sheep, goats, and cattle.

This supplies us with a variety of possible deprivation measures:

1. Total sheep units before reduction, minus total reported permit.
2. Total sheep units before reduction, minus total official permit.
3. Residual holdings before reduction, minus residual reported permit.
4. Residual holdings before reduction, minus residual official permit.
5. Total sheep units before reduction (the reasons for considering this equivalent to a measure of deprivation have been discussed above).
6. Residual holdings before reduction (by the same logic).
7. Sheep and goats before reduction (by the same logic).
8. Cattle before reduction (by the same logic).
9. Horses before reduction (by the same logic).
10. Horses before reduction, minus reported horse permit.
11. Horses before reduction, minus official horse permit.

In point of fact, there is no statistical association between any of the measures using horses alone (measures 9, 10, and 11) and peyotism, or between cattle holdings before reduction and peyotism (measure 8). Scores and tests of significance have not been supplied in the tables. Furthermore, cattle holdings make up so small a portion of pre-reduction holdings and affect rankings so little that a separate test for sheep and goats alone was not made (measure 7). Tests of significance for measures 1–6 are given. In fact, all the remaining measures of livestock loss are highly correlated. Rank-order correlations among these measures range between .91 and .999, so that the measures are virtually identical (Table 26).

All the measures distinguish peyotists and non-peyotists. In column 2 of Tables 23 and 24, each individual's "peyote status" is recorded. Current members of the peyote cult (in 1953) are designated "P." Non-members are labeled "NP." They are further subdivided: (1) those who have tried peyote but have stopped using it, after one, several, or many meetings—"NP(T)"; (2) those Aneth Navahos who use peyote privately as a medicine but have never attended a cult meeting and are uninterested in the religion—"NP(Pr)"; and (3) those who have never attended a meeting or used peyote privately, designated simply "NP."

Results are considered significant if (a) the trend is in the same direction in both communities; (b) the *combined* probability on any measure is .05 or better. The test employed is the summed ranks test. The probabilities are combined by the Stouffer method (Chart I). Rank-orders on all six measures are significantly associated with peyotism, the combined probabilities reaching .01 in every case (Table 27). Also, in every case, the findings for Mexican Springs are significant at the .01 level, whereas those for Aneth range from .14 to .07 at best—partly because of sample size. These findings appear in Table 27, as items 1, 2, 7, 8, 9, and 10. To give some idea of the magnitude of the difference between peyotists and non-peyotists in the two communities, the median loss (or median past holding) for peyotists and non-peyotists in Aneth and Mexican Springs is shown in Table 27. These figures show marked differences between peyotists and non-peyotists in both communities.

Thus these figures show an association between deprivation in livestock and peyotism. They do not, however, account for the gross difference in membership between the two communities. It could be said that in Aneth, only the people who lost fewest stock stayed *out* of the cult, whereas at Mexican Springs, only the people who lost most stock *entered* it. This difference is undoubtedly in part a matter of length of exposure to the cult, but only in part. Membership in the cult seems to have reached 75 per cent at Aneth some years ago, whereas it stayed low at Mexican Springs for some time. I have no explanation for this.

DEPRIVATION AND DATE OF JOINING THE CULT

If membership in the cult is stimulated by livestock losses, it should follow that those who lost most stock would join the cult first. With due qualifications, this seems to be true. We asked each respondent when he joined the cult (column 3, Tables 23 and 24). The dates may not be absolutely accurate, but in several cases they cross-check well with estimates by other informants.

The rank-order of entering the cult was compared with the rank-order for four measures of livestock loss: reported residual loss, reported total loss, official residual loss, and official total loss. For Mexican Springs, the rank-order correlations are positive: the earlier the date, the larger the loss. They are significant at better than

TABLE 27

DIFFERENCES BETWEEN PEYOTISTS AND NON-PEYOTISTS ON STOCK MEASURES

STOCK MEASURE	COMMU-NITY	PEYOTE		NON-PEYOTE		z	p	CM-BINED p
		Median	N	Median	N			
1. SG&C holdings before reduction...	A	400	17	139	6	1.50	.07	
	MS	575	9	175	26	2.74	.01	.01
2. Total holdings before reduction...	A	500	17	229	6	1.29	.10	
	MS	600	9	228	26	2.70	.01	.01
3. Reported permit, residual (SG&C)...	A	50	17	7	6	1.50	.07	
	MS	36	9	31	26	.89	......	.05
4. Reported permit, total.....	A	75	17	37	6	.80	......	
	MS	61	9	53	26	1.28	.10	.07
5. Official permit, residual (SG&C)...	A	50	17	9	6	1.54	.06	
	MS	52	9	34	26	2.06	.02	.01
6. Official permit, total......	A	75	17	40	6	.66	......	
	MS	76	9	53	26	2.30	.01	.02
7. Reported loss, SG&C......	A	340	17	137	6	1.29	.10	
	MS	332	9	143	26	2.32	.01	.01
8. Reported loss, total.......	A	396	17	199	6	1.15	.13	
	MS	399	9	170	26	2.62	.01	.01
9. Official loss, SG&C.......	A	340	17	136	6	1.29	.10	
	MS	439	9	139	26	2.70	.01	.01
10. Official loss, total.........	A	396	17	199	6	1.08	.14	
	MS	439	9	173	26	2.62	.01	.01
11. Present SG&C holdings (1953)	A	26	17	22	5	1.33	.09	
	MS	34	9	30	26	1.32	.09	.05
12. Present total holdings (1953).	A	43	17	22	5	1.60	.05	
	MS	57	9	43	26	1.23	.11	.02
13. Present total holdings minus reported permit...........	A	10	17	− 30	5	1.80	.04	
	MS	0	9	4	26	.09	......	.09
14. Present total holdings minus official permit.............	A	3	17	− 30	5	1.48	.07	
	MS	11	9	0	26	.38	......	.09

NOTES: All z-scores are normal deviate approximations for the summed ranks test. All p-values are one-tailed. All livestock figures are converted to sheep units. Rank-orders utilized for the summed ranks test are all derived from livestock figures in Basic Data Tables 23 and 24, as follows:

ITEM No.	BASIC DATA TABLES	ITEM No.	BASIC DATA TABLES
1.	Col. 5 + Col. 6	8.	Col. 8 − Col. 9
2.	Col. 8	9.	(Col. 5 + Col. 6) − (Col. 11 − Col 12)
3.	Col. 9 − Col. 10	10.	Col. 8 − Col. 11
4.	Col. 9	11.	Col. 13 + Col. 14
5.	Col. 11 − Col. 12	12.	Col. 16
6.	Col. 11	13.	Col. 16 − Col. 9
7.	(Col. 5 + Col. 6) − (Col. 9 − Col. 10)	14.	Col. 16 − Col. 11

the .05 level for all except reported loss in sheep, goats, and cattle (Table 28). For Aneth, however, the relationship is non-significant, and the trend is, if anything, reversed: all correlations, however small, are negative (Table 28).

This led to speculations about the special position of Aneth in the spread of the cult. Aneth is the Navaho community nearest to the Southern Ute group at Towaoc, the source of the Navaho cult. To reach the rest of the reservation by road, Aneth Navahos must pass through Towaoc. Aneth was exposed to the Ute cult and to Oklahoma peyotists visiting Towaoc very early. And Aneth is near Mancos Creek, where the first five Navaho peyote priests came from. These men had Aneth connections. These facts imply different opportunities for exposure to

TABLE 28

SPEARMAN RANK-ORDER CORRELATIONS OF FIRST USE OF
PEYOTE (ALL MEMBERS) AND LOSS OF STOCK

	REPORTED LOSS				OFFICIAL LOSS				
	SG&C		Total		SG&C		Total		N
	rho	p	rho	p	rho	p	rho	p	
Aneth, all members......	−.15	....	−.18	....	−.13	....	−.16	....	17
Aneth, contact-affected...	−.50	....	−.50	....	−.50	....	−.50	....	9
Aneth, pure.............	.61	.062	.61	.062	.61	.062	.61	.062	8
Mexican Springs, all members..................	.53	.0745	.62	.044	.78	.01	.75	.014	9
Combined probabilities, Aneth pure and Mex. Spgs..................	....	.021	....	.011	....	.003	....	.005	......

NOTE: Positive correlation indicates association between early first use of peyote and large losses.

peyotism than exist in most other Navaho communities, and certainly different from the exposure conditions at Mexican Springs.

We therefore made certain a priori assumptions about the Aneth Navahos, to weed out those whose use of peyotism may have grown out of special opportunities rather than special need. In this latter group we included all English-speakers, on the assumption that they had better opportunities for close relations with Utes. We also included individuals who said that they first used peyote through Ute or Oklahoma Indian influence, rather than as a result of contact with Navahos, on the assumption that they may have had especially close connections with the Utes. And last, we included in this group those who first used peyote through the offices of the Mancos Creek priests, on the assumption of especially close contacts there. These people, then, were considered to be individuals whose social relationships facilitated their contacts with the cult and thus tended to make for earlier membership. This classification was done a priori and not by inspecting the tables of correlation. These people were called "contact-affected," and are labeled "CA" in column 4 of the Basic Data Table for Aneth (Table 23). The remainder were called "pure" peyotists ("PP"). Mexican Springs peyotists were not so classified.

The contact-affected show a *negative* relationship between size of loss and date of joining: the smaller the loss, the earlier the membership (Table 28). The "pure" group shows a positive association for all four measures (Table 28). This is not significant at the .05 level but is close to this level. We combined the significances for the "pure" Aneth group and the Mexican Springs group, for each loss measure. The combined p is better than .05 in each case. Thus it may be said that there is an association between magnitude of loss and early membership.

This analysis was done after the work reported in Table 27 had been completed. Otherwise, it might have been possible to achieve better significance levels for the Aneth sample, by eliminating all the "contact-affected" peyotists. The median pre-

TABLE 29

STOCK LOSS MEASURES AND PEYOTISM IN THREE ADDITIONAL AREAS

	PEYOTE		NON-PEYOTE		z	p
	Median	N	Median	N		
1. Tohatchi, reported sheep and goats before reduction........	1,078	3	200	11	2.26	.01
2a. Greasewood, official loss, SG&C.....................	80	8	27	10	.97	.17
2b. Official loss, horses.........	8	8	2	10	1.59	.06

	Mean	Sigma	N	Mean	Sigma	N	z	p
3. District 4, official sheep and goats, before reduction.......	157	161	39	101	97	293	2.11	.02

4. Combined probability for items 2a and 3, $p = .02$.

NOTES: The z-scores for items 1 and 2 are normal deviate approximations for the summed ranks test. The z-score for item 3 is the normal deviate approximation for the test of the significance of the difference of two means. All p-values are one-tailed. All livestock figures are converted to sheep units.

reduction holdings for "pure" peyotists is 597; for "contact-affected," it is 267; and for non-peyotists, it is 229. The median for all peyotists is 500. Further analysis along these lines, however, was not carried out, first because it is not claimed that the "contact-affected" joined the cult *only* because of its superior availability, and second, because of the labor involved.

We have shown that there is a positive association between a number of highly inter-correlated measures of livestock loss and cult membership for the Aneth and Mexican Springs groups, and between size of loss (using some of these measures) and date of joining the cult, when effects of contact are controlled for. Even though findings are parallel for the two communities, it could be argued that they arise by chance out of the multiplicity of tables tested for significance. Hence it is critical to show that the relationship between deprivation and cult membership obtains for other areas.

PARALLEL TESTS FOR OTHER AREAS

Data for such a test are available for Tohatchi, Greasewood, and District 4 (Table 29). Analysis of the data supports the deprivation hypothesis. Since the data were not initially assembled with the aim of testing this hypothesis, they are not of the same sort in the three areas, nor do they correspond precisely with the kinds of figures collected in Aneth and Mexican Springs. They were gathered at various times, on the assumption that information about livestock was important. Although they do not represent random samples, there is nothing in the way that they were gathered that would seem to bias results in favor of the hypothesis. Indeed, the fact that they are not random samples is more likely to weaken any association of livestock loss and cult membership than to strengthen it. Hence positive findings would seem to buttress the theory.

For Tohatchi, the data were gathered by Moore in 1952, from a supposed cross-section of the community. The interviews supply information only on re-ported sheep and goat holdings prior to livestock reduction. Only in three cases were we able to locate the official permit figures, and we did not ask for the respondent's report of his permit. Hence the sheep and goat holdings prior to reduction must be used as the measure of loss. Like Mexican Springs, Tohatchi is in District 14. Hence the levelling process described earlier is operative in this community. As has been said, the association between rank-order for size of sheep, goats, and cattle holdings before reduction and the various measures using re-ported or official permit is almost perfect (Table 26). Cattle make up so small a proportion of pre-reduction holdings as to have little impact on the measure. Hence for Tohatchi, total sheep and goat holdings will be considered a valid measure of livestock losses.

When the summed ranks test is applied, it shows that peyotists had significantly larger holdings before reduction than non-peyotists (Table 29). Thus the relation-ship discovered for Aneth and Mexican Springs obtains at Tohatchi as well.

Greasewood data consist of official records of 1936 holdings and official records of permits. Consistent with previous measures of loss, one might at Greasewood use either 1936 holdings, or 1936 holdings minus official permit. But the use of 1936 holdings as a measure of loss is not legitimate for Greasewood. There the maximum regular permit is 275 sheep units, so that the levelling effect was less marked there. The use of 1936, rather than 1933 holdings is perhaps questionable, but these, at least, are figures for the year preceding systematic reduction, when the largest losses began, and they are also figures which precede the introduction of peyotism to Greasewood. This occurred in 1938 or 1939 (Aberle and Stewart, 1957, p. 80). We have already presented a justification for equating past holdings as reported by respondents with past holdings as listed by official records: rank-orders on the two measures are reasonably and significantly correlated. So the loss measure to be used for Greasewood is 1936 official holdings minus official permit.

The data for Greasewood were assembled as follows. In 1949, the chapter head supplied me with a list of all families in the community, classified as peyotist, non-peyotist, or divided. The list was rechecked against the opinions of peyotists in the community and against my own information on a number of families. It was re-checked again in 1954 with a leading peyotist to discover who had entered or left the cult in the intervening period. There were few changes.

The list of family names was then compared with the Government livestock roster for 1936 and the Government permit roster for 1949. Out of 99 families, 18 people were identified on both these lists. The rate of attrition when three rosters must be used is even greater than that observed for Aneth and Mexican Springs. But there is no reason to think that the final list is biased in favor of the hypothesis.

Because horses had not proved significant in other communities, horse figures were omitted. When the summed ranks test was applied, the results in terms of residual loss were significant only at the .17 level, but were in the anticipated direction: peyotists showed larger losses. For reasons discussed below, this result was combined with that for District 4, giving a significant combined probability (Table 29). For reasons of curiosity, a separate check on loss of horses showed a borderline significance, larger losses being associated with cult membership (.06– Table 29). This result was not paralleled in Aneth or Mexican Springs.

In District 4 there was no information on permits or reported holdings, but only a record of Government stock tallies for 1936. As has been said, we are justified in using Government figures for 1936 because of their rank-order correlation with reported figures, described earlier. In addition, District 4 is another area where the regular permit is low (75 sheep units), so that it is proper to assume that a very large number of people were given small permits. Hence the magnitude of loss can be effectively measured by the magnitude of prior holdings.

District 4 is a large area not clearly divided into local groups. It was impossible to secure a list of all families in the area and to label them peyotist and non-peyotist. Instead, in 1950, I assembled a list of peyotist families, which was begun by a peyotist, checked with a non-peyotist, and then checked with the District Supervisor, a Navaho, who knew the area well. The list was gone over in 1954 with the same peyotist and an active peyote priest from the area, and was sizably enlarged, principally because the cult had grown rapidly since 1950. This total list of more than 200 names was then compared with the 1936 stock census. Thirty-nine individuals, including a few widows of individuals listed in 1936, were common to both lists. But the 1936 roster contained nearly 340 names. I did not have a list of non-peyotists. It was therefore necessary to assume that everyone on the stock roster *not* known to be a peyotist was a non-peyotist. Since some of them were probably peyotists, this tends to bias the test against the hypothesis.

A test of the difference between the means was run to discover whether the mean stock holdings for the 39 known peyotists and the remainder of the people on the roster were significantly different. The results were in the predicted direction and significant. Peyotists had larger holdings than non-peyotists (Table 29).

Since official figures for 1936 holdings were used as a basis for loss measures in District 4 and Greasewood, the probabilities for the two areas were combined, and the combined probability was significant (Table 29).

For District 4, the relationship between horse holdings in 1936 and peyotism was checked but was not significant (no table).

District 4 provided a further opportunity to test the relationship between loss and date of joining the cult, since some peyotists had joined by 1950 and some between 1950 and 1954. Of the 39 for whom livestock figures were available, 27 joined by 1950 and 10 joined after 1950. The two remaining individuals joined before 1950, left the cult before 1950 as well, and rejoined by 1954. These two cases were omitted. There was a tendency for early joiners to have had larger holdings in 1936 than late joiners, but the probability value is only about .16 (no table).

Thus, three separate tests (Aneth-Mexican Springs, Tohatchi, Greasewood-District 4) provide support for the connection between livestock losses and peyotism. There is also an association between the date of joining the cult and magnitude of loss in Aneth and Mexican Springs (combined) and a tendency in the same direction in District 4.

Before we turn to the theoretical significance of these findings, some additional problems remain for discussion.

HORSE REDUCTION

First, in view of the disturbance created by horse reduction, and the widespread opinion among many whites that the Navahos were more concerned about horse reduction than about sheep and goat reduction, it is interesting that only at Greasewood, and only at a borderline level of significance is any connection found between loss in horses and peyotism. I am inclined to believe that great though the symbolic value of large horse herds may have been, it was not as great as the value of sheep and goats: in maintaining customary standards of living, relationships of reciprocity, and high status for large livestock owners.

ATTITUDES

Second, it is unfortunate that I have so little systematic information on attitudes toward reduction, or attitudes explicitly linking livestock losses and cult membership, to buttress the theory presented here. There are scattered data on a few interviews where the issue came up spontaneously. A trader from District 9 said that people in that area joined the cult in order to try to ward off livestock reduction. A well-to-do man from District 4 said that he joined the peyote cult as a result of his concern about taking care of his children after livestock reduction. And a Tribal Councilman from Teec Nos Pas told a Council meeting in 1956 that he joined the cult for comfort after livestock reduction.

There was only one question in the 1953 interviews at Aneth and Mexican Springs that bore on this issue: "Are you better off now, or were you better off before stock reduction?" This is a very crude measuring device. Most Navahos, of course, believed that they were worse off in 1953. In each sample, 83 per cent made this assertion. Indeed, the only way to group the answers to the question is to lump together all those who say they are better off now, or about the same now, or better off in some ways and worse off in others, or who say they do not know. We can then examine the relationship between attitudes toward pre- and post-reduction livelihood and peyote cult membership. In both communities there is a trend for peyotists to be disproportionately represented among those who claim to have been better off before—very weak for Aneth, close to significant for Mexican Springs. The combined probability for the two tables, using the Stouffer method, is only .11, which can be called a trend (Table 30). It was decided for methodological reasons to recheck the combined probability, using the Wallis method, since this was the only set of tables in this chapter to which this method could be applied without excessive difficulty. We were not trying to "squeeze" the data. The combined probability by this method was slightly better than .05.

There is, then, a significant, if equivocal, association between attitudes toward livelihood, pre- and post-reduction, and peyotism, which is in the predicted direction and which further supports the deprivation hypothesis.

Efforts at examining the effects of attitude on peyotism controlling for livestock, of livestock deprivation on peyotism controlling for attitude, and of livestock deprivation on attitude controlling for peyotism, are disappointing, because of the small number of cases and peculiarities of the distributions. No tables are presented. With no controls applied, there is an association between attitudes toward livelihood and livestock measures: those better off in terms of livestock are more likely to claim that they were better off before livestock reduction. This is a trend for Mexican Springs, significant for Aneth, and significant combined, using the summed ranks test.

TABLE 30

RELATIONSHIP OF PEYOTISM AND FEELING BETTER OFF
BEFORE STOCK REDUCTION

	ANETH		MEXICAN SPRINGS	
	P	NP	P	NP
Better off before reduction............	14	4	9	18
Other........................	3	2	0	8
	p .392		p .066	

Combined p, Stouffer method = .104   Combined p, Wallis method = .0484

NOTES: "Other" includes "better off now," "about the same," "better off in some ways, worse off in others," "don't know." In Aneth, one case of "Not Ascertained" omitted from table. Separate probabilities done by Fisher's Exact Test. Combined probabilities initially done by Stouffer method, consonant with other tables. As a check, Wallis' method was also used to combine probabilities for this table, with results shown above.

Furthermore, among those who claim to have been better off before livestock reduction, there is an association between peyotism and livestock losses—a trend at Aneth, significant at Mexican Springs, and significant for the combined probabilities, using the summed ranks test.

Various other possibilities permit of no conclusive statements. Thus we may examine the relationship between peyotism and livelihood attitudes separately for those who have above the median on livestock measures, and below. In three out of four tables the result is no variance in one or another row or column. In the case of people low on livestock measures at Aneth, the association is in the right direction but very far from being significant. As for attitudes toward livelihood and livestock measures, among peyotists, at Aneth there is a trend but at Mexican Springs there is no variance: all peyotists claim to have been better off before. Among non-peyotists the relationships are in the right direction but very far from being significant. Under these circumstances, efforts to build interpretations using the attitude measure as an intervening variable or any more complex interpretations seem doomed to failure.

In sum, peyotists are more likely to claim that their livelihood before reduction was better than are non-peyotists; people with high pre-reduction holdings and consequent losses are more likely to claim to have been better off before reduction than those with low pre-reduction figures and loss measures; and among those who claim to have been better off before livestock reduction, there is an association between high pre-reduction holdings and losses on the one hand and peyotism on the other, just as there is for the total sample.

PSYCHOLOGICAL VARIABLES

Third, the work of Dittmann and Moore on disturbance in dreams and peyotism merits discussion and an effort to relate it to the results here presented on livestock losses (Dittmann and Moore, 1957). In 1952, Moore collected materials on Navaho dreams in three communities. Respondents were asked whether they ever dreamed, what was a bad dream, and what was a good dream. The dreams were later rated on a scale of "disturbance" devised by Allen T. Dittmann. Peyotists proved to supply a far greater proportion of bad dreams connected with illness and death than did non-peyotists (significant at better than .01, one-tailed). They had slightly more bad dreams connected with economic problems than non-peyotists, but not significantly so. Global ratings of over-all "disturbance" were also carried out. Two of the three judges had highly correlated ratings, and these ratings differentiated peyotists from non-peyotists, using a t-test, at the .03 level. Reasons were given for placing less reliance on the third judge's ratings. The "disturbance" score was treated as a possible sign of difficulty in adaptation to the present conditions of Navaho life, rather than as an indication of overt psychopathology.

After this work was finished, Dittmann was given information on the pre-reduction livestock holdings of those respondents for whom data were available (based on their own reports). All cases were then dichotomized by Dittmann on the rating for over-all dream disturbance and on livestock holdings. The results appear in Table 31. At the time the livestock data were given to Dittmann, and before the results were available to me, I hypothesized that there would be a disproportionate number of peyotists among cases that combined disturbance and high pre-reduction holdings (a deprivation measure). There would be a disproportionate number of non-peyotists in all other categories, the smallest proportion in the cell that combined low pre-reduction holdings and low disturbance. Although the logic of these predictions was not fully spelled out at the time, it rests on the conception that objective deprivation is an experience that some people cope with better than others and that those with dream disturbance might be among those more vulnerable to acute subjective deprivation. I then tested the significance of various fourfold tables derived from the master table (Table 31) which Dittmann provided.

The general prediction that peyotists would be disproportionately represented in the "deprived-disturbed" group and non-peyotists in all other groups was tested by collapsing the first four columns of Table 31 into the relevant fourfold table. It was strongly supported (Table 31, 1). It can be seen by inspection that the non-peyotists do not cluster in any particular sub-category (high holdings, low disturbance; low holdings, high disturbance; low holdings, low disturbance).

But the relationship between livestock holdings and peyotism in these same four columns, reduced to a fourfold table, is not quite significant (Table 31, 2). Indeed, for these four columns, the relationship that Dittmann and Moore found for the entire sample, between disturbance in dreams and peyotism, is not quite significant (Table 31, 3). Nor is the relationship between disturbance in dreams and peyotism for the entire sample quite significant (Table 31, 4). It should be remembered that Dittmann and Moore used a rating scale, from which the dichotomous table used here was compiled, and hence that they were able to use a t-test, whereas one of the tests here (Table 31, 3) was done with only part of their sample, using Fisher's exact test, while the other, using their entire sample, used the less sensitive chi-square test on a dichotomous break.

The trend in the data, then, accords with the Dittmann and Moore analysis, but the combination of dream disturbance and high pre-reduction holdings provides the best prediction of peyotism by far.

TABLE 31

DISTURBANCE IN DREAMS, PRE-REDUCTION LIVESTOCK, AND PEYOTISM

	High Holdings		Low Holdings		Holdings Unknown	
	High Dist.	Low Dist.	High Dist.	Low Dist.	High Dist.	Low Dist.
Peyotists............	5	1	1	1	3	1
Non-peyotists........	1	9	9	7	12	9

NOTES TO TABLE 31

1. First four columns: peyotism vs. non-peyotism; high holdings, high disturbance, vs. all other combinations, Fisher's Exact Test, p .001.
2. First four columns: peyotism and livestock holdings, Fisher's Exact Test, p .079.
3. First four columns: peyotism and disturbance, Fisher's Exact Test, p .079.
4. All cases, peyotism and disturbance, chi-square, p between .10 and .05, one-tailed.
5. First two columns: peyotism and disturbance among high holders, Fisher's Exact Test, p .025.
6. Third and fourth columns: peyotism and disturbance among low holders, N.S.
7. Peyotists: livestock holdings and disturbance, N.S.
8. Non-peyotists: livestock holdings and disturbance, negative association, Fisher's Exact Test, p .023.
9. High disturbance cases: peyotism and livestock holdings, Fisher's Exact Test, p .025.
10. Low disturbance cases: peyotism and livestock holdings, N.S.
11. First four columns: pre-reduction holdings and disturbance, N.S.

If all the various fourfold tables that can be assembled from Table 31 are dealt with, the results are not very clear. Among Navahos with high pre-reduction holdings there is a significant relationship between peyotism and dream disturbance (Table 31, 5). This relationship is not found among those with low pre-reduction holdings, who include almost no peyotists (Table 31, 6). Among peyotists, there is no relationship between disturbance and livestock holdings. There is almost no variance (Table 31, 7). But among non-peyotists, there is a significant negative association between pre-reduction holdings and dream disturbance. The larger the holdings, the less the disturbance (Table 31, 8). Among Navahos with high dream disturbance, there is an association between peyotism and large pre-reduction holdings (Table 31, 9), but among those with low dream disturbance there is no association—there are almost no peyotists (Table 31, 10). Finally, there is no overall association between pre-reduction holdings and disturbance (Table 31, 11).

In sum, the prediction that peyotists would be found disproportionately among those with high dream disturbance and high pre-reduction holdings, by comparison with all other categories, was supported. The rest of the findings are tantalizing and suggest a variety of *post hoc* interpretative efforts, but are difficult to deal with in any simple way.

PEYOTISM AND LIVESTOCK DEPRIVATION: SUMMARY

The results of the statistical analysis presented thus far will be briefly reviewed. After many unsuccessful efforts to find statistical associations between peyotism and various plausible factors in two random samples drawn at Aneth and Mexican Springs, we found significant associations only with various measures based primarily on pre-reduction livestock holdings. These findings were interpreted in terms of relative deprivation. Those Navahos in the two communities who had once been wealthiest tended to join the peyote cult in greater numbers than did other Navahos. Because of marked levelling effects in both communities, there was a very close association between past holdings and any measure of livestock loss we could devise. Furthermore, with certain qualifications, those peyotists who lost most stock tended to be among the earliest to join the cult. Since these findings might have been the accidental product of innumerable tallies, additional data were brought to bear from Tohatchi, Greasewood, and District 4. Although different measures of loss had to be used in each area, significant results emerged associating large livestock losses with cult membership in Tohatchi, and (for the combined probability) in Greasewood and District 4.

There was no evidence that horse reduction had been of special significance in promoting peyotism. Negative attitudes toward present by comparison with pre-reduction livelihood were associated with peyotism. Disturbance in dreams is associated with peyotism. Disturbance, combined with livestock holdings, predicts cult membership better than either measure alone in one sample.

WEALTH AND PEYOTISM: AN ALTERNATIVE HYPOTHESIS

Many non-peyotists have suggested that road men are greedy for gain, and a few have claimed that they tend to make special efforts to attract well-to-do Navahos. Even some peyotists are willing to say that certain road men are strongly interested in financial gain. It is therefore necessary to consider the possibility that the entire association between pre-reduction livestock holdings and our measures of loss on the one hand, and peyotism on the other, merely reflect the tendency of road men to try to attract a well-to-do clientele. In this case, differential involvement with peyotism would be merely a result of differential access or exposure. (I have already said that greed does not seem to me to be characteristic of the average road man, but the idea must be explored.)

There are no statistical data at hand to refute this argument. Nevertheless, there are reasons for considering it implausible. The first, and most important, has to do with the negative attitude of most Navahos to peyotism. The peyotist is, to an important degree, rejected by the non-peyotist. In most communities, the peyotists are in a minority. Among the communities described earlier, this is true for Mexican Springs, Tohatchi, Greasewood, and (at least until recently) District 4. The wealth theory would demand that the more comfortably situated (and ordinarily more prominent and respected) members of the community should join and remain in a religious movement which destroys their standing in the community, just because a peyote priest sought them out. Furthermore, it is not the case that all the wealthy join and all the poor remain non-members. On the contrary, although we will see that peyotists are slightly better off than non-peyotists in terms of livestock holdings, it is a minority of the wealthy who join—as it is a minority of the poor—in communities where the cult is numerically small. Thus those who join cut themselves off from their peers and unite themselves with men of different status.

Second, the cult spread after wealth differences themselves were very much decreased by livestock reduction. Only a few people at Aneth, and none at Mexican Springs, had joined the cult before 1937, when systematic livestock reduction plans were very much in the air. The cult reached Tohatchi about 1937, but it did not even reach Greasewood or District 4 until reduction was well under way and wealth differences much reduced.

Third, it is hard to see why the wealthy were attracted to peyotism, a religion which sees man as helpless and dependent on an all-powerful God who provides for man in his desperate crises, unless they were experiencing some serious tension, strain, or deprivation. It is not sufficient to view peyotism as merely a sort of conspicuous consumption.

Be that as it may, the statistical data are not sufficient to refute the explanation in terms of wealth. Ideally, we should have a measure of wealth which has at least two characteristics. First, it should be independent of the loss measures, since any association of loss measures and wealth measures may make it difficult to choose between relative deprivation and wealth as explanatory variables. Second, it should provide an evaluation of individuals' fortunes shortly before they joined the cult. Neither of these conditions can be met.

There are three possible measures of wealth available from the current data. The first is, of course, pre-reduction livestock holdings. These have already been used as a measure of deprivation. Furthermore, since most Navahos joined the cult after systematic reduction began, they are not a good measure for evaluating the probable effects of available wealth on tendencies to join the cult.

The second measure is reported or official permit. This is a reasonable measure of a man's wealth immediately after reduction, although not necessarily of his holdings when he joined the cult. By and large, men with the largest permits began their post-reduction economic life with the largest herds. Some people held on to additional stock until they succeeded in securing special permits, but these permits are included in our figures.

The third measure is present holdings in livestock, as of 1953. This measure suffers from the defect that it does not show holdings as of the time of joining the cult.

The first measure, pre-reduction holdings, has already been shown to be associated with cult membership, in the detailed analysis of loss measures (Table 27). The second measure, reported or official permit, shows significant or nearly significant associations with peyotism in a number of forms: reported residual permit (.05), official residual permit (.01), total official permit (.02), and total reported permit (.07, nearly significant—Table 27). The third measure, 1953 holdings, shows a significant association between peyotism and present holdings in sheep, goats, and cattle and with total holdings (Table 27).

Of these three wealth measures, one has already been used as a measure of loss (pre-reduction holdings). Hence its association with peyotism provides no basis for choice between hypotheses. The other measures (permit and present holdings) are also significantly correlated with many of the loss measures for Mexican Springs data, but not for Aneth.

It should be noted that peyotists are differentiated from non-peyotists less effectively by the measures using present permit and present holdings than by those using pre-reduction holdings or various other loss measures. This can be seen by inspecting the combined probability levels. These, in turn, are a function of the sum of z-scores for Aneth and Mexican Springs, which can be regarded as a measure of the degree to which peyotists and non-peyotists differ in rank-order with respect to the measures in question. (Probabilities are combined by summing the z-scores and dividing by the square root of the number of probabilities summed. The resulting figure is used as a new z-score, from which the combined probability is derived. See Chart I.) Loss measures (items 1, 2, 7–10 in Table 25) all have probability levels of .01. Present holdings measures (items 11 and 12) have probability levels of .02 and .05. Permit measures (items 3, 4, 5, and 6) have probability levels of .05, .07, .01, and .02. This trend in the data and the implausibility of the wealth theory somewhat favor rejecting it.

PEYOTISM AND THE MANAGEMENT OF PROPERTY

Non-peyotists, peyotists, and Indian Service employees are all concerned about the economic effects of peyotism. Non-peyotists charge that the peyotists do not look after their affairs, or sell off their livestock to pay for peyote ceremonies. Peyotists claim that traditional Navahos sell off *their* livestock to pay for Navaho ceremonies. They also claim to work harder to be more "progressive" in educating their children and to plan their livelihood better. Indian Service employees worry lest the new religion and its attendant consumption of peyote somehow impair economic responsibility. The data at hand afford some information on this practical issue.

For a full understanding of the association between peyotism and various types of economic behavior, it would be necessary to have information on job performance, income from wage work, income from sales of livestock, meat, and wool, and income in kind. In addition, one should know about savings, herd size, property in the form of consumer goods, and jewelry. Since the attack on peyotists and the defense by peyotists include claims and counterclaims about seeking employment, educational level, actual education of children, and plans for children's future education, a general evaluation of the practical behavior of peyotists and non-peyotists would have to cover these topics. Data are available for only a few of them.

It has already been shown that peyotists and non-peyotists are indistinguishable in the random samples as respects job history, education, education of children, plans for children's education, or possession of such material objects as cars or radios. Full data on income and savings are not available. But there is information on current livestock holdings. Since so many accusations and counter-accusations center precisely on this topic, it is worth while to deal with it extensively.

First, in terms of livestock holdings as of 1953, peyotists are slightly better off than non-peyotists (Table 27, items 11 and 12). Hence it cannot be argued that, as a result of using peyote, cult members have become the poorest members of the tribe in terms of livestock. Nor can it be argued, as I was inclined to do when I first went to the Navaho country, that peyotism attracts the poorest members of the tribe. (Henceforth in this discussion, "rich" and "poor" will be used only with reference to livestock.)

Although peyotist holdings are larger than non-peyotist, the median holdings of the two groups differ far less than the median pre-reduction holdings—as might be expected when it is considered that the distribution pyramid for livestock was flattened by reduction.

It might well be argued that peyotists have larger holdings now only because they had larger holdings in the past, received larger permits, and therefore have larger herds. But if this argument is maintained, then there can be no dispute about the "good" economic behavior of either peyotists or non-peyotists. That is, if each group has remained at or near permit level, the management of livestock by the two groups must be similar. On the whole, there is fair support for this argument. There is indeed a very strong and significant correlation between rank-order on permit size and on present holdings, whether we examine reported or official permit, residual or total, and whether we examine holdings in sheep, goats, and cattle or total holdings (Table 26). But the correlation between pre-reduction holdings and permits is not so strong. At Aneth, indeed, there is almost no significant correlation between rank-order of reported pre-reduction holdings and reported or official permit (one correlation alone is close to significant). At Mexican Springs, the correlations, though significant, are modest, ranging from .34 to .51 (Table 26). On the other hand, the rank-order correlation between *official* pre-reduction holdings (for 1936) and official permit is significant and fairly high for the 16 cases where data are available from Aneth, Mexican Springs, and Tohatchi, and for the 18 cases at Greasewood where data are at hand. They range from .57 to .66 (Table 25). It must be remembered that permits were based on these official figures and that the official figures were influenced by such haphazard factors as mis-assignment of stock to the man who happened to bring in any herds at all. From what is known of the history of reactions to livestock reduction, it seems quite fair to assume that under-reporting and failure to bring herds in at all were commoner at Aneth than at Mexican Springs, which may account for the difference between the two communities as respects rank-order correlations of reported or official permit and reported pre-reduction holdings. It should also be pointed out that the rank-order correlations for Aneth, though non-significant, are at least in the right direction (they range from .10 to .33—Table 26). Hence, on the whole, it seems fair to assume that there is at least a tendency for peyotists, who held the largest herds before reduction, to have the largest permits after reduction, and hence the largest herds today.

The non-peyotists might argue, however, that although the peyotist has larger herds because he has a larger permit, he is "running these flocks down." That is, through mismanagement or sale of livestock he is dissipating his herds. If this is the case, the peyotist's herds should less often be at or above the level of his permit and should more often fall below his permit than is the case for the non-peyotist. To test this idea, permit, both reported and official, has been subtracted from present holdings. If a person holds more stock than his permit allows, the result is a positive figure. If a person holds less stock, the result is a negative figure. It is then possible to rank-order all cases from the individual who has the largest number over his permit to the individual furthest below his permit and to see whether peyotists are disproportionately represented among those high or low on this rank-order. If peyotists are consuming their wealth or failing to care for it, they should have holdings below their permit size more often than non-peyotists. In fact, what tendency there is, is in the opposite direction. There is a tendency of borderline significance for peyotists to hold more stock than the permit allows more often than is the case for non-peyotists (Table 27, items 13 and 14). Both groups are very close to permit size. So there is no visible tendency for peyotists to expend their herds.[1]

It might be argued on the basis of these findings that peyotists tend to disobey the livestock regulations more often than non-peyotists. But since these figures were gathered before the autumn sales, when people attempt to adjust holdings to permit size, no such conclusion can be drawn.

A rather more complicated argument could be made against the peyotist. It might be argued that small permits are so uneconomical that they cannot be maintained. Since peyotists have larger permits than non-peyotists, it would there-fore be easier for them to remain at or above permit level than for non-peyotists. Now in fact there is no doubt whatsoever that very small permits are uneconom-ical and difficult to maintain. It must be remembered, however, that in Aneth and Mexican Springs almost all permits are very small. It is only in other districts that permits of up to 275 sheep units are a regular feature. So almost all these permits can be regarded as small. There are only three permits of over 120 in the two communities. Operating within this narrow range, we examined the rank-order correlation between holding stock over, at, or below permit level on the one hand and permit size on the other. If, in these communities, relatively small permits force people to reduce their herds through consumption, there should be an association between these two factors. Whether reported or official permit figures are used, either there is no correlation between these two variables or it is very low and non-significant (Table 32).

Peyotists, then, have larger permits and larger flocks than non-peyotists. Prob-ably they have both because of larger pre-reduction holdings. They are managing their flocks at least as well as non-peyotists, to judge by their tendency to maxi-mize their holdings by comparison with permit size.

On the whole, there is no reason to assume that peyotists are more, or less enter-prising, careful, or foresighted than non-peyotists. It is possible, of course, that

[1] In item 13 of Table 27, it can be seen that there is almost no difference between peyotists and non-peyotists at Mexican Springs. Furthermore, the median overage figure for non-peyotists is larger than the median for peyotists (4 versus 0), whereas in Aneth the median figure for peyotists is larger. In spite of this reversal in the medians, the mean rank-order for peyotists is fractionally higher than the mean rank-order for non-peyotists in the Mexican Springs sample for this measure. Hence combining the probabilities is legitimate, since even in this item the criterion is met: the relationship must be in the same direction for both communities.

painstaking before and after studies would indicate that some peyotists have become more careful, hardworking, and successful, since joining the cult, and others less so. There is no doubt that peyotists believe firmly that cult membership helps them in managing their livelihood problems. Without further study, no more can be said.

A NOTE ON STATISTICS

The use of one-tailed tests of significance throughout this chapter requires brief discussion. The idea of using livestock figures as measures of deprivation arose out of the observation of trends in the livestock data from Tohatchi and Teec Nos Pas (combined), and from Aneth and Mexican Springs (separately), when these data were still being analyzed in a way which failed to reveal significant associations: the data were then grouped in such a way that considerable information was lost. The measures of loss were then constructed, but at the time they were constructed,

TABLE 32

SPEARMAN RANK-ORDER CORRELATIONS BETWEEN OVERAGE
AND PERMIT SIZE

		Reported Permit	Official Permit
Reported Overage......	A	.09	.01
	MS	−.13	.01
Official Overage........	A	.07	−.04
	MS	.21	.00

NOTES: (1) Aneth N 22; Mexican Springs N 35. (2) Overage is present holdings minus permit. (3) Cattle in Mexican Springs Cattle Association (Table 24, col. 16, figures in parentheses) disregarded because not counted against permit. (4) None of the correlations is significant at the .05 level.

it was not known that all loss measures were highly intercorrelated, and specifically it was not known that all loss measures correlated highly with pre-reduction holdings (one measure of loss). The prediction was that loss measures would be associated with peyotism, and thus, logically, a one-tailed test is legitimate. Nevertheless, it might be argued that for Aneth, Mexican Springs, and Tohatchi the prediction was based on a known trend in the data so that a two-tailed test should have been used.

If a two-tailed test is used, the results do not suffer appreciably. In Table 27, if the 5 per cent level is taken as a cutting point, the use of two-tailed tests drops significance levels from the 5 per cent level or better to worse than the 5 per cent level in only two cases for individual communities: Aneth, present total holdings (item 12), and Aneth, present total holdings minus reported permit (item 13). Neither of these affects the deprivation hypothesis. They bear on the wealth hypothesis, which is regarded as weaker than the deprivation hypothesis in any case, and the question of prudential management of livestock, where the argument is that differences between peyotists and non-peyotists are slightly favorable to peyotists but are minor at best.

Combined probabilities for a two-tailed test drop below the acceptable level by comparison with one-tailed tests for reported residual permit (item 3), and present sheep, goats, and cattle holdings (item 11). Again the deprivation hypothesis is

unaffected. The argument that peyotism affected the wealthy beca͟
wealthy is weakened, and differences between peyotists and non-peyotist͟
of current holdings become less conspicuous. Thus, in sum, use of a two-tailed
does not change the nature of the argument presented earlier.

Tohatchi findings (Table 29) are unaffected by the use of a two-tailed test.

In Tables 25, 26, 28, 30, and 31 predictions are clearly unidirectional so that one-tailed tests are legitimate. In Table 29, the data from Greasewood and District 4 were not inspected before the deprivation hypothesis had been formulated so that the use of one-tailed tests is legitimate. In Table 32, all correlations are weak and non-significant, whether the test is one-tailed or two-tailed. In other chapters, the basis for the use of one-tailed or two-tailed tests of significance is evident in most instances and is discussed in a few others.

SUMMARY: PEYOTISM AND LIVESTOCK

1. In Aneth and Mexican Springs combined, Tohatchi, and Greasewood and District 4 combined, there is an association between cult membership and large past holdings and large losses of livestock.

2. In the light of these data, peyotism is interpreted as a response to relative deprivation in the area of livestock, a deprivation which resulted from the Government livestock reduction program.

3. There is also an association, with certain limitations, between the size of past holdings and of loss, on the one hand, and date of joining the cult, on the other, for Aneth and for Mexican Springs.

4. Horse reduction does not seem to be significant for the acceptance of peyotism.

5. Negative reactions toward present, by comparison with pre-reduction livelihood, are associated with peyotism.

6. Disturbance in dreams is associated with peyotism.

7. Disturbance in dreams and large livestock holdings in the past predict cult membership better in combination than does either measure alone for the cases where this information is available.

8. It could be argued that peyotists are merely those who have the wherewithal in the form of livestock that makes it possible for them to afford peyote ceremonies. The data are consistent with this theory, but the probability values for these associations are lower than those for the various loss measures. Furthermore, there are non-statistical reasons for rejecting the theory.

9. There is no evidence that peyotists have managed their livestock holdings worse than non-peyotists. The best conclusion on this score is that peyotists, with larger pre-reduction holdings, have larger permits and bigger flocks than non-peyotists, but that management of livestock is about equal for the two groups.

10. Although use of one-tailed tests is logically defensible throughout, the bulk of the findings where the a priori character of the hypothesis might be disputed would not be altered if a two-tailed test were used.

11. Findings that relate various livestock measures to peyotism proved to be significant in many instances, whereas the large number of variables discussed in Chapter 16 failed to show significant association with peyotism.

Chapter 18

ʹY AND DISTRICT DIFFERENCES
AND PEYOTISM

ATION may account in part for individuals' joining or not join-
ative American Church. Evidently, however, it will not account
differences in the percentage of peyotists in Aneth and Mexican
Springs. ʌeth, all but the least deprived joined the cult, whereas at Mexican
Springs, only a few of the most deprived joined. Apparently, there is no simple
deprivation threshold that accounts for this variation. Yet differences in the percentage of members from community to community are a striking feature of the
Navaho scene, and efforts to account for this variation began with the start of the
research.

As work progressed, it became evident that in order to attempt to account for
variation in the percentage of peyotists among communities, it was necessary to
gather information on a large number of communities. Although a long study
using a small number of investigators or a short study using a very large number
of investigators might have provided surveys of enough communities for these
purposes, neither of these expedients was employed. Instead, we attempted to
assess certain characteristics of Navaho communities by asking Agency employees
to rate the communities. It is to the results of this analysis that we now turn.

The level of peyotism was treated as one dependent variable. Five variables were
used as independent variables to account for the level of peyotism found in a series
of Navaho communities. These variables were (1) availability of the cult; (2) level
of acculturation; (3) level of trouble; (4) amount of disturbance over livestock
reduction and grazing control; (5) strength of local political organization.

The amount of disturbance occurring in these communities as a result of the
introduction of peyotism was a second dependent variable. All the foregoing independent variables were used as independent variables, but, in addition, the level
of peyotism became an independent variable in accounting for the amount of
disturbance over peyotism.

We turn now to the reasons for the selection of these variables, the hypotheses
about their effects, the nature of the data collected, and the mode of analysis selected. Then the results of the analysis will be discussed and interpreted. Finally,
certain district differences will be briefly mentioned.

INITIAL RATIONALE OF HYPOTHESES

From the very beginning of field work, I had tried to discover differences between communities that might account for the differential acceptance of peyotism.
It was this interest that led to my attempting to work in a number of communities.

278

As has been said, I was eventually overwhelmed by the sheer size of the Navaho reservation and decided that some sort of rough survey methods were desirable for over-all perspective. The result was the peyote questionnaire in the spring of 1951 and Moore's interviews with Indian Service employees in the summer of 1951.

The *questionnaire* gave information about the percentage of peyotists in each district and the relative number of peyotists in each community in a district. The *interview* gave us ratings on all the other variables mentioned above except availability. The choice of these variables had emerged from previous field work and efforts at the analysis of the community data I had in hand. I believed that "tension" and hostility to livestock reduction should promote the acceptance of peyotism. My notes do not indicate what hypothesis I held regarding acculturation prior to the beginning of Moore's work. The normal hypothesis would have been that acculturation was also positively associated with peyotism. But before Moore's materials had been examined, I had come to regard acculturation as in some way an inhibitory force in the spread of peyotism, in the Navaho case. This approach dominated the analysis of the community ratings from first to last.

The choice of strength of political organization as a variable resulted from the repeated comments by Navahos that a "strong" local leadership tended to keep the cult at a low level. I believed that probably *post hoc* reasoning underlay this theory: that if peyotism rose to high levels in spite of the opposition of local leaders (who were normally in opposition, initially), this leadership was thought of as weak, whereas if the cult had few members, local leadership was thought of as strong. Nevertheless, the opinion was expressed often enough to merit exploration.

Finally, since both Navahos and the Office of Indian Affairs expressed concern over the bitterness, factionalism, and occasional violence that sometimes accompanied the spread of peyotism, it seemed worthwhile to see whether this could be accounted for in any way.

But always complicating the picture, was the problem of availability. Peyotism is not a symptom like migraine or hives, such that it can be generated by individuals under stress, even though they have never heard of migraine or hives. It is a religious movement. If we *could* identify predisposing factors, individual or group, which would lead to rapid acceptance of peyotism, we might nevertheless find a situation where a community with strong predisposing factors had no peyotism because its members had had no opportunity to come in contact with the cult. Worse than that, we might not be sure, in any given case, whether there had been an opportunity. If so, it would be possible to overlook significant predisposing factors, because many of the communities under examination had not in fact been exposed.

Furthermore, it is possible that the availability factor might be prepotent, masking the effects of predisposing factors. That is, a community "disposed" to peyotism might be far from centers of cult development, and a community not so disposed might be near at hand. Under these circumstances, the availability factor might well obscure the other factors.

In addition, I had the impression that there was some association between cult availability and the other factors in which I was interested. Thus peyotism entered the Navaho country from the north, but the northern Navaho country is, by and large, less acculturated and more "troubled," and (during the 1940's) was more hostile to livestock reduction than the south. So the task of dealing with factors promoting and inhibiting acceptance of peyotism was a complex one from the beginning, since there was a distinct possibility that the possible causative factors were themselves associated, rather than independent. But "from the beginning" means from the time we first began to analyze the data, not from the time that data collection began. We now turn to the question of data collection.

DATA COLLECTION

There were two basic instruments of data collection: a questionnaire dealing with levels of peyotism and an interview dealing with reactions to livestock reduction, acculturation, trouble, political organization, and trouble over peyotism. These have been briefly described in Chapter 15 (Work, 1951–1952). In both cases the end-products were a series of ratings.

The questionnaire, which I prepared after consultation with John Clausen and Henry A. Riecken, was circulated by the Window Rock Area Office to certain personnel of the Navajo Agency. The recipient was asked to list each District in which he had worked, to show the dates when he had worked there, to sub-divide the District into communities, using the divisions he was accustomed to use when he worked there, and for each community to enter a rating, using the following scale: None, almost none, considerably less than half, about half, considerably more than half, almost all (peyotists). This was subsequently converted to a six-point scale, in which 0 was equivalent to none and 5 to almost all. The rater was also permitted to indicate that he had no information on the community in question. He was asked when peyotism had entered the community and what the percentage of peyotists was in the entire district. (The information was subsequently analyzed in Aberle and Stewart, 1957, pp. 87–92 and pp. 123–125.) (See Map 3.)[1a]

The interview, prepared after consultation with Clausen and Riecken, was emended in consultation with Harvey C. Moore. Moore then interviewed certain Agency personnel. Each was asked to describe the community he felt he knew best, in a particular District selected by Moore and me. The nature of the interview is described in detail in Appendix F. In brief, the meaning of the five variables

[1a] Map 3 is explained in Aberle and Stewart, 1957, p. 123. A brief summary is provided here. Some ratings in Aberle and Stewart, 1957, pp. 124–125, used in the preparation of Map 3, do not appear in Table 34 of Chapter 18 of this volume. In some instances, where ratings for the late time-period are entirely lacking, extrapolations from adjoining areas appear on the map. A uniform, low level of peyotism is shown for District 16, because of spotty data. Levels for Dinnehotso in District 8 and Lukachukai in District 11 are based on field work, not on Agency ratings. Values of "none or negligible" for Districts 1, 2, most of 3, 5, and most of 8 are based on Navahos' reports, not on Agency raters. It seemed undesirable to alter the ratings and then manipulate them statistically, but permissible and desirable to alter the map to provide the best distributional data available. Community boundaries are arbitrary.

In Map 3, ratings of 4.5 to 4.0 are reflected in the category, "considerably more than half"; ratings of 3.5 to 3.0 are "about half"; ratings of 2.5 to 2.0 are "considerably less than half"; ratings of 1.5 to 0.5 are "almost none"; ratings of 0 and doubtful reports where we have reason to assume no adherents or only a handful are classified as "negligible or none."

A map for 1965 would show some peyotists in virtually every community and higher levels in many. This map shows the situation in 1951.

MAP 3

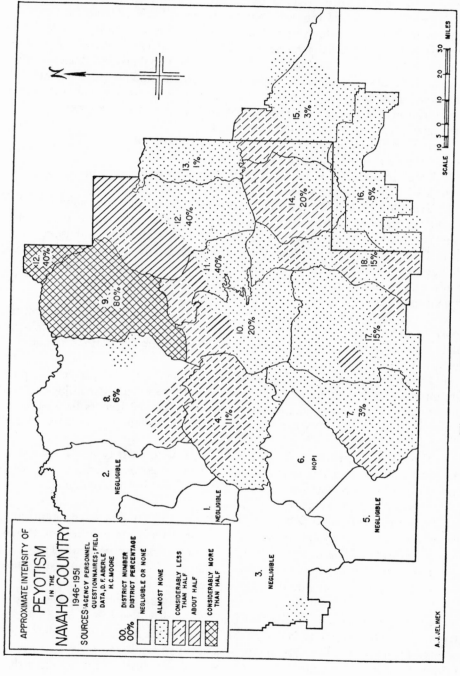

APPROXIMATE INTENSITY OF
PEYOTISM
IN THE
NAVAHO COUNTRY
1946-1951
SOURCES: AGENCY PERSONNEL
QUESTIONNAIRES; FIELD
DATA, D. F. ABERLE
H. C. MOORE

00.   DISTRICT NUMBER
00%   DISTRICT PERCENTAGE

☐ NEGLIGIBLE OR NONE
⬚ ALMOST NONE
▨ CONSIDERABLY LESS
    THAN HALF
▨ ABOUT HALF
▨ CONSIDERABLY MORE
    THAN HALF

1.
NEGLIGIBLE

2.
NEGLIGIBLE

3.
NEGLIGIBLE

4.
11%

5.
NEGLIGIBLE

6.
HOPI

7.
3%

8.
6%

9.
80%

10.
20%

11.
40%

12.
40%

13.
1%

14.
20%

15.
3%

16.
5%

17.
15%

18.
15%

A. J. JELINEK

SCALE
10 5 0   10   20   30
MILES

These maps reflect the situation as of 1951

that appeared in the interview was supplied to the respondents not by attempting to define the variable but by a series of detailed questions about certain character-istics of the community selected by the respondent. After these questions, the respondent was asked to rate the community he had selected and then to rate the other communities in which he had worked. To take acculturation as an example, the respondent was asked a number of specific questions about educational level, use of English, dress, hair-style, adherence to certain Navaho customs, religious practice, education of children, outside employment, and so on. Then, with these questions as background, he was asked to rate on a five-point scale the degree to which the people in the community chosen had "taken on American ways." He then rated other communities in the same way.

A brief statement of the general content of each of the five variables is supplied here. (For details, see Appendix F.)

1. Acculturation. As has been said, this dealt with acceptance of American ways, or lack of acceptance, in a variety of areas of life.

2. Trouble. This dealt both with trouble within the community—including trouble in the family—and trouble between Navahos and Agency personnel. It touched on anti-white sentiment in general and on such signs of tension as witch-craft fears and drinking. Although I had intended to delineate an area that I thought of as signs of tension, the final interview brought out Navaho-Navaho and Navaho-Agency overt hostility most clearly. "Overt disturbance" would be an equally good label.

3. Reactions to stock reduction—or grazing regulations, for respondents whose work in an area had followed the period of intensive reduction. This dealt princi-pally with opposition to livestock reduction or grazing regulations, including ma-jor crises.

4. Political organization. This discussed whether there was a central political organization in the community; if so, whether there were other influential leaders or groups in the community; if not, who the influential leaders or groups in the community were; and to what degree the various leaders or groups worked with or against each other.

5. Trouble over peyotism. This dealt directly with most types of overt conflict between peyotists and anti-peyotists and with the question whether this issue pene-trated other types of factional divisions, if any, within the community.

The actual order of topics in the interview was political organization, trouble, reactions to livestock reduction, acculturation, and trouble over peyotism. The detailed questions prepared the way for ratings on all communities for which the respondent was willing to supply them. These questions were intended to minimize the possibility that our conception of the nature of the relevant variables and the respondents' conception would diverge radically.

Since every respondent had filled out a peyote questionnaire, it was possible to make a list in advance of all the communities he was likely to know and to select from among the Districts in which he had worked the one on which we most wanted information. The respondent was always permitted to say that he had no information on a particular community or topic. It should be made clear that the interview was presented as an interview on general conditions, not an interview about peyotism. In order to avoid biasing responses, questions about peyotism came last.

RESPONDENTS

Final selection of respondents for the peyote questionnaire was determined by the Window Rock Area Office, in Spring of 1951. Arrangements had to be completed by mail and under time pressure. Although it would have been desirable to circularize traders, as well as Agency employees, it was impracticable to do so for at least two reasons. First, circulation of a questionnaire dealing with peyotism might have led to the expectation that the Agency was about to take some action. Agency personnel could not be dissuaded from this opinion, if they formed it, but they could be asked to keep the circulation confidential. Traders could not. (Most Agency personnel did respect this request.) Second, the Agency was in a position to put pressure on slow respondents to complete the questionnaire. It had no leverage with traders.

I asked the Agency to circulate the questionnaire to four categories of personnel:

1. To all district supervisors, and, preferably, to all former district supervisors who held other positions on the reservation in 1951. In addition, certain ex-supervisors no longer in the Navajo Agency were suggested as respondents.
2. Preferably, to all agricultural extension workers, government farmers, and government stockmen.
3. Preferably, to all school principals.
4. Preferably, to all school teachers.

The basis for selection of these categories was experience: my conversations with people in each of these positions convinced me that, in many instances, they had a great deal of information about the communities in which they worked. Medical personnel, on the other hand, were not suggested, since their work confined them so closely to hospitals and clinics as to give them little information about the areas in which they worked.

The list of employees prepared at Window Rock on the basis of my suggestions included all these categories but not all personnel in each category. Unfortunately, the Agency's basis for inclusion and exclusion of respondents on the final list was not made perfectly explicit, although reasonably evident from the list itself:

1. All district Supervisors, all former district supervisors still working in the Navajo Agency, and one former district supervisor working elsewhere received questionnaires.
2. A number of farm management supervisors, agricultural aides, stockmen, and range examiners received questionnaires, but I am not certain how many, if any, were excluded.
3. All, or almost all, school principals were reached.
4. Some teachers were circularized. But apparently, if a principal was reached in any given school, no teacher was used as a respondent. And there were respondents in only about half of the Agency schools. In some instances, omissions along these lines reflect the fact that a position was not manned and in others, the fact that the teacher was too recent an employee to have information. Only one respondent per school among 28 schools was secured.

This procedure, then, represented the Agency's adaptation of my list of suggestions. The failure to utilize the total list creates two problems: fewer ratings per area and fewer areas rated.

Both Navaho and non-Navaho employees received the questionnaire.

Sixty-eight employees and former employees (2 cases) received the questionnaire. Only 4 failed to reply—a response rate of 94 per cent. Of the 4, one was a teacher whose husband was also a teacher, who must have assumed that one form would do for both of them. Fourteen claimed to have no relevant information, and 3 sent in unusable or uninterpretable replies. There remained 47 usable questionnaires, or 69 per cent of the original group.[1]

The final distribution of employees providing usable questionnaires is shown in Chart J. At least 8 of the total of 47 were Navahos, including 3 district supervisors, 2 teachers, 1 farm management supervisor, and 2 agricultural aides.

Of those who provided unusable replies, had no information, or did not reply, 12 were in the field of education, 7 were in field jobs, 1 was a Headquarters em-

CHART J

AGENCY RESPONDENTS SUPPLYING QUESTIONNAIRE DATA

Field personnel:

District supervisors..............	11	
Former district supervisors........	3	
Stockmen, range examiners, etc.....	3	
Farm management supervisors......	6	
Irrigation engineers, irrigation operation and management foremen...	5	
Agricultural aides, gardeners.......	3	
Subtotal..............................		31

School personnel:

Principals, principal-teachers, area principals.....................	8	
Former principals................	1	
Teachers........................	7	
Subtotal..............................		16
Total.....................	47........	47

ployee, and 1 was a former district supervisor no longer with the Agency. Of the 21, at least 3 were Navahos. (Employees were not asked to identify their ethnic background; hence the number of Navahos providing useful forms, as well as the number supplying usable information may be slightly underestimated. Identifications are based on Aberle's information, which is reasonably complete.)[2]

The questionnaires supplied a basis for selecting respondents for Moore's interview. They told us who had worked where and for how long. They were used to select a group of employees with as wide an areal coverage and with as many years' experience as possible. The result was a group of 33 employees, the composition of which appears in Chart K.

Of the 33 selected, 2 were individuals with no information about peyote, but valuable for areal representation, and 1 was the man whose division of communities,

---

[1] One respondent misunderstood the instructions. One grouped communities in his area differently from all other respondents in the area. One provided information so much at variance from that received from other respondents and from information derived from field work that it was discarded.

[2] This summary of questionnaires supersedes and corrects that supplied in Aberle and Stewart, 1957, p. 87, which mentions 64 original questionnaires and 52 usable replies.

we later discovered, made his questionnaire unusable. By the same token, his rating sheets were also unusable. Hence there were 32 usable sets of rating sheets. The employees interviewed were distributed like those who returned usable questionnaires: about two-thirds field employees and one-third education employees.

Since there were 17 or 18 land management units, depending on whether District 19 is counted or not (Agency practice varies), it may be surprising that there were only 12 district supervisors to serve as sources of information. This occurred because, especially in the west, several Districts were placed under a single supervisor.

DATA PROCESSING

The procedures in collating the ratings from questionnaires and interviews for each community must now be described. Agency employees had variable lengths of service and had worked in different numbers of areas. Some had spent many years in one place and others only a few. Each was asked to give us information

CHART K

AGENCY RESPONDENTS SELECTED FOR INTERVIEW

Field personnel:

District supervisors and former district supervisors (all)	14	
Farm management supervisors and irrigation foremen	8	
Subtotal		22

School personnel:

Principals and former principals	6	
Teachers	4	
Other:	1	
Subtotal		11
Total	33	33

about each community where he had worked "when he was there," a somewhat indefinite instruction.

It seemed most undesirable to lump all the ratings for one community, regardless of the time-period to which they applied. On the other hand, if very small time-periods were to be used, we might find very few raters for a particular time. Furthermore, the earlier the time-period, the fewer the raters, since there is turnover in Agency personnel. Hence it was decided to use relatively large time-intervals. Given this decision, it was necessary to decide how to allocate a rater to a particular time-period.

There were three obvious possibilities—all with disadvantages. One was to assume that a man's ratings were valid for the entire period of his stay. This would mean that, after the total span of years covered by all the ratings had been divided into two or more time-periods, people in residence for many years would be listed in every time-period of their residence, which would inflate their influence. This procedure was not followed. The second was to assume that the rating reflected the median year of a man's stay. This assumption was made in some of the early work done with these ratings. The third assumption was that a man's more recent impressions would be dominant in his ratings, so that the best way to assign him to a time-period was on the basis of the year when he was last in any given area. This last procedure was followed, although clearly it is an arbitrary decision whether to use the last or second.[3]

The communities of the reservation were rostered, and the dates when each rater had been there were entered. The decision as to how many time-intervals there should be and what years would be used to divide the ratings was based entirely on an effort to get as many communities as possible rated for each time-period selected. This ultimately led to the selection of 1945–1946 as a break-point. All raters in a community who had been there and left there before the end of 1945 were assigned to the *early* time-period; all those who were still there at the beginning of 1946 were assigned to the *late* time-period. It would have been desirable to divide the raters at about 1941, but this would have put few communities in the early time-period.

TABLE 33

HYPOTHETICAL RATING SHEET FOR A COMMUNITY

	ACCULTURATION RATINGS	
	Early (before 1946)	Late (1946 and after)
Rater 1 (1933–1936).	2	. . . .
Rater 2 (1939–1942).	1	. . . .
Rater 3 (1943–1945).	2	. . . .
Rater 4 (1941–1947).	. . . .	3
Rater 5 (1945–1950).	. . . .	2
	Median 2	Median 2.5

After every rating had been assigned to one time-period or the other, the median rating for each time-period was determined. (In cases with an odd number of ratings, the middle rating was selected; in cases with an even number, a rating mid-way between the central two ratings was chosen.) The basis for selecting a median rather than a mean rating was to minimize the effects of extreme ratings, given the small number of raters.

These procedures are illustrated in Table 33, where five raters are shown. Each rater would also appear on the rating sheet of any other community he rated and for the time-period appropriate to his stay there.

Not all employees divided the communities in the same way. Some indicated that they lumped communities which others separated. We eventually lumped or separated such units depending on the preponderance of raters' views. Agreement was surprising, considering that in the peyote questionnaires no a priori division of the reservation was supplied as regards communities.

DATA ELIMINATION

After the rating sheets had been tabulated and ratings for each community prepared, it was decided to eliminate from consideration a group of districts in the

[3] This procedure was worked out in discussions with John Caylor and Walter H. Crockett.

northwest and west (Districts 1, 2, 3, and 8) and in the east and south (Districts 15 and 16). District 6, which is mainly Hopi, is a separate jurisdiction, from which no ratings were secured, although some Navahos reside there.

There were three basic reasons for this decision. First, we wished to exclude from consideration districts that had had little or no exposure to peyotism. Second, we wished to work with communities where there were ratings for both time-

TABLE 34

MEDIAN RATINGS OF NAVAHO COMMUNITIES

CO	MI	PE	PL	DE	DL	AE	AL	TE	TL	SE	SL	OE	OL
1. RATINGS USED FOR REGRESSION EQUATIONS													
9-1	51	2.5	4.0	2.5	3.0	2.5	2.0	4.5	3.0	5.0	4.0	2.5	3.0
9-2	51	3.0	4.0	2.0	2.0	2.0	1.0	3.5	5.0	4.5	3.0	1.5	2.0
9-3	58	3.0	4.0	2.0	2.0	2.0	1.5	4.0	3.5	4.0	4.0	2.0	2.5
9-4	74	2.0	4.0	1.5	2.0	2.0	1.0	3.5	3.0	4.0	3.0	2.0	2.0
9-5	79	2.0	4.0	1.0	2.0	1.5	1.0	3.5	3.5	4.0	4.0	2.0	2.0
11-1	84	2.0	2.0	3.0	1.5	2.5	4.0	2.5	2.0	1.0	2.0	4.5	4.0
11-2	101	0.5	2.0	1.0	2.0	2.0	3.5	2.5	2.5	1.0	3.0	3.0	3.5
11-3	89	0.5	1.0	1.0	1.0	2.0	3.5	2.5	2.5	1.0	3.0	3.0	3.0
12-1	33	2.0	3.0	2.0	3.0	3.5	4.0	3.5	2.0	4.5	4.0	4.0	4.0
12-2	67	2.0	3.0	.....	2.5	2.0	3.0	3.0	2.5	4.0	4.0	4.0	4.0
12-3	64	1.0	1.0	.....	1.0	2.5	3.0	3.0	2.5	4.5	3.5	3.0	3.0
12-6	55	2.0	2.0	2.0	3.5	2.0	3.0	3.0	3.0	4.0	3.0	2.0	4.0
12-7	33	3.0	4.5	3.0	2.0	1.0	1.5	4.0	2.5	5.0	4.5	4.0	4.0
13-1	56	2.0	1.5	2.0	1.0	2.0	4.0	3.0	2.0	1.0	2.0	3.0	3.0
14-2	84	1.0	2.0	.....	3.0	3.0	3.0	2.0	2.0	3.0	3.0	4.0	3.0
14-3	111	1.0	2.0	.....	1.5	2.0	4.0	2.0	3.0	5.0	3.0	4.0	4.0
14-4	121	1.0	1.0	.....	1.0	2.0	3.0	2.5	2.0	5.0	3.0	4.0	3.0
14-5	112	1.0	2.0	.....	1.0	2.5	3.0	3.0	4.0	5.0	3.0	4.5	2.0
18-1	146	1.0	1.5	1.5	1.5	3.0	4.0	2.0	3.0	4.0	2.5	4.0	3.0
18-2	139	1.0	2.0	2.0	3.0	3.0	3.0	2.0	3.0	3.5	3.0	3.0	1.0
18-4	97	1.0	1.0	3.0	1.0	3.0	4.0	2.0	2.0	4.0	2.5	4.0	4.5
18-5	145	0.5	2.0	1.5	2.0	3.0	3.0	2.0	3.0	3.5	3.0	3.0	4.0
18-6	170	0.5	1.0	1.0	2.0	2.5	2.5	2.0	3.0	4.0	3.0	3.5	4.0
18-7	159	0.5	2.0	1.0	2.0	3.0	3.0	2.5	4.0	3.5	3.0	3.0	1.0
18-8	140	0.5	0.0	2.0	1.0	2.5	3.5	2.0	4.0	4.0	3.0	3.0	3.0
4-1	144	1.0	2.0	2.0	3.0	2.0	3.5	3.0	2.5	3.0	2.5	2.0	2.0
4-2	158	1.0	1.0	2.0	2.0	2.0	3.5	3.0	2.0	3.0	3.5	3.0	2.5
4-3	158	1.0	2.0	1.5	3.0	1.0	3.0	3.0	2.5	4.0	2.0	2.0	1.0
4-8	155	1.0	2.5	3.0	3.5	2.0	3.0	3.0	2.0	4.0	3.0	2.0	2.5
10-1	132	0.5	1.0	1.0	1.0	2.0	3.0	2.0	3.0	4.5	1.0	3.0	3.0
10-2	122	0.0	3.0	1.0	4.0	2.0	3.0	3.0	2.5	4.0	1.5	3.0	2.5
10-3	109	0.0	2.0	1.0	3.0	2.0	2.0	3.0	3.0	4.5	2.0	3.0	2.0
10-4	157	0.0	1.0	1.0	1.0	2.0	2.5	3.0	3.0	4.0	2.0	3.0	2.5
10-5	165	0.5	1.0	1.0	1.0	2.0	3.0	3.0	2.0	3.5	2.0	4.0	3.0
17-1	184	1.0	1.5	1.0	1.0	3.0	4.0	2.0	1.0	2.0	1.5	4.0	5.0
17-2	191	1.0	2.0	1.0	1.0	3.0	3.0	3.0	1.0	2.0	1.0	3.0	5.0
17-4	167	1.0	1.5	.....	1.0	3.0	4.5	2.0	2.0	2.0	1.5	4.0	1.0
17-5	164	0.5	1.0	.....	1.0	2.0	3.0	2.0	2.0	2.0	1.0	3.0	4.0
17-6	178	1.0	1.5	2.0	1.5	2.5	3.0	2.0	1.0	2.0	1.0	4.0	5.0
17-7	195	1.5	3.0	3.0	3.0	2.0	2.0	2.0	2.0	2.0	1.0	3.0	3.0
17-8	189	1.0	1.0	1.0	1.0	3.0	2.0	2.0	1.0	2.0	1.0	3.0	5.0

TABLE 34—*Continued*

CO	MI	PE	PL	DE	DL	AE	AL	TE	TL	SE	SL	OE	OL
							2. OTHER RATINGS						
12-4	74	......	1.0	......	1.0	3.0	3.5	3.0	1.5	4.5	2.5	3.0	3.5
12-5	78	......	1.0	......	1.0	3.0	2.5	3.0	2.5	4.5	3.5	2.0	3.5
13-2	77	......	1.0	1.5	1.0	2.0	2.5	2.5	2.0	2.5	3.0	3.0	3.0
14-1	102	......	2.0	......	2.0	2.5	4.0	3.0	3.0	5.0	3.0	4.5	3.0
18-3	130	0.0	......	1.0	1.5	3.0	3.0	2.0	3.0	3.5	3.0	4.0	4.0
4-4	160	1.5	......	2.0	1.5	1.0	2.5	3.0	2.5	3.0	2.0	2.0	1.5
4-5	124	1.5	......	3.0	3.0	1.0	2.5	3.0	2.5	4.0	3.0	3.0	2.5
4-6	160	......	1.0	2.0	1.5	1.0	2.0	3.0	3.0	3.0	3.0	2.0	2.0
4-7	155	2.0	......	2.0	5.0	1.0	2.0	3.0	......	4.0	3.0	2.0	.....
4-9	167	2.0	......	2.0	......	2.0	......	3.0	......	4.0	......	4.0	.....
7-1	233	......	1.0	2.0	1.0	2.0	3.0	1.0	3.0	3.0	2.0	4.0	3.0
7-2	240	......	2.0	2.0	1.0	2.0	3.0	2.0	3.0	3.0	......	4.0	3.0
7-3	219	......	1.0	1.0	1.0	2.0	3.0	1.5	4.0	3.0	2.0	4.5	4.0
7-4	221	......	1.0	1.0	1.0	1.5	3.0	2.0	3.0	2.0	2.0	4.0	4.0
17-3	172	1.0	......	2.0	1.0	2.0	2.0	3.0	1.0	2.0	1.0	2.0	4.0

NOTES TO TABLE 34

1. *Variables.*—CO, community number; MI, distance from Towaoc (availability); P, peyote; D, disturbance over peyote; A, acculturation; T, trouble; S, reactions to livestock reduction; O, political organization; E, early (1945 and before); L, late (1946–1951).

2. *Assignment of Ratings.*—Rating is assigned to early or late time-period on the basis of rater's latest date of service in the area.

3. *Log transformations.*—To find availability figures for prediction equation, find the natural logarithm of the MI figure and multiply by ten.

4. *Communities.*—Each community has a two-part code. Figures before the hyphen show District number; after the hyphen is an arbitrary number for the community. Districts fall into two sets, an eastern (9, 11, 12, 13, 14, and 18) and a western (4, 7, 10, and 17). Within each set the districts are placed in numerical, rather than geographical order. Communities not used in the regression equation are separated from others. Such communities lack at least one peyote rating, early or late, and may lack other information as well. Identification of communities is supplied below.

4-1: Piñon
4-2: Hard Rocks, Oraibi Valley
4-3: Big Mountain
4-4: Burnt Corn
4-5: Forest Lake
4-6: Low Mountain
4-7: Sagebrush
4-8: Black Mountain, Kitseely
4-9: Dinnebito

7-1: Dilcon, Castle Butte, Cedar Springs
7-2: Teastoh, Seba Dalkai, Finger Point
7-3: Indian Wells, Na-ha-tee Canyon
7-4: White Cone, Jeddito, Low Star Mountain

9-1: Teec Nos Pas
9-2: Red Mesa
9-3: Sweet Water
9-4: Mexican Water
9-5: Rock Point

10-1: Chinle, Canyon de Chelly, Canyon del Muerto
10-2: Frazier, Many Farms, Valley Post
10-3: Rough Rock
10-4: Black Mountain, Salina
10-5: Nazlini

11-1: Lukachukai
11-2: Round Rock
11-3: Greasewood, Tsalee, Wheatfields

12-1: Shiprock
12-2: Red Rock, Cove

12-3: Sanastee, Tocito
12-4: Nava, Newcomb, Two Gray Hills, Toadlena
12-5: Sheep Springs
12-6: Beclabito
12-7: Aneth, Montezuma, Mancos Creek, Hatches'

13-1: Fruitlands (all)
13-2: Burnhams'

14-1: Tohatchi
14-2: Naschiti
14-3: Mexican Springs
14-4: Coyote Canyon
14-5: Twin Lakes, Tohlikai

17-1: Klagetoh
17-2: Wide Ruins
17-3: Pine Springs
17-4: Ganado
17-5: Kin-li-chee (Red House)
17-6: Corn Fields, Sunrise
17-7: Greasewood
17-8: Steamboat

18-1: Fort Defiance
18-2: Sawmill
18-3: Red Lake
18-4: Crystal
18-5: St. Michael's, Hunters Point
18-6: Oak Springs, Pine Springs
18-7: Saunders', Houck, Lupton
18-8: Window Rock, Coalmine

periods so that changes over time could be examined. Hence communities (or districts) where ratings for two time-periods were lacking were eliminated. Third, issues of face validity further reinforced our decision to eliminate some of the western districts.

In the case of the western districts (1, 2, 3, and 8), the primary basis for the decision was that inquiries pursued in the course of field work indicated that there was little or no exposure to peyotism in this area, except for the eastern part of District 8 and a small area in District 3. In addition, in District 1, there were no ratings on peyotism for the first time-period. Raters for the second time-period claimed that there was peyotism in the area, but my own information indicated almost no contact with peyotism as late as 1953. In District 2, there were slightly higher ratings for peyotism, but again field information failed to support the ratings. In District 3, early raters claimed that there was "considerably less than half" cult membership in several communities, whereas later ones claimed no peyotism for most of the area. The same pattern was found for District 5. But we have no reason to believe that such a decline has occurred anywhere in the Navaho country, so that the validity of these ratings is in doubt. For District 8, there were almost no ratings on most variables for the early time-period.

As for Districts 15 and 16, although there was certainly peyotism in parts of both areas, and probably in most of District 16, either early or late ratings were not available for at least one variable for every community.

After this pruning had taken place, there were 41 communities for which we had ratings on all variables except trouble over peyotism, missing in 8 cases for the early period, and a few more for which some ratings were available. These ratings are presented in Table 34.

CONSIDERATIONS OF VALIDITY

Quite evidently, a series of ratings by Agency personnel, however well-informed and sensitive to the issues involved, is a very rough measure of the variables in question. Furthermore, the division of raters into two time-periods is arbitrary, as is the selection of median ratings. It is therefore worth examining the final product to see whether there is any evidence for validity in it. On the whole, the results show a certain consistency and, where data are available, provide information equivalent to that gathered by other means.

First, there are only two instances in which the ratings indicate that peyotism has declined in the communities: 13–1 and 18–8. In both cases the decline shown is small. This is important, since there is general consensus among peyotists, non-peyotists, and Government employees that up to 1951 the peyote cult was not declining in membership anywhere: it was either static or rising. (The level of activity of the cult was sometimes said to have declined in some areas.) My own field work failed to turn up any instance of declining membership. Thus the ratings fit the common opinion and the available data. (This consistency did not obtain in the western area, which was entirely eliminated.)

Second, the levels of cult membership defined for the late time-period fit well with my own impressions from field work and, more important, in two instances correspond well with the results of the random samples. In Aneth, 75 per cent of the sample is peyotist, and the rating is between "considerably more than half" and "almost all." In Mexican Springs, 19 per cent of the sample is peyotist and the rating is "considerably less than half."

The acculturation ratings by and large show rising or static acculturation. In 6 out of 41 cases, or 16 per cent, however, the level is shown as falling. It is patent to any observer of the Navaho scene that the level of acculturation for any time-period in any community is either static or rising. The rarity of declining levels of acculturation in the ratings is, then, evidence in favor of their validity. (It must be remembered that *different* raters are involved for each community for the two time-periods: it is not a matter of asking a rater to evaluate acculturation levels at two different times in the same community.)

In the case of reactions to livestock reduction, there is no doubt that, in fact, they are less intense in general since World War II than they were earlier, although this may not be the case everywhere. The ratings show a drop in negative reactions in most cases. In 4 cases, the level is static; in 5, it rises.

In the case of trouble level, there is no general basis for any particular expectation. The ratings show a general decline. In the case of political organization, again there is no basis for any particular expectation. Rising and static cases predominate. In the case of peyote trouble, there is no particular expectation. Rising and static cases predominate.

The level of acculturation indicated for the late time-period may also be considered in connection with other data. The random samples show clear and marked differences between Aneth and Mexican Springs, with Mexican Springs much more acculturated. The ratings show Aneth somewhere between "not very" and "almost not at all" acculturated and Mexican Springs acculturated "to a considerable extent." On the other hand, among communities of any size, Shiprock would be considered by most observers in the late time-period to be the most acculturated. Nevertheless, its rating is only equal to that of Mexican Springs and a few others, whereas Ganado gets the top rating.

Thus, in spite of the fact that the judgments for the early and for the late time-period are made by different judges, there is a consistency in the results as respects the general tendency of peyote level ratings and of acculturation ratings to rise. Both these tendencies conform to the general perception of reality in the area, as does the tendency of ratings of hostility to stock reduction to decline. Where field experience and sample results are available, they tend to fit with the ratings.

For all of these reasons, the ratings will be regarded in the treatment that follows as rough and approxmiate measures of the actual state of affairs for two time-periods as respects these variables for a portion of the Navajo Reservation.

STATISTICAL TECHNIQUES

The independent variables for predicting peyotism are availability of the cult, acculturation, trouble, reactions to livestock reduction, and strength of political organization. The question of an availability measure is discussed in Aberle and Stewart (1957). Fundamentally, as has been said, the problem is that the level of peyotism in any given community should be a function of the ease of contact of that community with cult disseminators. All anthropological concepts of diffusion patterns and rates rest in part on a postulate of this nature, however great may be the perturbations introduced by other factors. Desirable though it would be to have a map of the frequency, duration, and intensity of contacts among communities, and specifically between communities with peyote priests and those without, no such data exist, except for a minimum amount of information about visiting between communities, utilized in Aberle and Stewart (1957). In default of such information, the measure of availability used is mileage from Towaoc, the place from which the Navaho cult originated, through contact with Ute Mountain Utes. Mileage is figured by the shortest practicable route for Navahos. Thus roads over the mountains, often impassable for automobiles, are considered practicable, since in the early days of cult diffusion, many Navahos travelled by horseback. This measure, reasonable enough for the early time-period, becomes a poorer measure for the later time-period, when there were several centers of cult activity and spread. No other simple measure seemed possible, so this one has been used. The dependent variable, of course, is peyotism.

Since there is some interest in the amount of disturbance created by the entry of peyotism into a community, trouble over peyotism has also been treated as a dependent variable; when this is done, the independent variables listed above are treated as independent variables, but, in addition, the level of peyotism in the community is also used as an independent variable, since it seems reasonable to assume that there is some tendency for trouble over peyotism to co-vary with the level of peyotism.

Given the dichotomy of ratings into early and late, thirteen variables emerge.

The model used for analysis of these ratings is that of linear multiple regression (cf. Blalock, 1960, pp. 326–346). Fundamentally, the analysis tells us how much change in the dependent variable will result from a change of one unit in each independent variable, with all the other independent variables held constant. It is thus analogous to, but not identical with, an analysis in terms of partial correlations, where the co-variation of each independent variable with the dependent variable is determined with all other variables controlled. The result of the regression analysis is a prediction equation which tells us what numerical values to use as constants to predict (in this case) the peyote score for each community. These constants are used as multipliers, the multiplicand being the amount by which the community rating on each variable departs from the sample mean for the variable. If, for example, the raw score regression weight for "trouble" is 1, this means that a change of one step (one whole rating point) in trouble level predicts a change of one step in peyote level. If the raw score regression weight is .5, then a change of one step in trouble level predicts a change of a half-step in the peyote score. If the regression weight is plus .5, then in communities with "trouble" scores which are one step above the mean, we expect the peyote scores to be one half-step above the mean. In communities which are one step below the mean, we expect the peyote scores to be one half-step below the mean. This weight, however, would be only one of many involved in the prediction equation and might be supplemented by, or more than compensated by, the raw score weight and its multiplicand for the other variables in any particular instance.

Examination of raw score weights, however, can be confusing. If one variable—for example mileage—has a very large variance, with a mean of 119 and a standard deviation of 48, whereas another has a very small variance—say, a mean of 2.3 and a standard deviation of .6, the variable with very large variance may have a very small weight but be exerting a great influence in the regression equation, whereas the other variable may have a much more sizable weight but be exerting a small influence.

Again, to be concrete, mileage for these communities has a range of about 160 miles. A weight of .008 would mean that the dependent variable changes by .008 for every change of a mile's distance away from the mean. Other things being equal, as we move from the community nearest to Towaoc to the community furthest away, the peyote score would shift by .008 × 160, or 1.28 points. On the other hand, the variable with the smaller variance might have a weight of .2. If its range were from 1 to 4, other things being equal, as we moved from 1 to 4, the shift in the peyote score would be .2 × 4, or .8. Thus the much smaller raw weight for mileage would exercise a larger influence on the final prediction score than would the larger weight for the variable with less variance.

To make assessment of the relative importance of the raw weights, a transformation to standard weights is necessary. This involves a transformation of each variable so that it has a mean of zero and a standard deviation of 1. Under these circumstances, variables with the largest standard weights can be regarded as having the largest impact in the regression equation.

Needless to say, the regression equation predicts for each case only approximately. Furthermore, when it is developed on a small sample, it may fail in predicting cases not in the sample. It is simply the best fit for the sample in question.

The assumptions underlying the use of a multiple regression model are threefold. First, it is assumed that the data are equal-interval data. The use of a rating scale is questionable in this regard but by no means outrageous. Second, it is assumed that the relationships among variables are linear, which is reasonable in this case. Third, if inferences are to be made from this sample to a larger universe of Navaho or Indian communities, using readily available techniques, it is necessary to assume that the variables have a normal distribution. For a sample of 41 communities, this is an assumption impossible to prove or to disprove.

The reason for choosing this model lay in the character of the data and the problem. The model that probably requires minimal assumptions is that of doing chi-square tests of each independent variable against each dependent variable, without making assumptions of equal intervals. If (as is the case) a number of independent variables prove to be associated with the dependent variables (peyote and disturbance over peyote), the question at once arises whether the independent variables are also associated, and if so, whether the association between any one independent variable and a dependent variable is mediated by another independent variable. This leads very quickly to a problem of non-parametric correlation coefficients and partial correlations, which, with a large number of independent variables, leads to a great many first, second, third, etc., order partial correlations, with corresponding complexities both of computation and of interpretation. Furthermore, for such correlation measures as phi, the character of the basic variables raises problems. Phi is sensitive to the smallest row or column frequencies. If all variables can be neatly dichotomized, no problem arises: phi coefficients of different magnitudes can be interpreted straightforwardly. But if some can be and some cannot, problems arise.

Under these circumstances, it seemed best to make the additional assumptions and use the multiple regression model, rather than to make fewer assumptions and be confronted with an exceedingly unwieldy analytic problem.

In the case of the mileage figures, mileage and peyote levels were graphed for the early and the late time-period. It was decided that transformation of mileage figures to logarithms fitted the character of this distribution better than the use of the raw mileage figures. In the tables that follow, the logarithmic figures that appear represent $10 \times \log_e$—a multiplication which avoids the use of very small decimal fractions. Experiment indicates that wherever mileage (distance from Towaoc) has a large weight in a prediction equation, the correlation between predicted and actual scores is improved by the use of the logarithmic transformation by comparison with raw mileage.

The assumption of linear relationships was subjected to gross empirical check: the cross-tabulations for all correlations were examined. For the most part, they fitted the assumption of linearity well enough, although in a few instances there is a possibility of a curvilinear relationship. These include early peyotism and early reactions to livestock reduction, late trouble over peyotism and late political organization, early acculturation and early reactions to livestock reduction, and late trouble and late political organization. Since in a large number of tallies a small number of weak curvilinear patterns might occur by chance, it was decided not to attempt any further refinements in data analysis.

It should be remembered in the discussion which follows that there are 41 cases for which we have ratings on all variables except early disturbance over peyotism but only 33 where we have ratings for early disturbance over peyotism. This means that discussions of this variable provide us with only a part of the total sample of 41 so that means, standard deviations, correlations, etc., all differ slightly from the total sample.

The data are presented in Table 34. These ratings and mileage figures (transformed to logarithms) were used to compute linear coefficients of correlation for each pair of variables. These in turn were used to provide raw score regression weights, standard errors of these partial regression weights, t-tests of the significance level of the raw score regression weights, standard score regression weights, and the multiple correlation between the predicted and actual score for the dependent variable. The approach was suggested by Manard Stewart, who programmed the analysis. The Statistical Laboratory and Computing Center of the University of Oregon supplied computer facilities and computer time.

RESULTS: PREDICTION OF PEYOTE LEVELS

We will begin with the correlation matrix which shows the relationships among all the variables except early peyote trouble (see Table 35). The initial theory specified that there should be a positive correlation between availability and peyotism—which means a negative correlation between distance from Towaoc and peyotism—the further from the center of distribution, the lower the level of peyotism. It hypothesized that acculturation should be negatively associated with peyotism, since acculturation supplied instrumentalities or modes of coping with current problems other than religious or magical ones. It hypothesized that trouble in the community or marked reactions to livestock reduction should be positively associated with peyotism. And it elected to accept for testing the common-sense hypothesis widely prevalent on the reservation that strong political organization should be negatively associated with peyotism. No special hypotheses about peyote trouble were developed. Furthermore, these hypotheses were developed before it had been decided that ratings must be divided into two time-periods, and no a priori refinements of these hypotheses were subsequently developed. It seems reasonable to assume that (*a*) early peyotism and early peyote trouble may be

TABLE 35

INTERCORRELATION MATRIX, ALL VARIABLES EXCEPT EARLY DISTURBANCE OVER PEYOTISM

	MI	PE	PL	AE	AL	TE	TL	SE	SL	OE	OL	DL
MI...	1.00	-.72*	-.58*	.19	.25	-.66*	-.29	-.31*	-.67*	.10	-.02	-.21
PE...	-.72*	1.00	.73*	-.19	-.40*	.62*	.17	.16	.50*	-.20	.05	.16
PL...	-.58*	.73*	1.00	-.29	-.62*	.71*	.29	.30	.46*	-.33*	-.17	.52*
AE...	.19	-.19	-.29	1.00	.43*	-.41*	-.20	-.17	-.14	.40*	.25	-.16
AL...	.25	-.40*	-.62*	.43*	1.00	-.51*	-.37*	-.34*	-.23	.54*	.18	-.22
TE...	-.66*	.62*	.71*	-.41*	-.51*	1.00	.28	.39*	.56*	-.41*	-.22	.32*
TL...	-.29	.17	.29	-.20	-.37*	.28	1.00	.54*	.48*	-.36*	-.55*	.14
SE...	-.31*	.16	.30	-.17	-.34*	.39*	.54*	1.00	.51*	-.08	-.23	.25
SL...	-.67*	.50*	.46*	-.14	-.23	.56*	.48*	.51*	1.00	-.10	-.18	.26
OE...	.10	-.20	-.33*	.40*	.54*	-.41*	-.36*	-.08	-.10	1.00	.39*	-.38*
OL...	-.02	.05	-.17	.25	.18	-.22	-.55*	-.23	-.18	.39*	1.00	-.27
DL...	-.21	.16	.52*	-.16	-.22	.32*	.14	.25	.26	-.38*	-.27	1.00

NOTE: 41 cases.
* Significant at the .05 level or better.

influenced by the state of other early variables and that (*b*) later peyotism and later peyote trouble may be influenced by the state of early or later other variables. We will examine the correlation matrix in the light of these hypotheses, omitting peyote trouble for the time being.

It is evident that the matrix fits these hypotheses. Early peyotism is negatively related to mileage,[4] early acculturation, and early political organization. It is positively related to early trouble and early reactions to livestock reduction. Late

[4] The log mile correlations with peyotism are —.72 for early peyotism and —.58 for late peyotism (the shorter the distance from Towaoc, the higher the peyotism levels). The raw mile correlations with peyotism are —.65 for early peyotism and —.53 for late peyotism. The non-parametric tests in Aberle and Stewart, 1957, p. 95, show the same tendencies, but the number of communities used is larger. For early peyotism, communities were classified as less than 90 miles from Towaoc and 90 or more miles, and as less than 1, 1, and more than 1, in peyote rating. A significant negative association was found. Fifty-five communities were used: many cases eliminated from the present treatment were not cast out of the earlier analysis. For late peyotism, with the same mileage classification and a classification of communities with ratings of less than 2, or 2 or more, with 63 communities used, there was no significant association, but the trend was for a negative association. Undoubtedly, part of the difference between the 1957 analysis and the present one results from the use of the larger sample in 1957 and part from the less sensitive statistical techniques used in 1957. The trends in both analyses are the same: negative associations, weaker in the second than in the first time-period.

peyotism is negatively related to mileage, early and late acculturation, and early and late political organization. It is positively related to early and late trouble and early and late reactions to livestock reduction.

Nevertheless, some of these relationships are non-significant and some of only borderline significance. Early peyotism is significantly related only to mileage and early trouble; late peyotism to mileage, late acculturation, early trouble, late reactions to livestock reduction, early political organization, and early peyotism itself. Relationships slightly worse than the 5 per cent level are found for late peyotism with early acculturation (negative), early reactions to livestock reduction, and late trouble.

Furthermore, if we examine the relationships among independent variables, we find problems that cry for more careful analysis. A simple example is to be found in the relationships between mileage and other independent variables. As we move away from Towaoc, communities apparently become less troubled and less disturbed over livestock reduction. Is the association between peyotism and trouble mediated by distance from Towaoc, or vice versa, or do both variables make a contribution? The same question might be asked for reactions to livestock reduction. Early trouble is associated significantly with reactions to livestock reduction. Does each of these variables have an impact on peyotism, or is the relationship of one to peyotism largely or entirely a function of its relationship with the other? And so on. How curious it is that late acculturation is more strongly associated with early peyotism than early acculturation is with early peyotism. How can this be? (The answer to this is not supplied by the regression analysis, but in fact the relationship between late acculturation and early peyotism is mediated by the strong relationship between early and late peyotism. We have not carried out a systematic analysis of all of the relationships of late predictors and early states of the dependent variable, but several, at least, yield to this interpretation through partial correlational analysis.)

Needless to say, analysis of first-order partial correlations to answer questions such as these raises further problems of second-order partials, and so on, because of the very large number of significant associations among independent variables. Here the multiple regression weights come into play as a quicker mode of analysis.

This approach reveals a fairly simple structure (see Table 36). For the early time-period, the only significant regression weight is that for availability—for the log of mileage from Towaoc. More remote communities have lower peyote scores. Early trouble has a positive weight significant at better than the 10 per cent level, but we have opted for the 5 per cent level throughout this work. This result will be regarded as borderline—of some possible importance. Furthermore, the standard scores indicate that availability has a weight about two and a half times that for trouble. All the predictor variables (MI, AE, TE, SE, and OE) account for .588 per cent of the variance of early peyotism scores, a respectable figure. It corresponds to a multiple correlation of nearly .77. (We must assume that some combination of errors of measurement and factors other than those studied account for the remainder of the variance.)

In sum, by far the most important determinant of the level of peyotism in these 41 communities is the availability of the cult (assuming that the log of mileage from Towaoc is a valid, rough index of availability). This is not a startling conclusion, but it gives us some confidence in the results. If availability had no impact on peyotism, the finding would be challenged by virtually every diffusion study ever carried out. The tentative finding that more troubled communities are more likely to have high levels of peyotism is of theoretical and practical interest, but, alas, it is not secure enough for any further elaboration.

Non-significant correlations provide non-significant weights (AE, SE, OE), but curiously enough the direction of the weights for early acculturation and early reactions to livestock reduction reverses the direction of the correlations.

It should be noted that raw weights that appear quite small (in the case of mileage) can be quite important—as can be seen by examining the standard weights, where the dominance of mileage is clearly expressed.

TABLE 36

EARLY PEYOTE: WEIGHTS

Independent Variable	Mean	Sigma	Raw Regression Weights	Standard errors of Weights	Standard Weights
MI..............	46.79	4.893	−.099*	.023	−.614
AE..............	2.30	.558	.031	.165	.022
TE..............	2.71	.671	.288†	.193	.243
SE..............	3.43	1.233	−.086	.071	−.133
OE..............	3.16	.794	−.065	.118	−.065

Dependent Variable	Mean	Sigma	R Sq.
PE..............	1.18	.797	.588*

NOTE: 41 cases.
* Significant at the .05 level or better.
† Significant between .10 and .05.

Finally, the results for early peyotism are similar to but more limited than those derived solely from examining the matrix.

The results for late peyotism are simple (see Table 37). The significant weights, in the order of magnitude of the standard weights, are, first, a positive weight for early peyotism and, second, a negative weight for late acculturation. The weighting for mileage becomes trivial. Early trouble has a moderate positive weight of borderline significance, and late political organization has a rather small negative weight of borderline significance. The significant associations in the matrix with mileage, reactions to livestock reduction, and early political organization are not echoed in the weights. Late political organization, non-significant in the matrix, is of borderline significance in the weights, and early trouble drops from a strong and significant association to a borderline weight. Here, then, there is simplification and change. The ten predictors account for .721 per cent of the variance, a much higher figure than for early peyotism, but a rise is expectable when the number of predictors is increased. The multiple correlation is nearly .85.

Thus for late peyotism, early peyotism plays somewhat the same role as a predictor that availability plays for early peyotism. This might be thought of as an internal diffusion factor: communities that were above the mean for the first time-period tend to gain converts and remain above the mean for the second. Another way of looking at it is that peyotism grows fairly rapidly in the second time-period in communities where a certain "critical mass" of converts was in existence by the end of the first time-period.

On the other hand, availability—mileage from Towaoc—is no longer of any significance in accounting for peyotism. Probably this results from the fact that by 1946 there were numerous distributing centers for peyotism, and not just a northern center.

The only other significant weight is acculturation. This finding, that high acculturation levels predict low peyotism levels among Navaho communities (and vice versa), is of considerable theoretical interest and will be taken up in some detail below.

TABLE 37

LATE PEYOTE: WEIGHTS

Independent Variable	Mean	Sigma	Raw Regression Weights	Standard Errors of Weights	Standard Weights
MI	46.79	4.893	−.012	.036	−.056
PE	1.18	.797	.595*	.184	.439
AE	2.30	.558	.105	.188	.054
AL	2.93	.884	−.441*	.149	−.361
TE	2.71	.671	.386†	.246	.240
TL	2.56	.860	−.067	.171	−.054
SE	3.43	1.233	−.003	.100	−.004
SL	2.60	.982	.002	.144	.002
OE	3.16	.794	.093	.156	.068
OL	3.06	1.125	−.149†	.110	−.156

Dependent Variable	Mean	Sigma	R Sq.		
PL	2.04	1.080	.721*		

NOTE: 41 cases.

* Significant at the .05 level or better.

† Significant between .10 and .05.

The two borderline weights—early trouble (positive) and late political organization (negative)—are borderline, so that, although they, too, conform to theory, it seems unwise to rely very heavily on them.

RESULTS: PREDICTING DISTURBANCE OVER PEYOTISM

We turn now to the task of accounting for disturbance over peyotism. For the early time-period, significant correlations between disturbance and other variables are found for mileage (negative) and early peyotism (positive), the correlation with early peyotism being the strongest (see Table 38). The regression weights produce the same story, although the weight for early trouble (negative) is of borderline significance (see Table 39). The contribution of early peyotism is far larger, as can be seen from the standard weights. The first point is obvious. The more peyotism, the more disturbance in the community over peyotism. (One would expect that this relationship would eventually become curvilinear, when most members of the community had joined.) The negative association with trouble, however, is superficially confusing. Early trouble tends to promote peyotism but to inhibit disturbance over peyotism. The simplest explanation for this is that where peyotism spreads to peyote-prone communities (those with a high "trouble" score), there is less disturbance over its spread because the community *is* peyote-prone, whereas when it spreads to communities with a low "trouble" score, it meets more opposition because the community is not peyote-prone. This interpretation receives further confirmation when we examine the late peyote trouble matrix and regression weights.

For late peyote trouble, we find significant correlations with late peyotism, early trouble (both positive), and early political organization (negative) (see Table 35). The largest correlation is with late peyotism. The regression weights, again, tell a different story (see Table 40). Disturbance over peyotism is significantly predicted by late peyote, late acculturation, early reactions to livestock reduction (all positive weights) and by early peyotism, early trouble, late trouble, and early political organization (all negative weights). Of these, late peyotism has by far the largest

TABLE 38

INTERCORRELATION MATRIX, EARLY DISTURBANCE OVER PEYOTISM
AND OTHER EARLY VARIABLES

	MI	PE	AE	TE	SE	OE	DE
MI.....	1.00	− .74*	.21	− .68*	− .29	.12	− .35*
PE.....	− .74*	1.00	− .19	.63*	.17	− .22	.55*
AE.....	.21	− .19	1.00	− .44*	− .14	.43*	− .07
TE.....	− .68*	.63*	− .44*	1.00	.41*	− .41*	.18
SE.....	− .29	.17	− .14	.41*	1.00	− .25	.09
OE.....	.12	− .22	.43*	− .41*	− .25	1.00	.07
DE.....	− .35*	.55*	− .07	.18	.09	.07	1.00

NOTE: 33 cases.
* Significant at the .05 level or better.

TABLE 39

EARLY DISTURBANCE OVER PEYOTISM: WEIGHTS

Independent Variable	Mean	Sigma	Raw Regression Weights	Standard Errors of Weights	Standard Weights
MI................	46.85	5.193	.010	.033	.078
PE................	1.21	.866	.658*	.180	.794
AE................	2.29	.587	− .166	.196	− .136
TE................	2.77	.697	− .298	.239	− .290
SE................	3.33	1.216	.078	.090	.132
OE................	3.00	.771	.202†	.153	.218

Dependent Variable	Mean	Sigma	R Sq.
DE................	1.71	.718	.396*

NOTE: 33 cases.
* Significant at the .05 level or better.
† Significant between .10 and .05.

weight, with early peyotism, early political organization, late trouble, early trouble, late acculturation, and early reactions to livestock reduction following in that order.

This picture makes no immediate sense in terms of these specific variables.

It is through a comparison of this pattern with that for early peyotism, early disturbance over peyotism, and late peyotism that its meaning emerges. This comparison is presented in Table 41.

Although the rank-order of the predictors shifts, the direction of the predictors is contrastive for peyote and peyote trouble, with few exceptions. Mileage remains

TABLE 40

LATE DISTURBANCE OVER PEYOTISM: WEIGHTS

Independent Variable	Mean	Sigma	Raw Regression Weights	Standard Errors of Weights	Standard Weights
MI.................	46.79	4.893	−.039	.036	−.212
PE.................	1.18	.797	−.589*	.207	−.521
PL.................	2.04	1.080	.842*	.156	1.010
AE.................	2.30	.558	−.009	.189	−.006
AL.................	2.93	.884	.350*	.164	.344
TE.................	2.71	.671	−.502*	.253	−.374
TL.................	2.56	.860	−.427*	.171	−.409
SE.................	3.43	1.233	.202*	.100	.277
SL.................	2.60	.982	.156	.144	.170
OE.................	3.16	.794	−.590*	.157	−.520
OL.................	3.06	1.125	−.121	.112	−.152

Dependent Variable	Mean	Sigma	R Sq.		
DL.................	1.91	.901	.598*		

NOTE: 41 cases.

* Significant at the .05 level or better.

TABLE 41

FOUR PREDICTION PATTERNS COMPARED

Variable	Early Peyotism	Early Disturbance over Peyotism	Late Peyotism	Late Disturbance over Peyotism
MI.....	1−*	6+	6−	8−
PE.....		1+*	1+*	2−*
PL.....				1+*
AE.....	5+	4−	7+	11−
AL.....			2−*	6+*
TE.....	2+†	2−	3+†	5−*
TL.....			8−	4−*
SE.....	3−	5+	9−	7+*
SL.....			10+	9+
OE.....	4−	3+†	5+	3−*
OL.....			4−†	10−

KEY: Numbers refer to rank-orders of standard partial weights for each prediction equation. Minus and plus refer to direction of prediction.

* Results significant at the .05 level.

† Indicates results significant at the .10 level but not at the .05 level.

consistently negative but becomes of less and less importance. The direction of the weighting for every other variable in predicting early peyotism is changed in predicting early disturbance over peyotism—a finding already interpreted. With one exception, early political organization, the direction of weights for early peyotism and of the same variables for late peyotism, is identical. Except for mileage, late trouble, and late political organization, the weights for predicting the late peyotism are reversed in the predictors for late disturbance of peyotism. Fundamentally, then, the major predictor, and by far the major predictor for late peyotism is the level of peyotism in the community: the more peyotism, the more disturbance. In addition, however, communities likely to have high disturbance over peyotism are those which are *not* most likely to be peyote-prone: communities with high initial peyotism, low early and high late acculturation, high early trouble level, considerable reaction to livestock reduction, and weak early political organization. Again the interpretation is justified that whereas peyotism itself is the primary cause of reactions against it, these reactions are most strongly developed in communities least prone to peyotism.

VALIDITY AGAIN

Admitted that the interpretation of these findings is tentative, are, then, the findings themselves to be regarded merely as interesting manipulations of a correlation matrix, or as having some reference to reality? It is possible to develop a theoretical structure which would account for a large number of associations on the basis of the structuring of the raters' outlook. Thus, if we assume that raters can perceive disturbance over peyotism, they might be led to infer a high level of membership from high level of disturbance. They might regard peyotism as non-Western and hence be inclined to rate such communities as having low levels of acculturation. Their perception of disturbance over peyotism might lead to the perception of a great deal of trouble, which in turn might influence their views on reactions to livestock regulation. Since disturbance is often manifest in factionalism, they might be inclined to rate high disturbance communities low on political organization. Only the availability measure is immune from this style of interpretation. There is no final way of disposing of this alternative approach. It is, however, open to two objections. First, it requires that 32 raters have the same interpretation to achieve these results. And it requires that this perception influence them throughout an interview which dealt with peyotism only incidentally until the end, and never as a central topic. Ratings on peyotism had been submitted to the Agency, not to Moore, months before. Second, it ignores the rough and approximate fit of the ratings on several variables with information derived from field work, observation, historical data, and so on. Hence the ratings are taken as an approximation to an evaluation of 41 Navaho communities.

INTERPRETATION

Thus far we have outlined, rather than interpreted, the results. Interpretation raises a number of problems. (1) How can the predictors that have the largest effect be best understood? (2) What shall we make of the predictors that have little effect but might be expected to have more? (3) How shall we understand the fact that the variables associated with individual acceptance of peyotism have little enough to do with acceptance at the community level, and vice versa? (4) What is the relationship between these findings and other work and theories respecting peyotism? Although it is not possible to organize the interpretative section so as to answer these questions *seriatim*, all must be dealt with in this section.

INDIVIDUAL, AGGREGATE, AND UNIT RELATIONSHIPS

We will begin with a general discussion of the relationship between individual associations, aggregate associations, unit associations, and mixed associations. An individual association obtains when individuals with attribute A are more likely to have attribute X than individuals without attribute A.[5] The association between livestock measures and cult membership are individual associations. An aggregate association obtains when, among a set of populations, greater amounts of attribute X are accompanied by greater amounts of attribute Y. Thus we might find that in a set of populations those with the highest percentages of college-educated members also had the highest percentage of participants in voluntary membership groups. There are no aggregate associations in the data at hand. The nearest thing to these are the ratings for acculturation level and the ratings for peyotism.

If we assume that high ratings on acculturation reflect a high percentage of educated Navahos, by community, then we might argue that these ratings *reflect* aggregate associations—a negative association between percentage of educated Navahos and peyotism. They are not aggregate measures, however, since these involve actual frequency counts and a population count.

A unit association obtains when two attributes of units tend to be associated. Thus a set of school districts might be characterized as having elective or appointive school boards and as having consolidated or other high schools. A unit association would involve the association, or lack of it, of type of school board and type of high school.

Mixed patterns of association are frequently examined. Thus we might inquire about unit-aggregate associations: associations between type of school board and percentage of satisfied P.-T.A. members, for example.

The ratings used here tend, on the whole, to be unit characteristics. This can be argued easily for trouble, reactions to livestock reduction, trouble over peyotism, and strength of political organization. Each demands, whatever else, an over-all assessment of the community. The various types of measures of trouble and disturbance all fail to distinguish whether there were lots of upset or disturbing people or a few, dealing instead with a global assessment of whether the impression made on the rater was of a very disturbed or disturbing community or a not very disturbed one. Hence they are not aggregate measures. Political organization in its nature has much of the unit character, since assessment depends on the nature, strength, and cohesiveness of leadership at least as much as on individual participation. Availability is a unit character: it is a matter of the geographical placement of the community.

[5] For the purposes of this discussion, we will avoid the complications created by the fact that some variables can be treated as continuous, some as scalar, some as dichotomous, and so on. A discussion of the effects of all these possibilities with respect to all these types of variables takes us too far afield.

In the case of acculturation and of the ratings on level of peyotism, the ratings may be said to reflect aggregate characteristics, rather than being unit measures.

What I have called individual associations are usually called by this term in the literature; what I have called aggregate associations are often called ecological correlations in the literature; what I have called unit attributes are often called unit attributes and sometimes system attributes in the literature.

It is important to note that only under special conditions do individual correlations imply particular aggregate correlations, and vice versa. It is quite possible for individual correlations (say between illiteracy and foreign origin) to be positive and for aggregate correlations (between percentage of illiterates in a set of districts and percentage of foreign born) to be negative; or for both correlations to have the same direction; or for one to be strong and the other to be absent. This problem has been discussed for a variety of particular instances, but the general argument is most clearly stated in Robinson (1950), Menzel (1950), Duncan and Davis (1953), Goodman (1953, 1959), and Selvin (1958). The situation for unit-aggregate versus individual associations is also complex, although it has received less elaborate treatment. (See Lazarsfeld and Kendall [1950] and Selvin [1958]).

In sum, there is no particular reason to anticipate that there will be precise correspondences between the individual associations described in Chapter 17 and the community rating correlations and regression formulae described in Chapter 18. Instead, there are general reasons for saying that such correspondences are not necessarily to be expected.

DIFFUSION

There is no effort to argue that peyotism "just diffused," independent of the situation at the time of the diffusion, the orientations of individuals within communities, or the characteristics of the communities. On the contrary, it has been argued that livestock reduction had a great deal to do with accelerating the spread of peyotism, available in the north at the time that reduction began (cf. Aberle and Stewart, 1957, pp. 85–105, for a detailed discussion of the importance of availability).

Nevertheless, the pattern for the *early* time-period comes very close to the limiting condition mentioned by Aberle and Stewart: "Only if we can show that a knowledge of the availability factor permits us to predict the level of adherence for all communities does it become possible to treat all other factors promoting adherence as insignificant or as constants" (1957, p. 87). Availability—miles from Towaoc—when converted to logarithms shows a very high correlation with peyotism and is the only significant weight for the prediction equation. The total variance accounted for by the prediction equation is only .588, so that other, unmeasured factors or errors of measurement must be invoked. We have not reached the goal of a perfect prediction via availability, but it is our most potent predictor. And for the late time-period something else in the availability-diffusion area is very powerful: the early level of peyotism. We might say that for the later period, a certain critical mass of peyotists, developed in the early time-period, accounts best for the new levels of peyotism. These variables—communications, diffusion, availability, etc., then, do predict a good deal.

TROUBLE MEASURES

Since trouble in the community during the early time-period carries a moderate amount of weight for both early and late peyotism prediction formulae, although of only borderline significance, it is a variable worth discussing, but not belaboring.

A high trouble rating would seem to reflect a community with a lot of internal trouble and/or a difficult relationship with the administration. We cannot be sure which of these two kinds of trouble, internal and external, contributes most to a rater's judgment. Nor can we know whether a "troubled" community is one where many people make some trouble, or some people make a lot of trouble, or a lot of people make a lot of trouble. We are not entitled to infer that a community with a high "trouble" score has a lot of "disturbed" people in it, or that the most "disturbed" or "disturbing" people are most likely to be cult members. All we can say is that perhaps the "disturbed" or "disturbing" communities are likely to have higher ratings on peyotism. What would explain such a pattern?

The interpretation most compatible with the general approach of this work is that the "trouble" score is a reflection of the degree to which Navaho culture no longer works. There is ample evidence that traditional Navaho culture does *not* operate satisfactorily today and that in most areas it has not since the 1930's. Perhaps, then, communities in which this operational failure was most evident were more likely to accept peyotism in the early time-period and, still responding to this operational failure, to gain new converts in the later time-period. The fact that the prediction weight is of borderline significance suggests that further elaboration of this theme is unnecessary.

There is no evident reason why early trouble level should contribute both to early and to late peyotism, whereas late trouble level makes virtually no contribution.

POLITICAL ORGANIZATION

This variable requires no special ingenuity for interpretation. High ratings reflect a reasonably cohesive and effective local political organization. It can be questioned, however, why there is a borderline impact of late political organization on late peyotism. The simplest interpretation, prevalent in the Navaho country, assumes that local leadership tends to oppose peyotism, and that if it is strong, this reduces the opportunity for peyotism to penetrate a community. This theory is perfectly compatible with the negative weight for late political organization. It is possible, however, that communities most effectively organized to cope with local problems are least likely to feel helpless and dependent and least likely to feel a need for a new religion like peyotism. No resolution between these interpretations seems possible.

VARIABLES THAT HAVE LITTLE PREDICTIVE VALUE

For some of these no particular pattern emerges. There seems no special reason why late trouble should have a very small standard weight and early trouble a much larger one, why early acculturation should have a very small standard weight and late acculturation a very large one, or why early political organization should have little predictive value and late political organization some.

It is striking and surprising, however, that early and late reactions to livestock reduction have non-significant weights and low standard weights, the largest being for early reactions and early levels of peyotism. It is not a logical corollary nor a necessary statistical implication that our findings on livestock measures for individuals should be echoed in our ratings on reactions to livestock reduction for groups, but it would be a more comfortable situation if this were the case. These measures differ, however, not only in being individual measures (livestock measures) and unit measures (ratings on reactions to reduction), but measures about different things: deprivation versus overt reactions to reduction. There is, perhaps, some tendency for overt, organized hostility to reduction to involve primarily people who did not join the peyote cult, if the situation at Teec Nos Pas is any guide. There those who kidnapped the District Supervisor were not peyotists, with few exceptions, although there were many peyotists in the area. But perhaps this dichotomy results from the fact that peyotists and non-peyotists were not capable of cooperation in those days. At any rate, even though there is an association between hostility to reduction and level of peyotism, reactions to livestock reduction make almost no contribution to the prediction equation when other things are controlled for.

PEYOTE TROUBLE

Thus far we have discussed the prediction of peyotism—a discussion which is completed below in connection with the results for acculturation. Let us first, however, dispose of the question of predicting trouble over peyotism. Here the patterns seem quite straightforward. The best predictor is the sheer level of peyotism—and the best by a very large margin. After that, we can say that the most "fuss" occurs in the communities which, on other grounds, one would be least likely to predict for high peyotism.

From the point of view of the practical value of this prediction, it should be said that empirically this direct association between amount of peyotism and amount of trouble becomes curvilinear over time. Communities where peyotists constitute over half of the community, and where peyotism has been for some time, are not in 1964 communities with a lot of disturbance over peyotism. But this state of affairs is reflected in later information about some of these communities, not in the ratings used in this chapter.

ACCULTURATION

Except for availability factors (mileage, early peyotism), late acculturation is the only variable that supplies a large and significant weight in the prediction equations for peyotism—late peyotism. And this weight is negative.

How is the negative weight to be interpreted? A number of alternatives seem reasonable, with no choice among them possible on the basis of the ratings alone. One interpretation is that acculturated communities are more secularized, so that peyotism, a religious response, has relatively little appeal. This interpretation was entertained early in the history of this project. But the general level of education achieved by Navahos in the late 1940's makes this interpretation rather implausible. One would expect that a much more thorough penetration of Navaho life by certain modes of Western thought would be necessary before inhibition of peyotism for this reason could be effective.

A second possibility is that "acculturated" communities are those where a good deal of Indian Service activity went on in the 1940's; thereby jobs were provided and morale was improved. Hence a turning to novel religious answers to questions arising out of despair was less likely. There are some grounds for accepting this interpretation. Among 13 communities above the mean for late acculturation, 5 were District headquarters and 1 was the Agency headquarters. Among 17 at the mean, 1 was a District headquarters. Among 11 below the mean, 1 was a District headquarters.

A third possibility is that in communities with many acculturated individuals, there is a better chance of solving contemporary problems than in other communities: jobs are easier to get for those who speak English; families (including older, non-English speakers) are more easily supported; kin have more opportunity to help each other; dealing with the trader and the Agent is easier, and so on. A fourth possibility is a combination of the second and third. Doubtless other interpretations could be devised.

The tentative interpretation made here is that some combination of easier problem solutions through acculturation and improvement of conditions through Agency endeavor is reflected in acculturation ratings.

In this connection, it should be noted that when everything else is held constant, early acculturation level makes a slight positive contribution to the prediction equation for early peyotism, whereas late acculturation level makes a large negative contribution for late peyotism. This finding is consonant with the tentative interpretation made above. Until they lost their livestock—and indeed for some years thereafter—efforts to increase Navaho education, certainly one of the prime modes of acculturation, met with considerable resistance. The reasons for this have been discussed before: for a people with a viable native economy, acculturation was a distraction and a nuisance. Shortly after the war the situation changed, at least as respects desires for children's education. There is no doubt that this change resulted from Navaho perception that the traditional mode of livelihood was shattered and that education was necessary to live. Such a view is quite conscious and articulate for many older Navahos today.

In the case of acculturation, there is a body of theory and of previous findings of other studies that should be discussed. In Chapter 16, I have cited and quoted various authors who have taken the position that peyotism is a religion of transition or of acculturation. Other instances could be found. There are, however, a number of difficulties about this theory. The first is its lack of specification. The level or type of acculturation necessary to promote or inhibit peyotism has never been made clear; nor has care been taken to state whether the theory is a theory about individuals, aggregates, units, or all of these. Under these circumstances, the theory becomes very difficult to disprove, and correspondingly to prove, since any proposition which cannot conceivably be proven false also cannot be proven true. Perhaps the most astonishing thing about this rather vague theory is that almost no one has seriously bothered about gathering data to attempt any rigorous proof of any part of it (which would, of course, require some more incisive statement of the theory or some part of it). We will later see that Spindler (1955) is a major exception. (Stewart [1944] attempts to discover whether peyotists differ significantly from non-peyotists for a series of attributes, but only a few of these bear directly on acculturation. He concludes that for these attributes peyotists do not differ significantly from non-peyotists. The analysis merits close attention.)

Approximately speaking, this theory must take a curvilinear form, both for acculturation as a quantitative attribute of individuals and for acculturation as a temporal attribute of populations or systems. No one has seriously argued that American Indians, non-peyotists in the traditional state, will become more and more peyotist as they become more and more acculturated, until finally, when they are fully Westernized in all other respects, they show the highest percentage of cult members. Rather, it is argued that peyotism "sets in" with acculturation, but it is implied that it will later disappear or diminish, for any given American Indian population. And it seems implied that the individuals who are intermediate in acculturation will be most peyote-prone (cf. Slotkin, who maintains, ". . . the most ardent adherents of the Peyote Religion were young men, and particularly those who were somewhat acculturated and marginal" [1956, p. 44; p. 115 cites a dozen studies in support of this point, but none is quantitative]).

Only one study with detailed quantitative data bearing on the "transition" theory has appeared: Spindler's work on the Menomini (1955). We turn now to the question whether his data and those in the present study are consonant or contradictory.

Spindler defined five groups: the Medicine-Lodge–Dream-Dance group, the peyote cult group, the transitional group, the lower-status acculturated group, and the elite acculturated group. Four of these (all except the transitional group) were defined on the basis of group membership criteria. The criteria for the first two categories are self-evident. Lower-status acculturated individuals are characterized by membership in the Catholic Church but not in the Holy Name society; elite acculturated individuals are Catholics and members of the Holy Name society (with two exceptions). The transitional group is a residual category: individuals not firmly associated with any of these groups. A variety of measures of acculturation indicate that, in general, there is a progression from least to most acculturated as one passes from the first group through the others to the fifth. Thus the peyotists represent the second of five levels of acculturation.

In the present Navaho study, however, no measure of acculturation reliably differentiated peyotists from non-peyotists. At first blush, therefore, the Spindler study and the present one seem to arrive at different conclusions. Probably, however, it would be more reasonable to say that we do not know whether they are contradictory or not.

We might ask, first of all, how the Navahos compare with Spindler's five levels of acculturation. In most respects, both the Aneth and Mexican Springs samples are less acculturated than any of Spindler's groups, including his most traditional group. Reasonably direct comparisons can be made for language, occupation, education, radio ownership, and church attendance. For the first three, both Aneth and Mexican Springs are less acculturated than the Medicine-Lodge–Dream-Dance Menomini. Aneth radio ownership is at a lower level than this group, but Mexican

Springs radio ownership is at about the level of Spindler's "transitional" group. *Claimed* regular church attendance for both Navaho groups is very low, but it is above Menomini transitionals and lower status acculturated. Actual Navaho attendance is probably below both. For certain traits of material culture that Spindler uses as indices of acculturation—use of piped water, gas, and electricity—the Navajo Reservation in 1953 afforded no options for most Navahos. By and large, only Government employees living on reservation could have any of these things. The use of space heaters or simply fires for heating was universal among Navahos at Aneth and Mexican Springs, as it was for traditional Menomini.

The direct comparison has one disadvantage: Spindler's samples are all male; mine include men and women. Use of an all-male Navaho sample would slightly raise the educational level, but it would not affect the comparisons of these Navahos and Menominis as respects occupation, knowledge of Navaho, radio ownership, or church attendance.

Thus Navahos who fall at or below Spindler's most traditional level are nevertheless drawn to peyotism. If the "transition" theory has validity, it must rest on something other than absolute level of acculturation.

In one respect, however, Navaho data afford some support for Spindler's work. In 1953, when extensive field work stopped, I did not know one peyotist who corresponded in his acculturation level to Spindler's "elite acculturated." The corresponding Navaho category could not be defined on the basis of church membership, but it would be possible to define an on-reservation Navaho elite by reference to occupation. No peyotist occupied a clerical, administrative, or semi-professional position in the Tribal or the Window Rock Area Office structure. As examples of such occupations, I have in mind clerk, accountant, typist, census office clerk, trained forester, draftsman, surveyor, nurse, Tribal manager, or District Supervisor. By 1953, some Navahos could be found in all these positions. But none of them were peyotists. Some peyotists did hold regular civil service positions: teacher-interpreter, matron, school janitor, etc. But these were the highest positions reached in 1953. By 1964, however, this clear dichotomy was obscured. Peyotists did hold good jobs in the Tribal structure, and some had moved up in the Indian Service structure. I do not have sufficient information to say whether peyotists were proportionately represented in these echelons. My impression is that their numbers are growing.

In sum, the comparison of Spindler's data and the Navaho data is a bit difficult, since the span of acculturation represented is so different. We might note that if Spindler had used only his "traditional" and peyotist group, the two categories nearest to the Navahos in their level of acculturation, he would have been forced to conclude that, in terms of acculturation, there were few differences between the two categories. To be exact, of 23 measures of acculturation used by Spindler, the most traditional group differed significantly from the peyotists on only 3 (Spindler, 1955, pp. 114–115). The quantitative Navaho data do not show any relationship between peyotism and acculturation, curvilinear or other. Additional nonquantitative data suggest the possibility of a curvilinear pattern.

We might now ask whether the findings in the present study that the most acculturated communities have fewest peyotists have any parallel in the Spindler study. Roughly speaking, they do. Spindler contrasts Zoar, the conservative community, with Neopit and Keshena, the more acculturated communities. No precise rating of acculturation as between Neopit and Keshena is provided. There are proportionately more peyotists in and about Zoar than in and about Neopit and Keshena.

In sum, individual associations between acculturation and partial acculturation discovered by Spindler are not supported by the present study, but the nature of the data prevent our saying that the two studies are contradictory. Associations between a high level of acculturation for a community and a low level of peyotism found for the Navaho are found for three Menomini communities, although Spindler did not analyze his data in this fashion.

ACCULTURATION OVER TIME

The plausibility of the "transition" theory led me to attempt to see whether there was some connection between Navaho acculturation over time and peyotism. The only possible way of assessing aggregate Navaho acculturation over time was to trace the percentage of educated members of the Navaho population over the years. And the data for a direct count of this sort were lacking. This led to my seeking the help of Denis F. Johnston, who constructed the cohort analysis of Navaho education that appears in Appendix A. Since no one has ever stated what the critical point in acculturation might be, the hypothesis had to be that an association between peyotism and aggregate acculturation should be manifested by a marked change in the percentage of adult, educated Navahos at, or a reasonable time before the point at which the cult began to flourish. The major break in the percentage of educated Navahos occurs after 1915, when the pace steps up sharply, slowing again after 1940 (Graph 3, Appendix A). Whereas undoubtedly it would be possible to think of a connection between the acceleration after 1915 and the flowering of the peyote cult after 1936, there is no greater reason to connect such an acceleration with peyotism than a shift in 1920, 1925, 1930, or 1935. Unless someone is prepared to assert that the critical point is reached when the percentage of educated individuals passes the 40 per cent level, there is no clear link between aggregate acculturation and peyotism shown in the figures in Appendix A.

There are other grounds than these data for skepticism about the aggregate theory, and, for that matter, the individual theory. So far as I know, the level of educational accomplishment in every Pueblo group is above that for the Navaho country as a whole. Yet the Pueblos are conspicuously low in their adherence to peyotism. Taos, often mentioned as an exception, shows a considerably slower growth rate than that for the Navahos.[6] Some other Rio Grande Pueblos have some

---

[6] The data on Taos peyotists are not entirely consistent over the years. There were said to be 52 cult members in 1923, in a population of 635 (La Barre, 1938, p. 111). In 1936, the number is reported as 130 (Survey of Conditions, Part 34, p. 18221), or 30 families and about 110 Indians (Survey of Conditions, Part 34, p. 18223). The second figure is based on John Collier's count at a meeting between Taos peyotists and Bureau officials. According to Agency records, the population in 1936 was 772; Survey of Conditions, Part 34, p. 18221 mentions 750. (I am indebted to Mr. Walter O. Olson, Superintendent of the United Pueblo Agency, for the Agency figures in this note.) In 1950, Fenton estimated 50–70 peyotists in a population of 921, of whom 800 lived in the Pueblo (Fenton, 1957, pp. 328, 307). Agency figures show 192 families and 963 individuals for the enrolled population of Taos. According to Dustin, there were 300 peyotists in a popula-

members, but my sources say that there are very few. According to Dustin (1960, p. 15), Santo Domingo, Acoma, and other Pueblo Indians attend Taos peyote meetings. It can be argued that the Pueblos are really not "acculturated," or that they are only "superficially" acculturated, or that they are enculturated in two cultures, and thus that they are not in any essential sense more acculturated than the Navaho. (Few theorists would be likely to grasp the other horn of the dilemma and say that they are so highly acculturated that they do not "need" peyote.) The difficulty with this style of answer is that unless we are willing to state what kind and degree of acculturation *is* congenial to acceptance of the peyote cult, we can develop *ad hoc* theories forever.

One plausible answer to the Pueblo-Navaho difference, congenial to the approach taken here, is to be found in systemic differences between the two situations. The Pueblos are, or were until recently, in a situation where their traditional system works, more or less. The Navahos since the 1930's have been in a situation where their traditional system does not work and where their involvement with the larger society provides minimal satisfactions.

To return to our three ways of looking at acculturation, it appears to me likely that the measurement of individuals, aggregates, or units on an acculturation continuum will not, in fact, provide us with a thermometer for predicting a boiling point where conversion to peyotism is likely to occur. What is common to the groups to which peyotism appeals is a native system that no longer works, combined with limited and inadequate access to the goods of the larger society.

Insofar as a semi-educated sector of the population finds it difficult to find satisfactions in a dislocated traditional system but difficult to find them elsewhere as well, peyotism may indeed be a religion of transition. Insofar as education and other factors promote access to the larger society or secure a niche in the new reservation society, they may reduce the attractions of peyotism. For peyotism is a mode of expressing rejection of the traditional system and of the American system, a mode of coping with feelings of helplessness, and a way of engendering a total re-orientation which assists in adjusting to wage work and cash cropping.

THE TRANSITION THEORY: GENERAL COMMENTS

In spite of general acceptance of the transition theory as an explanation for membership in the peyote cult, no one has attempted to specify the amount of

---

tion of 900 in 1960 (Dustin, 1960, p. 12). Agency figures show a total population of 256 families, and 1278 individuals.

It seems likely that the figures for 1936 are more or less right, but probably a bit low. For 1950 and 1960, the average number of members in a family is 5. So if there were 30 families, the number of peyotists may have reached 150 in 1936. It seems unlikely, however, that peyotists decreased between 1936 and 1950. Perhaps Fenton counted only adults; perhaps he undercounted. At any rate, if we use Agency population figures where they are available, and the highest figure for peyotists supplied by each source, the percentages for Taos are: 1923, 8 per cent; 1936, 17 per cent; 1950, 7 per cent (dubious); 1960, 23 per cent. The Navaho cult seems to have grown from 12–14 per cent in 1951 to more than 35 per cent in 1965. Although there may well be error in all of these estimates for Taos and Navaho, the general trend of the data favors the interpretation that the Taos cult has grown more slowly than the Navaho.

There has been a dramatic change in the position of the cult at Taos. In 1936, its members were a persecuted minority. In 1960, they held major religious and civic offices, including that of Governor (Survey of Conditions, Part 34, pp. 18164–18320; Dustin, 1960, pp. 12–13).

acculturation necessary or whether the theory is a theory about individuals, aggregates, or units. There are almost no efforts to provide quantitative data bearing on
the transition problem. Spindler's data, together with the Navaho data, suggest to
me the necessity for a certain caution. It would appear that for some reason Navaho communities which are *relatively* acculturated by Navaho standards are likely
to have fewer peyotists, although even these communities would be relatively unacculturated by Menomini standards. Navahos who would be "traditional" in
every respect except peyote cult membership by Menomini standards are peyotists.
Many do not fit our ordinary ideas of "marginal" or "transitional" individuals.

TABLE 42

DISTRICT PERMIT SIZE AND PERCENTAGE
OF PEYOTISTS

District	Permit Size	Percentage of Peyotists[a]
1.......	225	b
2.......	161	b
3.......	280	b
4.......	72[c]	11
5......	280	b
6[d]......	....	....
7......	237	3
8......	154	6
9......	83[c]	80
10......	153	20
11......	105	40
12......	104[c]	40
13......	200	1
14......	61[c]	20
15[d]......	88[c]	3
16[d]......	....	5
17......	275	15
18......	238	15

[a] Percentages are median estimates of raters for each
District for time-period 2 (1946–1951).

[b] Small percentages or none claimed; doubtful whether
peyotism had more than entered the area at time of survey.

[c] Special grazing permits in force.

[d] Entirely or largely off-reservation. No separate information on District 19. District 6, Hopi reservation.

For reasons developed in the next section of this work, I am inclined to see the
causes for acceptance or rejection of peyotism not so much in the levels of acculturation reached by individuals as in the nature of the situation in which American
Indian groups find themselves—in the effects of external relations on the reservation
community, rather than the effects of education, missionization, and so on, on individuals.

DISTRICT DIFFERENCES

Districts, too, differ in percentage of peyotists, and in permit size. There is some
tendency for a low maximum permit to imply that more people were severely
affected by livestock reduction, by comparison with a high maximum permit, although this tendency is slightly disrupted by the issuing of special permits in low
permit Districts. It is some interest to see whether there is any rank-order corre-

lation between permit size and percentage of peyotists. But it must be recalled that, as in the previous section, it is not proper to infer individual associations from this correlation. Table 42 presents a list of Districts, permit size, and percentage of peyotists. We may then ask whether there is a negative correlation between permit size and percentage of peyotists. Although in fact there is a significant over-all rank-order correlation (Spearman's rho), this is not a valid test of the situation. Just as certain Districts were deleted from the sample of communities because it was probable that there was little or no exposure to peyotism, so they should be deleted from this list: Districts 1, 2, 3, and 5. For District 15, the permit is not a clear measure, since individuals may also have livestock off-reservation. For Districts 16 and 19, all stock is held off-reservation, and we have no permit data. Hence a rigorous test demands that a correlation be run in 11 Districts—for Districts 4, 7 through 14, 17, and 18. The correlation is —.499, corrected for ties, but a correlation of better than .506 is required for 11 cases for significance at the .05 level. Thus we can claim only a tendency in the expected direction.

SUMMARY

1. The best predictor for early peyotism is the availability measure—mileage from Towaoc, in a logarithmic transformation. The shorter the distance, the higher the level of peyotism. Early trouble level is a positive predictor of borderline significance.

2. The best predictors for late peyotism are early peyotism (positive) and late acculturation (negative). Early trouble (positive) and late political organization (negative) are predictors of borderline significance.

3. The findings with reference to availability and early peyotism as predictors are interpreted as indicating the power of inter- and intra-community diffusional factors for the time-periods under consideration.

4. The finding with reference to acculturation is interpreted in terms of acculturation as affording answers to current Navaho problems. A discussion of acculturation as an explanatory variable in the study of peyotism is supplied.

5. No extensive interpretation of the borderline predictors is supplied.

6. Other variables, including reactions to livestock reduction, have little weight as predictors.

7. These findings apply to units or aggregates, not to individuals. Individual reactions are discussed in the previous chapter.

8. Disturbance over peyotism is best predicted by the amount of peyotism in the community, and secondarily by the "peyote-prone-ness" of the community: the less the community has of attributes which would tend to predict a high level of peyotism, the greater the amount of disturbance over peyotism.

9. There is a nearly significant negative correlation between size of permit and percentage of peyotists for 11 Districts.

PART V
PEYOTISM AS A REDEMPTIVE MOVEMENT

Chapter 19

A CLASSIFICATION OF SOCIAL MOVEMENTS[1]

ALTHOUGH RELATIVE DEPRIVATION has been used to explain the findings in Chapter 17, it has not been dealt with in general theoretical terms. Nor has there been any effort to place the peyote cult among the group of movements with which it is ordinarily classified. This is the central effort of Part V of this work. It seems best to begin with a general classification of social movements. This will involve a discussion of relative deprivation. Subsequently, peyotism will be dealt with in terms of this classificaton.

A social movement is an organized effort by a group of human beings to effect change in the face of resistance by other human beings. By this definition, a social movement is differentiated from purely individual efforts, from unorganized group efforts such as crowd action (if indeed these efforts are truly unorganized), and from efforts at technological change which proceed only against the resistance of

[1] This chapter was drafted in 1960–1961. In terms of the ideas presented it stands substantially as it was then written. It rests on the following bases: (1) a classification of social movements; (2) the interlocked concepts of reference field and relative deprivation; (3) a typology of deprivations; (4) a theory of the combination of context and type of deprivation which attempts to account for the choice of various types of movements and for certain elements in movements. Insofar as possible, I should like to acknowledge indebtedness and awareness of the work of others under these headings.

1. *Classification.*—The classification arose mainly out of efforts to revise Linton (1943), to subdivide Wallace's revitalization movements (1956b), and to deal with Slotkin's differentiation between opposition and accommodation (1956). It was stimulated in part by many discussions with Louis Guttman in 1955–1956. He attempted to help me make a facet analysis of responses to culture contact. The characteristics of transformative movements and some of the phrases used to describe them owe something to Cohn (1962, esp. p. 32). The classification shows parallels with Voget (1956), Ames (1957), Hobsbawm (1959), Smith (1959), Wallace, Voget, and Smith (1959), Wilson (1959, 1963), Clemhout (1964), and, I am sure, many others. I also consulted Schlosser (1949) and Guariglia (1959), but I used their materials rather than their classifications. The works of Ames (1957), Hobsbawm (1959), Wilson (1963), and Clemhout (1964) were examined after this chapter was drafted.

2. *Relative Deprivation and Reference Group.*—The concept of relative deprivation implies that of reference group. One obvious way for individuals and groups to appraise themselves is that of comparison with a reference group. The literature on relative deprivation and on reference groups is far too extensive for review, or even for enumeration here; nor will there be an attempt to provide an extensive genealogy of either concept. Both concepts undoubtedly take us back to lines of thought which precede the development of systematic sociology, social psychology, or anthropology. Bernard Barber first made me aware of the concept of deprivation, in conversation and through his articles (1941a and 1941b). His pedigree for the concept of deprivation is Lasswell (1935) and Nash (1937). All three define or use the concept in ways that make it clear that at least one component for them is that of relative deprivation. In the case of Lasswell and Nash, it might be argued that for them, relative deprivation is only a special case of a more general category of traumatic or dysphoric experience. Merton and Kitt (1950) brought together the uses of the concept of relative deprivation found in The American Soldier and joined the concept explicitly to that of reference group. My earliest contact with the explicit concept of reference group was through the work of Hyman (1942) and through discussions with him. (He uses the term "reference point," which I use, without giving it a technical status—1942, p. 26.) Influential in my thinking was Merton (1949), which affected

the material world.[2] Under the heading of resistance by other human beings is included passive resistance or apathy. It should be noted that the definition does not require that the resistance be organized. Religious movements constitute one type of social movement. Since we have a minimum of interest at this point in differentiating religious movements from other social movements, no definition of religious movements is supplied.

There are many ways of classifying social movements, and no review of these ways will be attempted here. The classification presented below is exhaustive in its own terms, but it is certainly not the only possible classification.

Social movements may be classified by reference to two dimensions. One is the dimension of the *locus* of the change sought. The other is the dimension of the *amount* of change sought. As to locus, a movement may aim to change individuals or some supra-individual system—the economic order, the technological order, the political order, the law, a total society or culture, the world, or indeed the cosmos. As to amount of change, movements may aim at total or partial change. These two dimensions give rise to four types, represented in Chart L.

CHART L

A CLASSIFICATION OF SOCIAL MOVEMENTS

| | | LOCUS OF CHANGE | |
		Supra-individual	Individual
AMOUNT OF CHANGE	Total	Transformative	Redemptive
	Partial	Reformative	Alterative

---

my definition of relative deprivation. Also relevant in this connection is Merton (1957a). To read Merton and Kitt (1950), Merton (1957b), and Hyman (1960) is to despair of listing all the formulations of these and related concepts. The reader is referred to these sources.

With respect to relative deprivation, the tradition of considering nativistic, revitalistic, messianic, cult, sect, millenarian, cargo, and various other social movements as products of dysphoria, dysnomia, anomie, trouble, misery, oppression, opposition, resistance, anxiety, and so on, is so old as to be unpatentable. In this connection among recent works I have benefitted particularly from Wallace (1956b), Cohn (1957), Worsley (1957), Burridge (1960), and Thrupp, ed. (1962). The opportunity to participate in a 1960 symposium on millenarian movements arranged by Thrupp, the results of which appear in Thrupp, ed. (1962), was most rewarding (cf. Aberle, 1962).

3. *Typology of Deprivations.*—I am indebted primarily to Louis Guttman for efforts at a facet analysis of types of deprivation, in 1955–1956. The differentiation of deprivation in goods and in status was influenced by Lipset (1955); see also Hofstadter (1955).

4. *Context.*—The work of Mooney (1896), Wallis (1943), Stanner (1953), Mead (1956), Cohn (1957), Worsley (1957), Schwartz (1962), Talmon (1962), and Thrupp, ed. (1962) has been influential, sometimes polemically, but much more often not. I find parallels in Mair (1958), Lanternari (1963), and Wilson (1963).

The work of various authorities on peyote has also affected this chapter in many ways, but since all of these receive mention elsewhere, they will not be listed here.

[2] This definition is deliberately broad. It does not try to distinguish a social movement from a transitory organized effort or from a highly specific organized effort, or even from political parties and their activities under some condition. Cf., for example, King (1961, pp. 27–28) and Heberle (1951) for more circumscribed definitions.

1. *Transformative movements* aim at a total change in supra-individual systems. The Ghost Dance, millenarian movements, and revolutionary movements (by contrast with rebellions) are examples.

2. *Reformative movements* aim at a partial change in supra-individual systems. The women's suffrage movement, movements in favor of compulsory vaccination, the child labor law movement, and rebellions are all examples.

3. *Redemptive movements* aim at a total change in individuals. Many sectarian movements aiming at a state of grace, among them, it will later be shown, the peyote cult, are examples.

4. *Alterative movements* aim at a partial change in individuals. Various birth control movements are examples, insofar as they do not involve efforts to change anti-birth control legislation (in that case they are reformative).

Some movements are probably close to pure types of one or another of these four classes. Others can ordinarily be classified as predominantly of one or another major type, with less emphasis on a different type. Thus redemptive elements are common in transformative movements. In still other cases, however, a movement is better described by reference to its particular blend of transformative, reformative, redemptive, and alterative elements, without being forced into one or another major category.

More important by far, however, any given movement may change in type over time. A transformative movement may shift to the quest for individual salvation and thereby fall into the redemptive class. An alterative movement may despair of achieving its ends by changing individuals and move toward efforts at new legislation, thereby becoming reformative, and so on. Any concrete historical instance may change radically, so that the appropriate classification at one time may be quite inappropriate later. It is an empirical question whether every type may be transformed in one step to every other type. Logically, it seems doubtful that a movement would move directly from alterative to transformative efforts without passing through a redemptive or a reformative stage, and a direct shift from transformation to alteration seems equally unlikely. Not only is a change in type of movement possible, it is very common, and the shift in the history of a particular movement from one type to another affords a strategic opportunity for research.

Classification of movements demands attention to the directing ideology and program of a group, and not merely to official ideology. Officially, all of Christianity is transformative: it awaits the millennium. But in fact relatively few Christian sects live in the tense expectation of the millennium. Only those that do can be considered transformative in their preparations for the new age.

A final caution: not everything that starts as a social movement finishes as one. A movement may succeed and turn into the Establishment. A religious group which once aimed at conversion and proselytized actively may turn instead to the maintenance of membership and the socializing of the new generation. When it does so, it stops being a movement. Many churches are best conceived of as having a "movement" and a "non-movement" sector: they have a mission area where their clergy are active in the pursuit of souls, and a home area which is stabilized. This is true of some political movements as well.

The principal interest of this book is in the difference between transformative and redemptive movements, and in variations in transformative and redemptive movements. Many of the nativistic, revitalistic, millenarian, cargo, and other movements studied by anthropologists may be classified as transformative or redemptive, and further categorized by reference to variations in transformative and redemptive movements. We will therefore proceed by delineating constants and variables of transformative and redemptive movements. Little further attention will be given to reformative and alterative movements.

Transformative movements consist of organized groups of people who actively seek, by whatever means, ritual or practical, a transformation of the socio-cultural, or indeed the natural order, including the socio-cultural—and this in their own lifetimes. Such movements involve a radical rejection of things as they are, and a perception of the enormous force necessary to make the shift from things as they are to things as they should be. Their constant characteristics stem from these facts.

CONSTANT CHARACTERISTICS OF TRANSFORMATIVE MOVEMENTS

1. *Time perspective.*—The desired change is expected to be imminent and cataclysmic—to begin soon and be completed speedily. Such beliefs aid men in withdrawing their energy from normal concerns and activities and turning it to the task of transformation, by prayer or struggle or both. Imminence promises immediate rewards; cataclysm foreshortens the task of reorganization implicit in the conception of transformation.

2. *Theory of history.*—These movements are teleological, in the sense that the transformation is viewed as destined, willed by God, or the outcome of entelechous forces. That is, the transformation may be seen as part of God's total plan for mankind, or as the product of his disapproval of current life, or, in the case of modern, secular movements, as the product of such forces as evolution, the dialectic process, the long course of history, the destiny of the race, and so on. This teleological element is a strong ideological support for the transformative effort, which, otherwise, seems to run in opposition to very large, if not overwhelming odds. If God, destiny, or history is on the side of the movement, how can its members lose?

3. *Leadership.*—Almost by tautology from what has been said, transformative movements are led by charismatic figures—those who regard themselves and are regarded by their followers as in touch with superior forces or as having superior knowledge of the forces of destiny. In a movement with a teleological ideology, someone must be capable of interpreting the telos in a situation fraught with uncertainty and of translating the interpretation into prescriptions for action. The gift of grace of the charismatic leader is the capacity to interpret the telos. Some charismatic leaders are believed to communicate with supernatural forces. They will be described as having sacred charisma. Others claim special capacities to discern the drift or plan of the empirical world—for example, to understand the forces of history. They will be described as having secular charisma.

A charismatic leader may be primarily an interpreter of what is happening, primarily a prophet of what is going to happen, or primarily a deliverer who will bring about what is to happen. The deliverer with sacred charisma is a messiah.

Thus in terms of this classification a messianic movement is a sub-category of the class of transformative movements, categorized by reference to its leadership. Indeed, it is a sub-sub-category, since the nature of leadership is not taken here as a major variable.

4. *Disengagement.*—Transformative movements seem to involve efforts at increased social or spatial segregation of their members from the larger society. The ideological reasons for this vary. Sometimes the members must seek higher ground to avoid a flood, sometimes a separate place to carry out a ritual, sometimes a separate location to prepare the transformation, sometimes social separation to avoid the contamination of the ungodly, and so on. Underlying all these there seems to be an effort to withdraw energy from the larger society and its routines so as to will, or work for the transformation.

In sum, transformative movements view the process of change as cataclysmic, the time of change as imminent, the direction of change as teleologically guided, the appropriate supervision of the movement as charismatic, and at some point move to increase the separation of their members from the larger social sphere. This cluster of traits is related to the vision of the enormous discrepancy between things as they are and things as they should be, and of the tremendous obstacles which impede transformation. These features may not all be maximized in every transformative movement, but they are, in theory, all minimally visible in each instance. They characterize both religious and secular transformative movements.

In addition to these constants, there are a number of variable features.

VARIABLE FEATURES OF TRANSFORMATIVE MOVEMENTS

1. *Means.*—At one extreme are found the revolutionary movements, which depend on men's practical actions in this world. At the other are religious movements that depend on prayer and ritual alone. Many combinations are possible. Sometimes, for example, it is expected that God will act, but man is also enjoined to take practical steps. Along this continuum, means may be classified as predominantly magical or predominantly empirical.

2. *Model.*—A transformative movement has a desired end-state in view. Broadly speaking, there are three types of end-states, or models: restorative, imitative, and innovative. Restorative movements seek to return to a vision of the past. Some restorative movements look for an ethnic paradise. Such was the Ghost Dance, which promised a restoration of all that was best in Indian life. Others seek what the members believe to be the past of the human race, the golden age of all mankind. Imitative movements are those which borrow their models quite frankly from a group considered to be foreign. Many cargo cults are imitative. Innovative models are those which are believed to correspond to no previously known state of affairs. Most millennial movements are of this character.

There are pure type models, models that can be typed as predominantly of one or another sort, and models best described as a blend. Among the commonest blends is a fusion of innovative and restorative elements. The re-creation of the golden age with modern technology is one such seductive image. Talmon believes that such a fusion is a particularly energizing one (Talmon, 1962).

3. *Scope.*—The definition of the beneficiaries of the transformation ranges from particularistic to universalistic. Some movements promise benefits only to, say,

American Indians. Others promise them to all humanity, or perhaps all except the wicked. It should be noted that at some point in their history, all transformative movements deny their future benefits to their opponents and to passive non-believers. This device attempts to secure commitment in the face of the obstacles posed by the status quo. But over and above this, movements are still relatively universalistic or particularistic.

4. *Relationship to existing systems.*—Sometimes the old world is to be destroyed utterly by supernatural intervention. Sometimes it is to be absorbed by the new system. Sometimes it is to continue, with the transformed system now in success-ful competition with it. Sometimes the new system is to be isolated from the old and corrupt one, and sometimes the new system is to achieve a more satisfactory integration with some larger social order.

In sum, transformative movements vary as to means, models, scope, and rela-tionship with existing systems.

These constants and variables serve to classify some of the plethora of types and instances of transformative movements which we now recognize. A messianic movement would not be a major subcategory in these terms: it would require classification according to means, models, scope, and relationship with existing systems. Many cargo cults are transformative, magical, imitative, particularistic, and anticipate competition with existing systems. (Since the term "cargo cult" has been used for a great variety of movements, however, not all will fit into these particular boxes.) The Ghost Dance is a transformative movement which differs from these cargo cults in being restorative and in expecting the disappearance of the existing system—at least in some versions of Wovoka's prophecy (cf. Mooney, 1896). It resembles cargo cults in being magical and particularistic. Communism as an ideology before the Russian Revolution was a transformative movement that was empirical, innovative, universal in long-time perspective, and expected to replace the existing system. (There is some tautology in the variables: a universal-istic system necessarily anticipates replacement of the existing system in some way or other. But a particularistic one may anticipate replacement of the existing sys-tem or any of several other possible outcomes.) Finally, it should be emphasized that many of the movements in which anthropologists have been interested are not transformative, but rather, redemptive.

CONSTANT CHARACTERISTICS OF
REDEMPTIVE MOVEMENTS

A redemptive movement aims at a state of grace in a human soul, psyche, or person. The defining characteristic is the search for a new inner state. Changes in behavior are sought as a path to such an inner state, or, more commonly, it is believed that changes in behavior can result only from a new state of grace—that alterations of behavior require change of heart. Not every religion which promises a heavenly hereafter is redemptive. Religions promising other worldly happiness may place reliance on rules of conduct, on obedience to ritual prescriptions, or on participation in ritual occasions conducted by ritually appropriate figures. Such religions are not redemptive. And there are redemptive movements which are secular in orientation. The psychoanalytic movement may be considered redemp-tive.

Virtually all redemptive movements, like the transformative movements, reject at least some features of the current society. They find evil in the world, not merely in the sinner. Although they put their energies into achieving a total change in persons rather than societies, they also castigate the society. (Sometimes their ideology holds that when enough people are redeemed the socio-cultural order will finally improve.) Insofar as a movement aims only to achieve a state of grace which permits the person to live more happily in the world, without criticizing that world, it falls outside the scope of this discussion. Few redemptive movements do. A possible example is that branch of the psychoanalytic movement which is interested solely in the adjustment of the person to the world. But Freud, Horney, and Fromm, for example, are leaders of the psychoanalytic movement who are critical of the current social order, different though their criticisms may be.

From the stress on achieving a state of grace and the rejection of the validity of some features of the existing system stem certain constants of redemptive movements.

1. *Overcoming resistance.*—The individual's resistance to change, or apathy toward being changed, must be overcome in order for the change to occur. He must become aware of his unfortunate condition and must be given an opportunity for self-evaluation. This process, however, can occur over a long period of time or a very short one. At one extreme, overcoming of conscious resistance is followed by prolonged self-evaluation and examination of the condition of redemption and the path to it, until finally redemption is achieved. At another, unwitting and witting resistance may vanish simultaneously and instantly, as when those who came to scoff remain to pray.

2. *Changed relationships.*—Either during and after, or after the change, the candidate for redemption must be buttressed against the obstacles to redemption created by his relationships with a social system partly rejected by the movement. He must either increase his contact with the redeemed, or decrease his contact with the non-redeemed, or both.

VARIABLE FEATURES OF REDEMPTIVE MOVEMENTS

The variables in redemptive movements are manifold, and this treatment will not attempt to be exhaustive. At least one of the originators of a redemptive movement is a charismatic figure, if only because new interpretations of the path to grace require confirmation through charismatic authority. This, however, is not necessarily the case where transformative movements become redemptive through re-interpretation: new charisma may here be a minor and insignificant phenomenon. The distribution of charisma in subsequent stages of redemptive movements is highly variable. The agent of redemption as defined in the movement may be supernatural, a human leader of a movement, an adept in the movement, or the person's own inner forces. The potential subject of redemption may be all of humanity, members of a particular group, or an elect. More important, the candidate for redemption may be required eventually to live in the world and struggle against it, or to withdraw from it. And the characteristic state of mind and code of conduct of the redeemed person varies very widely (cf. Weber, 1946, pp. 267–359).

However widely the code of conduct varies, redemptive movements are more likely to be concerned with immediate interpersonal relationships and day-to-day behavior than are transformative movements. Transformative movements are especially concerned with the future; redemptive movements are likely to define appropriate attitudes toward family, kin, friends, non-believers, work, leisure, sexuality, appetites, aggression, and immediate economic and political relationships. The definition of what is appropriate is highly variable. For Buddhism, these are all matters to be left behind—but this, too, is a matter of defining appropriate attitudes. For peyotism, we have already seen that most, if not all, of these areas are dealt with. A transformative movement with postponed or ebbing millennial hopes may turn increasingly to an emphasis on day-to-day rules of conduct, usually as the path to election after the millennium begins. Where the stress is on ritual to bring about the millennium or practical efforts in the same direction, daily rules receive less attention.

When the directive is to live in this world, rather than to withdraw from it, it is notable that the clusters of behavior defined as bad or good in redemptive movements would often seem to the casual observer to be fit candidates for merely alterative efforts. Indeed they are often bits of behavior which are the subject of moral preaching or education in other groups and at other times. In these other groups the same kinds of behavior are seen as achievable without a personal transformation.

On inspection, however, we often find that in his current social orbit the individual would have great difficulty in changing one thing without changing many others, or indeed without changing social orbits. Thus, if the results of hard work are likely to be drained off through the claims of kin, it may be impossible to inspire people to change their work habits unless they are given a new ethical interpretation which limits their responsibility to kinsmen and are provided with a new group to provide moral support —when their kin become upset. Linking both work habits and the new ethic to a state of grace and to divine commandment and altering the social orbit, may make the change in work habits possible. The same sort of linkage of items applies, of course, in the case of transformative movements (cf. Mead, 1956).

RELATIVE DEPRIVATION AND REFERENCE FIELD

So much for typology. The question is whether the classification can be included in a theory which attempts to account for the choice of one or another type of movement. Two links will be used for this purpose: relative deprivation, and the context of the group in which the movement occurs.

Social movements are, almost by definition, associated with some notion of distress, deprivation, dysphoria, or discontent. Unless we assume that humanity ceaselessly strives for perfection, we are obliged to assume that the goals of transformation, reformation, redemption, or alteration have roots in some negative evaluation of the current state of affairs. There is, however, one major dichotomy to be noted. In some reformative and alterative movements, and in the missionary branches of some churches, viewed as redemptive movements, the effort is to improve things for someone else. These disinterested movements are not the focus of attention here. Transformative efforts by one group solely on behalf of another are unknown. In movements where the beneficiaries of change are to be the members of the group which constitutes the social movement, even if others are to benefit as well, we must, I think, assume that there are subjective feelings of distress connected with the experiences of the members of the group. This assumption, although rejected by some who have written about the Ghost Dance and the Prophet Dance (e.g., Spier, 1935; Herskovits, 1938; Spier, Suttles and Herskovits, 1959; cf. Aberle, 1959 and 1962 for an opposite point of view), is central to virtually all theories and descriptive treatments of such movements. The core of the distress seems to be the experience of relative deprivation.

Relative deprivation is defined as a negative discrepancy between legitimate expectation and actuality, or between legitimate expectation and anticipated actuality, or both. A man who thinks he is suited to be a plant manager and is chained to a clerical job, experiences relative deprivation. A man who congratulates himself on having achieved a clerical job in spite of deficiencies in his earlier training does not. A man who expects the Government to increase his taxes by 20 per cent next year and who does not accept the Government's claim to this amount is relatively deprived. A man who has accepted his present taxes and does not anticipate an increase is not.

Relative deprivation, then, is a social and cultural phenomenon, not necessarily identical with such phenomena as physiologically induced pain, hunger, thirst, stress, suffering from cold, etc. These experiences may often involve relative deprivation, when they are regarded as experiences not legitimately to be expected, but they may not. Thus the suffering involved in the self-torture of the Sun Dance or the hunger and thirst of the vision quest are physiologically extremely dysphoric, but are not depriving experiences if we speak of relative deprivation. On the other hand, to a multimillionaire the loss of a million dollars *may* be a relative deprivation.

The concept of relative deprivation rests on three assumptions: the potentially limitless character of human wants; the approximate definition of legitimate expectations by the socio-cultural system; and the potential for disruption of these definitions by socio-cultural change. I follow Durkheim (1951) in the assumption that since man's wants, unlike those of other animals, are not merely biopsychologically determined, they are potentially limitless. Any given society—even a relatively open-class society—defines at least roughly the wants appropriate to the various statuses in that society. In no society, however simple, are all statuses equal, and correspondingly the legitimate expectations of individuals occupying different statuses in a given society differ. Even if there is an enormous hierarchy of statuses with theoretical complete mobility, different segments of the population have different legitimate expectations. Some low-status individuals are quite happy about their positions because they base their self-assessment on comparison with a limited number of people whose condition does not invite their envy (Hyman, 1942). The concept of "reference groups" has been used recently to account for the content or discontent of individuals in a variety of situations. Here, however, we will use instead the concepts of reference points and reference field. A reference point is anything used as a basis for measuring legitimate expectation. Such points are often found in reference groups, but they need not be. A person may feel that he "ought" to be as well off as members of groups or social categories to which he does belong (his colleagues, members of his kin-group, etc.), or that he "ought" to be as well off as members of groups to which he does not belong (the faculty of another university, white workers [if he is a Negro], and so on). But the measuring points may be his own past condition, his own present condition, and so on, rather than some group. Or he may use a specific individual. Any such point of comparison is a reference point. The total set of reference points used by an individual makes up his reference field.

For heuristic purposes, we may imagine a completely stable society with all statuses fixed at birth save those dependent on age. Under these circumstances, given the fact that reference points are ultimately culturally defined, and given adequate socialization of the bulk of the population, the experience of relative deprivation would have a special character. It would depend largely on those frustrations of legitimate expectation endemic in the human condition. The annual fluctuations of temperature and moisture alone guarantee that the outcome of human labor will be disappointing from time to time, and the facts of human morbidity and mortality provide for similar disruptions of legitimate expectation. Such relative deprivations might impinge on the entire society or local segments of it, or more or less randomly on individuals. Under these circumstances, one might expect increased effort to compensate for the deprivations, or various compensatory and motivation-maintaining magical and religious activities to resolve the tensions resulting from relative deprivation. This interpretation resembles Malinowski's theory of magic, arising where empirical knowledge provides inadequate prediction and control (Malinowski, 1948, pp. 1–71; cf. Levy, 1952, pp. 243–244). One would not expect social movements.

But in fact, complete stability is unknown in human affairs. Change in human society, proceeding from exogenous or endogenous factors, is chronic. And with change comes change in the relationship between legitimate expectation and anticipated or actual outcome. This can arise for either of two reasons: first, because the reference field changes; second, because the actual outcome changes or, it is anticipated, will change. If a group makes contact with another group with radically higher standards of consumption, it may use the new group as its reference point and come to feel relatively deprived. If a group suffers a drop in actual goods consumed as a result of domination by another group, it may also come to feel relatively deprived. It is also possible for change to result in feelings of relative enhancement rather than relative deprivation, either through the discovery of others, worse off, or through an increase in, say, goods available. (My examples here are largely in terms of standards of consumption, but it will later be seen that my conception of types of deprivation includes these as only one type.)

The changes which result in alterations in the relationship between legitimate expectation and actuality are multifarious. Industrialization may lead to the creation of new statuses and new standards for measuring status, with changes in the relative ranking of old statuses. Trade between Western, market-based and non-Western pre-market societies may lead to similar results, with the rise of a merchant group and a decline in the rank, or the income, or both, of a former birth-right aristocracy. Groups may be crowded off territories they once enjoyed; they may be dominated through conquest; and so on. Many of the changes which result in relative deprivation arise directly from changed relations between groups, either groups within the same society, and participating in the same general cultural tradition, or groups which belong to (or constitute) separate societies with quite different cultural traditions. (It is possible that *all* such changes depend on changed relations between groups, but for present purposes it is not necessary to make so sweeping a claim.)

Such changes in intergroup relations as create relative deprivation provide only a few ostensibly satisfactory ways of coping with the situation. The three most obvious solutions are fight, amalgamation, or flight: beat 'em, join 'em, or leave 'em. There are at least two other solutions: additional effort, used to reach the same standards in the face of obstacles (or new standards if standards rise), and a drop in standards. These five solutions are open to individuals or to entire groups. If every individual were to choose his own solution, making no joint cause with others, there would be no social movement, by definition. But in the usual situation, not all members of a group have equal access to opportunities for individual solutions. Consequently, even if some people adopt individual solutions, there may be a residuum for whom some social movement is a likely course of action.

Often enough the three simplest solutions are empirically impossible. In the last quarter of the nineteenth century, the Plains Indians had come to the limit of any possibility of beating the Americans, had been penned up and prevented from leaving the field, and had had small success, for many reasons, in joining the majority. The fourth solution, attaining the standard by increased effort, is also often impossible: no additional effort will succeed. After hunting in some of the richest game country in the world, adequately armed and mounted, the Plains Indians could not subsequently achieve their old standards by farming what were, in many cases, marginal lands. The fifth solution, a downward shift in standards, is relatively uncommon, at least in the short run. It is not clear why this should be so, but such shifts are unusual, and especially where the deprivation is sudden.

Where successful competition, successful infiltration of the disturbing group, and physical withdrawal are alike realistically impossible, magical competition, magical withdrawal, magical infiltration (in a limited sense), and partial social isolation remain as potentialities for organized social movements. And there also remains the fantasy of total reorganization of the social field.

Sometimes, however, the actors in a changing situation are not clearly aware of the source of their deprivation. Then they may direct blame at the self or at members of their own group or at some of the members, or at an out-group which is in fact not responsible for the deprivation, or they may see the source as stemming exclusively from the supernatural realm.

Where the deprivation experience stems from, and is recognized as stemming from relations with a "foreign" group, the ideology of a movement of magical recouping or magical total reorganization or social withdrawal has a "cultural" flavor. That is, it focuses on coping with cultural diacriticals. Under various circumstances, it may focus on cultural purification, on "instant" acculturation, or on cargo cult expectations. Where the deprivation experience proceeds from, and is seen as proceeding from relations with one's "own" society, it may focus on the future golden age or on the restoration of the primeval state of nature, but it does not self-consciously state an ideology based on the creation, maintenance, sharpening, or obliteration of cultural differences. It is the cultural ideology, and not millenarianism or messianism, that distinguishes movements arising in culture contact conditions from those that arise in other contexts.

We may summarize the argument regarding relative deprivation as follows. Standards—legitimate expectations—are defined by the reference field. Relative deprivation is measured by a comparison of the actual or expected condition of an individual or a group with his, or its legitimate expectations. Under stable conditions, the negative discrepancy between legitimate expectation and actuality or anticipation, although endemic, may be slight. Among the most potent causes of major relative deprivation are changes in intergroup relations, either because these result in a change of standards or because they bring about a disturbance of the outcome of usual activities. (Changes leading to experiences of enhancement are disregarded for present purposes.) Among these changes, changes of relations between groups of widely differing cultures are a special case. But inasmuch as a new culture moving into an area may often have a superior technology, with all that follows from that in terms of competition, contacts between groups of radically different culture often involve deprivation for some or many members of one of these groups. Where individual solutions fail and no realistic group solution to the deprivation is possible, magical and religious movements are a potentiality. The content of these movements is related to the nature of the deprivation.

A TYPOLOGY OF RELATIVE DEPRIVATIONS

But relative deprivation as a global term to cover all dysphoric results of changing relations between groups is too broad for analytic purposes. It includes petty discomforts, loss of livelihood, humiliation, loss of power, etc. These various elements are hard to treat under one heading. On the other hand, a mere phenomenal listing of deprivations as they come to mind or appear in the data becomes both cumbersome, lengthy, and unsystematic. I shall therefore attempt a heuristic classification of types of deprivation. Four types of relative deprivation will be considered: the areas of possessions, status, behavior, and worth. Under the heading of possessions, are included all types of goods which can be enjoyed by an individual or a group, access to which can be regulated by an individual or a group. Thus certain "free goods" such as air are excluded. But territory, fields, flocks; the yield from collecting, agriculture, pastoralism, manufacture, wagework, etc., are in this sense possessions. Relative deprivation consists in the experience of receiving less of any of these items than is the legitimate right of the individual, the members of a social category, or the group concerned.

Status, which might well be considered a "possession," with a minimum of redefinition, is nevertheless important enough to merit a separate pigeonhole. A status is a socially defined position. All statuses are ranked in terms of the values prevailing in a cultural system. (I do not mean to say that these values are arbitrary or free-floating, but that in status inheres the concept of "higher" or "lower" positions, and that the concept of higher and lower refers to some value scale. There may or may not be a plurality of ranking systems in any given cultural unit.) Where individuals, categories, or groups do not acquire the statuses which they consider legitimately theirs, relative deprivation exists.

It should again be emphasized that the relative deprivation may be based on one of several measures of legitimate expectation. Thus individuals may not have the possessions that they once received, and feel that they should; they may anticipate the loss of possessions they now have, and feel that this is wrong; they may have less than members of some other group, and feel for the first time that they, too, should have possessions like those of the other group; members of a group may have less than other members of that same group, who once received the same, or less than they did, and feel deprived on this account, and so on. The same considerations apply to status.

These comments are pertinent for the consideration of behavior. If an individual, category, or group considers his (its) behavior to be "worse than it should be," then deprivation in the area of behavior exists. Under behavior we consider any and all of the following items: activities given a moral evaluation, such as sexual conduct, commercial activities, treatment of children or the aged, etc.; activities given an evaluation in terms of manners or etiquette; activities evaluated in the context of ritual appropriateness; activities (and the products of activities) evaluated aesthetically; modes of dress, hairstyle, body decoration, etc. This list is by no means exhaustive. If, by comparison with former behavior or the behavior of another group, one's own, or one's group's, or one's membership category's behavior is seen as distinctly below standard, this represents behavioral deprivation. When old Navahos complain of increasing sexual irresponsibility at Enemy Way ceremonies, or of increased drinking, they manifest relative deprivation in the area of behavior. If young Navahos regard mother-in-law avoidance as "superstitious and foolish," they take on the standards of the larger American society and manifest relative deprivation in the area of behavior—provided they still consider themselves to be Navahos. If young Navahos regard conservative Navahos only as "those others," no such deprivation can be claimed by the observer. The range of behaviors subjected to negative evaluation in this fashion is virtually endless.

Sometimes, however, instead of negative evaluation of the behavior of one's own group, there is defensive insistence on the rightness of its behavior in the face of known, or imagined opposition. This can occur either when a new reference group is beginning to impinge, but is being resisted, or as a secondary reaction to the disapproval of significant others. Where this sort of reaction can be shown to be defensive, we may speak of relative deprivation in the behavioral area. On the other hand, unmixed pride in the standards of one's own group accompanied by sharp disapproval of the ways of others may involve only a trivial deprivation: anxiety over a possible shift of conduct in the direction of the behavior of the disapproved group.

Particularly in the case of magical and religious movements that represent reactions to contact, ambivalence is characteristic. This follows from the fact that so often no realistic solution for the deprivation is open, so that any solution is a compromise.

The last area of relative deprivation to be considered is that of worth. The concept of worth is residual. It includes the evaluation of a person, category, or group made by significant others, on the basis of those characteristics which are not subject to change, even in theory. Factors such as race, ethnicity, age, and sex fall in this class. If, regardless of his possessions, status, or behavior, a person is denied that degree of acceptance or positive evaluation by others which he considers to accrue to him by virtue of his possessions, his status, his behavior, or his human-ness, he thereby suffers relative deprivation in the area of worth. If an American Indian, regardless of education, income, or performance is looked on as inferior, dirty, worthless, savage, or untrustworthy simply because he is an Indian, he is deprived as respects his worth.

It is possible that a fifth type of deprivation, associated with loss of power and autonomy might be profitably considered. I have, however, preferred to consider the loss of positions of power or the inability to have access to them as features of status deprivation. Strivings of a group for political autonomy or for the reversal of present power relations I have preferred to treat as consequent on deprivation in the other areas mentioned. It is thus assumed that power is not sought for its own sake but for what it brings in its train, and that the striving for autonomy is closely associated with constraints connected with possessions, status, behavior, and worth. Since there is no logical way of proving that the set of categories I have used is exhaustive, the question of a fifth, or of additional other categories, remains open.

It seems to me that there is a certain normal sequence of types of deprivation arising in contacts between the West and those areas of the world it has successfully, and successively dominated. Deprivation in the area of possessions seems to be the first to arise. In many instances, the reasons for this are patent. A group is conquered or pressed back, and its access to previous sources of livelihood adversely affected. Or there is early exposure to new wants, through trade, which are not easily satisfied. Or the economic relations between the Western nation and the group it dominates are such as to siphon off goods without adequate replacement.

Status deprivation is likely to follow, or accompany these changes. It may proceed from any of four sources: the levelling of previous differences in status, often the result of territorial confinement on a smaller land-base than heretofore; the expansion of previous differences; the development of differences in a previously highly egalitarian, small-scale society; and the creation of new status positions which adversely affect the prior holders of high status in the previous system. In the ordinary case, it is some time before the members of the dominated group begin to aspire to positions within the status hierarchy of the dominant group; at that point they very often suffer additional status deprivation. This time lag results from the fact, quite evident to the dominated, that possession of these positions rests, in the ordinary case, on literacy and special skills not yet known to the members of the dominated group.

Deprivation in the area of behavior can follow closely on the heels of the previous ones, as respects decline in the performance of behavior thought desirable according to the standards of the system prior to change. Thus the moral standards of kinship obligations may no longer be closely adhered to, as political domination removes the kin group's political significance in cases of compensation or feud. Or wage-work and corresponding individuation may reduce the significance of kinship bonds. New forms of property may weaken the cohesion of the kinship unit, and alter the behavior of its members, if this cohesion has been based on the joint control of property.

This, however, is only one type of relative deprivation associated with the area of behavior. The other involves dissatisfaction with the behavior of one's own group by reference to the standards of another group. In order for this to occur, the other group must have become significant as a source of approval, which implies a longer and closer interaction than is necessary for some of the types of deprivation thus far described to arise.

By the same token, deprivation in the area of worth requires that the other group become a significant source of approval. Even today there are Navahos who do not know that whites consider them inferior, and others who do not care. For young men who have been to school and men who have worked off-reservation, however, such opinions are a significant source of deprivation.

Thus far we have discussed the origins, nature, and types of relative deprivation. We have furthermore implied throughout that these deprivations are the seed-bed for social movements. It would seem to follow from this that a knowledge of the severity and type of deprivation, and of the date and place of its occurrence, would make it possible to predict when, where, and with what ideology a social movement would arise. Such a claim cannot be sustained.

Empirically we know that severe relative deprivation occurs in many instances without the development of social movements. Thus the conditions of a number of Apachean groups had been worsening for several decades in the mid-nineteenth century, from the 1850's until the settlement of the Apaches on reservations in the early 1870's, and thereafter (Spicer, 1962, pp. 246–255). Yet only some of these groups became actively involved in rebellion in the reservation period, and only one in the (probably) nativistic and revitalistic movement led by Nakai-doklini in 1881 (Spicer, 1962, p. 254; Mooney, 1896, pp. 704–705; Bourke, 1892, p. 505; RCIA 1851–1881).[3] This movement itself involved an uprising. Furthermore, there is no current theory that specifies how long after deprivation begins—or reaches its most extreme development—a social movement is likely to occur, if it does occur.

CONTEXT OF SOCIAL MOVEMENTS

One reason for the difficulty of associating deprivation with the occurrence and timing of social movements is our lack of an adequate theory of such movements. Deprivation is only one element in such a theory, in my view. The other elements include the context of social relationships of the deprived group with others, and the deprived group's diagnosis of the source of its deprivations. And undoubtedly other elements are also crucial. The question of context has been touched on before. Under this heading are included such matters as power relationships, spatial segregation of the group in question, nature and degree of involvement of the group with the groups which are the source of its deprivations, and other factors.

[3] Interestingly, although my sources provide no information on this score, Spicer states that this group was under particularly severe pressure from Anglo settlers. His work was not available to me when this manuscript was drafted (Spicer, 1962, p. 254). The fact remains that all Apache groups suffered greatly during these years.

It is the context in part that determines what magical or practical solution seems sensible to the deprived group. The question of the group's diagnosis of the source of deprivation, however, also is related to its conception of an appropriate solution.

It would be premature to attempt to write a complete, general theory to predict the occurrence of social movements. I should like, however, to outline some features of such a theory. I will confine myself largely to transformative and redemptive movements.

The choice of type of movement—transformative, redemptive, reformative, or alterative—is conditioned by the social context of the deprived group. Transformative and redemptive movements involve not only considerable magnitudes of deprivation but also a lack of access to the locus of power. Some transformative movements arise when the group in question is a politically subordinate unit in a larger body politic. Some, however, arise in groups which are still separate political entities but are hard pressed by groups which promise to conquer and subordinate them. The locus of power in both instances lies outside the group and inaccessible to it. Reformative and alterative movements involve less deprivation and a greater consciousness of access to the sources of power.

As between transformation and redemption, transformative goals are most likely when a deprived group is segregated spatially or socially and when its involvement with the larger social order is either slight or decreasing, or both (cf. McLeod, 1928, pp. 507–508, for a parallel interpretation). Such is the condition of those whose conquest at the hands of a superior technology seems assured; of recently conquered primitives placed on reservations where the role of the larger society is to confine, dominate, and dole them; and of lower strata in complex societies that are both uprooted and unemployed. This results from the fact that the vision of transformation, often accompanied by the fantasy of the disappearance of major dominant groups, is the more difficult to maintain, the greater the number of links that the most deprived elements of a population have with the larger social network—through employment, position in a status economy, political participation, kinship, friendship, or voluntary association.

In sum, transformative movements seem to appeal to people who have been, or are being extruded from their niche—in terms of location, economic position, political position, etc., into more marginal niches, and who cannot foresee another niche which offers reasonable security—not to mention happiness. This was the condition of the Plains Indians in 1890 and of the groups that participated in millennial movements in medieval Europe (for the Plains, no specific reference; for Europe, Cohn, 1957, esp. pp. 27–32).

Those redemptive movements with a focus on living in the world, rather than withdrawing from it, seem to appeal to groups which are being pressed to occupy a new niche, sometimes new to them, sometimes new in the society—one regarded ambivalently, or even negatively, but not hopelessly. Such new niches are those of wage work, urban versus rural occupations, and so on. The people involved may be ethnic groups, social strata, occupational groups, etc. Being engaged actively in the total system through occupancy of the new niche—often engaged more economically than politically or socially—they do not tend to fantasy the dissolution of the entire system and its transformation. Whereas the transformative ideology aids in withdrawing energy from the system, the redemptive ideology of these movements serves both as a form of protest against the system and as a means of adjusting to it. The world of the non-redeemed is depicted as evil; the solidarity and virtue of the redeemed are stressed; but the code of ethics often promotes those attitudes toward work, leisure, the pleasures of the senses, and kinship which facilitate adjustment to the new niche—say the asceticism, individualism, and fore-sight demanded by the entrepreneurial role, or the sobriety, industry, and prompt-ness demanded by the industrial order.

As for those redemptive movements which do stress withdrawal from the world, like Buddhism, I do not even have suggestions as to what factors might promote adherence to them. My concern with peyotism has led to a preoccupation with the other type of redemptive movement.

Different sets of contexts, then, seem to be related to the choice between trans-formation and redemption on the one hand, and reformation and alteration on the other. Amount of engagement in the system seems to account for the choice be-tween transformative and certain redemptive movements. Further comments may be made as to the relationship of various external variables to certain additional features of these social movements.

As for the model selected by transformative movements, it seems to be based on the reference points used for measuring deprivation, which rest in turn on the group's experience. Restorative movements are most likely where a prior group of satisfactions has been lost: the present condition of the group is worse than the past. Where, in addition, the deprivation is seen as coming from an alien group, "restorative nativism" seems likely (Linton, 1943).

Where the deprivation stems from the larger society of which the group in question is a part—where the "deprived" group does not regard this society as alien or foreign—return to a golden age is an appealing model. Imitative move-ments are likely when the group has been exposed to new wants by another group —wants which cannot be satisfied. This seems to be the situation for many cargo cults (cf. Worsley, 1957, Firth, 1955, and, for a modification of this view, Bur-ridge, 1960). Innovative movements seem to arise among lower-status elements in a stratified society when they see their problems as endogenous and rooted in the nature of the society, rather than located in their changed relations with some specific sub-group in the society.

As for means, magical or empirical, the choice for transformative and reform-ative movements rests both on the general evolutionary level of the society and on the degree to which the obstacles confronting the group are seen as tremendous. In the case of some reformative movements, even in preliterate cultures, a relatively empirical approach may prevail. Thus kingdoms have rebellions which can be regarded as reformative, in that their aim seems to be a better-functioning or less tyrannical kingdom, or one less inimical to some local sector. And groups attempt to deal with alien groups by warfare. The goals are limited, and the movements may be called reformative in many instances. And the means are empirical.

In the case of transformative movements, only in the post-industrial world (although often in its less industrialized sectors) have there been transformative movements with no element of reliance on what the observer would ordinarily call supernatural force. And even among these secular transformative movements, there are functional analogues of supernatural forces, like "the forces of history," "national destiny," and so on. And even in these secular movements, there is a reliance on what might be called "omens." In transformative movements frankly oriented to supernatural forces, such things as natural catastrophes and dreams may be seized on as portents of success. In the secular movements, something similar occurs. Interpretations of the imminence of the revolution, for example, may be based on relatively trivial disturbances in social relationships in the larger society —small-scale protests, for example.

Thus reformative movements, where by and large the obstacles seem less overwhelming, often contain a most pragmatic and empirical orientation to means, even in preliterate societies. Transformative movements, where the power obstacles seem great, are oriented to supernatural forces in all instances except recent ones, where there is an effort at explanations which do not involve personified supernatural force. Even there, however, analogues creep in through the interpretation of teleological forces and of supposedly diagnostic events.

Deprivation, basic to the genesis of these movements but not to the type of movement, affects their ideology. Transformative movements tend, on the whole, to be restitutive in character. What was lost through deprivation will be restored through transformation. The evildoers and their evil will be removed, so that every man may sit under his own vine and his own fig tree, so that the buffalo may again roam the plains, so that the last may be first and the first last, or so that all may at last enjoy abundance. But redemptive movements tend more to reject restitution and offer compensation. Thus wealth may be derogated and poverty regarded as a blessed state. Instead of offering social recognition in the larger world, these movements may scorn it and offer, instead, the recognition of the elect.

This is not a complete theory. No effort will be made here to describe or account for various features of reformative and alterative movements, to account for such matters as the scope of transformative movements or their expected relationship with existing systems, or the orientation to living in the world or views on the elect of redemptive movements. What is presented is a typology of social movements, with some suggestions as to the circumstances under which they may arise and the possible sources of some elements of two types.

It must be stressed that a movement arising as one type has no fixed and immutable sequence of events to pass through, nor is it fixed in type. Arising out of change and operating in fluid situations, these movements respond to new changes in context and to new potentialities arising in the course of the movements themselves. As Worsley has pointed out, some religious movements succeed in uniting previously separate social units (Worsley, 1957, esp. pp. 227-243). As a result of this success there may be a sufficient change in the potential power of these groups to turn them from magical to empirical solutions for their problems (cf. the Delaware prophet and Pontiac's confederation; the Shawano prophet and Tecumtha's confederation, Mooney, 1896, pp. 662-691).

Furthermore, the social condition of the groups engaged in these movements can be sufficiently complex in character and sufficiently fluid so that more than one type of movement can be meaningful at any given time. The Manus were affected by two cargo cults, transformative movements of a swiftly epidemic character, while carrying on the Paliau movements, itself transformative in origin but largely empirical in means, and becoming more reformative as time passed (Mead, 1956, Schwartz, 1962). Peyotism began its spread before the Ghost Dance among Plains Indians and continued to spread during and after the Ghost Dance. In many instances not only the same tribes but the same individuals were attracted to both movements. The swift succession and alternation of movements both in Manus and in the Plains, as well as in historically documented cases and among American Negroes today, is a problem requiring closer study than is permitted within the scope of the present work. It is important to bear in mind not only that situations sometimes change so rapidly that movements of quite different character can be almost simultaneously appealing but that situations can be sufficiently many-faceted and difficult to interpret so that movements of different types can exist side by side. Finally, in such situations, the same individual may entertain alternative interpretations and expectations and hence be drawn to more than one movement at a time.

In sum, I suggest that the *aims* of transformative and redemptive movements are closely related to the deprivation history of the groups to which they appeal. The choice among *types* of movements, and, in the case of transformative movements, of *models* of transformation, the choice of *means* for movements aiming at system change, and a variety of other features are related far more closely to the social context of the deprivation and are not in theory predictable only from a knowledge of the deprivation itself. It would seem that transformative movements are likely when groups are being forced out of the socio-economic or ecological niches they occupy into more marginal niches, whereas redemptive movements are likely to appeal when groups are forced into new niches in a larger social framework.

Chapter 20

PEYOTISM RE-EXAMINED

THE GENERAL APPROACH to social movements just developed has five basic elements: a definition of social movements, a classification of social movements, a theory regarding the coherence of clusters of attributes of transformative and redemptive movements, respectively, a classification of types of deprivation, and a theory as to the relationship between context and type of deprivation on the one hand, and choice of type of movement and of elements of movements on the other. It should be examined in the light of a large number of social movements, but such an effort lies beyond the scope of an attempt to describe and analyze Navaho peyotism.

At a minimum, however, two things may be demanded of this approach. First, the classification should emphasize certain features of peyotism not brought out quite so clearly by other approaches to the subject. Second, since it emerged in close conjunction with the effort to analyze Navaho peyotism, it should at least fit the Navaho data. This is not a test of the theory, although in point of fact certain details of Navaho history fell into place for me only after the theory was developed.

We will begin with the first topic, taking up the second in a subsequent chapter. In the context of the discussion of social movements, peyotism emerges as a redemptive movement. Its goal is not, and seems never to have been, a totally transformed social order. Rather, through moral reform, proper worship, illumination, association with fellow peyotists, and some reduction of the intimacy of relationships with non-peyotists, the members of the Native American Church desire to create a better way of life for themselves. They further hope to extend this way to other potential believers.

For the most part, peyotism is not concerned with an earthly paradise, created either by its members' efforts or by supernatural intervention, nor with the triumph of the Kingdom of God in the last days. Such elements are not entirely absent in peyotism, however. Some peyotists believe that when all Indians have eaten peyote, the Kingdom of God will come on earth. Before this, there will be a war of whites against each other, but Jesus commands that Indians remain aloof from the fight (Slotkin, 1956, p. 113). Some Navaho peyotists believe that the whites are headed for catastrophe because of their materialism, science, and war-like tendencies, and one told me that after a catastrophic world war brought on by whites, the Indians will survive and live happily. But by and large, peyotism seeks a more satisfying way of life for Indian individuals in this world, in spite of the difficulties that confront Indians.

Peyotism cannot be described as reformative, since its only organized efforts at institutional change are those aimed at altering the legal status of the cult itself.

Groups like the Navajo Rights Association, the National Congress of American Indians, and the Indian Rights Association are reformative movements among Indians.

Peyotism also is not alterative. It does not believe in changes of individual habits alone, although actively interested in a number of such habits, but sees changes of belief, custom, behavior, and style of life as proceeding from a change of inner state.

Although undoubtedly some people come to peyote meetings only to be cured, there is ample testimony in anthropological studies that an inner transformation is one of the major goals of the Native American Church. This often occurs through sudden illuminations, but it is also thought of as continuing throughout life. This goal identifies peyotism as a redemptive movement. Whether the individual believes in the importance of visions, illuminations, or ruminative reflection, it is eating peyote that brings about the state of mind that permits redemption. It permits right thought, clear thought, and communication with God. It would be incorrect to assume that in every case redemption involves the experiencing of severe guilt, the rejection of past sin, and the liquidation of guilt. This is one kind of inner transformation, but not the only one. Where relevant, reflection on past sins and rejection of them is expected, but in any case self-evaluation and re-direction is expected of the ideologically committed peyotist. Much of the process of self-evaluation and re-direction takes place in a relationship with redeemed individuals: through discussion of experiences with other peyotists after a meeting. Reduction of interaction with non-peyotists is a fairly marked feature of peyotism and one which occasions much bitterness among non-members. As membership stabilizes in a community and the individual's new outlook is also stabilized, this reduction of interaction may become less evident. Nevertheless, there is always some feeling on the part of the peyotist that he cannot really communicate the nature of his experience to the non-peyotist, and that the non-peyotist can learn and understand only through eating peyote. Hence anthropologists studying the cult are under heavy pressure to eat peyote.

The redeemed are other peyotists. At least in theory, they are valued irrespective of tribal affiliation. Peyote meetings with intertribal participation are common where the situation makes this easy. Navaho meetings are seldom intertribal, because of relatively infrequent contact with other peyotist tribes, but road men from other tribes are accorded high prestige. Navahos visiting other tribes take pleasure in participating in peyote meetings there. (There are, of course, signs of critical attitudes between groups, tribal or other, which have different ritual practices or beliefs.) Furthermore, since peyotism is meant for Indians, the potential redeemed are conceived of as mainly, although not absolutely exclusively, Indians. Both in terms of practice and ideology, peyotism is pan-Indian (cf. Slotkin, 1956, p. 7; Newcomb, 1956).

Peyotism rejects at least these values of the dominant society: its emphasis on the goals of full acculturation and assimilation; its assumption that non-Western ways are inferior; its emphasis on materialism; its emphasis on learning rather than on insight as a technique of understanding the world. (Cult members have never been able entirely to give up the hope of gaining white acceptance, however. This is demonstrated by the warm welcome given to most white observers who indicate a lack of antagonism to the cult, by the appeal to the newspapers made by Navahos hard-pressed by their own tribesmen, and by the occasional efforts of peyotist groups to be accepted among the Protestant churches.)

Although in this sense peyotism turns its face from the white world, it has an ethic that is adaptive for the present condition of many American Indian groups. Its stress on abstinence from alcohol, on work, and on responsibility for one's family is adaptive for groups partially integrated into a market economy. Its stress on limited generosity, mutual aid, and sexual morality, is suited to the partially egalitarian community where social controls have partly broken down, in which so many Indians live or on which they ultimately depend in economic crises. Its emphasis on an internalized ethic is suited to the breakdown of traditional social controls.

Slotkin considers the ethical core of peyotism to involve the stress on hard work, self-support, care of family, and abstinence from alcohol (1956, p. 71). My most articulate Navaho informants and respondents repeatedly stressed these same issues. For that reason I shall emphasize these elements of the moral code, which are clearly adaptive for contemporary Indians. Nevertheless, it should be mentioned that some workers do not find these elements strongly developed, or at all developed in the groups with which they have worked. In describing the Antlers, Mead, for example, brings out the rejection of drinking, gambling, and illicit sexual activities, but also says that peyotism led to neglect of poultry and stock and made men unfit for work after a meeting (Mead, 1932, pp. 106–112). And there is a complaint in the Indian Service files from an agent who claimed that his most indigent, immoral, and ne'er-do-well charges were peyotists—alongside a report from another agent that in his area, peyotists were his most outstanding citizens.

Peyotism, then, is a redemptive movement with an ideology suited to its context. This ideology is also suited to the deprivations encountered by American Indians.

Deprivation of possessions is apparent for American Indians. Whether they take a long-range perspective and recall—as many do—that "once Indians owned all this land," or a shorter-range perspective and recall events as recent as Navaho livestock reduction, or even compare themselves with neighboring whites, they are, in the majority of cases, on the losing end as regards possessions. The ideology of peyotism as respects this deprivation has the best of two worlds. On the one hand, there is derogation of white preoccupation with material possessions and an identification of material poverty with spiritual wealth. On the other, appropriate prayer may bring the individual material welfare through God's blessing. (Although not every group uses peyote as a ritual means of getting material goods—for example the Delaware do not—this use of peyote seems to have been early, among the Arapaho at the turn of the century, for example—Petrullo, 1934, p. 127; Kroeber, 1907, p. 408. Navahos certainly pray at peyote meetings for material prosperity.)

Deprivation of status is variable among American Indian groups. In the Plains in the 1880's it was acute, as the means to validate or perpetuate old statuses disappeared with the going of raiding and hunting. For previously wealthy Navahos in the 1930's and thereafter, it was also acute. For groups longer stabilized in their mode of livelihood, it is not necessarily severe. For younger Indians, it may be insofar as they do not feel they can attain the position, either within or outside the tribe, to which their education entitles them. Peyotism offers positions of status within the group as compensation for those who have lost status outside it, or who cannot gain the status they think they should have. The organizational roles of the Native American Church and the ritual roles of road chief, particularly, and to a lesser degree of cedar chief, fire chief, and drummer chief, afford positions ensuring social recognition within the group. The relatively modest financial costs of putting up a peyote meeting leave it as a mechanism for securing social recognition, as well. (Again there are exceptions; the costs of peyotism among the Antlers were high—Mead, 1932, pp. 106–112.)

As for behavioral deprivation, peyotism responds both to the decline of morality (we do not behave as well as we once did) and to censure by whites (we do not behave as well as other groups do). I have already discussed how the internalized morality of peyotism acts as a counter to a condition where a morality reinforced by group pressure and interdependence is weakened as group ties break down. In addition, peyotism accepts the criticism of the outside world in its rejection of some native beliefs and practices as "superstitious" or "backward" or ineffective. Thus peyotists reject Navaho beliefs about the spirits of the dead and about burial, and tend to accept some white criticisms of Navaho hygiene. Needless to say this acceptance of outside criticism does not earn white respect, because of the insistence of peyotists on Indian rather than Western ritual forms and on the consumption of peyote.

With reference to worth, it is fair to say that Indians are regarded unfavorably in American society just because they are Indians. If they are perfectly acculturated, they are far more fully and easily accepted than Negroes, but there is prejudice directed against them. (It is in general weaker against mixed-bloods to the degree that they resemble the dominant white majority in appearance.) Thus there is deprivation in the area of worth. The response to this is, of course, the assertion of the worth of the Indian, phrased in terms of culture and of blood. There is also a counter-exclusion in some instances. Petrullo, for instance, was told that he would not have been permitted to attend a peyote meeting in one community had it not been believed that he was an American Indian (Petrullo, 1934, pp. v–vi). That this attitude is not universal is demonstrated by Slotkin's election to the position of Delegate at Large in the Native American Church of North America (Slotkin, 1956, p. 64). The assertion of worth, combined with constant interaction of peyotists, provides a counter to external prejudice and gives the individual a social context where his high worth is repeatedly underscored.

Peyotism, then, is a redemptive movement, a religion of Indians involved in, but not full participants in the white world. It provides a validation of their partial separation and identity, an ethic adaptive to their social position, and a set of compensations for their most pressing deprivations.

Before we turn to examine some of the implications of this classification of peyotism, one qualification should be noted. There are undoubtedly groups for which peyotism is no longer a movement—where, far from proselytizing, it attempts at most to hold the younger generation and to resist efforts to eliminate the cult. This seems to have been the case among the Antlers in 1929 (Mead, 1932, p. 109), whatever the situation may be there today, and for the Menomini in the early

1950's (Slotkin, 1952, p. 575). A static or declining cult is a redemptive religion, but by definition it is no longer a redemptive movement. This is so because the basic goal of a redemptive movement is the cure of souls, accomplished against the resistance of the potential candidate for redemption and the resistance of the unredeemed. A redemptive movement that stops proselytizing stops being a movement.

To call peyotism a redemptive movement does not change its nature, but may result in a fresh perspective on it. First, it puts the Native American Church in the context of other redemptive movements, whether or not they have nativistic ideologies, and hence may result in new theories about peyotism or about such movements in general. One such theory has been advanced earlier and will be examined in the light of Navaho data: the theory that many redemptive movements have an element of protest and that those which do not practice withdrawal from the world have an ethic adaptive for people being forced into a new and ambivalently regarded niche. It permits the exploration of these commonalities, rather than forcing the comparison of peyotism with other nativistic movements.

Second, it distinguishes peyotism as a redemptive movement from other movements with transformative goals, whether nativistic or not, and raises the question of the circumstances under which redemptive or transformative goals are sought. This topic, too, will be examined in the light of Navaho data.

Third, it points toward a re-examination of more familiar classifications for peyotism. Peyotism is usually considered a nativistic movement; it has been called a revitalization movement; its orientation has been described as accommodative or passive, by contrast with active, oppositional, or militant movements. Each of these characterizations is illuminating, but each also obscures some features of peyotism.

If peyotism is a nativistic movement, the problem is, What meaning shall we attach to the word "nativism"? Before we turn to this question, there is one major fact about peyotism that deserves attention: in most groups it seems to have spread against the opposition of traditionalists. As a sample, traditional opposition has occurred in at least the following tribes: Taos, Kiowa, Comanche, Northern and Southern Cheyenne, Menomini, Omaha, Pawnee, Arikara, Sauk, Yankton, and Sioux (all from La Barre, 1938, pp. 110–121; use of other sources would vastly multiply the instances). Indeed it is probably fair to say that the day-to-day opposition that peyotists have met in tribe after tribe comes primarily from traditionalist members of these tribes, rather than from whites. (In tribes with strong Christian groups, it would be a nice decision as to whether most day-to-day opposition came from Christian or from traditional Indians.) The Navaho case is not unique.

Peyotism, then, is a movement which most anthropologists would call nativistic; yet one of its principal enemies has been the native population most desirous of perpetuating traditional cultural forms. Under these circumstances, it seems worthwhile to examine some definitions of nativistic movements.

Linton defined a nativistic movement as "Any conscious, organized attempt on the part of a society's members to revive or perpetuate selected aspects of its culture" (1943, p. 230). In this sense, peyotism as it enters each new Indian group is not a nativistic movement—nor, in fact, did Linton ever use peyotism as an example in his article. It is a conscious, organized attempt on the part of Indians to perpetuate a cultural component which many of them interpret as part of the *Indian* past, but which is emphatically not a part of the past culture of the groups which it newly penetrates. After peyotism has been established for a generation, however, the effort to *retain* peyotism may be termed a perpetuative nativistic movement, in Linton's terms. But to do so is to make the assumption that the primary goal of peyotism is retention of peyotism, whereas it seems more reasonable to infer that its primary goal is the cure of souls and bodies through the vehicle of peyotism.

Voget includes peyotism in his category of "reformative" nativism. Reformative nativism is a "relatively conscious attempt on the part of a subordinated group to attain a personal and social reintegration through a selective rejection, modification, and synthesis of both traditional and alien (dominant) cultural components" (1956, p. 250). Again peyotism seems to fit this category with only a little cramming. Peyotists, of course, do not aim completely to replace the native culture, but only certain features of, or the whole of the religio-magical complex. Hence it may be argued that selective rejection and modification of traditional cultural components is involved. Peyotists also do not aim at total rejection of all white culture. Hence the same argument may be advanced as respects selective rejection and modification of alien (dominant) cultural components. And from the point of view of the observer, at least, there is a synthesis of some native and some dominant cultural components. But the definition omits the fact that peyotism involves the importation of alien (non-dominant) cultural components—peyote ritual and belief—and it is this set of components that so often creates a storm among traditionalists and modernists when peyotism enters a new tribe. Nevertheless, Voget's treatment of "reformative" movements is quite similar to mine of redemptive movements, and his stress elsewhere in his article on the innovative character of the reformative movement aligns his views and mine fairly closely. The only issue is the problem of definition.

Here Slotkin perhaps comes closest to the position taken here. "The subordinate ethnic group attempts to overthrow the domination-subordination relation culturally by means of *nativistic nationalism*. In the first place, a culture is created as a symbol of the ethnic group. I say 'created' because it is self-conscious and deliberate, and because acculturation has produced such a degree of culture change that it is impossible to revive the traditional culture" (1956, p. 6, italics supplied). His further analysis has parallels with Voget's treatment of the place of reformative nativism, concluding that peyotism "socially is an example of accommodation rather that militancy; culturally . . . it is a case of Pan-Indian nativism" (1956, p. 7). Thus for Slotkin the core elements are that certain created cultural features stand for the ethnic group, and that they are used in a context of protest against dominance-submission relationships. Slotkin does not require the culture thus created to be the real past or present traditional culture of the group involved, although in some of his examples it is part of the real past of at least one sub-group of a larger nativistic protest group. The only difficulty with Slotkin's formulation is that it does not seem proper to characterize peyotism as a culture, rather than as a component of culture or a culture complex.

The point of view set forth by Voget and Slotkin contrasts with certain earlier perspectives on peyotism, for example those quoted at the beginning of Chapter 16.

These statements, too, contain important truths. Modern peyotism is a blend of Indian prototypes and Christian elements, and it is a religion of transition in that the generations of peyotists in each tribe stand between non-peyotist traditionalists and more Westernized types. But what should be brought out sharply is the peculiar character of peyotist nativism. For the first-generation peyotist, peyotism is not an effort to retain traditional culture. It involves a sharp break with this culture, often with belittling of traditional religio-magical figures and practices—as Voget points out. It is not an effort to retain the past because it is familiar. Nor is it a self-conscious effort at achieving a transitional stage. It is an effort at personal integration, achieved through a ritual and symbol system which is self-consciously *not* that of the dominant culture, and *not* that of the peyotist's native culture. It cannot be that of the dominant culture, because that culture is rejected in significant aspects. It cannot be that of the native culture because it no longer works: the old integration of subsistence technology, social organization, and ideology cannot operate, for reasons having to do with relationships to the dominant culture. It can be Christian, because from the peyotist perspective the universalism of Christian ideology is accepted: Jesus was a savior for all mankind, and God is the God of all human beings—He created man with five fingers.

The tendency to look on peyotism more in terms of cultural retention than in terms of cultural innovation used in the service of opposition seems to stem from two sources. The first is that most anthropologists studied peyotism after it had been long established in an area. By the time the cult has been established for thirty years or so, its adherents are indeed upholding a traditional element against the opposition of modernists. But when peyotism is introduced, its proponents must take up what is foreign and uphold it against what is traditional.

The second is that, beginning with Shonle (1925), anthropologists have been impressed by the similarities between peyotism and the Plains vision quest and between peyote ritual and Plains ritual in general—this in spite of the fact that the specific antecedents of peyotist ritual—except where it is Christian—have yet to be discovered. This approach leads easily to the assumption that peyotism is accepted and retained because it resembles a familiar prototype, rather than accepted and retained because of or in spite of the fact that it seems alien. Only Stewart has raised the question of the basis for judging two cultural phenomena to be similar or dissimilar (1944), and his challenge has not been taken up. The controversy regarding the importance of the vision in Plains religion and peyotism requires close analysis, but I shall not attempt to provide it here (cf. La Barre [1960] for a review of the problem). It should be said, however, that there are two perspectives for judging degree of similarity, the anthropologist's and the Indian's. Indians, at least, differ in their judgments. Some Navaho cult members, and especially singers, claim that peyotism is "just like" Navaho ceremonialism, only better; many peyotists and all non-peyotists find it utterly different. It is highly probable that parallel reactions are to be found in other tribes.

So long as nativism is conceived of as a matter of opposition, which may attempt to use actual present or past culture as a vehicle for expression, or which may attempt to use cultural diacriticals which are essentially new materials, the label seems perfectly appropriate. But if the stress is on retention of the familiar or revival of the group's own past, the word does not properly describe first-generation peyotism. For those who have grown up as peyotists, the cult is properly labelled perpetuative nativism.

Peyotism has also been called a revitalization movement. The problem with this classification is that if peyotism is, so is virtually any social movement. For Wallace, a revitalization movement is a "deliberate, organized, conscious effort by members of a society to construct a more satisfying culture" (Wallace, 1956b, p. 265). As in the case of Slotkin's comments on nativistic nationalism, the claim that peyotism is an effort "to construct a more satisfying culture" is too great. Peyotism has a ritual, an ethic, an organization, and a goal—the achieving of a state of bodily health and personal grace. If this is an effort to create a more satisfying culture, so, surely, is the movement for the secret ballot, for city management, for phonemic script, and so on. Although Wallace explicitly includes peyotism among the revitalization movements, the thrust of his article is the analysis of transformative movements and of movements like that of Handsome Lake, which blend reformation and redemption. The label does us the service of bringing many kinds of movements under one head, but this very breadth demands sub-categories, those supplied here or others.

Various writers speak of peyotism as passive (e.g., Barber, 1941b). Slotkin calls it accommodative, saying that it had a "program of accommodation, as opposed to the Ghost Dance's program of opposition . . ." (1956, p. 21). The difficulties here have to do with the separation of actor's and observer's point of view, and of aim and activity.

Again both Barber's and Slotkin's labels are illuminating and helpful. It is quite true, as both argue, that the Ghost Dance did expect the disappearance of the white man and was interpreted as a threat, whereas peyotism does not expect this disappearance—or not at once—and is seen as obnoxious rather than as threatening. And it is probable, but not certain, that this difference does have to do with the collapse of the Ghost Dance and the continued vitality of peyotism. (The Ghost Dance, like many another transformative movement, might have undergone reinterpretation and emerged as an effective redemptive movement. It did not, perhaps because peyotism had already assumed the place that such a re-worked Ghost Dance might have taken.) But the labels, again, fail to do complete justice to the facts. With minor exceptions, the Ghost Dance had a *program* of accommodation, quite specifically. Its adherents were counseled to do nothing unfriendly to the whites. The final end was to be accomplished magically, after which the white man would be eliminated, or driven beyond this continent, or the Indian and the white man would dwell together in perfect peace—versions vary. It had an *aim* of opposition: it utterly opposed Western civilization and sought through magical means to eliminate it completely (Mooney, 1896). Peyotism does not have an *aim* of accommodation, nor does it have a *program* of accommodation. Its aim is a state of grace; its attitude toward the dominant culture is one of rejection; it responds to efforts to eliminate the use of peyote with opposition; and many of its members express a generalized antagonism to whites and white ways. (At various times Navaho peyotists have discussed with me their distrust of whites, their hostility to white values, their rejection of Navaho ceremonies and ceremonialists, and their hostility to the Indian Service, the Navajo Tribal Council, local [non-peyotist] chapter officers, and livestock reduction.) The program of peyotism is the cure of souls and bodies, the gaining of new members, the proper socialization of the young, and activity to combat those who would eliminate it. It is accommodative not because it has a program of accommodation but because it does *not* have an aim or a program of elimination of whites. The *effect* of its program is accommodation. As a redemptive, not a transformative or reformative movement, it lacks such an aim or program almost by definition.

The classification of peyotism as a redemptive movement, then, highlights the oppositional character of its choice of symbols and values, joins it with non-ethnic redemptive movements, and separates it from transformative movements, the other major class with which anthropologists have been most concerned.

Chapter 21

SOCIAL MOVEMENTS AMONG THE NAVAHO: PEYOTISM RE-EXAMINED

THE FINAL APPLICATION of the approach outlined in Chapter 19 is a re-examination of the Navaho case. This re-examination asks three questions: What major deprivations have the Navaho experienced since 1864 and when have deprivations been lacking? What has been the context of Navaho life—the relationship of the Navaho system to that of the dominant society since 1864? What movements, quasi-movements, and transitory excitements have occurred since 1864? The examination, however, will not proceed through a separate treatment of each question, but by means of a running narrative and analysis.

In terms of deprivation, the Navaho captivity at Fort Sumner must be ranked as a cataclysmic deprivation in every area of life. Yet no transformative movement is known to have arisen at the time. The Mescalero, confined at Fort Sumner at the same time, did have a transitory prophetic excitement. Toward the end of a flu epidemic which did not result in Apache fatalities, a medicine man told the Mescalero that the Great Spirit would exterminate them through disease if they did not leave Fort Sumner—their punishment for remaining as prisoners of the Americans (Cremony, 1954, pp. 233–236; I am indebted to Kunstadter, 1960, p. 35 for the reference). It is not clear when the epidemic occurred, or whether the Navahos were already at Fort Sumner, or whether they were also affected. Probably they were there and were affected; at any rate they experienced some illness while the Apache were at Fort Sumner and had a mild panic over illness while en route to Fort Sumner (*Condition of the Indian Tribes, 1867*, esp. pp. 337–355). The entire tenor of Cremony's account indicates that the medicine man seized upon the flu epidemic as a device to encourage Apache departure. It is evident that among the most serious pressures the Apaches faced at Fort Sumner, whether then or later, was the presence of large numbers of Navahos. The two groups were quite hostile to each other (Cremony, 1954; RCIA 1863–1866). Eventually the Apaches decamped—in November of 1865 (RCIA 1866, p. 133). It is not surprising that the Navahos did not imitate the Apaches, considering relations between the two groups, but an independent Navaho movement of the same sort could have arisen. The Navahos had a measles epidemic, which they attributed to the unhealthy locale at Fort Sumner (Reeve, 1938, p. 20). The Apache affair cannot be classified as transformative; a simple reformative effort, getting out from under, is involved, and the prophecy did not constitute a movement. According to Cremony, the prophet was discredited (1954, p. 236).

There are several possible reasons why a transformative movement did not develop among the Navaho. The first is that the theory is inadequate. The second is that it takes a while for reactions to deprivations to be translated into a social movement (cf. Wallace, 1956b on Delaware reactions). The third is that such a movement is unlikely to occur during a period of literal captivity—but the Mescalero prophecy indicates that at least stirrings might occur. The fourth is that transitory prophetic stirrings might have occurred among the Navaho but might not have been recorded—only Cremony, so far as I have been able to discover, mentions the Apache case.

The fifth, and by far the most probable in this instance, is that, for good and sufficient reasons the Navahos never ceased to hope and expect that they would be returned to their homeland. There was a serious division in the Indian Office in New Mexico, and among the citizens of New Mexico, as to the wisdom of the Fort Sumner experiment. One party wanted the Navahos returned to a portion of their homeland (RCIA 1863–68). It is impossible that the Navahos could have been kept from knowing that some people favored their return. By 1868, they seem to have been preparing to decamp in any case: they planted no grain that spring (RCIA 1868, p. 621). Whatever the explanation, the devastating captivity at Fort Sumner failed to produce a transformative movement. There may have been an organized reformative movement—to decamp—which would parallel the Mescalero instance.

From 1868, the release from Fort Sumner, to 1933, the beginnings of livestock reduction, the Navaho situation was a relatively unusual and favorable one for a group of Indians in the United States. They were permitted to return to their old territory after American domination, where their technology and social organization permitted them to adapt to conquest without radical changes.

Furthermore, unlike any other Indian group in the United States known to me, their history after domination was one of expansion of tribal lands, rather than of cession. Unlike most groups, they did not experience the typical sequence of cession, individual allotment, and further loss of land. And unlike many, they did not suffer repeated relocations. After Fort Sumner they were never relocated; instead they expanded into one adjoining area after another. The Reservation remains unallotted. These features of the Navaho condition rest on several bases. Their own territory and the surrounding area were marginal from the point of view of American agriculture and herding, so that white competition for the land was slight for many decades after conquest. (They did lose irrevocably the eastern and best part of their former territory.) No mineral wealth of any consequence was discovered in the Navaho country until after the period of speedy expropriation of Indians had terminated. The surrounding area did not lend itself easily to urbanization and industrialization. All these features can be summarized under one heading: alternative and more productive uses of the land by members of the dominant society did not exist when expropriation would have been easy.

In addition, in spite of many subsistence crises, the technology, gradually supplemented by American tools, provided a base in agriculture and herding sufficient to maintain life and to provide a surplus for acquiring tools, wagons, cloth, household utensils, and so on. Except for the expansion of territory, the Navahos share these conditions and characteristics with the Pueblo Indians and a few other Southwestern tribes. (There was, of course, a serious threat to the Pueblos in the 1920's in the Bursum Bill.) These conditions account for the fact that the Southwest retains more "aboriginal culture" than any other area of the United States.

After the Fort Sumner captivity, in spite of settler pressures and many very bad seasons of near-starvation, the Navahos continued to grow in numbers, territory, and wealth, for many decades. During the early years they seem to have compared themselves favorably in some respects with the Apaches and Utes, who received more goods from the United States Government. But they seem to have regarded any possibility of loss of their territory as a much more serious matter, so that it was fairly easy for agents to discourage them from attempting to gain more issue from the Government by means of a major outbreak. For a number of years, small groups of Navahos tended to respond to deprivation or threatened deprivation by settler incursion or stock raiding by counter-violence, and not by magical means. Direct action was a typical Navaho response in other areas of life as well. In some instances, violence appears to have been used against traders, but rarely in any organized form involving more than two or three men. Local, organized opposition, sometimes by forceful means, was used against the Government from at least as early as the expulsion of Agent Arny in the 1870's to as late as the kidnapping of the District Supervisor in District 9 in the 1940's. In the 1890's and early 1900's there were signs of anti-acculturative local movements, in Black Horse's resistance to children's schooling, on two occasions, in the resistance to arrest of a polygynist at Beautiful Mountain, and in the By-a-lil-le disturbance of 1907. The first episode involving Black Horse was directed at Agent Shipley; the other three were directed at Agent Shelton, who became prominent at the San Juan Agency in the early 1900's. Shelton was an exceptionally vigorous and inflexible proponent of Americanization. Rejecting polygyny, long hair, casual divorce, failure of men to support children by previous marriages, and paganism, he stood for education, improved agriculture, monogamy, Protestant Christianity, and sobriety. In the Shiprock area, where material progress occurred because of his energy, he was regarded with ambivalence and with some admiration. Indeed a Tribal tourist court at Shiprock was named Nat'aani Nez, Tall Leader, after him. In more outlying areas like Aneth and the Carrizos, where By-a-lil-le and Black Horse lived, his strong arm was probably felt, but the benefits of his approach were not so visible. Even there, however, one man told Dyk with evident pleasure how he secured agricultural implements from Shelton by being willing to speak up and to demonstrate genuine willingness to use them (Dyk, 1947, p. 99).

In the action against Agent Shipley by Black Horse and in the By-a-lil-le case, there is at least a suggestion of the use of traditional magic against whites. Black Horse's men seem to have used customary war magic against the Agent as an enemy with whom they were preparing to do battle. They did not stop with magic: they barricaded the Agent and his party in a trading post and seemed prepared to go further. As has been said before, it is not clear whether By-a-lil-le attempted to work witchcraft against his enemies, Navaho and American. Black Horse seems to have been a fairly effective leader; By-a-lil-le, more of a terrorist, with a limited following. Both may properly be called leaders of evanescent reformative anti-acculturative efforts, wishing to return to no education and (in By-a-lil-le's case) to unrestricted polygyny. The uprising at Beautiful Mountain does not merit the term "movement"; it was a marvelously complicated case of resistance to arrest and fear of violent action by soldiery.

Black Horse and By-a-lil-le, then, presumably in response to the threat of loss of children (for Black Horse) and of behavioral deprivation (enforced and undesired change of customs) in By-a-lil-le's case, were leaders of small reformative movements, using empirical means supplemented by magic. No other organized, activist anti-acculturative movement is known to me, although there has always been a strain of passive resistance to schooling (until after World War II) and change of customs among the Navahos.

Indeed, between 1864 and the 1930's, there is only one approach to a transformative movement recorded for the Navaho. This episode occurred between 1920 and 1922.

It had more of the character of a mass panic than an organized movement, but it was associated with a transformative message. The information is scanty but interesting.

> Warned by an old medicine man, that on the third day of July, 1920, a great deluge would destroy all the white people and all Indians who remained on the desert, they [the Navahos in the Chaco Canyon area] packed up, bag and baggage, and broke for the western mountains. Horses and sheep were driven headlong, many cattle were left behind, crops abandoned at a considerable loss. As the great catastrophe did not come off according to schedule we witnessed them drifting back, rather sheepishly for some weeks (Hewett, 1936, p. 139).

Hewett does not say that this occurred in the Chaco, but he does say he witnessed it—and he worked in that area. Kluckhohn says that the same story "was told and believed by many, among the Ramah Navaho (two hundred odd miles away) at the same time" (1942, p. 59). He does not amplify the story. He collected it some years after the event, at a time when he was working with Alexander and Dorothea Leighton, a collaboration that began in the late 1930's or by 1940 (personal communication from Kluckhohn as to the circumstances of collecting; cf. Leighton and Leighton [1949, pp. v, xi] for early collaboration).

Fr. Berard supplies an abbreviated version, without date or location. He gives the visionary's name, Mexican John, says that he "dreamed of a flood which would wipe out the tribe," and implies that because the prophecy was not fulfilled, Mexican John was killed (Haile, 1940).

Another account, dated as summer of 1922, has been collected for the Kayenta area. At that time the Wetherills, traders at Kayenta, and their guests were surprised to see the Navahos fleeing past their trading post. The Navahos said they were going to Black Mountain to escape a flood. An old man from near Oljeto, who had been struck by lightning, had risen from apparent death to prophesy a coming flood. It was coming "from the great water to the east," they said, and went on, "You are a Navajo; come with us" (Gillmor and Wetherill, 1934, p. 234).

Mrs. Wetherill dissuaded many people by telling them that the Rocky Mountains were higher than Black Mountain. Hence they would act as a dam for a flood coming from the east. And if the flood washed over the Rockies, Black Mountain would be no help. A Navaho who had once traveled east with her supported her view. But others who did not pass by the Wetherill post did flee, and many cornfields were ruined for lack of care during the flight. Later, Mrs. Wetherill discovered that a "missionary had told the Navajos about Noah's Ark and a great flood that had come because of men's sins" (1934, p. 235). He had warned the Navahos that they were sinful and would be punished, and this, Mrs. Wetherill believed, had stimulated the old man's prophecy.

Subsequent correspondence with Frances Gillmor and with Mrs. Wetherill's sister, Nellie V. Coston (Mrs. Wetherill is dead) provided additional information. Mrs. Coston discussed the question of the date and distribution of the flood scare with her nephew, Jack J. Wade, whose father, Mrs. Coston's brother, operated a trading post at Sweetwater (Tolacon) near the Carrizo Mountains. She confirmed the 1922 date, but she referred to Gillmor and Wetherill (1934) in doing so. She said that the flood scare was reservation-wide. In some areas, Navahos fled to the Carrizo and Lukachukai Mountains; from Kayenta, they went to Black Mountain. At both Sweetwater and Kayenta, the Indians urged the Wades and the Wetherills, respectively, to join them, saying, "you are our friends."

The Hewett and Wetherill-Gillmor-Coston versions are broadly similar but differ in certain curious ways. In the first place, they are dated two years apart. It is hard to imagine that a catastrophic prophecy kept running about the reservation for two years—from Hewett's 1920 to Mrs. Wetherill's 1922, confirmed by Mrs. Coston. Hewett's date is likely to be right, since he worked in Chaco Canyon from 1919 to 1921—at any rate, it would be difficult for him to have witnessed the episode in 1922 if he left in 1921 (cf. Hewett, 1936, p. 65). Either the excitement did continue off and on for two years, or Mrs. Wetherill and Mrs. Coston are slightly in error. In the second place, it is curious that the Oljeto prophet should have believed that he originated the prophecy if the flight in the Kayenta-Oljeto area followed the Chaco Canyon flight by two years. Such vivid convictions of originality among prophets do, however, occur. The problem of chronology must be left there.

I suggested to Miss Gillmor that the phrase, "You are a Navajo; come along with us" seemed to imply an anti-white reaction. She replied that when Mrs. Wetherill told the story, she (Miss Gillmor) had no awareness of an anti-white reaction, and that Mrs. Wetherill's remark can be explained by her tendency to emphasize the strength of the Navahos' undoubted affection for her in all her stories of life as a trader. At any rate, the Hewett version is anti-white; the Wetherill version sounds as if it *could* be anti-white, but this interpretation is rejected by the person in the best position to know (Gillmor, personal communication). Miss Gillmor used this episode in a novel in which no element of antagonism to whites appears (Gillmor, 1930).

It seems reasonable to conclude that some time between 1920 and 1922, perhaps repeatedly, or just possibly in 1920 only, a good many Navahos from many parts of the reservation heard a prophecy of an imminent flood. As Gillmor points out in her novel, such floods are associated in Navaho mythology with removal to another world. At least some Navahos believed that all whites would be destroyed by the flood and at least some that the flood was a punishment to Navahos for their sins. This kind of prophecy is transformative in tendency, but there was no further development of organization, leadership, ritual, or movement. The only known sequelae were damaged crops and livestock.

In terms of symbolism, two features require attention. First, although Navahos know of the Pacific and of the Atlantic, the flood was to come from the waters to the east. It seems possible that eastern waters had some symbolic connection with whites. Second, in the Hewett version, the flood was to occur on July 3. (We do not know, of course, whether the prophet set it for July 3 or merely, say, for four days hence.) A flood that would destroy whites the day before the Fourth of July further suggests anti-white sentiment—attested, in any case, for this prophet.

The ordinary deprivations with which we have been concerned in this work do not seem to have been operating at this time. There is no evidence of special economic hardship or of special pressure from the administration.[1]

There was, however, one quite different and disturbing catastrophe in 1918–1919: the flu epidemic, which raged among the Navahos and killed unknown numbers. It made so powerful an impression on them that for many years it was one of two incidents used to estimate people's ages. The other was the Fort Sumner captivity. It is conceivable that so catastrophic an event could lead to a world-end fantasy, and that the knowledge that the disease came from the whites might have given an anti-white tinge to the fantasy. This interpretation must remain speculative at present. It would still be possible to gather recollections of this flight from older Navahos. Whatever its causes, it is the only known approach to a transformative movement among the Navahos prior to 1936.

As late as 1931, the Navaho response to overcrowding on the land remained empirical in orientation: in that year they went on at some length at Congressional hearings about their needs for more land and for water development.

The general picture from 1864 to 1933, then, is one of a group of Indians whose conditions improved, for the most part, during these sixty years. After release from captivity, they succeeded repeatedly in enlarging their lands until the 1910's, their herds until a later date, although we cannot be quite sure on this score, and their population, continually. They could sell livestock, wool, silver, piñons, and labor. Their trajectory was upward for many years; there may have been a flattening in the 1910's and even a downturn in the 1920's and early 1930's, but it is evident that the Navaho expectation was of more land, more water, and more stock until 1933. A comparison of past and present condition, or present and future condition during those years would not have given rise to feelings of deprivation. That some poor Navahos felt deprived, there can be little doubt. But since the Government for the most part ruled lightly, since when it did not, Navahos did not seem to feel powerless, and since the poverty of some Navahos did not appear to result from relations with whites (except perhaps in the eastern off-reservation area), deprivations were seen as personal, not as stemming from some alien irresistible force. Such, at least, seems to be a legitimate inference. To the degree that Navahos compared themselves with other Indian groups with which they were in contact, the comparison during most of these years, would have led to feelings of enhancement, not deprivation.

[1] In early 1922, Albert B. Fall, Harding's Secretary of Interior, had taken the position that executive orders reserving land for Indians were completely revokable; subsequently, in 1922, the Bursum Bill, which would have had disastrous effects on Pueblo land and water rights—but not Navaho—was introduced in Congress but was defeated in 1923 (Collier, 1963, pp. 128–135). These events, which might possibly have had repercussions on the Navaho, came too late to be connected with the first prophecy in 1920.

Although, early on, they may have felt they got less issue from the Government than Utes or Apaches, they would presumably notice—if they had opportunity for any observations—that there was no land expansion in these areas, nor in the Pueblos, that for many of these years populations among these groups were static or decreasing, and that some of these groups suffered unhappy relocations, and in the case of some Apaches, imprisonment.

Beginning in 1933, deprivation and the anticipation of deprivation in the area of goods and of status (for the better-off Navahos) became features of the scene. The source of this deprivation was unmistakably the Bureau of Indian Affairs and the new consolidated Navajo Agency of 1935. Quite specifically, the personal agents of deprivation were seen as John Collier, the Commissioner, and E. Reeseman Fryer, the head of the consolidated agency from 1936 on.

Furthermore, in certain respects, these deprivations were set in a context of disengagement from the larger society. The depression had begun; prices for livestock, meat, and wool, and presumably for silver, blankets, and piñon nuts had dropped. And it can be assumed that the job market, which did not then engage too many Navahos in any case, must have been affected, with fewer jobs and lower wages. Furthermore, as resistance to livestock reduction increased, the role of the chapters, which had given Navahos a means of expression, was decreased by the Agency. Under these circumstances—a catastrophic deprivation in the areas of goods and status, and a reduced involvement in the market for goods and labor in the larger society—the stage would appear to be set for social movements, including transformative ones. Decreased involvement in the larger society would make it possible for some Navahos to imagine the disappearance of the whites.

But other elements must be considered. First, Collier's job program resulted in new involvements with the larger society for many Navahos—not necessarily, as they pointed out, the same ones who lost their livestock and their market for livestock. Second, Collier worked for an enlarged and more representative Tribal Council. Whatever the distrust of many Navahos for the new Council and its mechanisms, it did involve them more in Tribal affairs, counterbalancing somewhat the exclusion of chapters from decision-making. Third, in the early years, some Navahos who had not yet felt the full weight of Government pressure, could think in terms of direct, empirical action to resist reduction. Fourth, Navahos with experience of white ways could think in terms of organized protest through normal channels and formal organization.[2]

Under these circumstances, where disengagement in some respects and heightened engagement in others occurred almost simultaneously, where various experiences led to various thoughts of counteraction, a number of alternative responses seem to have been engendered.

At some point during these years, Jacob C. Morgan organized the Navajo Rights

[2] There is no intention to make livestock reduction as such, John Collier, or the Bureau of Indian Affairs the villains of this piece. Livestock reduction would have had a different impact had other alternatives existed for Navahos, but they were trained for none and none existed. It would have had a different impact had it occurred more slowly and with genuine consultation of Navahos. As a distinguished fighter for Indian rights, Collier needs no defense here. And the ambit of actions open to the Indian Service is circumscribed by Congress, by the American economic system, and by the fact that Indians exert minuscule power by comparison with whites.

Association, a secular, empirically oriented reformative organization. I have not been able to gather enough information to know how it was organized, or when, or exactly what its program was. Its principal support was northern and eastern—in Districts 9, 12, 13, and down Highway 666 through Districts 14 and 16. It also drew support in District 15, hard-pressed by ranchers who were eager for more land. Its program was undoubtedly anti-reduction, anti-Collier, anti-Fryer, and anti-"Government socialism, communism, collectivism, and atheism," anti–day-school, anti–consolidated agency. It was undoubtedly pro-livestock, pro–enlargement of the reservation, pro–six-agency system, pro–boarding school, and pro–twenty-, rather than pro–ten-acre allotments of irrigated land at Fruitland. It operated through letter-writing to Congressmen, through Morgan's appearances at Congressional hearings, through campaigns to elect Morgan chairman, and (I assume) through protest meetings. Morgan also got publicity in newspapers.

Organized resistance to the taking of stock records and to reduction occurred, but was episodic in character. Each such episode might be termed a small reformative movement in the empirical mode, aimed at eliminating permits or reduction or both. One almost terminated in the death of a Superintendent. Threats against Fryer's life were uttered by a group on at least one occasion.

The Tribal Council's actions throughout the period after 1935 and until today may be seen as a continuous reformative movement, aimed at ameliorating the conditions of reduction, grazing regulation, and livestock control. There has been some slight success.

In addition to all these reformative efforts, there were elements suggestive of the beginnings of transformative movements, and there was one major redemptive movement—peyotism.

The transformative features have been described in Chapter 5. In one case in 1936 or 1937 a woman had a vision in which she was told that the whole world was in a decline because people did not live right or think right. A revised version of Blessing Way was to be held to improve rainfall and grass and to promote increase of livestock. This was done. The decline and renewal of the world have a transformative cast. The adjuration to hold new ceremonies suggests the faint beginnings of a magical, transformative movement. There is nothing anti-white in the movement—the woman's second vision told her that the Government's work would have a good outcome sooner or later. A vision of Jesus Christ during livestock reduction is anti-white and also suggests transformation: Jesus promised to lead the Navahos out of the troubles made for them by whites—although he was, in the vision, a Caucasian. The first visionary had a ritual program; we know of none in the second case, so that it cannot be called a movement. A third vision of a field of skulls of white men killed by the Japanese, the sons of Changing Woman, is clearly anti-white and has a transformative character—there is certainly more than a hint of the elimination of the whites. But again no movement is known to have ensued. There may have been two other visionaries, but there are no data sufficient to characterize the visions. Only one of these events led to even a transitory movement; nothing further has been heard publicly of either visionaries or ritual innovations. If livestock reduction had not been accompanied by a variety of ameliorative efforts that increasingly involved Navahos in Government-directed work programs, it seems possible that the reduction might have led to a magical transformative movement. The conditions for wishing away the whites were present in slight degree, but other conditions developed early and strong, so that transformative reactions were weak and other types of reactions prominent.

Peyotism began its spread south of the San Juan in 1936. At least in District 9 it was early employed as a magical defense against livestock reduction: a technique for discovering the plans of Washington and Window Rock. It has continued to spread since then, but not as a magical technique for dealing with Government. Its appeal up to 1953 was especially, but not exclusively, to those who were deprived of possessions and status through livestock reduction.[3]

But the context in which it has been spreading is one in which the Navaho economy has at last begun to resemble that of so many other reservation groups. The Navahos, too, can survive neither wholly on, nor wholly off the reservation. They cannot gain a living from subsistence activities. They can rarely move fully into stable wage-labor in cities. And they cannot forego their subsistence activities, lest they should have to fall back on these resources. Old ways of gaining status are no longer available. New ways are available only to a few. The bonds of kinship and reciprocity are weakened by the individuation of wage labor, but they are not dissolved because of needs for mutual aid. And, in increasing numbers, Navahos meet anti-Indian prejudice in forms more damaging than the hostility they often encountered in making trips to town for enjoyment or for purchasing. Navahos today are deprived in goods, status, behavior, and worth. An ethic of work and family responsibility is needed in a situation where so many adult men (and quite a few women) must take jobs for at least part of the year.

Peyotism, for seventy years a redemptive movement adapted to, and adaptive for, just such contexts, has once again been accepted by a portion of an American Indian tribe. The more sophisticated peyotists have thereby chosen an Indian, not a Navaho, identity. Through the Native American Church, its Navaho members find guidance in life, a new identity, a new reference group for assessing status, assurance of worth, and an ethic appropriate to their present mode of existence. Possibly the mineral assets of the Navaho country may provide Navahos with a livelihood more satisfying materially than their present one, but the multiple appeal of peyotism makes it likely that Navahos will continue to be attracted to the cult for some time to come.

[3] It is notable that both visions and peyotism followed so closely on reduction. Peyotism, of course, was "waiting in the wings" across the San Juan, but the visions were local innovations.

Chapter 22

CONCLUSION

THE NATIVE AMERICAN CHURCH OF NORTH AMERICA has proved itself to be a durable movement of great vitality, whose spread to new Indian groups continues today. It arose in more or less its present form during the early reservation period on the Plains—during a period when Indians not only found themselves confined to reservations but also found their older subsistence technologies and economies inadequate to cope with the size and character of their shrunken and changed resources. Unlike many supernaturally-oriented movements generated by American Indian groups after conquest, the church is redemptive, rather than transformative, or even reformative. In Lanternari's apt phrase, it is a religion of the oppressed. It rejects local traditional culture and is rejected by cultural conservatives; it rejects major features of our own culture and is rejected by it. And it seems to provide an ethic adjustive for people in the condition of American Indians.

Its use of a cactus that produces unusual physiological and psychological reactions has stimulated great interest and great opposition by Indians and whites alike. This cactus is best understood as a religious adjunct which endows the user with the feeling that his experiences during the peyote ritual are rich in personal significance. In addition, the experience of taking a "powerful" substance probably contributes to the expectation of cure and to the tendency to attribute cure to peyote. At present there is no evidence of addiction to peyote, or any satisfactory evidence of harm from it or physical benefit from it. Testimony amply supports the existence of feelings of spiritual, physical, and psychological benefit in most users.

The Navahos, who make up the largest Indian tribe in the United States, have had a fate unlike that of most American Indian groups. Living after conquest in an area which represented part of their old domain, they have seen their property, land, and population increase over many years. Correlatively, from 1868, when they returned to their home territory, until the 1930's, they manifested no genuine, full-blown social movement attempting to deal with the post-conquest situation— which distinguishes them from many, but certainly by no means all, of the other American Indian groups. Beginning in 1933, livestock reduction, imposed by the Government as a response to overgrazing and erosion which continued for many years, created a profound disturbance among the Navaho.

The peyote cult, already available among the Southern Utes for some years, and known to some Navahos north of the San Juan for a few years, spread south of the San Juan in 1936, at more or less the same time that systematic, as opposed to spasmodic, reduction began. By 1951, it had reached perhaps 14 per cent of the tribe. It continues to spread, reaching new adherents in new and old areas. Estimates by peyotists in 1964 ranged from 25 per cent to nearly 50 per cent of the tribe. Although it cannot be proved that the initial spread of peyotism was promoted by the profound dislocation that resulted from livestock reduction and control, such an interpretation is supported by the lack of similar movements among the Navaho during the previous 65 years and by the minor religious innovations that occurred concurrently in the northern Navaho country in the late 1930's and early 1940's. In effect, the Navahos, although they possessed one of the most complete traditional cultural inventories in the United States in 1933—second only to the Pueblos—had been suddenly propelled into the classic reservation situation of American Indians, one in which a native economy no longer worked but in which new alternatives were underdeveloped. The peyote cult, with its protesting ideology and adjusting ethic, "made sense" to people whose traditional culture could no longer operate effectively, and who were forced to accommodate to the new situation.

The ideology of peyotism differed from traditional Navaho views in its emphasis on a transcendent God, and on power through peyote and inspiration rather than through formula and ritual. It promised cure for witchcraft-caused disease and rejected fear of spirits of the dead, or at least of the peyotist dead. Individual moral responsibility received great emphasis, where traditional Navaho life had depended on lateral sanctions on misconduct within a diffuse web of mutual interdependence, now shattered by economic changes. It gloried in the curative powers of peyote and derogated the value of traditional ceremonies.

Strong opposition to peyotism began before it became illegal in 1940 and has continued ever since. A peak of extra-legal actions against peyotists was reached in the mid-1940's; arrests under Tribal law probably reached their height in the mid-1950's. Legal and extra-legal action against peyotism reached the lowest point for many years in 1964. Opposition follows the same pattern that has been observed in many other areas: traditionalists object because peyotism is non-traditional; Christians because it is not standard Christianity; people fear, in varying intensity, its supposed addictive properties, supposed effects on health, and supposed behavioral effects. As in so many other tribes, opposition does not prevent the cult from spreading, and many peyotists would argue that the cult is stronger when it is opposed than when times are peaceful. The Navaho struggle was particularly bitter because of the existence since 1940 of a Tribal law forbidding the sale, use, or possession of peyote. Relatively few tribal groups have such laws.

In the past history of peyote studies, it has often been claimed that peyotists are transitional in acculturation level. Clear supporting data exist only for the Menomini case (Spindler, 1955). The Navaho data do not conform to this expectation, except, perhaps, in the sense that the most successful highly acculturated Navahos were not likely to be peyotists in the years up to 1953—and even this tendency may be breaking down. Instead, Navaho peyotists are distinguished from non-peyotists by various measures of livestock deprivation, by dream characteristics, or by both.

There has been almost no work attempting to account for community or tribal differences in level of acceptance of peyotism. Stewart pointed this out in his discussion of tribal differences (1944). The exceptions are Driver (1939) and the

Stewart-Opler controversy respecting acceptance of peyotism at Ignacio and Towaoc (Stewart, 1941, 1948; M. K. Opler, 1940, 1942). The Navaho data provide additional information and interpretations of community differences. Needless to say, diffusion factors turn out to be powerful variables in accounting for the pattern of distribution: availability for the early time-period (up to 1946); prior level of peyotism (in and after 1946). The other powerful factor is acculturation level; a high level of acculturation predicts a low level of peyotism. This finding is tentatively interpreted by reference to acculturation as a process that provides solutions to problems for contemporary Navahos. The importance of other predictive factors is questionable. Communities with a high level of peyotism are more likely to have trouble over peyotism than communities with a low level—not a startling finding. Communities which are, on other grounds, not very "peyote prone" react with more disturbance to the introduction of peyotism than do other communities. Ratings on Navaho communities support these findings. Recent information indicates that trouble over peyotism tends to subside over time.

Understanding of peyotism might be furthered if it were compared with other redemptive movements, whether these have "nativistic" coloring or not, and contrasted with transformative movements, whether "nativistic" or not. Tentatively, it is suggested that redemptive movements which do not preach withdrawal from the world flourish where groups are pushed into new, ambivalently regarded niches, where their engagement with a larger economico-political system is increased, whereas transformative ones flourish where groups are encapsulated or extruded from an old niche without obvious minimally satisfactory alternatives and with a general decrement in or lack of involvement in the larger system. The spread of Navaho peyotism against opposition fits this interpretation.

No evidence has been discovered that supports the interpretation that the practices of the Native American Church of North America, including its use of peyote, have damaging effects on the health, welfare, or morality of its members. Much evidence has been discovered that indicates that members of the Native American Church are seriously and strongly committed to their religion, including its use of peyote, and that if necessary they will suffer imprisonment rather than abandon the church and will fight cases through the courts, whether Tribal, State, or Federal, so long as they experience legal restrictions.

APPENDIXES

Appendix A

TRENDS IN NAVAHO POPULATION AND EDUCATION, 1870–1955

DENIS F. JOHNSTON

PART I

THIS APPENDIX traces the diffusion of formal, Western education among the Navaho since the Fort Sumner period ending in 1867.[1] The primary data utilized consist of the officially reported enrollment figures of Navaho children in Western schools and the official estimates of the total Navaho population, by five-year intervals, from 1870 to 1955.[2] An attempt is made to measure the cumulative impact of the educational process upon Navaho society by estimating numbers of survivors of successive cohorts of Navaho adults who experienced some degree of Western formal education during their childhood.

The impressive increases both of the total Navaho population and of the numbers of school enrollees since 1870 are shown in Graphs 1 and 2 (Graph 1 is based on Table 43, cols. 2 and 5; official school enrollments in Graph 2 are based on Table 43, col. 4). Graph 2 indicates a slow and sporadic increase in school enrollments until about 1910, and an accelerating growth, in general, since then. In order to study the impact of education on the Navaho population, a cohort analysis

[1] This analysis was prepared at my request by Denis F. Johnston, in an effort to evaluate the impact of acculturation on peyotism. The underlying hypothesis was that if it was to be argued that aggregate acculturation (see Chapter 18) had an important impact on the acceptance of peyotism, education was the best measure of aggregate acculturation over time. The argument would have to take one of two forms. Either one would have to argue that some particular percentage of educated persons was a necessary precondition for peyotism—and no one has stated what this percentage might be—or one would have to argue that a rapid rise in the percentage not too long before peyotism began its spread could account in part for that spread. As will be seen, the slope of the curve for percentage of adults with some education (Graph 3) shows a change in about 1915 and is fairly close to a straight line from then on. If this change can be connected with peyotism, probably any change can be. The analysis is presented here for three reasons. (1) It bears on the aggregate acculturation argument. (2) It has considerable methodological interest. (3) It affords the promise that similar cohort analyses for other groups can supply us with measures of aggregate acculturation over time. The text, tables, and all unsigned footnotes are the work of Denis F. Johnston. Johnston (1961) is the best source of information on Navaho population from the Spanish period to the present. This work is to be published as a Bulletin of the Bureau of American Ethnology.—D. F. A.

[2] The basic source for these figures is RCIA, 1870 and following years. Both the population and the education data are commonly reported by school and tribe. Earlier reports merely divide the population into "minors" and "adults," and fail to indicate the exact ages included in the category "children of school age." In 1927, the reports defined this latter category as children aged 6 through 18. It has been assumed that school enrollees fall within this group throughout the period under consideration, unless otherwise specified. The totals for both population and school-age enrollees were obtained by summing the figures for all schools reported to be Navaho schools.

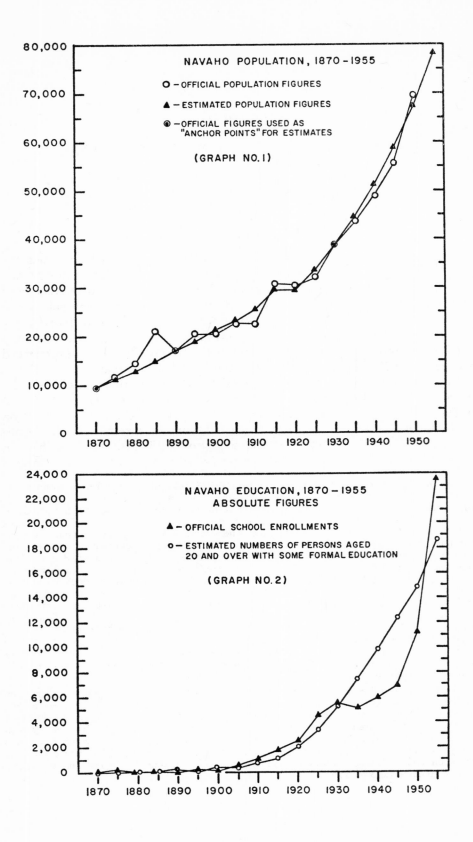

NAVAHO POPULATION, 1870-1955

O – OFFICIAL POPULATION FIGURES

▲ – ESTIMATED POPULATION FIGURES

◉ – OFFICIAL FIGURES USED AS
"ANCHOR POINTS" FOR ESTIMATES

(GRAPH NO. 1)

NAVAHO EDUCATION, 1870 – 1955
ABSOLUTE FIGURES

▲ – OFFICIAL SCHOOL ENROLLMENTS

o – ESTIMATED NUMBERS OF PERSONS AGED
20 AND OVER WITH SOME FORMAL EDUCATION

(GRAPH NO. 2)

was carried out. The results are presented in Graph 2, which depicts estimated numbers of persons aged 20 and over with some formal education (this is based on Table 47, col. 5). The number of educated persons begins to rise perceptibly from 1915 on, and from 1925 on the absolute rise is rapid and more or less even, with a further shift in the slope between 1950 and 1955.

The data of Graphs 1 and 2 are summarized in Graph 3, which shows the percentage of children in school from 1870 to 1955, and percentage of persons over 20 with some education for the same period (based on Table 43, cols. 4 and 6, and Table 47, col. 7). This indicates clearly the failure of educational facilities to

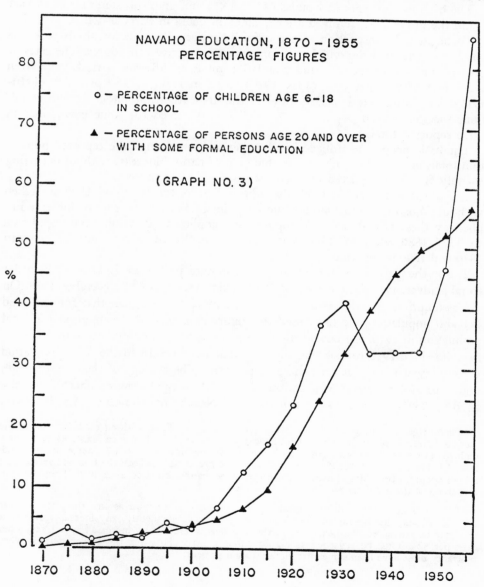

NAVAHO EDUCATION, 1870 – 1955
PERCENTAGE FIGURES

o — PERCENTAGE OF CHILDREN AGE 6–18
     IN SCHOOL

▲ — PERCENTAGE OF PERSONS AGE 20 AND OVER
     WITH SOME FORMAL EDUCATION

(GRAPH NO. 3)

keep pace with rising school-age population during the years from 1935 through 1945, partly as a result of little school construction during the war years.[3] It also shows the tremendous acceleration on a percentage basis for the years 1950–1955 —almost as great as for the preceding 70 years. The impact of this rise in Navaho children attending school will not, of course, be felt for another twenty years, until educated children become mature adults.

The percentage of adults with education shows essentially the same pattern as absolute figures: there is a change in the slope of the curve between 1910 and 1915; after 1915 the rise is a fairly straight-line function.

The basis for the summary tables (43 and 47) and graphs is summarized in Part I, and the procedures involved are explained in detail in Parts II–VI.

To begin with, inspection of the officially reported population totals reveals a number of irregularities which call for certain corrective procedures. The rates of growth implied by the reported population totals at different periods vary from a decrease of 0.26 per cent (1915–1920) to an increase of 6.57 per cent (1910–1915). The latter rate is clearly beyond the limit attainable under known conditions for any human population and indicates the need for some corrections in these reported totals.[4]

The basic procedure utilized in adjusting or "smoothing" the reported population totals in order to produce plausible rates of natural increase without departing entirely from the reported data can be summarized as follows.

1. For the period 1870–1890, the official reports for 1870 and 1890 are taken without adjustment and used as "anchor points." The natural rate of increase implied by these two figures is computed and applied to determine the population for 1875, 1880, and 1885. This assumes, of course, that the rate of increase between 1870 and 1890 is constant.

2. For the period 1890–1910, a more elaborate procedure is adopted in order to take advantage of the census of 1910, which reported 9,082 Navahos 6–18. On the assumption that this estimate would be more reliable than that for the total Navaho population, we have used this figure as a basis for computing the total population in 1910. An examination of several age distributions computed for the Navaho since 1940 reveals that the proportion aged 6–18 to the total population varies between 33.4 per cent and 36.5 per cent. The average of these percentages comes to 35.4 per cent. Application of this percentage to the number of Navaho aged 6–18 in 1910 gives us an estimated total Navaho population of 25,655 in 1910.

[3] Percentages of children in school were computed by D. F. A. without consideration of the fact that some children in school are below 6 or over 18 (cf. "Notes to Table 43"). If these children are omitted, percentages drop by the following amounts: 1930, 2.1 per cent; 1935, 1.6; 1940, 1.1; 1945, 0.4; 1950, 0.8; 1955, 3.4. The last figure presumably reflects the Bureau's accelerated school program for older children with no prior education, initiated after 1950. Thus the general trend of the graphs is not importantly altered.—D. F. A.

[4] Since our concern is with the total Navaho population, we must assume the population to be "closed"—i.e., having no immigration or emigration. Consequently, any increases over time can only be attributed to an excess of births over deaths. Hence any increase beyond, say, 3 per cent per year must be regarded as highly dubious, particularly for the earlier periods when mortality must have been somewhat higher than at present.

The "anchor points" for the 1890–1910 period are thus established.[5] The computed rate of natural increase between 1890 and 1910 is then used to determine the population totals for 1895, 1900, and 1905, again assuming a constant rate of increase throughout this period.

3. For the period 1910–1930, the census figure for 1930 is accepted without adjustment. However, the impact of the influenza pandemic in 1918–1919 is reflected in a very small net loss of population between 1915 and 1920, according to official reports. Therefore, in computing the rate of increase from 1910 to 1930, we assume that the population in 1920 is equal to that in 1915, which corresponds closely to the officially reported figures at this time.

4. For the period 1930–1950, the procedure outlined in (2) above is repeated. The school census of 1950 reports 24,025 Navaho aged 6–18. Assuming that this group constitutes 35.4 per cent of the total population at this time, we arrive at a total population of 67,867 in 1950. The rate of increase implied by the growth between 1930 and 1950 is then used to compute the total population for the intermediate five-year intervals in the usual manner.[6]

5. The estimated population for 1955, finally, is again based upon the number of Navaho aged 6–18 reported in the school census of 1955.

Table 43 shows the official population totals, numbers aged 6–18 when given, and the reported school enrollment figures. It then lists the adjusted population totals and computed numbers aged 6–18, by five-year intervals, from 1870 to 1955. The crude rates of natural increase implied by these figures are also included. The reader should note that while the adjusted totals do not depart markedly from the official estimates, they are consonant with plausible rates of natural increase. Detailed explanations of the computations involved in estimating the proportions aged 6–18 and 5–19 in the total Navaho population are described in Part II; the procedure for smoothing the reported population totals by five-year intervals is described in Part III.

A comparison of the school enrollment figures at any given time with the population at that time would provide us with a crude estimate of the significance of

[5] This procedure assumes that the proportion aged 6–18 remains constant for the Navaho population throughout the period in question. Although some shifts in this proportion have undoubtedly occurred, the following considerations suggest that this assumption is not unrealistic as a basis for our computations: First, we should note that the range in the proportions aged 6–18 for the several Navaho age distributions available to us was quite narrow, although one of these age distributions was based upon Ramah data extending back to 1880. Second, it has recently been demonstrated that in the long run, the general age distribution of a population is only slightly altered by variations in mortality, provided that fertility remains fairly constant and migration is negligible. The Navaho population appears to satisfy these conditions in the period dealt with. In regard to the relative impact of variations in fertility and mortality upon the age distribution of a population, see Lorimer, 1951. A more exact quantitative formulation of the same idea is presented in Coale, 1956.

[6] Two advantages to this procedure should be noted: (1) It is likely that the school census is somewhat more accurate than the estimates of total Navaho population, in view of the careful efforts made to locate children of school age, and (2) the census reports of 1950 provide two population totals, one for resident population and one for enrolled population. It is believed that a single figure based upon the reported school-age population provides a more realistic basis for our analysis.

education among the Navaho people. Such a comparison, however, does not constitute an adequate indication of the true impact of education, since it fails to take into account the adults living in Navaho society who have experienced some education in their youth. The next step, therefore, is to estimate numbers of survivors of original cohorts having once experienced some formal education, as they progress to the later ages.

TABLE 43

OFFICIAL AND COMPUTED ESTIMATES OF TOTAL NAVAHO POPULATION, NUMBERS AGED 6–18, AND REPORTED SCHOOL ENROLLMENTS, AT FIVE-YEAR INTERVALS, 1870–1955

(1)	(2)	(3)	(4)	(5)	(6)	(7)
	DATA FROM OFFICIAL REPORTS			COMPUTED TOTALS[a]		
DATE (x)	Total Population	Number Aged 6–18	Number Enrolled in School (All Ages)[b]	Total Population	Number Aged 6–18	Crude Rates of Natural Increase (Per Cent) (x to $x+5$)
1870.........	9,790	....	30	9,790	3,466	2.86
1875.........	11,768	....	123	11,272	3,990	2.86
1880.........	14,800	....	45	12,978	4,594	2.86
1885.........	21,003	....	100	14,942	5,284	2.86
1890.........	17,204	....	89	17,204	6,090	2.02
1895.........	20,500	....	270	19,011	6,730	2.02
1900.........	20,500	....	230	21,009	7,437	2.02
1905.........	23,000	....	558	23,216	8,218	2.02
1910.........	22,455	9,082	1,122	25,655	9,082	2.79
1915.........	30,871	....	1,761	29,445	10,424	0.00
1920.........	30,473	....	2,484	29,445	10,424	2.79
1925.........	31,985	....	4,408	33,795	11,963	2.79
1930.........	38,787	11,363	5,555	38,787	13,731	2.84
1935.........	43,514	12,724	5,159	44,610	15,792	2.84
1940.........	48,796	12,421	5,962	51,306	18,162	2.84
1945.........	55,458	19,867	6,869	59,009	20,889	2.84
1950.........	69,167[c]	24,025	11,202	67,867	24,025	2.93
1955.........	....	27,752	23,679[d]	78,395	27,752	....

[a] The underlined values are taken without adjustment from official reports as "anchor points" in calculating the remaining values. See Parts II and III for procedure.

[b] Prior to 1930, enrollees are assumed to fall within the age-group 6–18. From 1930 on, the figures in col. 4 include the following numbers of enrollees aged "under 6 or over 18": 1930: 295; 1935: 255; 1940: 206; 1945: 88; 1950: 191; 1955: 938.

[c] This figure pertains to the enrolled population of the Navajo Agency. The resident population on the reservation in 1950 was reported as 54,997. See U.S. Department of Health, Education, and Welfare, 1954, p. 18.

[d] From Statistics Concerning Indian Education, Fiscal Year 1955, Table 1, Annual School Census Report of Indian Children —Fiscal Year 1955, p. 6.

In order to estimate survivorship rates of successive cohorts as they proceed through life, we must apply a series of age-specific mortality rates to each cohort, reducing its numbers in accordance with the indicated rates of attrition. This requires, ideally, a set of age-specific death rates for each cohort under consideration. In the case of the Navaho, of course, no such mortality data exist for any period prior to 1940.[7] Consequently, it is necessary to estimate Navaho mortality by comparing the limited empirical data on mortality among the Navaho to a set

[7] Even the mortality rates computed from registration data in the past few years reflect serious deficiencies in death registration. See, for example, the comments of Hadley, 1951.

of "model" life table values. The empirical data available for this purpose consist of a year-by-year count of the members of the Ramah band of Navaho, by single years of age, from 1880 to 1948. These data were accumulated by Clyde Kluckhohn and associates as a part of an intensive study of the Ramah community. The model life table values to which the Ramah data are compared were developed to serve as guides in arriving at plausible approximations of age-specific mortality among populations for whom only the mortality at the early years of life is known.[8]

If we could assume that the Ramah Navaho mortality rates were typical of the rates for the total Navaho population, our problem would be solved once the indicated Ramah mortality rates had been established. Unfortunately, the mortality rates computed from the Ramah data contain a number of peculiarities that militate against their acceptance as typical of the Navaho as a whole. Two of these peculiarities deserve particular mention in this connection (see Table 44). First, the indicated death rates from birth to age 5 ($_4q_0$) are far too low when compared with the indicated death rates for the Ramah population at higher ages. The early death rates for Ramah, as reported, would fall below the levels attained by any population on earth at the present time. Second, the frequent absence of any mortality whatever for specific age-groups over considerable periods of time could not occur in any large population.[9]

Therefore, instead of applying the indicated Ramah mortality rates directly to the total Navaho age-groups, these rates are compared to the rates provided in the model life tables, and the model rates that correspond most closely to the Ramah rates, on the average, are then applied to the Navaho population as a whole.[10]

In Table 45, the "closest" model life tables reflected in the Ramah death rates for each of three periods, 1880–1900, 1900–1925, and 1925–1945, are indicated. The "average" model indicated by the Ramah death rates during each of these three periods is determined, and the age-specific mortality rates corresponding to these three average models are listed in Table 46. The first of these models is then used in determining the survivorship rates of Navahos at all ages from 1870 to 1900, the second model is applied to Navahos at all ages from 1900 to 1925, and the third model is used thereafter. The detailed procedure for estimating these three sets of age-specific mortality rates for the total Navaho population is described in Part IV.

[8] Calculation of mortality rates from the Ramah data as given assumes that in-or-out migration is negligible, which does in fact appear to have been the case. See Kluckhohn, 1956. Kluckhohn reports a total immigration of 72 persons and a total emigration of 74 persons to and from Ramah between 1890 and 1950.

[9] The evident under-estimation of mortality from birth to age 5 may be due to the common tendency of older persons to "forget" infant deaths that occurred at an earlier period. As for the complete absence of mortality for specific cohorts over considerable periods of time, we should note that this could indeed occur within a small group purely by chance. However, zero mortality at any age is implausible for any large population, since deaths occur at all ages. In other words, the reported variations in mortality among the Ramah band must be regarded as peculiarities of their small numbers and cannot be projected to the total Navaho population without adjustment.

[10] These model life tables were developed by John V. Grauman and others, and are based upon 158 life tables pertaining to mortality variations for some 50 different countries (see *Age and Sex Patterns of Mortality*, 1955).

TABLE 44

Ramah Navaho Population and Implied Mortality Rates ($_4q_x$), by Five-Year Age Groupings at Five-Year Intervals, 1880–1945[a]

(1) Age-Group	(2) l_x 1880	(3) l_{x+5} '85	(4) $_4q_x$ '80-'85	(5) l_x '85	(6) l_{x+5} '90	(7) $_4q_x$ '85-'90	(8) l_x '90	(9) l_{x+5} '95	(10) $_4q_x$ '90-'95	(11) l_x '95	(12) l_{x+5} '00	(13) $_4q_x$ '95-'00	(14) l_x '00	(15) l_{x+5} '05	(16) $_4q_x$ '00-'05	(17) l_x '05	(18) l_{x+5} '10	(19) $_4q_x$ '05-'10	(20) l_x '10	(21) l_{x+5} '15	(22) $_4q_x$ '10-'15
0–4	11	11	0	13	13	0	19	19	0	34	33	29	42	41	24	44	44	0	48	46	42
5–9	13	13	0	11	11	0	13	13	0	19	18	53	33	32	30	41	40	24	44	40	91
10–14	8	8	0	13	13	125	11	11	0	13	13	0	18	18	0	32	31	31	40	38	50
15–19	4	4	0	8	7	0	13	13	0	11	11	77	13	13	91	18	18	0	31	29	64
20–24	5	5	0	4	4	0	7	7	0	13	12	0	11	10	0	13	11	154	18	17	56
25–29	6	6	0	5	5	0	4	4	0	7	7	0	12	12	0	10	8	200	11	11	0
30–34	6	6	0	6	6	0	5	5	0	4	4	0	7	7	0	12	12	0	8	8	0
35–39	0	0	0	6	6	0	6	6	0	5	5	167	7	7	0	7	7	0	12	11	83
40–44	1	1	0	0	0	1,000[b]	6	6	0	6	6	0	4	4	0	4	4	0	7	7	0
45–49	0	0	0	1	0	0	0	0	0	6	6	0	5	5	167	5	5	0	4	4	0
50–54	1	1	0	1	1	0	0	0	0	6	6	0	6	5	0	5	5	200	5	5	0
55–59	2	2	0	2	2	0	0	0	0	0	0	0	0	0	0	5	5	0	4	5	0
60–64	1	1	0	1	1	0	1	1	0	1	1	0	0	0	0	0	0	0	5	5	0
65–69	0	0	0	1	1	0	2	2	0	2	2	0	1	1	0	0	0	0	0	0	0
70–74	0	0	0	0	0	0	1	1	0	1	1	0	3	3	0	4	4	0	4	2	0
75–	0	0	0	0	0	0	0	0	0	1	1	0	3	3	0	4	4	0	4	2	500
Unknowns	16	16	0	16	16	0	16	16	0	16	16	0	16	8	500	8	7	125	7	6	143

[a] These data were provided through the courtesy of the late Clyde Kluckhohn. The original data were by single years of age; they were grouped into five-year groups as shown. The "l_x" columns are the numbers of Ramah Navahos in the respective age-groups who were alive at the time indicated. The "l_{x+5}" columns are the numbers of the *same* original age-groups or "cohorts" who were still living five years later. The "$_4q_x$" columns show the rate of mortality of the respective groups. These values are obtained by the formula:

$$_4q_x = \frac{l_x - l_{x+5}}{l_x} \cdot 1,000 .$$

Although the above symbols are those used in denoting conventional life table functions, their values are derived in this case from actual numbers of people, by age, rather than from an hypothetical stationary life table population.

[b] This value was omitted in computing the average q_{40} for the period 1880–1900, since it would greatly distort the result.

TABLE 44—*Continued*

(1) Age-Group	(23) l_x 1915	(24) l_{x+5} '20	(25) $4q_x$ '15-'20	(26) l_x '20	(27) l_{x+5} '25	(28) $4q_x$ '20-'25	(29) l_x '25	(30) l_{x+5} '30	(31) $4q_x$ '25-'30	(32) l_x '30	(33) l_{x+5} '35	(34) $4q_x$ '30-'35	(35) l_x '35	(36) l_{x+5} '40	(37) $4q_x$ '35-'40	(38) l_x '40	(39) l_{x+5} '45	(40) $4q_x$ '40-'45
0–4	41	39	49	74	69	68	74	70	54	57	56	18	77	73	52	96	90	62
5–9	46	42	87	39	39	0	69	63	87	70	68	28	56	52	71	73	73	0
10–14	40	36	100	42	37	119	39	37	51	63	61	32	68	67	15	52	51	19
15–19	38	33	132	36	31	139	37	36	27	37	32	135	61	57	66	67	64	45
20–24	29	27	69	33	32	30	31	27	129	36	31	139	32	31	31	57	55	35
25–29	17	16	59	27	27	0	32	29	94	27	26	37	31	30	32	31	29	64
30–34	11	11	0	16	15	62	27	26	37	29	25	103	26	25	38	30	27	100
35–39	8	8	0	11	11	0	15	14	67	26	25	38	26	25	38	25	23	80
40–44	11	11	0	8	8	0	11	11	0	14	13	71	25	23	80	25	24	40
45–49	7	7	250	11	9	182	8	7	125	11	11	0	13	11	154	23	21	87
50–54	4	3	0	7	6	148	9	7	222	7	7	0	11	10	91	11	8	273
55–59	5	5	250	3	3	0	6	5	167	7	5	0	7	7	0	10	8	200
60–64	4	3	0	5	5	0	3	3	0	5	3	333	7	6	143	7	5	286
65–69	5	5	0	3	2	333	5	5	0	3	2	400	5	5	0	6	5	167
70–74	0	0	500	5	4	200	2	2	0	5	3	500	2	1	500	5	4	0
75–	2	1	500	1	1	0	5	2	600	4	2	200	5	5		6	2	200
Unknowns	6	3		3	4	......	4	5	......	5	4		4	5	......	5	5	667

365

One further calculation is necessary before we can carry out our cohort analysis of Navahos with some education. The official reports of Navaho school enrollment do not indicate the precise age distribution of the enrollees, except to distinguish those aged 6–18 from those aged under 6 or over 18. We must distribute these enrollees among the appropriate five-year age-groups. This can be accomplished with sufficient accuracy for our purposes by assuming that the age distribution of the school enrollees corresponds to that of the general population of Navaho children and youth. Accordingly, the average age distribution of the total Navaho

TABLE 45

AVERAGE RAMAH NAVAHO MORTALITY RATES FOR THE THREE PERIODS 1880–1900, 1900–1925, AND 1925–1945, WITH THE CLOSEST MODEL LIFE TABLE INDICATED BY THESE RATES[a]

(1) Age-Group	(2) Aver. Ramah $_4q_x$ (1880–1900)	(3) Corresp. Model	(4) Aver. Ramah $_4q_x$ (1900–1925)	(5) Corresp. Model	(6) Aver. Ramah $_4q_x$ (1925–1945)	(7) Corresp. Model
0– 4.......	29	2	46	4	46	4
5– 9.......	53	31	58	32	62	33
10–14.......	....	....	75	40+	29	28
15–19.......	125	40+	112	40+	68	37
20–24.......	77	35	80	36	84	37
25–29.......	....	....	130	40+	57	27
30–34.......	....	....	62	27	70	29
35–39.......	....	....	83	30	56	25
40–44.......	167	38	....	....	64	25
45–49.......	....	....	182	37	122	30
50–54.......	....	....	190	35	195	35
55–59.......	....	....	....	....	184	30
60–64.......	....	....	250	32	214	28
65–69.......	....	....	333	32	250	25
70–74.......	....	....	200	1–	367	26
75 and over..	....	....	(500)	....	....	....
Aver. Model[b]		34.67		32.62		29.64

[a] The Ramah values are simple (unweighted) averages of the mortality rates shown in Table 44 for the period in question. All zero values and one value of 1,000 were omitted from consideration as being erroneous or due to the small numbers in the Ramah population.

[b] The numbers in cols. 3, 5, and 7 pertain to the model life table whose $_4q_x$ value corresponds most closely to the indicated Ramah mortality rate. The model values are presented in *Age and Sex Patterns of Mortality*, 1955, Table 5, pp. 14 f. All values have been rounded to the nearest whole number. In computing the "average model," for each period, all models over no. 40 and below no. 10 were omitted as implausible.

population is used as a basis for distributing the school population into the three age-groups 5–9, 10–14, and 15–19. It is assumed that none of the enrollees falls outside these three groups. For an explanation of the exact procedure utilized at this step, see Part V.

With the completion of this final adjustment, we are prepared to apply the appropriate age-specific mortality rates in Table 46 to successive cohorts of Navaho children and youth enrolled in school. The result gives us an estimate of numbers of successive cohorts of adult Navahos who are still living and have experienced some education in their youth. Summing the several cohorts at any given period gives us an "in-time" picture of the numbers of educated Navahos

TABLE 46

AGE-SPECIFIC MORTALITY RATES DERIVED FROM MODEL LIFE TABLES FOR THE THREE PERIODS 1870–1900, 1900–1925, AND 1925–1945[a]

(1) Age-Group	(2) $_4q_x$ Model 35	(3) $_4q_x$ Model 34	(4) $_4q_x$ Model 34.67	(5) $_4q_x$ Model 33	(6) $_4q_x$ Model 32	(7) $_4q_x$ Model 32.62	(8) $_4q_x$ Model 30	(9) $_4q_x$ Model 29	(10) $_4q_x$ Model 29.64
0– 4.....	431.7	413.9	426	396.3	378.8	390	344.4	327.5	338
5– 9.....	70.1	65.4	68	60.9	56.6	59	48.6	44.8	47
10–14.....	46.8	43.9	46	41.1	38.3	40	33.2	30.7	32
15–19.....	60.9	57.9	60	54.9	52.0	54	46.1	43.2	45
20–24.....	78.3	75.0	77	71.7	68.4	70	61.6	58.1	60
25–29.....	90.4	86.1	89	81.8	77.5	80	68.8	64.6	67
30–34.....	103.8	98.1	102	92.5	87.0	90	76.2	71.0	74
35–39.....	120.6	113.1	118	106.0	99.1	103	85.8	79.4	84
40–44.....	140.6	131.5	138	123.0	114.6	120	98.8	91.4	96
45–49.....	165.4	155.0	162	145.3	135.8	142	117.8	109.4	115
50–54.....	195.2	184.1	192	173.7	163.4	170	143.7	134.4	140
55–59.....	234.4	223.0	231	212.1	201.2	208	180.0	169.8	176
60–64.....	288.4	277.2	285	266.4	255.3	262	233.1	222.2	229
65–69.....	363.0	352.3	360	341.7	330.6	338	307.9	296.3	304
70–74.....	473.1	462.4	470	451.6	440.2	447	416.2	403.9	412
75 and over	....	....	....	....	....	....	....	....	....

[a] Model values are obtained from *Age and Sex Patterns of Mortality*, 1955, Table 5, pp. 14 f. Values in cols. 4, 7, and 10 are rounded to the nearest whole number. These values are then applied to successive cohorts of Navahos enrolled in school to obtain numbers of survivors at later ages.

TABLE 47

GROWTH OF POPULATION AND THE IMPACT OF EDUCATION AMONG THE NAVAHO, 1870–1955

(1) Date	(2) Total Population (Smoothed)[a]	(3) Estimated Population Aged 20 and Over[b]	(4) Numbers with Some Education, All Ages[c]	(5) Numbers with Some Education, 20 and Over[d]	(6) Percentage with Some Education All Ages (4)/(2)	(7) Percentage with Some Education 20 and Over (5)/(3)
1870.......	9,790	4,112	30	0	0.31	0.00
1875.......	11,272	4,734	130	7	1.15	0.15
1880.......	12,978	5,451	90	45	0.69	0.83
1885.......	14,942	6,276	201	101	1.35	1.61
1890.......	17,204	7,226	259	170	1.51	2.35
1895.......	19,011	7,985	496	226	2.61	2.83
1900.......	21,009	8,824	560	330	2.67	3.74
1905.......	23,216	9,751	1,034	476	4.45	4.88
1910.......	25,655	10,775	1,853	731	7.22	6.78
1915.......	29,445	12,367	2,955	1,194	10.04	9.65
1920.......	29,445	12,367	4,550	2,066	15.45	16.70
1925.......	33,795	14,194	7,847	3,439	23.22	24.23
1930.......	38,787	16,291	10,796	5,241	27.83	32.17
1935.......	44,610	18,736	12,582	7,423	28.20	39.62
1940.......	51,306	21,549	15,765	9,803	30.73	45.49
1945.......	59,009	24,784	19,172	12,303	32.49	49.64
1950.......	67,867	28,504	26,047	14,845	38.38	52.08
1955.......	78,395	32,926	42,373	18,694	54.05	56.78

[a] From Table 43, col. 5.

[b] Assuming that 42.0 per cent of the total population is aged 20 and over. See Table 48, col. 12.

[c],[d] Data from Part VI, Table 50.

in Navaho society at that time. The results of this computation are shown in Table 47. The detailed procedure is explained in Part VI.

In conclusion, it is apparent that Navaho society has experienced a steady and rapid increase in the proportions of Navahos with some degree of formal, Western education. This growth has been fairly continuous since the beginning of this century, as is indicated in the percentages in Table 47, column 7. A comparison of the percentages shown in column 6 with those in column 7 suggests that despite occasional lapses in the growth of school enrollments (especially between 1930 and 1935), the impact of previously educated adult Navahos upon their society has been growing steadily during the last 50 years.

In estimating the social significance of these trends, we should bear in mind a number of qualifications. In the first place, these data do not reflect either the level or the quality of the education that has been experienced. We have no precise information regarding the rate of drop-outs among officially enrolled students; nor do we know how long, on the average, a Navaho student tends to remain in school, once enrolled. As explained in Part VI, it was assumed that the average length of attendance at school was 5 years or less prior to 1925, and 7.5 years thereafter. Where figures on average attendance were reported (prior to 1930), these figures lagged behind the official enrollment figures by as much as 40 per cent, indicating much absenteeism.

Second, it should be emphasized that the above figures represent a "maximum" estimate of the impact of education among the Navaho. Application of a more stringent criterion, such as "functional literacy," would doubtless produce considerably lower percentages of "educated" Navaho at all periods.

We should note, finally, that the very considerable increase in school enrollments since 1950 gives promise of even more rapid diffusion of education among the Navaho in the future. It remains to be seen whether the increased opportunities provided by this rise in education can compensate adequately for the increased economic pressures implicit in the tremendous growth in Navaho population.

PART II. PROCEDURE FOR ESTIMATING THE AVERAGE AGE DISTRIBUTION AND THE POPULATION AGED 6–18, OF THE TOTAL NAVAHO POPULATION

If we examine a number of available age distributions for several Navaho populations, we can omit those having apparent discrepancies and calculate an average age distribution from those that remain. Table 48 gives the numbers and percentage age distributions of those populations which were selected as a basis for computing a single "typical" age distribution for the Navaho. Column 12 in this table indicates the resultant distribution.

It should be noted that these distributions, save for the Ramah data, are derived from relatively recent surveys and censuses. Even the Ramah data are weighted heavily toward more recent periods. As is noted in Part I, it is believed that the application of this single distribution to Navaho populations throughout the period under consideration is justifiable on the grounds that whatever variations have occurred have been relatively minor.

In estimating the average percentage aged 6–18 inclusive for the Navaho population, we utilized the following formula:

$$_{12}l_6 = {}_4l_5 + {}_4l_{10} + {}_4l_{15} - \frac{{}_4l_5 + {}_4l_{15}}{5},$$

where $_nl_x$ denotes the actual population in the age-group x to $x + n$.

This formula gives a rough estimate of the number aged 6–18 by merely subtracting one-fifth of those aged 5–9 and 15–19 from the group aged 5–19. This implies a slight under-estimation of the number aged 5–6, and a slight over-estimation of the number aged 18–19. Since these two errors tend to offset each other, the resultant should be a satisfactory approximation to the number aged 6–18.

Table 49 shows the application of the above formula to each of the five populations in Table 48. Dividing the number aged 6–18 by the total population in each case gives the percentage aged 6–18. Summing the five percentages and taking a simple average gives us 35.3 per cent aged 6–18. However, in view of the rather low percentage derived from the Ramah data, it was decided to give the other four

TABLE 48

AGE DISTRIBUTIONS OF SELECTED NAVAHO POPULATIONS, BY FIVE-YEAR GROUPINGS, BOTH SEXES

(1) Age-Group	(2) No.[a]	(3) Per Cent	(4) No.[b]	(5) Per Cent	(6) No.[c]	(7) Per Cent	(8) No.[d]	(9) Per Cent	(10) No.[e]	(11) Per Cent	(12) Per Cent[f]
0–4	10,531	16.5	3,014	17.2	4,906	17.2	10,081	17.1	864	19.0	17.5
5–9	9,318	14.6	2,859	16.3	4,864	17.1	9,508	16.2	721	15.9	16.0
10–14	8,552	13.4	2,379	13.6	3,805	13.3	7,935	13.5	600	13.2	13.4
15–19	7,978	12.5	2,029	11.6	3,106	10.9	6,567	11.2	488	10.7	11.1
20–24	4,276	6.7	1,584	9.0	2,555	9.0	5,184	8.8	408	9.0	9.0
25–29	4,787	7.5	1,130	6.4	1,953	6.9	6,631	11.3	322	7.1	6.8
30–34	3,893	6.1	869	5.0	1,568	5.5			271	6.0	5.6
35–39	3,319	5.2	830	4.7	1,282	4.5	4,846	8.2	204	4.5	4.7
40–44	2,681	4.2	629	3.6	1,056	3.7			172	3.8	3.8
45–49	2,170	3.4	600	3.4	895	3.1	3,489	5.9	137	3.0	3.2
50–54	1,723	2.7	404	2.3	726	2.5			111	2.4	2.5
55–59	1,276	2.0	322	1.8	510	1.8	2,135	3.6	71	1.6	1.8
60–64	1,021	1.6	277	1.6	453	1.6			56	1.2	1.5
65–69	830	1.3	240	1.4	409	1.4	886	1.5	40	0.9	1.2
70–74	766	1.2	159	0.9	187	0.7	598	1.0	32	0.7	0.9
75 and over	702	1.1	209	1.2	217	0.8	997	1.7	48	1.0	1.0
Totals[g]	63,823	100.0	17,534	100.0	28,492	100.0	58,857	100.0	4,545	100.0	100.0
Unknown			88				238		132		

[a] Estimated population in 1950 by age and sex, Navajo Reservation, adjusted on the basis of the age distribution of the population as enumerated in 1940.

[b] Estimated population by age and sex of Navajo Indians on the reservation, New Mexico, 1940.

[c] Hulsizer, 1940, Table IX b. This distribution is based upon an extensive survey conducted in 1938.

[d] Hadley, 1954, Table 4.

[e] Derived from a synthetic age distribution obtained by summing the population in each age-group at quinquennial intervals, 1880–1945, plus 1948. The original data were provided by Clyde Kluckhohn.

[f] Obtained by taking the simple (unweighted) average of the distributions shown in cols. 3, 5, 7, and 11. The distributions shown in col. 9 was omitted because of its ten-year age groupings. The percentages in col. 3 for the age groups 15–19, 20–24, and 25–29 were omitted in computing the average distribution in col. 12 because of their atypical variation.

[g] All totals exclude persons of unknown ages, if any.

percentages twice the weight of the Ramah percentage.[11] The resultant average is 35.4 per cent. This percentage is used throughout in estimating both the total population from those reported to be in the 6–18 group, and in estimating the 6–18 group from the total population when given.

TABLE 49

COMPUTATION OF AVERAGE PROPORTION AGED 6–18

(1) Age-Groups	(2) a	(3) b	(4) c	(5) d	(6) e
5– 9..........	9,318	2,859	4,864	9,508	721
10–14..........	8,552	2,379	3,805	7,935	600
15–19..........	7,978	2,029	3,106	6,567	488
Total.........	25,848	7,267	11,775	24,010	1,809
1/5 (5–9).......	−1,864	−572	−973	−1,902	−144
1/5 (15–19)......	−1,596	−406	−621	−1,313	− 98
No. 6–18.........	22,388	6,289	10,181	20,795	1,567
No. all ages......	63,823	17,534	28,492	58,857	4,545
Per cent 6–18.....	35.1	35.9	35.7	35.3	34.5

a to e. See notes for Table 48.
"Average" percentage aged 6–18 = 2(35.1) + 2(35.9) + 2(35.7) + 2(35.3) + 34.5 divided by 9 = 35.4 per cent.

PART III. GRADUATION OF REPORTED NAVAHO POPULATION TOTALS, AT FIVE-YEAR INTERVALS, 1870 TO 1955

Our initial step is to select certain population totals as reported, utilizing them as "anchor points" and interpolating the population at intermediate points in time. For this purpose, the six underlined values shown in Table 43 were taken without adjustment. The reader should note that three of the six values chosen give the estimated number aged 6–18. These figures were translated into total population figures by assuming that the 6–18 group is 35.4 per cent of the total population, as computed in Part II.

A word should be added regarding our acceptance of these particular values without adjustment. The first figure chosen, for 1870, was accepted because it agrees roughly with the estimates made by recent studies.[12]

The reported figures for 1890 and 1930 are based upon special censuses of the Indian population conducted at those dates. Despite possible errors in census procedures, especially in the census of 1890, these figures are taken as reported since they are probably more accurate than the estimates of the period made by agents in the field.

[11] The lower proportion aged 6–18 among the Ramah group suggests possibly lower fertility than that of the general Navaho population. This consideration, together with the small numbers involved, indicate the desirability of giving the Ramah data less weight than those of the larger populations reported.

[12] The actual report estimated that there were 7,790 Navaho on the reservation in 1869, plus an estimated 2,000 Navahos "roaming with other tribes" (RCIA 1874, Document No. 124: Statistics of Education, etc.). Van Valkenburg estimated the population at this time as about 11,000, while Young's recent estimates would imply a population of about 7,800 in 1870 (see Van Valkenburg, 1938, and Young in TNY 1954, p. 104).

The school-age figure for 1910 is taken in preference to the total population reported for that year because the latter figure appears too low when compared with preceding and subsequent estimates. The school-age figures reported for 1950 and 1955 are used on the assumption that the school censuses are more accurate, in general, than estimates of total population.[13]

Having thus obtained our anchor points, the next step is to compute the rates of natural increase between them. The formula used here is the standard "compound interest" formula:

$$\frac{P_n}{P_0} = (1 + r)^n$$

hence

$$\log(1 + r) = \frac{\log P_n - \log P_0}{n},$$

where P_0 = the population at the start of a time interval; P_n = the population at the end of that interval; n = the length of the interval in years; and r = the rate of natural increase during the interval.

Applying this formula to the population figures for 1870 and 1890 gives us a rate of natural increase of 2.86 per cent per year. This percentage is then used by the same formula to compute the intermediate populations for 1875, 1880, and 1885. The same procedure is used for the remaining periods, except for the period 1910–1930. Here, the rate of increase was computed on the assumption of no increase in population between 1915 and 1920. This takes into account the effects of the influenza pandemic of 1918–1920, as evident in column 2 of Table 43.

PART IV. COMPUTATION OF AGE-SPECIFIC MORTALITY RATES FOR THE TOTAL NAVAHO POPULATION AT THREE PERIODS: 1870–1900, 1900–1925, AND 1925–1945

The only age-specific mortality data for the Navaho which reach back into the nineteenth century are those of the Ramah community (as shown in Table 44). The first step in our procedure is to compute a simple average from the age-specific rates for three periods: 1880–1900, 1900–1925, and 1925–1945. The result of that computation is shown in Table 45. As was observed previously, these rates cannot be applied to the total Navaho population without some adjustment, particularly for the 0–4 age-group and all age-groups reporting zero mortality. The next step, accordingly, is to compare the indicated rates to the age-specific mortality rates of the 40 model life tables prepared by John V. Grauman and others. The model whose age-specific mortality rate corresponds most nearly to that of the Ramah community is also indicated in Table 45. Models above 40 imply rates of mortality exceeding those of any known population on earth, while those below 10 imply lower mortality rates than those found anywhere on earth as yet. The reader should note that all the models indicated in Table 45 fall above 20, excepting those for age 0–4 and one for age 70–74. Therefore, in estimating a single "typical"

[13] The 1890 estimate is from U.S. Census Office, 1894, Table V, pp. 82 ff. The 1910 estimate is from RCIA 1911, Table 24, Total Scholastic Population, etc., pp. 159 ff. The 1930 estimate is from U.S. Bureau of the Census, 1937. The 1950 school-age figure is from RCIA 1950; that for 1955 is from Statistics Concerning Indian Education, Fiscal Year 1955, Table 1.

model for each period, we have omitted any model above 40 or below 20. The average model for each of the three periods is thus a simple average of the age-specific models between 20 and 40 for that period.

In Table 46 are given the mortality rates ($_4q_x$) of the models which correspond most nearly to the "average" model for each period. The age-specific mortality rates for these three typical models are obtained by interpolation, and are shown in columns 4, 7, and 10 of Table 46. Using the mortality rates in these three columns, we can estimate the numbers of survivors of successive groups or cohorts of Navahos at all ages and at any given period. The rates in column 4 are used to estimate survivors at all ages 1870–1900; those in column 7 are applied at all ages 1900–1925; those in column 10 are applied at all ages thereafter.

PART V. PROCEDURE FOR DISTRIBUTING SCHOOL ENROLLEES AGED 6–18 AND BELOW 6 OR OVER 18 AMONG THE THREE AGE-GROUPS 5–9, 10–14, AND 15–19

1. According to the "typical" Navaho age distribution computed in Part II (Table 48, col. 12) we have:

Age-Group	Percentage of All Ages
5–9	16.0
10–14	13.4
15–19	11.1

2. Assuming an even distribution of persons within age-groups 5–9 and 15–19, we can roughly estimate the percentages aged 6–9 and 15–18 as follows:

Per cent aged   6–9 $= 16.0 \times .8 = 12.8$

Per cent aged 15–18 $= 11.1 \times .8 = 8.9$

Thus, the per cent ages 6–18 = (approximately) $12.8 + 13.4 + 8.9 = 35.1$

3. The proportion of the 6–18 group falling into each of the three age-groups 6–9, 10–14, and 15–18 can now be approximated as follows:

Prop.   6–9   of the 6–18 group $= \dfrac{12.8}{35.1} = 36.5$ per cent

Prop. 10–14 of the 6–18 group $= \dfrac{13.4}{35.1} = 38.2$ per cent

Prop. 15–18 of the 6–18 group $= \dfrac{8.9}{35.1} = 25.3$ per cent

The above proportions can be approximated with sufficient accuracy for our purposes by assigning one-fourth of the total enrollment (aged 6–18) to age-group 15–19 and dividing the remaining three-fourths evenly between the age-groups 5–9 and 10–14. Hence we have distributed the reported school enrollment figures among the three age-groups by assigning 25 per cent to age-group 15–19 and 37.5 per cent to each of the other two age-groups. This is shown in Table 50.

One final adjustment remains before we can compute the survivors of successive cohorts of Navahos experiencing some formal education. Beginning in 1930, the official reports of school enrollments indicate small numbers of school enrollees aged "below 6" and "above 18." (The actual numbers so reported are listed in Table 43, note.) We have merely divided these enrollees evenly between the two age-groups 5–9 and 15–19, since we lack any evidence as to their precise ages. This assumes, further, that none of the enrollees is under 5 or over 19. While this assumption may under-estimate the enrollment of adult Navahos in schools, the numbers involved are too small to materially affect our results, at least prior to 1955.

PART VI. PROCEDURE FOR ESTIMATING NUMBERS OF SURVIVORS OF SUCCESSIVE COHORTS OF NAVAHOS WITH SOME EDUCATION, AT FIVE-YEAR INTERVALS, 1870–1955

Table 50 presents the basic data from which the proportions of Navahos with some formal, Western education can be estimated. The reported school enrollments are first distributed among the three age-groups 5–9, 10–14, and 15–19, as described in Part V. This gives us three cohorts of school enrollees for each period, at five-year intervals, 1870–1955.

To estimate numbers of survivors of each cohort to different ages, we simply apply the mortality rate which corresponds to that particular age-group and time-period. These rates are given in Table 46. For example, Table 50 indicates 46 school enrollees aged 5–9 in 1875. The mortality rate for that group and period is given in Table 46 as 68 per 1,000. Therefore, on the average, 3 of these 46 persons would fail to survive to the next interval. Thus we have 43 survivors aged 10–14 in 1880. This identical procedure is applied to every age-group throughout the period in question, giving us the frequencies as shown in Table 50. Summing these frequencies for any given period gives us the total number of Navahos with some amount of education at that period. These totals are shown at the bottom of Table 50 and in Table 47.

One further explanation is in order at this point: we have assumed, prior to 1925, that *none* of the school enrollees in a given five-year age-group would still be in school, on the average, five years later. This is roughly equivalent to assuming that the average duration of school attendance prior to 1925 was five years or less. This implies that the survivors of any given cohort of school enrollees should be added to those of the next cohort five years later, in computing the total number with some education. From 1925 on, however, it has been suggested that the average length of school attendance has risen above five years. If so, this would imply some "overlap" from one five-year period to the next. That is, some of the enrollees aged 5–9 in 1930, for example, would still be found among the enrollees aged 10–14 in 1935. Therefore, in computing the survivors of successive cohorts of school enrollees after 1920, we assume that *one-half* the survivors of enrollees in a given age-group are still enrolled in the succeeding age-group five years later. For example, we find, in Table 50, 1,653 enrollees aged 5–9 in 1925. The mortality rate

TABLE 50

COHORT ANALYSIS OF NAVAHO SCHOOL ENROLLEES, BY FIVE-YEAR AGE GROUPINGS, AT FIVE-YEAR INTERVALS, BOTH SEXES, 1870–1955

(1) Age-Group	(2) 1870	(3) 1875	(4) 1880	(5) 1885	(6) 1890	(7) 1895	(8) 1900	(9) 1905	(10) 1910	(11) 1915	(12) 1920	(13) 1925	(14) 1930	(15) 1935	(16) 1940	(17) 1945	(18) 1950	(19) 1955
Number Enrolled in School[a]																		
6–18	30	123	45	100	89	270	230	558	1,122	1,761	2,484	4,408	5,260	4,904	5,756	6,781	11,011	22,741
<6+ >18													295	255	206	88	191	938
5–9	11	46	17	37	33	101	86	209	421	660	931	1,653	2,119	1,966	2,261	2,587	4,224	8,997
10–14	12	46	17	38	34	101	86	209	421	661	932	1,653	1,973	1,889	2,159	2,543	4,130	8,528
	(10)	(10)	(43)	(16)	(34)	(31)	(94)	(81)	(197)	(396)	(621)	(439)	(788)	(1,010)	(937)	(1,077)	…	…
15–19	7	31	11	25	22	68	58	140	280	440	621	1,102	1,463	1,354	1,542	1,739	2,848	6,154
	(11)	(11)	(53)	(57)	(52)	(65)	(126)	(173)	(278)	(593)	(1,015)	(1,044)	(1,225)	(1,718)	(1,868)	(1,952)	(2,274)	…
Survivors with Some Education[b]																		
20–24		7	39	60	77	70	125	174	296	528	977	1,548	2,049	2,567	2,934	3,257	3,525	4,892
25–29			6	36	55	71	65	116	162	275	491	909	1,455	1,926	2,413	2,758	3,062	3,313
30–34				5	33	50	65	60	107	149	253	452	848	1,358	1,797	2,251	2,573	2,857
35–39					5	30	45	59	55	97	136	230	419	785	1,258	1,664	2,084	2,383
40–44						5	26	40	53	49	87	122	211	384	719	1,152	1,524	1,909
45–49							4	23	35	47	43	77	110	191	347	650	1,041	1,378
50–54								4	20	30	40	37	68	97	169	307	575	921
55–59									3	17	25	37	32	58	83	145	264	695
60–64										2	13	33	27	26	48	68	119	218
65–69											1	20	15	21	20	37	52	92
70–74												1	7	10	15	14	26	36
5–74	30	130	90	201	259	496	560	1,034	1,853	2,955	4,550	7,847	10,796	12,582	15,765	19,172	26,047	42,373
20–74	0	7	45	101	170	226	330	476	731	1,194	2,066	3,439	5,241	7,423	9,803	12,303	14,845	18,694

a The original enrollment figures are obtained from Table 48, col. 4. Numbers in parentheses are estimated survivors of persons previously enrolled in school but no longer attending school.

b These values indicate the survivors, at the ages specified, of original cohorts enrolled in school.

for that group (see Table 46) is 47 per 1,000. Hence the survivors in 1930 (aged 10–14) would be 1,576. One-half this number gives us 788, which is the number of "educated" Navaho in the 10–14 age-group in 1930 *in addition to* the actual enrollees at that time. This procedure, followed for all cohorts of actual enrollees after 1920, is roughly equivalent to assuming an average duration of school attendance, after 1920, of about seven and one-half years.[14]

[14] These estimates of the average duration of school attendance among Navaho children are based upon discussions with Mrs. Hildegarde Thompson and others of the Branch of Education, Bureau of Indian Affairs, Department of the Interior.

Appendix B

VOCABULARY

I. WORDS FOR GOD

diyin 'ayóí 'át'éii, literally, *diyin* (he is supernatural, holy); *'ayóí* (remarkable); *'át'éii* (the specific one who is); freely, the Supreme Being. (I am indebted to Robert W. Young for these and following transcriptions and translations. The comments are my own.) This term was coined for the Franciscan Fathers, as early as 1905, by older Navahos, to designate the God of foreigners. The word *diyin*, which is ordinarily translated "holy," for traditional Navahos meant sacred as opposed to secular, supernatural as opposed to natural, but the word had no traditional connotation of moral sanctity. Young suggests "Super-men" for *diyin dine'é*, usually translated "Holy people." The coiners thought that in time this phrase might come to carry a conception of moral sanctity. It seems to indicate *the* supernatural, not *a* supernatural (cf. Haile, 1937, pp. 33, 42). Fr. Berard told me that he had never been happy over the question of translating "God" into Navaho and found especially that the conceptions of uniqueness and omnipotence were difficult to carry over. Nevertheless, this coinage of the turn of the century seems to have caught on sufficiently to be used by the peyotists. (It appears in Haile's transcription, altered to Young and Morgan symbols, as *dighin 'ayoit'éi*.)

diyin binant'a'i, literally, holy their-leader; freely, the leader of all spiritual entities. Here the idea of uniqueness is more weakly developed, and the conception of what is meant by "leader" may vary widely for individual Navahos—from the idea of absolute power to the idea of one who is *primus inter pares*. Formerly a leader (*naat'áanii* or *binant'a'i*) had few powers. Today, however, the term is used in compounds which designate figures of considerable authority. So, at a minimum, God as expressed by this phrase is at least the influencer of all spiritual beings, and probably for most peyotist Navahos, the authority over all spiritual beings. Cf. *kráisd nixinant'a'i*, Christ our Lord who is (Haile, 1937, p. 173).

diyin 'aláají', literally, holy (being) foremost. Here a sense of precedence is found, but the connotation of supremacy is weaker than in the case of previous terms.

diyin bóhólníihii, holy one in charge (Rapoport, 1954, p. 137).

nilch'i diyini, literally, spirit (wind) holy; freely, Holy Spirit. Although Fr. Berard claims that *nilch'i* is a term too closely associated with the winds who are supernatural beings in Navaho mythology to be used for spirit, he had nevertheless used it himself in a compound for Holy Ghost, *diyin'ayoit'ei binilch'i*, or Supreme Being's Spirit (Wind) (Haile, 1937, p. 108, for example). The term has no necessary conception of supremacy or uniqueness, but since peyotists use it in alternation with the other terms mentioned above, it may well have achieved these connotations. It is used for God, not for the Holy Ghost.

nihitaa' diyin yisdá'iiníłi, literally our-father holy the one who saves people, or more freely, Our Father and Savior. But Savior is a bit too free: Saver would be better. Fr. Berard notes that the idea is that of being saved from danger, not saved from or redeemed from sin (Rapoport, 1954, p. 138). The *-taa'* of "our father" is a stem meaning "father" which is obsolescent, if not obsolete, in the sphere of kinship, but found both in Navaho prayers and in Fr. Berard's Catechism and Guide throughout (Haile, 1937). It thus has dignity and a sense of fatherhood transcending the familial. The phrase is used in prayer and should be compared with the next item, also used in prayer.

shimá dóó shizhé'é, literally, my mother and my father. Used often in prayers, this phrase is likely to be uttered in emotional tones. The man who delivers it is likely to call himself, or the group present, "Your infant(s)" or "Your child(ren)." The *-zhé'é* stem for "father" is ordinarily used in addressing one's own father.

II. WORDS FOR PEYOTE

'azee' diyiní, Holy Medicine.

'azee', medicine. For traditional Navahos this word would refer to any medicinal substance or material used in a curing ceremony.

These terms are used both in ordinary discourse and in ceremonies. Three that follow are used in ceremonies.

ni'ilníí' siźíinii, that which stands in the middle of the earth.

yak'ashbąąh doo bínií'ohí, nothing is hidden from it from horizon to horizon.

nihook'eh doo bínií'ohí, nothing is hidden from it (even) in a storage crypt.

The last two terms imply that peyote sees everything.

'azee' yit'aałii, chewing medicine, a term used by non-peyotists.

'azee' ch'įįdii. Although translated "Devil medicine" in the 1940 Tribal Council hearings, this is in fact "ghost medicine." It is a non-peyotist's term and highly derogatory.

III. WORDS FOR SOUL, GHOST, AND IN-STANDING THING

niłch'i hwii' siźíinii, literally spirit or wind inside of the specific one that stands; freely, in-standing spirit. This term is used by peyotists for man's immortal soul, which goes to a heavenly dwelling place when a man dies—or perhaps to a new life on earth. This term also has its parallel in Fr. Berard's translations: he uses *siźíini* for soul in his Catechism and Guide (Haile, 1937, pp. 40–41). So here we find another usage apparently influenced by the Franciscans' choice of terms.

The traditional meaning of *siźíini*, however, differs from the Catholic or the peyotist meaning, whether we follow Fr. Berard or Reichard. Fr. Berard claims that in traditional lore, *'ii' siźíini*, in-standing one, is a term referring to the "directing or life principle within living beings," whether these are spiritual, human, or animal. The term has a connotation of wind, since Dawn Woman sends colored winds into the bodies of newborn infants. The in-standing one becomes a homunculus as the child matures and is the cause of physical and personality traits, desirable and undesirable. Hence a person is not fully responsible for his own behavior, which is a product of his in-standing one—which was given to him. Fr.

Berard believes that the traditional attitude is shifting in the direction of moral responsibility and chose the term to mean Christian soul at the suggestion of Navahos (Haile, 1937, pp. 40–41; Haile, 1951, pp. 169–170). Reichard, however, says that the in-standing thing is an image of turquoise in a man's chest which makes him strong if it stands upright. It is found only in Navahos who have undergone particular ceremonies (1950, pp. 32–33). Haile, however, says that the in-standing one is not affected by ceremonies. Whatever the case, both Catholic and peyotist usage seem to have sublimated the homunculus.

ch'įįdii, ordinarily translated "ghost," according to Fr. Berard may be translated as "deprived thing," and refers both to the corpse and its clothes and to a shadowy and harmful entity which remains about the country after death. Fr. Berard asserts that this ghost is not to be confused with the in-standing one, which returns to Dawn Woman and perhaps is used again. But he says that the in-standing one may remain about the premises for four days after burial and in this sense may be called a ghost—yet he criticizes Navahos who confuse the two concepts. To me his very remarks would indicate that the two ideas are in fact intertwined for Navahos. A person who dies of old age, says Fr. Berard, has no ghost, but only an in-standing one, which goes to the place "where old age exists" (1951, pp. 309–310). Reichard prefers to translate *ch'įįdii* as "potentiality for evil" or "the contamination of the dead" (1950, pp. 48–49).

There is evidence of lack of unanimity among Navahos regarding the spirit and the ghost in Ladd, 1957, p. 417, and Wyman, Hill, and Osanai, 1942.

IV. WORDS FOR OFFICIANTS

'aláaji' hoołáligíí, road chief, literally, foremost one who carries on a ceremony. *hoołááł*, he makes things progress; he carries on a ceremony (Progressive mode).

'asaa' yee hoołáligíí, drummer chief, literally, drum with the one who performs: the one who performs with a drum.

'ayah didi'nił yee hoołáligíí, cedar chief (*'ayah didi'nił*, incense, literally *yah*, under, *didi'nił*, put them into fire, a standard term in traditional Navaho ceremonialism), the one who performs with incense.

ko yee hoołáligíí, fire chief, the one who performs with the fire.

'azee' deiyání, peyote cult members, literally medicine those who eat it, medicine eaters.

doo 'azee' deiyání, non-members, those who do not eat medicine.

'azee' bee hoogáałii, Native American Church, or more literally, medicine, its movement, and hence, in context, peyote movement.

V. GENERAL COMMENTS

The term for Supreme Being and in part the word for soul have been borrowed from the Franciscans. On the other hand, the word for "Savior" has a Protestant derivation. Some terms for God seem to imply both the ascendancy of God and the existence of other spiritual beings—the Leader of all spiritual entities, the Foremost Holy Being.

The terms for the four ritual leaders do not include any element which can be translated "chief." On the other hand, in the standard English vocabulary of peyotism, road chief, drummer chief, cedar chief, and fire chief are as often called road man, drummer man, etc., which puts the stress on performance rather than on leadership.

Postscript, 1965. There are additional, common words for God which I failed to record. One, for example, is usually translated, "Our Heavenly Father."

Appendix C

FOUR INTERVIEWS

OUT OF A LARGE NUMBER OF INTERVIEWS, four have been selected to give some idea of the views of individual Navahos. The first is with a northern road chief; the second, with a southern. These give an idea of sophisticated peyotism and also permit the comparison of northern and southern orientations. The third interview is with a northern woman with a simple devotion to peyotism but little concern with ideology, the fourth with a southern woman of comparable attitudes. These interviews show quite similar outlooks. In addition, they bring out the tendency for men to be the ideologues of peyotism and for women not to be. Parentheses are the speakers'; brackets are my questions or explanatory comments.

A NORTHERN ROAD CHIEF

The northern road chief is *Ben Eastman,[1] born in about 1900. He completed only first grade, but was in the Army in World War I, though not overseas. He has some background in the Presbyterian Church. He speaks some English. He was trained as a singer, and claims to know "all the chants." Asked for a list, he supplied Chiricahua Apache Wind Way, Evil Way, Shooting Way (Male Branch), Flint Way, Blessing Way, and Enemy Way (translations drawn from Wyman and Kluckhohn, 1938; he did not specify which branch of Flint Way he knew). This is a very large repertory, but it is possible that he knows only portions of some of these; I did not inquire more closely. In addition, he states that he used to do Hand Trembling Divination (*n'dilniih*) and Star Gazing Divination (*déest'įį'*, which involves looking at a star through a rock crystal or prism). He gave up Star Gazing when he got paint in his eyes and they were injured, and he simply abandoned Hand Trembling. He owns a canvas teepee, which he uses for peyote meetings. He was given Alfred Wilson's brass kettle for a drum—I believe after Wilson's death. He lives in District 9, north of Red Mesa, on the San Juan, and keeps close contact with Aneth, which he reaches by fording the river. He was born at Aneth and grew up near the Carrizo Mountains. He was interviewed on August 25, 1950, before a peyote meeting near Emmanuel Mission. The interview was carried out through an interpreter.

[I asked him how he had come to take up peyotism.] Eleven years ago [1939], around the Carrizos, I was very sick. And *Ernie Finch came over. At that time he was living at Beclabito. I went to visit *Ernie and on the way I became very ill. *Ernie boiled three peyote buttons for me, and that was the first time I saw peyote. And it seemed to quiet down the pain the next day. And that day, *Dan Pritchard came and boiled nine more peyote buttons for me, and I drank that.

---

[1] Asterisk preceding a proper name indicates a pseudonym.

And the medicine took effect, and I became conscious of its effects. I heard a voice saying, "This medicine is the rays of the sun and air," and under this influence I also heard that the Jewish people had written the Bible—that's how I knew about that. And I realized that there was such a thing as the Almighty. So in its teachings I found out that the medicine was used in prayer, and not often to cure, but especially for prayer, to be in communion with the Lord or Almighty.

So I figured that the purpose of the sickness was to enable me to recognize how I became sick. The teaching of the Almighty made me realize I had a father, a mother, a sister, and relatives. In the past I had not realized my position [i.e., he now realized the significance of these relationships]. And then I realized that my body is of earth, that I breathe through the rays of the sun and the air, and that is how I live. And I started thinking of my relatives, and I realized that the people of the world had different tongues [languages] and names, but they are the same in having five fingers, but their skins are different. They all breathe the same air. And this Church had the same teaching as children learning in school [i.e., it educates as a school does]. I think a great deal of this Church, even though I have been in jail [on account of practicing peyotism], and I depend on the Almighty and I have no fear while I am walking on this earth. And so in this way I keep up with the Church.

We have schoolchildren, but Indians of all tribes in the United States lack education and have no science of their own to realize what their white brothers have learned. Their white brothers have education and have scientists, working on what the earth and the air contain. And so I realized that there must have been something wrong against the Almighty: that earth people are not intended to do that, and perhaps that's why there is a war [the Korean War]. Maybe the Almighty is doing it, and maybe the earth people are doing wrong. Before the white man came to this country, it belonged to the Indians, and the whites came as immigrants, and took control of all this land, without the consent of the natives, and up to date they have not considered the natives or helped them in their welfare, and in this country when there is a war, they call on the natives to take up arms. That's the only time they need their help. What about in peacetime? Even Congress, or the President of the United States, I figure, in the true sense is not the creator or the superior of this land, but God Almighty is. That is what peyote is teaching me.

So today I think by the use of peyote that before the whites came this land belonged to the Indians, and when the whites had wars, our boys joined and helped them, but the people in Washington have not expressed thanks for our help in fighting for freedom. And all the minerals from this land go into war machinery [there are vanadium mines in the northern Navaho area], into what they fight with across the ocean, and all this is borrowed from the Indians. We are made of earth, and they don't come round and apologize for that. [Probably he refers to an apology to mother earth.]

I have two boys over in Korea. And I keep on considering that we are mistreated and not helped. Many of our boys went across in the last war and some died there, fighting for freedom, and now, speaking of our religion, I consider also how this church will run without interference from non-users [of peyote], the government, or people from different organizations.

Today I have a clear consciousness from thinking of all these things, that when we are not at war they turn away from us. They take our boys in war. Why are there wars? Because the people in the world don't know about the Almighty, or because the people do wrong? I think of these things today. And that's how I use peyote at this time. Let me show you this. [Letter dated June 29, 1949, to the Commissioner of Indian Affairs. It comments that the origin of the American Indian is unknown and goes on to request and comment on a series of things. It requests religious freedom, especially since American Indians fight in wars for freedom. It observes that the Indians once owned all the land. It says that there is need for a Navaho program for livelihood. There should be no livestock reduction. Indian Service employees should be reduced in number. There should be well-drilling with the money saved. Loans should be administered better; at present the Loan Committee makes loans on a political basis. It asks for removal of the Tribal Attorney. It concludes by citing a Statute regarding Indians passed by the U.S. Assembly of July 13, 1797, which is not familiar to me. The letter is signed by *Ben Eastman and his wife, *Bertha. A second letter of June 29, 1950, states that it is necessary for the Native American Church to take action against slanderers. It is signed by the President, Vice-President, Secretary, and one other member of the Native American Church of Utah.]

Is it possible that if the Church existed without interference, a man like you [DFA] would take fees? [I think that the intent of the question is that since I am making a study of peyote in which the Indian Office is interested, I might claim a fee if I reported sympathetically and the legal status of peyotism was improved. My answer is not recorded, but I assume I denied such an intention.]

[Had you heard of peyote before you took it?] Yes, over on the Ute reservation. [When did it first come to the Navahos?] Fifteen years ago [1935]. [At this point the interview passed briefly into questions about the history of peyotism which have been dealt with in Aberle and Stewart, 1957.] [When did you learn to put up a meeting?] Nine years ago [1941], a year after I first used peyote [slightly inconsistent—by a year]. [From whom did you learn?] Sam Standing Water [Cheyenne] first taught me, and then Alfred Wilson. I use the big moon.

[We then briefly discussed the fact that trouble over peyotism had first arisen in the Lukachukai area, and that then there had been a Tribal Council resolution. I then asked about the history of troubles in District 9. *Eastman listed ten principal opponents, including a local Tribal Councilman, *Eastman's own wife's father and brothers, and an uncle of *Eastman. I asked what happened.] They ran around looking for meetings and disturbing them, at Beclabito, Teec Nos Pas, and at Black Mesa, and three miles from here—that was the last time. The people in the meeting got four disturbers and tied them up at midnight and turned them loose in the morning. That was four years ago [actually it was in early 1947]. I was there. I just stayed in the meeting. There were sixty or seventy members there, with a guard out, and they came about two in the morning, four of them; others stayed back. They were caught and tied. [Names them.] We just tied them. The next morning we asked [their leader] how he came to do it. He said that [the

Chairman of the Council] and [the Head of Law and Order] told him to do it. [There is no evidence to support this allegation.] We let them go the next morning. They complained to the Agency. The police picked up some boys and took them to jail—twenty members. They stayed in jail two days and then they were released.

Look at this. [He showed documents and letters. The documents recorded his own arrests of 3 April 1941, 21 January 1944, and 1 May 1945. In 1944 he had been fined $200.00, and in 1945, $90.00. The maximum *legal* fine is $100.00. There was a letter of May 10, 1950, written on official stationery of the Native American Church of the State of Utah. The letterhead is printed. On the left side of the letterhead is a picture of soldiers marching under the American flag, underneath which is the motto, "We Are Fighting to Preserve Religious Freedom." On the left side is a picture of soldiers with rifles raised to fire a volley over a grave (cemetery crosses in the background; American flag also in the background). Underneath this is the motto, All Men Are Created Equal. In the lower left-hand corner is printed a torch of liberty, underneath which appears the motto, "Constitutional Liberty." The letter deals with some very complex local chapter election problems of 1950 and is signed by *Ben Eastman, President (of the NAC of Utah), *Dick Monroe, Vice-President, and *Bertha Eastman, Secretary-Treasurer. An undated petition asks for freedom of worship in their own way and accuses non-users of peyote of drinking and doing evil and harmful things. It is signed by ten members of the Native American Church from the general area, including two Tribal Delegates and one chapter officer. *Bertha is a signatory, but in this case, not *Ben.

A letter of November 30, 1943, from a Navaho soldier in the American Army speaks of providing help if the trouble over peyote continues. It asks whether the Germans and the Japanese are behind the opposition to the Native American Church. A letter of December 7, 1948, contains a patriotic statement by *Ben. A letter states that in 1946 the same soldier, together with *Ben, was arrested by the Tribal Police, and put in jail at Shiprock. The arrest occurred at a peyote meeting. The meeting was, in fact, a peyote wedding, and the soldier was the groom.]

[I asked him whether members had ever broken up Navaho ceremonies. He denied this and also said that the kidnapping of the Superintendent at Teec Nos Pas in 1945 had been done by non-members. I asked him whether things were as bad for members of the Church as they had been.] No, the opposition has quieted down. I talk to [two of the leaders], and it seems that there are no hard feelings.

[I told him that I had heard that if a witch took peyote, he would be compelled by its power to confess his witchcraft and give up witching. He said he knew nothing about this, but on another occasion, during a peyote meeting, he pointed out to me a man who, he said, had done just that.]

[We continued with relationships in the community.] I have no hard feelings against the non-members, even against my relatives who are non-members. We shake hands. But I don't know how they feel toward me. We are not very close. [Are many of your relatives still non-members?] My uncle is the only one who stayed out. All his children and family joined.

[We then discussed a famous case of a woman alleged to have gone insane from taking peyote. This and other allegations are discussed elsewhere; so the details of *Ben's view of the history are omitted here. It emerged in the course of the talk that *Ben believed that if peyote were improperly administered it might cause pain or mental effects. I asked what he meant by this.] If the person who gives the medicine is not initiated in the full use of it, and if he has bad thoughts or something against a person and is not using it right, it will work like that. It's like a quack. [DFA: It is far more like Navaho beliefs in the power of singers to harm people in the course of carrying out ostensible curing rituals. The apparent difference is that a peyotist who would do this would be one not fully instructed, in *Ben's view. Hence he would apparently hold that a fully instructed priest could not and would not do this.]

[The discussion continued with comments about numbers of peyotists in various areas. These materials have already been used in Aberle and Stewart, 1957. One comment is of interest, however. *Ben said that there were less peyotists in Shiprock than in Aneth and District 9, because Shiprock is close to town and people go to town on Saturday nights when peyote meetings are often held.]

[We then discussed his knowledge of Navaho ceremonies. I asked him whether he still sang Evil Way. He said that he did. I then asked him whether he believed in ghosts or in a soul that went to heaven. He said he believed in the soul. I asked why he still sang Evil Way.] If a non-member dies, his spirit is a ghost, but a member's spirit is not. [Do you still carry on Navaho ceremonials in general?] Yes. [For non-members only?] No, for members as well. The sole purpose of the ceremony is to cure the patient, and whoever needs help, I give it to them.

[How do you feel about the Navaho spiritual beings and the God you learned about from the Church?] Our bodies are of earth, and the chants are for the purpose of healing the bodies. In the Native American Church you pray for the spirit. And if a person is sick in the hospital, they give him a remedy. The remedy comes from the earth, and they apply it without speaking of God. [I asked for further explanation.] The remedies all come from the earth. Washington is a headquarters, and it has its agent. And if something is wrong on the Navaho reservation, and we try to go to Washington about it, they ask us if we saw the District Supervisor. For a sticker in your finger you don't call on the Almighty. [Then do you use Navaho ceremonies for lesser ills and the Native American Church for greater ones?] Yes. [How about you, do you ever use the hospital?] Yes, I have, since I joined the Native American Church.

[There is a lot of discussion about which costs more, chants or peyote ceremonies. You do them both, perhaps you can tell me.] The chants cost you more. A meeting costs you less than a button. [Well, I thought a peyote meeting cost something to run.] The Native American Church has no fee. The chant does have a fee. [Well, what about the contributions at the peyote meeting?] If you run a meeting, one way of people's expressing gratitude is by the contributions they make. The road man spends money on his car, and so on. And so they give you money—or they may not. It depends on whether the patient is rich or poor.

[Well, what do you think should be done about the conflict over peyotism in the Navaho country, to settle the troubles?] "Amend" [change] the law. It's been set in Washington. We will put up $10,000 to take it to the Supreme Court. The loser will have to pay $10,000. This month when the Council meets it will discuss peyote and do away with this law. Three Oklahoma Indians and lawyers will bring it up—Robert Yellow Tail [then a Delegate at Large of the Native American Church, a Crow], Allen Dale [then President of the Church, Omaha], and Frank Takes Gun [then Vice-President, Crow]. It will be brought up at the Tribal Council meeting next month. And the Secretary, Woodrow Wilson [Southern Cheyenne], and White Cloud [?]. [I must have expressed some doubt that these men would be able to appear before the Council; at any rate, *Ben remarked that the Secretary of the Interior supervises the Tribal Council and that *somebody* would discuss it. Nothing was scheduled to occur, nor was the issued raised in the Council at this time.]

[I then asked for certain biographical data, *Eastman remarked that he had learned hardly any English in school, had spoken a little in the Army, and had really learned English through using peyote. He closed by remarking ironically that the police at Shiprock used peyote, arrests or no, and that Fryer had been good to the Native American Church.]

This terminated the interview. The end was characterized by a good deal of conversation between *Ben and me on the legal status of peyote, and only certain portions of this were recorded by me.

Next day, after the meeting, two of the group present expressed a great deal of hostility and suspicion of me. One was the Vice-President of the Native American Church of Utah. They suggested that somehow I was out to make money out of my work and out of them, that I would publish something unsuitable, that the names I took down would be used for arrests, etc. They also commented that it was whites who were behind the Tribal Council that voted the resolution against peyote. In the course of all this, the Vice-President remarked, "Hitler was a good thing. Before the war, people wasted things. During the war they didn't." *Ben continued, "And he killed people off and made more room."

In spite of the vigor of his anti-white feelings, *Ben has been kind and cooperative in all my dealings with him.

The ideological keynote of this interview seems to be intense nativism, and correspondingly strong hostility to whites. Hostility to non-peyotists is nearly as marked. He both competes with the whites for knowledge and asserts that man was not intended to know as much as the white man is trying to find out. He regards the Indian as a victim of exploitation whose contribution remains unrecognized. He has typical attitudes toward Navaho livelihood: if we keep our stock, get rid of the Indian Service, and get enough water, everything will be all right. I do not know why he opposes the Tribal Attorney. He receives voices and illuminations immediately from peyote. He minimizes curing in his discussion, but actually conducts a great many curing ceremonies. He does not express antagonism toward Navaho ceremonials, being himself a ceremonial practitioner. He comments, not in the least unreasonably, about the very serious history of conflict in his area. He displays a wide circle of acquaintanceship with the national organization and has had enough contact with two Cheyenne peyotists to learn the ritual from each. This has occurred in spite of a fairly marked linguistic handicap. He is an "organization" man as well as a road man. The two roles do not necessarily coincide. (*Ben and *Bertha both died in the early 1960's after this was written.)

A SOUTHERN ROAD CHIEF

The southern road chief is *Barney Strong of Piñon. Born in about 1919, he started life in the Piñon area as the son of one of the wealthier Navahos of Black Mountain. He spent seven years in the Government school at Keams Canyon, and 6 years at Fort Wingate Vocational High School, completing high school there. He is Catholic in terms of formal religious affiliation. According to the Supervisor of District 4 during and before World War II, *Barney's written English was only fair when he went into the Army but improved rapidly and remarkably during that time. His spoken and written English were good in 1950, when I interviewed him (July 29, 1950), and have continued to show marked improvement ever since. The interview was in English. The circumstances were roughly comparable with my meeting with *Ben Eastman. It was a first encounter, and it preceded any occasion on which both of us attended the same peyote meeting—an occasion which often facilitates subsequent discussions. The interview, like that with *Eastman, began with a relatively unstructured phase and continued to specific points that I wished to cover.

[To begin with, I asked him how he had happened to start using peyote.] In 1943, I think, I went to my first meeting. It wasn't a regular meeting; there was no altar, people were just eating the medicine. I wasn't sick; I just wanted to see how it looked. My folks were in it, and they liked it and said it was good. I tried it, and it was all strange, the singing, and the praying, and felt good, and all right too. The singing and the praying were good. And so I happened to attend one or two more. Most people at that time had not gone far, we were all beginners, starting to use this medicine.

I kept using the medicine, and the war was on, and I was selected for the armed forces and was inducted April 28, 1944, into the Marines. And I got a strange pain below my abdomen, in my pelvic region. Perhaps I strained myself. The doctors said I was OK, but at Guadalcanal I got worse and was given pills, but nothing else. And then I landed in Okinawa on Easter Sunday, and went through the campaign and was wounded there. I was sent back to Guam, and then to Japan. I got worse and reported to the doctor and was put to bed at Yokosuka. I spent fifteen days there, and then was taken to a hospital ship in an ambulance. I spent a week there with pills and nothing else. I couldn't sleep. I would imagine things. I thought I would be dead. I went back to the States one month after World War II ended, to San Lorenzo Naval Hospital. I spent two months there, still feeling the same. It affected my mind and thinking [i.e., it worried him terribly]. They couldn't find out the trouble. I was discharged from San Diego and came back here to my home. And they put up a Native American Church meeting for me. It didn't have much effect. And they had Navaho sings also, and they didn't have much effect. I went back to Fort Defiance Hospital [in November, 1948]. The doctor found something wrong with my prostate, and gave me penicillin and drugs, but I still had the same feeling. And I went to Oklahoma to see Native American Church members four years ago [1946]. There was a meeting there, with medicine, praying and singing, and boy, I felt all right again, and I brought back lots of medicine and used it at home. I would eat it and rest—up to 20, 30, 40, or 100 a day, and I seemed to be getting all right, and my bad feelings were getting out. I went back to Oklahoma again. An Oto man named Truman Dailey—we call each other brother—he wanted me to use his fire-place and way, and he gave me his ways, and I am using it that way, and I try to help people that way, and that's how I do, and I know I help lots of people. Some were sick and got helped. Some couldn't be helped. They were too far gone, and I don't have [know] enough.

Before, I couldn't work, but now I can. I worked from November until June at Piñon School. Then I had my annual leave, and I will go back Monday, and I am all right. The white doctors tried everything, at the Naval hospitals and Fort Defiance, but even though I got better for a short time, I had trouble again later on. I used the medicine every day. There is something—some part of good in this medicine. What little I have found out I explain to other people about this medicine. It's what you *think*. We talk to God, to our Creator, through this medicine, and in that way we get well and understand things. That's the main. part. [Any further pain?] A little pain still. I can do a lot of work, though.

Even under this threat, the Tribal Council at Window Rock, we don't think there is anything wrong. We use it. We don't care if the police come in. So long as the Government has the law of freedom of worship, the Constitution, that's why we want to have this church. That's the truth.

[Have there been any arrests up here?] No. [Any trouble in the community?] No trouble. My brother was arrested through some one telling that he used peyote. He was sentenced to eight months in jail but he spent only a month there. I went over there [to the jail at Fort Defiance] a couple of times and got the case repealed. That was three years ago. A woman might have been spying on us; maybe she hid a couple of buttons and took them to the police as evidence. My brother was running the meeting. [Any breaking into meetings?] No. There were other arrests, but I don't know who.

[What do you mean, your mind was upset when you were ill?] It makes you think you may die right away. That's the worst thing I ever encountered. I pray through the medicine, like in church, and I want to think good and go straight. I might have got sick through my own [bad] ways. And it came out that way so far. [Things went well.]

[He was a rifleman in the Marines, a Pfc with a good record. He was 26 when he went in. Although he had occasional combat dreams, he gave no history resembling a combat neurosis. His major participation in the Church began after the war. The local chairman of the Native American Church speaks no English. The vice-chairman does. *Strong is secretary.] They wanted me in the Church here because I talk English. I have made many good and honest friends, Oklahoma people, through that. I have stopped whiskey and unnecessary bad stuff [bad behavior]. [What did you do when you got drunk?] I gave away a lot of stuff—I didn't get into fights. [When did you stop drinking?] I haven't drunk since before I went into the Marines.

[How did peyote come to this area?] *Mal Hancock was the first. At first there was no altar; the drum, rattle, and [prayer] cigarettes were for the leader only.

There was no whistle, no [midnight and morning] water [ceremony], and no [ceremonial] foods in the morning. [And then?] After I came back from the Marines, *Walter Abbott ran meetings. [And *Bill Conroy?] Yes. Me and *Bill have the same ways [of running a meeting]. [Have the Oto boys been over here to visit? (The phrase "Oto boys" is used by many of the Navahos who have been trained by Otos.)] Yes. [Proceeds spontaneously:]

In Navaho ceremonies you find people sleeping and drinking [there is a vigil the last night of Navaho ceremonies, during which no one is supposed to sleep.] There is none of that in the Native American Church. Evil Way and Enemy Way don't help. There was a squaw dance [Enemy Way] for a service man, and the people were drunk. There was a knife fight. The same boy three or four years later killed a Hopi. And he went to the penitentiary. But there was no execution and he got back in the service. The ceremony is supposed to be sacred and reverent, but it was done with drunks and fighting, and so the boy had all this trouble [i.e., the fighting at his ceremony caused him later to fight and kill someone, the cause being a disruption of supernatural power]. If they held them in the right way they would be OK, but if they are held in the wrong way they are no good. They put up an Enemy Way for me. [Well, aside from the drinking and bad behavior, what do you think of the old Navaho ceremonies?] The old medicine men teach the younger men how to act. They say you should be careful. If you ever miss [make a mistake], something will go wrong. I don't want to use it if something might go wrong, and I might get finished off; so I stick to the Native American Church. There you can say what you want. The prayers aren't fixed. [There is a prayer which both singer and patient must say word-perfect if the ceremony is to work, according to Navaho ceremonial theory.] [Well, what if you *do* make mistakes, in a peyote meeting; after all there are some things that are supposed to be done just so.] If you make a mistake, it's up to you what attitude you take. If you think its bad, it's bad; if you think not, it isn't. [Are there many young people learning Navaho ceremonies? Will they go on?] There are not many young people learning. They are missing a lot. In ten or fifteen or twenty years, most of it will be gone. And that's why Almighty God has put the Church in the middle of it. If we are without our ceremonies, we must have something to live by, something to pray to, and so the Creator He put the Native American Church among us.

[What about the missionaries?] They say, "You must do this, pray this," and so on. We can't understand this. I am a Catholic myself, and I was once a helper to a Catholic priest, but through the Native American Church we don't say to *live* this way, *do* this, *know* this, we let the *medicine* do it. If we tell them that way, we might be doing it wrong ourselves, and so we don't advise people. [i.e., an ordinary mortal advises others at his peril; he may himself err in his standards of conduct and teaching. It is best for a person to receive his illuminations directly, through peyote experience, and receive his guidance from supernatural, not human sources.] [We then discussed his educational and religious history briefly. I asked whether he still took peyote daily.]

No, I take it quite rarely, at meetings. [Well, what happened when you took it in these quantities every day?] I felt nothing in me, I felt as if a feather was stroking me. I didn't imagine things, though I took almost a hundred medicines [pieces of peyote]. I thought about good. Eating medicine all day and the night before, I thought of my past up to then, and I humbled myself and burst into tears. Then I sure felt good. [Any visions?] No vision. If you had bad actions, bad words, you will see your wrongs. Then you feel bad, and pray and sing, and then get out of it, and leave these things behind and get better. And make confession and smoke. [In sum, if your mind is right, you do not get visions.] [What do you call God?] Almighty God, *diyin 'ayói 'át 'éii*. [Note that as a Catholic he was exposed to this term.] [What is the relationship between the *diyin dine'é*, holy people of Navaho stories, and *diyin 'ayói 'át 'éii?*] The Navaho holy figures and this are something different. God made everything, and he made the Navahos and put these gods among the Navahos to pray to. [What is the word for soul?] *Nílch'i hwii' sizínii*. [Note again that this term, though not identical with the Catholic *sizíinii* overlaps with it.] [I returned to the issue of daily consumption of peyote. If a man takes peyote, can he just go around anywhere?] No, he should stay home and rest. [Returning to the theme of Navaho religion, I asked whether any Navaho ritual elements were used in a peyote meeting, or whether peyote could be used in a Navaho ceremony. The answer was, "No." We then continued with a discussion of Navaho singers' attitudes toward peyote. *Strong said that if the singers came in and saw the meeting they liked peyotism, but if they heard only the rumors about it, they distrusted it. There were a few who attended meetings. He named three, all of whom are in fact singers in District 4 and members of the peyote cult. I have interviewed them. He also said that in his view the members of the cult were more or less a cross-section of the community— as regards age, sex, education, etc. I asked whether his becoming a peyotist had caused him to lose friends.] At first I did, but now things have quieted down. At first they didn't like me because I used it, but now they see it doesn't do me any harm. I have good relations now. [We then discussed his own present situation.] I have a wife, a boy and a girl. The kids are both in school. My wife has been sick these last two months, but now she is all right; they had a sing for her, but she would not go to the hospital—she has no education. [Well, what do you think of the doctors?] They are good. [Does peyote cure?] I have seen cures—you have seen that boy [some one who lives in *Barney's family group]. He was 12 or 14 years old and sick, and in a brush hogan, ready to die. [Peyote cured him.] I have no father and no mother, that's one reason why I attend church and am a member, because I have no one to depend on. [What about your more remote kin, do they belong?] My grandmother and my mother's sister both belong, and my wife.

[I keep on hearing rumors about sexual misbehavior in peyote meetings. What do you think is responsible for them?] A woman who might have been nasty [misbehaving] with the men-folks—the medicine might bring out what she had done, and that's how it happens. [I.e., she would have a vision concerned with sexual misbehavior and talk afterward as if people had done such things.] That's how the rumors start.

[How about you—did you ever have much background in Navaho ceremonials?] I never tried to learn the sings. [What about stories (Navaho myths) or songs or prayers?] I was not told any of these things.

[The discussion terminated, but we began to talk again the following morning, July 30. In the meantime I had attended a peyote meeting run by *Strong. In the morning I addressed myself largely to ritual symbolism. The remainder of the interview is transcribed or summarized not only for the materials, but for the attitudes revealed.] The drum? The Oklahoma Indians have their ways. We don't know much about it. They tell us just to do this, this is the way it goes. Truman Dailey said nothing about the drum. I have a lot to learn. I don't know the purpose of the drum. He said, like in last night's meeting, I should place the whistle in the water in his way. It has something to do with clans. Truman is Eagle Clan. There must be an eagle at the fire place: an eagle feather. I can't tell you about the gourd, and the rest of the equipment. What I tell you is all I know. The whistle should be an eagle leg bone. I use bamboo. There is a legend that goes with it, but I can't remember it—I don't recall much. [How did peyotism start?] I wasn't there at the time. [He then told a variant of the story of the woman alone and starving who found peyote. After she ate it and it "worked on her" she felt all right, and "whether she imagined, or whatever, no one knows, a scissor-tail bird spoke to her" and told her that she should go nearby where there was a ceremony. She was seated to the right of the priest at the ceremony, which was going on in a teepee, and asked for help to return to her people. The priest (or chief) said it could be done, he thought.] That's all I know. From here on I don't remember much; the rest I forgot. I'm not old, I'm just learning. I don't ask, they [the Otos] just tell me. That's the way it is. [This ended the interview.]

Subsequently, in 1954, *Barney told me much more about symbolism. It would be very hard to know whether on this first occasion he felt he had told me enough for one time, since there is a common belief that one learns about peyote gradually (and never learns everything) or whether he had reached his own limits, since he was undoubtedly also being taught little by little.

*Strong, who had held a job in the school since the previous November, continued with Government jobs thereafter—at Piñon, Brigham City, and Tuba City, largely connected with the schools but briefly at least he was employed as a policeman. He finally went to work for a business firm in Tuba City. Things may have been "quiet" in Piñon when I was there, but subsequently he was repeatedly arrested in connection with peyotism. There were four such arrests in 1955, one apparently for annoying the police by telling them that there was no law against the use of peyote and that they had no authority for arrest, once for possession of peyote at a peyote meeting and for resisting arrest, and twice presumably for running meetings and possessing peyote. There was also an arrest in 1956. I do not have a later record. He informed me that he had decided not to resist arrest in the future. He became a figure in a *habeas corpus* case entered by the Native American Church in an effort to challenge the law against peyote. I do not have details on this case.

Since I have known *Strong for several years, a short comment on his personal qualities might be of some help before we turn to the content of the interview. He is a big, dignified, slow-spoken, soft-spoken, soft-voiced man of excellent intelligence, intense but steady in emotional tone. He is what I call a "local" priest, in that his interest is not in travelling to far places to supply his ritual to strangers, but in taking care, as he sees it, of local people, and, so far as I can see, uninterested in financial gain from running a meeting. There is (or was, when last we spoke) a lack of any real bitterness, but a burning conviction of the rightness of his position which has undoubtedly been the spur to his repeated legal infractions. (He may have regarded himself as a convenient "goat" in addition, since on several occasions he was released from jail so as to avoid interruptions of maintenance and janitorial services at the school where he worked. Subsequently, however, there were difficulties over his government job which I have been unable to follow up. He was dismissed but complained and was ultimately given full back pay.) He is an unusually loyal friend, and I would say a most honorable man.

In the summer of 1962, he and I had a brief discussion respecting the probable content of my projected book on Navaho peyotism. At that time, he expressed profound disappointment to hear that I did not plan to state that I knew peyote to be a powerful curative agent. He asked, in effect, why I was not using his testimony and that of other members for this purpose. When I put it to him that testimony was not evidence, he understood the difference, but, naturally, he remained very unhappy that peyotists' experiences of the curative powers of peyote would not be used as he had hoped in this work.

In the summer of 1965, *Strong and I talked again about this book. He commented that more and more people were joining the Native American Church. Then he asked me whether I had surely noted in my book that many of those who join the cult are people who once bitterly opposed it, people who tried other ways of getting well and then turned to peyote, where, they felt, they succeeded. On re-reading the manuscript, I found that the discussion of entry into the cult did not bring out this point sufficiently. One might think, for example, from reading Chapter 12, that those who join the cult move mainly from neutrality or lack of interest to a positive attitude, rather than mainly from an initially negative attitude. I therefore use this opportunity to enter *Strong's correction of the record.

The ideological keynote of this interview seems to be the search for God's guidance through thought, prayer, and reflection on one's own conduct. This is the key to physical, mental, and spiritual health. No one else can guide a man or dare to be responsible for him. As in *Eastman's case there is a health crisis.

Visions occur, he seems to believe, only as a result of serious misbehavior, and he expects them to be disturbing. In spite of the consumption of unusually large quantities of peyote, he denies ever having had a vision, whereas *Eastman had one immediately after a much smaller quantity. *Barney's attitude is found among other southern peyotists as well, though by no means among all of them.

He expresses largely negative attitudes toward Navaho ceremonials, on two grounds: that a supernatural power which can be misdirected through a minor mistake is too untrustworthy, whereas one that allows spontaneity is agreeable, and that Navaho rituals are improperly run. There is some ambivalence, as if he were saying that, properly conducted, Navaho ceremonies might have kept their place in Navaho life. He seems to find missionaries rigid and uncompromising. Nativism makes no explicit appearance, although it does when he talks in ceremonies and in subsequent discussions with him, but not in the bitter form which *Eastman's takes. Pan-Indianism is evident but not marked. Curing is very important to him, while *Eastman maintains that it is only a minor aspect of peyotism. There is no rejection of science and no evidence of a need to compete with the white man for superior knowledge.

Two meetings with *Barney as road chief resulted in the expression of some of the themes absent in his interview. He spoke often of "us poor Indians" and commented that during a drought in the community the teacher had asked him not to give water from the school well to local people (the school water supply is a perennial problem in many parts of the Navaho country). He asked the teacher what she wanted to do—kill off the Navahos? They had been here first and had a right to the land. She could not tell him that the water was only for education, etc. She replied that the Navahos hadn't started from Arizona, either: they had come from Asia. He asked me whether this was true, and then asked how anyone knew, and why did they care about the past—they should be planning for the future. He subsequently remarked that it didn't look as if "Uncle Sam" should be in Korea. He asked whether Russia had the A-bomb and good scientists, remarking that Russia was powerful and had lots of man-power. These attitudes, including the concern about the Korean War, parallel some of *Eastman's.

There was also, in these meetings, a good deal of dwelling on "Indianism" and on the Indian-ness of the ritual.

Personal relationships were particularly agreeable throughout my visit in this area.

A NORTHERN NON-SOPHISTICATE

We will now deal with a northern and a southern interview with "non-sophisticates." The subjects will be people with no Western education who have not been trained as peyote priests. The first of these is a woman from Sweetwater, elderly, and without education. She does not know her age; I estimated it at 75 years, in 1950. She was interviewed on August 24 of that year. The interpreter was her son's daughter's husband.

[How did you happen to come to use peyote?] About eight or nine years ago I heard of this religion around the San Juan area, and I heard so much about it, and my husband was still living, and my grand-daughter [interpreter's wife's sister] was very sick. And a singer from around here had another patient at his home and was telling her that he had heard of this medicine in the San Juan area, and he said he was going for peyote, and so she gave him a sack of wool for the Sweetwater Trading Post. He took the wool to the store and traded it for money and went to the San Juan area. He found *Ed Lyons and bought some peyote, and *Ed said he would come two or three days later, and when the singer returned, he brought peyote, and I had never seen it, and two or three days later I heard there was to be a meeting at his house, and I took my grand-daughter to the meeting. During that meeting I ate peyote, and they knew—those who were at the meeting—that she was sick and that she would be well, and that the best thing was to have a sing for her—Evil Way. And so they sang over her and from then on she got better. At that time on the reservation the police were looking for this peyote, and other people were scared, but I was not, because my grand-daughter had gotten well on it, and so I felt it was good. And I took it ever since then.

And all that time I was using it, and then my grandson became very sick, and I nursed him with this peyote, and he also got well on this medicine, and even though the police were after this medicine, so many people were getting well on it. And when my grandson was sick, sings were administered, but they did no good. *Ben Eastman brought me some peyote, and I nursed him and took peyote, and when my son was sick I took quite a few of these buttons and started to think who was behind all that—even witchcraft—and I was treating him day and night and had very little sleep. And in the morning I saw a vision, a moon shape, and that was about all. I heard that *Ben was planning a meeting, and I and my husband were caring for my grandson, and there was no one else around. I said I was going to that meeting for help, but my grandson would not let me go. And I said, "I must have help," and I went anyhow, by horseback late in the afternoon in the deep snow. Close to Red Mesa, it all went white, and I was lost. I found a trail, and at sunset I came to a hogan, and I was going toward the mountain [the Carrizos, presumably], and I knew where I was, and I came to the house, and a man there said, "Where are you going?" and I said, "To the meeting." And he said, "The store is still open and two people are still there—hurry and you can catch them. And I followed the track all the way to the store, and there were two men at the Trading Post [Red Mesa], and I knew them, and I told them where I was going, and got warm and went on my way and arrived there [at the house where the meeting was to be] and it was 9:00. The meeting had not yet started. I went in next to the door. There were many people. *Ben and *Bertha Eastman were there, and I sat down between them after shaking hands, and while I sat, I began my story and told them how I was lost in the snow and having a hard time and my grandson was sick and needed help, and I begged for help for him and told the whole story, and about my son's condition, and they said, "We will pray for him at the meeting." So the meeting began and after the meeting was in session, *Ben followed the procedure of explaining the purpose of the meeting, and then he explained about me and how I came there, and asked for prayers for my grandson, and told how I hoped for help through prayers. The meeting went well, and I stayed all night, and I prayed with a cigarette [i.e., she was one of those who made a special, public prayer], and good prayers were given, and I asked *Ben to come to my place and give a meeting for my grandson. A few days later there was a meeting entirely for my grandson, and after that I ate plenty of peyote, and that's how I started in and I am still a member. So you see I have told you all about myself and as I told you my two sons got well, and I think it is good medicine for us and for me, too, and that's how it happened.

And only last winter I got sick. The year before last I went to the mountains with my two grand-daughters and gathered piñons until late in the winter, and I returned with my grandson and felt like eating medicine, and I took one to make me feel good [well] because I was not feeling well, and my side was aching. Something was wrong. And I took more medicine, and it kept on aching, but I thought maybe something was wrong, or maybe it was the effect of the peyote [?], and I let it ride, and two or three days later I had a pain again. And it got me down. I was in bed, and day by day getting worse, and I was sick one entire week, and finally my grandson came and asked me was I really sick, and I said, "Yes," and he asked for a meeting for myself, and still I was sick and felt bad, and so it went for days. I was sick and lying in bed and couldn't get around. And then my grandson came again and another woman was sick too, and so my grandson said they will hold a meeting for you both, and so there was a meeting, and at that meeting I had pretty near visualized what was ailing me—a chant or something, Evil Way, or something else [she probably means the effects of some improper performance of an Evil Way ceremony, or improper ritual contact with such a ceremony, but she might mean she was being injured by a ghost—a less likely meaning]. And the other woman was very sick too, and after the meeting I was better but the other woman was worse, and I got a little better each day, and I was towards getting well, and then after my grandson had a meeting they got to talking that I needed a chant over me, Plume Way said my grandson [that is, efforts at diagnosis were made at this second meeting], I thought it was Evil Way. A sing was held over me by the singer I mentioned before, and I felt better. It was Plume Way. After I got well, I found that this medicine was the best I had ever taken, and I have great respect for this church and this religion because I got well and both my grandsons got well, and my grand-daughters got sick and then got well on peyote, and I appreciate your coming here and asking all these questions, even though you have lots of business back East, and I sure hope that after all these troubles [over peyote] it will be settled and everyone will be happy.

And as you see I am now a widow and alone, with two grandsons to care for me, and I am a poor woman trying to care for myself and my children, and nevertheless I keep thinking that through some spirit, my husband's spirit, I have strength with the help of the Almighty [she burst into tears]. And I am thankful that you came and glad to tell that story. Even though other old people get [Federal] relief, I put in an application and got no help. I have only a few head of sheep and goats. That's how I make a living with the help of peyote. If it was not for these peyote meetings I would not be here. And I thank the Almighty through peyote that I am here. And a meeting is to be held in my hogan, and at that very spot I need help. And give it [the meeting] the best that you can. Also I am thankful for all the white people at Washington, D.C., and the plans they have given for the Navahos. And I appreciate it very much.

[She has heard of open conflict over peyote in the area but has had none herself. She has never used Western medicine, never having been near the hospital.] Taking this peyote and using the hospital are almost the same to my way of thinking.

This concluded the interview. It is notable for running almost continuously at considerable length, without questioning. It was held in the afternoon, and immediately afterward a peyote meeting began in one of the hogans of the cluster in which she lived. It was conducted by her grand-daughter's husband to bless some returning school children and to cure his wife, who, it developed, had St. Vitus' dance. Although I did not fully realize it, she was asking me to pray for the girl. It was on this occasion that I diagnosed the girl's trouble, to the delight of her father, and also of the old lady, who then asked me if I knew why she had low back pains. She accepted my view that they might be caused by old age but that I was unable to diagnose her condition.

The interview is plainly intended to be a testimonial to the power of peyote, but secondary themes are the support which she feels from God, peyote, and (most unusual among Navahos) from her dead husband's spirit—also gained through peyote. In her straitened circumstances, it is a miracle to her that she is alive, and peyote is to be blessed. (It is only fair to add that she is the oldest member of a large household with three young employable men in it, who take many off-reservation jobs.) It is evident that she does think of a Supreme Power, but no less evident that Navaho ceremonies have power for her, and that witchcraft is a force she feels she has to reckon with. Nativism and pan-Indianism play no role in her discussion whatever.

Her polite comment about the Indian Service can be taken more as a gesture toward me than as an expression of deeply felt sentiment—not a gesture of ingratiation, but one designed to give me pleasure. Relations with this family became very close.

In sum, this is a woman of exclusively Navaho background and considerable age, whose sole concern is with the power of peyote and of God as it helps her to cope with misfortune. She seems to want a vision, but so far has managed only a small one whose significance, if any, she does not mention. Reflection and illumination are also sought.

A SOUTHERN NON-SOPHISTICATE

For a comparable interview I use one with a somewhat younger woman from District 4, aged 57, with no schooling. The interview differs in that I asked more questions and elicited material that might have come up in talking to the previous woman, had it not been that in the northern interview I was dazed by the flow of materials and surrounded by other people eager to talk to me. The informant had attended Catholic and Protestant church services, but only rarely. She is not a "pure" southern case, because she has attended *Mal Hancock's and other northern meetings, but she has had extensive southern contacts as well. The interview was held through an interpreter.

[How did you first come to use peyote?] Seven years ago my sister's son was sick all the time. He had an earache and was having it pretty hard, and we tried Navaho ceremonies and they had no effect. My husband was worried about that and asked about the Native American Church as a possibility for the boy, and they told him how it worked, how it helped out the sick. He persuaded *Mal Hancock to run a meeting for the boy in a log cabin [unusual], and about midnight after the midnight water was taken out he was relieved of his pain and could hear. And in the morning it was OK. I too was sick with swellings in my joints, my arms, legs, hands, and face, and I too got better. And it was discovered at the meeting that *Verne Oridon should run a Blessing Way for the boy. [*Oridon is a singer, Chairman of the Native American Church in the area, and a Tribal Councilman.] And it was discovered that they should take turquoise and "jewels" up to the mountain [Black Mountain] and have a ceremony. [She subsequently explained that there were songs and prayers in the mountain, "like a sacrifice." The word used for "jewels" was ntl'iz, which the interpreter translated as "pearls." According to Fr. Berard, it designates hard, as opposed to soft goods, and is a collective term to designate jewel stones. Pearls are among the jewel stones and hence might lead to this translation. Compare Kluckhohn and Wyman, 1940, pp. 29, 88–89, Franciscan Fathers, 1910, pp. 394, 410.] And there was to be another meeting near Kitseely, and we took the boy with us and went to the meeting the day after the Blessing Way. At that meeting my swellings disappeared and I felt in better health than ever before. My husband attended a meeting at Many Farms, his third, and then a year after that they put up a meeting for him here, and we both got all right and the pains were all gone. And a couple of years later there was another meeting here. And from then on we have been doing all right.

And we have meetings about once a year (at our house). There was another meeting for my nephew at my older sister's place three miles from here. And we have been doing OK until last fall, when my husband had a hemorrhage for some time—a nosebleed—and he was taken to Fort Defiance for a transfusion, but they didn't help much and he didn't get back to normal while he was at the hospital, and he had Navaho sings, and on January 2 there was a meeting for him, *Barney Strong ran it, and from then on he regained some of his mind and the feeling he had in his body and made good progress in health. So a month and a half later there was another meeting, *Bill Conroy ran it, and from then on he came back to normal and could do his work in time to plant down at Chinle. It seems in this way the Native American Church has helped me out up to now. It is doing all right by us.

We had those meetings, and last fall one boy, my husband's sister's son (also my brother's son), whose mother had died—he does chores around here—he was thrown from a horse, and he was pretty sick. There was a Navaho sing for him and he got all right but still not back to normal—something bothered him, and he hemorrhaged from his lungs, and last winter he was that way, and at *Conroy's meeting he improved. But he still was not normal, and two weeks ago *Mal Hancock ran a meeting and he got OK, back to normal, and he could do his chores without any trouble. That's how I think of the Native American Church and how it helps me. I think a *lot* of it, since it has helped me out, as I have said.

I don't know what I would have done without the Church. My husband thinks the same. I try to remember what it has done for me, my husband, my son, and my nephew. In this way it has helped me out. And in this way we live a normal life, just as we did before we had all these troubles, and I think highly of it.

They tell me to take care of myself and my relatives, and they tell me how to carry on my life more easily by doing the right things around the home. That's what I meant by saying I'll tell you what little I do know. [During my first introductory discussion. "They" probably refers to people who teach or suggest things in the meetings.]

[I'm not quite sure I understand in what order things were done for the boy with the ear trouble.] First there was a peyote meeting, then a Blessing Way for two nights, then there was a peyote meeting for four nights in a row. [From the discussion, I assume that the jewel offering occurred in conjunction with the Blessing Way.]

[Well, which do you prefer—the Native American Church, Navaho ceremonies, or the hospital?] I like all three. I have used them all, and the white man's medicine as well—liniment—and I like this Blessing Way, which our old people used, and they made it possible for us to go on today. And I can't choose one as the best; I like all three. [Do you think the Navaho ceremonies are declining?] For my part, I think it's going to go on, because many people use it, and they don't know about the Native American Church. I myself use both. As generations go, one thing upholding Blessing Way is this: when a young girl becomes a woman, they have Blessing Way. That upholds it, and so I don't think we will forget about the ceremonies, and they will go on for a long time. Many people use only Navaho ceremonies. And as I see it, I use both, and it would be stupid to cut off one—it is better to use both.

[Well, how often do you attend Church meetings?] I am far from the other members, and so it's hard for me to attend unless the meeting is here, when my sister joins with me. If it's convenient I go, but it's hard; I'm alone, without children to care for things while I am away, but I do go when it is convenient, and so I do so about three or four times a year. [Continues spontaneously:]

People around here talk about my using the Native American Church, but they can say what they want, since I know for myself what it does. My husband goes round more often than I do myself. [Do people say things against you?] They do, but also they come round and talk good to me, they don't say it to my face—but they argue with my husband and the boy doing the chores, but in the long run I get along with them. They come to us for help; so I think they are all right toward me.

[How much peyote do you use at a meeting?] The first time I took twenty-nine, and from then on I can't take that many. Sometimes it's hard to get, so on average, about four or five. [Did you ever have a vision?] No. It never happened that way to me; perhaps I never took enough, or perhaps I haven't the brains. I have tried hand-trembling [divination] and star-gazing [divination] but it never worked on me. [I am no longer certain whether she meant that the techniques did not work when applied to her case, or that she was never able to divine in these ways— probably the latter.] [Well, when you take peyote, how does it make you feel?] I have a lot of pep, like when I was young. I have energy, I can move around and do anything I want to. My ailment goes away. That's the way it is.

[Would you explain to me a little more about how you have learned to do the right things around the home?] One thing that causes me to do things better is that my ailments are gone, and since that happened I can care for things better. I could hardly do housework, and after that I could try to improve [my work around the house].

[Did you ever go to the hospital for your joint trouble?] I never did. The doctors took out all my teeth. My teeth take me to the dentist. So there is no question of one [way of curing] being better than the other.

[Did you ever go to school?] No. I wanted to, but my mother and father didn't want me to, and I do not blame them for that. They didn't want me to leave them. And now I'm all alone [i.e., she has no children to help her and no education]. [Did you ever go to church, Catholic or Protestant?] I have attended both, when I was around and there were services.

[Well, you use both Navaho sings and the peyote Church. How do you fit together these two things—the Holy People and God?] The Catholic and Protestant Church among the whites name their Gods and pray; they speak of God Almighty, and so on—and we have our *own* [Navaho] names, due to the fact of two different languages—and so I think they are the same people with different names. [Further discussion indicates that she applies this line of thinking both to Navaho holy beings vis-à-vis those who are mentioned in Catholic and Protestant services, and vis-à-vis these mentioned in Native American Church services.] This terminates the interview.

This interview very closely resembles the one from Sweetwater. The primary preoccupation is with the cures achieved through peyote and the sense of support it gives her. There is some effort to indicate that she has "learned" something through peyote about caring for her household, but this seems to be about half physical facilitation of household activities. Medical facilities seem far more accessible to her, although in fact Fort Defiance hospital is a great deal further from Piñon than is Shiprock hospital from Sweetwater. But medical centers at Keams Canyon (opened in 1913) and at Chinle (opened in 1932) may have facilitated her use, and make transportation to a major medical center easier. Both Keams Canyon and Chinle are nearer to her home than is Shiprock to Sweetwater. She is happy with a wide range of curing techniques, does not seem to see any fundamental conflict between Navaho religion and peyotism, and certainly does not think that Navaho religion is declining. There is no note of pan-Indianism or nativism, no tendency to make anti-white comments, no special search for illuminations or visions, but perhaps a slight disappointment that she has had no visions. Her commitment is strong enough to make her disregard public opinion, even though her level of participation in ceremonies is low.

Appendix D

PEYOTE AND HEALTH

NAVAHO NON-PEYOTISTS are much concerned as to whether peyote has harmful mental or physical effects. They badly want information on the subject. Peyotists are eager for evidence to support their claims of the physical and mental benefits of peyote. But there are almost no properly controlled studies bearing on these problems, and most of the carefully controlled research has been on animals (cf. Seevers, 1954). In spite of the existence of various psychiatric studies, there is certainly nothing conclusive in the literature as respects either beneficial or harmful mental or physical effects of peyote in the doses normally used by American Indians (cf., for example, Wikler, 1957; La Barre, 1960; a new periodical, the *Psychedelic Review*, has recently emerged as a strong defender of mescalin, LSD, and psylocibin). When one considers the wealth of medical and lay opinions on the subject, the lack of research adequate for any policy decision is particularly disturbing. Under these circumstances, it is worth emphasizing that a medical *opinion* that peyote is harmful or helpful is of no particular value. The history of medicine reveals many cases where substances now known to be damaging were viewed as harmless or helpful, and where substances now known to be harmless or helpful were once regarded as damaging.

The issue of "drug addiction" is the most difficult one to present clearly, although it is also the one on which the most work has been done. It must be kept in mind that there is no one valid definition of addiction. Many definitions have been phrased with legal rather than medical considerations in mind. They were created to make it possible to outlaw the use of some substances believed to be harmful and still permit the use of other substances regarded as acceptable in the society. Physiological and legal definitions may be at odds with each other. I have chosen a physiological definition, since many legal definitions are phrased primarily with a view to legal action, rather than by reference to physiological and psychological effects. My own definition of addiction is based on Lindesmith (1947), and was presented earlier (Chapter 2). For purposes of medical discussion, however, I will adopt the definition of Tatum and Seevers, because of its straightforward physiological interest: "Addiction is a condition developed through the effects of repeated actions of a drug such that its use becomes necessary and cessation of its action causes mental and physical disturbances" (Seevers, 1954, p. 2). The term "drug" is not defined, except by example. Thus among "drugs" not causing addiction Seevers includes caffeine (in coffee or tea), nicotine (in tobacco), salicylates (of which aspirin is one), and alcohol (in modest quantities). It is clear that Seevers uses the word "drug" broadly, and that he does not regard all substances labeled as "drugs" as unusual, medicinal, or even harmful.

In an extensive discussion of various substances from the point of view of addiction, Seevers points out that studies on animals indicate the following conclusions. (1) Tolerance to peyote is found. Tolerance refers to "the fact that more and more of a drug must be used to produce equivalent effects" (Seevers, 1954, p. 5). Specifically, in the case of dogs, heavy doses of peyote given over twelve months resulted in the dogs' no longer becoming nauseated when they ate peyote. (Peyote users report to me that if they take peyote with some frequency they tend to become less likely to be nauseated, but that this effect disappears after a few weeks of abstinence from peyote.) No tolerance for the effects of peyote on the central nervous system was observed. That is, the only way in which increased doses were necessary to maintain the same effects was to maintain nausea. There was no evidence for a decrease in the other effects of peyote. (2) No physical dependence is developed. Thus, in the sense of Tatum's and Seevers' definition, no addiction occurs. (3) Peyote did not attract former opiate addicts at the Federal hospital at Lexington. (4) Seevers concludes, "In the absence of clearly defined emotional dependence or of significant harm to the individual or to society, there exists no possible basis for categorizing peyote as an addicting drug" (Seevers, 1954, p. 14). Furthermore, in spite of legislation which permits "peyote addicts" to be incarcerated in Federal hospitals for the cure of drug addiction, "No peyotist has ever applied, or been admitted, to the U.S. Public Health Service Hospital at Lexington" (Seevers, 1954, p. 14). Thus far Seevers.

No research report can be found that supplies evidence of physiological dependence in man, and therefore there is none which supplies evidence of addiction. There is no research evidence of emotional dependence or of significant harm to the individual or to society. Many, many people have expressed *opinions* as to the harm done by peyote, but evidence supporting these opinions satisfactory to a scientist has never been provided.

We turn now to other physical and mental problems. It is impossible for a person like the writer, without medical training, to evaluate these problems satisfactorily. Nevertheless, I have taken the following steps, which supply some information of value. (1) Where it was asserted that a person had died, become ill, or become insane as a result of using peyote, and where that person had been given medical study at a medical center, I endeavored to get information about the case. I could do this only in the case of Government medical facilities, and then only on the promise that the names of patients would not be revealed. Where the charge of damage through peyote was made and there had been no medical study, it was hopeless to attempt any evaluation. (2) When an individual claimed medical benefits from peyote, and where medical data were available in Government medical facilities, I secured them. Where benefits were claimed but there had been no diagnosis of the condition before or after using peyote, it was impossible to evaluate the claim.

I shall attempt to show that the data so far collected provide no evidence that peyote did harm in the instances where it was alleged to have done so and provide no evidence that it improved the health or cured the diseases of individuals who claimed it had.

I shall also try to show that the rumor process greatly affects the accuracy of reports by laymen about the negative effects of peyote.

CHART M

I. Alleged insanity or other mental disturbance resulting from use of peyote

Case No.	Sex	Known to use peyote	Used peyote before onset of symptoms	Diagnosis and Comments	Outcome	Source of diagnosis
1	M	Yes	Uncertain	Psychosis due to central nervous system syphilis	Death	State Hosp.
2	M	Yes	Uncertain	Blindness due to syphilis; psychosis due to central nervous system syphilis	Permanently blind; psychosis remitted; dischgd.	State Hosp.
3	M	Yes	Yes	Brain malignancy	Death	BIA Hosp.
4	F	Yes	Yes	Psychosis, severe depression with melancholia	Unknown	BIA Hosp.
5	M	Yes	Disputed	Schizophrenia	Improved, dischgd.	BIA Hosp.
6	F	Yes	Yes	Psychosis resulting from epileptic clouded state	Improved, dischgd.	State Hosp.
7	F	Yes	Yes	Alcoholic intoxication	Unknown	BIA Hosp.
8	F	Yes	Uncertain	None; described as psychotic	Remitted; dischgd.	BIA Hosp.
9	M	Uncertain	Uncertain	Grand mal epilepsy with psychosis. BIA physician believes he took jimson weed	Suicide	BIA Hosp.
10	M	Doubtful	Unknown	Paranoid schizophrenia	Unknown	State Hosp.
11	M	Doubtful	Unknown	Senile psychosis	Unknown	State Hosp.
12	F	Doubtful	Unknown	Behavior disorder	Remitted; dischgd.	State Hosp.
13	M	Doubtful	Unknown	Schizophrenia, catatonic type	Unknown	State Hosp.

II. Alleged death resulting from use of peyote

Case 14. Shortly after a peyote ceremony patient (male) was taken to a hospital and from there removed to a larger hospital. Operation disclosed massive peritoneal gangrene, probably the result of a ruptured appendix.

Case 15. Subject (male) died shortly after eating peyote, age 71. Autopsy revealed cause of death as heart failure, caused by coronary insufficiency related to an atherosclerotic plaque on the anterior descending branch of the left coronary artery (hardening of the arteries). Alkaloids of peyote found in blood (as would be the case for anyone shortly after using peyote), but physician unwilling to attribute death to use of peyote.

III. Alleged cures resulting from use of peyote

Case 16. Subject (male), in his early forties in 1950, claimed entire relief from diabetes through use of peyote. Uses large quantities of soda pop. Diagnosis verified through Veterans Hospital. BIA physician states that at this man's age and given the mild character of his diabetic condition, he would be symptom-free regardless of peyote. Later symptoms expected. Subject died about 1960, cause unknown.

Case 17. Subject (male), in his late 30's in 1951, claims relief from severe back pains through peyote. Medical record of prostatitis, evaluated by BIA physician, who states that cause of back pains is not prostatitis. Prostatitis treated and improved in hospital. Cause of back pains remains undetermined; effects of peyote also remain undetermined.

The data collected consist of 17 cases, shown in Chart M. Thirteen of these involve allegations of insanity or other mental disturbance caused by peyote, 2 of death, and 2 of cure. It must be again emphasized that other cases where allegations of insanity or death were made are known to me, but that in these cases there are no medical data. There are at least a half-dozen such instances. In at least 100 cases Navahos have testified to me at length that peyote has cured them of a variety of unfortunate physical and mental afflictions—almost all of these physical— but again, no medical records are available.

In the first 8 cases, there is no question about the use of peyote. Either the subject attested that he used peyote, or those close to him, or peyotists, or all of these. Four of these cases (Nos. 1, 2, 3, and 6) involve organic brain conditions— syphilis, brain tumor, or epilepsy. All are familiar in populations not using peyote; there is no reason to believe that Navahos are ordinarily immune from these conditions; and it would be a rash physician who claimed peyote as a contributing cause. Two of these cases (Nos. 4 and 5) involve functional psychoses, severe depression and schizophrenia, again conditions familiar in populations not using peyote. There are no data suggesting that peyote is a causal agent in relatively long-enduring states of insanity. In one case (No. 7) the woman had an outbreak of excited behavior in the hospital. She was known to have been given peyote, in the hospital, and antipeyotists became animated in their discussion of the case. The attending physician said that she had also had alcohol and that her behavior was consistent with alcoholic intoxication. In one case (No. 8), it remains unclear (a) whether a psychotic state of a few weeks duration began before or after she first used peyote; (b) how much peyote she took. She may have taken almost none. A psychotic episode triggered by peyote is a possibility; so is a psychotic episode preceding the use of peyote. An interview with the subject some years after the event failed utterly to clear up these issues. She held a responsible post as a school matron when interviewed.

The remaining cases (Nos. 9–13) are more significant in illustrating the rumor process than in the light they cast on the effects of peyote. Case No. 9 is believed by some Navahos to have used peyote, but by a BIA physician to have used jimson weed (datura metalloides). Peyotists deny that he used peyote. So do members of his kin-group. In cases 10–13 the sole basis for the claim that the subjects used peyote is the assertion of the head of the Navajo Law and Order Office. No notation respecting use of peyote appears anywhere in their case records. As in cases 1–7, a familiar array of organic and functional conditions is found, like that in any other population.

With the exception of case 8, where the data are most unclear, there is nothing in any of these cases to suggest peyote as a triggering, exacerbating, or contributory element in the diseases from which these people suffered.

Case 14 again illustrates the rumor process. Navahos in the man's home community alleged that the surgeon who operated on him said that peyote had caused his intestinal condition and death. The surgeon was interviewed. He said that such a statement would be irresponsible, that he had no reason to suspect that peyote could have any such effects, and that he had never commented on the role of peyote in this case. It was his belief that if this man, or any other man with acute appendicitis, delayed hospitalization, whether to go to a peyote ceremony, to attend a Navaho ceremony, or for any other reason, peritonitis could set in and terminate fatally. This was, he believed, the only sense in which peyote could conceivably be a contributory factor.

Case 15 involves an autopsy performed because the subject died shortly after a peyote ceremony. Specifically, it was hoped that the autopsy would deal with local anxieties and hostilities aroused by the death, either by confirming or denying the importance of peyote in causing death. Fundamentally, it is a case of an elderly man with hardening of the arteries dying of a heart attack.

Cases 16 and 17 require little comment. We have two instances in which major benefits are claimed from the use of peyote. In the case of the diabetic, there were no such benefits. In the other case, the cause of the symptoms being unclear, the effects of peyote must remain equally unclear. The analgesic effects of peyote are probably not at stake, since subject claims permanent improvement.

I have no other cases where there is a good medical history and a claim of cure through peyote. The reason for this is fairly plain. Individuals whose health improves while they are taking peyote are unlikely to go to the physician simply to record the fact of their improvement.

(Postscript, 1965. There are many more cases today where there has been a medical diagnosis, and where a cure through peyote is claimed, than I could gather earlier. Far more work could be done to evaluate these cases than I was able to manage.)

The cases presented here provide no evidence to support the claims of those who hold peyote is damaging; nor of those who believe it to be curative. It is clear that many Navahos have experienced subjective reactions of physical and mental well-being after using peyote. Without detailed studies, it will be impossible to come to any conclusion other than that presented here: no evidence. It is clear, however, that the illness or death of a person who is known to use peyote becomes an occasion for non-peyotists to blame peyote, and that illness and death sometimes become the occasion to suspect the use of peyote where no such use is known. On the basis of such suspicions, it is not proper to make claims. It is equally evident that remissions or supposed remissions of symptoms are always believed by peyotists to result from peyote. This also affords no sound evidence.

I turn now to the complicated subject of "the American Medical Association" report on peyote. Let it be said to start with that the American Medical Association has never taken a policy position on peyote; nor has it carried out any systematic investigation of the subject. A Survey of Medical Care Among the Upper Midwest Indians in 1949 does contain an opinion regarding peyote, which appeared in the *Journal of the American Medical Association* in 1949 (Braasch, Branton, and Chesley, 1949). On one page of this report (p. 225) appears the following statement.

Drug Habits.—The drug most frequently used by the Indian is peyote ("mescal button") which is obtained from the tops of a small narcotic cactus grown in the Rio Grande section of the United States and in Mexico. It is eaten by the Indian tribes of the Southwest in religious ceremonials, for the sense of well-being which it induces and to promote trances and hallucinations. The use of peyote has been a problem among

Indians for many years. It has gradually spread so as to involve many of the Indians in the Northwest [presumably the authors refer to the northern middle-west]. Unfortunately, the Indian Bureau permitted use of peyote among the Indians several years ago on the grounds that it was part of an Indian religious ceremony. We are informed by the Narcotics Bureau of the United States Treasury Department that peyote is not covered by the Harrison Narcotic Act, but that its use is prohibited by law in some of the southwestern states. It is high time that the sale and possession of this drug be restricted by a national law. It is a habit-forming drug and acts on the nervous system as a stimulant and narcotic. The drug usually is taken prior to festival dances and causes excessive stimulation for several hours. The following day the addict is left in an exhausted condition and is incapable of physical exercise or labor.

This quotation is the *entire* statement of these doctors. In the Navaho country, knowledge of the study, rumors of the statement, and knowledge of the statement were built into a theory that the American Medical Association has made, or is making, a study of peyote which will supply information about its effects. Other than this study, none has been done or is being done.

There are a few problems about the statement as it stands. First, it is misleading to state that the Indian Bureau "permitted" use of peyote several years ago. Although the Indian Bureau prior to the administration of John Collier did what it could to stop the use of peyote, by efforts to confiscate peyote, to use local agents' pressure to discourage ceremonies, and to secure Federal legislation to forbid the use of peyote, the fact remains that the Bureau was never in a legal position to forbid peyote, and hence can scarcely be said to have started to permit its use a few years before. Specifically, Collier's action was to order agents to stop interfering with peyote ritual and peyote consumption, such interference never having had clear-cut legal support in any event.

Second, the statement asserts that peyote is "a habit-forming drug." No evidence is produced to support this statement, and none is available. If by habit-forming the doctors mean that peyote causes physiological dependency, the statement is incorrect. No evidence of such dependency has ever been found, although Seevers' research employed the techniques ordinarily used to discover whether physiological dependency can be developed in animal subjects. It is possible to prove that a substance does cause dependency; it is difficult to prove that it does not. The fact that peyote has been used for seventy or more years in the United States by Indians without any evidence of addiction is, however, *prima facie* evidence against its addictive properties. During that same time, many other substances have been shown to be addictive.

If by "habit-forming" the doctors mean that obsessive craving for peyote exists, again there is no evidence from any source to support this statement.

If by "habit-forming" the doctors mean that use tends to be fairly regular and that users have a positive attitude toward taking peyote, peyote use then falls into the very large class of human habits which include eating a given number of meals a day, sleeping about eight hours a night, going to church regularly, etc.: of things called "habits" because of the repetitive character of the behavior. This type of habit, however, is not normally the subject of legislation.

The doctors assert that peyote is a stimulant and a narcotic. These terms are technical, and according to certain definitions of the terms, peyote is certainly both. So are a large number of other substances, by no means all of which are subject to prohibitive legislation, and some of which are subject to none. The caffeine in coffee is a stimulant, for example, and alcohol is a narcotic. The use of neither is prohibited by Federal law.

It is also said that peyote causes "excessive" stimulation for several hours. Unless some content is given to the phrase "excessive stimulation," so that we can decide what is excessive and what sufficient stimulation, it seems difficult to judge the accuracy of this statement.

Last, the doctors charge that the "addict" (no peyote addicts are known) is left exhausted the day following a peyote meeting and is unable to work. No evidence as to how often this occurs, for how many people, is supplied. No evidence is supplied to show whether peyotists manage more or less working days per year than non-peyotists, or whether after becoming peyotists they work more or less than before. Without such data, it seems very difficult to judge whether this vague charge can be substantiated and whether the problem thus created (if it exists) merits restrictive legislation.

In sum, three doctors who surveyed medical conditions in the upper midwest over a period of a few months made a recommendation that peyote should be the subject of Federal restrictive laws, on the basis of statements some of which are inaccurate, some of which do not in and of themselves justify legislation in any case, and some of which are not supported by evidence. Dr. Seevers, a pharmacologist, on the other hand, after surveying the literature and carrying out detailed research on the physiology of peyote reactions, and after a lifetime of work on drugs and drug-control problems, is unwilling to make any such recommendation.

The available evidence on the effects of peyote and peyotism seems inadequate to justify restrictive legislation—unless the position is taken that everything must be forbidden which might turn out to be harmful. Physicians who do detailed work on peyote seem chary of making any restrictive recommendations, whereas those whose experience is more superficial seem eager to make them. The only possible medical recommendation which seems reasonable is a plea for more research.

Appendix E

THE LEADERSHIP OF THE NATIVE AMERICAN
CHURCH IN THE NAVAHO COUNTRY

THIS APPENDIX will describe the characteristics of organizational and ceremonial leaders of the Native American Church among the Navaho. In part,
it is an attempt to answer a question asked by Bernard Barber in 1941. He
listed certain "adaptive functions" of the cult in other areas. In his view these
included the bestowing of prestige, status, and social advancement on cult leaders;
liquidation of anxieties and social control functions through public confession; and
integrative functions through the cult's serving as a center for tribal ceremonial
and social activity. He continued, "An opportunity for further testing of this
hypothesis [regarding the adaptive functions mentioned] exists among the Navaho.
Although they have known about it for at least two generations, the Navaho have
had recourse to Peyote only recently, under the impulsion of the incipient cultural
disorganization that is now affecting them. Further research should seek to answer
the following questions, among others: Do the leaders of the new cult come from
among the old elite? What satisfactions accrue to its adherents? In what ways does
the cult help the group adjust, contribute to its stability?" (1941b, p. 675).[1]

The issues raised by Barber's second and third questions have been given consideration at various points in this book. But his first question has not been dealt
with directly. Insofar as it can be answered, the answer would appear to be that
a portion of the "old elite" tended to join the cult in disproportionate numbers,
but as members, not as leaders.

Defining the "old elite" is not easy. In traditional Navaho society there were
presumably three major modes of achieving an elite position. The first was that of
political influential: headman or head of a major kin-group. The second was that
of wealth, through livestock—and often the political influential was also a man of
wealth. The third was that of ceremonial knowledge. Singers were not necessarily
wealthy and indeed, according to Kluckhohn were often not very wealthy (Kluckhohn, 1944). They might, however, be political influentials, and where the role
of the headman was clearly structured, the headman was supposed to know
Blessing Way (Hill, 1940). But by 1936, a convenient date for the beginning of
the rapid spread of the peyote cult, there were certainly other elite positions. One

---

[1] It is extraordinarily doubtful that in 1941 the Navaho had known about peyote for at least
two generations. That would mean 40–60 years before 1941, or in 1880–1900. Aberle and Stewart
(1957) were unable to demonstrate any Navaho contact with the peyote cult prior to the 1920's.
It is possible, of course, that a few schoolboys might have learned about the cult from Oklahoma
Indians in off-reservation boarding schools, but if so, no trace of such knowledge has yet been
discovered. These schoolchildren might also have been given anti-peyote information by mission or Bureau personnel, but this would be unlikely to promote interest in the cult.

of these was the intercultural intermediary—who might also be wealthy. Chee Dodge was one of the earliest and most impressive of these. Not all such intermediaries, however, had high prestige. A second, which emerged in 1937, was that of Delegate or Chairman of the reorganized Navajo Tribal Council. The first delegates to the new Council were selected from among a group of influential figures from all over the Reservation (TNY 1961, pp. 378–379). Finally, everything to do with an "elite" was undoubtedly fluid and uncrystallized, from what we know of Navaho society then and now.

With respect to local figures who were politically influential and their tendency to join or reject the cult, I have no information. With respect to the wealthy, we have already seen that there is a significant tendency for large pre-reduction owners to join the cult more frequently than small pre-reduction owners. But this is only a tendency, and it does not tell us whether the most respected wealthy joined, or rejected the cult. In its early days at Greasewood and Piñon, some wealthy and respected men joined the cult, and most did not. Furthermore, those who did join unquestionably lost respect among those who did not.

With respect to ceremonialists, my data from Greasewood and Piñon, although not detailed enough for statistical check, suggest that ceremonialists joined the cult in disproportionately small numbers between its introduction into these communities and the years 1949–1950, when I worked there.

With respect to the "old" Tribal Council, whose status in the elite category is questionable, no, or almost no delegates joined.

With respect to the "new" Tribal Council, which certainly included a number of elite figures, by 1940 there was only one peyotist on the Council. It is possible that this proportion (slightly over 1 per cent) is about equivalent to the proportion of peyotists then in the Navaho country, but probably there were more peyotists than that. Since then, the character of the Council has shifted, with an increasing emphasis on education as a criterion for election—still another elite. The percentage of peyotist Council members, so far as can be judged, has grown as the cult has grown, or a little slower—certainly no faster.

Barber's question seems to be based on a theoretical assumption very like the deprivation theory advanced in this book. He seems to imply that the "old elite" would be most likely to seek prestige, status, and social advancement through a new nativistic movement. And perhaps there is an implication that the elite would be in the best position to afford leadership to the peyote cult. As has been pointed out, his assumption is partly correct. Those most deprived of status and wealth were more likely to join the cult than others, and to join it earlier than others. Barber seems not to have anticipated that the cult would provoke so much antagonism among Navahos, so that joining the cult often re~~~~~~ ~~ ~~~~ ~~ ~~~~~~~~ in the larger community of Navahos. Nor did he foresee ~~~~~~~~~~~~~~~~~ ship qualities that would be needed in the Navaho Nativ~~~~~~~~~~~

We now turn to the nature of the leadership of the Chu~~~~~~~~~~~~~ of leadership positions in the Native American Church ~~~~~~~~~~~~ first I call "organization man," although there is no genera~~~~~~~~~~ for this position. These men are concerned with dealing ~~~~~~~~~~ opposition to the use of peyote, in ways that will be ~~~~~~~~~

below. The second is that of road man, or leader of peyote ritual. Some leaders occupy only one of these positions; some occupy both.

From the point of view of the observer—and again there are no native terms—each of these major categories may be subdivided: into supra-community and community organization men, and supra-community and community road men.

A supra-community organization man is actively concerned with the organization of the Native American Church above the community level and at the community level on the Navaho Reservation, and with the legal battles over peyotism. He may serve as an officer of the Church in the states of New Mexico, Arizona, or Utah. Earlier, he participated in the organization of these branches and with their incorporation according to the laws of these states. He tries to deal with the Tribal organization, to assist those arrested under the Tribal resolution of 1940, and to secure the repeal of that law or to exert pressure to keep it from being strengthened. He is involved in various legal efforts to change the Tribal and State laws not only through legislation, but also through court cases. In some instances, he works directly with the national organization of the Native American Church, and in one case, a Navaho is a major official of that Church: vice-president. He may work with local community organizations of the Church or attempt to develop or improve them. And he may be active in the local organization of his home community. In sum, he organizes the Church for legal purposes and confronts authority as necessary in short-term skirmishes or long-term battles. In the 1940's, he sometimes protested to the Agency Superintendent when anti-peyotists took direct, illegal action in raiding meetings.

A community organization man attempts to maintain a local organization in his home community, or to build one, collects dues, attends supra-community organization meetings when and where he can, deals with the law in case of local arrests, sometimes had to resort to direct action when meetings were raided, and sometimes appealed to Window Rock when these extra-legal raids occurred.

Many organization men are officers of the Church, local and State, but some active organization men are not officers.

A supra-community road man is a road man who is in demand in large numbers of communities—in an area larger than that which includes his home community and immediately adjacent communities.

A community road man performs only locally—in his home community and adjacent communities. Sometimes this restricted sphere results from the fact that his reputation has not yet spread very far, sometimes from a lack of personal qualities that "draw" a larger clientele, and sometimes merely from the fact that he does not wish to take on the burden of travelling over a large area.

The functional dividing line between the supra-community and the community leader is a fine line at any one point in time and a shifting line over time. Nevertheless, these observer's labels define types of activities and spheres of activities of leaders.

It should be made clear that we are talking about very different kinds of positions. The road man knows a lot about peyote, a lot about the ritual, and is viewed as a curer—although the curative powers of some men are believed to be greater than those of others. He may or may not be regarded as arbiter and teacher of morality. He is a charismatic figure, but he does not necessarily speak with authority in matters of organization. Organization men need not be able to run a peyote meeting; they are regarded as having a good understanding of the substance of peyotism; they are sought out for help in organizational and legal matters; in point of fact, all those I have known had exceptionally clearly articulated views on the ideology of peyotism. I have already pointed out that as an organization the Native American Church is not, for the most part, concerned with theological or liturgical matters, but, whether among the Navaho or elsewhere, with the legal status of peyotism. From this derives the non-schismatic character of the Church, in spite of differences of opinion as respects theology and ritual among road men and their followers.

I have some idea of the number of Navaho road men serving Navaho peyotists in 1954, but a realistic appraisal of the number of organization men is impossible. In early summer of 1954, I worked with a well-informed peyotist who was a local road man and a supra-community organization man. Together we listed some 43 road men then operating in the Navaho country. (This omits from consideration non-Navaho road men who appeared from time to time, mainly from Oklahoma. [See Aberle and Stewart, 1957].) My own notes add 4 cases to this list, of whom one probably became a road man after 1954. Of this total of 47, 6 practice only V-way or one or another special way, rather than standard peyote ritual. Probably we overlooked some, but it is likely that there were not more than 55 road men in 1954. Furthermore, the men who practiced only V-way and other special rituals probably received little or no recognition as road men outside Red Rock, Cove, Little Shiprock, and adjacent communities. This appendix is written in 1964. I do not know how many road men are now operating. Some of those listed for 1954 have died, but undoubtedly there are many new ones. An estimate of 65 to 100 appears reasonable. (*Postscript, 1965.* This estimate is undoubtedly too low.)

Of the 47 operating in 1954, at least 17 can be considered supra-community road men, on the basis of the fact that I heard of their performing in communities other than their own and adjacent communities. About 14 can be characterized as local road men in 1954. For the rest, I cannot say.

In 1954, there were at least 9 supra-community organization men who were not road men, and an additional 4 community organization men who were not road men. My information is quite deficient on community organization men: I did not hear of them unless I visited a community. Not every community had a local organization of the Native American Church, and articulation with the State-wide organization was loose and personal.

At least 7 supra-community road men were also supra-community organization men.

At least 9 supra-community road men played little role in organizational matters. Most of the local road men played little role in organizational matters.

From these figures it seems possible to draw the following tentative conclusions. A good deal of the organization of the Native American Church in 1954 lay in the hands of non-road men, and a good many road men played no role in organizational matters. Supra-local road men were more likely than local road men to be organizationally important, and non-road men were more likely to be organizationally active than road men.

Since then the situation has shifted somewhat. Most of the men who were then organizationally active are still active, but at least 4 who were not road men in 1954 are now road men. (One of these had learned in 1954 but had never practiced.)

With this background, we may turn to the question of the recruitment of men for both types of roles.

The year 1936 is one dividing mark in the history of Navaho peyotism. Before that date peyotism was largely confined north of the San Juan; thereafter, it moved south. The first *de facto* leaders of the cult were the "pioneers," the five or six men from Mancos Creek who were the first, by common acknowledgment, to learn the peyote ritual. Whether or not they knew the ceremonial well when they began to move widely, they learned soon after, since by 1938 Alfred Wilson was with them on some of their trips. One of these men spoke fair English. He became, and remains a major organizational figure. Three of the remainder spoke little English (one case) or none. For the remaining one or two men (and I am not sure whether it was one or two), I have no information. Four of the five or six were active proselytizers for years. They were early supplemented by a Shiprock Navaho with seven years of experience as an interperter for a Protestant mission. With six years' schooling, he had a fine vocabulary and remarkable fluency and precision as an interpreter. He had been active in Tribal and local politics and now turned to peyotism as the future salvation of the Navaho. He had a truck and transported the pioneers; later, when opposition developed, he became a major organizational figure, although he has recently left peyotism for a Protestant church. Not surprisingly, he was one of the first of a similar set of figures. Most of them were characterized by above-average skills in the use of English, given the general level of education in the Navaho country at the time. Unfortunately I do not have precise figures on the education of these men. Some of them I met very early, under conditions not conducive to formal interviews, and in many such cases I never returned to the issue of their level of education, since we became engrossed in discussions of peyotism and of the Navaho situation, as I came to know them better.

In a few instances, however, although they were major organizational figures, they spoke little or no English. One such case was a Tribal Delegate, whose chief importance to peyotism was that of a voice on the Council. Three others were road men. There was a tendency, then, for those Navahos who became peyotists and who had a good command of English and leadership skills to gravitate quickly to major organizational affairs, and for a few road men and others without the linguistic skills to do likewise. English language skills made it possible for Navahos to serve as intermediaries for all Navaho peyotists with Oklahoma Indians, with Indian Service personnel, with white opponents, and with the lawyers whose assistance they have repeatedly required.

Some idea of the concentration of supra-community organizational affairs can be gathered from the overlapping of roles in certain instances. Of three officials of the New Mexico organization of the Native American Church (chairman, vice-chairman, and secretary), two were among the signers of the charter for Arizona. (I have not seen the New Mexico charter, so that similar overlaps cannot be noted.) The secretary for the Arizona church is the vice-president of the Utah church. A further analysis of the Utah and New Mexico charters would undoubt-edly show similar features.

As might be expected, although officers of the Church sometimes speak no, or almost no English, the secretary is always some one who speaks and writes English reasonably well. The chairman for New Mexico, the president for Arizona (later superseded by an English-speaking chairman), and the president for Utah in the 1950's spoke relatively little English. The same was true for some local presidents (often called "chapter" presidents, since the Native American Church has tended to follow Navaho organizational patterns at the local level).

In religion, more road and/or organization men are Catholic than are Protestant, in those cases where religious affiliation is known, but affiliation is known in only 13 cases, or a small fraction of the total.

One difference between the pure organization men of 1954 and the road men is the greater tendency of the organization men to hold steady jobs. Of all the road men in 1954, organization or not, only 2 held regular, year-round jobs. Of 13 organization men, 5 held steady jobs. In addition, 2 were Tribal Delegates, one of whom ran a trading post. Of the 6 remaining, 1 was the educated wife of a supra-community road man. By 1964, among the 12 survivors of this organization group, 6 held steady jobs and the two who had been Delegates remained Delegates. I do not have the figures on comparable shifts among the original group of road men, but it is my impression that they remain primarily oriented to a combination of herding, farming, and wage-work.

There would seem to be two reasons for this difference. If a person is heavily committed to the role of road man, it is difficult for him to meet the demands of his clientele and the demands of a five-day-a-week job. An organization man can meet the demands of organizational work, and because his educational level is often above average, he can secure steady wage work. If he begins in the Church as an organization man with a job, even if he later learns to be a road man, he is unlikely to run meetings with great frequency.

Indeed, among peyotists whom I have known longest and best, who are, for the most part, organization men with a good command of English, the job histories are impressive. They would differentiate this group not only from road men, but also from the average Navaho, although I cannot be sure that they would differen-tiate this group from its non-peyotist equivalent in terms of education. One is a garage mechanic and has been ever since I have known him, moving from a gov-ernment position to a private garage (in order to send his children to school in Gallup), and back again. One began as a stock boy in a tribal industry and today holds a position of considerable responsibility. He has recently refused a job for about $12,000 per annum outside the reservation. One, working in the bean fields in 1950 in spite of a high-school education and some business school, is today work-ing in adult education in a Bureau school. One, with a minor agency job in the schools in 1949, is now providing occupational training to students in a large Bu-reau school and has done so for more than ten years, living several hundred miles off-reservation. One has worked as a truck driver for a tribal enterprise ever since I first knew him. One has worked for the Bureau for at least a dozen years, and probably more. One works for a vanadium company, after a number of years working for the Bureau in the schools in a semi-skilled position. Of these 7 men, 3 are road men, and 2 more are probably road men. All began as organization men.

Two additional organization men are Tribal Delegates. Another, a recent and youthful figure, is a Tribal employee, as are two men who have been organizationally significant, but the extent of whose present participation in organizational matters I do not know. The employment status of one man I do not know. Several others make reasonable livings through some combination of herding, farming, wage work, and (in one case) trucking, a more standard Navaho pattern. The condition of the rest I do not know.[2]

It is worth noting that in the case of those peyotists whom I have known longest, I find their general outlook more serene, more differentiated and sophisticated, and more cheerful than when I first knew them. Perhaps it cannot be argued that peyotism is responsible for their present economic condition and general outlook, especially since their education has surely helped their economic adjustment, but it would be exceedingly hard to argue that this agreeable state of affairs has come about in spite of peyotism. And for each of them, the Native American Church appears as the focal factor in their personal adjustment and general outlook. Finally, of all of the central figures I have known, only one has left the peyote cult.

I have mentioned age. The median year of birth for organization men, road men or not, falls in the interval 1905–1909. These ages are, however, estimated in some cases. Only one was born more recently than 1924, the new central figure referred to above. The median age for road men who are not organization men, where known, is about five years younger. But this group has a bimodal distribution, with a cluster born before and another born after 1914. On the whole, then, when peyotism first met serious opposition, in 1940, the organization men were mainly 40 and below. (This would not be true of cult members, whose ages are far more widely spread.)

These figures and analyses, however, convey no picture of the organizational and ceremonial elite of the Native American Church in the Navaho country. A composite picture of the organizatonal group can be drawn. They have at least some education; they have had to struggle for a living; they speak of periods of personal disorganization prior to joining the cult. They have had to build an organization from scratch, and it is gradually emerging. They have had to learn the exceedingly complex legal situation of the cult, and they are doing so. They are deadly serious about peyotism, and exceedingly tenacious in the face of opposition. They are suspicious, but not unrealistically so in most cases. In many cases they are very sensitive to slights. In many cases, a hilarious sense of humor about matters other than peyotism and its enemies is characteristic.

Road men are a far more diverse group. For some, being a road man seems but a seal on their commitment to peyotism, rather than a career. Peyotism is a center of gravity in a difficult world. Such are some of the Aneth road men, who, along with other members of the Aneth community, have been fighting a battle over

---

[2] Although it is not relevant to the issue of old elites, it is of interest to note that one man, who was a teen-ager attending peyote meetings when I first knew him, in 1949, too young to be either an organization man or a road man, has recently been elected to public office in one of the Southwestern states.

land for decades. Some are true mystics. Some are preoccupied with healing. Some are concerned with ethical teachings. Some, consciously or unconsciously, are attracted, among other things, by the fame of their position and the opportunities it brings, among them economic opportunities. I cannot say that many belong in this last group. The same attitudes—tenacity, deadly seriousness about peyote, suspiciousness well-tempered by attention to reality, and in many, but not all cases, humor in other matters—seem characteristic. Although many of them speak some English, few of those I have met speak English well, so that I have come to know them less intimately than the organization men.

In sum, there was some tendency for the elite of wealth among the Navaho before reduction to join the cult, but its leadership, both organizational and cere-monial, seems not to have been drawn from the old elite. English-language skills characterize organizational leaders, who, for the most part, emerged as leaders first and became road men later. On the whole, long-time organizational leaders who are not, or only later became, road men, are characterized by more participation in steady wage-labor and salaried jobs than are pure road men. Organization men show not only organizational skills and leadership ability but a type and level of economic adjustment unusual in the Navaho country today.

THE INTERVIEW ON NAVAHO
COMMUNITIES

C HAPTER 18 presented the analysis of ratings for 41 communities, the median ratings of 32 Window Rock Area Office employees. Prior to being asked to rate the communities in which he worked, each respondent was asked a series of questions intended to clarify for him the nature of the general variable with respect to which he was asked to make the ratings. This appendix makes clear the general character of the interview and the nature of the questions asked for each variable. To begin with, the respondent was told by Harvey C. Moore, who did all of this interviewing, that he had a list from Window Rock of all the districts and communities where the man had worked. He pointed out that the respondent had been selected because of his knowledge of one or more parts of the reservation and then asked the respondent to talk about some community in a particular district—the community in the district that he knew best. (In a few cases, the respondent was asked to discuss a particular community about which we wanted information; in a few, the respondent rejected the district or community under consideration and asked to substitute another one.) Moore went on, "For the kind of questions I'd like to talk to you about, the best thing would be to pick just one community and stick to it for all these questions." Later, he said, "Now remember that it's [names the community] that we're talking about, for the time period [mentions dates when the employee worked there]." If the respondent were to ask what a community was, Moore replied that the respondent might think of the district as he usually did, divided by chapters, or by trading posts, or by school areas. If necessary, a list of communities representing general consensus among respondents to the peyote questionnaire—including this respondent—was presented, with the comment that the respondent was free to depart from this list and make a different subdivision. Respondents were told that the aim was to cover various conditions on the Navaho Reservation for as wide an area as possible, over a number of years. Hence many respondents were needed.

As was pointed out in Chapter 18, the topics were presented in the following order: political organization, trouble, reactions to livestock reduction, acculturation, and disturbance over peyotism. The order of listing in Chapter 18 and below is that followed in the statistical tables.

1. *Acculturation (A)*.—This section began with a request that the respondent discuss how much the Navaho in the community he knew best were (or are) "taking on American ways." A series of check-list questions followed, respecting education, competence in English, clothing, hair-style, automobile ownership, improved housing, moving out of houses when some one died in them, mother-

in-law avoidance, attention to children's education and desire for it, preference for off-reservation, public, and mission schooling, Christian religious adherence, part-time off-reservation employment, and families living off-reservation most of the year. There was a short discussion of the effects of off-reservation labor on funds available and attitudes. The interview continued with use of medical facilities and traditional ceremonialists. It asked about the existence of local missions and Navaho reaction to them and about whether the number of ceremonialists and of ceremonials seemed to be increasing or decreasing. It inquired about Indian-owned trading posts and their success in the area. Thus it discussed the degree of adherence to customary ways versus adherence to American ways in a variety of areas which have been the focus of attention in the Navaho country. It concluded, "Well, all in all, if you were asked to compare this community to others, would you say the people had taken on American ways: (5) almost completely; (4) to a considerable extent; (3) to a moderate degree; (2) not very much; (1) almost not at all?" The same question was asked for other communities where the employee had worked.

2. *Trouble* (*T*).—This section opened with a discussion of the fact that some communities are fairly quiet; "people behave themselves well, and there's very little trouble. Other places are different." For the community in question, "I thought we might start off by talking about some sort of signs of trouble . . . and go on to other subjects along that line. Just for example, [how was the community under consideration] about drinking—was there very much? I mean, compared to the other communities you know, did it strike you as outstandingly high or outstandingly low or neither in the amount of drinking?" The same question was asked about bootlegging, manufacture of liquor in the community; fights at sings; talk about or signs of fear of witches, accusations of witchcraft, threats against people thought to be witches, or efforts at witch trials. (This list was shortened if the answers to the first two questions resulted in answers of "don't know" or "low" in talk about witches or fear of witches.) It went on to ask about wife-beating, separations (since these are hard to distinguish from divorces), theft, physical fights between individuals, and mass violence. It also inquired about reactions to livestock reduction and to grazing regulations over time. The interview went on to a general discussion of morale, optimism and pessimism, cooperation, and industriousness. It then turned to anti–Indian Service feelings and actions and anti-white feeling and activity. From there it went to general cooperation of the community with the employee, to conspicuous failure of cooperation or opposition, and, where relevant, to concrete acts such as non-cooperation in livestock dipping and letting water out of stock tanks. It is evident, then, that the "trouble" area is defined by a variety of elements: troubles within the community and within the family; trouble with the Indian Service and hostility to whites in general; illegal activity; and such signs of tension as concern about witchcraft, a very high level of ceremonialism, and drinking. The section concluded, "All in all, would you say that compared to the others you've known, [the community under discussion] was a particuarly troubled, or 'hot' or 'tense' or disturbed community, or not? Was the trouble among themselves or mostly in their dealings with the government, or both? Taking that a little further, would you call it: (5) very

disturbed, (4) quite disturbed, (3) about average, (2) not very disturbed, (1) hardly at all disturbed." The respondent was then asked to rate the other communities where he had worked.

3. *Reactions to livestock reduction* (S).—This section began with a discussion of the maximum regular and special permit (if any), of the range of size of livestock holdings and of whether any permits were unused. It went on to ask whether people with special permits seemed to expect to keep them, or raise them, or have them cut, and whether those with regular permits had one or another of these expectations. Then it took up the livelihood condition of those with insufficient sheep to make a living and of Navahos in the area in general. It went on to ask how the people felt about the future of livestock raising as a way of making a living and then took up livestock reduction. It asked how much reduction there had been in the area in question, and whether there had been any special crises over reduction. It asked who was most opposed to reduction (in the past) or grazing regulation (at present), and whether any group supported either reduction or regulation. It concluded, "Well, taking it all in all, compared to the other places you know, how much trouble was there over stock reduction (or grazing regulation) [in the community under discussion]? (5) a great deal; (4) quite a lot; (3) a fair amount; (2) not very much; (1) hardly any." The respondent was asked to select the rating that corresponded with his evaluation. "Well, let's take the other communities you know." For each one, "Was there a great deal of trouble, quite a lot, a fair amount, not very much, hardly any?"

4. *Political Organization* (O).—This section opened with a discussion of local organization in the community in question. If necessary, the respondent was asked whether there was a chapter organization, whether it was confined to the community in question or included others, and whether it had regular elections and meetings. He was then asked whether the chapter was the effective organization in the community or not, whether there were other important sources of leadership, and whether they worked with or against the chapter. Various possible sources of leadership were then mentioned and the respondent asked whether they were of any importance: Tribal delegates, head men (in addition to, or instead of chapter officers), old, respected men, wealthy men, young educated men, heads of important families, and ceremonialists. Local whites as possible leaders were discussed: traders, missionaries, doctors, government personnel. The respondent was asked about organizations as potential foci of leadership: the Navajo Rights Association, the Native American Church, or any others. He was then asked about opposition among any of these sources of leadership, and, if there was any, over what issues it arose. He was asked about which leaders cooperated with each other and to whom one went in order to get community support. And he was asked where most trouble for him originated. He was then told, "Well, by asking you these questions that we just finished with . . . I've been trying to get a picture of whether this community was pretty well-organized politically or not. So let me ask you—what do you think, as compared to other communities you've been in on the reservation, do you think it was pretty well-organized, pretty tightly organized as a local community, from the political point of view, or not? Well, going on a little further, if you were asked to compare [the community in question] with

all the other communities you've known, would you say that from the point of view of the local political set-up it was: (5) highly organized; (4) quite organized; (3) moderately organized; (2) not very organized; (1) almost not at all organized?" He was then asked to rate other communities he knew on the same five-point scale.

5. *Disturbance over peyotism* (D).—This section began with a question as to whether there was peyote in the community under consideration when the respondent was there, going on to ask about what per cent of the population belonged and how he made the estimate—as a cross-check on the earlier peyote questionnaires (although the respondent did not know this). He was then asked how the presence of the peyote church affected life in the community in general and with specific reference to the political organization, or lack of organization, which the respondent had described earlier (see 4 above). The question of factional developments was touched on, the leadership of factions, their correspondence or lack of correspondence with factions described before, and the involvement of the peyote issue with other issues like attitudes toward the school or livestock reduction or tribal politics. The general issue of whether the community was "more upset" as a result of the entry of peyotism, and the question of physical fights, if any, were then raised. Finally, the respondent was asked, "Well, how much trouble do you think there has been in [the community under discussion] between the peyote side and the anti-peyote side: (5) a great deal; (4) quite a lot; (3) a moderate amount; (2) not very much; (1) almost none at all?" If the interview had not yet clarified the type of trouble, the respondent was asked to explain further. He then rated other communities on the same scale.

6. *General comments.*—The wisdom of seeking ratings on complex variables is open to question, although the orderly character of the final list of median ratings secured gives some reassurance on this score. At least two other comments on dubious methodology should be made. The initial rating, for the community selected, combines both relative and absolute features. That is, the respondent is asked "Compared to the other places you know, how much trouble was there over stock reduction?" Surely this is a relative question, but it is followed at once by the rating scale, which runs from "a great deal" to "hardly any," which tends toward an absolute scale. The reason for this curious split, manifest in four out of five of the variables, is simple enough. We felt that if the respondent were asked in the abstract to state "how much" of one or another quality was present in a community, he would say, "compared to what?" Since his frame of reference had to be his experience in diverse Navaho communities in any case, we made this frame of reference explicit but tried to make the labels for our five-point rating scale as absolute as we could. There is a certain lack of methodological purity in this procedure. Nevertheless, it is probable that the impact of the procedure was, in the end, on the absolute side. Thus each respondent was handed a card showing the verbal descriptions for each of the five points on the scale, to hold while he rated a considerable list of communities. The card omitted the relative element, asking only, "For each community mentioned, would you say that it was. . . ." The five-point scale and verbal descriptions of the scale followed.

Second, the definition of the variables for the respondents involved some minimal contamination of variables. The discussion of political organization adverted to the question of leadership exerted by the Native American Church and to factionalism centering about the Native American Church. The discussion of trouble in general adverted to reactions to livestock reduction. Although these questions may have been undesirable from a methodological point of view, their omission would have given a certain quality of unreality to discussions of political organization and trouble for people working in communities where peyotism and livestock reduction were particularly lively issues. It is evident that leadership vested in the Native American Church and peyotist factionalism represent only a small part of the area of inquiry regarding political organization, and trouble over livestock reduction only a small part of the inquiry regarding trouble. We must leave the problem there.

Appendix G

POSTSCRIPT, 1965

Field work in District 4 in the summer of 1965 brought me back into close contact with peyotists in the area whom I had known in 1950, as well as allowing me to get to know others, old and young. The subject of inquiry was Navaho kinship, but of course there was a great deal of discussion of the Native American Church, and I attended four peyote meetings. In reading copy for this publication, I found some points that needed amplification, more recent information, or correction, and I have indicated these through footnotes or inserts in the text. A few additional points need to be made.

First, I have become painfully aware that a book written for social scientists, for peyotists, and for non-peyotists must necessarily fail to meet the needs of at least part of its audience. In particular, I think that this book might have been more evocative than it is. I am not sure that I have conveyed the dignified and serious atmosphere of a peyote meeting, the passionate and zealous religious conviction that inspires so many peyotists, or their certainty that through peyote they have indeed found a cure of souls and bodies. I have not made it sufficiently clear that many of those who are now strong peyotists were equally strong in opposition until a health crisis, or a personal one, led them to try peyote and to find benefits in it. It is too late to remedy these deficits; I can only mention them.

Second, as I had foreseen, there is, today, a generation of young members of the Native American Church who have grown up in that church and hold to it. One might expect that their adherence would be more routine than that of their parents, yet for many of them the process of discovery, of "learning through peyote," is as characteristic as it is for older peyotists. The educational level of peyotists, like that of the general Navaho population, is rising. In District 4, there are a number of high-school graduates who are members, and some who have attended or are now attending college.

Third, arrests have begun again, although there are not many. Peyotists continue to plan to remove the legal restrictions on the use of peyote by members of the Native American Church, either through getting the Tribal Council to change its position, through a suit in the Supreme Court, or through the effects of a proposed congressional bill "of Indian rights" (S. 961). This is a bill "to protect the constitutional rights of American Indians from being infringed upon by Indian tribes exercising powers of self-government." It proposes that "any Indian tribe in exercising its powers of local self-government shall be subject to the same limitations and restraints as those which are imposed on the Government of the United States by the United States Constitution." (I am indebted to the Honorable Robert B. Duncan, Fourth Congressional District, Oregon, for the text.) As

Navaho peyotists understand the intent of this bill, it would nullify the Tribal law on peyote, because of the First Amendment to the Constitution.

Fourth, "talking against" peyote is no longer so popular among non-peyotists. There is far less visible bitterness at the community level.

Fifth, at the Tribal level peyote is still a "hot" issue. Raymond Nakai, the present Chairman, has taken a position favoring tolerance for the Native American Church. His opponents, labeled "the Old Guard," are, in the main, opposed to it. It is probable that, if peyote becomes a matter for Council discussion, the cleavages will follow these lines, and, unless the issue is settled in the near future, a candidate for the chairmanship or for the Council will undoubtedly be evaluated by peyotists and non-peyotists in part by reference to his stand on peyote.

Sixth, some peyotists have expressed the opinion that, as vigorous local opposition has waned, some younger members have been attracted to the Native American Church because of the opportunity it affords for competing in singing and drumming in meetings rather than out of serious conviction and concern for the religious beliefs and ethic.

Seventh, in the body of this book I have said that the ethic of peyotism serves as a legitimation for individuals who feel the need to concentrate more on family obligations and less on those of the wider network of kinship. Field work in District 4 has made me reconsider this interpretation. I believe that peyotism *can* provide this justification, but in District 4 peyote meetings mobilize the larger kin group in the same way that traditional Navaho ceremonies do. Furthermore, in that area, with the spread of peyotism, sibling groups once divided at least as repects involvement in peyotist activities are again reunited. District 4, however, does not afford a fair test of the proposition regarding kinship bonds, because of its relatively traditional character.

Eighth, in District 4, a number of people who had left the cult in 1950, during my first visit, had rejoined it by 1965. Of the active peyotists I knew in 1950, none had left the cult.

Ninth, in District 4, I was impressed by the psychological security and economic adequacy of those peyotists whom I had first come to know in 1950.

Tenth, in my discussion of the use of peyote in curing ceremonies, I have neglected to lay sufficient stress on the importance of a peyote ceremony in allaying anxiety. The psychological and physiological effects of peyote itself, the assembling of friends and relatives who contribute toward carrying out the ceremony, participate in it, and pray in it, the content of the prayers—all these tell the patient that something is being done for him. As Jerrold Levy has suggested to me, the consequent allaying of anxiety in peyote ceremonies, as in other curing ceremonies, is probably therapeutic for the patient and not merely psychotherapeutic.

BIBLIOGRAPHY

REFERENCES CITED

Many United States Government publications, and certain others, are referred to in the text by convenient mnemonic titles or by author. These titles and authors appear in the bibliography below with cross-references to the correct, full citation. Newspaper items were sent to me as clippings or were discovered as clippings in files. Hence page and column references are not available. They are therefore cited by the name of the newspaper and the date of the article, with a brief description of the contents or a listing of the headline. This is not a full bibliography on peyotism, but only a list of references cited. Extensive bibliographies are to be found in La Barre, 1938 and 1960, Slotkin, 1952, and Survey of Conditions, Part 34.

ABERLE, DAVID F.
1959 The prophet dance and reactions to white contact. Southwestern Journal of Anthropology, 15:74–83.
1961 Navaho. *In* Matrilineal kinship, ed. David M. Schneider and Kathleen Gough. Berkeley: University of California Press. Pp. 96–201.
1962 A note on relative deprivation theory as applied to millenarian and other cult movements. Pp. 209–214 in Thrupp, 1962 (*q.v.*).
1963 Some sources of flexibility in Navaho social organization. Southwestern Journal of Anthropology, 19:1–8.
1965 The Navaho singer's "fee": payment or prestation? *In* Studies in Southwestern Ethnolinguistics, ed. Dell H. Hymes with William E. Bittle. Studies in General Anthropology, No. 3. The Hague: Mouton & Co. Pp. 15–32. (Published in 1967.)

ABERLE, DAVID F., and OMER C. STEWART
1957 Navaho and Ute peyotism: a chronological and distributional study. University of Colorado Studies, Series in Anthropology, No. 6. Boulder, Colo.: University of Colorado Press.

ADAMS, WILLIAM Y.
1963 Shonto: a study of the role of the trader in a modern Navaho community. Bureau of American Ethnology Bulletin 188. Washington, D.C.: U.S. Government Printing Office.

ADDITION TO WESTERN NAVAJO INDIAN RESERVATION
See U.S. Congress. Senate. Committee on Indian Affairs (1930).

AGE AND SEX PATTERNS OF MORTALITY, 1955
See United Nations, Department of Economic and Social Affairs, Population Division, Age and Sex.

AMES, MICHAEL M.
1957 Reaction to stress: a comparative study of nativism. Davidson Journal of Anthropology, 3, No. 1.

AMSDEN, CHARLES A.
1949 Navaho weaving, its technic and history. Albuquerque: University of New Mexico Press.

ARIZONA DAILY STAR
1962 Issue of November 15. Deals with trial of Navaho members of the Native American Church in California.

ARIZONA DAILY SUN
1956 Issue of August 5. Deals with suit by members of the Native American Church.

ARIZONA REPUBLIC
    1954 Issue of July 11. Deals with peyotism; provides picture of peyote ceremony.
BARBER, BERNARD
    1941a Acculturation and messianic movements. American Sociological Review, 6:663–669.
    1941b A socio-cultural interpretation of the peyote cult. American Anthropologist, 43:673–675.
BARBER, CARROLL G.
    1959 Peyote and the definition of narcotic. American Anthropologist, 61:641–646.
BELL, DANIEL, ed.
    1963 The radical right, the new American right, expanded and updated. Garden City, N.Y.: Doubleday & Co., Inc.
BERINGER, K.
    1927 Der Meskalinrausch, Seine Geschichte und Erscheinungsweise. Monographie aus dem Gesamtegebiete der Neurologie und Psychiatrie, 49:35–89, 119–315.
BLALOCK, HUBERT M., JR.
    1960 Social statistics. New York: McGraw-Hill Book Co., Inc.
BOURKE, JOHN G.
    1892 The medicine-men of the Apaches. Ninth Annual Report of the Bureau of Ethnology, 1887–1888, pp. 443–617. Washington, D.C.: U.S. Government Printing Office.
BRAASCH, W. F., B. J. BRANTON, and A. J. CHESLEY
    1949 Survey of medical care among the Upper Midwest Indians. Journal of the American Medical Association, 139, No. 4, Jan. 22, 1949, pp. 220–226. (Also circulated in mimeographed form, for release November 26, 1948, by the Office of Indian Affairs.)
BURRIDGE, KENELM O. L.
    1960 Mambu, a Melanesian millennium. London: Methuen & Co., Ltd.
CLEMHOUT, SIMONE
    1964 Typology of nativistic movements. Man, 64:14–15 (Article 7).
COALE, ANSLEY J.
    1956 The effects of changes in mortality and fertility on age composition. Milbank Memorial Fund Quarterly, 34, No. 1, pp. 79–114.
COHEN, FELIX
    1942 Handbook of federal Indian law. Washington, D.C.: U.S. Government Printing Office.
COHN, NORMAN
    1957 The pursuit of the millennium. London: Secker and Warburg.
    1962 Medieval millenarism: its bearing on the comparative study of millenarian movements. Pp. 31–43 in Thrupp, 1962 (q.v.).
COLLIER, JOHN
    1952 The peyote cult. Letter. Science, 115:503–504.
    1962 On the gleaming way. Denver, Colo.: Sage Books.
    1963 From every zenith. Denver, Colo.: Sage Books.
CONDITION OF THE INDIAN TRIBES, 1867
    See U.S. Congress. Joint Special Committee on the Condition of the Indian Tribes, 1867.
CREMONY, JOHN C.
    1954 Life among the Apaches. Tucson, Arizona: Arizona Silhouettes. (Facsimile of the first edition. San Francisco: A. Roman & Co., 1868.)
DE HUFF, ELIZABETH WILLIS, and HOMER GRUNN
    1924 From desert and pueblo; five authentic Navajo and Tewa Indian songs, the lyrics based on the Indian text by Elizabeth Willis De Huff, the Indian melodies transcribed and harmonized by Homer Grunn, the illustrations and cover design by Nah-ka-voh-ma (Fred Kabotie) of the Hopi Tribe. Boston: Oliver Ditson Co.

DITTMANN, ALLEN T., and HARVEY C. MOORE
    1957 Disturbance in dreams as related to peyotism among the Navaho. American
    Anthropologist, **59**:642–649.
DIXON, WILFRID J., and FRANK J. MASSEY, JR.
    1957 Introduction to statistical analysis. New York: McGraw-Hill Book Co., Inc.
    2d ed.
DOCUMENTS ON PEYOTE
    1937 Part 1. Table of Contents: Senate Bill 1399, February 8, 1937, and Departmental
    report of May 18, 1937. Statements by: Dr. Franz Boas, Dr. A. L. Kroeber, Dr. Ales
    Hrdlicka, Dr. John P. Harrington, Dr. Weston La Barre, Dr. Vincenzo Petrullo,
    Mr. Richard E. Schultes, Mrs. Elna Smith, Chief Fred Lookout, Osage Tribe.
    Mimeographed, 137817. Washington, D.C.: U.S. Government Printing Office.
DOWNS, JAMES F.
    1964 Animal husbandry in Navajo society and culture. University of California
    Publications in Anthropology, Vol. 1. Berkeley: University of California Press.
DRIVER, HAROLD E.
    1939 The measurement of geographical distribution form. American Anthropologist,
    41:583–588.
DUNCAN, OTIS DUDLEY, and BEVERLY DAVIS
    1953 An alternative to ecological correlation. American Sociological Review,
    18:665–666.
DURKHEIM, ÉMILE
    1951 Suicide, a study in sociology; trans. John A. Spaulding and George Simpson;
    ed. with an intro. by George Simpson. Glencoe, Ill.: Free Press.
DUSTIN, C. BURTON
    1960 Peyotism and New Mexico. Santa Fe: Vergara Printing Co.
DYK, WALTER
    1938 Son of Old Man Hat, a Navaho autobiography recorded by Walter Dyk.
    New York: Harcourt, Brace & Co.
    1947 A Navaho autobiography. Viking Fund Publications in Anthropology, No. 8.
ESTIMATED POPULATION BY AGE AND SEX OF NAVAJO INDIANS ON THE RESERVATION, NEW
    MEXICO, 1940
    See U.S. Department of Health, Education, and Welfare, Branch of Indian Health,
    Estimated population by age and sex of Navajo Indians.
ESTIMATED POPULATION IN 1950 BY AGE AND SEX, NAVAJO RESERVATION, ADJUSTED ON
    THE BASIS OF THE AGE DISTRIBUTION OF THE POPULATION AS ENUMERATED IN 1940
    See U.S. Department of Health, Education, and Welfare, Branch of Indian Health,
    Estimated population in 1950.
EXECUTIVE ORDER OF MARCH 10, 1905
    In U.S. Laws, Statutes, etc. Indian Affairs, p. 690.
EXECUTIVE ORDER OF MAY 15, 1905
    In U.S. Laws, Statutes, etc. Indian Affairs, p. 690.
FARMINGTON TIMES-HUSTLER
    1937 Issue of February 21. Referred to by Clyde Kluckhohn in personal communi-
    cation but not examined. Deals with a visionary woman in the Huerfano district.
FENTON, WILLIAM N.
    1957 Factionalism at Taos Pueblo, New Mexico. Anthropological Paper No. 56,
    Bureau of American Ethnology Bulletin No. 164, pp. 297-344. Washington, D.C.:
    U.S. Government Printing Office.
FIRTH, RAYMOND
    1955 The theory of 'Cargo' cults: a note on Tikopia. Man, **55**:130–132 (Article 142).
FORBES, JACK D.
    1960 Apache Navaho and Spaniard. Norman: University of Oklahoma Press.
THE FRANCISCAN FATHERS
    1910 An ethnologic dictionary of the Navaho language. St. Michaels, Ariz.

FRANCISCO, MANUEL
    1952   Man's most potent drink. Sir! A Magazine for Males, Vol. 7 No. 11, August,
    1952, pp. 22–23, 54–55.
GALLUP GAZETTE
    Issues of January 26, 1940; March 11, 1943; March 16, 1944. No systematic use was
    made of this newspaper; certain clippings appeared in various files. Articles on live-
    stock reduction and control and Navaho reactions.
GILLMOR, FRANCES
    1930   Windsinger. New York: Minton, Balch & Co.
GILLMOR, FRANCES, and LOUISA WADE WETHERILL
    1934   Traders to the Navajos, the story of the Wetherills of Kayenta. New York:
    Houghton Mifflin Co.
GODDARD, PLINY E.
    1933   Navajo texts. Anthropological Papers of the American Museum of Natural
    History, No. 34, Pt. 1.
GOODMAN, LEO A.
    1953   Ecological regression and the behavior of individuals. American Sociological
    Review, 18:663–664.
    1959   Some alternatives to ecological correlation. American Journal of Sociology,
    64:610-625.
GOODY, JACK
    1957   Anomie in Ashanti? Africa, 27:356–363.
GUARIGLIA, GUGLIELMO
    1959   Prophetismus und Heilserwartungs-Bewegungen als völkerkundliches und
    religiongeschichtliches Problem. Wiener Beiträge zur Kulturgeschichte und Linguis-
    tik. Band 13. Horn-Wien: Verlag Ferdinand Berger.
GUNNERSON, DOLORES A.
    1956   The Southern Athabascans: their arrival in the Southwest. El Palacio,
    63:346–365.
HADLEY, J. NIXON
    1951   Indian registration in Arizona and New Mexico. October 5, 1948. National
    Office of Vital Statistics. Mimeo., Oct. 12, 1951. Washington, D.C.
    1954   See U.S. Department of Health, Education, and Welfare, 1954.
HAILE, BERARD
    1937   A catechism and guide, Navaho-English. St. Michaels, Ariz.: St. Michaels Press.
    1938   Origin legend of the Navaho Enemy Way. Yale University Publications in
    Anthropology, No. 17.
    1940   A note on the Navaho visionary. American Anthropologist, 42:359.
    1943   Origin legend of the Navaho Flintway: text and translation. University of
    Chicago Publications in Anthropology, Linguistic Series. Chicago: University of
    Chicago Press.
    1947a   Prayer stick cutting in a five night Navaho ceremonial of the Male Branch of
    Shootingway. Chicago: University of Chicago Press.
    1947b   Navaho sacrificial figurines. Chicago: University of Chicago Press.
    1950a   Legend of the Ghostway ritual in the Male Branch of Shootingway, Part 1;
    Suckingway, its legend and practice, Part 2. St. Michaels, Ariz.: St. Michaels Press.
    1950b   A stem vocabulary of the Navaho language. Vol. 1, Navaho-English. St.
    Michaels, Ariz.: St. Michaels Press.
    1951   A stem vocabulary of the Navaho language. Vol. 2, English-Navaho. St.
    Michaels, Ariz.: St. Michaels Press.
HALL, EDWARD TWITCHELL, JR.
    1944   Recent clues to Athabascan prehistory in the Southwest. American Anthro-
    pologist, 46:98–105.
HANDBOOK OF AMERICAN INDIANS
    See Hodge, Frederick W.

HEBERLE, RUDOLPH
1951 Social movements, an introduction to political sociology. New York: Appleton-Century-Crofts, Inc.

HERSKOVITS, MELVILLE J.
1938 Acculturation: the study of culture contact. New York: J. J. Augustin.

HEWETT, EDGAR L.
1936 The Chaco Canyon and its monuments. Handbooks of Archaeological History. Publication of the University of New Mexico and the School of American Research. Albuquerque: University of New Mexico Press.

HILL, WILLARD W.
1938 Navajo use of jimsonweed. New Mexico Anthropologist, 3:19–21.
1940 Some aspects of Navaho political structure. Plateau, 13:23–28.

HOBSBAWM, E. J.
1959 Primitive rebels, studies in archaic forms of social movement in the 19th and 20th centuries. Manchester: Manchester University Press.

HODGE, FREDERICK W. (ed.)
1907 and 1912 Handbook of American Indians north of Mexico. Bureau of American Ethnology Bulletin No. 30, 2 vols. Washington, D.C.: U.S. Government Printing Office.

HOFSTADTER, RICHARD
1955 The pseudo-conservative revolt—1955. In Bell (ed.), 1963, pp. 63–80 (q.v.).

HR 11735, MARCH 1, 1933
See U.S. Laws, Statutes, etc. (1933).

HR 5390, SEPTEMBER 7, 1949
See U.S. Laws, Statutes, etc. (1950).

HULSIZER, ALLAN
1940 Region and culture in the curriculum of the Navajo and the Dakota. Federalsburg, Md.: J. W. Stowell Co.

HURT, WESLEY R.
n.d. The persistence of peyote in the Dakotas. Ms.

HUXLEY, ALDOUS
1954 The doors of perception. New York: Harper & Bros.

HYMAN, HERBERT
1942 The psychology of status. Archives of Psychology, No. 269.
1960 Reflections on reference groups. Public Opinion Quarterly, 24:383–396.

INDIAN AFFAIRS, LAWS AND TREATIES
See U.S. Laws, Statutes, etc., Indian Affairs (1913).

INSTITUTE FOR GOVERNMENT RESEARCH, WASHINGTON, D.C.
1928 The problem of Indian administration. . . . Survey staff: Lewis Meriam, technical director. . . . Baltimore: Johns Hopkins Press.

JOHNSTON, DENIS F.
1961 An analysis of sources of information on the population of the Navajo. Ann Arbor, Mich.: University Microfilms. To appear as Bureau of American Ethnology Bulletin 197. Washington, D.C.: U.S. Government Printing Office, 1966.

KENDALL, PATRICIA L., and PAUL F. LAZARSFELD
1950 Problems of survey analysis. In Continuities in social research, studies in the scope and method of "The American Soldier," ed. Robert K. Merton and Paul F. Lazarsfeld. Glencoe, Ill.: Free Press, pp. 133–196.

KIMBALL, SOLON T.
1950 Future problems in Navajo administration. Human Organization, 9:21–24.

KING, C. WENDELL
1961 Social movements in the United States. Fifth printing. New York: Random House.

KLUCKHOHN, CLYDE
1942 Myths and rituals: a general theory. Harvard Theological Review, 35:45–79.

1944 Navaho witchcraft. Papers of the Peabody Museum of American Archaeology and Ethnology, Harvard University, Vol. 22, No. 2.

1945 A Navaho personal document with a brief Paretian analysis. Southwestern Journal of Anthropology, 1:260–283.

1956 Aspects of the demographic history of a small population. *In* Estudios Antropológicos Publicados en Homenaje al Doctor Manuel Gamio. Mexico, D.F.: Dirección General de Publicationes.

1962 Culture and behavior: collected essays of Clyde Kluckhohn, ed. Richard Kluckhohn. New York: Free Press of Glencoe.

KLUCKHOHN, CLYDE, and DOROTHEA LEIGHTON
1946. The Navaho. Cambridge: Harvard University Press.

KLUCKHOHN, CLYDE, and KATHERINE SPENCER
1940 A bibliography of the Navaho Indians. New York: J. J. Augustin.

KLUCKHOHN, CLYDE, and LELAND C. WYMAN
1940 An introduction to Navaho chant practice, with an account of the behaviors observed in four chants. Memoirs of the American Anthropological Association, No. 53.

KLUCKHOHN, FLORENCE R.
1961 Dominant and variant value orientations. *In* Personality in nature, society, and culture, ed. Clyde Kluckhohn, Henry A. Murray, and David M. Schneider. New York: Alfred A. Knopf, pp. 342–357.

KROEBER, ALFRED L.
1907 The Arapaho. IV. Religion. Bulletin of the American Museum of Natural History, Vol. 18, Pt. IV, pp. 279–454.

KUNSTADTER, PETER
1960 Culture change, social structure, and health behavior: a quantitative study of clinic use among the Apaches of the Mescalero Reservation. A dissertation submitted in partial fulfillment of the requirements for the degree of Doctor of Philosophy in the University of Michigan. Ann Arbor: University Microfilms.

LA BARRE, WESTON
1938 The peyote cult. Yale University Publications in Anthropology, No. 19.

1939 Note on Richard Schultes' "The appeal of peyote." American Anthropologist, 41:340–342.

1960 Twenty years of peyote studies. Current Anthropology, 1:45–60.

LA BARRE, WESTON, DAVID P. MCALLESTER, J. S. SLOTKIN, OMER C. STEWART, and SOL TAX
1951 Statement on Peyote. Science, 114:582–583.

LADD, JOHN
1957 The structure of a moral code. Cambridge: Harvard University Press.

LANTERNARI, VITTORIO
1963 The religions of the oppressed, a study of modern messianic cults. Trans. Lisa Sergio. New York: Alfred A. Knopf.

LASSWELL, HAROLD D.
1935 Collective autism as a consequence of culture contact: notes on religious training and the peyote cult at Taos. Zeitschrift für Sozialforschung, 4:232–247.

LAW AND ORDER FILES
Maintained in the office of the Head of Law and Order for the Navajo Agency in Ft. Defiance during the period of my field work. I was not permitted to examine them and did not seek to. Information relevant for the history of peyotism was supplied by the Law and Order staff, respecting early arrests for possession of peyote, provided that no names would be used in publication (cf. Aberle and Stewart, 1957, p. 58).

LEIGHTON, ALEXANDER H., and DOROTHEA LEIGHTON
1949 Gregorio, the hand-trembler, a psycho-biological personality study of a Navaho Indian. Reports of the Ramah Project, Report No. 1. Papers of the Peabody

Museum of American Archaeology and Ethnology, Harvard University, Vol. 40, No. 1.

LEIGHTON, DOROTHEA, and CLYDE KLUCKHOHN
1947   Children of the People. Cambridge, Mass.: Harvard University Press.

LEVY, MARION J., JR.
1952   The structure of society. Princeton, N.J.: Princeton University Press.

LINDESMITH, ALFRED R.
1947   Opiate addiction. Bloomington, Ind.: Principia Press.

LINTON, RALPH
1943   Nativistic movements. American Anthropologist, 45:230–240.

LIPSET, SEYMOUR MARTIN
1955   The sources of the radical right—1955. In Bell (ed.), 1963, pp. 259–312 (q.v.).

LORIMER, FRANK
1951   Dynamics of age structure in a population with initially high fertility and mortality. UN Population Bulletin, No. 1, December, 1951, pp. 31–41.

McLEOD, WILLIAM CHRISTIE
1928.   The American Indian frontier. New York: Alfred A. Knopf.

McNITT, FRANK
1962   The Indian traders. Norman: University of Oklahoma Press.

MAIR, LUCY P.
1958   Independent religious movements in three continents. Comparative Studies in Society and History, 1:111–136.

MALINOWSKI, BRONISLAW
1948   Magic, science and religion and other essays, selected, and with an introduction by Robert Redfield. Glencoe, Ill.: Free Press.

MARWICK, MAX G.
1952   The social context of Cewa witch beliefs. Africa, 22:120–135; 215–233.
1958   The continuance of witchcraft beliefs. In Africa in transition, ed. Prudence Smith. London: Max Reinhardt.

MATTHEWS, WASHINGTON
1887   The Mountain Chant; a Navajo ceremony. Annual Reports of the Bureau of American Ethnology, 1883–4, No. 5, pp. 379–467. Washington, D.C.: U.S. Government Printing Office.
1889   Noqoilpi, the gambler: a Navaho myth. Journal of American Folklore, 2:89–94.
1897   Navaho legends. Memoirs of the American Folklore Society, No. 5.
1902   The Night Chant, a Navaho ceremony. Memoirs of the American Museum of Natural History, Vol. 6 (whole series, Vol. 6, Anthropology, Vol. 5).

MAURER, DAVID W., and VICTOR H. VOGEL
1954   Narcotics and narcotic addiction. Springfield, Ill.: Charles C Thomas.

MEAD, MARGARET
1932   The changing culture of an Indian tribe. New York: Columbia University Press.
1956   New lives for old, cultural transformation—Manus, 1928–53. New York: William Morrow & Co.

MENZEL, HERBERT
1950   Comment on Robinson's "ecological correlations and the behavior of individuals." American Sociological Review, 15:674.

MERIAM REPORT
See Institute for Governmental Research, Washington, D.C. (1928).

MERTON, ROBERT K.
1949   Social structure and anomie. In Robert K. Merton, Social theory and social structure. Glencoe, Ill.: Free Press, pp. 125–150.
1957a   Continuities in the theory of social structure and anomie. In Robert K. Merton, Social theory and social structure, revised and enlarged edition. Glencoe, Ill.: Free Press, pp. 161–194.

1957b   Continuities in the theory of reference groups and social structure. *In* Robert K. Merton, Social theory and social structure, revised and enlarged edition, Glencoe, Ill.: Free Press, pp. 281–386.

MERTON, ROBERT K., and ALICE S. KITT
1950   Contributions to the theory of reference group behavior. *In* Robert K. Merton and Paul F. Lazarsfeld, eds., Continuities in social research: studies in the scope and method of the American Soldier. Glencoe, Ill.: Free Press, pp. 40–105.

MIDDLETON, JOHN, and E. H. WINTER (eds.)
1963   Witchcraft and sorcery in East Africa. New York: Frederick A. Praeger, Inc.

MINUTES, NAVAJO TRIBAL COUNCIL
See Navajo Tribal Council, Proceedings of Meetings.

MOONEY, JAMES
1896   The Ghost-Dance religion and the Sioux outbreak of 1890. Fourteenth Annual Report of the Bureau of Ethnology, 1892–93, Pt. 2, pp. 641–1136. Washington, D.C.: U.S. Government Printing Office.
1897   The Kiowa peyote ritual. Der Urquell (new ser.), **1**:329–333.

MOSTELLER, FREDERICK, and ROBERT R. BUSH
1954   Selected quantitative techniques. *In* Gardner Lindzey (ed.), Handbook of Social Psychology, **I**:289–334. Reading, Mass.: Addison Wesley Publishing Co.

NASH, PHILLEO
1937   The place of religious revivalism in the formation of the intercultural community on Klamath Reservation. *In* Social anthropology of North American tribes, ed. Fred Eggan. Chicago: University of Chicago Press, pp. 375–449.

NAVAJO TRIBAL COUNCIL, PROCEEDINGS OF MEETINGS
Mimeo., Window Rock, Ariz.

NAVAJO TRIBAL COUNCIL RESOLUTIONS, 1922–1951
n.d. Mimeo., Window Rock, Ariz.

THE NAVAJO YEARBOOK
1954   The Navajo yearbook of planning in action. Report No. 4. Compiled by Robert W. Young. Pub. 1955. Window Rock, Ariz.: Navajo Agency.
1957   The Navajo yearbook. Report No. 6. Compiled and edited, with articles by Robert W. Young. Pub. 1957. Window Rock, Ariz.: Navajo Agency.
1958   The Navajo yearbook. Report No. 7. Compiled and edited, with articles by Robert W. Young. Pub. 1958. Window Rock, Ariz.: Navajo Agency.
1961   The Navajo yearbook. Report No. 8. Compiled, with articles by Robert W. Young. Pub. 1961. Window Rock, Ariz.: Navajo Agency.

NEW YORK SUNDAY NEWS
1945   Issue of January 28. Deals with the kidnapping of a District Supervisor in District 9.

NEW YORK TIMES
1962   Issue of November 30. Deals with trial of Navaho members of the Native American Church in California.
1964   Issue of August 25. Coast Navajos win right to use peyote in religious rites.

NEWBERNE, ROBERT E. L. (prep.), and CHARLES H. BURKE (directed)
1925   Peyote, an abridged compilation from the files of the Bureau of Indian Affairs. Third edition, revised and corrected. Lawrence, Kansas: Haskell Printing Dept., Haskell Institute.

NEWCOMB, WILLIAM W.
1956   The peyote cult of the Delaware Indians. Texas Journal of Science, **8**:202–211.

NTCR
See Navajo Tribal Council Resolutions.

OPLER, MARVIN K.
1940   The character and history of the Southern Ute peyote rite. American Anthropologist, **42**:463–478.
1942   Fact and fancy in Ute peyotism. American Anthropologist, **44**:151–159.

PETRULLO, VINCENZO
1934 The diabolic root, a study of peyotism, the new Indian religion, among the Delawares. Philadelphia: University of Pennsylvania Press, The University Museum.
1940 Peyotism as an emergent Indian culture. Indians at Work, Vol. 7, No. 8, April, 1940, pp. 51–60. (This issue is numbered Vol. 8 but is actually Vol. 7.)

POLANYI, KARL, CONRAD M. ARENSBERG, and HARRY W. PEARSON (eds.)
1957 Trade and market in the early empires, economies in history and theory. Glencoe, Ill.: Free Press.

PROCEEDINGS OF THE MEETINGS OF THE NAVAJO TRIBAL COUNCIL
See Navajo Tribal Council, Proceedings of Meetings.

PROCEEDINGS OF THE MEETING OF THE ADVISORY COMMITTEE, NAVAJO TRIBAL COUNCIL
1950 (That part of the minutes of the Meeting dealing with The Native American Church), Window Rock, Ariz., May 16–18 (mimeo.).

PSYCHEDELIC REVIEW
1963—Published in Cambridge, Mass.; Vol. 1, No. 1 appeared in June.

QUARTERLY BULLETIN OF THE NATIVE AMERICAN CHURCH
This mimeographed publication was edited by J. S. Slotkin from 1955, when it first appeared, to 1958, when it was discontinued.

RAPOPORT, ROBERT N.
1954 Changing Navaho religious values: a study of Christian missions to the Rimrock Navahos. Reports of the Rimrock Project Values Series, No. 2. Papers of Peabody Museum of American Archaeology and Ethnology, Harvard University, Vol. 41, No. 2.

RCIA
See U.S. Commissioner of Indian Affairs.

REEVE, FRANK D.
1937–1938 Federal Indian Policy in New Mexico, 1858–1880. New Mexico Historical Review, **12** (1937): 218–269; **13** (1938): 14–62, 146–191, 261–313.

REICHARD, GLADYS A.
1928 Social life of the Navajo Indians, with some attention to minor ceremonies. Columbia University Contributions to Anthropology, No. 7. New York: Columbia University Press.
1939 Dezba: woman of the desert. New York: J. J. Augustin.
1944 Prayer: the compulsive word. Monographs of the American Ethnological Society, Vol. 7.
1949 The Navaho and Christianity. American Anthropologist, **51**:66–71.
1950 Navaho religion, a study of symbolism. 2 vols. Bollingen Series 18. New York: Pantheon.

REPORTS OF THE BOARD OF INDIAN COMMISSIONERS
See U.S. Board of Indian Commissioners.

REPORTS OF THE COMMISSIONER OF INDIAN AFFAIRS
See U.S. Commissioner of Indian Affairs.

RHODES, WILLARD
1958 A study of musical diffusion based on the wandering of the opening peyote song. Journal of the International Folk Music Council, **10**:42–49.

ROBINSON, W. S.
1950 Ecological correlations and the behavior of individuals. American Sociological Review, **15**:351–357.

ROUHIER, ALEXANDRE
1927 La Plante qui fait les yeux émerveillés: le peyotl. Paris: Gaston Doin et Cie.

ROYCE, CHARLES C.
1899 Indian land cessions in the United States. Annual Reports of the Bureau of American Ethnology, 1896–7, No. 18, Pt. 2. Washington, D.C.: U.S. Government Printing Office.

St. Paul Sunday Pioneer Press
    1964 Issue of August 30. Dreamy drug promotes Navajos' new religion. By Dan L. Thrapp.

Santa Fe New Mexican
    1954 Issue of July 14. Deals with peyotism; provides picture of peyote ceremony.

Schlosser, Katesa
    1949 Propheten in Afrika. Kulturgeschichtliche Forschungen, Band 3. Braunschweig: Albert Limbach Verlag.

Schultes, Richard E.
    1938 The appeal of peyote (lophophora williamsii) as a medicine. American Anthropologist, **40**:698–715.

Schwartz, Theodore
    1962 The Paliau Movement in the Admiralty Islands, 1946–1954. Anthropological Papers of the American Museum of Natural History, Vol. 49, Pt. 2.

Seevers, Maurice H.
    1954 Drug addictions. Chap. 19 *in* Pharmacology in medicine: a collaborative textbook, ed. Victor A. Drill. New York: McGraw-Hill Book Co., Inc.

Selvin, Hanan C.
    1958 Durkheim's "Suicide" and problems of empirical research. American Journal of Sociology, **63**:615–618.

Shepardson, Mary
    1963 Navajo ways in government: a study in political process. American Anthropological Association, Vol. 65, No. 3, Pt. 2, June, 1963. Memoir 96.

Shonle, Ruth
    1925 Peyote, the giver of visions. American Anthropologist, **27**:53–75.

Siegel, Sidney
    1956 Nonparametric statistics for the behavioral sciences. New York: McGraw-Hill Book Co., Inc.

Slotkin, J. S.
    1952 Menomini peyotism: a study of individual variation in a primary group with homogeneous culture. Transactions of the American Philosophical Society, Vol. 42, Pt. 4.
    1956 The peyote religion, a study in Indian-White relations. Glencoe, Ill.: Free Press.

Smith, Marian W.
    1959 Towards a classification of cult movements. Man, **51**:8–12 (Article 2).

Spencer, Katherine
    1957 Mythology and values, an analysis of Navaho chantway myths. Memoirs of the American Folklore Society, No. 48.

Spicer, Edward H. (ed.)
    1952 Human problems in technological change. New York: Russell Sage Foundation.

Spicer, Edward H.
    1962 Cycles of conquest, the impact of Spain, Mexico, and the United States on the Indians of the Southwest, 1533–1960. Tucson: University of Arizona Press.

Spier, Leslie
    1935 The prophet dance of the Northwest and its derivatives: the source of the Ghost Dance. General Series in Anthropology, No. 1. Menasha, Wis.: George Banta Publishing Co.

Spier, Leslie, Wayne Suttles, and Melville J. Herskovits
    1959 Comment on Aberle's theory of deprivation. Southwestern Journal of Anthropology, **15**:84–88.

Spindler, George D.
    1952 Personality and peyotism in Menomini Indian acculturation. Psychiatry, **15**:151–159.
    1955 Sociocultural and psychological processes in Menomini acculturation. Uni-

versity of California Publications in Culture and Society, Vol. 5. Berkeley: University of California Press.

SPINDLER, GEORGE D., and WALTER GOLDSCHMIDT
1952 Experimental design in the study of culture change. Southwestern Journal of Anthropology, **8**:68–83.

STANNER, W. E. H.
1953 The South Seas in transition. Sydney: Austral-Asian Publishing Co.

STATISTICS CONCERNING INDIAN EDUCATION, FISCAL YEAR 1955
See U.S. Bureau of Indian Affairs, Statistics concerning. . . .

STEVENSON, JAMES
1891 Ceremonial of Hasjelti Dailjis and mythical sand painting of the Navajo Indians. Annual Reports of the Bureau of American Ethnology, 1886–7, No. 8, pp. 229–285. Washington, D.C.: U.S. Government Printing Office.

STEWART, OMER C.
1941 The Southern Ute peyote cult. American Anthropologist, **43**:303–308.
1944 Washo-Northern Paiute peyotism: a study in acculturation. University of California Publications in American Archaeology and Ethnology, No. 3, **40**:63–141.
1948 Ute peyotism. University of Colorado Studies, Series in Anthropology, 1. Boulder, Colo.: University of Colorado Press.
1961 The Native American Church (peyote cult) and the law. Denver Westerners Monthly Roundup. Vol. 17, No. 1, January, 1961, pp. 5–18.

SURVEY OF CONDITIONS, PART 18
See U.S. Congress. Senate. Committee on Indian Affairs (1932).

SURVEY OF CONDITIONS, PART 34
See U.S. Congress. Committee on Indian Affairs (1937).

SWANSON, GUY E.
1960. The birth of the gods: the origin of primitive beliefs. Ann Arbor: University of Michigan Press.

TALMON, YONINA
1962 Pursuit of the millennium: the relation between religious and social change. European Journal of Sociology, **3**:125–148.

TC
See Navajo Tribal Council, Proceedings of Meetings.

THRUPP, SYLVIA L. (ed.)
1962 Millennial dreams in action, essays in comparative study. Comparative Studies in Society and History, Supplement II. The Hague: Mouton & Co.

TIME MAGAZINE
1951 Issue of June 18. Deals with Dr. Clarence G. Salsbury's comments on peyotism and with the peyote cult.
1954 Issue of August 9. Deals with peyotism and provides a picture of a peyote ceremony.

TNY
See The Navajo Yearbook.

UNDERHILL, RUTH
n.d. Here come the Navaho. Indian Life and Customs, No. 8. U.S. Indian Service.
1956 The Navajos. Norman: University of Oklahoma Press.

UNITED NATIONS, DEPARTMENT OF ECONOMIC AND SOCIAL AFFAIRS, POPULATION DIVISION
1955 Age and sex patterns of mortality. Population Studies No. 22. By John V. Grauman and others.

U.S. BOARD OF INDIAN COMMISSIONERS
Reports of the Board of Indian Commissioners. Washington, D.C.: U.S. Government Printing Office.

U.S. BUREAU OF THE CENSUS
1937 Fifteenth census of the United States: 1930. The Indian population of the United States and Alaska. Washington, D.C.: U.S. Government Printing Office.

U.S. BUREAU OF INDIAN AFFAIRS
Statistics concerning Indian education. . . . Published, Lawrence, Kans.: Haskell Press. Haskell Institute.

U.S. CENSUS OFFICE. ELEVENTH CENSUS, 1890.
1894   Report on Indians taxed and Indians not taxed in the United States at the 11th Census, 1890. [Vol. 10.] Washington, D.C.: U.S. Government Printing Office.

U.S. COMMISSIONER OF INDIAN AFFAIRS
Reports of the Commissioner of Indian Affairs. Washington, D.C.: U.S. Government Printing Office.

U.S. CONGRESS. JOINT SPECIAL COMMITTEE ON THE CONDITION OF THE INDIAN TRIBES
1867   Condition of the Indian Tribes, Report of the Joint Special Committee Appointed under Joint Resolution of March 3, 1865, with an Appendix. Washington, D.C.: U.S. Government Printing Office.

U.S. CONGRESS. SENATE. COMMITTEE ON INDIAN AFFAIRS
1930   Addition to western Navajo Indian Reservation, hearing, 71st Cong., 2d Sess., on S. 3782, to permanently set aside public lands in Utah as addition to western Navajo Indian Reservation, March 12, 1930. Washington, D.C.: U.S. Government Printing Office.
1932   Survey of conditions of the Indians in the United States. Part 18, Navajos in Arizona and New Mexico. Hearings before a subcommittee of the Committee on Indian Affairs, United States Senate, 71st Cong., 1st Sess. (Pursuant to S. Res. 79, a resolution directing the Committee on Indian Affairs of the United States Senate to make a general survey of the conditions of the Indians of the United States.) Washington, D.C.: U.S. Government Printing Office.
1937   Survey of conditions of the Indians in the United States. Part 34, Navajo boundary and Pueblos in New Mexico. Hearings before a subcommittee of the Committee on Indian Affairs, United States Senate, 75th Cong., 1st Sess. (Pursuant to S. Res. 79, a resolution directing the Committee on Indian Affairs of the United States Senate to make a general survey of the conditions of the Indians of the United States.) Washington, D.C.: U.S. Government Printing Office.

U.S. DEPARTMENT OF HEALTH, EDUCATION, AND WELFARE. BRANCH OF INDIAN HEALTH
Estimated population by age and sex of Navajo Indians on the reservation, New Mexico, 1940. Mimeographed report prepared by Francis Felsman.

U.S. DEPARTMENT OF HEALTH, EDUCATION, AND WELFARE. BRANCH OF INDIAN HEALTH
Estimated population in 1950 by age and sex, Navajo Reservation, adjusted on the basis of the age distribution of the population as enumerated in 1940. Mimeographed report prepared by Francis Felsman.
1954   Indian population of continental United States: 1950 (mimeo.), prepared by J. Nixon Hadley and others. July 27. Washington, D.C.: U.S. Government Printing Office.

U.S. LAWS, STATUTES, ETC.
1913   Indian affairs. Laws and treaties. Vol. 3 (laws) comp. to December 1, 1913, comp., annot., and ed. by Charles J. Kappler. 62d Cong., 2d Sess., Senate Document no. 719. Washington, D.C.: U.S. Government Printing Office.
1933   An act to permanently set aside certain lands in Utah as an addition to the Navajo Indian Reservation, and for other purposes. Approved March 1, 1933. (Public Law 403, 72d Cong., 47 Stat. 1418.) [HR 11735.] Washington, D.C.: U.S. Government Printing Office.
1950   An act to authorize the Secretary of the Interior to exchange certain Navajo tribal Indian land for certain Utah State land. Approved Sept. 7, 1949. (Public Law 302, 81st Cong., 63 Stat. 695.) [HR 5390.] Washington, D.C.: U.S. Government Printing Office.

VAN VALKENBURG, RICHARD
1938   A short history of the Navajo People. U.S. Department of Interior, Navajo Service, Window Rock, Arizona (mimeo.).

VOGET, FRED W.
  1956 The American Indian in transition: reformation and accommodation. American Anthropologist, **58**:249-263.
WALLACE, ANTHONY F. C.
  1965a New religions among the Delaware Indians, 1600–1900. Southwestern Journal of Anthropology, **12**:1-21.
  1956b Revitalization movements. American Anthropologist, **58**:264-281.
WALLACE, ANTHONY F. C., FRED W. VOGET, and MARIAN W. SMITH
  1959 Towards a classification of cult movements: some further contributions. Man, **51**:25-28 (Articles 25-27). Article 25 by Wallace; Article 26 by Voget; Article 27 by Smith.
WALLIS, W. A.
  1942 Compounding probabilities from independent significance tests. Econometrica, **10**:229-248.
WALLIS, WILSON D.
  1943 Messiahs: their role in civilization. Washington, D.C.: American Council on Public Affairs.
WATSON, DON
  1937 Navahos pray for the good of the world. Mesa Verde Notes, 7, No. 1, pp. 16-18.
WEBER, MAX
  1946 From Max Weber: essays in sociology, translated, edited, and with an introduction by H. H. Gerth and C. Wright Mills. New York: Oxford University Press.
WETHERILL, LULU W., and BYRON CUMMINGS
  1922 A Navaho folk tale of Pueblo Bonito. Art and Archaeology, **14**:132-136.
WIKLER, ABRAHAM
  1957 The relation of psychiatry to pharmacology. Baltimore: Williams & Wilkins.
WILSON, BRYAN R.
  1959 An analysis of sect development. American Sociological Review, **24**:3-15.
  1963 Millennialism in comparative perspective. Comparative Studies in Society and History, **6**:93-114.
WINDOW ROCK AREA OFFICE FILES
  Files on peyotism, livestock reduction, the land use survey of the 1930's, and various topics germane to my research were made available.
WOLF, ERIC R.
  1955 Types of Latin American peasantry: a preliminary discussion. American Anthropologist, **57**:452-471.
WORSLEY, PETER
  1957 The trumpet shall sound, a study of 'Cargo' cults in Melanesia. London: MacGibbon & Kee.
WYMAN, LELAND C. (ed. and comment.)
  1957 Beautyway, a Navaho ceremonial. Myth recorded and translated by Fr. Berard Haile, with a variant myth recorded by Maud Oakes, and sandpaintings recorded by Laura A. Armer, Franc J. Newcomb, and Maud Oakes. Bollingen Series 53. New York: Pantheon.
WYMAN, LELAND C., and STUART K. HARRIS
  1941 Navajo Indian medical ethnobotany. University of New Mexico Bulletin, Whole Number 366, Anthropological Series, Vol. 3, No. 5. Albuquerque: University of New Mexico Press.
  1951 The ethnobotany of the Kayenta Navaho, an analysis of the John and Louisa Wetherill ethnobotanical collection. University of New Mexico Publications in Biology, No. 5. Albuquerque: University of New Mexico Press.
WYMAN, LELAND C., W. W. HILL, and IVA OSANAI
  1942 Navajo eschatology. University of New Mexico Bulletin, Anthropological Series, Vol. 4, No. 1. Albuquerque: University of New Mexico Press.

WYMAN, LELAND C., and CLYDE KLUCKHOHN
   1938 Navaho classification of their song ceremonials. Memoirs of the American Anthropological Association, No. 50.
YOUNG, 1952
   See Young and Morgan, 1952.
YOUNG, 1954
   See Young and Morgan, 1954.
YOUNG, ROBERT W., and WILLIAM MORGAN
   n.d. The Navaho language. A Publication of the Education Division. U.S. Indian Service. (No publisher, no place, no date.)
YOUNG, ROBERT W., and WILLIAM MORGAN (eds.)
   1952 The trouble at Round Rock, by Left-Handed Mexican Clansman with related anecdotes by Howard Gorman and the Nephew of Former Big Man. Part I by Robert W. Young and William Morgan. Navajo Historical Series, 2. U.S. Indian Service. Printed at Phoenix Indian School, Phoenix, Ariz.
YOUNG, ROBERT W., and WILLIAM MORGAN (comp., ed., transl.)
   1954 Navajo Historical Selections. Navajo Historical Series, 3. Bureau of Indian Affairs. Printed at Phoenix Indian School, Phoenix, Ariz.

Weston La Barre's *The Peyote Cult, New Enlarged Edition* (Hamden, Conn.: The Shoe String Press, Inc., 1964) was not used in the preparation of the present work but should be listed as a major bibliographic resource and source of new information on peyote and peyotism.

INDEXES

INDEX OF NAMES, PSEUDONYMS, ORGANIZATIONS, PLACES, AND TRIBES

[NOTE: Native American Church has not been indexed. See Subject Index under appropriate topics. Entries under "Navaho" and "Navajo" have been kept to a minimum. See appropriate topical headings, e.g., "Religion, Navaho." Names preceded by an asterisk are the author's pseudonyms for various Navahos.]

SUBJECT INDEX

Accommodation and peyotism, 339, 341–42, 353
Acculturation
  attitudes toward, Navaho, 95–96, 99, 103
  and disturbance over peyotism, 298–99
  increased, and peyotism, 308
  interview on, 282, 414–15
  Navaho, 50–51, 92, 97
  and peyotism, 233, 235, 236–38, 241, 244, 245, 278–80, 294–97, 303, 304–10, 354, 357
  see also Anti-traditionalism; Deculturation; Education; Interview on acculturation; Nativism; Traditionalism; Transition
Addiction, defined, 10, 399
Addiction to peyote
  absence of, 9–11, 399–400, 404–5
  anti-peyotist beliefs about, 213
  see also Craving; Dependence; Tolerance; Withdrawal symptoms
Affines, Navaho, 44
Agriculture, Navaho, 32
Alcohol; see Drinking
Alteration and peyotism, 335
Alterative movements, 317–18
  and power, 330
  and redemptive movements compared, 322
American Medical Association and peyote, 115, 403–4
Anthropological issues, peyote, 117–18
Anthropologist
  and peyote, 115–16, 156
  role of, 227–31, 233, 235–36
Anti-peyotism, 205–23
  beliefs versus facts, 221–23
  ideology, 111–13, 118, 119, 205
  interpreted, 221–23
  in 1965, 420
Anti-traditionalism, peyotist, 341; see also Acculturation; Deculturation; Education; Interview on acculturation; Nativism; Traditionalism; Transition
Anti-white reactions, peyotist, 152, 341, 381–82, 385, 391–92, 398
Appeal of peyotism, 14–17, 199–200
  ostensible, 193–94
  sustaining, 187–89
Appeals of peyotism, multiple, 351
Arrest of peyotists, 110, 114–16, 119, 120, 121, 123, 160, 163, 383, 387, 390, 419
Availability
  and disturbance over peyotism, 297–300
  and peyotism, 235, 237, 278–80, 293–97, 302

Blizzards of 1948–49, Navaho, 78
Burials, fear of, and anti-peyotism, 217; see also Dead; Ghosts; Souls

Cargo cults, 317, 320, 331
Carrying capacity, Navaho range, 66, 69, 83; see also Livestock reduction
Cattle; see Livestock
Cattle cooperative, Navaho, 92, 101, 105
Cedar chief, Navaho words for, 378
Ceremonies; see Meeting(s); Religion, Navaho; Ritual
Chapter system, Navaho, 42–43
Cheyenne influence on Navaho peyotism, 191
Christian beliefs, peyotist view of, 178
Christian churches
  and Navaho religion, 397–98
  and peyotism, 397–98
Christian-Indian blend and peyotism, 340
Christianity
  and anti-peyotism, 223
  attitudes toward, Navaho, 207
  and peyotism, 153, 166–67, 204, 244, 353, 378–79
  see also Missionaries
Clan, Navaho, 43, 44
Clans, linked, Navaho, 44
Classification of various movements, 315; see also under specific types of movements
Cohort analysis, 362–75
Communications, Navaho, 91
Communism, 320
Communities
  interview on, 414–18
  Navaho, 1953, compared, 91–106
Community cooperation, Navaho, 101
Community differences and peyote levels, summary, 311
Community and peyote, 353
Community peyote levels, prediction of, 293–97
Community ratings, basis for, 280
Conservation and Navaho, 55; see also Erosion; Over-grazing
Context
  of peyotism as social movement, 351
  of social movements, 316, 322, 329–33
Converts, peyotist, 391, 419
Costs
  of Navaho sings, peyotist beliefs about, 214
  of peyote, 215–17
  of peyote meetings, 128–29, 215–17, 384
  anti-peyotist beliefs about, 214